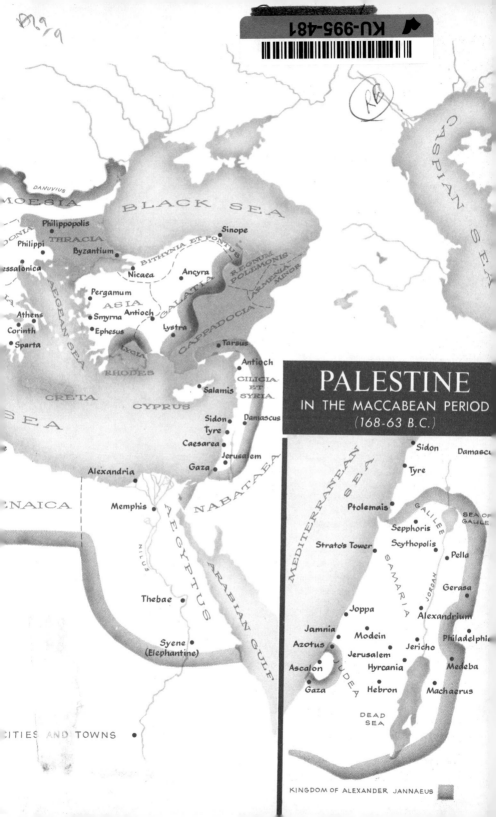

PALESTINE
IN THE MACCABEAN PERIOD
(168-63 B.C.)

DANUVIUS

MOESIA

BLACK SEA

CASPIAN SEA

Philippopolis

THRACIA

Philippi

Byzantium

Sinope

essalonica

BITHYNIA ET PONTUS

Nicaea

Ancyra

REGNUM POLEMONIS

ARMENIA

Pergamum

ASIA

GALATIA

CAPPADOCIA

MINOR

Athens

Smyrna

Antioch

Corinth

Ephesus

Lystra

Sparta

LYCIA

Tarsus

RHODES

Antioch

CILICIA ET SYRIA

AEGEAN SEA

Salamis

CRETA

CYPRUS

Damascus

SEA

Sidon

Tyre

Caesarea

Jerusalem

Alexandria

Gaza

NABATAEA

NAICA

Memphis

AEGYPTUS

NILUS

ARABIAN GULF

Thebae

Syene
(Elephantine)

Palestine inset

MEDITERRANEAN SEA

Sidon

Damascu

Tyre

Ptolemais

GALILEE

SEA OF GALILEE

Sepphoris

Strato's Tower

Scythopolis

Pella

SAMARIA

JORDAN

Gerasa

Joppa

Alexandrium

Jamnia

Modein

Philadelphie

Azotus

Jericho

Ascalon

Jerusalem

Hyrcania

Medeba

Gaza

JUDEA

Hebron

Machaerus

DEAD SEA

CITIES AND TOWNS ●

KINGDOM OF ALEXANDER JANNAEUS

THE LIVING WORLD
OF
THE NEW TESTAMENT

THE LIVING WORLD
OF
THE NEW TESTAMENT

Howard Clark Kee
The Theological School, Drew University

Franklin W. Young
The Episcopal Theological Seminary of the Southwest

DARTON, LONGMAN & TODD
LONDON

Published in the U.S.A. under the title of *Understanding the New Testament* and © Copyright 1957 by PRENTICE-HALL, INC., Englewood Cliffs, New Jersey. All rights reserved. No part of this book may be reproduced in any form, by mimeograph or any other means, without permission in writing from the publisher.

This edition published 1960

Reprinted 1961

Third impression 1962

Fourth impression 1966

Fifth impression 1969

232 48033 8

PRINTED IN GREAT BRITAIN BY
LOWE AND BRYDONE (PRINTERS) LIMITED, LONDON, N.W.10

To
Janet, Clark, and Chris
Jean, Franklin, and David

≫≪

PREFACE

The fact that the Bible continues to be a runaway best-seller year after year provides no guarantee that it is easily understood by those who read it. It is the task of each generation to examine the Bible afresh in an effort to discover its significance for the contemporary scene. Biblical interpretation is not an exact science; rather, it is a dynamic process, influenced by new historical and archaeological discoveries as well as by changing cultural and theological emphases. This book, and its companion volume, *Understanding the Old Testament*,[1] have been written in order to help modern readers understand the Bible by enabling them in some measure to enter into the life of the communities that produced the Old and New Testaments.

To enter the thought world of the people who produced the Bible, we must study the life situations in which their convictions came to them, and out of which they responded to those convictions. Their ideas cannot be studied in isolation from their sphere of life, nor is there any point in trying to reconstruct their history without recognizing the power of the faith that helped to shape that history. Since these people lived in an unfamiliar part of the world, we have supplemented the story with illustrations of the land, the art, and the architecture of New Testament times. We have inserted maps to show the reader how the dynamic faith of these people moved them from land to

[1] Published in England as *The Living World of the Old Testament* (Longmans).

land in fulfilment of what they were convinced was their mission under God. The thread around which this book is woven is the narrative of the rise and spread of the Christian faith, as seen through the eyes of those among whom it developed. But our examination of the New Testament must be more than antiquarian research into ancient modes of life and thought; we must seek to understand the power that continues to operate through the New Testament down to our own time.

In writing an introductory study of the New Testament, it is inevitable that many questions of justifiable concern to specialists must be passed by. The line of argument by which certain conclusions are reached often cannot be traced. And the indebtedness to the many scholarly researches by others on which a book of this type must rest cannot always be acknowledged. Among those who are directly responsible for aiding in the publication of this book, we should like to mention the following: the Committee on Projects and Research of the National Council on Religion in Higher Education, for initiating the preparation of these volumes on the Old and New Testaments; Mr. James T. Stewart for his work in preparing photographs; Dr. Robert J. Bull and Mr. Edward Lincoln for the loan of coins from their collections; the Harvard University Press for permission to quote extensively from Kirsopp Lake's translation of the *Apostolic Fathers*, Loeb Classical Library; Professor Leland Jamison, Dr. Henry J. Cadbury, and Dean Bernhard Anderson for their suggestions and corrections; to Mr. James Guiher and Mr. Walter Behnke for their work in preparing the maps and illustrations; and finally, to Mr. Everett Sims for his patient and perceptive editorial aid.

HOWARD CLARK KEE
FRANKLIN W. YOUNG

CONTENTS

ix

2 *The Community and Its Convictions* 46

3 *The Conduct of Jesus' Ministry* 77

4 *The Content of Jesus' Teaching* 108

PART THREE

THE COMMUNITY MATURES

14 The Community in Rapprochement with the World: II

❀

ILLUSTRATIONS

xvi

❧❦

MAPS

End-paper maps and all maps listed above, except *Plan of the Temple Area* and *Ancient Rome*, are based on maps in *The Westminster Historical Atlas to the Bible* (Revised Edition), edited by George Ernest Wright and Floyd Vivian Filson, copyright 1946 by W. L. Jenkins, published by the SCM, and are used by permission.

Plan of the Temple Area is based on the plan in *Sacred Sites and Ways*, by Gustav Dalman, copyright 1935 by S.P.C.K., and is used by permission.

THE LIVING WORLD
OF
THE NEW TESTAMENT

INTRODUCTION

There is no book in the English language that we quote oftener and understand less than we do the New Testament. The Prodigal Son, the Good Samaritan, "turn the other cheek," "the second mile" are part of the language. Not long ago, Paul's phrase about faith, hope, and charity was resounding from juke boxes across the nation. But why did the original disciples desert Judaism and follow Jesus? How did Christianity develop from the seemingly simple teachings of Jesus into the theological complexities of Paul and the Gospel of John? These are troublesome questions, and their answers must be pieced together from many scraps of evidence.

When a modern reader picks up the New Testament and leafs through the four Gospels—Matthew, Mark, Luke, and John—he tends to choose one of them as the basis for his knowledge of the life of Jesus. Or else he reads at random among the four, settling on those parts that happen to strike his fancy. But why are there four Gospels instead of just one? And why do they differ so strikingly from one another? The short historical work called Acts is the only direct account in the New Testament of the rise of Christianity, and yet it leaves many questions unanswered. Why does it concentrate so heavily on Paul's activities? Were not the other apostles important too? And still other questions bother the serious reader of the New Testament: Why was this miscellaneous collection of writings, most of them epistles or letters, brought together in a single book? Why were these particular writings included rather than others? What was going on in the Christian church while these books were being written?

One way to approach the New Testament is to study each book by itself, or in connection with other closely related books—for example, I, II, and III John might be studied together. Although this approach does introduce the reader to the background of a particular book or group of books, it gives him no feeling for the dynamic, advancing life of the church that produced these writings. Studying the New Testament book by book may throw light on the immediate situation out of which each book emerged, but it fails to place the book in the larger setting of the experiences that the emerging Christian community was living through.

Another way of approaching the New Testament is to concentrate on the important themes that run through the various books. And this is an important part of any serious approach to the New Testament. But it often leaves out of account the variety of viewpoints and emphases that crowd the pages of the New Testament, and gives a false impression that most of the writers were pretty much in agreement on major points. For example, on the question of how the early Christians should behave toward the Roman empire, Jesus is reported to have urged men to "render to Caesar what is Caesar's"; but Paul insisted that Rome's authority was ordained by God and was not to be defied; and the book of Revelation pictures the Roman emperor as the devil incarnate. Only when we understand the different situations that confronted Jesus, Paul, and John can we account for the differences in their reactions to Rome.

A third possible approach to the New Testament is to stress the historical situation in which early Christianity took form, and to describe Christianity as a movement that developed against this background. And this approach too is necessary to any real understanding of the New Testament. But it has two weaknesses: (1) Christianity arose not merely out of a historical process, but also out of a powerful set of convictions shared by a zealous religious group who came to be called Christians; (2) too heavy a stress on history and chronology may lead us to neglect the basic concern of anyone who really seeks to understand the New Testament: *its content.*

With these aims and precautions in mind, in the chapters that follow we shall try to provide the modern reader with information on the historical setting and the sequence of events connected with the emergence of Christianity, and on the situations that led the writers of the New Testament to produce their respective books. But in addition we hope to help the reader to enter with sympathy and understanding into the faith that provided the dynamic for the early Christian community. Some readers will share this faith; others will not. But this book will aim at increasing both groups' understanding of that faith.

Our task would be a good bit easier if the early church had left behind some detailed biographical, chronological, or simple factual records. The plain fact is that we cannot tell with certainty just when Jesus was born, or what the circumstances of his early life were, or what the sequence of events was in his public ministry. Nor do we know much about Paul's youth and training; there are blanks in our knowledge of his life even after he was converted to Christianity. About the other leaders of the early church we have even less information. So any attempt to reconstruct the life of the early church is necessarily a mixture of certainties and probabilities. We make no claim that what follows in this book is the only defensible reconstruction of the events and beliefs of which the New Testament speaks, but it does attempt to set forth a plausible reconstruction to help the reader understand the collection of writings that are our primary source for the rise of Christianity.

We shall begin with a survey of the world at the time of the birth of Christ, paying particular attention to the religious hopes and aspirations of Jews and Gentiles in the age of anxiety with which the Christian era opened. Among the men and women who were searching for a faith that would give meaning to their life, and for a group with which they could identify themselves, was the tiny band of Christians. We shall try to reconstruct what it was this community of Christians believed and how they acted under the impulse of their faith. Recognizing that all the evidence we have for the life and teaching of Jesus comes from records prepared and preserved by this community, we shall examine that evidence in order to see how the words and deeds of Jesus gave rise to Christianity.

As we trace the spread of the Christian faith from the nucleus of believers around Jerusalem out into the Roman world, we shall look closely at the writings that grew out of this rapid, dramatic period of expansion. From Paul's letters we shall try to learn how he fought the exclusiveness of his fellow Jewish Christians, how he dealt with moral crises that arose in churches made up for the most part from heathendom, how he translated a basically Jewish message in order to make it meaningful to non-Jews. In the final section of the book we shall see how the church organized itself as it grew, how it met the challenge of pagan intellectuals, and how it combated false teaching from within and official opposition from without.

As we move along, we shall examine in some detail all the books of the New Testament. But we shall examine them, not as isolated literary products, or as miscellaneous writings that by some chance were brought together in a single collection, but as records of the living faith that gave rise to the Christian church. Only when we understand that faith and the situations in which it was formulated can we arrive at a real understanding of the New Testament.

PART ONE

THE
COMMUNITY EMERGES

⚜

CHAPTER ONE

THE

SEARCH FOR COMMUNITY

Every age is an age of transition, for the world never stands still. But in some ages the rate of change seems to speed up. Ideas move swiftly from place to place, the population shifts about restlessly, social classes become more mobile, loyalties are made and unmade overnight, and political and economic institutions are dramatically reshaped. Rapid changes of this sort always dislocate groups and individuals, creating an atmosphere of uneasiness or even of anxiety. Life seems to be open at both ends; the past seems to be crumbling and the shape of the future has not yet become clear. Fascination

with new developments breeds insecurity, and men and women tend
to cling uncertainly to the discredited beliefs of the past or else grasp
frantically at any new proposal that offers a solution to the perennial
problems of life. It is as though some sinister hand had written across
the face of the present: "Subject to change without notice."

Unsettled by the insecurity of such an age, men search for certainty.
Some seek for a more profound understanding of the nature of the
universe and the ultimate meaning of life. Others may shun the search,
preferring rather to put their confidence in the fantastic promises of
would-be saviours or in the secret formulas of those who purvey quick
and easy answers. An age of transition is a flourishing time for religions
and philosophies that promise security and for governments that
promise stability. When the old patterns of society break up and men
are set adrift in a hostile, unpredictable world, they seek for security
in some group that is bound together by common concerns and
common aspirations. They search for true community—that is, for
community of interest, for a common destiny, and for a sense of
belonging.

It was in such an age of transition and search that the New Testament
was written. To understand these writings, we must try to feel ourselves back into the anxieties and aspirations of the age, and to see
how the writers of the New Testament spoke to men's needs. These
writers spoke, not as isolated individuals proposing solutions of their
own, but as the spokesmen for a group, a tiny minority struggling
for existence in the vast Roman empire at the opening of the Christian
era. Although the events that gave rise to the convictions recorded in
the New Testament took place among the Jews of Palestine, the
community that arose around these convictions soon spread across
Asia Minor and into Europe, where it welcomed Jew and Gentile
alike into its membership, and where it grew with astonishing speed.

The community that produced the New Testament began, not in
a vacuum, but in an age of conflicting social, political, philosophical,
and religious forces. So we must look closely at the state of the world
in New Testament times if we are to understand how the Christian
community came into being. Our effort to understand the New
Testament begins, then, with a sketch of the Roman world at the
opening of the Christian era. Then we shall focus somewhat more
sharply on the Jewish world out of which the Christian community
emerged.

Augustus, the first emperor. It was during his reign that Jesus was born.

War and Peace:
From Alexander to Augustus

One of the most familiar stories in the New Testament—the birth of Jesus according to the Gospel of Luke (Luke 2:1 ff.)—reminds us that Christianity began during the reign of Octavian (27 B.C.-A.D. 14), better known by his title of Caesar Augustus, the first and in many ways the greatest of the Roman emperors. "In those days a decree went out from Caesar Augustus that all the world should be en-

rolled." Augustus was acclaimed by many throughout the empire as
a deliverer and saviour. And it is true that he had brought to an
end the power struggle among the Roman leaders that had led to the
murder of Julius Caesar in 44 B.C. He had driven the pirates from the
seas, making them safe once more for travel and commerce. He had
quelled Rome's enemies, some of whom had harassed her borders for
decades. Above all, he had managed to create an atmosphere of peace
and unity throughout the far reaches of the empire. On landing at
ports, sailors gave thanks to Augustus that they had been able to sail
unmolested by pirates. The Italian peasants, with their strong sense of
morality, were profoundly grateful to Augustus for combating the
immorality that had become rampant among the upper classes of
Rome in the years before his rise.

CAESAR AS SAVIOUR AND DIVINE KING

The people of the empire acclaimed Augustus not merely as
a human deliverer from conflict and struggle, but as a divine saviour-
king. Temples were erected in his honour; sacrifices were made and
incense was burned on the altars. In Palestine, for example, the fawning
puppet king, Herod, built an imposing seaport in honour of Augustus.
From it one could see glistening on the distant Samaritan hills the
white limestone columns of the Temple of Augustus, which stood at
the west gate of the city that Herod had built on the site of ancient
Samaria and had named Sebaste (the Greek equivalent of Augusta).
Although the Jews themselves did not pay divine honours to Augustus,
most of the other eastern peoples accepted him as divine, in keeping
with their ancient tradition of regarding the king as a god. Augustus
carefully avoided accepting the title of king, and even tried to preserve
the fiction that he was no more than the leading citizen (*princeps*)
among equals in the empire.

The world-wide acclaim given Augustus was not without precedent:
in the fourth century before Christ a young Macedonian prince named
Alexander had been hailed as a divine king in Egypt, in Asia Minor,
and throughout much of western Asia. The military conquests of
Alexander the Great, as he came to be called, were aided by the
popular belief that he was a divine ruler before whom resistance would
be useless and impious.

Although Augustus did not publicly seek divine honours as had
Alexander the Great (356-323 B.C.), he benefited from Alexander's
success in establishing himself in the minds of men from the Mediterranean basin to the borders of India as a divine king destined to unify
the civilized world. Even the three centuries that intervened between

the time of Alexander and that of Augustus had not tarnished the popular image of the divine ruler; so Augustus took on a familiar role when he set about extending the empire from the Nile to the Seine and from Gibraltar to Jerusalem.

CAESAR RE-CREATES
ALEXANDER'S ONE WORLD

But Augustus inherited from Alexander more than the tradition of divine kingship; the atmosphere of outward peace and inner unrest that characterized the age of Augustus was a direct development of forces that had been set in motion in the time of Alexander.

Alexander the Great, on a silver coin (tetradrachm) minted during his reign.

Alexander's conquests had begun in Greece at a time when the city-states were in decline (336 B.C.). The weakening of the Greek social and political structure resulted in both military weakness and a breakdown in the sense of group loyalty that had reached its height in the golden age of the city-states. Although Alexander managed to build up an administrative unity among the Greek cities, he failed to create a common allegiance to himself to take the place of the old devotion to the city-states. In the eastern territories, however, where the tradition of divine kingship reached back for centuries, Alexander did succeed in winning great personal devotion from the conquered peoples.

A story arose that the tide along the coast of Asia Minor had retreated at his coming to enable him to pass along a narrow beach between sea and cliff. Since there was an ancient legend that the sea would recede at this point to herald the coming of a world ruler, word of the event sped before him and prepared the way for his acceptance in the East as a divine king. Had Alexander lived, there is little doubt that he could have developed tremendous support and affection—even veneration—from the peoples he had conquered, for legends of his divinity had begun to flourish even during his brief lifetime. But his efforts to create a politically unified world were cut short by his death in 323 B.C.

Alexander's vision of one world stretched far beyond the political sphere, however; he took with him a small army of scholars to record descriptions of the peoples, customs, animals, plant life, and terrain that he and his armies encountered. He had caught from his old teacher, Aristotle, a love of knowledge and an insatiable curiosity about the world around him. And he shared Aristotle's conviction that Greek learning was superior to all other, and that it was his responsibility as a leader of men to spread Greek culture wherever he went. This process of "Greek-izing" the world became known as *hellenizing,* since the Greeks called their own land *Hellas* and themselves *Hellenes.* In their intensive efforts to disseminate Greek culture, Alexander and his followers established Greek-style cities as far east as the Indus Valley and as far north as the territory now included in the Central Asia states of the Soviet Union. Reports have come down to us of petty monarchs in Central Asia who staged Greek tragedies as entertainments for their courtiers.

Yet hellenization never succeeded in laying more than a thin veneer of Greek culture over the oriental parts of Alexander's realm, either during his reign or after his death. The mass of the people in the subject lands remained faithful to their native customs and ways of life. Among the aristocracy, however, there was a strong desire to ape the ways of the Greeks. The aristocrats changed the names of their temples to honour local gods under new Greek titles. They built gymnasia and hippodromes and theatres to provide a setting for Greek-style entertainments. The upper classes even adopted Greek dress. But most of the people in these conquered lands continued to live and amuse themselves much as they had before Alexander began his hellenizing conquests.

In one area of life, however, hellenization had a profound and lasting effect, for Greek was widely accepted as the common language of commerce and international correspondence. Although men continued to speak their native language among themselves, Greek became the *lingua franca* of the hellenistic world. So readily did it gain acceptance that some colonies of expatriates—such as the Jews living in Alexandria—stopped using their native tongues altogether and spoke only Greek. The Alexandrian Jews finally had to translate their Hebrew Bible into Greek so that their own people could understand it. This translation, known as the Septuagint (i.e., seventy, since a Jewish legend claimed that seventy men had prepared independent

translations that miraculously turned out to be identical), was widely
used by Jews and was known to educated Gentiles throughout the
world.

With Alexander's death in 323 B.C., all appearances of political unity
vanished. His generals vied with one another to gain power over
their dead leader's domain, and conflict among them and their successors raged on until the rise of Rome in the middle of the first
century B.C. Only two relatively stable centres of power remained in
the hellenistic empires: one was Syria, where the Seleucids (successors
of Seleucus, one of Alexander's generals) ruled, and the other was
Egypt, where Ptolemy (another general) established the Ptolemaic
dynasty. But in Asia Minor and Greece there was an unending series
of wars and dynastic disputes.

In spite of the widespread disruption created by the continuing
struggles, important centres of learning managed to grow up during
the period between Alexander and Augustus. Athens had already begun
to decline as the centre of philosophical thought, although the
Academy founded by Plato (427-347 B.C.) continued to exist for two
centuries after his death. Tarsus, on the southern coast of Asia Minor,
however, became an important university city. But most significant
of all was Alexandria, the city that Alexander had founded at the
western edge of the Nile Delta as a centre for commercial and cultural
interchange between East and West. There Alexander had founded the
Museum, by definition a shrine to the Muses, but in actuality a great
library with more than half a million volumes, and a centre of learning
and research unparalleled in the ancient world. It was there that
Euclid developed his principles of plane geometry, that Archimedes
performed his famous experiments with water, and that Eratosthenes
discovered the formula by which he was able to calculate the size of
the earth.

At the eastern end of the Mediterranean Sea there was continual
conflict between the Seleucids and the Ptolemies. As we shall see
later, one victim of this conflict was the Jewish nation, situated as it
was in the buffer zone between the two great centres of power. The
Ptolemaic kingdom enjoyed a high degree of stability because of the
great desert that protected it on three sides and because of the immense
wealth that it acquired, both through the agricultural produce of its
own lush valley and through the luxuries that were shipped across it on
the way from India to the Mediterranean cities. The Seleucids, on
the other hand, had vast territories to the east over which they exercised
only feeble control and beyond which lived powerful hostile tribes
who constantly threatened to engulf them. Except for a century of

B

14   THE COMMUNITY EMERGES

relative independence, Palestine, from the time of Alexander until the coming of the Romans in 63 B.C., was subject to either Egypt or Syria, the one rich and indolent, and the other aggressive but insecure.

THE FAILURE TO CREATE UNITY

In spite of the efforts of Alexander's successors to bring unity to their realms, they succeeded only in creating profound unrest. The simpler units of society, like the Greek city-states and the petty oriental kingdoms, had been ruined by the military and cultural conquests of Alexander and his successors. And nothing had risen to fill the void. Merchants could no longer look ahead in the certainty that their business would continue as usual. Villagers never knew when a pillaging army might sweep through and leave them impoverished. The old worship of local gods had been disrupted by attempts to make all men worship universal deities, or at least to give new and unfamiliar names to the old ones. Politically, a man's allegiance to his city or to his petty prince was irreparably shaken; religiously, the world revealed by his widening horizons was too vast to be controlled by local gods.

In Rome itself the ancient gods of the Latin people were still worshipped after a fashion, but the daily round of sacrifices and incantations had become increasingly pointless. Moreover, the Romans had been subjected to powerful influences from Greece and the Orient which on the one hand increased scepticism about the traditional gods and on the other introduced an emotional kind of religion that was far more colourful and satisfying than the formal worship of the state gods.

Rome's contact with the religious philosophy of Greece and the gods of the East was an outcome of her commercial and military operations in the eastern Mediterranean. For centuries, Romans had modestly busied themselves developing and safeguarding agriculture and commerce within the limits of the Italian peninsula. But in the process of extending their power over all of Italy, they fell into conflict with the Phoenicians, who dominated the sea from their capital, Carthage, across the Mediterranean in North Africa. In the course of her long struggle with Carthage (264-146 B.C.), Rome gained control of the southern coast of France and Spain, and became mistress of the western Mediterranean. Only then was she ready to extend her power to the east.

Rome's sympathy with the democratic ideals of the Greek city-states moved her to aid Greece in her struggles during the early second century B.C. against the Macedonians and other hellenistic kingdoms that were competing for the opportunity to absorb her. But Rome's motives in turning to the aid of Greece were not altogether unselfish, for her commercial success in the west had led her to cast ambitious eyes toward the east. When a Seleucid ruler (Antiochus the Great) intervened to support Macedonia in an invasion of Greece, he was defeated by the Roman army and driven back into Syria (192-190 B.C.). Now Rome was in control of Greece, Illyria (modern Yugoslavia), and Asia Minor as far east as the Taurus Mountains. By treaty and military conquest, her expansion continued steadily for more than a century (200-63 B.C.), until at last Syria herself, including Palestine, became a Roman province. Egypt continued her independence under the Ptolemies, although Rome had to intervene in 168 to keep the Seleucids from taking over. The final round in Rome's battle for the East came in 30 B.C., when, following the defeat of Antony by Octavian (Augustus) and the suicide of Cleopatra, Egypt too became a part of the Roman empire. Augustus' victory was the crowning one; the Mediterranean had become a Roman lake; what began as a defence of democracy had ended in the establishment of the most powerful empire the world had ever seen.

The calm that fell after Augustus' destruction of his enemies brought peace to the empire but not peace of mind to its peoples. In the long struggle for power, the Roman ideals of democracy had been crushed. Public and private morality had declined appallingly in the presence of new wealth and power. The local Roman gods had been offered up on the altar of political expediency, for over and over again the Roman leaders had honoured foreign gods in order to win the favour of subject peoples. The strict moral philosophy that the Roman ruling classes had borrowed from the Greeks had withered away. And, in spite of efforts to create a kind of universal religion by identifying the Greek and Roman gods with those, for example, of Egypt, men everywhere were left with no sense of religious certainty. Instead of worshipping the gods who were meant to keep things as they were, men searched for a religion that would deliver them from the evils of this world and would provide a promise of new life in the next.

The Decline of Philosophy

Although the Greeks tried hard to spread their culture throughout the civilized world, the rich tradition of Greek philosophy degenerated on foreign soil. And even at home, the lofty heights of philosophy reached by Plato were never attained by any of his successors in the

Academy (the famous school that he founded, and that continued to exist until 129 B.C.).

THE DECLINE OF PLATONISM

In the golden age of Greek philosophy, Plato (427-347 B.C.) had taught that reality does not consist of specific, tangible objects or observable activities like houses, men, and good or evil deeds. Rather, reality consists of the idea or universal pattern of any particular class of objects. For example, the *idea* of house exists independently of whether or not a particular house exists; the *idea* of goodness exists independently of whether or not men do in fact perform good deeds. These "ideas," Plato suggested, exist eternally; they are not concepts that exist only in men's minds; they are the true and perfect realities of which the objects and actions we know in this world are only imperfect copies. Even though by the beginning of the Christian era philosophers who claimed to subscribe to Plato's thought had debased his system, his understanding of reality had an important influence on Christian thinking almost from the start.

THE APPEAL OF STOICISM

The name Stoic was originally given to the philosophical school founded by Zeno (336-264 B.C.), who instead of giving his lectures in a hall, as did other teachers of the day, gathered his pupils around him in one of the colonnades, or *Stoa*, adjoining the public marketplace of Athens. During Zeno's lifetime, and for centuries after his death, the Stoic way of life continued to attract a large following among both aristocrats and the common people. Perhaps the chief appeal of the great Stoic figures was their personal character and quality of mind, for they were earnest men of great moral integrity. Their outlook on life was one of quiet joy and serenity, and they accepted suffering and tragedy with calmness. Although their ascetic ways discouraged pleasure-seekers from following them, their ability to discipline themselves appealed to many in an age when the moral standards of public officials and private individuals were notoriously low.

The Stoics rejected the Platonic belief that ideas exist independently of man and of the physical universe, and affirmed instead that the real world is the world of material bodies acting and reacting upon one another. They believed that the universe is a single organism energized by a world-soul, just as man is a body energized by a human soul. Soul itself is an extremely fine bodily substance that penetrates everything and is to be found in greater degree in man, in lesser degree in

The Agora at Athens, with the reconstructed Stoa of Attalos in the centre. The Theseum, a temple of the god of fire and the best-preserved ancient temple in Greece, is visible at left centre.

animals and inanimate objects. This world-soul is Reason, an impersonal force that operates throughout the universe, shaping its destiny, and bringing it to its predetermined goal. Then evil will be overcome, and great happiness unknown since the legendary past will again prevail. The true unity of man will be realized in the establishment of a great brotherhood of mankind. The world will be absorbed by God, who is all in all; a great conflagration will purge the universe, and a new cycle of the ages will begin.

Critics of the Stoics scoffed at the notion that the history of the world is the unfolding of a divine purpose, claiming instead that man is free to make his own decisions on the basis of what serves his natural desires, and that there are, after all, no certainties in this world, only degrees of probability.

In spite of critical attacks, Stoicism continued to exert a powerful influence down into the Christian era. The two greatest figures in the later period of Stoic thought were Epictetus, a contemporary of Paul the Apostle, and Marcus Aurelius, the philosophizing Roman emperor of the second century A.D.

EPICURUS' VISION OF THE PLEASANT LIFE

A more sophisticated philosophy than Stoicism was that of Epicurus (342-270 B.C.), whose views were adopted by such outstanding Roman thinkers of the first century B.C. as Lucretius and Cicero, and by Latin poets like Vergil and Horace. Epicureanism never exercised a wide popular appeal, however, largely because it pictured the gods as far removed from the world and utterly indifferent to human affairs. Contrary to popular misconception, Epicureanism did not teach self-indulgence; rather, it taught peace of mind based on the conviction that the universe operates according to fixed laws over which man has no control, and in which the gods have no interest. Its chief concern was to free man from anxieties over the terrors of hell, and from fear of the acts of capricious gods. Although the scientific treatises of the Epicureans (like Lucretius' *On the Nature of Things*) are filled with quaint and fascinating speculations on the natural world, their ethical and religious statements sound like commonplaces from the pen of some contemporary writer telling his readers how to stop worrying, how to find inner peace, how to live bravely in the face of adversity, and so on.

THE HYBRID PHILOSOPHIES

None of these philosophies continued for long in a pure form. For as the years passed elements from all of them were merged into a kind of generalized religious philosophy, which became immensely popular among self-styled intellectuals during the last century B.C. and the first Christian century. To this philosophical mixture each of the philosophical schools contributed some facet of its thought. Stoicism provided its stress on reason, thereby permitting the hybrid philosophers to claim that they were essentially rational in their approach to truth. From Platonism came the yearning for a vision of the eternal world. But Platonism itself provided no mediators to bridge the gap between the finite world known to human senses and the eternal world. Accordingly, the popular philosophies developed hypotheses about ways of mediation through which men might attain direct knowledge of the eternal. From Stoicism and Epicureanism came curiosity about the physical world; so the composite philosophy had its quasi-scientific interests as well.

One of the best-known of the eclectics (*i.e.*, a thinker who chooses what suits his fancy from a variety of philosophical systems) was Seneca (4 B.C.-A.D. 65), a chief adviser at the court of the emperor Nero. Even though he called himself a Stoic, Seneca drew heavily on Plato and Epicurus and on anyone else whose moral teachings happened to appeal to him at the moment.

Perhaps the most prolific of the eclectic philosophers of the first Christian century was a Jew named Philo. Born into a prominent

family among the nearly third of a million Jews of Alexandria, Philo
distinguished himself in public affairs as leader of an embassy to the
court of the emperor Gaius Caligula (A.D. 37-41), and in intellectual
circles as the first thinker to join together in thoroughgoing fashion
rational philosophy and the revealed religion of the Jews.

Philo's voluminous writings consist chiefly of long treatises on the
spiritual (i.e., philosophical) meaning of the narratives and laws included in the Hebrew Bible. For example, Abraham's journey from
Ur in Mesopotamia to Hebron in Palestine is really not a narrative of
ancient Semitic nomads, but a description of the spiritual journey of
the seeker after truth, who moves from the world of the senses (Ur)
to the place where he has a direct vision of God (the promised land
of Palestine). By fanciful explanations of Old Testament stories, names,
and numbers, Philo tried to show that the sacred books of the Old
Testament were really saying the same things as the religious philosophers of his own day. Although we have no evidence that Philo's
writings attracted a wide following among Gentiles, they do show
how eager the Jews of the first century A.D. were to find in the Bible
some knowledge of God that would be rationally defensible and that
would at the same time provide an experience of God's living presence.
In his interpretations of the Old Testament, Philo uses many of the
commonplaces of Stoic and Platonic philosophy as they had come
to be understood in his time.

Growing rapidly alongside these movements in philosophy, and at
times overlapping them, were three other closely related approaches
to the universe: astrology, magic, and gnosticism.

Efforts to control a hostile universe

Astrology developed in Mesopotamia, where men had observed and recorded the orderly movements of the stars and planets for
centuries. At last they had come to the conclusion that the stars possessed power over human affairs, and that the particular configuration
of the stars at the time of a man's birth shaped his destiny. To gain happiness in life, therefore, man must try to understand and, if necessary, to
placate the star spirits. Plato's belief that the stars were gods (Timaeus,
section 40) had provided a link between those astrological speculations
and the Greek philosophical tradition. Other hellenistic philosophers,
by combining astrology with Greek mathematics, heightened the sense
of order and precision with which the stars moved. As a result, men
of the late Hellenic and early Roman periods grew apprehensive about
the power of the stars, and more eager than ever to learn their secrets
in order to gain the favour of the star spirits. Only in this way could

men guarantee that the fate ordained for them by the stars would be a happy one.

The intense desire to curry the favour of the star spirits, and of other seemingly hostile forces of nature, gave rise to formulas by which one could ward off evil or drive away pain and accidents. Societies sprang up that claimed to possess such secrets as astral knowledge, or the trick of staying on the right side of Asclepius, the god of healing. The magic formulas invoked the names of as many deities as possible in order to assure a happy outcome. One crudely written manuscript has been discovered in which the name of Jehovah (or Yahweh), the God of the Hebrews, is linked with Zeus, the chief god of the Greeks, and with the Egyptian god, Serapis. Presumably the man who knew the most magical words and how to invoke the greatest number of deities stood the best chance of gaining happiness in this world and the next.

As kingdoms fell and as life grew more uncertain, people of every class became more interested in life beyond the grave and more anxious to escape the catastrophes of life on this side of it. Even the magic formulas fell into disrepute, and many people turned elsewhere in their search for the secrets of life and death. Some believed that they possessed superior knowledge of history and secrets of the universe that had been revealed to them through visions of divine oracles. They claimed that they could help a man to learn his own fate, or, better still, to secure a happier one; they offered to teach the topography of the underworld to aid men on their journey back from death to the next life. This claim to superior, hidden knowledge is known today as gnosticism, from the Greek word for knowledge, *gnosis*.

There arose gnostic secret societies, into which one must seek initiation in order to attain to true "knowledge." Those so initiated were considered to be "enlightened" and fit to walk the path that leads to an understanding of this life, of the future, and of life beyond the grave. Through membership in one of these societies, even the humblest workman could gain some sense of status, even a feeling of cosmic importance, for he felt that he was one of the select few who knew what the world was all about. By the second century of the Christian era, gnosticism had developed into elaborate systems of theology and cosmic speculation. But the basic elements were present long before the beginning of Christianity.

The Rise of the Mystery Religions

Closely related to the gnostic societies were the groups of worshippers who made up the so-called mystery cults. Through participation in religious dramas and other ceremonies, the initiates of these cults believed that they could share in the life of the gods. The myths on which the mysteries were based varied from country to country, but the basic intent and the general pattern of the myths were common to all. In each case there is a wife (or mother) who grieves for her lost husband (or child). After a period of suffering, the son or daughter is restored to the mother—usually from the dead—and begins a new life.

THE MYSTERY OF OSIRIS

In the Egyptian cults, the myth tells of Isis and her consort, Osiris, a divine king of ancient Egypt. Osiris was seized by his enemies, killed, and dismembered, and Isis wandered over the earth searching for his body, burying each part as she found it. Part of Osiris' corpse

The Telesterion, or great assembly hall, at Eleusis, where the mystery rites of Demeter, the goddess of grain, were annually enacted.

was eaten by the fish in the Nile, which the Egyptians believed to
flow into the underworld; as a result, Osiris became god of the underworld, where he ruled over the dead. In a series of elaborate ceremonies, described in detail in the *Metamorphoses* of Apuleius, a Latin
writer of the second century A.D., an initiate re-enacts the suffering and
journey to death that Osiris experienced. As a result of the initiate's
union with Osiris, the king of the dead, death has no more fears for
him and he is assured of life beyond death. The dignity of the cultic
ritual, the splendour of the robes worn by the priests, and the awesome-
ness of the drama combined to give the worship of Isis and Osiris a
tremendous appeal, not only in Egypt but in Rome and throughout
the empire as well.

GREEK MYSTIC SAVIOURS

In Greece, the mystery cults developed around the myth of
Dionysus, the god of wine, and Demeter, the goddess of grain.
Dionysus was the son of Zeus, the father of the gods, and was destroyed and devoured by the Titans. His heart, however, was snatched
from them and given to Semele, one of the wives of Zeus, who bore
another Dionysus to the father of the gods. Since the race of man
sprang from the Titans, the divine spark that the Titans took in by
eating Dionysus was also present in man. Through mystical union
with Dionysus, man could purge away the earthly aspect of his
existence and, by rekindling the divine spark, could enter more closely
into the life of the gods. From the classical era of Greece down into
the Roman period, union with Dionysus was sought by groups of
people—especially women—who through night-long ceremonies and
the drinking of wine entered into a state of frenzy in which the god
allegedly appeared to them. A gruesome account of one such ecstasy
is preserved in *The Bacchae*, by Euripides (480-406 B.C.), one of
classical Greece's greatest dramatists.

In the cluster of myths that have survived, Demeter is pictured as
the goddess of earth, whose daughter, Persephone, was stolen from
her by the god of the underworld. In her grief, she neglects the earth,
and all vegetation withers and dies. Through the intervention of other
gods, Persephone is restored to her, but since Persephone has eaten
food in the lower world she must return there for a part of each year.
During the months of the year when mother and daughter are united,
the earth rejoices and vegetation flourishes; but during the winter
months Demeter mourns her lost child. While Demeter was searching
for her daughter, she disguised herself as a child's nurse and stayed at
Eleusis, a town about twelve miles from Athens. From early Greek

A Greek vase painting showing Bacchus, the god of wine, with a procession of his worshippers.

times, a series of ceremonies was conducted here every year, beginning with a procession from Athens, and including the re-enactment of the mourning of Demeter, the journey of Persephone into the underworld, and her joyous return.

Only the general outline of the Eleusinian and other mysteries is known, but we know they were attended by thousands every year from all over the civilized world. From the time of Caligula (A.D. 37-41), who granted permission for the worship of Isis to be carried on in Rome, to the initiation of Julian (A.D. 331-363) into the cult of Attis, the mysteries found support in high places in the empire.

Scholars have offered various theories to account for the origin of the mysteries. The fact that one of the most important of the sacred objects displayed to the initiates at Eleusis was a stalk of grain suggests that the rites originated as a magical means of guaranteeing good grain crops. This conjecture is confirmed by the way in which the sacred mystery dramas follow the pattern of recurrent death (sowing), mourning (the winter period when seeds are dormant), and life from the dead (growth and harvest). In one of the cultic liturgies, the priest shouted at the sky, "Hu-eh" (meaning "rain"), and at the earth, "Ku-eh" (meaning "bring forth") The myth of Isis was clearly associated with the annual flooding by the Nile, which was the sole source of fertility for the land of Egypt.

But it is obvious that by hellenistic times the ceremonies had become far more than rituals performed to ensure good crops. The crops' cycle of life and death had become a symbol of man's cycle of life and death, and the intent of the mystery drama was to assure new life, not for the crops, but for the worshipper. In an age when the future held so little promise, and when the old order had broken down, men turned with enthusiasm to these cults with their secrets of life beyond death and their guarantees of immortality.

The mystery religions had another strong appeal: The initiates of each cult were united in a brotherhood from which the barriers of race and social standing were erased. All presented themselves to the deity on the same level, and through participation in the sacramental rites all were united into a fellowship that was to endure forever. That the mysteries were ridden with superstition, that the myths on which they were based were jumbled and contradictory, and that they provided no basis for social or individual morality seem to have mattered only to cynics and critical satirists. Slaves and freedmen, middle-class merchants and artisans, men and women of the upper classes—all flocked to the mystery cults in their search for security and a sense of community in an age of uncertainty.

The Community of Israel

There was one community in the Graeco-Roman world which, more than any other, shared a common life and thought. This was the community of Israel—the Jews—who looked to Palestine as their homeland and to Jerusalem as their capital city. And yet Jerusalem was not a political capital for the Jews, for they had been without political power for the better part of five centuries. Rather, it was a religious capital for a people who were indissolubly bound together by a religious faith and a history that reached back into the distant past. After their political community was wiped out, the Jews succeeded in developing a remarkably homogeneous religious community which, though it looked to Palestine as its homeland, was scattered throughout the Graeco-Roman world. At the beginning of the first century A.D., there were more Jews living outside Palestine than in it; large Jewish settlements were thriving in the major cities, such as Rome and Alexandria, and in many smaller cities as well. Jews had continued to live in Mesopotamia since the sixth century B.C., when they were carried there as captives by the Babylonians. In spite of their being scattered over the civilized world, the Jews were forced by historical circumstances and by religious convictions into a tightly knit community.

THE JEWS UNDER FOREIGN DOMINATION

In the late sixth century, Persia overthrew the Babylonians who had led the Jews into slavery, and granted the exiles permission to return to their homeland (538 B.C.). Many of them were content to remain where they were, but others began a slow migration homeward that continued for a century. By 516 B.C., the Temple in Jerusalem (destroyed by the Babylonians in 586 B.C.) had been reconstructed and work had been started on rebuilding the city and its walls. Because of opposition from hostile neighbours, however, the walls were not completed until shortly after 450 B.C.

By the end of the fifth century B.C., then, Jerusalem had once again become the centre of Jewish national and religious life, even though the Jews were the political subjects of Persia. Though stripped of political power, the Jews were free to develop their religious life and thought with little interference from the Persian authorities. Under the leadership of their High Priest they developed into a small theocracy set within the confines of the Persian empire.

When the Greeks under Alexander made their conquest of Persia and her territories, the Jews, like most of the oriental subjects of Persia, welcomed him as a liberator. During the period following Alexander's death, when the Jews were subjected first to the Ptolemies and then to the Seleucids, they enjoyed the same religious toleration they had experienced under Persia. So long as they paid their tribute and offered no resistance to their rulers this condition continued—until the reign of the Seleucid king, Antiochus IV Epiphanes (175-164 B.C.). It was at this time that the Jewish people experienced the most serious threat to their existence that had arisen since the Babylonian captivity.

THE MACCABEAN REVOLT

Ancient and modern historians have offered many reasons for Antiochus IV's attack on the Jews. Among them was a very practical economic reason. For some time, the Seleucids had been hard pressed for funds not only to carry on their feud with the Ptolemies but also to maintain control over their vast holdings in the East. One of their sources of revenue was the Jewish nation. In addition to increasing the taxes levied on the Jews, Antiochus decided to offer the Jewish office of High Priest to the highest bidder. He deposed the rightful High Priest, Onias, and in his place appointed a man named Jason, who offered large sums of money for the office and agreed to support Antiochus in the hellenization of the Jewish nation. Antiochus, who fancied himself a true representative of hellenistic culture, was eager to force this culture upon all his subjects. It was this effort, in which Jason joined, that led to conflict between Antiochus and the Jews.

Jason built a gymnasium in the heart of Jerusalem in which young Jews, some of them from priestly families, exercised in the nude, according to Greek custom. Some Jews even submitted to surgery to remove the distinctive marks of circumcision. These Greek practices horrified many of the Jews, who regarded them as contrary to their Law and in violation of their covenant with God. Consequently, a strong opposition party called the Hasidim (pious ones) arose in opposition to Jason and to the Jews who were sympathetic to hellenization. The Hasidim fought against all efforts to adopt Greek ways, for to them these customs were inseparably bound up with the idolatry and immorality that they associated with the Greek religion and way of life.

Antiochus finally realized that he could not bend the Jews to his will until he had first destroyed their religion. So in 168 B.C. he issued an edict of proscription. Under penalty of death all Jews were forbidden to circumcise, to celebrate religious festivals, or to observe the Sabbath. He ordered all copies of the Law to be destroyed, and anyone found in possession of it to be punished. Antiochus' men set up a Greek altar to Zeus in the Temple in Jerusalem, and sacrificed swine upon it. Heathen altars were erected throughout the land, and the Jews were compelled to worship heathen gods. To enforce his edict, Antiochus stationed troops throughout Israel.

Although the Jews who had favoured hellenization in the first place acceded to Antiochus' demands, the stubborn Hasidim refused to comply with the edict even though they were faced with martyrdom. Finally, the Jews revolted under the leadership of a priest named Mattathias (from the Hasmon family—Hasmonaeans), who came from the village of Modin. After killing a Jew who was in the act of sacrificing on a pagan altar, Mattathias fled with his five sons to the rugged hill country outside Jerusalem. There they gathered around them followers who were ready to fight the Syrian oppressors in the name of God and in defence of their right to live according to their Law.

This action marked the beginning of the Maccabean Revolt, named from Judas Maccabeus, Mattathias' oldest son, who assumed command of the forces when his father died. The Syrians were little disturbed by the uprising, for the Jews had no trained militia, no arms, and almost no financial backing. But Antiochus underestimated their religious zeal,

their bravery, and their ingenuity. Since the Jews were greatly out-
numbered and had only crude weapons, they turned to guerrilla tactics
against the Syrians in the rugged hill country of Judea. After suffering
a number of discouraging defeats, Judas and his men made a heroic
effort and finally managed to win a peace treaty from Antiochus' general, Lysias. In December, 165 B.C., Judas entered the Temple at Jerusalem, cleansed it, and re-established the traditional Jewish worship. To
the present day, Jews commemorate this triumphant event in the
festival of Hanukkah (Rededication), the Feast of Lights.

Now that religious liberty had been restored, many of the Hasidim
were apparently ready to withdraw from the revolt. But Judas and his
followers carried on raids against the Ammonites and Idumeans, traditional enemies of the Jews, and led expeditions to Galilee and Gilead
to rescue Jews who were suffering retaliation at the hands of Gentiles.
The fact that the Syrians still were in control of strong fortifications in
Judaea and in Jerusalem itself (the Acra) also must have increased
Judas' reluctance to disband his forces. Furthermore, there was still an
active hellenizing party among the Jews that continued to seek the high
priestly office and was quite ready to call upon the Seleucid king for
assistance.

What had begun as a revolt for religious liberty now became a
struggle for political freedom, a struggle that was carried on by the
brothers of Judas after his death. Under the leadership of Simon (142-
135 B.C.), the Jews took several strategic Syrian fortresses, including
the Acra in Jerusalem, and thereby gained virtual independence. The
people acknowledged Simon's success by naming him the legitimate
High Priest, even though he was not a member of a high priestly family.
As the years passed, efforts were made to enlarge the boundaries of the
kingdom, and the Hasmonaean rule became more obviously political.
John Hyrcanus (135-104 B.C.), Simon's son, made notable strides toward his goal of restoring the boundaries of the former kingdom of
David. This ambition was more nearly realized by Simon's son, Alexander Jannaeus (103-76 B.C.), who was more ambitious than his father
and more ruthless in his tactics. Using mercenary troops, he even attacked fellow Jews who opposed his insatiable desire for expansion,
and put to death many of the Jewish leaders. Under Alexander Jannaeus, the religious aims of the original Maccabean revolt were all but
obliterated, and most Jews looked upon him as disloyal to the cause of
the original Maccabean heroes.

After Alexander Jannaeus' death, his widow Alexandra (76-67 B.C.)
restored some degree of stability to the Jewish nation. But when she
died, a dispute sprang up between her two sons over the succession.

Each had his following among the Jews, and each sent an embassy to Pompey, in Syria, to seek Roman support. A third embassy, representing the Jewish people, requested that Pompey reject the monarchy altogether and restore the Jewish nation to its pre-Maccabean non-political status.

UNDER ROMAN RULE: THE HERODIANS

In 63 B.C., with Pompey's arrival in Jerusalem, the political independence of the Jews was cut off once again. The territory now passed under Roman rule, and was made subject to Rome's representative in the territory of Syria. Hyrcanus II, a son of Alexandra who was appointed High Priest by Pompey, faithfully carried out Rome's policy with the help of his minister, Antipater, an Idumean who was clearly motivated by personal ambition. During the long period of disturbances in Rome at the close of the Republican period, Antipater and his son Herod, through political astuteness and cunning, managed to stay in favour with a succession of Roman leaders. In 40 B.C., Rome named Herod ruler of both Judea and Samaria, with the title of king, although disturbances in Jerusalem made it impossible for him to ascend the throne until 37 B.C. Herod's rule (37-4 B.C.) was confirmed by Augustus Caesar in 30 B.C. Before Herod died, his kingdom had come to include not only Idumea, Judea, and Samaria, but also Peraea in Transjordan, Galilee, and a territory north and east of the Sea of Galilee. It was this Herod who was ruler at the time of Jesus' birth.

Herod proved one of the most successful of Rome's puppet rulers, and he was given the title of Herod the Great. He restored some degree of law and order to troubled Palestine and set it up as a buffer state between Rome's territories and the marauding Arab peoples who constantly threatened the peace and Rome's lines of communication. Furthermore, in the fashion of a true hellenistic monarch, he tried to foster in his kingdom Augustus' hopes for a common Graeco-Roman culture throughout the Roman empire. Herod, as we noted above, gave support to the imperial cult and built temples honouring Augustus in many cities (see also Chapter 11). He rebuilt many old cities according to the hellenistic pattern, and throughout the land he constructed gymnasia, theatres, and stadia to encourage the hellenistic way of life.

But most of the Jews despised Herod for his Idumean ancestry and for his tireless efforts to hellenize the kingdom. Furthermore, his ambitious building programmes cost money that had to be raised by excessive taxation. Desperately jealous of his power and fearful lest he lose it, Herod filled the land with secret police and severely punished any Jew who aroused the least suspicion of disloyalty. He went so far as to have

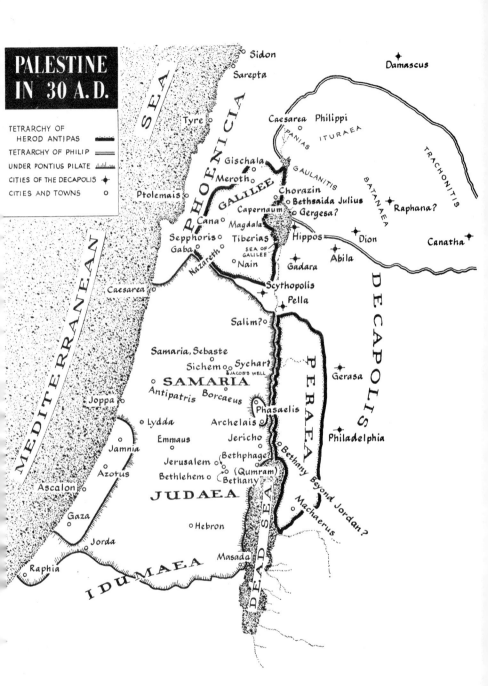

PALESTINE IN 30 A.D.

TETRARCHY OF HEROD ANTIPAS
TETRARCHY OF PHILIP
UNDER PONTIUS PILATE
CITIES OF THE DECAPOLIS
CITIES AND TOWNS

Sidon
Damascus
Sarepta
Tyre
Caesarea Philippi
PANIAS
ITURAEA
PHOENICIA
Gischala
TRACHONITIS
Meroth
GALILEE
GAULANITIS
Chorazin
BATANAEA
Ptolemais
Capernaum
Bethsaida Julius
Raphana?
Cana
Magdala
Gergesa?
Sepphoris
Tiberias
Hippos
Dion
Canatha
Gaba
SEA OF GALILEE
Nazareth
Nain
Abila
Caesarea
Gadara
Scythopolis
DECAPOLIS
Pella
Salim?
MEDITERRANEAN SEA
Samaria, Sebaste
Sichem
Sychar?
JACOB'S WELL
Gerasa
SAMARIA
PERAEA
Antipatris
Borcaeus
Joppa
Phasaelis
Lydda
Archelais
Emmaus
Jericho
Philadelphia
Jamnia
Bethphage?
Jerusalem
(Qumram)
Azotus
Bethlehem
Bethany
Ascalon
JUDAEA
DEAD SEA
Gaza
Hebron
Bethany Beyond Jordan?
Jorda
Machaerus
Raphia
Masada
IDUMAEA

29

his mother-in-law, two of his sons, and his favourite wife (he had nine others) murdered because he suspected their loyalty. Herod did try, though in vain, to conciliate the Jews, for in hard times he eased their taxes and during famine he provided food. And he began the construction of a beautiful new temple in Jerusalem (20 B.C.), though it was not completed until after his death. But all these efforts were of no avail. The land was seething with parties of dissatisfaction, and there is evidence that Herod shrewdly played one off against the other to heighten the internal unrest.

It is not surprising, then, that when Herod died in 4 B.C. the Jews sent an embassy to Augustus imploring that Rome refuse to execute Herod's will, in which he had appointed his sons as successors. When riots broke out in Judea, Varus, the Roman governor of Syria, was sent to quell them, and Augustus shortly approved Herod's will dividing the kingdom among his three sons. Archelaus was appointed ethnarch in Judea (4 B.C.-A.D. 6), Herod Antipas tetrarch of Galilee, Perea (4 B.C.-A.D. 39), and Philip tetrarch of Iturea, Trachonitis, Batanea, Auranitis, Gaulinitis, and Panias. Philip, most of whose subjects were Gentile, enjoyed a very successful rule. Herod Antipas was relatively successful in the eyes of Rome but distasteful to the Jews; it was under his rule that John the Baptist and Jesus carried on their ministries (see Chapters 3 and 5). Archelaus, who proved totally incompetent, was deposed after offending both Jews and Romans. Following Archelaus' deposition, Jerusalem and Judea passed under direct Roman rule administered by a succession of procurators. There was just one short break in the administration (from A.D. 41 to 44), when Herod Agrippa I, Herod the Great's grandson, was granted the rule of his grandfather's entire territory. Since the welfare of the Jewish nation during the years of Roman rule depended directly on the relations between the people and the procurators, we must consider more carefully the events of this period.

THE PROCURATORS (A.D. 6-66)

No less than 14 procurators were sent to Judaea during the 60-year period from A.D. 6 to 66. As the years passed, tension between Rome and the Jewish people increased steadily, partly because of the character of the procurators themselves. With few exceptions, these men failed to measure up to the highest standards of Roman administrative personnel, and their caliber seemed to decline with each successive appointment. Repeatedly, they made foolish judgments in administration, and often they were guilty of inordinate cruelty in carrying out official policies.

But the lot of the procurators was not easy, for they were appointed to govern one of the most troublesome territories under Roman rule— a territory that had grown increasingly resentful under years of alien control. Furthermore, they could not understand the Jews' stubborn resistance to hellenistic religion and customs, and their persistent loyalty to their own religious faith—a faith that the procurators looked upon as superstitious and barbarous. In the name of that faith, minor figures arose time and time again promising release from Roman rule. To the Romans, such promises carried with them the threat of political treason. A good example of the procurators' failure to understand the Jews occurred under Pontius Pilate (A.D. 26-36), before whom Jesus stood trial. On one occasion, in order to build a new aqueduct, Pilate appropriated funds from the temple treasury in Jerusalem that were specifically designated for maintaining sacrifices. Then, when the people protested at this outrage against their religion, he turned them away by force of arms. On another occasion, he offended the religious sensitivity of the Jews by bringing military insignia bearing the emperor's image into the city of Jerusalem. Pilate finally had to be removed from office when he commanded his soldiers to attack a crowd of defenceless Samaritans who had gathered to watch a self-styled prophet perform a miracle on Mt. Gerizim.

As time went by, an increasing number of Jews were drawn into groups (Zealots) that openly or secretly favoured armed rebellion. Open hostility often flared up. Under Felix (A.D. 51-60), before whom the Apostle Paul was brought for a hearing, the Jewish reactionary groups became even more fanatical, and assassinations on both sides were common. Felix's ruthless reaction to his opponents drove still more Jews to adopt radical ways of showing their hatred. Albinus (A.D. 62-64), who was recalled by Rome because of his graft and his maltreatment of innocent people, emptied the jails of prisoners before he left Judaea, flooding the country with brigands who added to the confusion of the times. By the time of Florus (A.D. 64-66), the last of the procurators, open fighting had become common. To add to the fury, Florus plundered the temple treasury, and when the people demonstrated against his action he ordered many of them to be crucified. By A.D. 66, the situation had become so critical and the promise of improvement so remote that organized revolt against Rome finally broke out.

But the rebellion of the Jews against the Romans was lost before it began, for the trained and powerful forces of Rome could not be overcome. Under the Roman generals Vespasian and Titus, the war was successfully concluded by Rome in A.D. 70, though the last remnants of resistance were not wiped out until A.D. 73. The city of Jerusalem suffered heavy damage during the fighting, and the Temple itself was destroyed. For the third time in their history, the Jews had suffered what appeared to be annihilating defeat; yet once again they managed to survive.

Although political, social, and economic factors contributed to the outbreak of the Jewish war, the desperate venture sprang primarily from religious motives. Most of the leaders of the revolt saw themselves as the true successors of the Maccabean heroes, and they fought the enemy for the sake of their faith. Like the revolt itself, the Jews' survival as a community can be understood only in terms of faith. And, since it was the religious development within the community that determined to a large degree the community's development, we must turn now to the faith of the Jewish community that sustained its life through these decisive periods in its history.

THE FAITH OF THE JEWISH COMMUNITY

After the calamity wrought by the Babylonians in 587 B.C., it was a resurgence of religious faith that had brought about the reconstitution of the Jewish community. The Jewish prophets and leaders during the exile boldly declared that the victory of the Babylonians was not a sign of the weakness of their God Jehovah, but rather the means whereby he had revealed his judgment on his people for their sins. Looking back to the words of the great prophets, Amos, Hosea, Isaiah, and Jeremiah, the Jews saw that through them God had repeatedly warned his people that continual refusal to obey his commands would lead to destruction. In the Exile, destruction had indeed come as testimony to the truth of all that the prophets had said.

The prophet whose words are found in the last chapters of the book of Isaiah (40-66) saw in Cyrus' permission to the Jews to return to their homeland a sign of God's continuing concern for his people. By granting them an opportunity to renew their loyalty to him, God had provided the Jews with further evidence that he was not only their God but the only true God in all the universe. It was the mission of his people to bear witness to him to all the nations through their loyalty and obedience.

When the leaders of the returning Jews tried to understand just how the people had sinned and had brought down the judgment of God, they emphasized three major failures: First, the Jews had succumbed to idolatry and had turned to foreign gods rather than to Jehovah alone. Second, they had not worshipped Jehovah in purity but had permitted their worship to become corrupted by all manner of foreign practices. Third, they had not obeyed the commandments that he had given them.

With these failures in mind, the post-exilic Jews determined to guard against any intrusion into their religious belief and life that might turn them from worshipping God as he ought to be worshipped. They realized that all through their history God had been seeking to lead them to what they fully came to understand only through the Babylonian captivity. They had been chosen by the one true God to know him, to worship him, and to live according to his commandments.

These convictions led to what has been called Jewish "particularism" or "exclusivism." It was not merely their belief that they were God's chosen people that set the Jews apart from all other people. Given their firm conviction that belief, conduct, and worship were all of one piece, it was inevitable that they would seek to separate themselves from any mode of life that threatened the purity of any of the three. The book of Ezra shows the lengths to which this particularism was carried, for in it the Jews returning to Judea after the captivity are forbidden to marry foreigners, and those who have married non-Jews are asked to put them aside. Such exclusivism can be understood only in the light of the religious zeal that prompted it—the earnest desire to avoid at all costs the disloyalty of their fathers. And since loyalty to Jehovah involved every aspect of life, it was dangerous to enter into close relations with those who lived in accordance with other ways. This exclusivism at its worst could become a cloak for the derision and hatred of other peoples. But at its best it was the Jews' testimony to the reality of the God they worshipped and the way of life into which faithfulness to him inescapably led them.

In the hellenistic age, when polytheism and idolatry were commonplace, and when religion and morality were not so clearly related as they were in Judaism, the exclusivism of the Jews stood out sharply against the pagan world. Concerted efforts to hellenize the Jews, by such rulers as Antiochus Epiphanes, drove loyal Jews to defiance, since they felt that their way of life had been given by God himself, in the form of the Jewish Law. More than anything else, it was the Law that provided the bond between Jews and that distinguished them as a community from all other people.

The Centrality of the Law

The Jews were convinced that to avoid the recurrence of such a tragedy as the Babylonian exile, they must know God's will as revealed in the Law of Moses and live in accordance with it. The Jews fervently believed that his Law had been given by divine revelation through

Moses and was contained in the Pentateuch (the first five books of the Old Testament). It is now common knowledge that these books contain materials that were gradually brought together over many centuries and that it was not until the end of the fifth century B.C. that they reached their present state.

By the end of the third century B.C., the prophetic books (Amos, Hosea, Isaiah, and so forth) had also assumed the form in which they now appear and had been accepted as part of God's divine revelation to his people. In the New Testament, the phrase "the Law and the Prophets" is a reference to God's revelation to his people as it was contained in these holy scriptures. By the end of the first century B.C., all the books in the Old Testament, except for a very few, were regarded as divine revelation.

The English term "Law" is not a precise equivalent of the Hebrew word *Torah* (Law), a fact that is obvious to anyone who reads the Pentateuch carefully. For the Pentateuch contains a great deal of legend, history, and myth, as well as specific rules or regulations. To the Jews, Torah was a very inclusive term that referred to all that God had revealed about himself, their history, and the conduct that was required of them. In time, the entire written revelation came to be referred to as Torah, though in the more narrow sense Torah always meant the Pentateuch, and often specifically God's commandments.

It is this centrality of the Torah in Judaism that accounts for the rise of a body of Jewish scholars known as the Scribes (*Sopherim*). Since knowledge of the Torah was so essential, there had to be authorities who were competent to interpret the meaning of Torah to the people. In the early post-exilic period, the priests had been the learned men who were looked to as authorities. By the end of the third century B.C., some laymen had become Scribes charged with the responsibility of preserving the writings and giving the official interpretation of them. The conviction had arisen by that time that God was no longer revealing his will through the prophets but that the authority for understanding and interpreting God's will now resided largely with the Scribes, who accordingly thought of themselves as the successors to the prophets. In the New Testament, the Scribes are mentioned in relation both to the Sadducees and the Pharisees, since both groups included among them men who were trained in the interpretation of Torah. The Sadducees, as we shall see, represented the priestly school, and the Pharisees were laymen.

The Torah, then, provided the basis for the common belief and conduct that characterized Jewish life and bound Jews together wherever they might be. But no institution in Judaism was more important

in transmitting knowledge of the Torah and in nurturing deep reverence for it than the synagogue. It is impossible to speak with certainty
of the precise origins of the synagogue. It may have had its inception
during the exile in Babylonia, when the Temple no longer stood and
the Jews, far from their home, came together for worship, deliberation,
and mutual support. Long before the end of the first century B.C., the
synagogue had become a well-established institution, though its significance had evolved gradually. Not only in Palestine, but wherever Jews
lived throughout the Graeco-Roman world, the synagogue served as
the centre of Jewish life and thought. Indeed, the term synagogue
referred not so much to a place of meeting as to the coming together
of Jews in any locality. It was an assembly for worship for Jews who
had no temple, an occasion to read and interpret the Torah in the
presence of the community. And it was in the synagogue that the
"elders," the respected counsellors of the local Jewish community,
sought ways in which the Jews could conform themselves to an alien
environment without being unfaithful to the Torah. When the
Romans destroyed the Temple in A.D. 70, the synagogue continued as
the vital centre of Jewish faith and life.

The Temple and the Priesthood

When the Jews returned to Jerusalem from the exile after 538 B.C.,
one of the first things they did was to rebuild the Temple. This step
was in keeping with their strong desire to re-institute the proper worship of God. The priests who did the final editing of the Law of
Moses (Torah) were careful to include specific instructions on the
temple structure and the form of temple worship. The Temple itself
consisted of a series of courts; the innermost court was the Holy of
Holies, which only the High Priest was permitted to enter. This secret
chamber was the place where God dwelled, and it symbolized his
presence with his people. Naturally enough, the Holy of Holies pro-
voked endless curiosity among non-Jews, who circulated scandalous
rumours about the contents of the room and what went on inside.

The heart of the temple worship consisted of sacrificial offerings,
including daily sacrifices morning and evening, and special sacrifices
and more elaborate rituals on festival occasions. Then there were daily
private offerings by individuals to cover the multitude of sacrifices
required by Torah. Consequently, the temple area was constantly
crowded with priests and Jews making offerings, and with the sacrificial animals and the men who sold them. In addition, money-changers

were always on hand, since Torah required that financial transactions in the Temple could be carried on only with a particular kind of coin.

It is hard to tell just what meaning the sacrifices had for the average Jew at the end of the first century B.C. But there is no doubt about one point: The whole sacrificial system was essential to Jewish worship, for it was required by Torah itself.

To officiate at the numerous sacrificial rites there were multitudes of priests from a long line of priestly families whose genealogies were recorded in the Torah. Admission to the priesthood was carefully controlled, since the Jews were determined that worship be conducted only by properly qualified men. Only descendants from the sons of Aaron could be priests, although descendants from the line of Levi could perform restricted functions alongside the priests. The Torah's regulations to ensure the purity of the priests were meticulously observed, as was the Torah's requirement that the priests and the Levites be supported from offerings made by the people.

At the head of the priesthood was the High Priest, an office that seems to have emerged during the Persian period. As the titular head of the Jewish people, the High Priest carried on negotiations with the various governments to which the Jews were subject. From the beginning, this meant that the High Priest, together with the other priests whom he represented, exercised unusual authority in the community. By the second century B.C., and perhaps earlier, he served as head of the Sanhedrin, a court that handled cases involving infraction of the Torah. Since the Jews made no distinction between civil and religious law, the Sanhedrin could control every aspect of the daily life of the Jewish people. In practice, however, the Sanhedrin concerned itself with only the most obvious infractions of Torah. Since the Romans recognized the Sanhedrin as the ruling body over the Jews, except in matters of treason, the Sanhedrin with the High Priest at its head wielded a great deal of authority.

In the Temple itself, the High Priest's importance was most dramatically symbolized on the Day of Atonement (Yom Kippur), when he entered into the Holy of Holies, into the very presence of God, as the representative of all the Jews. There he offered sacrifices for all the unwitting sins committed by the people during the year, and in response God assured the Jews of his continuing presence and love.

Although the High Priest and the priesthood continued to occupy a place of great importance up to the time of the destruction of the Temple in A.D. 70, their influence had begun to wane. Since the families from which the High Priests came were typically wealthy and aristocratic, they were separated in sympathy and understanding from the

masses of the people. Probably the most important factor in the decline
of the priesthood was the rising influence of the Pharisees, who were
in dispute with the priests on many points of interpreting the Torah
and who usually represented a position more sympathetic toward the
people.

Nevertheless, as long as the Temple stood it provided a unifying
bond among all Jews. Whether in Palestine or the Diaspora, the Jew
looked to the Temple as a symbol of his status as one of God's people.
Every year, Jews throughout the world sent their contribution to the
Temple, and most Jews longed to make a pilgrimage to the Temple in
Jerusalem at least once in their lives. When the Temple was destroyed,
it was only a remarkable resurgence of religious faith and the centrality
of the Torah that enabled the community to survive.

The Hope of the Jewish Community

Underlying the growth and development of a strong Jewish community lay a hopefulness that came to play an increasingly important role
in its life. Paradoxically, the greater the hardships and calamities the
Jewish people suffered, the more fervent became their hope for the
future.

Although the expectations of the Jews were expressed in many ways,
two concepts were basic to all others in popular thought. The first
expectation, which had its roots in pre-exilic times, was for the coming
of an ideal ruler who would establish a reign of righteousness and peace
throughout the world. As time passed, the Jews came to believe that
this ruler would be a descendant of David and that he would restore
the kingdom of David, which the Jews increasingly tended to idealize.
This expectation obviously implied that the Jewish nation would regain the political prestige it had once enjoyed, but its ultimate meaning
was that the nation's resurgence would vindicate the faith of the Jews
and the righteousness of God.

The second expectation was that God himself would establish his
heavenly rule throughout all the world, a hope that gradually found
expression in the concept of the kingdom of God, God's perfectly
righteous rule that one day would supplant the imperfect rule of man.
During the last two centuries B.C., this concept received particular emphasis, for two principal reasons. First, as the result of repeated defeats
by the Seleucids and the subjection of the Jewish nation to Rome, the
Jews came to believe that only through some act of God himself could
they ever be vindicated and their oppressors brought under judgment.

Second, there was a growing belief that the world lay in the power of evil spirits who could not be defeated by human agencies alone. Under the influence of Persian religious thought, the Jews had developed dualistic tendencies in their thinking. They conceived of the world as the battleground of two opposing realms, the realm of God and the realm of Satan, with all men divided between those who fought in faithfulness for God and those who served Satan. Although the powers of evil seemed to have the upper hand for the time being, the Jews were confident that God was still in control. The day was coming when he would once and for all destroy the realm of Satan and bring in a new age in which his people would be vindicated.

During the last two centuries B.C. there emerged a whole body of literature dealing with the conflict between the kingdom of God and the kingdom of Satan, and with the great victory that God would eventually bring about. In general, the struggle was portrayed as growing increasingly worse until a violent conflict broke out among mankind, accompanied by violent disruptions in the whole natural order. Finally, in a totally renewed order of existence, God's kingdom would prevail, God's faithful servants who had died would be raised up to live in joy and peace, and God's purposes in creating the world would be brought to fulfilment.

Although the Jews felt that it was God himself who would bring about this final renewal, there was a growing tendency to think that it would be accomplished by the Messiah, one anointed by God as his agent in carrying out his purposes. Not all the Jews thought of the Messiah in the same way. Some expected him to be a human being who would emerge from the Jewish people, perhaps the long-expected ruler from the Davidic line. Others expected him to be a divine being who would descend from heaven and lead the righteous to a transformed life in a heavenly kingdom. But most Jews agreed that the Messiah's coming would mark the beginning of God's victory over the powers of evil.

This type of thinking about the events related to God's final judgment on evil is referred to technically as *eschatological*, a term that comes from the Greek word meaning "final" or "end." Another term used to describe such speculative thought is *apocalyptic*, derived from a Greek term meaning "revelation." Writers who dealt with eschatology presented revelations regarding the end that purported to have been given to ancient worthies such as Enoch, Noah, and Abraham. Although the various apocalyptic and eschatological writers made use of a wide range of mythological images, they were all interested in making one point: that God would triumph over evil and bring to completion his purposes.

Throughout the period from the Maccabean Revolt to the end of the war with Rome, the eschatological hopes of the Jews fanned the flames of their religious zeal and held them firm in their resistance to any violation of the Torah. Soon after the Maccabean war broke out, the apocalyptic book of Daniel was written, urging the Jews to stand firm in their faith since God's kingdom was at hand and the kingdom of evil was about to be destroyed. Appropriately, evil was personified in the Seleucid kingdom. Later, under Roman domination, other apocalyptic writings appeared in which Rome was identified with the reign of evil. The sharper the crisis, the more brightly the Jewish hopes flamed.

When the final battle with Rome took place in A.D. 66, these hopes undoubtedly played a major role in rallying the Jews to action. Those who thought of God's victory in political terms stood side by side with those who looked for some cataclysmic transformation of the world and a renewed order of existence. For Rome was both the political enemy of the Jewish nation and a personification of the evil that thwarted the rule of God himself. But it was primarily the religious hope that led the Jews to throw themselves into conflict with Rome. This was a hope common to all Jews, for all had been nourished on the conviction that God would vindicate their faithfulness to him before the eyes of the whole world.

Jewish Sectarian Groups

Although the world-wide Jewish community was bound together by a genuine unity of faith, certain differences did spring up in the interpretation of that faith. The most obvious disagreements arose between the Jews of Palestine and those of the Diaspora, such as Philo of Alexandria (see pp. 18-19). Under the influence of hellenistic thinking, the non-Palestinian Jews began to make various modifications and accommodations in their religious thought. But even within the confines of Palestine, certain differences developed. These differences are clearly illustrated by three sectarian groups that originated in Palestine: the Sadducees, the Pharisees, and the Essenes.

The Sadducees were the most conservative segment of the Jewish population, both politically and religiously. Consisting mainly of members from wealthy, aristocratic, priestly families, they were in close touch with the political problems of the harassed nation. In the Roman period, they were anxious to stay on peaceful terms with Rome, for preservation of the status quo was to their advantage both socially and

economically. From the religious point of view, their conservative attitude showed itself in their concern with the temple cultus and the
proper administration of the sacrificial rites. They stressed the importance of the Law of Moses, especially the regulations governing the
priesthood and the sacrificial system.

The Sadducees were particularly opposed to apocalyptic and eschatological thought, on the grounds that such speculation was not compatible with the Torah. For the same reason, they disavowed the
popular belief in angels, demons, and evil spirits. That the Sadducees
were unrepresentative of Judaism and the Jews in general is clearly
shown by their disappearance from Jewish history after the destruction
of the Temple. Their view of the Torah was so narrowly restricted to
the temple cult that once the cult was destroyed their reason for existence came to an end. The disappearance of the Sadducees marked the
triumph of their chief rivals, the Pharisees.

The origin of the Pharisees was probably closely related to the
revolt of the Hasidim in the Maccabean period. Like the Hasidim, they
were rigorous supporters of the Torah. But unlike the Sadducees, they
did not concentrate exclusively on its priestly regulations. They paid
equal respect to the prophetic writings and to the other books that
were gradually being accepted into the Old Testament. But the Pharisees went a step further, for they also acknowledged the existence and
validity of an Oral Torah (Oral Tradition), which they claimed had
its inception with Moses himself. On this point they were in radical
conflict with the Sadducees, who rejected the Oral Torah and all
doctrines not found in the written Law.

In their insistence on the validity of the Oral Torah, the Pharisees
exercised a liberalizing influence on Judaism, for through the Oral
Torah it was possible for Judaism to keep the Written Torah relevant
to changing conditions. The Pharisees believed that God had fully revealed his will in the Written Torah, but that new rules of conduct
had to be worked out if the Written Torah were to be kept relevant
to the changing needs of the people. It was their firm conviction that
every decision in life must be governed by Torah that led them to
develop elaborate principles of interpretation whereby they could derive specific rules to govern conduct in every conceivable situation.
This approach resulted in an endless multiplication of rules of conduct
(*halakah*) for those who desired to live in strict accordance with Torah.
In addition to *halakah*, the Oral Torah also contained many stories,
legends, and other types of material (*hagadah*) to illustrate the ethical
and doctrinal truths contained in the Written Torah. It was through
the freedom of interpretation allowed by the Oral Tradition that the

Pharisees, in contrast to the Sadducees, came to accept the doctrine of the resurrection and the eschatological concept of the kingdom of God even though these concepts were not specifically taught in the Written Torah. Many of the apocalyptic writings produced in the post-biblical period were from the hand of the Pharisees.

And yet the Pharisees' zeal for the Torah and their vigorous effort to govern their whole lives by it led them into a rigorous legalism. Believing as they did that faithfulness to God was expressed through faithfulness to the Torah, they set a standard of rigid adherence that few could follow. So although on the one hand the Oral Torah brought religious faith and practice nearer to the average Jew—for example, the synagogue, and its worship and practice, were validated by the Oral and not the Written Torah—on the other hand the elaborate rules of the Pharisees cut them off from many of their fellow Jews. Their attitude inevitably brought with it the danger of self-righteousness, a danger that they repeatedly combated in their writings.

It was the Pharisees who led the Jewish community to recovery after the fall of Jerusalem and the destruction of the Temple. Although they had no love for Rome or her puppet rulers in Palestine, most of their leaders cautioned against open revolt. They were not motivated by political or economic ambitions as the Sadducees were, but by their understanding of Torah and by their firm belief that the destiny of the Jews was religious rather than political. By applying the Oral Torah to the new situation that arose after the destruction of the Temple, they were able to withstand the shock and proceed to create an even greater unity of life in the Jewish community—a unity that has persisted to the present day.

The Essenes were the third important sectarian group to develop in the Jewish community during the last two centuries B.C. Although the Essenes are not mentioned in the New Testament, they have long been known from the writings of Philo and of Flavius Josephus, the Jewish historian of the first century A.D. According to these writers, the Essenes withdrew from normal social intercourse in order to live apart in isolated communities. They were particularly numerous on the western shores of the Dead Sea, but they also had community houses in the villages of Judea. At the head of each community was an official to whom all members owed obedience. Admission to the community was possible only after a three-year novitiate, at the end of which those who had proved themselves worthy were given full status under oath that they keep the community teachings secret. The members of the community met together for their meals, which held a place of great importance; they all worked; and all brought their wages to a common

The excavated ruins of the monastery at Qumran, with the Dead Sea in the background. The cave in the cliff in the right centre foreground contained manuscript fragments of the Dead Sea Scrolls.

treasury, from which each was supported. The sect frowned on marriage and depended on new converts for its continuation and growth. The Essenes held the Torah in high esteem, studying it continually and interpreting it allegorically, but they also valued many writings outside the Torah. They observed the Sabbath scrupulously, and although they sent gifts to the Temple they did not offer animal sacrifices.

Many questions regarding the origin of the Essenes have never been answered. But recently a new flood of light has been thrown on the Essene movement with the discovery of the now famous Dead Sea Scrolls, more recently called the Qumran Scrolls after the name of the site (Khirbet Qumran) of the community dwelling in which they were kept. Scholars generally agree that there was a close relation between the Essenes described by Josephus and Philo and the sect of Qumran, though it is too early to define the nature of that relationship precisely.

Archaeological explorations of the site at Khirbet Qumran have uncovered structures that undoubtedly are the remains of a community centre for the sect. A large central building housed a refectory, a kitchen, and a scriptorium where members of the community apparently copied their sacred writings. A series of pools or cisterns were used by the sect for purificatory baths and ablutions. A cemetery nearby contains the graves of about 1,000 persons, indicating that the population was considerable over a period of years. With the exception of a few years, the site at Khirbet Qumran was inhabited by the sect from the end of the second century B.C. until the period of the war with Rome (A.D. 66-70).

Although many of the scrolls that have been recovered from surrounding caves have not yet been published, we do have a good bit of information on the beliefs and practices of this group. The sect looked upon itself as the community of the new covenant that had been called by God to cut itself off from wicked men and to live in purity according to the true understanding of the Torah. We are still uncertain about when the sect originated, although many scholars believe it received great impetus during the Maccabean Revolt, when its members joined the Hasidim in resisting hellenization. At some point in its history, one of its leaders, known as the Teacher of Righteousness, suffered at the hands of a wicked priest and ruler. Whether this reference is to events at the time of the Maccabean Revolt or to a later period, such as the time of Alexander Jannaeus, is still an open question. But by the end of the first century B.C. the community thought of itself as the true remnant of God's people who alone lived in obedience to the Torah.

The pools at the Qumran monastery used for baptisms.

One of the most important of the scrolls, the *Manual of Discipline*, contains specific information on the rules of the sect. These rules often parallel the descriptions of the Essenes in Philo and Josephus, on such points as regular worship, common meals, and frequent ablutions. The *Manual of Discipline* indicates that the community was steeped in eschatological thought. Indeed, the members believed they were the true people of God waiting patiently for the final triumph of God's kingdom over the kingdom of Belial (Satan). Although it appears that they awaited the coming of a Messiah, there is still considerable disagreement among scholars over what they thought his nature and function would be. It is clear that their Teacher of Righteousness had introduced them to certain new interpretations of the Torah and of the prophets, interpretations that were undoubtedly eschatological. The discovery of several apocalyptic writings among the scrolls suggests that some of them may actually have been composed by its members.

Our knowledge of how the Essenes were related to other movements in Judaism is still far from complete, but we do know that they differed radically from the Pharisees in many interpretations of the Torah. Further, their emphasis on a spiritual interpretation of sacrifice indicates definite disagreement if not conflict with the Sadducees and the temple priests. And their insistence on the central importance of the

The remains of a table on which scribes copied manuscripts for the Qumran sect. Traces of dried ink were found in inkwells on the table, and at the far end is a ceremonial basin in which the scribes washed their hands before copying the sacred writings.

Torah, accompanied by a tendency to spiritualize its meaning, both relates and distinguishes the sect from the other two parties.

The existence of these sectarian movements shows a degree of flexibility in Judaism that is often overlooked. Although each movement in its own way claimed the Torah as the basis of its life, common loyalty to Torah helped to give the Jewish community its sense of unity. This unity of life and thought must have attracted non-Jews by its religious and ethical fervour, and must have repelled them by its exclusiveness. Other men and women in the hellenistic age were still seeking for the security of a religious community, but the Jews seemed to have been born into such a community. The Jews had made efforts to share their religious life with Gentiles, but with little success. Now, however, there arose out of Judaism a new movement that succeeded where the parent had failed. We turn next to a consideration of this new community—the Christian church.

C

☙❧

CHAPTER TWO

THE COMMUNITY
AND ITS CONVICTIONS

In the days of the newly established Roman empire, there was a restlessness among the people of Judea that Rome could neither condone nor control. Augustus had tried to pacify them by naming an ambitious Palestinian named Herod as puppet king, but the Jews detested Herod for his pagan habits and his mixed ancestry. Tiberius had despaired of controlling the country through petty dynasts, and had put Judea under direct imperial control by appointing a series of procurators, of whom the most famous was Pontius Pilate. But the Jews were determined to resist everything that threatened observance of the Law of Moses, their most sacred heritage. They could never forget the success with which Judas Maccabeus and his followers had thrown off the yoke of foreign domination when the Seleucids ruled the entire Fertile Crescent (see pp. 25-27). Furthermore, the writings of the Hebrew prophets were filled with assurances that God would deliver his people again, as he had delivered them from bondage in Egypt. So long as this hope lived on in their hearts, the people of Judea could not submit to Roman rule.

The Rise of the Community

But not all the Jews resisted the Romans: Many of the aristocrats basked in the *pax romana* and winked at or even enjoyed the pagan pleasures of the occupying foreigners. These were the exceptions, however, for the vast majority of the people resisted the Romans, either actively or passively. The passivists looked to God alone to defeat his enemies and to establish his rule over his people in his own way and by his own means. Many Pharisees took this passive attitude. The activists were convinced that only by armed insurrection could the land be freed from Roman domination. Still others awaited the coming of a Messiah—one anointed of God to fulfil his purposes, like the kings of ancient Israel—who would overthrow the enemies of God. Some believed that the Messiah would be chosen from among the descendants of David; others that he would be a figure of supernatural origin, like the Son of Man described in a popular Jewish book of apocalyptic speculation called the Book of Enoch.

THE DISTINCTIVENESS OF THE COMMUNITY

There was one group, however, that stood apart from all the rest. Like many others, their chief concern was with the coming of the Messiah, but unlike the others they were convinced that he had already come. They admitted freely that he had recently died, but far from spelling defeat for their movement they felt that his death was essential to his messianic role. His disciples were convinced that he had triumphed over death. This did not imply that he had merely been resuscitated to lead them in a military uprising against Rome. As a matter of fact, they carried on their work daily in the temple enclosure in Jerusalem, where the Roman garrison was always at hand to disperse or even imprison them as disturbers of the peace if they exhibited the slightest tendency to revolt.

At the outset, no spectacular claims were made about this man's birth.

His followers were frank to acknowledge his humble origins: he had left a workshop in the insignificant village of Nazareth in Galilee to carry on his brief public career of preaching and healing. At least one member of his immediate family was included in the circle of adherents. He had carried on his activities quite openly, and had at first attracted wide attention in his own region of Galilee. His habit of associating with people who were considered socially and religiously unacceptable had scandalized the Pharisees, and his broad and sometimes radical interpretation of Torah made him *persona non grata* with the Sadducees as well. Even though the religious leaders of the nation had spurned this man and had plotted successfully to have him executed by the Roman authorities, his followers did not hesitate to hold meetings and carry on street preaching where all might see. They proclaimed the doom of the present age, but they did not withdraw into seclusion as did the communities of ascetics who had retreated from the evil world to live the pure life in isolated settlements in the Jordan Valley (see p. 41). Unlike the devotees of the mystery cults, this group made

The eastern hill of Jerusalem, with the Mount of Olives on the horizon. The domed structure is the Dome of the Rock—a Muslim shrine erected in the seventh century A.D.—which stands on the site of the altar of sacrifice of the Jewish Temple.

no secret of what it believed: its evangelists were in the Temple every day trying to persuade all who would listen of the truth of their message. The method by which they sought to win adherents resembled both the tactics of the Hebrew prophets, who summoned their contemporaries to repentance, and those of the Stoic teachers of popular philosophy, who harangued the passers-by in the marketplaces of the Greek cities.

THE COMMUNITY'S CONVICTIONS ABOUT JESUS

The central theme in the preaching of this group was, of course, the significance of Jesus of Nazareth. It was only in the last years of his life that Jesus had become known outside his obscure Galilean village. His early association with John the Baptist, the latter-day prophet of the Jordan Valley, had passed all but unnoticed by the throngs that responded to John's call to repentance. Moreover, Jesus' activities as teacher and proclaimer of the kingdom in the traditionally turbulent province of Galilee had attracted little attention in the Judean metropolis of Jerusalem. Later, however, Jesus had created serious disturbances: first, when he seemed to be usurping the messianic role described by the prophet Zechariah (Zech. 9:9) by riding into Jerusalem on an ass; second, when he forcibly drove the vendors and money-changers from the Temple precincts. The reaction of Jerusalem's civil and religious leaders to these acts made the Roman authorities even more suspicious that the followers of Jesus were potential rebels. Clearly, they felt, the leader himself should be imprisoned and executed as a threat to the *status quo*. In the final hours of Jesus' life, his band of followers—never large—shrank to a handful, and even they withdrew into seclusion after his death.

The Practices of the Community

THE COMMON GOODS

According to Acts, however, the group had soon reunited, and with growing strength was seeking to enlarge its circle. It had become a new and distinctive religious community, sharing certain common convictions, and participating in common experience, even though it remained closely allied to the Jewish faith and life in Jerusalem. The most striking of these communal aspects—though perhaps the most short-lived—was the pooling of resources by the group, so that the needs of all might be met regardless of economic status. As might be expected, this sharing arrangement gave rise to misunderstandings, and led to the setting up of a simple organization with specific duties. (This development is described in some detail in Chapter 6.)

THE COMMON MEALS

Closely related to the sharing of earthly goods was the eating together of common meals. The group believed that the end of the age was imminent, and that the members had no further need for property or money-making. The impending transformation of the world by divine intervention, which had been announced by John the Baptist and Jesus, was to result in the coming of the kingdom of God, in which the people of God would share in an age of peace and joy, in fellowship with Jesus the Messiah. In anticipation of this event, and in remembrance of the last meal that Jesus had shared with his disciples, the community ate together a common meal—an act that was to retain a sacramental significance into future ages and in one form or another was practised from the first.

THE COMMON SPIRIT

Of great significance in this common meal, and indeed in all the life of the community members, was the presence and activity in their midst of what they referred to simply as "the Spirit." This manner of describing God's working is, of course, widely used in the Old Testament: it is the Spirit of God that moves over the face of the deep in the creation stories of Genesis (1:2), and it is for a double portion of the Spirit that Elisha prays (II Kings 2:9). But to the new community gathered in Jerusalem, the presence of the Spirit was taken as a further sign that the new age had already dawned. By means of the Spirit, God was enabling them to do the same kind of healings and exorcisms as those performed by Jesus and identified by him as signs that the kingdom was already present (Lk. 11:20). In the letters of Paul, as we shall see, the Spirit is at times identified with the Lord himself (II Cor. 3:17-18). The coming of this Spirit in such a powerful way was interpreted both as a fulfilment of the promise of God (Joel 2:28-32; Acts 2) and as an assurance that the transforming work that God initiated with the coming of Jesus would be consummated in the new age, which had now begun but which would come in its fullness in the future. This is the significance behind Paul's reference to the Spirit as an "earnest," or pledge (II Cor. 5:5). The ecstatic joy of the group while experiencing this transforming power of the Spirit was so great that hostile critics interpreted it as drunkenness (Acts 2:13). Later on, the possession of the Spirit was taken as a kind of badge of bona fide membership in the Christian community. Even at the beginning, however, the Spirit's presence was a common experience, and exerted a unifying force as the members shared the meal.

The Common Tradition about Jesus

The practices of the early community will be dealt with at greater length in Chapter 6, in which the life of the Judean church is discussed. There is, however, one element that constituted this group as a community which we must now consider in some detail: the community's common conviction about the religious significance of Jesus. There was no one official position on the meaning of Jesus; rather, the New Testament itself supplies ample evidence of the many ways in which Jesus was interpreted by the early Christians. Yet there are certain common strands running through the announcements of the various Christian writers and preachers about the significance of Jesus for man's redemption. These basic convictions about Jesus are as old as the community itself. There is no evidence that the community created them; rather, it rallied around them.

PAUL'S LETTERS AND THE BOOK OF ACTS

The first summary of the faith of the early community to which a date can be assigned is found in Paul's first letter to the Corinthians, 15:3-8. This letter, as we shall see later in this chapter, was written between the years 52 and 54, or approximately twenty years after the events described. Paul makes clear that what he is passing along in this concise credo did not originate with him. For a man like Paul, who insisted on the divine origin of the gospel he preached, this was an amazing confession. He wrote to the Galatians when his authority as an apostle was called into question, ". . . The gospel which was preached by me is not man's gospel. For I did not receive it from man, nor was I taught it, but it came through a revelation of Jesus Christ" (Gal. 1:11, 12). In spite of this denial that the gospel was passed on by human beings, Paul admits that when it comes to the facts about Jesus and his basic meaning for faith, he has simply passed on to his converts what had been passed on to him, in apparently an already fixed form. The noun corresponding to the verb that Paul uses when he says "I delivered, etc.," is *paradosis*, the Greek equivalent of the Latin term *traditio*.

The word "tradition" has a connotation in present-day usage quite distinct from what it had in the first century. To us, tradition has come to mean a story or belief of somewhat dubious origin. Since its source is lost in the unknown past, its reliability is questionable. *Paradosis,* however, as used by Paul in relation to the community's stories and beliefs about Jesus, emphasizes the chain of transmission linking the accounts, as he passes them on, with the original observers of the events described. The appeal to the traditional, therefore, is not a dependence on shaky evidence for lack of anything more reliable; it is rather a claim that the heart of Paul's message goes straight back to the very beginning of the Christian community. (The process by which this transmission took place will be discussed later in this chapter.) Paul is simply transmitting to the Corinthian church a tradition regarding Jesus that had come to be accepted by the churches of Palestine and Syria. Paul did not think of himself as an innovator, but as a preserver of the traditional interpretation of Jesus that had come to him from the Jerusalem community of which Jesus' former disciples were the founders and of which Jesus' brother James was the acknowledged leader.

When we compare these words of Paul with the sermons that the author of Acts ascribes to the apostles, we find that Paul was outlining the same conviction that is elaborated in the apostolic sermons. The proclamation of the early church about Jesus has been called the *kerygma,* a Greek term for the message announced by a herald. The cognate verb, *kerussein,* is the normal one used in the New Testament to express the meaning "preach." One way to account for the uniform viewpoint among these sermons is to regard them as wholly artificial—a literary invention of the author of Acts. It was, in fact, the custom for historians of Greek and Roman times to compose speeches for their heroes and to put them on the lips of the speaker as though they were authentic. Similarly, Plato, when he records the speeches of Socrates, does not distinguish between statements that Socrates actually made and convictions that he is ascribing to Socrates. In Acts, however, it appears that the sermons recorded in the first ten chapters of the book represent a very early form of Christian proclamation, antedating the oldest Gospel (Mark) and almost certainly representing the convictions of the first generation of Christians.[1]

Some of the sermons in Acts, however, do seem more authentic than others. Stephen's address before the Sanhedrin gives evidence of having been translated from a Semitic original, which makes it fairly certain that the author of Acts did not invent the speech. Furthermore, its emphases and viewpoint are unlike those of the other speeches, which confirms the impression that the author has here reproduced an early

[1] For a somewhat more sceptical estimate of these speeches, see "The Speeches in Acts and Ancient Historiography," in *Studies in the Acts of the Apostles,* by M. Dibelius. London: SCM Press, 1956.

source, and has not composed a speech that puts his own words in the mouth of Stephen (Acts 7). On the other hand, Paul's sermon on the Areopagus in Athens (Acts 17) seems to be quite unrelated to his theological perspective as we can infer it from his letters. Now he may have been experimenting with ways of making his words more appealing to his hearers, although many students of Paul's thought find it impossible to believe that he would ever have accommodated himself to such a degree. (Both these speeches will be dealt with more fully in Chapters 7 and 8.) If, as has often been suggested, all these speeches had been invented by a follower of Paul in a piously fraudulent attempt to lend support to his theological position, they would probably sound more like Paul than they do. Such phrases as "Thy Holy Child Jesus" (Acts 4:30) are quite foreign to Paul. The emphasis on repentance in these sermons, rather than on faith as in Paul, gives further evidence of a viewpoint distinctly different from that of Paul. The similarity of this call to repentance to that ascribed to Jesus in the Gospels suggests further that these speeches echo the vocabulary and approach of the earliest Christian preachers.[2] Nevertheless, when we compare Paul's summary of the *kerygma* in I Corinthians 15 with one of the sermons— Peter's in Acts 10:34 ff., for example—it becomes apparent that the crucial emphases are identical: the repeated stress on the relation between the promises to Israel and the fulfilment in Jesus (according to the scriptures); the pivotal significance of the death; the triumphant and well-witnessed experience of the resurrected Jesus. Yet in spite of the basic similarity of the two statements, the attention given in Acts 10 to the earthly life of Jesus reminds us that this is not merely a disciple of Paul ascribing his master's thoughts to Peter in order to gain some of Peter's authority for Paul's point of view. Paul's letters evince relatively little interest in the earthly life of Jesus, in contrast to the writers of the Gospels, who regard the healings and the works of compassion during the days of his flesh as decisive evidence that in Jesus the powers of the new age had been launched. The differences of expression here give strong evidence of separate origins; the fundamental similarity reminds us that there was a common conviction among the members of the Christian community.

LATER NEW TESTAMENT WRITINGS

This consensus regarding the significance of Jesus is found in the later books of the New Testament as well as in Paul and in Acts.

---

[2] *Cf.* Foakes-Jackson, *Acts of the Apostles* (Moffat Commentary), pp. xv-xvi. London : Hodder, 1931.

Judged by the criteria of polish and sophistication, the Letter to the
Hebrews and the Gospel of Mark stand at opposite ends of the poles.
Mark is written in inelegant Greek, with constant repetition of favourite
words and stilted phrases. St. Augustine is reported to have counted the
barbarity of New Testament Greek (in contrast to the smooth style
of the classics he read and studied) as one of the major obstacles that
at first kept him out of the Christian church. At the other extreme,
Hebrews is not only polished in style, but it states the Christian faith in
terms that were then in current use among the intellectuals of the
Graeco-Roman world. Its points of similarity to the mystic philosopher
of Alexandria, Philo Judaeus, as well as the influence of a Platonic type
of thought are readily apparent.

But in both Mark and Hebrews we find the same basic interpretation
of Jesus that is shared by Paul and by Acts. The magnificent prologue
to the book of Hebrews makes it clear that what God said through the
prophets as a kind of preface has been spoken in completeness with
the coming of Jesus, especially through his sacrifice and subsequent
exaltation. Similarly, the Gospel of Mark begins with quotations from
the Old Testament to recount the events of Jesus' life and ministry,
and moves on to the description of the death and resurrection of Jesus.
In Mark's account, Jesus himself speaks of the redemptive significance
of his coming death (10:45; 12:7-11; 14:22-25), and announces his
resurrection in advance.

There is no escaping the fact, then, that the whole of the New Testament is informed by a common conviction regarding the redemptive
significance of Jesus. There are variations in the emphasis, in the vocabulary and metaphor by which the redemptive role is described or
anticipated, but the underlying facts are present throughout, from the
oldest strands of tradition embodied in the Gospels to the late first- or
early second-century writings. But just what are the specific elements
on which the community agreed?

The New Community and the Old

We have already hinted at the answer to this question in our comparison of the summary of the *kerygma* in the letters of Paul and the
sermons of Acts. But now let us look more closely at the individual
points.

The first point that strikes us in the community's proclamation is
the insistence that there is an unbroken continuity between Israel and
this newly established people of God. This means more than just that

the great majority of the first Christians were Jews. The Gospels, the epistles, and the sermons of Acts are crowded with allusions to the Hebrew scriptures. The Old Testament is the major authority for the community's faith and its understanding of itself. Quite literally, it is their Bible. It is these writings, which have come down to them from ancient Israel, that the preachers claim have been fulfilled in Jesus and in the people of the new covenant that he has called together. When anything is described as having been done "according to the scriptures," it is obviously the Jewish canon that is being appealed to. Even when the church moved out beyond the borders of Palestine into the Greek-speaking world, it still depended on the scriptures in translation for the preaching and moral instruction of the predominantly Gentile congregations. Conveniently, the Jewish scriptures had been translated into Greek in the third century before Christ, and by the beginning of the first century A.D. this translation was in common use throughout the entire Jewish dispersion. Surely one of the most potent forces in preparing the way for the acceptance of Christianity was the Septuagint, as this version of the Hebrew Bible was called (see pp. 12-13). The fact that most of the quotations from the Old Testament found in the New come from the Septuagint rather than from the Hebrew text itself indicates the popularity of this translation in the Christian church. The subtle transformation of Judaism that resulted from the translation of a Semitic document into Greek provided a friendly atmosphere for the revolutionary message that Christianity proclaimed to the world.

The Jewish scriptures, however, provided much more important material for the Christian community than just a vocabulary and a string of Bible verses to be used in establishing the messianic claims concerning Jesus. More importantly, they showed that the same God who had revealed himself in the events of history and through the prophets' interpretation of those events was now made known in a climactic act of self-disclosure. God had spoken in former times through Israel's leaders and prophets; he had acted on behalf of his people through men chosen for the purpose. When it was God's will to call the Hebrew nation into existence, for example, he had raised up Moses as their leader. When Pharaoh objected to their leaving for the Land of Promise, God had delivered them in a series of mighty acts. When Israel was a loosely organized confederation of tribes, subject to strife within and depredations from without, God had appointed David to unify his people under a single, effective government. After the end of Judah's punishment in the Exile, God had "anointed" Cyrus to give official permission for them to return to their land.

And along with these works of God on behalf of his people, God had sent his word to Israel by way of his chosen ones, the prophets. They had sought to warn the nation of the consequences of infidelity, and to lead the people back to the covenant relationship that had been established at the birth of the nation. They had denounced the popular worship of Yahweh, which had become either perfunctory or pagan, or both. The sense of community within the nation had been destroyed by the greed of the rulers and their oppression of the poor. And in times of national crisis Israel had come to rely on alliances with heathen nations, rather than on the God who had redeemed her from bondage in Egypt. By scathing condemnation, by touching appeal, and by symbolic acts, the prophets had sought to call Israel to repentance and to a return to her privileged status as the people of God.

Powerful as God's word and his acts in Israel's history had been, they had not succeeded in recalling all the people to their covenant responsibility. Most of the people either refused to heed or else vehemently rejected the message from God. What God had been speaking all through Israel's history had never been really comprehended by his people. Now, however, with the coming of Jesus, the final word was being spoken. The true significance of what even the prophets themselves had understood only imperfectly was now made known. The work of revealing God that Jesus had begun was now being carried on by the illuminating work of the Spirit which the Risen Lord (as the community called him) had sent in their midst. It is wholly appropriate, therefore, that Peter begins his sermon on the day of Pentecost (Acts 2; especially vs. 15) with the announcement that what the people of Jerusalem have seen taking place is in fact the manifestation of God's Spirit that was promised through the prophet Joel.

The Central Redemptive Act

The decisive point in the whole drama of divine redemption has now been reached: Jesus has triumphed over the forces of evil, and the deliverance promised through the prophets has become an actuality. Both the direction that human destiny will take and the assurance of God's ultimate victory over evil have now been irrevocably established through Christ. The power of evil will never again be so great, nor the impotence of man to combat it so hopeless, now that Jesus has died and risen.

But Jesus is not merely the last and greatest of the prophets, suffering a more tragic martyrdom than those before him. For this community.

Jesus is unique. He cannot be thought of as one Saviour among many; he cannot be identified with Osiris, or Orpheus, or Dionysus, even though titles and epithets similar to theirs are ascribed to him. Neither can it be admitted that other religions have any claim to true and full knowledge of God. The community regards even Judaism as an incomplete religion, distorted because of the people's unbelief. The chosen people has forfeited its right to the promises of God, and the new community is the true Israel and the heir of the promises. Judaism still stands in a place of special privilege as the channel of God's self-disclosure, but this privilege will be retained only by those of Israel who respond to the new word that God has spoken through Jesus Christ.

Misguided men had seized Jesus and had him put to death. Their intentions were good, since they were trying to preserve the true religion in Israel in the face of his denunciation of their religious institutions. But they failed to perceive God's real intention. By a curious paradox, their very misunderstanding had resulted in Jesus' redemptive death and subsequent resurrection. By their wilful opposition to God's anointed, they had unwittingly shared in the fulfilment of the divine plan of redemption. The Jewish leaders had thought that by getting Jesus out of the way they would put an end to another of the disruptive movements that kept Palestine in constant turmoil and periodically brought down the wrath of Rome. He was a real threat to the established religion and to the nation's continuing existence. After Jesus had been put to death, the leaders may have supposed that their plan had succeeded. After all, the followers of Jesus had scattered or had at least dropped out of sight, and the whole disturbance seemed to be at an end. Now, however, the followers were expressing a completely different interpretation of the events: seeming defeat had brought a decisive triumph. The doom of the evil powers was now certain, as was the long-awaited consummation of the rule of God.

Although the community agreed on the redemptive significance of the death of Jesus, it did not agree on the precise connection between his death and the defeat of evil. Evil is not to be thought of here as a philosophical abstraction: for the first-century man, it was a personal matter. That is to say, evil existed as personal forces with which the universe, the community, and the individual were all involved. In the Hebrew tradition (Gen. 3), evil was a personal being, called simply "the serpent," who introduced to Adam and Eve the idea of questioning the will of God, and then of rebelling against it. In late Judaism, the tempter was identified as Satan—i.e., the Adversary. In the Book of Daniel, interstellar space is peopled with demonic beings so powerful that they can delay the messengers of God (Dan. 10). This dualistic conception of evil, together with its elaborate notions about angels and demons, was probably adopted by the Hebrews during the period of contact with the Persians, whose religion was characterized by a sharp division of cosmic forces into the good and the evil, engaged in constant warfare. Whatever the source, it is certain that in the Palestine of Jesus' day evil was conceived in this way. Sin is thought of as transgression of the divine law or as rebellion against the divine will, but in both cases the sinner has taken his cue from Satan, the Adversary. So successful has Satan been in his God-defying programme that there is actually a kingdom of Satan, whose ruler can be described as "the god of this age" (II Cor. 4:4).

In addition to his demonic aides, Satan is assisted by men who submit themselves to his purposes and thereby gain extraordinary powers. Others are involuntarily possessed by one or more demons, and thus come compulsorily under Satan's control. The result of such seizure may be simple disobedience toward God, or it may take the form of mental or physical aberration: epilepsy, insanity, dumbness. When a qualified exorcist commands the demons to come out of such an individual, they must obey, however reluctantly. Jesus was pre-eminent as an exorcist, as the Gospels' emphasis on this aspect of his ministry attests. Jesus' words in Mark 3:27 clearly imply that before the constructive work of establishing the rule of God can be completed the kingdom of Satan must be destroyed. And in order to accomplish this, Satan himself must be overcome and rendered impotent; hence the statement about first binding the strong man and then plundering his house. In the wonderful works that Jesus performed, the community recognized the power of God. To the extent that the rule of Satan was being overcome, the rule of God was already making itself evident in their midst. As Jesus phrased it, "If it is by the finger of God that I cast out demons, then the kingdom of God has come upon you." It was the conviction of the community that Jesus did accomplish his marvellous acts by the power of God at work through him, and that therefore his coming brought about the dawn of the long-awaited new age.

Yet the works of healing and exorcism, important though they were in checking Satan's activities, did not deal with the root of the matter—the defeat of Satan himself. To achieve this, Jesus had to die as the decisive factor in the messianic woes that would bring in the rule of God. Like a woman bringing forth a child, the new age could arrive only after much suffering.

The direct relation between Jesus' death and Satan's rout is implicit throughout the New Testament, but a variety of figures is used to spell out its meaning. In Mark's account (10:45), Jesus speaks of his coming death as a *ransom*, the implication being that he liberates men by the sacrifice of himself, and thereby makes possible their release from enslavement to the powers of the Evil One. Some scholars even translate the last phrase of the Lord's Prayer (as Matthew records it) as, "and deliver us from the Evil One." Sin is the result of an alliance with Satan. At first, the alliance is voluntary, but as it continues the victim becomes increasingly helpless under the diabolical domination. The kingdom of Satan is made up of the demons and men under his sway. Only in the act of total dedication to the will of God by which Jesus went to the cross was it possible for Satan's stranglehold on the human race to be broken. The community is convinced that the death of Jesus accomplished this, and that his resurrection demonstrates that deliverance—salvation—has been accomplished.

To the community, however, the death of Jesus meant more than just the destruction of Satan. It had great creative significance as well. One of the major elements of Hebrew faith was the conviction that sacrifice was essential to the establishment and maintenance of fellowship with God. This approach had been challenged and even rejected by some of the prophets—by Isaiah (1:12-15), for example, and Amos (5:21, 22)—but it remained a fundamental tenet of Jewish belief. And in the years following Israel's return from the exile in Babylon, the Jews had actually elaborated and expanded their system of sacrifice. The priestly viewpoint was that relationship with God had always been brought about through sacrifice. It was true of Abel (Gen. 4:4), of Noah (Gen. 8:20-21), and of Abraham (Gen. 15:7-11). The book of Leviticus develops this principle at length, and points out the significance of specific sacrifices in the complex cultic regulations. Behind this complicated system, however, there is one basic conviction: that sinful man can approach God and enjoy his blessing only through an appropriate and adequate sacrifice. This belief achieves its loftiest expression in the prophecies of Second Isaiah, who depicts the true servant of Yahweh as the one who dies as a sacrifice in order that benefits might come to his people. His act of complete self-giving effects an atonement—that is, an at-onement—which makes the people at one with their God, even though their rebelliousness has alienated them from him.

So it is in keeping with Hebrew tradition that the sacrificial significance of Jesus should be a major theme in the preaching of the early community. The simple kerygmatic statement was, "Christ died for us" (Rom. 5:8), but Paul elaborates this into a more complex theology of the cross (Rom. 3-5). Still other figures are used by later New Testament writers to spell out the meaning of Jesus' death. In the Letter to the Hebrews, for example, there is a remarkable synthesis of Greek and Hebrew modes of thought in explaining the significance of the cross. Here the basic motif is the Day of Atonement, ancient Israel's most solemn occasion, on which the High Priest entered the inner sanctuary to offer sacrifice for the sins of the people. The earthly sanctuary is contrasted with the true Holy of Holies (that is, the heavenly and eternal sanctuary), in a manner reminiscent of Plato. Just as earthly phenomena are but the shadow of the heavenly substance, according to Plato, so for the author of Hebrews the earthly temple is only a copy of the divine prototype in the heavens. It is to this perfect sanctuary that the ideal priest, Jesus, has brought his own perfect sacrifice—himself. Similarly, Hebrew and Greek elements are brought together in the Gospel of John, where Jesus is both the *Logos* (a familiar term in Greek philosophy to describe the rational principle inherent in the natural world) and the Lamb of God (common in Jewish sacrifices; see Chapters 13 and 14, below).

As priest and as *Logos*, Jesus must not only have access to God, but must be able to identify himself with man. Although both the Letter to the Hebrews and the Gospel of John appear to represent fairly advanced stages of theological development, they are equally insistent on the genuineness of Jesus' humanity. Hebrews stresses that Jesus was tempted as other men are, and the Gospel of John reminds us repeatedly that Jesus, like all men, was on occasion hungry, thirsty, joyous, and pained.

In spite of the differences in background among the New Testament writers, and the resulting differences in their explanations of the meaning of Jesus, these men remain true to the basic conviction that was transmitted to them in the *kerygma:* that the same Jesus who suffered and died under the Roman procurator, Pontius Pilate, is the risen and glorified Lord who has the paramount role in the divine plan by which man may be reconciled to God.

The Confident Hope of the Community

As the community understood it, there would have been no triumph in the death of Jesus if it had not been succeeded by the resurrection. The spark that had fanned into flame the dying zeal of the disillusioned disciples was the experience of meeting the resurrected Christ. It was upon this confrontation by the Risen Lord that their authority as apostles rested, for it was he who had charged them with the mission of preaching the gospel of the kingdom.

The tremendous significance that the community attached to the resurrection was not just that a man had come back from the grave: similar instances of resuscitation occur in the stories of the Old Testament (I Kings 17; II Kings 4) and in Jesus' own ministry (Mark 5:21-42; Luke 7:11-17). But this time, God, in raising Jesus from the dead, had attested his acceptance of the sacrificial death of Jesus on the cross. The resurrection is God's public witness to his designation of Jesus as Son of God. As such, it is not merely another sign that the new age had dawned with the coming of Jesus; it is the decisive act of God, demonstrating to all that the rejected Jesus of Nazareth has been declared Lord and Christ, triumphing over sin and death. The new age, anticipated in the mighty works that Jesus performed, has now begun. Its beginnings are small and unpretentious, but its final triumph will come in the Day of Consummation, when Jesus will return in glory and the kingdom of God will be established in its fullness.

Since the community expected this consummation in the very near future, no effort was made at first to relate the resurrection of Jesus to the resurrection of the faithful. It was only when the first generation of Christians had begun to die off, and the expectation had not yet been fulfilled, that the community had to think through this problem.

Yet, crucial as the resurrection was, it was not a matter of common knowledge. Jesus appeared, raised from the dead, only to "chosen witnesses" (Acts 10:41), and was visible only to those who would meet him with faith. The continuing manifestations of God through the Spirit at work in the community provided tangible proof that Jesus had been raised, since it was he who had sent the Spirit according to the promise of God (Acts 2 ; Joel 2). The belief in the resurrection was a contagious affair, transmitted by heart-to-heart contact with those who had seen the risen Lord. Most of the people who lived in the very city where the appearances had taken place scoffed at the claim that the members of the community were making. Lacking an eye to see and a heart to understand, the sceptics dismissed the report as nonsense or worse. The very fact that the members of the community did not agree entirely on the locale and circumstances of the resurrection appearances complicated things even further, as we shall see in the discussion of the Gospels. But to men of faith, this experience of Jesus raised from the dead provided the final seal of his Messiahship.

The community was persuaded that the redemptive role of Jesus would not come to an end with the resurrection, however. Rather, at the time of the consummation, he will appear as judge of all men, both those who are alive at the time and those who will have died before his coming. This theme appears widely in the Gospels and epistles. For example, the account of Paul's address in Athens, as recorded in Acts 17, reads, "God has fixed a day on which he will judge the world in righteousness by a man whom he has appointed, and of this he has given assurance by raising him from the dead." Even in the Gospel of John, in many ways so different from the other Gospels, it is the "word" of Jesus which will judge the dead (5:20-24). The early circle of Christians was convinced that this man who was wholly dedicated to the will of God would serve as the standard by whom God would judge all men.

This drama of redemption not only describes the destruction of the power of evil but also calls attention to man's moral condition and responsibilities. It assumes that man's sin constitutes a barrier between himself and God that can be removed only through God's initiative. As Paul makes plain explicitly, the death of Jesus is viewed as a sacrifice that removes the barrier of sin between man and God. Furthermore, through Jesus' death God discloses that he loves all men and forgives the sins of even the worst. Jesus had already stressed God's forgiveness in his teaching (Mt. 6:12, 14; Lk. 15:11-24), and that same forgiveness has now been demonstrated in the reconciling act of God through the death of Jesus. God is now promising to men in the here-and-now forgiveness of their sins, the Spirit to strengthen them for life and work, the defeat of the forces of evil, and a sense of oneness with others in the community of the new covenant. For the future, the offer of forgiveness means vindication of the righteous and punishment of the wicked, and the final transformation of all mankind and even of the creation itself in the new age of God's rule.

The Literature Produced by the Community

How could such extravagant claims ever have arisen? Or, to put it another way, what relation do these claims of the early community have to the teachings of Jesus? Was Jesus' original message one of simple piety that subsequently became overlaid with the theological embellishments of the early church, or did the community develop along lines already laid down by Jesus? To answer these questions, we must turn to the New Testament itself. Quite surprisingly, in view of the importance these events were to take on, non-biblical sources provide only fragmentary evidence on the beginning of Christianity, and none of them adds anything significant to our knowledge of Jesus.[3] We are limited, therefore, to the material preserved in the pages of the New Testament.

THE HISTORICAL ACCURACY OF THE WRITINGS

To a generation of students trained to search for truth objectively, the commitment of the New Testament writers to the Christian faith might seem to disqualify them as dependable reporters. Only when a man can detach himself from the events he is observing, it is claimed, is he in a position to make a reliable record of those events. In point of fact, however, neither historians nor reporters of the news in contemporary periodicals are content with "the bare facts." In addition to the events they describe, they are concerned with the larger meaning of each occurrence. To put it another way, only when an occurrence is supplemented by an interpretation does a happening become an event. Even the selection of the events to be reported calls for some amount of interpretation. A politician reporting to the people is always careful to omit the less happy aspects of his record. A nation at odds with a former ally will surely not publicize the more cordial relations of an earlier day. Selectivity is an inescapable part of reporting, and inevitably involves interpretation.

Similarly, the presuppositions of the historian influence the records he produces. A mad mathematician who thought that Euclidean plane geometry was ultimate truth could scarcely be relied on to review a treatise on solid figures and three-dimensional relationships. Frequently, when we reject evidence on the ground that it lacks objectivity, we do so, not because we have weighed the evidence and found it wanting, but because we do not accept the presupposition on which the evidence rests. This kind of difficulty is important to bear in mind when we are dealing with the rise of Christianity. Contemporary records of the crucifixion in Roman archives would interpret the death of Jesus in a far different light from what we find in the Gospels, but the Roman records would not automatically be more "objective" because they were non-Christian. The Jewish traditions recorded in the Talmud (the official collection of rabbinic commentary on the Torah) describe the death of Jesus as the execution of a criminal of whom the world was well rid, rather than as the revelation of "the power and wisdom of God" which Paul understood the crucifixion to be. Clearly, the Talmud's response to Jesus is just as much a matter of bias as is the favourable response of the early Christians.

---

[3] Cf. M. Goguel, *The Life of Jesus*, pp. 98, 99. London : Allen & Unwin, 1933.

The demand that the records of early Christianity be objective—in the sense of being uncommitted to a point of view—is a foolish one: no such records exist. Although historians of early Christianity would welcome other records relating to the life or death of Jesus, whether written from favourable or unfavourable viewpoints,they would still be written from *some* point of view. To acknowledge that all historical records are interpretative is not to put an end to all serious historical investigation, however; it simply reminds us that to understand any movement in history we must try to examine from the inside the convictions and practices of the group in which we are interested. Whether or not we share the presuppositions and conclusions of the group is quite another matter.

So in order to comprehend the beginnings of the Christian community we must try to enter into its life and thought. Although Jesus himself wrote nothing, so far as we know, the writings included in the New Testament are carefully preserved records of the impact of his message and actions on his associates and their followers. These writings constitute, therefore, the primary sources for the study of the rise of the Christian community.

A distinguishing characteristic of Hebrew-Christian faith is its conviction that God has revealed himself through history, through the concrete life-situations of human experience. "What happened" is of paramount importance, therefore, because the community recognizes that it is through historical events that the nature and purpose of God are revealed. It was because the Jewish and Christian communities had lived through these historical experiences that they had a basis for interpreting them as they did. The records, however, include what we would call "the facts," not because the community wanted to have an objective record of what happened, but because of the significance it attached to them. The deliverance of Israel from Egypt was given a place of prominence in the Hebrew scriptures, not to satisfy the curiosity of latter-day archaeologists, but because it was understood as revealing the mighty hand of God redeeming his people from bondage. Similarly, contemporary references in the New Testament—such as the names and territories of Roman governors in Palestine—though of great interest to the modern critical student, are included only incidentally by the writers, who are far more concerned with the religious significance of the events described. The traditional approach to history is to ask first, "What happened?" and then, "What does it mean?" In studying the New Testament, however, we must reverse this procedure. The writings furnish the interpretation, and the student must seek to discover the "what happened" that lies behind the records.

THE NATURE OF THE LITERATURE

A further complication in the study of the New Testament arises from the fact that it is not a single unified work, but an anthology of diverse writings serving a variety of objectives and originating in widely scattered parts of the empire over a range in time of about a century. There is no "plot" running from one section to another, as in a novel or biography. In fact, the first four books retell the same story four times in succession, with significant variations. These four writings (called *Gospels*, the Anglo-Saxon equivalent of the Greek root *euangelion*, meaning "good news") relate excerpts from the life and teachings of Jesus, but their lack of completeness and their obvious eagerness to convince the reader set them apart from ordinary biography.

To complicate matters still further, the writers of these fascinating little works begin their accounts at different points and differ somewhat on the order and circumstances of the events of Jesus' life. The first and third of this series, Matthew and Luke, start their narrative with the birth of Jesus in Bethlehem. Mark's Gospel, the second in the series, begins the account with Jesus as an adult submitting himself to baptism by John. The last of the four, John, opens with a magnificent, semi-philosophical prologue that relates Jesus to the eternal Word of God, which has existed from before the creation of the universe. Not only do the Gospels start at different points; they also differ in content, both in major matters and in details. Yet in spite of these differences, a good bit of the material is parallel in all four (e.g., the story of the Passion), and many narratives and sayings are recounted in almost identical form by the first three Gospels. Before discussing the probable origin of these books, and the reasons for their similarities and differences, we shall look briefly at the other types of writings found in the New Testament.

Immediately following the Gospels, as the books are arranged in our New Testament, comes a vividly written account of the beginnings of the community in Jerusalem and of those phases of its spread that are connected with Paul, the man who took Christianity to Europe. A comparison of the opening words of this book, called The Acts of the Apostles, with the third Gospel reveals that Luke and Acts are volumes one and two of what was originally a single work, and that Acts is simply a continuation of the narrative begun in Luke. It is written in excellent Greek, and provides our only source of knowledge about this earliest stage in the expansion of Christianity. We can, however, check its information against the letters of Paul, where parallel accounts of certain key events appear. Acts also gives us valuable summaries of the apostolic preaching referred to earlier in this chapter. Although these are obviously not verbatim reports of the speakers' words, they appear to reflect the themes and emphases of the original Christian preachers.

Following without transition upon Acts are the letters of Paul. "Epistle" is too formal a term to apply to these writings; they are informal missives from the founder of the Gentile churches, exhorting the members to serve more diligently, rebuking error and moral defection in their midst, and explaining to them the solutions to problems that had arisen in the course of their corporate life. So we must not expect elaborate or systematic treatments of either ethical or theological matters here; that sort of teaching had been carried on by Paul during his extended sojourns in the various cities where churches were established. Both the scope and content of Paul's thought, therefore, have to be inferred from his letters; they are not readily apparent to the casual reader who ignores the background situations that evoked them. The nearest approach to an ordered discussion of Paul's convictions is found in the Letter to the Romans, addressed to a church that Paul had not founded and had not yet visited at the time of writing. In the pages of Romans he deals in an orderly way with the relation of Christianity to Judaism—a controversial issue that he discussed at fever pitch in his letter to the Galatian church (Gal. 1, 2). In addition to discussing specific problems, Paul's writings include personal observations and recollections, prayers, and portions of early Christian hymns (Phil. 2:1-10). Although a modern analyst of Paul's thought might wish for a more systematic statement from him, these vivid letters have an immediacy and a warm personal quality that a theological treatise would almost certainly lack.

Earlier in this chapter, in our discussion of the *kerygma*, we assigned the date A.D. 52-53 to the first letter of Paul to the Corinthians. This approximate date is inferred from comparing the account in Acts 18 of Paul's trial before Gallio with an inscription found at Delphi, across the Gulf of Corinth from the city of Corinth itself. The inscription relates the proconsulship of Gallio to the reign of Claudius, and makes it almost certain that Gallio came to Corinth in the year 51. If, as is probable, Paul left Corinth not long after the trial, it must have been some time between 52 and 54 that he sent from Ephesus (I Cor. 16:8) his first letter to the church in Corinth. With this point of chronology relatively well fixed, we can infer the approximate dates of Paul's other letters: from about 50 to 60.[4]

---

[4] For a full discussion of the Pauline chronology, see Foakes-Jackson and Lake, *The Beginnings of Christianity*, Part I, Vol. 5, Note 34. For a reconstruction based

Closely allied with the thought of Paul and his mode of interpreting the Christian faith are four writings that, though they are called letters, seem to lack the personal warmth of the epistles that are unmistakably Paul's. These include Ephesians, I and II Timothy, and Titus, the last three of which are commonly grouped together and called the Pastorals. All of them seem to come from a community that was more highly organized than the church was during the lifetime of Paul. Some scholars believe that personal notes written by Paul while in prison are embedded by the unknown author—who shared Paul's point of view but not his vocabulary—in these writings that purport to come from the pen of Paul.[5] The power of Paul's understanding of the gospel and the influence of his epistolary style are strongly apparent in these writings. The practice of writing under the name of a bygone man of prominence is abhorrent to us who have been reared in a strict tradition of copyrights and safeguards against plagiarism. But these laws are of recent origin, and the ancients knew no such highly individualistic conception of authorship. Just as the Homeric hymns bear the great poet's name even though they come from a later time, so many of the late Jewish writings bear the honoured names of Baruch, Enoch, and Ezra, who lived centuries or even millennia earlier.

Among the later writings of the New Testament are several others that were also written under the names of the earliest leaders of the church; yet their style and content make it clear that they were written at a later date. The epistles of Peter and James are among this group. The three letters of John have traditionally been ascribed to the disciple John, but there is considerable doubt as to whether the John associated with these writings was the apostle John, a disciple of the apostle, or simply a leader in the church of Asia Minor by the name of John.[6] Even the Gospel of John does not identify its author, although it gives a prominent place to "the disciple whom Jesus loved," who may or may not have been John the apostle. In spite of the valuable historical data that this gospel gives us on the location of John the Baptist's activity, and on the chronology of the Passion week, the writer's interest is more theological and mystical than biographical. The dialogues between Jesus and his questioners, instead of coming to a conclusion, sometimes slip over almost imperceptibly into affirmations about Jesus. An example of this tendency is the interview of Jesus with

---

solely on the letters of Paul, see J. Knox, *Chapters in a Life of Paul*. London : A. & C. Black, 1954.

[5] For a technical discussion, see P. N. Harrison, *The Problem of the Pastorals*. London: Oxford, 1921.

[6] *Cf.* M. S. Enslin, *Christian Beginnings*, pp. 447-451. New York: Harpers, 1938.

Nicodemus, whose original questions are only partially answered before Jesus begins a discourse, which in turn gives way to an exposition by "John" of the significance of Jesus (Jn. 3). The claims of Jesus to Messiahship, which are usually only implied or indirectly stated in the first three Gospels, are boldly proclaimed in the fourth Gospel. It is clear, then, that the Gospel that bears the name of John is more concerned with the significance of Jesus for Christian faith than with what Jesus did and said. Because the Gospels of Matthew, Mark, and Luke share a common framework and great verbal similarity, they are often called the Synoptics—i.e., they represent a common perspective. Their relative freedom from the theologizing that marks the Gospel of John suggests that they were written earlier. But why would such basic documents not be written down at the very beginning of the movement? Since we lack any contemporary evidence of the beginnings of the community, we can only guess at the answer.

THE ORIGIN OF THE WRITINGS

There can be little doubt, however, that Paul's letters are the earliest of all the documents of the church that have come down to us. They make no mention of the Gospels, nor do they even hint at the existence of such writings. There are allusions to the words of Jesus (e.g., I Cor. 11:23 ff.), and on one occasion Paul is reported as quoting a saying of Jesus that is not preserved in the Gospels (Acts 20:35). Yet Paul apparently did not have access to any written records of Jesus' life and sayings, and what knowledge he did have was probably transmitted orally by the earliest followers of Jesus in the course of their preaching and instruction of converts to the new movement. From the amount of space devoted to it in the Gospels, the end of the present age and the coming in fullness of the new age was a major concern of the community. And, since this fulfilment was expected to come very soon, there seemed no point in making permanent records of the words and works of Jesus. Few could read and write, and the end of the present age was at hand. Clearly, the most efficient and effective way of preserving the recollections of the Messiah was by word of mouth.

To the modern mind, such an informal procedure seems quite unreliable, but in the Jewish tradition the disciples of any teacher would remember his teachings verbatim, and transmit them in turn to their own pupils. The literature of the Talmud was built up by this method, with the period of oral transmission extending in some cases for centuries. Apparently the materials that were later incorporated in the Gospels were used by the early missionaries sent out by the community

The "Wailing Wall," a part of the massive masonry built by Herod to enclose the area around the Jewish Temple. Sections of masonry like this are all that remain of the network of structures connected with the Temple in the time of Jesus.

to convert their hearers to belief in Jesus' messianic role, and to give ethical instruction to people in the newly established communities. Some critics suggest that the sayings ascribed to Jesus in the Gospels are at times simply a reflection of the needs and problems of the later church, and not a part of Jesus' teachings at all. They claim, for example, that Jesus would not have used the term "church" in counselling his disciples, since this designation of the Christian community did not come into use until a decade or two after the group had been established. Since the Aramaic word that Jesus would have used, *Qahal*, was often applied to the ancient community of Israel, it is possible that Jesus did use this word in referring to the new covenant community that he was calling into existence through the gospel.

In any event, it is certain that the Gospels achieved their present form at a later stage in the developing life of the church, probably after the catastrophic events connected with the destruction of the Temple and the scattering of the Jewish community in A.D. 70. This calamity seems to be behind the emphasis on the judgment that was to fall on the city as recorded in Mark 13 and in the parallels in Matthew 24 and Luke 21.

A careful comparison of the Greek text of the Synoptic Gospels makes it clear that Mark was the first of the three, and that the other two have used Mark as their base, together with certain supplementary material. The additional tradition about Jesus that Matthew and Luke share is usually designated simply as Q, from the German world *Quelle* (source). Both these Gospels include other material that is peculiarly their own. All the material that we find in the Synoptic Gospels presumably came from the common fund of oral tradition used by the Christian preachers, although Q may have been written down as a collection of the sayings of Jesus before the Gospels were composed.

Each of the writers of the Gospels wanted to preserve accounts of Jesus' teaching and the crux of his career. But each of them also had his own specific purposes in mind. Mark seems to be eager to show that the Messiahship of Jesus was kept a secret, and that it was for this reason that his own people did not receive him. Matthew describes Jesus as the giver of the New Law. His Gospel emphasizes moral responsibilities, and it is divided quite artificially into five sections (cf. 7:28; 11:1; 13:53; 19:1; 26:1), like the Five Books of Moses. Again like the ancient Torah of Israel, the heart of the New Law is given through God's chosen spokesman on the Mount (Mt. 5, 6, 7).

In addition to his interest in the New Law, Matthew has other special concerns. From the opening chapters, we are struck by his heavy emphasis on the ways in which Jesus fulfilled the Old Testament prophecies. So eager is the author to press home this point that on occasion he shapes scriptures to fit the facts of Jesus' life (Mt. 2:23), or modifies the facts to fit the prophecies (Mt. 21:2-5). Strange as this procedure seems to us today, this method of interpreting the scriptures was widely used in Jewish circles of the time. Some of the Dead Sea Scrolls have provided us with examples of this interpretative method.

Matthew is the only one of the Gospels in which the word "church" appears (16:18; 18:17), which suggests that the author had strong interests in the church as an institution. The way in which Matthew has used the word "church" gives to it certain organizational connotations that the Aramaic word in Jesus' original saying would not have had. Similarly, the sense of the nearness of the coming of God's kingdom is heightened in Matthew. When Matthew's version of Jesus' sayings about the future of Israel's hope is compared with the parallels in Mark or Luke, it is clear that Matthew wants to stress his conviction that the fulfilment is to be in the immediate future.

Luke too had his special interests. He was anxious, for example, to place the beginning of Christianity in the context of contemporary Gentile history; hence his frequent references to Augustus, Tiberius, and other Roman rulers and officials. More than any of the other Gospel writers, he points out that Jesus' mission was not just to the Jews, but to all men. Notice that when he records the Parable of the Good Samaritan it is a Samaritan, not a Jew, who fulfils the Jewish Law. This parable, along with the parable of the Prodigal Son, the Rich Man and Lazarus, and other familiar gospel materials, is recorded only by Luke, who apparently was drawing them from a special source, referred to by scholars simply as L. His account begins in Jerusalem, not Bethlehem, since he wants to show the movement of the gospel from the centre of the Jewish world (Jerusalem) to the centre of the Gentile world (Rome).

When we join the book of Acts to the Gospel of Luke, as it originally was, we see that the author has tried to give a running account of the beginning of Christianity from the announcement of the birth of Jesus to the close of the work of Paul, the church's greatest missionary. The account is by no means complete, but by correlating Acts with the letters of Paul we can reconstruct the main development of the Pauline wing of the early church as it moves out from the original Jerusalem community.

From as early as the second century, there has been a lively interest in the place of origin of each of the Gospels. All four were in use in the church at Rome by the middle of the second century, and Christian writers there were quoting from them all, although Matthew and Luke seem to have been the favourites. Ignatius, who was bishop of Antioch about A.D. 115, quotes extensively from the Gospel of Matthew, which suggests that it was popular in his city at an early date. Another bishop who lived in this period, Papias of Hierapolis in Asia Minor, reported that Matthew had written down in Hebrew (he should have said, Aramaic), a collection of Jesus' sayings, and that Mark had written the memoirs of Peter about the time of Peter's death in Rome. Papias' statement is often interpreted as referring to the Gospels that bear the names of Matthew and Mark, but this inference can hardly be correct. Although the Gospel of Matthew has a deep interest in relating Christianity to Judaism (by attention to the Law and by demonstrating that Jesus is the fulfilment of scripture), it quotes from the Greek Old Testament (the Septuagint) and is careful to interpret any Semitic words that it uses. Other conjectures about the place of origin of Matthew's Gospel have been Caesarea and Alexandria. Possibly Papias' remark should not be interpreted as applying to the Gospel at all, but rather to a collection of sayings of Jesus—possibly Q or a similar document now lost.

Papias' statement about Mark's connection with Peter fits in well with the evidence from the New Testament that Mark and Peter were together in Rome, although both the references to Mark's presence in Rome are from books of doubtful authorship (II Tim. 4:11 and I Peter 5:13). It would be foolish, therefore, to dogmatize, but all the evidence—slim as it is—points to Rome as the place of origin of the Gospel of Mark.

In trying to determine where the Book of Acts was written, we find some evidence that its author (or the author of one of its sources) was from Macedonia. On the strength of this assumption, Greece has been suggested as the place of writing of Luke-Acts, but just as strong a case can be made out for Rome, where, according to the Pastorals, Luke was aiding Paul during Paul's imprisonment (II Tim. 4:11). A third possibility for the place of origin of the book is Antioch, which figures so importantly in the narrative of Acts, and which was the home town of Luke, according to some of the early church fathers.

The persistent tradition concerning the Gospel of John is that it was written in Ephesus, the chief centre of Christianity in Asia in the second century. Papias, the bishop referred to above, speaks of an elder named John as the author of the fourth Gospel, distinguishing him from John the Apostle, but implying that the Elder John had also seen Jesus in the flesh. Other writers of the second century confirm that there was a leader of the church in Ephesus named John, and add that he was originally from the priestly caste in Jerusalem and that he lived to a great age. It may be that he was the leader of a circle at Ephesus that produced the Gospel and letters of "John," even though he may not have written all or any of the works associated with his name. The production of the collection of writings that bear the name of the apostle John but were written by members of a group is analogous to the process by which the Pastorals originated. Written by followers of Paul who knew well his concerns and modes of expression, it seemed the most natural thing to attach his name—and thereby his authority— to these later writings.

Certain cities seem to have shown a preference for one Gospel over another. For example, Antioch preferred Matthew; John was the favourite in Asia Minor. But some churches preferred to have all four Gospels woven into a single narrative. Tatian, a scholarly leader of the church in Syria in the latter part of the second century, prepared a composite version of the Greek Gospels, known as the Diatessaron, a fragment of which was found in 1933 in the ruins of a Roman military outpost called Dura-Europos on the banks of the Euphrates. In time, however, the authorities condemned the circulation of the condensed version of the Gospels, and the collection of four came into universal use.

THE WRITINGS ARE CONSOLIDATED

We shall see in the works of Paul and his associates how the early community tried to communicate its message to hearers outside Palestine. In the prologue of the Gospel of John, and especially in the Letter to the Hebrews we have evidence of the attempt to establish contacts between the Gospel and pagan intellectual thought. But as the community expanded, foreign influences began to find their way into Christian circles, and the leaders had to define somewhat sharply what was to be considered as truth and what must be rejected as error. This stiffening attitude against the perversion of the gospel gradually increases, from the first hints in the letters of Paul (especially in Colossians) to the fairly rigid outlook in the Pastoral Letters, to the firm stand against false teaching evident in Jude and II Peter. Throughout the history of the church, the orthodox position is defined over and over again in reaction against emerging heresy.

The New Testament canon closes with the Apocalypse, or Revelation. In spite of popular misconception, this book is primarily an encouragement and an appeal to fidelity addressed to those who are about to undergo severe persecution by the empire for their Christian faith. It does include a vivid account of the end of the present age, portrayed with elaborate symbolism and filled with descriptions of fantastic creatures and fearsome beasts, but the writer's chief concern is to comfort and strengthen, not to terrify. The historical situation that called forth Revelation seems to have been the impending persecution of Christians during the reign of Domitian as a result of their refusal to participate in the worship of the emperor. This would mean that the book was written about the year A.D. 95.

The date usually assigned to the letters of John, the letter of Jude, James, and first letter of Peter is the latter part of the first century. The second letter of Peter was probably written some time afterward, since the author seems to have depended on the Book of Jude, and the letters of Paul had already achieved the status of scripture (II Pet. 3:15-16).

The Literature Becomes Scripture

By the early years of the second century, therefore, the writings that were to constitute the Christian canon of scripture, on a par with the Torah of the Jews, had already been written and were in wide circulation. It was once fashionable for scholars to place the writing of the Gospel of John at A.D. 150 or later, but the discovery of a papyrus fragment of this book far up the Nile, written in a scribal style of the early second century, forced the revision of this theory.[7]

Various hypotheses have been advanced to account for the bringing together of these diverse writings into a single collection. Professor E. J. Goodspeed is convinced that the first New Testament writings to be circulated as a group were the letters of Paul.[8] According to this hypothesis, the letters were collected soon after Paul's death, in order to make available to all the churches these masterful writings that had been sent to individual congregations.

In the middle of the second century, a brilliant, though unorthodox, leader in the church by the name of Marcion published his own list of the Christian books that he thought worthy of the true faith. He was violently anti-Judaistic, and would admit as genuinely Christian only the letters of Paul and an expurgated edition of Luke-Acts. It was perhaps to counteract the influence of Marcion that the church began in the middle of the second century A.D. to make lists of the books that were to be considered authoritative for the life and faith of the church. Some books—such as James, Hebrews, and II Peter—were argued over for more than a century, but the core, consisting of the Gospels, Acts, and the letters of Paul, constituted what very soon came to be known as the New Testament. Lists of the accepted books are found in the writings of Clement of Alexandria and in a scrap of late-second-century manuscript called the Muratorian canon. In both cases the lists are basically the same as our New Testament, with a few additional books that we now exclude. The second-century fathers of the church quote from the new collection of sacred writing with the same sense of authority with which they refer to the ancient Torah of Israel.

It would be a mistake to assume that the writings included in the canon were the only important ones circulating in the early church, or that they are the only reliable ones for reconstructing the history of

---

[7] Cf. Sir Frederic Kenyon, *Our Bible and The Ancient Manuscripts*, p. 148. New York: Harper, 1940.

[8] Edgar J. Goodspeed, *Introduction to the New Testament*, pp. 210-221. Chicago: University of Chicago Press, 1937.

the spread of Christianity. Three examples of the types of writings that have come down to us from this period suggest the importance of this non-canonical literature.

The First Epistle of Clement, prompted by a dispute within the church at Corinth about A.D. 95, is a lengthy exhortation from the church of Rome to the brethren at Corinth, appealing to them to submit to ecclesiastical authority. In discussing the issues, the author of I Clement lays down clearly the lines along which the doctrine of apostolic succession (i.e., the transmission of spiritual authority within the church and from generation to generation) was to develop.

A second type of writing is the *Didache*, or Teaching of the Twelve Apostles, which consists of moral instruction and regulations for the administering of baptism and the Lord's Supper. This document, which is thought to have been written before A.D. 100, is the earliest treatise on ecclesiastical regulations that has survived, and may in fact be the first that was ever produced.

The third type of writing is the general exhortation to a church, as exemplified by the seven letters ascribed to Ignatius, bishop of Antioch in Syria. Although these letters purport to have been written by him as he was on his way to martyrdom in Rome, they are little more than

A fragment of the Gospel of John, written on papyrus in Egypt around 125 A.D. and found on an island in the Upper Nile.

a series of appeals to churches everywhere to submit to the authority of their bishops, and to allow moral exhortation to take the place of the exciting predictions about the future that were so popular in the church in times of persecution.

Although these writings are regarded as inferior in quality to those included in the canon, they nevertheless aid us greatly in filling in the details of the life of the Christian community at the close of the first century and the beginning of the second.

It is hard for us today to comprehend the tremendous changes that took place in the first hundred years of the Christian community's existence. Beginning, as an obscure Jewish sect in one of the border provinces, it came to have thriving groups of adherents in the major cities of the empire. Its voice was so strong that it could not be stilled even by imperial edict. Although its original leaders were "uneducated, common men" (Acts 4:13), it produced a literature that continues to exert a profound influence, and to appear in new editions on the lists of "best sellers" in our own day. The secret behind the incredible appeal of this community is the message it proclaimed, and the faith that its members shared in the significance of Jesus of Nazareth as the Messiah of God.

We must now turn back to our earlier question regarding the relation of the community's claims to Jesus himself. Are the extravagant claims of the community based on the mission in life to which Jesus had dedicated himself? To answer this question we must turn to our basic sources for knowledge of Jesus' life and his message: the Synoptic Gospels.

❧❦

THE CONDUCT
OF JESUS' MINISTRY

After the death of Jesus, the little community of disciples began to tell their unique story to the world. Their account began with the career of another figure in contemporary Jewish history—John, called "the Baptizer" (John the Baptist). All four of our Gospels acknowledge John's significance, and the traditions dealing with him emerged during

New Testament readings relevant to this chapter and the next two are the Gospels of Mark, Matthew, and Luke. For the present chapter, the following reading will be helpful: the entire Gospel of Mark; Matthew 1:1–4:11; and Luke 1:1–4:13. Other relevant passages are cited in the course of the chapter.

the earliest period of the oral tradition. An understanding of his mission
and message will help us to understand the mission and message of
Jesus Christ himself.

John the Baptist

John appeared on the restive scene of Jewish history during the
twenties of the first century A.D. (Lk. 3:1). He was only one of many
who emerged during the long, hard decades of Roman domination
claiming a special message from God for the Jewish nation. But none
of the others had such an immediate or permanent influence as John did,
an influence attested not only by our Gospels, but by the principal
Jewish historian of the period, Flavius Josephus.[1]

We first hear of John as a fiery preacher living and carrying on his
mission "in the wilderness." The Gospel of Matthew says it was the
"wilderness of Judea" (3:1), but it is more likely that the scene of
most of his activities was in transjordanian Peraea, in the territory of
the tetrarch Herod Antipas, who finally arrested him. The Gospel of

---

[1] Josephus has a very important reference to John in his *Antiquities*, Book XVIII,
5, 2, which provides a supplement to our gospel material.

The modern road from Jerusalem to Jericho in the "wilderness of Judea," with the Dead Sea and the delta of the Jordan River in the background.

John specifically mentions two sites of John's activity: Bethany across the Jordan, and Aenon near Salim (1:28; 10:40; 3:23). Archaeological discoveries have made it possible to locate both places—Bethany in Peraea on the east bank of the Jordan River near the ford between Jericho and Rabboth Ammon, and Aenon thirty miles north on the west bank of the Jordan, not far from Galilee.[2] Both sites are located near travel routes. Although John withdrew to the wilderness, he preferred places that were accessible to people from both Judea and Galilee, and to the many travellers who journeyed along these highways. The Gospel record tells us: "And there went out to him all the country of Judea, and all the people of Jerusalem" (Mk. 1:5; Matthew adds "and all the region about the Jordan," 3:5).

We have little specific information about John before he appeared in the wilderness. Chapter 1 of the Gospel of Luke deals with incidents that purport to relate the birth of John, but the reliability of this section has been seriously challenged. The section does show us, however, that John was an important enough figure to have become legendary, and it undoubtedly contains certain reliable historical data.[3] Which of the details have a historical basis is by no means clear, but one element is extremely difficult to explain in legendary terms: John's priestly

---

[2] For discussion and bibliography see Carl H. Kraeling, *John the Baptist*, pp. 8 ff. London : Scribners, 1955.

[3] The section in Luke dealing with John's birth is part of a larger body of tradition about John that was no doubt originated and treasured by his disciples. On the basis of literary criticism, a strong case can be made to demonstrate that the two birth stories, one of Jesus and the other of John, were brought together by Luke or by a source on which Luke was dependent. There was a tendency on the part of the early church to relate Jesus and John in every way possible.

79

descent. It has been suggested that this is the one specific detail of John's early years that gives us a clue to his subsequent career.[4] John's fiery attitude may be explained in part as revolt against some segment of the priestly group in Jerusalem, in the manner of the revolt of the Dead Sea Sect (see p. 43). Although there is no evidence that John was actually a member of this sect, its conflict with the Temple priests may shed light on John's own rebellion. We cannot account for John solely in negative terms, however, for his message and his whole demeanour suggest that he was a man driven by divine necessity to carry out a task commissioned by God.

THE PROCLAMATION OF JOHN

John the Baptist was burdened with a proclamation: He felt called upon to announce an imminent crisis in world history. The content of his message is preserved in the Q source (Mt. 3:7-10 = Lk. 3:7-9). Here such phrases as "wrath to come" and "axe is laid to the root of the trees" indicate that John was proclaiming the event that had long been awaited by the Jews: God's final judgment upon the evil of the world. That John was speaking in eschatological terms is further suggested by his reference to another one who "is mightier than I" (Mt. 3:11 = Lk. 3:16), who was about to appear. He is one whose "winnowing fork is in his hand to clear his threshing floor, and to gather the wheat into his granary; but the chaff he will burn with unquenchable fire" (Lk. 3:17 = Mt. 3:12). So superior is this Mightier One that John declares himself unworthy even to untie his sandals (Mk. 1:7; Mt. 3:11; Lk. 3:16). He is none other than the Messiah, through whom God is to execute his final judgment.

What could men do to prepare themselves for this impending crisis? The Gospels tell us that John was "preaching a baptism of repentance for the forgiveness of sins" (Mk. 1:4; Lk. 3:3), and that repentance was the one thing demanded of all men. Further, they were to demonstrate the sincerity of their belief in John's word and of their repentance by being baptized "confessing their sins." The call to repentance was all-inclusive; no one was excepted. For John to make such a proclamation to the Jewish people, in whose religious life repentance played so prominent a role, seems somewhat strange. The concept of repentance was central to the Temple sacrifice and was taught in every synagogue. In what sense, then, did John's call to repentance differ from traditional practice?

The answer must be found in John the Baptist's claim that his call to

---

[4] Kraeling, *ibid.*

repentance and baptism had behind it the immediate authority of God. His word by implication brought the whole of the institutional religion of the Jews under judgment, for, like the prophets of old, John challenged the adequacy of conventional religious life. Only those who believed that God was acting through John would sense the newness of the crisis and would respond to this new call to repentance in preparation for the imminent judgment that the "Coming One" was to usher in. And so John had to say to some complacent Jews: "Do not begin to say to yourselves, 'We have Abraham as our father'; for I tell you God is able from these stones to raise up children to Abraham" (Lk. 3:8; Mt. 3:9). Being a descendant of Abraham, one of the chosen race, or complying with the requirements of traditional religious practice, provided no exemption from the repentance preached by John. The traditional forms were being challenged, since John believed himself called by God to summon all men, particularly his fellow Jews, to a new act of repentance and faith. John called men to repentance in expectation of the judgment and the forgiveness of sins that God was to effect through the Mightier One who was soon to come in judgment. To turn expectantly to his coming, to fear his power to judge, and to hope in his power to forgive—these were the supreme needs of men.

THE BAPTISM OF JOHN

This repentance was consummated in an act of baptism, and the fact that John was popularly called "the Baptizer" indicates the importance of baptism in his mission. Many efforts have been made to explain the origin of John's emphasis on baptism.[5] A few have seen non-Jewish influences, but in general it has been explained on the basis of Jewish practices. Purificatory ablutions held an important place in Levitical law, and in John's own day proselytes were required to submit to a rite of baptism. We have already seen that the Dead Sea Sect and the Essenes paid particular attention to frequent baptisms. So ablutions and baptisms were not new to Judaism.

There were, however, three distinctive features of John's baptism that combined to make it a new phenomenon in Jewish religious history. First, it was to be received only once by each individual. Second, it was required of all men, Jews as well as Gentiles. Third, it was inextricably related to another baptism that would be administered through the Mightier One who was presently to appear. It is this third point that concerns us most. In the Gospel of Mark, John is reported to have

---

[5] For a thorough discussion see Kraeling, *John the Baptist*, pp. 95-122.

said: "I have baptized you with water; but he will baptize you with the Holy Spirit" (Mk. 1:8). Matthew and Luke, drawing on the Q source, add "and with fire" (Mt. 3:11; Lk. 3:16). It is probable that the words "with the Holy Spirit" are an addition to John's message springing from the later Christian understanding of baptism in Christ. Certainly a baptism "with fire" would be more in keeping with John's message of judgment, for fire was a familiar metaphor for judgment.

John's baptism in water anticipated a baptism that the Messiah would administer when he appeared for final judgment, and it was incomplete without the baptism of the Mightier One. Consequently, the forgiveness that John claimed for his baptism was to be consummated only in that coming baptism. Those who entered John's baptism confessing their sins in true repentance, and awaiting the imminent coming of the Messiah, had the assurance that in his coming baptism of "fire" their sins would be forgiven.

John exhorted those who came to him to be baptized to "bear fruit that befits repentance" (Mt. 3:8; Lk. 3:8). "Brood of vipers" he called them (Mt. 3:7; Lk. 3:7), implying their perverseness in thinking they could escape judgment without making a radical change in their life. John was a preacher of righteous living, and like the prophets of old he decried the unrighteousness of the nation. He spared no one. Matthew says he singled out in particular the Pharisees and Sadducees as "vipers," but Luke says John was referring to the multitudes. All three Gospels portray John as fearlessly attacking the wanton Herod Antipas. Perhaps it would be accurate to say that while he preached judgment upon the nation in general, he did not hesitate to be specific. John tested the sincerity of a man's repentance by the quality of ethical living that accompanied it.

The Gospel of Luke has preserved from its special source (L) in a brief summary what is no doubt a typical example of John's teaching:

> And the multitudes asked him, "What then shall we do?" And he answered them, "He who has two coats, let him share with him who has none; and he who has food, let him do likewise." Tax collectors also came to be baptized, and said to him, "Teacher, what shall we do?" And he said to them, "Collect no more than is appointed you." Soldiers also asked him, "And we, what shall we do?" And he said to them, "Rob no one by false accusation, and be content with your wages."
>
> —LUKE 3:10-14

How well organized a religious community John gathered about him we cannot say. The New Testament itself tells us that there was a John the Baptist sect after John's death,[6] and during his lifetime he was apparently surrounded by a close group of disciples to whom he gave a prayer (Lk. 11:1) and who practised a special type of fasting (Mk. 2:18; Mt. 9:14; Lk. 5:33). According to the Gospel of John, some of Jesus' first disciples were former followers of John (1:35-42). Chances are that only a few close disciples among the many who submitted to John's baptism gathered together in a closely knit community, and that the others were united only by their expectation of the coming of the Mightier One at the end of the present age.

In the prophetic voice of John many heard the Word of God with all its divine authority sounding forth anew. But now they stood on the threshold of a new age. In John's word the prophecies of old were finding their fulfilment.

JESUS AND JOHN THE BAPTIST

Among the multitudes attracted by the forceful message of John was a young Jew from the village of Nazareth in Galilee by the name of Jesus. In simple language, the Gospel of Mark records their meeting: "In those days Jesus came from Nazareth of Galilee and was baptized by John in the Jordan" (Mk. 1:9). On the basis of the account in Mark we would assume the two had never met. In the Gospel of Luke, on the other hand, we have a tradition in which the families of Jesus and John are described as being related. Matthew, like Mark, does not connect the families or births of Jesus and John, even though it includes a story of Jesus' birth.

Luke incorporates the tradition from a special source not available to Mark and Matthew. Even if the claim of family relationship is historically accurate, the reference found in these two chapters (Lk. 1 and 2) is full of legendary material. The early church was certain that John was the forerunner of Jesus and that God was at work in John the Baptist. As the two chapters now stand, they may best be understood as stories motivated by the desire of Christians to show that the life and work of John and Jesus must be seen as of one piece and one pattern. The Greek style and phraseology of these two chapters show dependence on a tradition that originated in the Aramaic language, and the traditions here go back to the Aramaic-speaking Christians— probably from an early period. Nevertheless, in these chapters we gain more certain information about the faith of the early church than about the relation of Jesus and John before the baptism. The stories are reminiscent of Jewish *hagadah*, which contain many delightfully

---

[6] Acts 18:25; 19:3. See Chapter 6.

The lower end of the Jordan Valley, looking toward the hills of Judea, near the traditional site of Jesus' baptism.

imaginative stories told about some important person to emphasize a salient truth about his life. In this sense they are legendary. It is significant that these two chapters contain materials that undoubtedly were used for purposes of worship and liturgy in the early church (see p. 375). Clearly, the content was not valued at first primarily as biographical data.

To understand the use to which the material in these two chapters was put saves us from one pitfall. For to read these chapters as literal history would demand a mechanical interpretation of the life and work of both Jesus and John. We would have to assume that what John and Jesus would do had been predetermined at birth, and that they were simply filling out a pattern of life. But this interpretation does violence to the whole picture of the ministry of both. The nature of their meeting and the subsequent relation between them contains all the elements of spontaneous encounter and response. Although the early church was right in its claim that John was the forerunner of Jesus, there is nothing in the record of that encounter to suggest that they were mechanical robots playing roles in a drama that they knew beforehand or that left no room for freedom of decision. What then, was it that brought Jesus to John? Our answer to this question will tell us something about Jesus as well as about John.

We have already seen that at the heart of John's message was his proclamation of the "day of wrath," the imminent coming of God's Messiah to pronounce judgment upon the world. It was to this proclamation that Jesus, along with many others, responded. The young Galilean saw in John the chosen herald of what was to be God's most decisive action in human history, the moment toward which all prophecy pointed. In John the voice of prophecy—which was believed to have been silenced since the last prophet, Malachi, had spoken—now sounded forth afresh. The Q source records a discourse between Jesus and certain unnamed persons whose curiosity had apparently been aroused by John's activity. Jesus says to them:

> What did you go out into the wilderness to behold? A reed shaken by the wind? What then did you go out to see? A man clothed in soft raiment? Behold, those who are gorgeously apparelled and live in luxury are in kings' courts. What then did you go out to see? A prophet? Yes, I tell you, and more than a prophet.
>
> —LUKE 7:24-26; MATTHEW 11:7-9

John was a prophet in the sense that he spoke with all the authority implicit in the prophetic office. The word that he spoke had already become an instrument of the judgment it anticipated. John was "more than a prophet" in that from the long line of prophets in Israel he had been chosen to be the immediate forerunner of the coming Messiah. That is why Jesus says, "I tell you, among those born of women none is greater than John" (Lk. 7:28; Mt. 11:11). John stood upon the threshold of "that day" foretold by the prophets in which God was to usher in a new age.

Because Jesus believed that John was the bearer of a God-given message, he went to him and sought baptism. This act of Jesus caused concern in the church from a relatively early date. That Jesus had been baptized by someone believed to be "lesser" than himself became an increasingly important factor as time went on and as the John the Baptist sect emerged in opposition to (or at least in competition with) the early church. Furthermore, John's baptism was for "the remission of sins." How could the church, which believed in its Master's sinlessness, accept Jesus' baptism?

In the Gospel of Mark there is no indication of these problems. In Matthew, on the other hand, John hesitates to baptize Jesus and tries to prevent him from being baptized, saying: "I need to be baptized by you, and do you come to me?" (Mt. 3:14). Matthew has Jesus explain why he is baptized—"for thus it is fitting for us to fulfil all righteousness" (Mt. 3:15). In other words, Jesus was baptized because it was

God's will as declared by Jesus himself. The Gospel of John shows a further development in the tradition (John 1:28-34). The author uses the baptism narrative primarily to announce publicly who Jesus is— "the Lamb of God who takes away the sin of the world." In both Matthew and John, we see the early church trying to deal with a difficult problem and trying to rewrite the story in such a way as to resolve that problem.

The doctrine of the sinlessness of Jesus involves far more than a historical analysis of the baptism, however. In reality, it is an article of faith that derives from the belief in the resurrection and Lordship of Jesus the Messiah rather than from any evidence concerning Jesus' own consciousness of sinlessness. Jesus never makes such a claim of sinlessness for himself. Quite the contrary, at one point he is reported to have answered someone who addressed him as "good teacher": "Why do you call me good? No one is good but God alone" (Mk. 10:17-18). It seems that in Mark it was not a consciousness of sinlessness or of sinfulness, but humility in the presence of the righteousness of God, that led Jesus to utter these words. On the basis of the record in the Gospels, Jesus' submission to John's baptism indicates his conviction that he must submit himself to the judgment and forgiveness of God preached by John. There can be no doubt that the author of Mark believed in the sinlessness of Jesus, and yet he saw no difficulty in the baptism. Perhaps the very fact that Jesus did not claim to be sinless was crucial to the Christian belief in his sinlessness. For the crucial point of sinlessness is the possession and enactment of positive virtues such as humility, and an active submission to the will of God.

But there is more to be said about Jesus' baptism. John's call to baptism was to all the nation, and in baptism Jesus identified himself with the sinful nation and with those in Israel who were anticipating God's decisive action in the imminent future. With them he looked beyond the formal channels of God's gracious activity to a direct and immediate revelation of his power in some new way.

The baptism by John was a moment of crisis and decision in Jesus' life, and it marked a vocational turning point. The cruciality of this event became embedded in the earlier tradition. In describing the baptism, the Gospel of Mark says: "And when he came up out of the water, immediately he saw the heavens opened and the Spirit descending upon him like a dove; and a voice came from heaven, Thou art my beloved Son; with thee I am well pleased" (Mk. 1:10-11; cf. Mt. 3:16-17; Lk. 3:21-22). In these words recorded in Mark we have an account of the way the early Christians described Jesus' anointing by God for his messianic office. From this moment on, he set out on the path of messianic ministry that culminated on the cross. The words "Thou art my Son" are taken from Psalm 2, which even in pre-Christian times had been interpreted as referring to the messianic king. And the phrase "with thee I am well pleased" is an allusion to a passage from one of the Servant Songs of Isaiah (42:1). To the early church, Jesus was designated by God as Messiah and Suffering Servant from the time of the baptism.

Was Jesus himself conscious of his messianic role at this point? There are those who say no, insisting that the account of the baptism is an invention of the early church and has no foundation in the experience of Jesus. These scholars argue that he was not conscious of his messianic office at the baptism, or, as some would say, at any point in his ministry. Others answer yes, but with this qualification: Jesus was conscious of his messianic role at the time of his baptism, but he had no clear idea of the direction it would follow. Instead, the meaning of his mission unfolded gradually to him throughout his ministry. Still others claim that not only was Jesus conscious of his messianic role, but also that he had a fairly clear understanding of the pattern it was to follow.

Obviously we are dealing here with a very difficult subject. It is always dangerous to say what transpired in the mind of another person, but that is exactly what Mark seems to do when he reports that the voice from heaven spoke directly to Jesus. The Gospel of Matthew changes the account somewhat by having the voice speak not to Jesus personally, as in Mark, but to the assembled crowds. Whereas in Mark the words are, "Thou art my Son," in Matthew we read, "This is my Son" (Mt. 3:17). In the latter version we have a public announcement of Jesus' Messiahship; this makes no appreciable difference in Matthew, since the story of Jesus' birth reveals from the beginning who he is. In Mark, however, we have what has been called the "messianic secret." From the beginning of the Gospel of Mark, only Jesus and the demons are aware of his messianic identity. Not until Peter's confession at Caesarea Philippi (Mk. 8:29) do the disciples even begin to understand, and they are still really ignorant of the full implications of his Messiahship until after his death and resurrection.

It is impossible to decide solely on the basis of the baptism narrative to what extent, if at all, Jesus was conscious of a unique mission at the time of his baptism, or what he conceived this mission to be.[7] To this

---

[7] It is possible that Jesus later on in the ministry actually told his disciples about his inner experiences at baptism, thus providing the basis for the traditional account in Mark. Although this is not impossible, it is hypothetical and has no basis in the Gospels. An hypothesis based on the evidence of the Gospels would seem more acceptable.

extent the early church was right: It understood the baptism not as an isolated event but in relation to Jesus' entire ministry, death, and resurrection. What can be said is that there is no clear evidence that John recognized Jesus as the Mightier One at the time of baptism. Later, when John was in prison, Luke records that he sent to Jesus asking: "Are you he who is to come or shall we look for another?" (Lk. 7:19). This would imply that subsequent events in Jesus' life led John at least to consider the possibility that Jesus was the one he expected.

These later events also suggest that the baptismal experience of Jesus was crucial for his subsequent mission, for he began his own public ministry shortly afterward. Few would contend that he spent much, if any, time as a disciple of John. All that intervened was the sojourn in the wilderness that is reflected in the temptation narratives found in Matthew and Luke.

So the baptism stands at the crossroads, and in it God laid upon Jesus a mission and a message. The nature of his message concerning the kingdom of God, his relation to that kingdom, his miracles, and his death all point to a unique line of travel from baptism to death. It is only by investigating all these aspects of the ministry that we can construct an adequate interpretation of the baptism, and come to an understanding of the messianic consciousness of Jesus in relation, not only to the baptism, but to his total ministry. When this is done, then perhaps it will appear that the early Christian interpretation of the baptism had a historical foundation in Jesus' submission to God and Jesus' intention at baptism—an intention that was meaningfully revealed in later developments.

The Ministry of Jesus

THE TEMPTATION

Each of the Synoptic Gospels records that after the baptism and before the beginning of his actual ministry Jesus underwent a period of temptation in the wilderness. The account in the Gospel of Mark merely mentions this experience. But an examination of the parallel passages in Matthew and Luke shows that the Q source had a far more lengthy account of it (Mt. 4:1-11; Lk. 4:1-13). Jesus emerged from the baptism with a question: What course of action was he to take in view of the impending crisis proclaimed by John and his new relationship to God that culminated in the baptism experience? It is not surprising that Jesus withdrew for solitary prayer and thought at the beginning of his ministry, as he was to do over and over again later on. He sought guidance for his course of action. Nor are we surprised that he was "tempted by Satan," as Mark says. It is clear that the Gospel writers understood the temptation experience as an encounter between the Messiah and the Prince of Evil, whose power he had come to destroy. Jesus' victory in the beginning was the first of a long sequence of victories over Satan that would ultimately end in the destruction of Satan's power by God through the death and resurrection of Christ.

No one else was present with Jesus during this period in the wilderness. If the lengthy description of what transpired (as found in Q) has any historical basis, it must have been confided by Jesus to his disciples at a later time. Although there is no specific mention of such a confidence, it is not impossible.

According to Matthew and Luke, the temptation consisted of three encounters with Satan. Each encounter involved a request and an offer on the part of Satan, and each was one aspect of a single choice that Jesus had to make in coming to an understanding of his mission in life. Would he identify himself with the Jews who hoped that God would establish an earthly kingdom by reviving Israel as a political and military power? Or would he identify himself with those who felt that God would establish his kingdom in a way unknown to the political connivings of man? The second alternative meant renouncing the claims of temporal power and glory as false and inadequate; it meant

The Mount of Temptation, identified by local tradition as the place where Jesus was tempted by Satan. The belt-like monastery on the side of the mountain contains a tiny chapel in a cave, which is supposed to be the place where Jesus spent forty days and nights in prayer.

trustful and expectant waiting for God to disclose his power in his own way and in his own time.

The Gospels tell us that Jesus took the latter course. But, although the temptation represents a crucial moment of decision for Jesus, the experience persists throughout his ministry. The decision that Jesus made in the wilderness was reaffirmed continually up to and including the very moment of death on the Cross, when the powers of evil threatened him with their final taunt. The dramatic presentation of the temptation in Q must not lead us to a mechanical interpretation of Jesus' battle with the forces of evil, or to the assumption that his triumph was automatic or the outcome inevitable.

THE BEGINNING OF THE MINISTRY

Mark tells us that "after John was arrested Jesus came into Galilee preaching the Gospel of God" (Mk. 1:14). This may mean that Jesus did not begin his own preaching mission until after John had been arrested; or it may mean that only after John's imprisonment did Jesus go into Galilee. From what the Synoptic Gospels tell us, it is difficult to decide just what the course of events was. Although they seem to say that the ministry began in Galilee, they do not exclude a prior ministry in Judea. The Gospel of John, in fact, actually records a ministry in Judea before Jesus' departure to Galilee (John 1:35-42). If there was such a Judean ministry, however, we have no reliable information about it.

John the Baptist was imprisoned by Herod Antipas in the fortress of Machaerus and was eventually executed for reasons more complicated than those given in the Synoptic Gospels. These Gospels tell the story that John attacked Herod Antipas for his marriage to his brother's wife, Herodias (Mk. 6:17-29; Mt. 14:3-12). Such a marriage was not legally valid from the Jewish point of view and offended Jewish sensitivities. But Herodias was even more offended by John's criticism, and during the course of a dinner party she connived to gain Herod's consent to execute John. This story, including Salome's famous dance, bristles with historical difficulties. It is very probable that John, along with other Jews, had indeed criticized Herod; however, it is highly improbable that this single act would have provided sufficient grounds for executing so popular a person as John. Josephus, in relating the death of John, implies a more serious cause. Here is what he has to say about Herod's attitude toward John:

> And when everybody turned to John—for they were profoundly stirred by what he said—Herod feared that John's so extensive influ-

ence over the people might lead to an uprising (for the people seemed likely to do everything he might counsel). He thought it much better, under the circumstances, to get John out of the way in advance, before any insurrection might develop, than for himself to get into trouble and be sorry not to have acted, once an insurrection had begun.[8]

In view of the unsettled conditions of the Jews and their tense relations with Rome, such language suggests only one thing: Herod feared that John might provide the motivation for a new revolt against Rome. And a rebellion would place Herod in an embarrassing situation with Rome, who looked to her subject rulers to keep peace at any price

Jesus undoubtedly regarded the death of John the Baptist with grave concern, and it must have had a profound influence on his understanding of his own mission. For he was beginning his ministry under the shadow of the death of John, who, if we can trust Josephus' account, soon became a martyr in the eyes of the people. When we read Mark's account, it is plain that his story of John's death is intended to sound a note of doom throughout his Gospel. But it is more than a literary device. For Jesus to take up the work of John was to court from the outset the same fate that John had met. Indeed, Jesus' words in Luke (13:34) refer to the tradition that the prophets and those sent from God were doomed to suffer abuse and humiliation. This theme, which must have been proverbial among the Jews, was further substantiated by John's death.

THE PLACE AND DATE OF THE MINISTRY

That was the situation, then, when Jesus came into Galilee preaching. According to Mark, the ministry of Jesus can be divided geographically into four parts: The first period was in the villages and countryside of Galilee (Mk. 1:14-7:23). Then came a brief journey to the northwest, to the borders of Tyre and Sidon, and then east to the neighbourhood of Caesarea Philippi in the territory of the tetrarch Philip (7:24-9:29). Next, there was the last journey to Jerusalem, beginning from Galilee and continuing through Judea (9:30-10:52). Finally, there was the ministry in Jerusalem (11:1-15:47) and the events leading up to his death.

Not all the Gospels follow this scheme exactly, however. Luke omits the journey to the northwest, but includes a lengthy passage called the "Peraean Section" or the "Great Interpolation," which has as its setting a journey to Jerusalem through Samaria and Peraea (Lk. 9:51-

---

[8] Josephus, *Antiquities*, XVIII, 5.

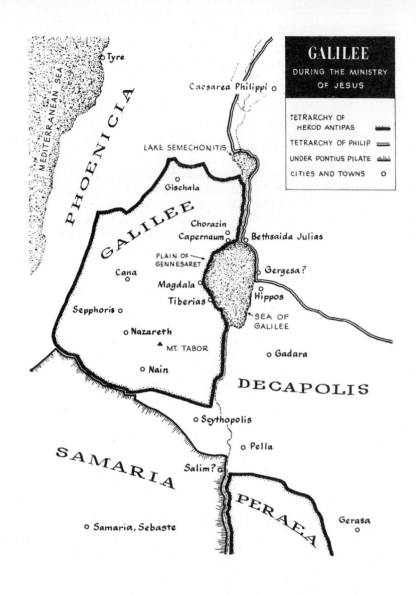

GALILEE

DURING THE MINISTRY
OF JESUS

TETRARCHY OF
HEROD ANTIPAS

TETRARCHY OF PHILIP

UNDER PONTIUS PILATE

CITIES AND TOWNS   o

MEDITERRANEAN SEA

o Tyre

PHOENICIA

Caesarea Philippi o

LAKE SEMECHONITIS

o
Gischala

GALILEE

Chorazin
Capernaum o

Bethsaida Julias

PLAIN OF
GENNESARET

Gergesa?

Cana
o

Magdala o

Hippos

Tiberias o

SEA OF
GALILEE

Sepphoris o

o Nazareth

▲ MT. TABOR

o Gadara

o Nain

DECAPOLIS

o Scythopolis

SAMARIA

o Pella

Salim? o

PERAEA

Gerasa
o

o Samaria, Sebaste

18:14). On the basis of a variant reading of the Greek text, it is possible to interpret Mark in such a way as to include this Peraean phase of the journey.[9] Since the Peraean section of Luke contains much of the author's special material (L), it is very probable that he used it as an opportunity to insert details that he could not fit in elsewhere. Nevertheless, both the journey through Peraea and the journey to the northwest can be strongly defended.

The length of Jesus' ministry has always been the subject of debate. The major problem is raised by the chronology of the Gospel of John, which refers to two, and probably three, successive Passover festivals in Jerusalem during Jesus' ministry. According to this account, then, the ministry must have lasted at least two or three years. Mark, followed by Matthew and Luke, on the other hand, includes only one journey to Jerusalem, one Passover, and leaves the impression of a short ministry of about a year. The Gospel of John, even more than the Synoptics, reflects a theologizing tendency.

In general, the Synoptic chronology of a shorter ministry of one to two years seems preferable, and this conclusion is substantiated by the political and psychological climate of the ministry. Jesus began his work as a marked man because of his relationship with John the Baptist. The atmosphere was explosive. Once his mission caught fire, it was not long before political and religious authorities were aware of it. Mark dates the gathering of strong opposition too early in the ministry (Mk. 3:6), but he is very persuasive in describing the speed with which it gained momentum.

When we try to ascribe actual dates to the ministry, we run into even more problems. The one specific date given in the Gospels is Luke's dating of the ministry of John the Baptist in the fifteenth year of Tiberius Caesar (Lk. 3:1). Since Tiberius' reign began on the 19th of August, A.D. 14, John's ministry would fall between the 19th of August in A.D. 28 and the 18th of August in A.D. 29. Some scholars have suggested that Luke wrote his Gospel in Syrian Antioch, where a variation in calculating imperial years occurred in the first century A.D. If so, these figures might be revised downward to between October 1, A.D. 27, and September 30, A.D. 28. The crucifixion of Jesus has been dated variously from A.D. 28 to A.D. 33 on the basis of the date that Luke gives.

---

[9] The reading in question is found in Mk. 10:1. This is a technical problem discussed in any reputable commentary on the Gospel of Mark.

The Preaching of the Kingdom

The Synoptics open their account of the ministry of Jesus with a description of his early activities in Galilee. Arriving there under the compulsion of a God-given commission, he set about his task of communicating his message to the people. According to Mark's outline, the one place that might be called Jesus' centre of operations was the little village of Capernaum, apparently the home of Peter and Andrew. Jesus spared no effort in seeking out the places where he could find the most people to listen to him. As a good Jew, he sought out the village synagogues, where, in keeping with the custom of the day, guests were given an opportunity to speak. But he did not limit himself to the synagogues. In the open countryside, beside the sea, on a Galilean hillside, in the homes of friends, old and new, even pausing in his travel along the way, he seized every opportunity to speak to all who came to hear.

We have already seen how difficult it is to determine with any certainty the sequence of events in the ministry of Jesus. The early church had no concern in preserving a detailed narrative account of the ministry, with each incident carefully fitted in chronologically and topographically. But many scholars feel that in Mark 1:21-39 we may have a historically dependable reminiscence of a day's activity in the village of Capernaum in this early period of the ministry. Here we find Jesus both teaching and healing in the synagogue on the Sabbath. Leaving the synagogue, he goes to the home of Simon Peter, no doubt to share in the customary Jewish meal that marked the close of the Sabbath observance. But he is followed by crowds of eager people who come bringing their sick to be healed while they themselves hear more of what this new teacher has to say. This early period, then, was characterized by teaching and healing, and by an enthusiastic response on the part of the people. But before we can understand this popularity, we must look more closely at the meaning of both the "teaching" and the "healing" to which Mark refers.

Mark makes use of two terms in referring to Jesus' message. Occasionally he uses "teaching" (1:21); but at other times he uses the expression "speaking the word" (2:2). Exactly what it was that Jesus was teaching, or what word he was speaking, Mark does not specifically report. Mark, in contrast to Matthew and Luke, records very little of the content of Jesus' teaching, and he is not primarily interested in Jesus as a teacher. In a brief summary, however, he gives the essence of the one all-encompassing message that Jesus sought to communicate

The Sea of Galilee with Mt. Hermon in the distance. Melting snow from the peak provides much of the water for the Jordan.

to the people in various ways. At the very outset, Mark says that the substance of Jesus' proclamation was this: "The time is fulfilled, and the kingdom of God is at hand; repent and believe in the gospel" (1:15). From the beginning to the end of his mission, Jesus sought to confront men with the kingdom of God. On this point all three Synoptic Gospels are in agreement. Most of Jesus' parables and many of his sayings have the kingdom of God as their primary subject, and those that make no specific mention of it can be understood only against the background of the dominant reality of the kingdom.

It was the substance of this message that brought the people in ever-increasing numbers to hear his word. News that a new voice was proclaiming the "kingdom of God" travelled quickly through the Galilean countryside. The ardor of the Galileans had not been extinguished simply because the promises of other messianic prophets had failed to materialize in recent years. No doubt it was already being rumoured about that Jesus had been associated with John the Baptist, and that report alone would have been enough to arouse curiosity. Here was a man who seemed to be taking up where the other had left off. Surely the bitter disappointment over John's fate was quickly dispelled in the minds of many by the prospects of this new proclaimer. When Jesus boldly announced that the time appointed by God for his decisive action had been fulfilled, his hearers, steeped in the popular religious beliefs of the day, recognized the language immediately. It meant only one thing: In a short time God would establish his divine kingdom in all the world. This message had particular appeal in Galilee, for it meant not only release from the iron rule of Rome but also from the hated Herod Antipas. Here, more than in any other place, the Jews had suffered from the economic pressures of alien rule, and for years Galilee had been a seed-bed of revolt against social and economic oppression.

95

To the people of Galilee the coming of the "kingdom" meant that the mighty of this world would be brought low and the poor and oppressed would be lifted up. Since most of those who heard Jesus came from the poor and lowly, it is no wonder that what he had to say aroused their interest and revived their hopes.

Jesus' listeners felt a note of intense urgency in the words of this young Galilean when he talked of the imminence of the kingdom. Time was foreshortened, and they were living in the days that the prophets and kings of old had longed to see (Mt. 13:17; Lk. 10:24). Some of the listeners, remembering an old tradition based on the words of Malachi (4:5), hesitated to accept his message, saying that the kingdom could not come until Elijah had first returned. In answer to them, Jesus boldly declared that Elijah had appeared in the person of John the Baptist and had been killed (Mk. 9:11-13). There could be no delay in deciding, for no man could tell in what hour the final bell would toll. Neutrality was impossible; all men were divided between those who were for the kingdom and those who were against it. Men could not serve two masters. While there was still time, men must seek this kingdom with all their hearts, for it is the only treasure worth having.[10]

And what was the way to the kingdom? "Repent and believe the good news" (Mk. 1:15). The actual word that Mark uses for "good news" is *euangelion*, which is usually translated "gospel." The "good news" obviously had a meaning for the author of Mark that it did not have for Jesus. When Mark wrote the "gospel," he included the death and resurrection of Jesus with all the meaning these events had for the faith of the early church. But that Jesus himself brought a message of good news is obvious in all his teaching.

What was this good news? It was that the imminence of the kingdom brought with it opportunity as well as threat, and that God in his love and mercy had delayed its consummation in order that all men might repent and believe. It is at this point that the message of Jesus differed notably from that of John the Baptist. The thought of judgment dominated John's preaching, but, though Jesus in no sense avoided the fact of judgment, he saw it only in relation to God's mercy. It was God's will that not one should be lost. As a shepherd will leave his flock to risk his life seeking for one lost sheep, so God withholds nothing in his search to bring men into the kingdom (Mt. 18:10-14). As a father awaits joyously the return of a son who has strayed afar and has wasted himself in profligate living, so God joyously awaits the return of every man to the kingdom (Lk. 15:11-32).

---

[10] A more detailed discussion of the meaning of the kingdom of God will be given in Chapter 4.

The key word here is "return," which is probably the best rendering of the Hebrew word that we translate "repent." Jesus called men to return to God, who had created them and who was the source of their life. They were to turn from all else that demanded a loyalty above their loyalty to God. But this return depended on their belief, which in turn involved trust in God's love for mankind. In Jesus' message, repentance and faith, return and trust, were inseparable. The one was absolutely dependent upon the other. Jesus proclaimed the nearness of the kingdom as "good news" for men with ears to hear and hearts and minds to receive his message in repentance and trust.

This was the heart of the message, then, that Jesus of Nazareth came preaching. We are told that those who heard it were amazed that he taught "as one who had authority, and not as the scribes" (Mk. 1:22; Mt. 7:28-29; Lk. 4:32). This question of authority was bound to be raised, because of the nature of the message itself: It was concerned with the divine act through which God was to bring to fulfilment his purposes for Israel and for all mankind. Such a message either was or was not authoritative. But inextricably related to the authority of the message was the authority of the one who conveyed it. How seriously the people received the message depended on whether or not they trusted Jesus himself. Either he had God's authority to speak or he had not. There was no possibility of accepting the message without acknowledging the person. The question of who he was and by what authority he spoke was to be the inevitable and decisive question from the day Jesus first proclaimed the "good news." His claim to speak a word about God's kingdom involved an implicit claim of divine authority and raised the question that was to pursue him to the cross: "By what authority?"

To the people, prone to think in terms of external evidence, even the way he spoke raised the question of authority. Although Jesus did not hesitate to use the sacred scriptures to reinforce and substantiate his message, he more frequently spoke and taught as though he were acting under the immediate aegis of the divine will. Unlike the Jewish teachers of his day, who dutifully sought to teach the divine law within the framework of the tradition, Jesus frequently speaks as though God would directly authenticate his words in the hearts of those who hear. Although the influence of the Old Testament permeates his teaching, he rarely seeks authority for his word by referring to it. As a result, he frequently broke with the formal, traditional, and authoritative methods of interpretation used by the scribes. The people were amazed, and rightly so, for Jesus was carrying on his mission in a way that was reminiscent of the prophets. But their line had long since ceased. In the popular mind, it would not be until the coming of the final days, when the Spirit would be poured forth anew, that God would again speak directly to his people. And so, from the very beginning, the question raised by Jesus' proclamation of the kingdom was not merely: What does it mean? Is it true? What must we do? The central question was: Who is he and by what authority does he speak this word?

The Mighty Works

It was not only Jesus' proclamation of the kingdom, the authority with which he spoke, and the urgency of his words that made his "fame spread everywhere throughout all the surrounding region of Galilee" (Mk. 1:28). All four Gospels record that Jesus performed "mighty works," the term used for miracles in the Synoptics.

Even the Jewish opponents of Jesus acknowledged his unique power (Mk. 3.22). The most critical of scholars today recognize that many of the miracle stories had their foundation in actual happenings during Jesus' ministry. On the basis of the Gospels the miracles were of four types: exorcisms (casting out demons), healing of physical ailments, raising the dead, and nature miracles such as walking on the water or stilling the storm. The Gospel of Mark leaves the impression that in the early ministry of Jesus the mighty works made a profound impression on the people of Galilee. In the first four chapters of Mark we find accounts of one exorcism, four healing miracles, and a reference to Jesus' healing many who were sick or demon-possessed.

It is not surprising, then, that the Gospels portray Jesus as a worker of miracles. Furthermore, this was an age that had an intense interest in anything miraculous. Miracle stories clustering about historical personages were common among the Jews as well as Gentiles. These stories were told to enhance the personal status of the hero. In fact, it was common practice to fabricate miraculous incidents for this purpose. A very good example of the importance given to miracles is to be found in the Life of Apollonius of Tyana, written in the third century A.D. by Philostratus, which narrates the journeys of a wandering preacher and wonder-worker whose fame spread around the Graeco-Roman world. In one sense, then, interest in the miracles of Jesus was part of a common interest in miracles shared by many in the Graeco-Roman world.

Study of these stories reveals that in the telling they came to possess a common literary form. For example, an introduction describes the circumstances surrounding the event; the means (often through sacred objects or magical language) by which the miracle is performed is described; and the story concludes with the reaction of witnesses and the results of the miracle.

In the Gospels, the miracle stories are preserved in two forms. Occasionally they provide a context for an important saying of Jesus that comes at the end of the account. In this type, the sayings are as important as the miracles. On the other hand, most of the stories are told as independent units in which the main interest is in the miracle story itself. Study of miracle stories has revealed that certain tendencies were at work controlling the development of the story in the re-telling. Since it is possible to study these developments by comparing Mark with the later Gospels of Matthew and Luke, we can see that the tendencies at work in the oral period continued to operate even after the traditions were written down. In general, three tendencies were at work: the total account was shortened, but explanatory points were added; specific names of persons and places were dropped; indirect discourse replaced direct.[11] Although there are exceptions, careful analysis on the basis of these tendencies usually make it possible to determine how much the stories have been modified, and, where two accounts of the same miracle are reported, which one is the older.

Although the miracle stories in the Gospels resemble the popular miracle stories in many ways, there are important differences. One is the Gospel's emphasis on the miracles as manifestations of the power of God. The "mighty works" were not ends in themselves; they were signs of the kingdom's power. They were told in order to glorify Jesus, but this was not the sole end, as it would have been in the popular miracle stories. Another important difference is the absence in the Synoptics of the use of magical words or sacred objects in the cure. Also, there is a repeated emphasis on faith, which is generally lacking in the secular miracle stories. As the miracle stories were transmitted by the early community, however, they were influenced by the secular form. Occasionally the miracle is heightened, as when Matthew has Jesus heal two blind men instead of the one reported in Mark (Mk. 10:46-52; Mt. 20:29-34). Moreover, there is evidence that the purpose for telling the story sometimes became to glorify Jesus rather than to give a sign of the power of God. Some miracles, such as the Cursing of the Fig Tree, were created by the community to serve this end of glorifying Jesus.

What was Jesus' own view of his mighty works? What did they

---

[11] See Vincent Taylor, *The Formation of the Gospel Tradition*, pp. 119-141. London : Macmillan, 1953.

mean to him? Since we have no grounds for supposing that he performed mighty works before he began his mission, he probably asked himself this same question at the outset of his mission. In the first place, it was out of his deep love and sympathy for human beings that he exerted himself to relieve suffering. To neglect this basic factor in studying the miracles would be as inexcusable as it would be to neglect it in any phase of his life's work. In fact, it provides one criterion for determining the historicity of the miracle stories. For example, the miracle of the Cursing of the Fig Tree (Mt. 24:32-33) raises this question: Is it possible to conceive of this act as consistent with Jesus' normal tendency to act only where human need is involved? Many scholars say no, and insist that the story is the product of the early community's imagination.

But Jesus saw his healing of the sick and exorcising of demons as only part of his total ministry. His preaching and teaching derived from his confidence in the power of God to act on behalf of men, and Jesus saw his miracles as evidences of that power already at work.

The Synoptic Gospels record an incident in which Jesus was accused of being helped by Satan in performing his miracles (Mk. 3:22-30; Mt. 12:24-29; Lk. 11:15-22). He tried to show his opponents the foolishness of this argument by pointing out how futile it would be for evil to assault evil, for the Prince of Evil to help him cast out evil demons. All three Synoptics report this statement: "But no one can enter a strong man's house and plunder his goods, unless he first binds the strong man; then indeed he may plunder his house." To a world that believed sickness to be the work of wicked demons, Jesus says that only if a greater power overcomes the demons can the sick be relieved. The Q source includes in the episode another saying of Jesus: "But if it is by the finger of God that I cast out demons, then the kingdom of God has come upon you" (Lk. 11:20; Mt. 12:28). Here Jesus specifically states that his miracles, accomplished through the power of God, are manifestations of the kingdom of God.

We see, then, that Jesus at no time sought to work miracles for the sake of glorifying himself or of enhancing his own prestige. We have further proof in Jesus' repeated refusal to perform miracles to demonstrate his power. On one occasion, when a miracle was demanded to prove his authority, he replied: "This generation is an evil generation; it seeks a sign, but no sign shall be given to it except the sign of Jonah" (Lk. 11:29; Mt. 12:39). Since Jonah preached repentance, Jesus seems to be saying that those who ask for a sign (in the form of a miracle) show that what they really need is to repent. They are asking for visible proof of God's power.

But, as we have seen, Jesus proclaimed that the power of the kingdom could be known only through trust in God's promise to establish his kingdom. This trust could not be established or proved by tangible signs, but only through repentance, through a return to God in expectation of his love and forgiveness. And so Jesus believed that only those who first trusted God and the power of his kingdom could understand the meaning of the miracles. As a matter of fact, one of the distinctive features of Jesus' miracles was his repeated emphasis on faith as the basis of healing. "Thy faith hath saved thee" is a common theme in the Gospels' miracle stories. And the end is never the miraculous cure but the manifestation of God's power in the inner life of the one who is healed. It is reported that when Jesus visited his home town of Nazareth "he could do no mighty work there except that he laid his hands upon a few sick people and healed them" (Mk. 6:5), to which this significant comment is added: "And he marvelled because of their unbelief."

We have now examined the meaning of the mighty works to both Jesus and the early community. But the question remains: What really happened? On the basis of sound historical judgment we can conclude that *something* happened, but we must keep in mind that in Jesus' day men did not have the knowledge of secondary causes that we have. There were two worlds: the invisible spiritual world, and the visible world of observable phenomena. But these two worlds were bound together by countless invisible creatures—demons, angels, and so on— who lived between the worlds. To Jesus' contemporaries, since all extraordinary events were evidence of the dominance of the invisible world over the visible world, a miracle did not mean the interruption of natural law.

The modern mind reacts in various ways to the different types of miracle. It seems certain that the most common in Jesus' ministry were exorcisms,[12] in which the subjects were people suffering some sort of mental derangement that today we would call a psychosis. In the light of modern psychiatric therapy, these miracles are fairly understandable, since we are dealing with cures that are not totally alien to our experience.

Perhaps the same could be said for the healing of physical ailments. In the Gospels, Jesus cures such diseases as paralysis, deafness, blindness, a withered hand, dumbness, fevers, epilepsy, and leprosy. Again, in the light of the developments in psychosomatic medicine we have a ground

---

[12] For an excellent discussion of the exorcisms of Jesus see S. Vernon McCasland, *By the Finger of God*. London : Macmillan, N. Y., 1951.

of experience that gives us some basis for understanding what might have happened.

But when it comes to the question of the miracles of raising the dead we confront greater difficulties, since none of us has seen a dead man restored to life. There are only two such accounts in the Synoptic Gospels: the raising of Jairus' daughter (Mk. 5:21-43; Mt. 9:18-26; Lk. 8:40-56) and the raising of the widow of Nain's son, recorded only in Luke (7:11-17). Since both persons had just died, we might explain the events by saying that a state resembling death was mistaken for death. But such a state, though detectable to modern medicine, was unknown in the ancient world, and there can be no question that the authors of the Gospels regarded the persons as actually dead.

Probably the most difficult of the miracles to understand are the nature miracles, of which there are three: the Feeding of the 5,000 (Mk. 6:31-45; Mt. 14:13-21; Lk. 9:10-17), the Stilling of the Storm (Mk. 4:35-41; Mt. 8:18-27; Lk. 8:22-25), and the Walking on the Water (Mk. 6:47-52; Mt. 14:23b-33). Although they are the rarest type in the Synoptic Gospels, they have been the subject of the greatest debate. In general, the nature miracles have been explained in two ways. In the first place, they have been rationalized. For example, it has been said that the Feeding of the 5,000 is based on an historic incident, when many people were gathered together and Jesus asked those who had food to share with those who had not. This incident, it is argued, provided the background for the miracle story in which Jesus fed the 5,000 by multiplying bread and fishes. In the second place, there are those who accept the nature miracles as they are. Denying that the stories can be rationalized, they accept them as literal fact and evidences of God's power over what modern man calls the "natural world." If Jesus was truly the Son of God, who would put a limitation on his power?

However we answer this question of what really happened, we must remember one thing: In the Gospels, and in Jesus' own mind, the miracles ultimately had no meaning apart from their being signs of the power of God. Although the honest historian cannot avoid trying to find out what happened, he will be deceived if he seeks the ultimate meaning of the miracles through a rational analysis of the events. Ultimately, any interpretation of the miracles depends on philosophical and theological presuppositions. And a world-view that has no place for a dimension of existence that in some sense transcends what we call the physical or natural world cannot possibly make room for the ultimate meaning that the miracles had for Jesus and the early church. In the last analysis, neither science nor historical research has the final word to say on the meaning of the miracles. For this meaning is found not in the analysis of the events but in the answer to the very question that confronted the people of Galilee two thousand years ago: "By what authority and power" did Jesus do these things? This was the same question that was raised in connection with the preaching of the kingdom. To paraphrase the question: Is it the authority and power of God that is manifested in these occurrences? The final judgment must be one of faith. An affirmative answer has been given both by those who have rationalized the miracles and by those who have accepted them literally. The interpretation of the miracle does not produce faith; rather, faith produces the interpretation of the miracle.

The early Christians, believing in a divine being whose power and purposes they encountered in Christ, saw the mighty works through the eyes of this faith. Early in Jesus' ministry, these works aroused the curiosity of the people in Galilee and contributed to his popularity as a wandering preacher.

The Call of the Disciples

When Jesus began his mission of preaching and healing, the urgency of his task forced him to give up his old pattern of life. He could no longer engage in the carpenter's trade by which he had supported himself and helped to support his family, and his life as an itinerant preacher made it impossible for him to live at home and engage in the family and community life he had known from early childhood. There are suggestions in the Gospels that his family and friends were doubtful about whether or not he should go on with his mission; it is even probable that they attempted to dissuade him from pursuing it further (Mk. 3:21). Nor were the other people in his home town of Nazareth any more enthusiastic about his activities. In fact, it was a mission to Nazareth, which brought a very meagre response, that seems to have occasioned one of Jesus' most familiar sayings: "A prophet is not without honour, except in his own country, and among his own kin, and in his own house" (Mk. 6:4; Mt. 13:57; Lk. 4:24).

Although Jesus' mission meant breaking off former ties, it brought him into a series of new relationships. In all his associations he showed a profound ability to identify himself with people, and he was acutely aware of the interrelatedness and interdependence of human beings. On one occasion, pointing to the crowds of men and women around him, Jesus said: "Here are my mother and my brothers" (Mk. 3:34). His awareness of the interrelatedness of all persons was more than just an intellectual attitude, for in his teaching and healing, in all his rela-

Nazareth in Galilee. An insignificant village in Jesus' day, it was expanded by the Crusaders and given the appearance of a provincial town of northern Italy.

tions, he entered deeply into the lives of others. Daily he took upon himself the sorrows, sufferings, and joys of others. We are not surprised at the later claim of his followers that he bore with them in their sins.

Once his mission had begun, then, Jesus found himself bound to all persons in a new way. But he was related to a few in a very special way, and some of the men and women with whom he came into contact became more than occasional hearers. Most of these "followers" who regularly were in the company of Jesus were from the lower economic and social strata of the Jews. There were a few exceptions, however, such as Joseph of Arimathea, who provided the tomb for Jesus' burial.

We might justifiably refer to this whole group of followers as disciples, for the word "disciple" means a "learner" or "pupil," a category into which all the followers of Jesus would fit. The early church, however, tended to restrict the use of this term to a group of twelve men

who were related to Jesus in a very intimate way almost from the beginning of his Galilean ministry. All the Gospels contain accounts of
the "call of the disciples" (Mk. 1:16-20; Mt. 4:18-22; Lk. 5:1-11). The
fact that there are variations in these accounts suggests some uncertainty about the circumstances of each call, and for most of the
disciples tradition preserved no record at all. But all the narratives
indicate that these "disciples" were summoned for the specific purpose
of sharing in Jesus' ministry. As Jesus put it: "Follow me and I will
make you become fishers of men" (Mk. 1:17).

Throughout much of his ministry Jesus was accompanied by some
or all of these disciples. Mark tells us that he "appointed twelve to be
with him and to be sent out to preach and have authority to cast out
demons" (Mk. 3:14-15). Three of the twelve disciples—Peter, James,
and John—came to play a more important role than the others in Mark's
account; this emphasis may be an accurate indication of the actual situation, and it may also account for the fact that we have very little
information about the rest of the disciples. But at best our information
about the background of any of the disciples is very slight. We know
that there were two sets of brothers, Peter and Andrew, James and
John, and that these four were fishermen. Another, Matthew, was a
tax-collector. About the remaining seven nothing is known, although
it seems safe to say that none of them came from the official circles of
Judaism.

That Jesus should have had a small group of close followers was not
unusual, for it was the custom among Jewish teachers (rabbis) to
gather around them a group of faithful disciples. But there the similarity ends. The rabbis and their disciples were concerned primarily
with the study of the scriptures and the oral tradition. They were eager
to master the proper principles for interpreting the Law. Although
Jesus always taught against the background of the scriptures, and on
occasion even made his own interpretations of it, his primary concern
and the primary concern of his disciples was not the study of the Law
but rather the coming of the kingdom of God.

The bond between Jesus and the twelve disciples grew stronger as
his ministry progressed. Although at first they stayed close to their
Master in his work, the time came when Jesus called them to go forth
to take a more active part in the great mission. A vivid picture of this
occasion is recorded in the Gospels (Mk. 6:7-13; Mt. 10:1, 5-23, 40-42;
Lk. 9:1-6), even though the account as we have it no doubt contains
certain additions of the later church. In substance, though, it represents
Jesus' counsel to his disciples, who were to journey in pairs, carrying
with them no food, money, clothing, or baggage. They were to accept

lodging wherever they were fortunate enough to receive an invitation. Nothing was to encumber them in their work. And so they went forth, trusting only in the power and support of God, whose kingdom they proclaimed, and in Jesus, who had given them their message. Sometimes they succeeded in their mission (Mk. 6:30; Lk. 9:10; 10:17-20); other times they failed miserably (Mk. 9:14-29; Mt. 17:14-21; Lk. 9:37-43). Jesus said when they failed it was because of their lack of faith.

As Jesus' ministry progressed and as his conflict with opponents grew more severe, he confided more and more in his disciples. At the end, when his death was imminent, he took upon himself the almost impossible task of convincing the disciples that his death was a part of the mission that God had laid upon him. He urged them to remain loyal. Jesus had never spoken of discipleship as an easy path, and his death spoke even more effectively of how great was the cost of faithfulness to the kingdom.

This little community of disciples—the men who had answered Jesus' call to the service of the kingdom of God—was one day to become the nucleus of the church. To be sure, their faith was to undergo a radical transformation in the meantime. But that transformation would have been impossible had it not been for their trust in Jesus, which, though halting, grew as they shared in the labours of his ministry.

Fishermen draw in their nets on the shore of the Sea of Galilee in much the same way as they did in the time of Christ.

By choosing twelve men to follow him, Jesus may have intended to symbolize the twelve tribes of the nation of Israel, whose obligations and responsibilities the small community was to assume. And it is true that the disciples were charged with the mission of recalling Israel to God's kingdom, which was at hand. With their Master, they regarded themselves as the faithful remnant of the people of Israel, gathered together to herald the dawn of a new day and a new life.

∿

CHAPTER FOUR

THE CONTENT
OF JESUS' TEACHING

Nnews of Jesus' activities travelled swiftly over the countryside. Wherever he journeyed, enthusiastic crowds converged upon him and his little band of followers. True, any unexpected event was enough to stir the interest of a suppressed people. But there was more here than just a break in the monotony. This man from Nazareth exercised extraordinary powers. In the very synagogue at Capernaum he had healed

New Testament readings relevant to this chapter are the Gospel of Mark, particularly chapter 4; Matthew 5-7, 13, 18, 25; Luke 8; 10:25-37; 15; 18. Other relevant passages are cited in the course of the chapter.

a demon-possessed man (Mk. 1:23 ff.) and a man with a crippled hand (Mk. 3:1 ff.). In that same village a paralytic had been carried to Jesus and the villagers had watched him rise up and walk away healed (Mk. 2:1 ff.). A Roman centurion's paralytic servant had been restored to health (Mt. 8:5 ff.), and it was reported that the daughter of Jairus, a man well known in official Jewish religious circles, had been brought back to life (Mk. 5:21 ff.).

Jesus the Teacher

Episodes such as these, which seemed particularly impressive to the people, were later to be preserved in the oral tradition and were eventually to find their way into one or more of the written Gospels. But undoubtedly there were other occurrences that were eventually lost to recorded memory. For people came from near and far seeking the healing touch of Jesus, sometimes for themselves, sometimes for their friends or relatives whom they brought to him (Mk. 1:32; 2:1 ff.; 3:7). Repeatedly the people exclaimed: "We never saw anything like this!" (Mk. 2:12). It is hardly surprising that "his fame spread everywhere throughout all the surrounding region of Galilee" (Mk. 1:28).

These "mighty works" were not the sole basis for Jesus' popularity, however, for he was joyously burdened with a message. The fires of conviction that burned within him warmed many who came to hear. The people exclaimed not only, "We never saw anything like this," but also, "What is this? A new teaching!" (Mk. 1:27). They gathered around him not only to be healed but also to hear him "preaching the word" (Mk. 2:2). Whether he was on a hillside (Mt. 5:1) or beside the sea (Mk. 2:13; 4:1), he paused to teach; and whenever he did, the people gathered around him. So great were the crowds that assembled along the seashore that sometimes he had to move offshore in a boat in order to teach them (Mk. 4:1). Such was the appeal of his message.

Some of the people called Jesus "rabbi" (Mk. 9:5; 10:51; 11:21; translated "Master" in R.S.V.), a title of respect and honour on the lips of his fellow Jews. The rabbis were respected teachers of the Law and interpreters of the scriptures to whom the Jewish people looked for guidance. The title, rabbi, was usually reserved for students of the Law who, having associated themselves with some well-known rabbi for training, finally became teachers in their own right. So far as we know, Jesus never had this sort of formal training; neither was he ever recognized by official circles as a rabbi. His teaching laid such an inescapable claim on people, however, that many quite spontaneously called him rabbi.

E

The Sea of Galilee, the surface of which is 685 feet below sea level. The Gospels tell us that Jesus taught on the sides of hills such as these.

The Synoptic Gospels contain materials drawn from a great wealth of remembered teachings of Jesus. A glance at an outline of the contents of the Synoptics will readily show that Matthew and Luke contain more of Jesus' teaching than Mark—and not just because they are longer Gospels. Mark was not primarily interested in presenting Jesus as a teacher, but rather as the Messiah, the Son of God, who had come to inaugurate God's kingdom. So Mark subordinates Jesus' teaching to this major purpose. Although Matthew and Luke also present Jesus as the Messiah, they emphasize his role as teacher. This is particularly true of Matthew, in which Jesus is the giver of a new law. And Luke, which shows a wider concern with Jesus as the Saviour of the world, is dominated by those teachings that tend to stress the universality of God's love and his kingdom. Here Jesus is not so much the teacher of Israel as he is the universal teacher of all mankind.

All three Synoptics convey the impression that Jesus was a teacher, but each author makes a different selection and use of the materials according to his special interests and purposes. This is important to remember whenever we read any specific passage dealing with Jesus' teaching, for often we must make a distinction between the way the Gospel writer understood the material and the original meaning of the teaching as spoken by Jesus.

When we are studying material that appears in all three Synoptics, it is often easy to identify the interpretations of the different authors— as in the use of Markan material by both Matthew and Luke, for example. We can also compare the uses to which Matthew and Luke put the Q material, although here we are handicapped somewhat because we do not have the original source on which Matthew and Luke depended (see p. 70). And when we come to the material that is peculiar to Matthew or Luke, the problem becomes even more difficult, for here we have tradition presented by only one author. Any effort to determine whether it bears the marks of interpretation is far more hypothetical, since we are dealing with the development not of the written but of the oral tradition, a study that is tentative at best.

THE TEACHINGS ARE PRESERVED AND INTERPRETED

All study of Jesus' teaching must begin with the written Gospels. But since there was a long period of oral transmission before his teachings were written down, we must first ask why and how they were preserved and transmitted in this oral stage. To deal with this question a useful method of study known as "form-criticism" has been employed. Form-critics emphasize that in the early period of oral transmission there was no continuous narrative of the life of Jesus, nor was there any strictly biographical interest in Jesus. The tradition about his life and teachings was of interest to the early community because he was the Messiah, and was valued because it disclosed the true meaning of God's kingdom, salvation, and will for the Christian community and consequently for all men. The teachings were relevant for the community primarily as they spoke to the needs and problems of their day.

Form-critics have emphasized the important role of the community in shaping the tradition of Jesus' teachings, and the ways in which the teachings were preserved, applied, and interpreted in order to meet the needs of the early church. The teachings were important to the church in its missionary activity, first to the Jews and then to the Gentiles, in preaching, in worship, and in teaching new converts. But the teachings were also applied to the problems raised by the church's running debate with the Jews and by the community's expansion out of Palestine into the Gentile world. As the church tried to carry on its activities and to adjust itself to an ever-changing environment, it applied the teachings of Jesus that it felt to be most relevant, and in doing so left its interpretation on the teachings in the very act of preserving them.

Here is a simple illustration of this process. Each of the Synoptic Gospels contains a teaching of Jesus regarding divorce:

> And he said to them, "Whoever divorces his wife and marries another, commits adultery against her; and if she divorces her husband and marries another, she commits adultery."
>
> —MARK 10:11-12

> But I say to you that every one who divorces his wife except on the ground of unchastity, makes her an adulteress; and whoever marries a divorced woman commits adultery.
>
> —MATTHEW 5:32

> Every one who divorces his wife and marries another commits adultery, and he who marries a woman divorced from her husband commits adultery.
>
> —LUKE 16:18

All three versions of this saying of Jesus agree that the man is forbidden to divorce his wife. Mark, however, adds another restriction: The woman cannot divorce her husband. This restriction does not make sense in the Jewish context of Jesus' teaching, for there was no provision in Jewish law for a woman to divorce her husband. She might go to court and ask that her husband be ordered to divorce her if he had certain diseases or on certain other grounds that she claimed were detrimental to her well-being. But she could not get a divorce. When Gentiles began to enter the church, however, the situation changed, for according to Roman law a woman could divorce her husband. So the last half of the saying in Mark reflects the community's interpretation of the saying; on the basis of a teaching of Jesus, a new community rule has been formulated to deal with the new situation.

As the traditions of Jesus' life and ministry were transmitted orally, they tended to take on various set forms, as we saw in discussing the stories of the mighty works in the last chapter. And in the written Gospels we find numerous stories about Jesus which the community valued because they illustrated some important truth about the Messiah and his mission—for example, the stories of the baptism, temptation, entry into Jerusalem, and crucifixion and burial. Frequently these stories clearly reflect a development in the tradition as the church interpreted them in the light of its needs and its new faith in Jesus after his death and resurrection. Some of them, such as that of the baptism, can be set chronologically in the ministry on the basis of their content. No one, for example, would deny that the baptism preceded the ministry. But most of the stories circulated as independent units with no chronological connection, and to use these stories in reconstructing the life and ministry of Jesus requires careful historical analysis.

The teachings of Jesus, as well as the stories about his life and ministry, were also preserved in definite forms. So we find that many of his sayings were preserved as climactic utterances at the conclusion of a story. The story itself is an account of some debate or discussion, and then at the end Jesus utters a saying that terminates the episode. These stories have been appropriately named Pronouncement Stories.[1] A very good example of this type of story is the well-known dispute over the tribute to Caesar recorded in Mark (12:13-17). The story describes a debate between Jesus and certain Pharisees over the propriety of the Jews' paying the Roman tax, but the whole episode leads up to the final utterance of Jesus: "Render to Caesar the things that are Caesar's and to God the things that are God's." The sayings found in these stories were highly valued by the community and probably suffered little change in transmission. They provide important material for any reconstruction of the teaching of Jesus, and often the setting reflects some actual incident that took place during his ministry.

This coin, a silver denarius of the reign of Tiberius Caesar, is like the one that Jesus held in his hand when he commanded the Pharisees to "Render to Caesar the things that are Caesar's."

Many other sayings of Jesus were preserved by themselves, without being brought into any narrative or historical context. But, at a very early time, collections of these sayings were gathered together as the community saw in them illustrations of a common theme or principle. Such collections of sayings are found in all the Gospels—there are several in Mark, for example (4:21-25; 8:34-9:1; 9:37-50), and the Q material common to Matthew and Luke contains a great many more. No doubt the Q material was only one of a number of such collections brought together by the church, probably for purposes of instruction. Since in most cases the sayings were not preserved in their actual historical context, the original meaning has been lost. Often, though, we can recover some of the original meaning by interpreting them in the light of the rest of Jesus' teaching. Finally, it is clear that some of the long series of sayings, such as portions of the Sermon on the Mount, were uttered by Jesus in connected form in the first place (Mt. 6:25-34).

Of all the forms in which Jesus' sayings were transmitted by tradition, none more nearly preserves the original teaching than the parable. Jesus was not alone in his use of parables, for they are found in the Old Testament, and the rabbis made use of them in their teaching. But scholars agree that the parables of Jesus have a unique character. (We shall discuss this point at greater length later on.) In the parables we come very close to the teaching of Jesus, and they shed much light on the meaning of many sayings whose specific historical setting has been lost in transmission.

THE FORM AND METHOD OF JESUS' TEACHING

Jesus' method of teaching was analogical—that is, he tried to stimulate men's imaginations to new insights by leading them to draw a comparison between a self-evident truth and a truth of another order of reality. The parable form was ideally suited to such a method.

What is a parable? It is a simple story of an incident that may or may not have actually occurred. The important point is that it speaks in familiar and lifelike terms, and conveys some vivid impression, some truth. But the parable achieves its end only when it serves as a window through which a truth of another order can be seen.

By way of illustration, let us consider one of Jesus' shorter parables:

> Or what woman, having ten silver coins, if she loses one coin, does not light a lamp and sweep the house and seek diligently until she finds it? And when she has found it, she calls together her friends and neighbours, saying, "Rejoice with me, for I have found the coin which I had lost."
>
> —LUKE 15:8-9

This parable of the Lost Coin, which is found only in Luke, is a perfect illustration of Jesus' parables. Notice the vivid and true-to-life situation: A poor woman loses a coin, searches frantically for it, and in her joy of finding it tells all her friends. All the details converge to leave a vivid image of a joyous woman who has found a lost coin.

What was it Jesus was seeking to teach through this parable? In Luke, it is grouped with two other parables that are concerned with the joy· of God when a sinner repents. So in this parable Jesus is saying that the concern of God for a sinner, and his joy over his repentance, is something like the concern of this woman for her lost coin and her joy over its discovery.

Many of Jesus' parables convey some truth about the kingdom of God, but they also deal with many other subjects, such as humility, sympathy, and forgiveness. The parables were originally uttered to answer some specific question or to teach some particular lesson raised by some actual historical episode; and the more certain we are of the actual context, the better chance we have of getting at the original meaning. Unfortunately, though, it is difficult to reconstruct the concrete situation that prompted many of Jesus' parables. Even so, they are so vivid that they seldom fail to strike the thoughtful reader, not only because of their lifelike quality, but also because they were intended to reveal something about the relation between God and man, or between man and his fellow man. Because these relationships are real and profound, the parables were capable of opening men's minds and hearts to new insights.

The early community did not always understand the meaning of the parables—in part because many of the original settings had been lost in oral transmission, and in part because the parables were a challenge to the imagination, which can always go astray. One of the chief sources of error was the belief that the parables were intended to convey some hidden or even esoteric teaching of Jesus. And in order to get at the hidden meaning the early church often interpreted the parables allegorically.

An allegory is a story in which one set of ideas is expressed by an entirely different set of ideas. Every detail of the story has a symbolical significance, and unless the reader knows what each detail symbolizes he cannot decode the true meaning of the story. But an allegory is quite a different form from a parable, for in a parable all the details have significance only as they lend concreteness and credibility to the actual setting for the story.

There are numerous examples of allegorizing in the Gospels. In one notable instance—the Parable of the Sower—a parable of Jesus is followed by an allegorical interpretation. The parable itself has all the characteristics of a genuine parable (Mk. 4:1-9; Mt. 13:1-9; Lk. 8:4-8), for it is the very lifelike story of a sower who sowed grain, most of which failed to produce but a small amount of which yielded abundantly. It strikes a note of encouragement, and was ap-

parently spoken by Jesus at a time when his followers had become
discouraged over the results of his ministry.[2]

The allegorical interpretation (Mk. 4:13-20; Mt. 13:18-23; Lk.
8:11-15) that follows this parable is placed on the lips of Jesus himself
(Mk. 4:13). Here the main point of the parable drops into the background and each detail is allegorized: The seed is the word, each soil
is symbolical of a type of human response to the word, each condition
of growth symbolizes some human situation, and so forth. Obviously
this allegorical interpretation has come from the early Christian community and reflects the historical circumstances and discouragement
of a later day. But allegorizing of this sort misses the whole point, for
Jesus spoke in parables in order to make his point clear, not in order
to confuse his listeners. Furthermore, he used this form in order to
draw forth a spontaneous response as the hearer drew his own conclusions, and to explain a parable would be to divest it of its intended
impact.

Jesus' parables provide the most vivid illustration of his analogical
method of teaching, but this same method pervades the rest of his
teaching as well. His sayings abound with metaphors and similes:
Herod Antipas is an "old fox" (Lk. 13:32); those who seek the kingdom of God are the "salt of the earth" (Mt. 5:13); Jesus sends the
disciples forth "as lambs in the midst of wolves" (Lk. 10:3). These
are only a few from the multitude of figures of speech that are found
in Jesus' teaching. In each case, he makes his real point by means of a
concrete example. And so the realms of ordinary human experience
and natural phenomena become vehicles for conveying unexpected
spiritual meaning.

In some instances Jesus taught through an action. For example, on
one occasion he placed a small child in the midst of his hearers (Mk.
9:36); he mounted and rode a donkey into Jerusalem (Mk. 11:4-8);
he drove salesmen and bankers out of the temple (Mk. 11:15-19); he
broke bread and passed it among the disciples (Mk. 14:22). Such
incidents, which have been called "enacted parables," convey a message far more eloquently than the words that accompany the action.
And they are reminiscent of similar acts of the Jewish prophets:
Jeremiah, for example, who took a jar outside the gates of Jerusalem
and broke it to pieces before the eyes of the people (Jer. 19:10 ff.),
thereby vividly disclosing the destruction that would befall them.[3]

In fact, Jesus' teaching reminded some people so much of the ancient

---

[2] For a fuller interpretation of this parable see Chapter 5 p. 143
[3] See also Ezek. 4:1 ff.; Isa. 30:3 ff.

prophets that they called him not only rabbi but "prophet" as well (e.g., Mt. 21:11; Mk. 6:15). In a sense, this title distinguished him from the rabbis, for the Jews believed that the prophetic office had ceased to exist in Israel with the last Jewish prophet, Malachi (fourth century B.C.). As teachers of the Law, the rabbis conceived of their role as didactic, not prophetic. They believed themselves to be the interpreters of the Law and of the prophets—but not lawgivers or prophets themselves. Hence, all their teaching was based on the scriptures, and could not contradict them (see p. 34). Jesus did not hesitate on occasion to meet the teachers of the Law on their own terms: He too could quote scripture to make a point (for example, see Mk. 12:26). But scripture-quoting was not characteristic of his method. (Jesus' understanding of the Law will be discussed later in the chapter.) Like the prophets of old, who frequently introduced their message with the words "thus saith the Lord," Jesus spoke directly, as in the Sermon on the Mount where he repeatedly says "but I say unto you" (Mt. 5:17-48). Here Jesus does not try to support his words by referring specifically to scripture; he actually challenges the literal meaning of scripture. He speaks as one who is under the immediate and direct authority of God.

Jesus' teaching is cast in forms that suggest the necessity for spontaneous and imaginative response. As we have seen in his use of the parable, the hearer is required to move from the truth of some familiar event to the disclosure of a higher truth with which it is compared. But the hearer must himself be struck and moved by the connection between meanings. The very form of Jesus' teaching is strikingly appropriate to its content, for the heart of all his teaching is the truth of the inescapable and immediate presence of God whom men can know only in a spontaneous and freely chosen response of trust. The originality and uniqueness of Jesus' teaching derive from the intensity of his own awareness of God's active presence in human history and the amazing way in which he adapted his mode of expression to the communication of this fact. Where his teaching failed, it was not because of the inadequacy of form but because of his listeners' blindness to the reality of the kingdom of God, the subject of all his teaching.

The Kingdom of God

The heart of Jesus' message was "The kingdom of God is at hand" (Mk. 1:15), and the burden of all his teaching was to lead men to an understanding of what this message meant. The Gospel of Mark records the story that on one occasion a Jewish scholar came to Jesus asking which of the commandments was the "first of all" (Mk. 12:28-34). Jesus is reported to have replied: "The first is, 'Hear, O Israel: The Lord our God, the Lord is one; and you shall love the Lord your God with all your heart, and with all your soul, and with all your mind, and with all your strength.' The second is this, 'You shall love your neighbour as yourself. There is no other commandment greater than these.' " The scholar agreed, adding that such love was "more than all whole burnt offerings and sacrifices." In spite of this apparent agreement, Jesus is then reported to have said, "You are *not far* from the kingdom of God."

In his answer to the scholar, Jesus went beyond the original question, for he states not only the first commandment but the second. Both are taken directly from the Old Testament. The first, from Deuteronomy (6:4), appears in the *Shema*, which every good Jew was expected to recite at least once a day. The second is from Leviticus (19:18). Jesus, like all good Jews, felt that these two commandments were at the heart of a man's duty and were central to God's revelation to Israel.

Nevertheless, Jesus boldly declared that the scholar who asked the question—even though he was conscious of this supreme truth—was still "not far" from the kingdom of God. Apparently Jesus did not equate knowledge of this truth with possession of the kingdom. In short, the kingdom was not to be equated with rules or laws, even the supreme law of love for God and for neighbour. What, then, is this kingdom which is so central to Jesus' teaching?

When Jesus spoke of the kingdom of God,[4] he was using a religious term that was well known to the Jews, who had long referred to God as King in recognition of his sovereign rule over all creation. The expression was obviously borrowed from the political sphere, and the point of the analogy was the supreme sovereignty of God or rule of God over man and all creation.

There had been a time in Israel's past when God as King had been inseparably related to Israel's king. But in the centuries following the destruction of Jerusalem by the Babylonians, the political kingdom had ceased to exist and the concept of the kingdom of God had changed. The Jews tended increasingly to conceive of the kingdom of God as the rule of righteousness that would be realized when God finally acted to defeat the forces of evil in the world. In an earlier chapter we saw that this belief appeared in a variety of

---

[4] The Gospel of Matthew prefers the term "kingdom of heaven," reflecting a Jewish tendency to refrain from using the "divine name."

forms, for there was no agreement on the way in which God would accomplish his purposes. Some believed it would be accomplished through the restoration of Israel to political power. They felt that the present world order would continue, but that Israel would be restored to world leadership and that foreign political powers would be subjected to her. Others believed that the coming of the kingdom would involve the complete dissolution of the present world order and the creation of a new one. Nature and human society would be radically transformed. To indicate the radical nature of such a change, these Jews used apocalyptic language in describing it: The heavens would be shaken; stars, moon, sun, and planets would vary in their courses. Heavens and earth would be completely transformed to become a fit environment for the establishment of the perfect and righteous rule of God. The righteous dead would be raised up to enjoy the blessings of the kingdom.

Regardless of the concepts through which this hope in the coming kingdom was expressed, the Jews of Jesus' day did agree on certain points: The kingdom had not yet come; it was to be established as an act of God; and its coming was to mark the triumph of God's purposes for man—the triumph of good over evil.

All Jesus' teaching about the kingdom of God presupposes the reality of God who exercises active sovereignty over the world. Jesus never offers an abstract definition of the kingdom; instead, he uses the language of metaphor, simile, prophetic utterance, and parable. He tries to teach what the rule of God is like but not what it *is*. Not that Jesus lacked faith in men's ability to know what God's rule is: rather, he seems convinced that it is only as men confront the rule of God in trust and obedience that they can know for themselves what it is. Teaching about the kingdom may be illuminating; it may prepare mind and heart. But the kingdom can really be understood only as the individual encounters the personal rule of God. As we have seen, even Jesus' method of teaching depended directly on the personal response of the hearer to the God about whom Jesus taught. The metaphor, "kingdom," designates the personal rule of God over man, and implies a personal relationship. The kingdom of God, then, inevitably implies a relationship of persons.

Although Jesus often spoke of the kingdom of God, he rarely followed the analogy through to the point of speaking of king and subjects. Apparently he did not feel that such terms gave an adequate description of the relationship between God and man. When Jesus wanted to speak of this relationship, he turned from the political analogy to that of the Father-son relationship. A consideration of what

Jesus meant by the Fatherhood of God is important for an understanding of the kingdom of God.

THE FATHERHOOD OF GOD

That Jesus should have spoken of God as Father was not unusual, for the Old Testament frequently refers to God as Father in the sense that he created the nation of Israel and made the Israelites his sons when he delivered them from the Egyptians (Deut. 32:6). Israel was to demonstrate its sonship to the Father through love and obedience to his will (Deut. 14:1). This Father-son analogy continued to be a common way of referring to God's relation to Israel in the period after the close of the Old Testament canon. To the present day, Jews praying in their synagogues say: "May the Father of mercy have mercy upon a people that have been born (sic) by him."

Jesus does not seem to have made casual use of the term Father. Study of the Synoptic Gospels shows that in Mark and Q the term occurs only in prayers and in intimate talks with his disciples. It is in the Gospel of Matthew that the term occurs most frequently, and it is generally agreed that in some of these passages the term was introduced by the author of the Gospel. There is little evidence to suggest that Jesus preached extensively about the Fatherhood in public, though the concept is deeply embedded in his teaching.

It is a reasonable assumption, then, that to Jesus the word Father suggested a very personal and intimate relationship. "Father" on the lips of Jesus, though he depended on Jewish tradition, was far more than a traditional term that he had received as a fitting designation of God. God was the Father not only as known through his relationship to Israel in the books of the Law, the prophets, and the Psalms; he was the Father whom Jesus had come to know in his own complete trust and in the commitment of his life—in his own mission, which he believed he had taken up in obedience to God.

Jesus teaches the meaning of the Fatherhood of God more clearly through what he does than what he says. His resolute obedience to God and his inexhaustible trust in God inevitably point to the One obeyed and trusted. When Jesus called men to a recognition of God as Father, he did not ground his summons in the traditional fact that they were Jews. Rather, God was their Father and they were true sons only as they responded to him in trusting obedience.

The terms "trust" and "obedience" are perhaps the best words to describe the human response in which the Fatherhood of God is both known and acknowledged, and in which sonship is realized and affirmed. In the last analysis, Jesus was not concerned with teaching an abstract concept of Fatherhood. God as Father was not a lesson to be learned, but a personal relationship that must be entered through obedient trust.

That Jesus tried to lead his disciples into a realization of this true Father-son relationship is made very evident in the Sermon on the Mount (Mt. 5-7), where we find a large collection of Jesus' teachings assembled by the author of Matthew. Much of the same material is found scattered throughout the Gospel of Luke. In these remarkable chapters the author of Matthew intended to bring together a long discourse that would be representative of the teaching of Jesus. Although the word "trust" does not occur in the Sermon, the theme recurs constantly. In the passage in which Jesus speaks of human anxieties (Mt. 6:25-34) he mentions the elemental human concerns: food, drink, clothing, and physical existence. In the key introductory phrase, Jesus says to the disciples: "Therefore, I tell you, do not be anxious about your life, what you shall eat or what you shall drink, nor about your body, what you shall put on." Why? Because your "heavenly Father knows that you need them all" (Mt. 6:32). Life is to be lived in complete trust in God, whose merciful providence supports all his creation. To live in such trust is to know the meaning of God as Father.

But Jesus was not suggesting blind trust in some vague "goodness of life." Each day has its own troubles and evil (Mt. 6:34), and he was not asking his disciples to believe that life in general is good but that God the Father is good. Neither does he suggest that to know God as Father is to escape hardship or deprivation, for he promised his disciples suffering and trouble. Instead, he is concerned to lead his disciples to trust that whatever circumstance befall them they are under the care of a loving Father who knows their needs better than they.

Here is the prayer commonly known as the Lord's prayer, which Jesus is reported to have taught his disciples (Mt. 6:9-13; Lk. 11:2-4):

> Our Father who art in heaven,
> Hallowed be thy name.
> Thy kingdom come,
> Thy will be done,
> On earth as it is in heaven.
> Give us this day our daily bread;
> And forgive us our debts,
> As we also have forgiven our debtors;
> And lead us not into temptation,
> But deliver us from evil.

Jesus urges his disciples to pray to God as Father, and the prayer itself fills the word Father with its own meaning. For to utter the words "Our Father" meaningfully involves delivering oneself in trust to the One who alone provides man with physical existence (daily bread) and a healthy inward or spiritual life (forgiveness and deliverance from evil), and creates the condition of mind and heart that will enable the speaker to forgive freely those who have harmed him or others. Prayer itself is an act of trust for the disciple; in it he acknowledges his utter dependence on the One who is Creator and sovereign of all that is (heavens and earth). In the trust that finds expression in such a prayer the disciple comes to know the meaning of God as Father.

What does Jesus' teaching about the Fatherhood of God have to do with the kingdom of God? Simply this: The God who is King and sovereign ruler of the universe is also the Father of mankind. He is One who may be known as Father now, and he is One whose kingdom may be known now, for the Father is King and the King is Father. In the Lord's prayer there is the petition "*Thy* kingdom come," and in Jesus' teaching on anxiety and trust there is the exhortation "to seek first *his* kingdom" (Mt. 6:33). It is the kingdom of "your Father in heaven who knows what you need before you ask." Nevertheless, though Jesus exhorts the disciples to "seek the kingdom," he also says that the kingdom is a gift: "Fear not, little flock, for it is your Father's good pleasure to give you the kingdom" (Lk. 12:32). Here we see the final expression of God's Fatherhood, for he gives his kingdom to those who seek it.

This emphasis on the kingdom as the gracious gift of the Father was new and strange to many of Jesus' listeners. The Pharisees, for example, though they surely believed that repentance was necessary to enter the kingdom, taught that through knowledge of the Law and good works men might earn their way into the kingdom. There were even some who felt that if the Jews would repent and keep the Law for just one sabbath they might force God to establish the kingdom. But Jesus constantly taught that man could neither build the kingdom nor earn it. Of the many parables that stress this point, none is more striking than that of the Labourers in the Vineyard (Mt. 20:1-16). The labourers who worked only an hour receive the same wage as those who worked many hours. The gift of the kingdom is not according to the work, for the Father gives to whom he will. So no one could predict who would enter the kingdom. Certainly entry was not a Jewish prerogative: "And men will come from east and west, and from north and south, and sit at table in the kingdom of God" (Lk. 13:29; Mt. 8:11-12).

THE KINGDOM AS COMING EVENT

There are numerous passages in the Gospels where Jesus speaks of the kingdom of God in language that suggests it has not come. For example, on one occasion he said to his disciples: "There are some standing here who will not taste death before they see the kingdom of God come with power" (Mk. 9:1). Again, on the last evening Jesus spent with his disciples he promised them: "I shall not drink again of the fruit of the vine until that day when I drink it new in the kingdom of God" (Mk. 14:25). Another time, rebuking those who rejected his message, he warned: "There you will weep and gnash your teeth, when you see Abraham and Isaac and Jacob and all the prophets in the kingdom of God and you yourselves thrust out. And men will come from east and west, and from north and south, and sit at table in the kingdom of God" (Lk. 13:28-29; Mt. 8:11-12). Each of these sayings, together with many others, looks to the coming of the kingdom as a future event.

Many of the parables too look to the future for the coming of the kingdom. A good example is the parable of the Ten Maidens found in the Gospel of Matthew (25:1-13), which conveys two closely related thoughts: the sudden and unexpected coming of the kingdom and the need to be prepared for its coming. The coming of the Bridegroom is the single important event in the parable that determines the Maidens' expectations. And the coming of the kingdom is the great event that determines the expectations of those who long for it. The theme of the kingdom as coming event is dominant in the parable.

The same emphasis on the kingdom as coming event is found in the parables that have judgment as their theme. The parable of the Last Judgment is an excellent illustration (Mt. 25:31-46). Jesus, like John the Baptist, often spoke of the coming of the kingdom as involving God's final judgment on evil. And in this parable Jesus uses the symbolism of Jewish eschatology when he portrays all the nations passing before the judgment throne of God. To some the King says: "Come, O blessed of my Father, inherit the kingdom prepared for you from the foundation of the world." To the rest the King says: "Depart from me, you cursed, into the eternal fire prepared for the devil and his angels." The fire is symbolic of the judgment on the evil nations. Here the judgment of evil and the inheritance of the kingdom by the blessed is an event that has not yet been consummated.

Additional passages in the Gospels reflect this same future expectation, such as those in which Jesus urges watchfulness (Lk. 12:35-46) and those in which he admonishes the people to agree with their adversaries before it is too late (Mt. 5:25-26; Lk. 12:57-59). Sayings that look forward to the coming of the Son of Man [5] in glory or in judgment also fall in this category, as does the dispute between Jesus and the Sadducees over the resurrection. Here Jesus by implication acknowledges his belief in a coming resurrection (Mk. 12:18-27; Mt. 22:23-33; Lk. 20:27-38), which he undoubtedly related to the coming of the kingdom.

On the basis of all these passages, it is clear that in some sense Jesus thought of the kingdom of God in terms of a coming event. The urgency with which he spoke and the way he expressed himself leave no doubt that he expected God's decisive action in the near future, before some of those who heard him had tasted death (Mk. 9:1). And there can be no doubt that Jesus broke with those who looked for the coming of the kingdom as the restoration of Israel as a political power in the present age. Rather, he insisted that the coming of the kingdom would mark the end of the present order of human history. Like many before him, Jesus anticipated a complete transformation of all things and a new order of life. But, unlike those who speculated at length on the conditions of life in that new age, Jesus was concerned only with the moral and spiritual consequences of its coming.

THE KINGDOM AS PRESENT REALITY

There are also many passages in the Gospels from which it can be inferred that the kingdom is in some sense a present reality. A few of the parables seem to form a bridge between the kingdom expected as future event and the kingdom known as present reality. We shall consider three of these: The Parable of the Seed Growing Secretly (Mk. 4:26-29), The Parable of the Mustard Seed (Mk. 4:30-32; Mt. 13:31-32; Lk. 13:18-19), and the Parable of the Leaven (Mt. 13:33; Lk. 13:20-21).

In each of these parables the coming of the kingdom is suggested by the completion of the action described—the coming of the sickle at harvest, the full-grown mustard seed, and the fully leavened loaf. Such an interpretation would make the coming of the kingdom strictly a future event, and some scholars would limit the parables to this meaning. But although the element of future fulfilment is undeniably present, this interpretation does not do full justice to the parables. The growing seed in the first two parables and the working leaven in the third are essential to the final result of the harvest, the fully grown mustard plant, and the leavened loaf. And in each parable

---

[5] The meaning of Son of Man will be discussed in the next chapter.

Jesus uses the idea of growth in close relation to the final product. So to interpret the parables as speaking of the hidden presence of the kingdom seems to be as accurate as to interpret them as speaking of the kingdom only as future event. It is not a case of either-or. The kingdom of God conceived as present reality seems to be an integral part of each comparison.

If we could be sure of the actual historical contexts in which these parables were originally spoken, we could determine more certainly in just what sense Jesus spoke of the kingdom as a present reality. The Gospel of Mark, by presenting the settings immediately after the explanation of the parables, undoubtedly intends to relate the parables to Jesus' ministry of teaching and preaching. For Mark the kingdom is present, though hidden, in the ministry of Jesus. Since one of the author's purposes in writing this Gospel was to declare that the power of the kingdom was present in Jesus, the unrecognized Messiah, some interpreters hesitate to accept the fact that Jesus himself thought of the kingdom as present in his ministry. They claim instead that this is just Mark's interpretation. Other scholars, however, believe that these parables refer to the ministry of Jesus as the present manifestation of the kingdom, though the final revelation of the kingdom is yet to come.

When we look more closely at the ministry, this latter interpretation seems the more valid of the two. In the last chapter, we saw that Jesus looked upon his "mighty works" as manifestations of God's power. This is the meaning of his saying: "If I by the finger of God cast out devils, then is the reign of God come upon you" (Lk. 11:20; Mt. 12:28). He saw his healing ministry as the present victory of the power of the kingdom over the powers of evil.

Another statement of Jesus acquires new significance if we take it as referring to the kingdom as present in his ministry. When John the Baptist, before his execution, sent to Jesus asking if he was the expected one, Jesus is reported to have answered: "Go and tell John what you have seen and heard: the blind receive their sight, the lame walk, lepers are cleansed, and the deaf hear, the dead are raised up, the poor have good news preached to them. And blessed is he who takes no offence at me" (Q; Lk. 7:22-23; Mt. 11:2-6). The substance of this answer comes from various passages from the prophet Isaiah which in Jesus' day were interpreted as describing the time of God's salvation and the coming of the kingdom. Jesus' answer, then, is a tacit acknowledgment that in his ministry he already saw evidences of the victory of God. The last portion of the answer makes reference to the "preaching to the poor," which would bring into focus Jesus' proclamation of the kingdom and the call to repentance and belief. For ultimately the sign of the presence of the kingdom's power was the fact that through Jesus' word men were already turning their eyes to the kingdom of God in repentance and trust. Already the poor and the dispossessed were entering into the kingdom and enjoying its blessings.

And it is in relation to the ministry that we must understand Jesus' words to his disciples:

> Blessed are the eyes which see what you see! For I tell you that many prophets and kings desired to see what you see, and did not see it, and to hear what you hear, and did not hear it.

> —LUKE 10:23-24; MATTHEW 13:16-17

The prophets and kings of Israel had looked forward to the coming of the kingdom of God, and those who are witnesses to the ministry of Jesus are seeing and hearing the first signs of the kingdom's coming.

How are we to reconcile these two aspects of the kingdom, the present and the future? No solution is possible apart from Jesus' concept of the Fatherhood of God and his own profound knowledge of the meaning of sonship. The Father who exercised his sovereign rule in mercy and love is the God whose rule is already revealed to those who trust him as Father. In Jesus' own case it was obedience to this rule that initiated and sustained his own ministry. All who responded to his proclamation of the kingdom and its rule could be spoken of as already entering the kingdom. But, although the actuality of God's rule was a present fact, it was not yet completely victorious, for the powers of evil still assailed the kingdom. There were still those who wilfully denied his call. And Jesus proclaimed the day when the rule that was already manifesting itself in his own life and ministry, and in the lives of those who responded to his word, would finally prevail over all the earth.

Many of Jesus' contemporaries were very pessimistic in their outlook toward this world. They believed that the world lay in helpless subjection to evil, and they saw relief only in a future coming of the kingdom. In contrast, there was a profound optimism in Jesus' teaching, for he taught that though evil was present and fearful the rule of God was already at work in this world, and he rejected the otherworldly view of the kingdom. Though he looked forward to a coming judgment and the complete manifestation of the rule of God in the future, he did so from the perspective of one who saw the judgment and mercy of God's rule already active and real in this world. This is clearly evident in all he taught.

It seems clear that Jesus expected the final consummation of the kingdom to come soon, and that this expectation conditioned his proclamation and gave urgency to his mission. Yet he denied any definite knowledge of exactly when the end would come: "But of that day or that hour no one knows, not even the angels in heaven, nor the Son, but only the Father" (Mk. 13:32). And unlike many of the apocalyptic writers he had no interest in speculating on the various catastrophic signs of the end-time. Although the Gospels include a discourse containing predictions of disaster as signs of the end (Mk. 13:5-27; Mt. 24:4-31; Lk. 21:8-28), they show Jesus more characteristically declaring that the only sign of the end would be his preaching and call to repentance. To him, the time when that end was to come was not ultimately significant.

But more important than this, the meaning of the kingdom's coming derived from his knowledge of God in the present and from his belief that men could know God's rule now. And so he taught men about the rule of God as it could be known and submitted to in the present. The final consummation did not come in the immediate future, but that did not invalidate the rule of God. The time of God's final act could not alter the character of his rule. The end—whenever it came— would confirm it.

Those, then, who responded to the message of the kingdom were called to its blessings through submitting themselves to its rule in their lives. And Jesus tried to describe that rule in terms of how it would manifest itself in the lives of those who submitted to it.

The New Life of the Kingdom

According to Jesus' urgent proclamation regarding the kingdom, the first response that God demanded was repentance and trust. To repent was to turn to God from all distractions that tended to obscure the primacy of God's judgment. Trust involved committing one's life to the mercy and goodness of God. Such repentance and trust were total: they involved every aspect of man's life. The judgment of God inevitably involved a shaking-down of mankind. But although a final judgment awaited all men, they were already being called into judgment now. How they responded to the call to repentance now determined what the future judgment would be. By their present judgment they would be judged. The call was for radical action and decision in the immediate present, for there could be no postponement of the decision; the demands of the kingdom could not be put off. Two

128 THE COMMUNITY EMERGES

variant sayings of Jesus found in the Gospels of Matthew and Luke convey the inclusive and radical nature of these demands:

> You, therefore, must be perfect as your heavenly Father is perfect.
>
> —MATTHEW 5:48
>
> Be merciful, even as your Father is merciful.
>
> —LUKE 6:36

These terse demands aptly summarize the content of all the ethical teaching of Jesus. The one and all-encompassing factor in the new life of the kingdom was the will of the perfectly good and loving Father, and to live under the dominion of his love and mercy was the sole criterion of the new life.

JESUS AND THE TORAH

In his teaching about this new life, Jesus by no means rejected the Torah as a source of knowledge. Jesus knew the sacred writings well and drew extensively from them. He undoubtedly believed that they contained the revelation of God's will for his people. In Matthew's Sermon on the Mount, for example, Jesus is reported to have said: "For truly, I say to you, till heaven and earth pass away, not an iota, not a dot, will pass from the law until all is accomplished" (Mt. 5:18). Even if this saying derives from the early community instead of from Jesus himself, it accurately represents Jesus' attitude. He did not set aside the scriptures. On another occasion, when a man came to him asking what he must do to inherit eternal life, Jesus told him to keep the Ten Commandments (Mk. 10:17 ff.). After healing a leper, Jesus commanded the man to go to the priest for ritual purification in accordance with Levitical law (Mk. 1:44). And earlier in this chapter we saw that Jesus agreed with a fellow Jew regarding the greatest commandments. All these incidents show the esteem Jesus had for the teachings of the Old Testament.

Nor, on the other hand, did Jesus reject outright the oral Law. The Gospels show that Jesus continually attended the synagogue for worship, even though the synagogue had no sanction in the written Law, only in oral tradition. And the prayer of blessing that Jesus uttered at the last meal with his disciples derived from a common practice of blessings before meals that had been established through oral tradition.

Nevertheless, it is also clear from the Gospels that Jesus repeatedly found himself in conflict with the Pharisees over the Law. Although we must be on guard against exaggerations in the Gospels resulting from the early church's conflict with the Jews, the fact that Jesus engaged in a running controversy with the Pharisees cannot be denied. One of the principal causes of this controversy was the observance of the sabbath. Jesus and his disciples were once criticized for breaking the sabbath by plucking grains from a wheat field and eating them (Mk. 2:23-28). According to strict Pharisaic definition, such activity was looked upon as work forbidden on the sabbath. In answer to the charges, Jesus admitted that he had laboured on the sabbath but he defended himself by referring to an incident in the Old Testament where David had acted similarly (I Sam. 21:3-6). On one occasion, David and his men had satisfied their hunger by eating the bread of the Presence, which was reserved for priests alone (Lev. 24:5-9). Jesus concluded his remarks with the saying: "The sabbath was made for man; not man for the sabbath" (Mk. 2:27). In drawing this conclusion he implied that the laws governing the sabbath must always be interpreted in the light of human need, and that human need took precedence over any clearly legal requirement.

Jesus applied this same principle in the case of healing on the sabbath (Mk. 3:1-6). Although Pharisaic law forbade healing on the sabbath, it allowed for exceptional cases where a life was in danger. In none of the sabbath healings recorded in the Gospels, however, was a life in danger. Since it was not a matter of saving a life, Jesus' opponents argued that one more day would not make any difference. Yet Jesus healed the persons at once, for as he saw it the will of a merciful God demanded that human suffering be relieved whenever possible even though it meant breaking literal laws. This was in keeping with the original intention of sabbath observance as found in the Deuteronomic version of the Ten Commandments (Deut. 5:12), which was to protect men from excessive work by providing a day of rest. But Jesus insisted that making conformity to the Law more important than the relief of human need annulled the original intention of sabbath legislation.

Other conflicts with the Pharisees over the matter of divorce law (Mk. 10:2-12) and the law of vows (Mk. 7:9-13) reveal Jesus seeking with the same probing spirit to discover what is right in accordance with God's ultimate will. At no other point does he differ so radically from the Pharisees as in his treatment of laws governing relations with sinners. The word "sinners," which occurs frequently in the Gospels, is a technical term used to designate those Jews who for one reason or another did not adhere strictly to the Law. The Pharisees believed that in order to escape defilement a man had to separate himself completely from sinners. But Jesus found himself constantly in contact with sinners—in fact, the most enthusiastic response to his proclamation and teaching came from them. He talked with them, healed them, lived with them, and ate with them. And when he was called upon to defend himself, he said: "Those who are well have no need of a physician, but those who are sick; I came not to call the righteous, but sinners" (Mk. 2:17). And he also said: "The Son of Man came to seek and to save the lost" (Lk. 19:10).

In the eyes of the Pharisees, Jesus' concern for sinners brought him into constant relationship with those who defiled him ritually. By eating with them, he was guilty of using cups and dishes that were not ritually pure according to Pharisaic law. But he answered: "There is nothing outside a man which by going into him can defile him; but the things which come out of a man are what defile him" (Mk. 7:15). Not that Jesus wanted to overthrow the whole ritual law; rather, he was combating those who would substitute ritual purity for inward purity of heart. And when men refused to associate with sinners because they feared ritual defilement, Jesus believed that ritual purity had supplanted purity from within.

Clearly, then, Jesus differed from the Pharisees in his understanding of the Torah. But there were also certain underlying agreements. Both agreed that the Torah was the revelation of God's will; both agreed that it must be interpreted; both sought to discover in it the righteousness of God; both began with the demand of the Torah: "You, therefore, must be perfect as your heavenly Father is perfect" (Mt. 5:48; Lev. 19:18). But even after we have noted these points of agreement, the differences remain. And the principal difference seems to have been in the understanding of "perfection." The Pharisees thought of perfection largely in terms of the literal fulfilment of laws; Jesus on the other hand thought of perfection in terms of God's mercy and goodness, which could not be attained by fulfilling literal rules but was an inward condition of the heart that only God could give.

Since Jesus believed that the Torah had been given to guide men to a love of God and their fellow men, he radically disagreed with those who had made it a barrier between men and between God and men. We have his attitude in the vivid contrast he once drew between two men at prayer—a Pharisee and a tax-collector (Lk. 18:9-14). The Pharisee was a student and a strict adherent to the Law, but to most Jews the tax-collector stood as a shocking symbol of the flaunting of the Law. Yet it was the tax-collector who found approval in the sight of God. Not that the Pharisee was not righteous in terms of keeping the literal requirements of the Law, but his righteousness had become an excuse for passing judgment on other men and for separating himself from them—and thereby from God. The tax-collector, on the other hand, claimed no righteousness, had no grounds for passing judgment on other men, and could look only to the mercy of God for his knowledge of righteousness.

Jesus attacked law-righteousness because it provided men with a specious ground for boasting of their relation with God and blinded them to the necessity for repentance in response to his proclamation of the kingdom and its righteousness. And to show the foolishness of their over-confidence, Jesus once said: "So you also, when you have done all that is commanded you, say, 'We are unworthy servants; we have only done what was our duty' " (Lk. 17:10).

It is sometimes believed that the Pharisees did not appreciate that God's mercy was the ultimate source of man's salvation, but this is an injustice to Pharisaism. The Pharisees did not deny that all men were sinners and that all depended on God's mercy for salvation. The radical difference between Jesus and the Pharisees was this: The Pharisees believed that as long as this age lasted righteousness consisted in the literal fulfilment of the Law; Jesus, believing that the kingdom was already coming, proclaimed that law-righteousness itself had come under the judgment of God. According to Matthew, Jesus said: "Unless your righteousness exceeds that of the scribes and Pharisees, you will never enter the kingdom of heaven" (Mt. 5:20). The whole import of Jesus' proclamation was to bring even the most faithful adherents of the Law to recognize their need for repentance, and to measure their lives not by the fulfilment of legal requirements but by the perfection of God. And here we have the clue to the Pharisees' failure to understand or accept Jesus. To accept his proclamation meant to acknowledge that in his words and deeds the kingdom was already manifesting itself, and this they failed to do.

It is clear, then, why we find no code of law or system of ethics in Jesus' teaching about the new life. Contemporary Jewish religious leaders, conscientious and undeniably devout, were making every effort to derive from the Torah precepts to guide human conduct in every imaginable situation. Jesus, on the other hand, was more concerned with laying men's motives and desires open to the perfect will of God. When this happened, he was sure that men's conduct would be acceptable to God. He once said: "Strive to enter by the narrow door; for many, I tell you, will seek to enter and will not be able" (Lk. 13:24; Mt. 7:13-14). "Entrance" undoubtedly refers to the kingdom, but the "narrow door" surely does not mean adherence to a rigid system of law. Rather, it is the door of radical judgment on any pride in conduct, the door of complete trust in the power of God to lead men into the new life.

Jesus did not propose to substitute a new code of law in place of the old one, nor did he issue injunctions to cover each and every kind of moral decision. His purpose was to make perfectly clear that the new life was to be lived not in a relationship to laws but to the living God— a person—and to one's fellow man.

CHARACTERISTICS OF THE NEW LIFE

Jesus' teaching about the new life centres around certain general principles. We have seen that Jesus, like every good Jew, set a two-fold requirement at the very centre of his teaching: love of God and love of man. But in doing so, he went far beyond any specific injunctions of the Law by expanding love to include sinners—and even enemies:

> But I say to you, Love your enemies and pray for those who persecute you, so that you may be sons of your Father who is in heaven; for he makes his sun rise on the evil and on the good, and sends rain on the just and on the unjust. For if you love those who love you, what reward have you? Do not even the tax collectors do the same? And if you salute only your brethren, what more are you doing than others? Do not even the Gentiles do the same?
>
> —MATTHEW 5:44-47; LUKE 6:27-28; 32-36

Notice that he does not put this principle of "love for enemy" in purely legal terms, for he makes no efforts to describe the conditions under which one must love, nor does he define the patterns of conduct that must be followed under such conditions. The question of the specific fulfilment is left open. Furthermore, his injunction to "love your enemies" is not a legal prescription; he does not say, do this because the Law says so. The fact that men should love their enemies is implied on the grounds of God's universal love: the love that daily manifests itself as the sun shines and as the rain falls on all mankind, both the evil and the good. Men must love their enemies because God already loves them. There are no qualifications or conditions on such love because there are no qualifications in God's love for men. The Pharisees, in an attempt to fulfil the injunction to love one's neighbour, had gone to great lengths to define the term "neighbour," and in many instances had made the term far more inclusive. But Jesus showed the futility of their attempts by extending the term to include *all* men, as in the Parable of the Good Samaritan (Lk. 10:29-37).

A second great principle of Jesus' teachings was his insistent emphasis on forgiveness in the new life of the kingdom. And here again he set

It was on this treacherous road that leads from Jerusalem down to Jericho that the traveller was attacked by robbers in Jesus' parable of the Good Samaritan.

about freeing the concept from legal shackles and extending it to include all men:

> Take heed to yourselves; if your brother sins, rebuke him, and if he repents, forgive him; and if he sins against you seven times in the day, and turns to you seven times, and says "I repent," you must forgive him.

—LUKE 17:3-4

This injunction is not to be taken as a law prescribing the number of times a person must forgive in order to fulfil a legal requirement. Matthew's addition of the words "seventy times seven" (Mt. 18:22) rightly interprets the saying. The disciple to whom Jesus was speaking is to forgive as often as forgiveness is sought. Notice that Jesus does not define specific conditions under which forgiveness is necessary. The requirement of forgiveness is rooted in the forgiveness of God himself. Knowledge of God's forgiveness of sins provides both the motivation and the power to forgive others, and Jesus teaches that the power to forgive springs inevitably from true knowledge of God's forgiveness. So Jesus teaches his disciples to pray: "Forgive us our sins, for we ourselves forgive everyone who is indebted to us" (Lk. 11:4). When Jesus wants to impress upon his hearers the inescapable need for a forgiving

133

spirit, he does not string out rules defining the precise conditions of forgiveness. Instead, he teaches by parable, as in the Prodigal Son (Lk. 15:11-32), the Lost Sheep (Mt. 18:10-14), and the Unmerciful Servant (Mt. 18:23-35). The perfect forgiveness of God is to be seen first as a divine act of God toward man, and only then as a demand placed upon man.

A third principle in Jesus' teachings is that the new life in the kingdom is characterized by humility. But at no point does Jesus lay down rules defining how men must act in order to be humble. When Jesus teaches about humility, he describes in a parable a self-righteous Pharisee looking in disdain on a tax-collector who in his heart feels unworthy to petition God for mercy (Lk. 18:10-14). Or he tells this parable of a banquet:

> When you are invited by anyone to a marriage feast, do not sit down in a place of honour, lest a more eminent man than you be invited by him; and he who invited you both will come and say to you, "Give place to this man," and then you will begin with shame to take the lowest place. But when you are invited, go and sit in the lowest place, so that when your host comes he may say to you "Friend, go up higher"; then you will be honoured in the presence of all who sit at table with you.
>
> —LUKE 14:8-10

Here Jesus is not trying to set down rules of etiquette; rather, he is drawing upon a common experience to suggest that self-seeking ambition and humility are incompatible with the new life in the kingdom. Nor does he end with the command: "Therefore, be humble." Instead, the parable is immediately followed by this prophetic declaration: "For everyone who exalts himself, will be humbled, and he who humbles himself will be exalted." But who will do the exalting and how does one humble oneself? Although no clue is given in the passage, it is clear from Jesus' teaching that God alone can exalt a man, and the "how" of humility cannot be spelled out in a set of rules. Jesus does, however, suggest indirectly the conditions of humility. Here is an exchange between Jesus and two of his disciples:

> And James and John, the sons of Zebedee, came forward to him, and said to him, "Teacher, we want you to do for us whatever we ask of you." And he said to them, "What do you want me to do for you?" And they said to him, "Grant us to sit, one at your right hand and one at your left, in your glory." But Jesus said to them, "You do not know what you are asking...." And when the ten heard it, they began to be indignant at James and

John. And Jesus called them to him and said to them: "You know that those who are supposed to rule over the Gentiles lord it over them, and their great men exercise authority over them. But it shall not be so among you; but whoever would be great among you must be your servant, and whoever would be first among you must be slave of all."

—MARK 10:35-38; 41-44

Jesus' concluding saying in this story, like the Parable of the Wedding Banquet (Lk. 14:7-14), deals with humility. Here, however, humility is portrayed as a positive quality of life that manifests itself when men are dedicated and committed wholeheartedly to the service of their fellow men. Humble men are so wholly dedicated that they are not even aware that their service is praiseworthy. This is made very clear in the Parable of the Last Judgment, in which those who are about to be rewarded for their devout service are completely unaware of when or where they have performed service worthy of such acclaim (Mt. 25:31-46).

Jesus' teaching, then, says that the new life in the kingdom is characterized by love, forgiveness, and humility that manifests itself in selfless service. This new life derives from a relationship with God. God loves, forgives, and alone exalts man; God provides both the motivation and power for human love, forgiveness, and that spontaneous service which is the hallmark of humility. But human love, forgiveness, and service mean that there must be other human beings to be loved, forgiven, and served. Clearly, then, the new life in the kingdom can be conceived only in social terms. It implies a community of life, a community of men without which the new life cannot be realized. As the new life is a social life, so the new ethic is a social ethic.

Jesus' mission, as we have seen, brought him into a new relationship with all men, but it brought him into a special relationship with those who answered his call to repentance and trust and opened their minds and hearts to the coming of the kingdom. This was because there was a common understanding and sharing of God's good gifts. Those who looked upon the active love of Jesus and the community for sinners as defiling could not understand this relationship, nor could those who preferred the adulation of men to divine approval. Men who valued material possessions and temporal power over the kingdom's blessings and power could only look upon Jesus and the community as poor, deluded fools. As Jesus taught, this scorn did not remove the obligation to love, forgive, and serve those who misunderstood, although the community to its own discredit often did reject this obligation. But it was

only to the community that accepted the promises as well as the demands of the kingdom that the teaching of Jesus made any sense.

Much of the popular response to Jesus arose among the dispossessed
and "sinners." Unblessed by material possessions, they were eager to
hear about the blessings of the kingdom. With no righteousness of
their own to claim, they were open to the righteousness of the kingdom. In Jesus' teaching about the coming kingdom he held out great
promise, nowhere more clearly than in the Beatitudes (Mt. 5:3-12),
the introduction to the Sermon on the Mount (Mt. 5-7). The poor
would inherit the kingdom; the hungry would be filled; the meek
would inherit the earth; the mourners would be comforted. Jesus
taught that the coming kingdom would bring its reward, and this was
a sanction, though not the primary one, for obeying the demands of
the kingdom. Already in this present age the children of the kingdom
are pronounced "blessed" in the Beatitudes, and they are blessed not
only because the future holds recompense but because they can know
the Father now and live in trust and obedience as his children. This
they could realize, not in isolation, but in the love and mercy shared
in the new community that Jesus was calling into being.

THE NEW LIFE IN THE WORLD

The author of Matthew concludes the Sermon on the Mount
with the observation that "the crowds were astonished at his teaching"
(Mt. 7:28-29). Succeeding generations have testified to the same astonishment. One of the reasons is that the radical nature of Jesus' teaching
is made so vivid in the Sermon. Jesus condemns not only harmful acts
against one's fellow man but anger itself (Mt. 5:21ff.). He condemns
not only adulterous acts but also the hidden lust that may never manifest itself (Mt. 5:27-30). Men are to love not only their friends but
also their enemies—especially their enemies (Mt. 5:43-48). Men are not
to pass judgment on friends or enemies (Mt. 7:1-5). The demand is
for unimpeachable integrity and singleness of purpose, purity of heart.
Discerning listeners—in Jesus' own day and ever since—have been
prompted to exclaim: "What man is capable of this?"

The same astonishment has been prompted by other words of Jesus.
He required that men resist evil with love instead of with retaliation;
when struck they are to turn the other cheek (Mt. 5:39). When a man
is sued for one garment, he must willingly surrender another too (Mt.
5:40). The man who comes borrowing must not be refused (Mt. 5:42).
Confronted with such demands, many have protested that to live like
this would mean the breakdown of all social order. They have claimed
that such teaching is utterly unrealistic in our world.

Many explanations have been offered to justify these teachings of Jesus. For example, some have said that we are not to take his demands literally. What Jesus meant to do was simply to illustrate the *ideal* attitude or spirit that we ought to have toward our fellow man. This attempt to rationalize the teachings is a very inadequate and dangerous procedure, however, for it robs the teachings of their concreteness and can lead only to highly subjective conclusions. Although Jesus laid great stress on the inward condition of man, he never intended to separate attitude or inward spiritual condition from action. Furthermore, it is impossible to avoid the conclusion that Jesus often meant exactly what he said. Only on these grounds can we account for his contemporaries' amazement at his teaching.

Others have insisted that Jesus' words must be understood literally, that they represent the absolute demands of God upon man, and that they are truly the demands of the kingdom, but that they cannot be complied with in this world. Rather, they are counsels of perfection, whose primary value is to bring man to his knees in repentance when he sees how impossible it is for him to comply with them in this world. They are the demands of the perfect will of God, but man can fulfil them only when God finally brings about the consummation of the kingdom.

This interpretation too has always created a certain uneasiness. To interpret Jesus' teaching in such a negative way does not square with the positive emphasis of his total mission. For again, we cannot escape the impression that Jesus optimistically expected that men ought to be capable of radical action *here and now.* He wanted to do more than show men how weak they were; he wanted them to realize that where there was a radical inward change radical outward conduct would follow.

Still others have sought to cope with the problem of Jesus' teachings by asserting that Jesus intended them to be taken literally, but that they are not practical, applicable, or even relevant to life in this world. They are to be understood only in terms of the coming of God's final judgment and the dissolution of the present world order. Jesus' ethic has been called an "interim ethic"—that is, it provides a way of living only for "the time being," for a short time of withdrawal from the affairs of this world in expectation of the immediate end of this world.

This interpretation has also been rejected as unsatisfactory, for it neglects Jesus' emphasis on the fact that the kingdom is more than a coming event. It is already coming with his ministry. Furthermore, this interpretation implies a certain irrelevance in the teaching of Jesus for the life of this world, which in a sense suggests an irrelevance in the message of Jesus. But certainly Jesus conceived of his message as of extreme relevance for man in the present order of existence.

The real danger in any attempt to explain away the problem of Jesus' teaching is that of oversimplification. In an effort to clarify the issues, we make one principle paramount. But there is no easy solution to this problem, any more than there is to the paradox of the kingdom as both future event and present reality. Indeed, the problem of Jesus' ethic is difficult just because it is so inextricably related to his teaching about the kingdom.

It is true, of course, that insofar as Jesus' teaching about the new life demands absolute conformity to God's will, then no man can hope to satisfy the demand in this world. In that sense, the demand of Jesus' teaching always stands as a judgment on man and leads him to repentance. The perfection demanded always awaits the final consummation of the kingdom and the final reformation of man. As long as we can speak of the kingdom as coming, the new life is never complete.

On the other hand, insofar as the kingdom is impinging on human life here and now, both its absolute demands and its power are present as well. As we have seen, this power was present even in the ministry of Jesus. Above all, it is a power for righteousness—not initiated by man but by God. Jesus' words, "You, therefore, must be perfect, as your heavenly Father is perfect" (Mt. 5:48), must not be understood merely as a demand of God but also as prophetic words proclaiming God's intention to bring men to perfection. The righteousness of God means God's moral perfection, particularly as revealed in his power to save men from sin. So it is only God who knows whether or when his righteousness may be revealed through man. Because men cannot help but be humble in the presence of the righteousness of the kingdom does not mean that God will not manifest that righteousness when and where he wills.

> Nothing is said in the Sermon [on the Mount] about the time when the rule, now discernible in nature, will be made evident in human affairs. It is taken for granted that it will become evident in crises such as the concluding parable indicates, but whether crisis occurs in individual life or in social history does not seem important; whether the pure in heart shall see God after their death or after some revolution in social history, whether those who hunger and thirst after justice will be satisfied when the kingdom of God will be manifest on earth or in a spiritual life beyond history is not the important matter.[6]

---

[6] W. Beach and H. R. Niebuhr, *Christian Ethics*, pp. 32-33. New York: Ronald, 1955.

All Jesus' teaching presupposes the repentance and faith of those who hear it and take it upon themselves. Its ultimate truth, validity, and relevance are not to be measured by how well it fits in with the conventional ethics in any particular age. Rather, the ethic of the new life presupposes the righteousness of the kingdom. Those who do not acknowledge the kingdom as proclaimed by Christ obviously cannot take the ethic seriously, but that does not mean that it is irrelevant to them. Rather, the ethic is a judgment on the world. The more radical the resentment and rejection of the kingdom and its demands, the more irrelevant the ethic will seem to be. That is the very meaning of the words "Strive to enter by the narrow door" (Lk. 13:24)—the door is narrow just because there is so much resentment against the demands. But to submit to judgment is to enter into the community of the new life.

> The Sermon on the Mount is directed to those who have already begun to enter into the new age and who have begun to share its new powers. It should never be forgotten that both its ethical teachings and its confidence in God are spoken in a context of salvation. The Beatitudes make that clear at the beginning. The standards set are otherwise both impracticable and implausible— and the trust in God naive.[7]

Finally, we must realize that the sayings of Jesus cannot all be lumped together indiscriminately and made into principles of universally valid law. In some cases it is likely that Jesus did not intend his commands literally. For example, he did not mean that people should actually remove their eyes and hands to enter the kingdom (Mt. 5:29-30). Then, too, many of his commands can be understood only in the context of the particular historical situation in which they were spoken. We have already seen that Jesus himself recognized that the precepts of the Old Testament were to be understood in relation to the concrete historical situations in which they were being interpreted. Where a literal interpretation of the specific requirements of the Law did violence to the present demand of the kingdom as he understood it, he refused to make that interpretation. It would be a violation of Jesus' own understanding of his imperatives to try to universalize them—to try to create a new legalism where he rejected the old one.

It is particularly important to keep this historical context in mind when we study the sayings of Jesus that were first spoken in the his-

---

[7] Amos N. Wilder, "The Teaching of Jesus: The Sermon on the Mount," in *The Interpreter's Bible*, ed. George A. Buttrick, Vol. 7, p. 163. New York: Abingdon-Cokesbury.

torical crisis of his own ministry—for example, the sayings spoken to
the disciples toward the end of the ministry when it was becoming
apparent that the mission was failing. The requirements of discipleship
were conditioned by the growing opposition of the time. An urgent
crisis had arisen, and it had to be met with drastic demands from Jesus.
We turn now to a consideration of this crisis in Jesus' life, a crisis that
also engulfed the new community of followers.

CHAPTER FIVE

❧❧

THE CRISIS
IN JESUS' MINISTRY

At some point in Jesus' Galilean ministry, he had a disappointing experience in his home town of Nazareth. Luke places the event at the beginning of Jesus' ministry (Lk. 4:16-30), whereas Mark, followed by Matthew, places it more accurately later in the Galilean ministry (Mk. 6:1-6). All three Synoptic Gospels report that it was on this occasion that Jesus spoke the words: "A prophet is not without honour,

New Testament readings relevant to this chapter are the Gospel of Mark, especially chapters 6-15; Matthew 21-27; Luke 19-23. Other relevant passages are cited in the chapter.

141

F

except in his own country, and among his own kin and in his own house" (Mk. 6:4; Mt. 13:57; Lk. 4:24). Mark concludes the episode with this comment: "And he could do no mighty work there, except that he laid his hands upon a few sick people and healed them. And he marvelled because of their unbelief" (Mk. 6:5-6). Luke reports that the villagers actually drove Jesus out of Nazareth, and threatened him with bodily harm (Lk. 4:28-29).

The Close of the Ministry in Galilee

As far as we know, Jesus never returned to Nazareth. The failure of his home village to receive his message was probably a deeply disturbing experience for him, and it may even have forced him to realize how few would enter by the "narrow door." Yet the rejection of his message by his home village failed to dampen the enthusiasm with which he continued to carry on his mission. If anything, he intensified his efforts after this experience.

Some time later, Jesus sent his disciples forth on a great mission. All the Synoptics contain accounts of this mission of the twelve disciples (Mk. 6:7-13; Mt. 9:35; 10:1, 5-42; Lk. 9:1-6), and all imply that it was one of the crucial events in the ministry of Jesus. The account in Mark impresses us with one thing in particular: that the mission was urgent. The disciples are to take nothing with them except a staff and the clothes they wear. They are to carry no food, money, or extra clothing. In each village they are to enter only one house. If the villagers refuse to receive them hospitably, they are to hasten on to the next village. What were they to do on this mission? All three Synoptics agree that they were to cast out unclean spirits and heal; they were to call the people to repentance (Mk. 6:12) and proclaim the kingdom of God (Lk. 9:6; Mt. 10:7). They were to share in the mission of Jesus by heralding the imminent coming of the kingdom.

The results of the mission were varied. The Gospel of Mark tells us that "the apostles returned to Jesus and told him all they had done and taught" (Mk. 6:30). In his variant account of the mission, Luke records that the disciples reported to Jesus: "Lord, even the demons are subject to us in your name" (Lk. 10:17). Both statements imply some degree of success. The passage in Luke is followed by these words of Jesus: "I saw Satan fall like lightning from heaven" (Lk. 10:18). The suggestion is that in the mission Jesus saw evidence of the overthrow of the power of evil and the ultimate victory of God's kingdom.

FAILURE AND GROWING OPPOSITION

But not everyone welcomed the mission of Jesus and his disciples. The reluctance of certain villages to heed their words led Jesus to prophesy:

> Woe to you, Chorazin! woe to you, Bethsaida! for if the mighty works done in you had been done in Tyre and Sidon, they would have repented long ago in sackcloth and ashes. But I tell you, it shall be more tolerable on the day of judgment for Tyre and Sidon than for you. And you, Capernaum, will you be exalted to heaven? You shall be brought down to Hades.
>
> —MATTHEW 11:21-23; LUKE 10:13-15

It was becoming more apparent that there was a stubborn resistance to the proclamation of the kingdom and its demands on men. Perhaps it was the disappointment over this resistance that led Jesus to tell the well-known Parable of the Sower (Mk. 4:3-9) to his disciples. In it Jesus tells them that not everyone who hears the word will respond favourably. The disciples are not to become discouraged. The power of the kingdom is not to be measured by their apparent lack of success. God, in his own time and in his own way, will bring his purposes to fulfilment, and in the meantime the disciples must continue to proclaim the kingdom in word and deed.

The Gospels also give the distinct impression of a growing and active opposition on the part of the Pharisees. The Gospel of Mark, for example, in three different passages (Mk. 2:1-3:6; 7:1-23; 12:12-37), records a series of disputes, some of which undoubtedly occurred during the Galilean ministry. We have already seen that Jesus' interpretation of the Law led to disputes with the Pharisees. And since we have no reason to believe that he retreated from his position, it is only logical to assume that his relations with a growing segment of the Pharisaic movement deteriorated as time went on.

This growing opposition from the religious authorities was accompanied by potential opposition from the political authorities. The Gospel of Mark suggests that the mission of the disciples attracted the attention of Herod Antipas, the tetrarch of Galilee and Peraea, who at this time resided in the city of Tiberias on the western shore of the Sea of Galilee (Mk. 6:14-16). It was in this general vicinity that the mission took place. According to Mark, Herod had heard reports about Jesus' work and had been informed that people were saying Jesus was John the Baptist come back to life.

As we saw earlier, Herod's motives in executing John had been largely political, for he could not tolerate potential agitation or insurrection. We do not know just when the activities of Jesus were first brought to Herod's attention, but the mission of the disciples may well have been the event that forced him to take a new measure of the situation. He must have known that Jesus was proclaiming the kingdom of God, and he had every reason to suspect that such a proclamation might at any moment incite the restless and depressed populace to insurrection. That Herod was actually hostile to Jesus is further suggested by a passage in Luke (Lk. 13:31-35), which reports that certain Pharisees came to Jesus and said: "Get away from here, for Herod wants to kill you." Jesus replied: "Go and tell that fox, 'Behold, I cast out demons and perform cures today and tomorrow, and the third day I finish my course.'" Obviously Herod's hostility did not deter Jesus from his mission.

CONTINUING POPULARITY
AND JOURNEYS TO THE NORTH

Along with this evidence of growing opposition to Jesus, there is also evidence of his continuing popularity. Soon after the mission of the disciples had been completed, Mark tells us that Jesus retired with his disciples to a wilderness place to "rest a while" (Mk. 6:30-44). If Mark is right in reporting that they went by boat, the destination must have been some uninhabited place on the shores of Lake Galilee. Before long, crowds had somehow discovered their presence and "ran on foot from all the towns." Jesus received them, and during the course of the day healed and taught them. Mark adds that Jesus "had compassion on them, because they were like sheep without a shepherd" (Mk. 6:34).

The day is remembered primarily for what happened at its close. The crowds had been assembled for many hours and they were tired and hungry. Since there was no food at hand, the disciples suggested that Jesus send the people away. But Jesus fed them with "five loaves" and "two fish" gathered from the crowd. The Gospel writers believed that on this occasion Jesus had performed a mighty work, and endless pages have been written to explain what happened (see p. 102). But however we explain it, one question remains: Did Jesus make this meal an occasion for teaching the people about the kingdom of God? We are told that he had been teaching all day, and according to Luke he "spoke to them of the kingdom of God" (Lk. 9:11). If Jesus did seek to teach through the feeding we may assume that the subject of his teaching was the kingdom.

The accounts of the Great Feeding as they stand in the Gospels show the tendency of the early church to interpret it as a foreshadowing of the Eucharist.[1] This is most clearly seen in the Gospel of John, where the author actually discusses the Eucharist in a long discourse following the story of the Feeding (see pp. 398 ff.). Although Jesus could not have had this Eucharistic meal in mind at the time of the Feeding, there is good reason to believe that he was thinking of another meal. In his teaching, Jesus frequently spoke of the coming of the kingdom through the symbolism of a great meal, and one of his parables may provide us with a clue to an understanding of the story of the Great Feeding. In this parable, Jesus tells of a man who prepares a great feast and then extends an invitation to all when the feast is ready (Lk. 14:16-24; Mt. 22:1-10). The metaphor of the feast as a symbol of the kingdom of God was familiar to the Jews; it had been implied in Isaiah and it became more explicit in later Jewish writings.[2] Jesus elsewhere refers to many who will "sit at table in the kingdom of God" (Lk. 13:29; Mt. 8:11), and at the Last Supper he speaks of the coming kingdom in terms of a feast (Mk. 14:25).

So it may be that Jesus intended the Great Feeding to be understood as a sign of the coming kingdom. To those who ate in repentance and faith, it was a pledge of the inevitable coming of the kingdom. Indeed, they already shared in its blessings. We might say that the Great Feeding was an "acted parable" similar to the parables that Jesus enacted on other occasions. Just as the crowds ate together in the wilderness, so those who repented and believed would one day share in the Great Feast in the consummation of God's kingdom.

After the Great Feeding, Jesus sought refuge from the crowds. Mark says "he went into the hills to pray" (Mk. 6:46). Both Mark and Matthew tell us that there ensued an eventful night on the stormy Sea of Galilee, and that Jesus and his disciples then landed on the plain of Gennesaret on the western side of the sea. Once again the people learned of Jesus' presence, and the whole neighbourhood brought their sick to be healed.

All these episodes confirm the fact that the fame and popularity of Jesus continued to increase in spite of growing opposition.

It was about this time that Jesus made a journey into the region of Tyre and Sidon, which lie to the north of Galilee on the Phoenician coast of the Mediterranean (Mk. 7:24; Mt. 15:21). The purpose of this trip has always been an enigma. Mark seems to imply that Jesus went

---

[1] For a discussion of the Eucharist or Lord's Supper see Chapter 6, p. 190.
[2] See Isaiah 25:6; also 4 Ezra 6:51 ff.; I Enoch 62:14 ff.; 2 Baruch 25:5 ff. Among the recently translated writings of the Dead Sea Sect is one passage that may refer to this messianic banquet. See Theodor H. Gaster, *The Dead Sea Scriptures*, pp. 309, 310. New York: Doubleday & Company, 1956.

to carry on a mission to the Gentiles, since Tyre and Sidon were in the non-Jewish territory of Phoenicia. But we must remember that the author of Mark wanted to write a Gospel for Gentile Christians, though there is nothing in the Gospels to suggest that Jesus himself conceived of his mission as directed to the Gentiles. On the contrary, he specifically says that his mission was directed only to the "lost sheep of the house of Israel" (Mt. 10:6). So a more plausible suggestion is that he withdrew at this time because Herod was threatening to interrupt his work. If so, Herod must have believed that Jesus was a menace to peace and order in Galilee. It is possible that the crowds who had gathered together at such times as the Great Feeding failed to understand Jesus' teaching about the kingdom, and read into his words their own nationalistic and materialistic hopes and dreams. Such a misunderstanding on the part of many people and the resulting apprehension on the part of Herod seem to be the best explanation for Jesus' northern journey, for he would have needed time to consider what steps he should take next.

Jesus did not remain in the region of Tyre and Sidon for very long, but it is difficult to trace his movements after he left. Not only is the itinerary in Mark (followed by Matthew) confusing (Mk. 7:31), but Mark (again followed by Matthew) includes in his Gospel a doublet of his first narrative of the Great Feeding (Mk. 8:1-21; Mt. 16:5-12).[3] In any event, not long after leaving Tyre Jesus and his disciples travelled north-east of Galilee to the region of Caesarea Philippi, in the territory of the tetrarch, Philip. It was here, our Gospels tell us, that Jesus began to teach his disciples of his impending death.

The question near caesarea philippi

According to the Gospels, a crucial conversation between Jesus and the disciples took place in the region of Caesarea Philippi (Mk. 8:27-33; Mt. 16:13-23; Lk. 9:18-22). Unfortunately, only a summary of this discussion is preserved, but from it we can infer that Jesus believed a crisis in his ministry was rapidly approaching, if it had not already arrived. In the first place, the conversation reflects Jesus' concern over the attitude of the people of Galilee toward his ministry. The disciples report that the people were calling him John the Baptist, Elijah, or one of the prophets—a sign that many were looking to him as the immediate forerunner of the coming kingdom. If these reports were true, and if widespread misunderstanding had developed over the

---

[3] Scholars agree that the second story of the feeding is a variant (doublet) of the first. Luke omits the second in his Gospel, but Mark had access to two accounts of the feeding and included them both.

nature of the kingdom he proclaimed, then Jesus' concern was well-founded. The excitement created by such gossip would undoubtedly have reached the ears of Herod, and there was no telling when he would put an end to Jesus' ministry just as he had terminated John the Baptist's.

Another significant point arose in that conversation. It is reported that Peter said to Jesus, "You are the Christ" (Mk. 8:29). The word "Christ" is derived from the Greek equivalent of the Hebrew word Messiah, and this was the first time that such a claim had been made by any of the disciples. Elsewhere in the Gospels the term is used only in the description of the hearing before the Jewish Sanhedrin (Mt. 26:63; Mk. 14:61; Lk. 22:67), in the accusation before Pilate as recorded by Luke (Lk. 23:2), and in Pilate's conversation with the crowds when they sought the release of Barabbas (Mt. 27:17, 22). In the Gospel record, Jesus neither refers to himself as Messiah nor discusses his mission in *specific* terms of Messiahship. According to Mark, when Peter called him Messiah, Jesus neither assented nor dissented, but told the disciples to speak to no one about the conversation.

The description of what happened on this occasion near Caesarea Philippi has caused no end of debate. Some scholars have argued that this story and the narrative of the Transfiguration that follows (Mk. 9:2-8) are post-resurrection stories of the early church read back into the period of the ministry. They point out that Jesus never claimed to be the Messiah and that nowhere else do the disciples make such a claim. This is seen as evidence that these stories must derive from the post-resurrection period, when for the first time Jesus was believed to be the Messiah. Others, on the basis of the same passages, argue quite the opposite. If Peter had not believed Jesus to be the Messiah, it would be impossible to explain his later belief in Jesus' resurrection and Messiahship. Any effort to deal with the problem must, however, take its start from a far more comprehensive view of Jesus' ministry.

We have seen that from the beginning Jesus conceived of his ministry as uniquely related to the coming of the kingdom. In the light of the record, then, the very least we can say is that his role was in some sense unique. The people sensed this strangeness, and the religious leaders were also aware of it. On at least one occasion his opponents accounted for it on the grounds that Jesus was demon-possessed. Some tried to express his uniqueness by calling him a prophet, but even the term prophet in Jesus' day designated an unusual role peculiarly related to the coming of the kingdom.

The one term that sheds light on Jesus' role is Son of Man, a designation that is found only on the lips of Jesus in the Synoptic Gospels.

The term "Son of Man" is a translation of the Semitic idiom, *ben adam* (Hebrew), or *bar nasha* (Aramaic), which could mean "man" in the generic sense. It is often used with this meaning in the Old Testament and at least once in Mark (Mk. 2:28). But generally the term Son of Man has a special religious significance in the Gospels.

There are a number of passages that speak of the Son of Man in connection with the final consummation of the kingdom. The most notable is Jesus' reply to the interrogation of the High Priest during the final questioning before his death: "I tell you, hereafter you will see the Son of Man seated at the right hand of Power, and coming on the clouds of heaven" (Mt. 26:64; Mk. 14:62). Elsewhere reference is made to the Son of Man coming in glory and power with the angels (Mk. 8:38; Mt. 25:31). In another saying, whose authenticity seems certain, Jesus prophesied to his disciples: "For truly, I say to you, you will not have gone through all the towns of Israel, before the Son of Man comes" (Mt. 10:23). Although a number of the passages referring to the coming of the Son of Man are interpretations of the early church, it is generally agreed that some of them go back to original sayings of Jesus. It must be said, however, that in these passages Jesus does not *explicitly* identify himself with the Son of Man.

These references to the Son of Man bear a striking similarity to one of the visions in the book of Daniel, in the seventh chapter of which the author paints a dramatic picture of the final triumph of God's kingdom:

> I saw in the night visions, and behold, with the clouds of heaven there came one like a *son of man*, and he came to the Ancient of Days and was presented before him. And to him was given dominion and glory and kingdom, that all peoples, nations, and languages should serve him; his dominion is an everlasting dominion, which shall not pass away, and his kingdom one that shall not be destroyed.
>
> —DANIEL 7:13-14

In this passage, *son of man* is used as a symbolic term to designate not an individual but the faithful remnant of Israel, vindicated by God on the day of his kingdom's triumph. Elsewhere the author calls them the "saints of the most high" (Dan. 7:22). It would seem that this imagery of Daniel influenced Jesus' sayings regarding the coming of the Son of Man in the consummation of the kingdom.

There is another group of sayings in the Gospels that refer not to the Son of Man's coming in triumph but rather to his suffering. At Caesarea Philippi, immediately after Peter's confession, Jesus "began to teach them that the Son of Man must suffer many things. . . ." (Mk. 8:31). Here are other sayings representative of this class:

> And how is it written of the Son of Man, that he should suffer many things and be treated with contempt?
>
> —MARK 9:12

> The Son of Man will be delivered into the hands of men, and they will kill him; and when he is killed, after three days he will rise.
>
> —MARK 9:31

> Behold, we are going up to Jerusalem; and the Son of Man will be delivered to the chief priests, and the scribes, and they will condemn him to death and deliver him to the Gentiles.
>
> —MARK 10:33

There are obvious differences between these two classes of sayings about the Son of Man. When Jesus refers to the final coming of the Son of Man, he does not make an *explicit* self-designation. When he refers to the suffering of the Son of Man, however, it is impossible to escape the conclusion that the suffering refers to his own, and that Son of Man is in some sense a self-designation. This has led some scholars to deny that Jesus ever uttered the sayings that deal with suffering, and that they were created by the early church under the influence of the Passion event. But this seems too arbitrary a conclusion, especially in the light of one Son of Man saying whose authenticity can be strongly defended and which does not specifically refer to death. In the Q source, Jesus is reported to have said: "Foxes have holes, and birds of the air have nests; but the Son of Man has nowhere to lay his head" (Lk. 9:58; Mt: 8:20). It would seem, then, that Jesus used the term Son of Man not only with reference to a future coming in glory but also as a self-designation in relation to his ministry.

In any event, Jesus' use of the term Son of Man raises two important questions: How do we account for the fact that when speaking of the coming Son of Man it is not an explicit self-designation, whereas in other instances it obviously is? What is the relation between the coming Son of Man and Jesus himself as the Son of Man? The answer to both these questions is to be found in Jesus' own understanding of his mission.

One of Jesus' sayings clearly shows that he saw his own mission in close relation to the coming Son of Man. He is reported to have said: "For whoever is ashamed of me and of my words in this adulterous and sinful generation, of him will the Son of Man also be ashamed, when he comes in the glory of his Father with the holy angels" (Mk. 8:38). In this passage Jesus seems to be saying that when the Son of Man comes men will be judged on the basis of the response they have made to the message of Jesus. We have seen that Jesus said the same thing in different terms elsewhere, when he proclaimed that men's status in the coming kingdom would be determined by their response to his call to repentance and belief in the good news. The difference here is not one of meaning but of language. The same event, referred to both as the coming of the Son of Man and the coming of the kingdom, is inextricably related to the mission of Jesus.

In Jesus' use of the term Son of Man as a self-designation, he implies that he is commissioned to give himself over completely to the task of calling Israel to the kingdom. A saying preserved in Luke has Jesus say: "For the Son of Man came to seek and to save the lost" (Lk. 19:10). And Mark reports that Jesus said: "For the Son of Man also came not to be served but to serve, and to give his life as a ransom for many" (Mk. 10:45). In both these sayings the mission of the Son of Man is described as the role of service, or the role of the servant. Even if we did not have these sayings, the life and teachings of Jesus would be enough to show that Jesus conceived of his mission as one of obedient service.

It is at this point that the prophetic book of Isaiah, rather than Daniel, helps us to understand Jesus' use of the term Son of Man. Centuries earlier, at the time of the return from the exile in Babylonia, an unknown Jewish prophet [4] spoke of the day when God would fulfil his purposes in Israel through the mission of a "servant." In a series of prophecies known as the "suffering servant" passages, he described the mission of this servant. At times the term "servant" seems to refer to an individual; at other times it seems to be a collective term. The most familiar passage, that found in Isaiah 53, gives us the most complete statement of the affliction and suffering involved in the servant's mission.

Many scholars are convinced that these prophecies in Isaiah are essential to a comprehension of Jesus' own understanding of his mission. No other section of the Old Testament seems to be closer in spirit and attitude to Jesus' teachings than Isaiah 40-66. According to Luke, when Jesus first preached in the synagogue at Nazareth his text was taken from this very section:

> The Spirit of the Lord is upon me, because he has anointed me
> to preach good news to the poor. He has sent me to proclaim re-

---

[4] His prophecies were eventually preserved in chapters 40-66 of the book of Isaiah. Some scholars believe that the prophecies of more than one man are contained in these chapters.

lease to the captives and recovering of sight to the blind, to set at
liberty those who are oppressed, to proclaim the acceptable year
of the Lord.

—LUKE 4:18-19; ISAIAH 61:1-2

Luke reports that after reading this passage Jesus said: "Today this
scripture has been fulfilled in your hearing" (Lk. 4:21). But even if
Luke had never reported this, a study of Jesus' words and deeds would
make it quite clear that these prophecies were finding fulfilment in
his ministry. That he himself found inspiration and guidance from the
great prophet of the exile is a logical deduction.[5]

Jesus would have been justified in using the term Son of Man as a
self-designation since his mission was the necessary prelude to the
coming of the Son of Man in triumph. So his reluctance to refer to
himself explicitly as the triumphant Son of Man remains something of a mystery. But two things can be said: First, as he saw it, he
was the Son of Man only insofar as he gave himself to the task of
proclaiming in word and deed the coming of the kingdom and the
triumphant Son of Man. Although his historic ministry foretold final
victory, it was not in itself the final victory. In using the term Son of
Man, Jesus was not making a claim on God; he did not seek from God
a manifestation of his power that would bring immediate and final
victory over the forces of evil gathered against him. Rather, he was
recognizing the utter claim of God on his life, and admitting that he
should give his life in the service that would bear witness to final victory.

In the second place, Jesus' reluctance to refer to himself explicitly
as the coming Son of Man may be accounted for by his own understanding of the great event that the coming signified. For the coming
of the Son of Man would mark the final gathering of all those who
had entered into the kingdom. As we have seen earlier, Daniel used
Son of Man as a collective term to refer to the redeemed of Israel. It
may be that by speaking of the coming Son of Man Jesus was referring
to the victory of all those who had responded to his call to the kingdom. The coming Son of Man was the coming of the whole company
of the kingdom to share in the victory he had proclaimed. Furthermore, Jesus expected men to enter into the sonship of God not only
through him but with him. The triumph he expected was not his
triumph alone but the triumph of all the children of the kingdom who
would share with him in God's victory.[6]

---

[5] See also the discussion of Jesus' words to John the Baptist, Chapter 4, p. 125.
[6] See T. W. Manson, *The Servant-Messiah*, pp. 65-79. Cambridge, England:
University Press, 1953.

So much for Jesus' use of the term Son of Man; but how do we account for Jesus' reluctance to use the title Messiah? The term Messiah had connotations that conflicted with Jesus' own understanding of his mission, for in popular opinion the Messiah was one through whom God would restore the kingdom of David. To many this meant an earthly kingdom. But, as we have seen, in Jesus' own understanding of the kingdom there was no place for the fulfilment of the political or nationalistic hopes of the Jews.

The term Son of Man, on the other hand, had none of these connotations, and it does not seem to have been a popular messianic title. It is true that in the book of Enoch, a compilation of writings dating from the first and second century B.C., Son of Man is used as a messianic title. But in Enoch the Son of Man is, to say the least, a mysterious figure who appears from heaven. He bears no resemblance to the usual picture of the triumphant Son of David—to say nothing of a suffering Son of Man.[7] Had Jesus referred to himself as Messiah he would only have beclouded the whole purpose of his mission, since he did not believe that the popular understanding of the Messiah's task adequately described it. Neither did he believe that the final victory of the Messiah, as it was understood by the popular mind, was within his power. In the last analysis only God could finally appoint his Messiah—when in his own time and in his own way he brought the consummation of the kingdom. This attitude would account for Jesus' entreaty to the disciples at Caesarea Philippi to say nothing about Peter's confession, and it would also explain Peter's reaction to Jesus' mention of his death.

According to Mark, Peter reacted violently to Jesus' reference to death at Caesarea Philippi (8:32), and actually rebuked him for it. Jesus replied to him in strong words: "Get behind me, Satan! For you are not on the side of God, but of men." In spite of Jesus' words, Peter could not accept the possibility that Jesus' mission might end in suffering and death. Peter was indeed on the side of men: he had not advanced beyond the popular way of thinking of the kingdom's coming only in terms of triumph and glory.

THE STORY OF THE TRANSFIGURATION

Not many days after Peter's confession (Mark says six; Luke, eight; Mk. 9:2; Lk. 9:28), another important incident, commonly

---

[7] There is reason to believe that the references to the Son of Man in Enoch are later Christian interpolations. For another viewpoint, see R. Otto, *The Kingdom of God and the Son of Man*, trans. by Filson and Lee-Woolf. London: Lutterworth Press, 1951.

called the Transfiguration, took place. Jesus and the disciples had journeyed north of Caesarea Philippi into the mountains, probably to the vicinity of Mt. Hermon, which lies about fifteen miles north of Caesarea Philippi. Jesus had taken Peter, James, and John to a mountain top, and there the three disciples had an unusual experience. According to the Gospel account, they saw Jesus transformed in appearance. His garments became glistening white, and "there appeared to them Elijah with Moses, and they were talking to Jesus" (Mk. 9:2-8).

This experience has been interpreted in many ways. Some have claimed that the narrative is a post-resurrection story that has been read back into the historical ministry of Jesus. On the other hand, many believe that the story, though elaborated by later tradition, is a reminiscence of some unusual experience that actually took place. The mention of the exact time of the event, which is unusual in the Gospels, and the crucial place it holds in Gospel tradition, point in this direction. Since it follows closely upon the Caesarea Philippi experience, its meaning must surely be related to the earlier event. No doubt for Jesus this was a time of intense agonizing over the direction that his mission should take, and it may even have been at this point that he decided to carry his mission to Jerusalem. The increased emphasis he put on his death in the following weeks suggests that the Transfiguration event marked the culmination of his own acceptance of death as the possible end of his ministry. For the disciples it must have been a time of discussion and debate over Jesus' teaching about his death. The mention of Elijah and Moses, symbols of the prophets and the Law, may indicate that they debated whether the scriptures in any way justified an expectation of death for the Messiah. Whatever the circumstances, the import of the Transfiguration story seems to be that the three disciples came out of the experience even more convinced of Jesus' unique role. Since the story has been so radically transformed by later tradition, nothing more than this is certain.[8]

In the period after the Caesarea Philippi experience, then, Jesus placed increasing emphasis on his own death, and at the same time he instructed the disciples that they too must expect suffering: "If any man would come after me, let him deny himself and take up his cross and follow me. For whoever would save his life will lose it; and whoever loses his life for my sake and the gospel's will save it" (Mk. 8:34-35). No one could share in the victory of the Son of Man unless he shared in the sufferings of the Son of Man on earth. The cost of

[8] For an excellent discussion, see Rollins and Rollins, *Jesus and His Ministry*, pp. 184-203. Greenwich: Seabury Press, 1954.

discipleship was high; it might even mean the disruption of family ties: "If anyone comes to me and does not hate his own father and mother and wife and children and brothers and sisters, yes, and even his own life, he cannot be my disciple" (Lk. 14:26). The ministry was heading toward a crisis: "Do not think I have come to bring peace on earth; I have not come to bring peace, but a sword" (Mt. 10:34). So each man must realize the cost of discipleship: "For which of you, desiring to build a tower, does not first sit down and count the cost, whether he has enough to complete it? Otherwise, when he has laid a foundation, and is not able to finish, all who see it begin to mock him saying, 'This man began to build, and was not able to finish' " (Lk. 14:28-30). There could be no turning back: "No one who puts his hand to the plow and looks back is fit for the kingdom of God" (Lk. 9:62).

Confronted by the expectation of death, Jesus became increasingly more pointed in his warnings to the disciples. They could expect no more than their leader: "A disciple is not above his teacher, nor a servant above his master" (Mt. 10:24). Although it is difficult to place specific sayings chronologically in the ministry of Jesus, many of those that foretell suffering for the disciples were probably uttered in this later period, when the crisis was drawing ever nearer.

The Mission to Jerusalem

After his sojourn in the region of Caesarea Philippi, Jesus returned for a brief period to Galilee (Mk. 9:30). According to Mark, he revisited the village of Capernaum, where he had spent so much time in the early days of his ministry (Mk. 9:33). Soon afterward, he left Galilee on his final journey to Jerusalem.

Why did Jesus go to Jerusalem? Some have said he went there to die, and this is certainly implied in the Gospels. It also seems to be implied in Jesus' reply to the Pharisees who warned him of Herod's ill-will: "Nevertheless I must go on my way today and tomorrow and the day following; for it cannot be that a prophet should perish away from Jerusalem" (Lk. 13:33). But Jesus' growing awareness of the possibility of death does not necessarily mean that this was the sole, or even the primary, reason for his going to Jerusalem. It would be more accurate to say that his purpose was to bring his message to the place that was the seat of the nation's religious life. There can be no doubt that he intended his message for the whole nation, and that would certainly call for a ministry in Judea, especially in Jerusalem.

The events in Jerusalem substantiate this conclusion. He did not go to court death, but to carry out his mission to Israel. Since his death marked the climax of this mission in the eyes of the early church, it is not surprising that the Gospel tradition puts unusual emphasis on this purpose in the Jerusalem journey.

We have no accurate record of the detailed events of this trip. The account in Mark reports that Jesus "went to the region of Judea and beyond the Jordan" (Mk. 10:1), which suggests that the trip south to Jerusalem took Jesus through Judea and into Peraea east of the Jordan River. Matthew agrees with Mark. Luke, on the other hand, describes a mission to the villages of Samaria and Peraea. The lengthy section of Luke in which this mission is described is referred to variously as "Luke's Special Section," "The Great Interpolation," or "The Travel Document" (Lk. 9:51-18:14). The author includes this sequence of events in order to work in a large quantity of special material from the Q and L sources which he could not fit into the Markan outline he was using. Although there is some evidence that Jesus passed through or near Samaritan villages, and that he had some contact with Samaritans (Lk. 9:51-56), there is no reason to accept Luke's suggestion that Jesus carried on an extended ministry in Samaria. It seems reasonably certain, however, that the trip took him near or through Samaria and involved a ministry in both Judea and Peraea.

Jesus came to Jerusalem by way of Jericho, a city located about five miles west of the Jordan and thirteen miles north-east of Jerusalem. Mark records the healing of a blind man in that village (Mk. 10:46ff.), and Luke records an encounter with a tax collector, Zacchaeus (Lk. 19:1ff.). Both incidents give evidence of Jesus' characteristic concern for the suffering. He heals a blind man of his infirmity, and he befriends a despised publican suffering from social and religious ostracism. When Jesus goes into the house of Zacchaeus to dine, a murmur springs up from the alarmed crowd: "He has gone in to be the guest of a man who is a sinner" (Lk. 19:7). In concluding his story, Luke tells us that Jesus said to Zacchaeus:"The Son of Man came to seek and to save the lost" (Lk. 19:10).

THE MISSION IN JERUSALEM

From Jericho, Jesus and his disciples made their way through the villages of Bethphage and Bethany (Mk. 11:1), a short distance to the south-east of Jerusalem, and stopped at the Mount of Olives. It was from this point that he entered the city of Jerusalem. Here again we are confronted with the problem of trying to work out an accurate sequence of events. According to the account in Mark, the well-known

Triumphal Entry took place when Jesus first came to Jerusalem. Mark tells us that the entry into the city, with the episodes leading up to the crucifixion, all happened within a week's time. But just as there was probably a longer ministry in Peraea and Judea than Mark implies, so the Jerusalem ministry probably lasted longer than a week. Mark himself says that Jesus had been teaching daily in the temple (Mk. 14:49), suggesting that Jesus spent a fairly long time in and around the city. That Jesus was on the move in and out of Jerusalem is certain, since incidents took place at Bethany (the anointing; Mk. 14:3ff.) and at the Mount of Olives (the arrest: Mk. 14:26ff.). Luke gives us this editorial note: "And every day he was teaching in the temple, but at night he went out and lodged on the Mount called Olivet" (Lk. 21:37). When we read between the lines, then, we find it difficult to fit the Jerusalem ministry into one week. Apparently Mark has created a sequence to satisfy his own purposes. Still it is impossible to speak with assurance of the order of events before the Last Supper and the beginning of the actual Passion Narrative (Mk. 14:17ff.).

This much we do know: At some time during this final period in Jerusalem, Jesus made an entry into the city that remained vivid in the memory of the early church and that is memorialized to this day

Modern Jericho and the Jordan Valley. The road paralleling the dry creek bed is the old Roman road that leads up to Jerusalem. The mound in the left foreground contains the ruins of a Hellenistic fortress alongside which the Herodian kings built an elaborate villa.

A telephoto picture, taken from the eastern edge of the Mount of Olives, showing the villages of Bethphage and Bethany, the Wilderness of Judea, and the depression of the Dead Sea.

in the celebration of Palm Sunday. On that occasion Jesus entered the city riding on an ass, an act that was charged with symbolic meaning. Matthew's Gospel (Mt. 21:4; *cf.* Zech. 9:9) tells us that it was done in order that a prophecy in Zechariah might be fulfilled:

> Tell the daughter of Zion,
> Behold your king is coming to you,
> Humble and mounted on an ass,
> And on a colt the foal of an ass.

Matthew's interpretation is probably valid, for by this act Jesus identified his mission with lowliness and peace rather than with earthly power and splendour. It was to be understood in terms of the prophecy of Zechariah rather than in terms of the contemporary longing for one who would usher in a new day of political power and economic

157

prosperity for Israel. Certainly this act was consistent with all Jesus' teaching about the kingdom and about his own mission.

Jesus entered Jerusalem near the season of Passover, when the city was crowded with pilgrims from all parts of Palestine and the Mediterranean world. If a crowd did gather and hail the entrance of Jesus, as the Gospels imply, it was no doubt led by Jesus' disciples and friends, along with Galileans who were in Jerusalem for the festivities. The people were in a festive mood; any excitement would have attracted their attention. Mark tells us that the crowds cried out:

> Hosanna! Blessed be he who comes in the name of the Lord! Blessed be the kingdom of our father David that is coming! Hosanna in the highest!
>
> —MARK 11:9-10

Although this has been called the "Triumphal" Entry, succeeding events were to prove the term a misnomer. The shout of Hosanna meant "Save now!" But it is likely that the salvation the crowds expected in the coming kingdom of David was a far cry from the kingdom in whose name Jesus had come. It was the practice of the Roman procurator to come from his residence in Caesarea with reinforcements of Roman soldiers to keep peace in Jerusalem during the festival. So the mood of the people was undoubtedly influenced by the presence of the hated Romans in the Holy City. Their hopes were filled with thoughts of revenge, and their desertion of Jesus during his last hours was proof of their disappointment in his mission.

During his stay in Jerusalem Jesus made repeated trips to the Temple. At least one visit made a vivid impression on the people gathered there. Jesus entered into the Temple precincts and drove out the money-changers and vendors of animals who were carrying on the commerce connected with the sacrificial rites (Mk. 11:15-19). This incident has been interpreted as a sign of Jesus' dissatisfaction with the way in which commerce had interfered with true worship. Again, it has been interpreted as a challenge to the priestly authorities, the Sadducees, to hear his message and to decide for or against the kingdom. Others have seen this act as an indication of Jesus' resentment over the desecration of the Court of the Gentiles, that place in the Temple to which the Gentiles had access. Jesus considered this practice a violation of God's will that his Temple should be "a house of prayer for all nations."

All these explanations shed light on the actual historical circumstances that prompted Jesus' action and on the meaning of his act. We cannot understand its full meaning, however, without taking into account a statement that Jesus made during his last days in Jerusalem. Referring to the Temple, Jesus said to his disciples: "Do you see these great buildings? There will not be left here one stone upon another, that will not be thrown down" (Mk. 13:2). Apparently the disciples were not the only people to know about this statement, for when Jesus was being questioned before the Jewish authorities he was accused of having threatened to destroy the Temple (Mk. 14:57).

How is this saying related to Jesus' total mission and message? First, it must be seen in terms of the actual historical situation. Many of the Jews were seething with a desire to revolt against the Romans, whom they looked upon as hated intruders; yet Jesus continually refused to give in to the popular hopes for revolt and revenge. Not that he was unaware of the oppression of his people. Rather, he seems to have been convinced that armed revolt was not the way out of their difficulties. It would lead only to destruction, motivated as it was by a desire fully as evil as the Romans' desire for power—the desire for revenge. The saying regarding the Temple's destruction may very well have been a prophecy of Jesus: unless the Jews heard his message and accepted the rule of the kingdom, a rule of peace and reconciliation, they could expect destruction. The destruction of the Temple would be the most vivid symbol of such a tragedy.

Second, the saying might have had even broader implications. Jesus may have meant to imply that with the coming of the kingdom of God the Temple cult would no longer exist. This would mean far more than a simple reformation of religious practice. In the Cleansing of the Temple, Jesus might have foretold by prophetic action the great day of reckoning when in the heavenly kingdom the earthly temple would no longer exist.

It is no wonder that Jesus' words and actions aroused the Sadducees, the ruling members of the priestly orders, for they regarded them as an attack on the traditional faith and on their own security. The priests derived their income from the sacrificial trade, but it was not only the threat to their financial well-being that disturbed them. They were very anxious to stay on good terms with the Romans, who could at any time close or even destroy the Temple (as they later did) if the priests failed to keep order in the land. Jesus' action was obviously a threat to their control, and as time goes on the exchanges between Jesus and the religious leaders reflect a mounting controversy.

Controversy accounts for a good bit of the material that the Synoptic authors have included in the Jerusalem ministry. But controversy was not a new thing for Jesus; he had known it all through his ministry. So it is difficult to know which of the episodes properly

MT. OF OLIVES

GETHSEMANE

KIDRON VALLEY

SILOAM

REMAINS OF HERODIAN WALL

LOWER CITY

TEMPLE AREA

TOWER OF ANTONIA

UPPER CITY

GARDEN TOMB

VALLEY OF HINNOM

CHURCH OF THE HOLY SEPULCHRE

CITADEL

PALACE OF HEROD

JERUSALEM IN THE TIME OF JESUS

OLD WALL ▬▬▬

ROADS ═══

To Samaria
To Bethlehem

Golgotha?
Bethzatha
Pool
Tower of Antonia
Altar
Temple
Suburb
Palace of Hasmoneans
House of the Sanhedrin
Present Wall
Citadel
Palace of Herod
Present Wall
Upper City
Lower City
Royal Porch
Pool of Siloam
Lower or Old Pool
Kidron Valley
Valley of Hinnom
Aceldama?
Mt. of Olives
Gethsemane
Bethphage
Bethany

Cross-Section West~East

West

East

PLAN OF THE TEMPLE AREA IN THE TIME OF JESUS

South

RAMPS

A. "THE HOUSE"
B. PORCH
C. ALTAR
D. LAVER
E. COURT OF THE PRIESTS
F. COURT OF ISRAEL
G. COURT OF WOMEN
H. ROYAL PORCH
I. SURROUNDING WALL
J. MOUNTAIN OF THE HOUSE

belong to this period. At least two of them, however, seem to fit into the last days in Jerusalem. In each of these incidents the religious authorities are eager to "entrap him in his talk" (Mk. 12:13).

The authorities made one attempt when they questioned Jesus about the payment of tribute to Caesar (Mk. 12:13ff.). Many of the more radical Jews smarted under this tax, for it was the most vexing symbol of their subjugation to Rome. Only when the tax had been wiped out would they feel that they were truly free from tyrannical rule. Jesus' questioners expected him to say something that would incriminate him in the eyes of the Roman authorities—something that would identify him with the radicals who threatened to revolt. In his answer, Jesus did not try to sidestep the issue: "Render to Caesar the things that are Caesar's, and to God the things that are God's" (Mk. 12:17). He merely meant to say that since the major problem of the Jews was not political, no political solution would be adequate for it. Rather, their major problem was one of religious decision: Would they or would they not accept the call to repentance that God was extending to them through Jesus' mission?

The religious authorities made another attempt to ensnare Jesus when they questioned him directly about his authority: "By what authority are you doing these things, or who gave you this authority to do them?" (Mk. 11:28). Here they were trying to entice him into making some broad personal claim that could be interpreted as blasphemy. But again his answer was consistent with all he had said throughout his ministry. Like John the Baptist, he had no other authority than what God gave him. They must decide for themselves whether his words and deeds had validity and authority in the sight of God.

These controversies and others, such as the debate with the Sadducees over the resurrection (Mk. 12:18-27), and with the Pharisees over the Davidic descent of the Messiah (Mk. 12:35ff.), probably occurred during the last days in Jerusalem. Each time, Jesus seems to have emerged the victor, if only temporarily. But his success further inflamed the resentment of his opponents.

FINAL TEACHING

Controversy did not absorb Jesus completely during the Jerusalem ministry, however. He spent a good bit of time with his disciples and friends, especially when he withdrew to Bethany and the Mount of Olives (Mk. 11:11; 14:3; Lk. 21:37; etc.). What was the subject of his teaching on these occasions? It is uncertain how much of the teaching found in the Gospel accounts of the Jerusalem ministry really belongs in that period. But it does seem certain that the major emphases reflected in the Gospel passages represent the main line of his teaching. In thinking about Jesus' teaching in Jerusalem we must keep in mind the mood of the disciples, of the religious leaders, and of the people. Both the priestly authorities and many of the Pharisees were plotting a showdown; the people did not seem to understand what Jesus was talking about; and his own disciples, though they followed him, were following in the dark—and were probably afraid.

In face of the opposition of the religious leaders and the lack of understanding of the people, Jesus dwelt on the rejection of his mission. Such parables as the Wicked Tenants (Mk. 12:1-12), the Marriage Feast (Mt. 22:1-14; Lk. 14:16-24), and the Talents (Mt. 25:14-30; Lk. 19:12-27) represent a persistent theme in Jesus' teaching even though they may not all be from this period. As Israel's rejection of his mission became more and more apparent, the situation must have weighed heavily on his mind. Here are the poignant words of Jesus' lament over Jerusalem:

> O Jerusalem, Jerusalem, killing the prophets and stoning those who are sent to you! How often would I have gathered your children together as a hen gathers her brood under her wings, and you would not! Behold your house is forsaken and desolate! For I tell you, you will not see me again until you say, "Blessed be he who comes in the name of the Lord."
>
> —MATTHEW 23:37 ff.; LUKE 13:34 ff.

These words clearly reveal how deep was Jesus' pathos over the rejection of his mission. There is no indication that he felt any personal offence, but his words reveal a profound spiritual agonizing over his conviction that the rejection of God's message would mean awful calamity for his nation. This same concern is evident in other words of Jesus: "Would that even today you knew the things that make for peace! But now they are hid from your eyes" (Lk. 19:42). The rest of this saying (19:43-44) shows obvious reworking by the early church under the influence of the actual destruction of Jerusalem in A.D. 70. But the final prophecy, "and they will not leave one stone upon another in you; because you did not know the time of your visitation," undoubtedly is Jesus' own. It is the awful thought of the destruction of his people that moves him to speak with such pathos.

We cannot always determine whether Jesus is referring to a political calamity or to the final judgment in these sayings. But to try to distinguish would be to miss the point of Jesus' message, for the judgment of God that would be executed in the end was the judgment of the God who already was sovereign of the world. It was not the mode of judgment that concerned Jesus. The real tragedy was the fact that Israel was rejecting both her mission and her sonship by failing to respond to God's call.

Jesus' criticism of the Pharisees probably grew more sharp and direct as time went on. Matthew and Luke, drawing on the Q source, include a series of strong rebukes against them. In Luke they are scattered throughout the Gospel (Lk. 20: 45-47; 11: 39-44, 46-52), but in Matthew they are brought together in one long section dated in the Jerusalem period (Mt. 23:1-36). In some of these passages Jesus attacks the hypocrisy of the Pharisees:

> Beware of the scribes, who like to go about in long robes, and love salutations in the market places and the best seats in the synagogues and the places of honour at feasts, who devour widows' houses and for a pretence make long prayers. They will receive the greater condemnation.
>
> —LUKE 20:46-47

The Pharisees looked upon themselves as the leaders of the nation; but instead of leading Israel to the fulfilment of her destiny by responding in faith and repentance to God's call, they refused to respond themselves and actually hindered others from responding: "But woe to you, scribes and Pharisees, hypocrites! because you shut the kingdom of heaven against men; for you neither enter yourselves, nor allow those who would enter to go in" (Mt. 23:13). Although in Matthew's day this passage undoubtedly reflected the Jews' refusal to enter the early church, in Jesus' day it must have referred to the Pharisees' attitude toward "sinners." But, as we saw in the last chapter, the Pharisees could not change their attitude unless they came to a new understanding of the mission of Israel in light of Jesus' proclamation of the kingdom.

In the face of impending death, Jesus' teaching of his disciples emphasized the inevitable coming of the kingdom. In Mark we find a long discourse that has been called the "Little Apocalypse" (Mk. 13) because of its apocalyptic language and ideas. Although many of the sections were added by the early church (see pp. 451 ff.), some of the sayings were actually uttered by Jesus—certainly those that call for watchfulness and preparedness. The end would come suddenly. Watchfulness and preparedness are the themes of the parables added by Matthew to the apocalypse of Mark: the Watchful Householder (Mt. 24:42-43), the Faithful and the Wise Servant (Mt. 24:45-51), the Ten Maidens (Mt. 25:1-13). The disciples were to be alert not only to the deception of false leaders (Mk. 13:5-6), but also to opportunities to do the will of their Master (Mt. 24:45ff.). They must be found faithful in the kingdom, as the Parable of the Talents implies (Mt. 25:14-30).

THE LAST SUPPER

At last the time came when the religious leaders could no longer tolerate the activities of Jesus. The Passover season was at hand, and they decided to make a decisive move before the day arrived. "And the chief priests and the scribes were seeking how to arrest him by stealth, and kill him; for they said, 'Not during the feast lest there be a tumult of the people' " (Mk. 14:1-2). These words of Mark appear at the beginning of the story of the final days and the events that led up to the crucifixion. This section, commonly called the Passion Narrative (Mk. 14:1-15:47), is one of the few extended sections in the Gospels whose chronology is dependable. Gospel studies have shown that it became fixed very early in the development of the oral tradition. Although the story as it now stands in each of the Synoptic Gospels contains various expansions by the early community, the principal events are present in each and in consistent sequence.

Jesus entered Jerusalem "on the first day of Unleavened Bread, when they sacrificed the Passover lamb..." (Mk. 14:12), and he apparently planned to be with his disciples for the opening festivities of the Passover season. Two disciples were sent ahead with instructions to find quarters in the crowded city where the disciples might be together with Jesus (Mk. 14:13-15). In the evening, after they had made the necessary arrangements, Jesus arrived and entered the "upper room" with them.

That evening, Jesus and his disciples shared in a memorable meal. The Synoptic accounts imply that it was a Passover meal, but scholars have debated this. According to the Gospel of John, the meal took place the evening before the Passover celebration (John 13:1). All four Gospels agree that the crucifixion occurred on Friday and the Last Supper on Thursday evening. John, however, indicates that the Passover fell on the sabbath day in that year, so both the sabbath and the Passover eve would have been Friday evening. Consequently the meal with the disciples on Thursday would have come before the Passover. Strongly supporting this dating by John is the argument that Jesus was crucified before the Passover. It is difficult to see how, even in the case of so controversial a person as Jesus, the Jewish authorities would have carried out his arrest and execution on the festival day. Even Mark makes it clear that the chief priests and scribes wanted to do away with Jesus before the Passover (Mk. 14:1-2). Many scholars, therefore, prefer John's chronology, and regard Mark's dating of the meal as a result of the early church's desire to relate the Lord's Supper to the Passover meal.

Whether or not it was the Passover meal, there can be no doubt that the memory and meaning of Passover were vivid in the minds of Jesus and his disciples. Each year, Passover intensified the Jews' memory of the mighty act of God in redeeming Israel from the iron hand of Egypt. It reinforced their faith that one day God would act for the salvation of his people. As he had once made a covenant with his people through Moses, so in a new day he would covenant with them again. Passover was an occasion not only for recollecting the past but also for looking forward to the future. Such were the thoughts that must have been in the air that evening. Jesus had proclaimed and taught about the new day that lay ahead, and had gathered together a handful of followers to share with him in proclaiming it.

Jesus and his disciples had joined together many times in fellowship meals. And the disciples had often heard Jesus offer thanksgiving and pronounce the blessing over bread and wine according to Jewish custom. The early church's practice of sharing in fellowship meals points back to this precedent. In the Orient, these meals had a highly symbolical meaning—they signified a close bond among those who ate together. But new factors were at work in this final meal, and the prospect of Jesus' death and the obvious rejection of his mission pervaded the thoughts of the disciples.

During the meal, Jesus shocked his disciples with the words: "Truly, I say to you, one of you will betray me, one who is eating with me" (Mk. 14:18). The bewilderment of the disciples reveals their ignorance of who this was to be (Mk. 14:19). According to Mark (Mk. 14:10-11), Judas, the betrayer, had already made his plans. Why he had decided to betray Jesus we cannot know. Mere financial gain seems too superficial a reason. The most likely explanation is that he had steadfastly hoped that Jesus would somehow exercise his powers as a political leader, and when he failed to do this, Judas, disappointed and disillusioned, reacted violently against him and offered to help in his capture. Neither are we given any hint of how Jesus knew the betrayer. But Judas was there, unknown except to one, sharing in the last meal.

Jesus spoke other words during the course of the meal that were to make the occasion memorable:

> And as they were eating, he took bread, and blessed, and broke it, and gave it to them, and said, "Take; this is my body." And he took a cup, and when he had given thanks he gave it to them, and they all drank of it. And he said to them, "This is my blood of the

covenant, which is poured out for many. Truly, I say to you, I shall not drink again of the fruit of the vine until that day when I drink it new in the kingdom of God."

—MARK 14:22-25

This is the simple account of the Last Supper, as recorded by Mark. Matthew's version, with the exception of a few phrases, follows Mark closely; there are somewhat different versions in Luke (Lk. 22:15-20), and in Paul's First Epistle to the Corinthians (I Cor. 11:23-26). Although the details vary, in general the accounts are the same. The continuation of the fellowship meal became central to the religious life of the early church, and its developing meaning will be taken up later.[9] But at this point we may ask: What did the Last Supper mean to Jesus?

Jesus' mention of the body in close connection with the breaking of the bread, and of the blood in close connection with the drinking of the wine, are prophetic of his imminent death. As on many other occasions, Jesus sought through an action to say a prophetic word. The fact that he mentioned the blood in connection with a "covenant" and the coming of the kingdom of God suggests that he was trying to convey to his disciples his confidence that his death would be used by God to establish his kingdom. Jesus believed it had been God's will for him to live for the proclamation of the kingdom; now he must die for the kingdom that God would establish through a new covenant with his people.

Nowhere else in Jesus' teaching does he refer to a covenant, but his mention of it here is not unexpected. All Jews knew of the great day prophesied by Jeremiah (Jer. 31:31 ff.) when God would establish a new covenant with his people, and the history of God's relation to Israel was a story of the making of covenants. As we have seen earlier, during Jesus' ministry one of the most vital sects of Judaism lived in the belief that it was the community of the "new covenant" (see p. 44). So it was not strange for Jesus to speak of his death in relation to God's establishment of the covenant of the kingdom. Furthermore, the mention of covenant in relation to blood suggests the Jewish belief that where there was a covenant there must be sacrificial blood (Ex. 24:8 ff.). It is impossible to say in what way Jesus regarded his death as a sacrifice. But this much we can say: As he gave his life in service for the kingdom, so now he gave his life in death for the kingdom. How it would be used, he left to the wisdom of God.

---

[9] See Chapter 6, p. 190; and Chapter 8, p. 260.

With his final words Jesus welded the disciples together in the expectation that he would eat with them again in the coming of the kingdom: "Truly I say to you, I shall not drink again of the fruit of the vine until that day when I drink it new in the kingdom of God." As their eating together had been an expression of the fellowship they had known during the ministry, so the promise of sharing in a common meal in the kingdom pointed toward a new fellowship with one another in the future. How this would be accomplished Jesus did not say. He simply prophesied that it would be.

Clearly, the disciples did not understand the full meaning of this fellowship meal, for it pointed to something that had not yet happened. In a few short hours they were to be in the depths of despair over Jesus' death. But the meal left one vivid impression in their minds: Whatever despair and confusion they experienced, Jesus had spoken of his death in hope, confidence, and trust. They still did not really understand how such an attitude could be justified, but the hope and trust in God that he revealed at that last meal must have gripped them more than at any other time during the ministry.

Arrest and crucifixion

Events moved swiftly after the last meal. Jesus and his disciples retired to the Mount of Olives, where Jesus made two painful predictions. To the disciples he said, "You will all fall away" (Mk. 14:27), and to Peter he predicted that before the cock crew he would deny him (Mk. 14:30). Peter, and all the disciples with him, protested: "If I must die with you, I will not deny you" (Mk. 14:31). Even though Jesus expected the disciples to waver, however, he still had confidence in them. According to Luke, Jesus is reported to have said to Peter: "Simon, Simon, behold, Satan demanded to have you, that he might sift you like wheat, but I have prayed for you that your faith may not fail; and when you have turned again, strengthen your brethren" (Lk. 22:31-32). Perhaps this saying, more than any other, discloses Jesus' hope that through Peter the little community of disciples would rally to a new understanding of the mission and to a new loyalty to the cause of the kingdom.

Then Jesus went with his disciples to a garden on the slopes of Olivet called Gethsemane. He was in great distress: "My soul is very sorrowful" (Mk. 14:34). He asked Peter, James, and John to keep watch while he went away to pray. Mark records his prayer: "Abba, Father, all things are possible to thee; remove this cup from me; yet not what I will but what thou wilt" (Mk. 14:36). If this was actually Jesus' prayer, the three disciples must have been close enough to have heard and remembered it. In any event, that it was a moment of agonizing prayer is signified by Jesus' use of the word "cup," which in Jewish thought frequently symbolized suffering and hardship. Jesus himself had once asked James and John if they were able "to drink the cup" that he was to drink, obviously referring to his sacrificial service, possibly his death (Mt. 20:22). Surely it would be wrong to think of the "cup" in Jesus' prayer as referring merely to his own physical suffering. Nothing in his ministry would lead us to believe that he would ask the Father to remove this. What, then, was the cup of suffering over which Jesus agonized? There are at least two possible answers. First, it may refer to the anguish he experienced over the people's rejection of his mission. We have already seen how deeply he mourned the consequences of this, and it is consistent with his deepest longings that to the very end he prayed that God would open their eyes. Second, the cup of suffering may refer to the concern Jesus felt for his disciples and followers. No matter how great his confidence and hope, it was still possible that they might abandon

The Garden of Gethsemane, where Jesus was arrested the night before his death. Beyond the garden is the Jewish cemetery on the Mount of Olives. Here the pious were buried to be near the Lord, who, according to Zechariah's prophecy, will stand on the mountain on the Day of Judgment.

their mission. The very fact that the disciples could have slept while he prayed must have been a vivid reminder of their frailty.

Whatever the meaning of the "cup," one thing is certain: The prayer discloses the profound humanity of Jesus, "a man of sorrows and acquainted with grief." It is the same man who says: "Yet not what I will, but what thou wilt" (Mk. 14:36). His resolute, courageous, and obedient submission to death, even though many issues remained unresolved in his own mind, gave these words their ultimate meaning. He could act only in the same trust that he had called for in the lives of others. This alone was the sign of Sonship.

The disciples fell asleep while Jesus was praying (Mk. 14:37). Meanwhile, Judas was coming through the darkness leading a group of servants from the High Priest to apprehend Jesus (Mk. 14:42-43). Judas, who knew where to find Jesus, came forward and kissed him—the sign that had been arranged to identify Jesus in the darkness. When the men seized Jesus he rebuked them for acting as though he were a common criminal who might try to escape (Mk. 14:48-49). As for the disciples, "they all forsook him and fled" (Mk. 14:50).

It was very late evening or early morning when Jesus was seized. The Gospel records are not entirely clear about what happened next. In Mark, Jesus is taken immediately to the home of the High Priest; a full-dress hearing before the Sanhedrin, the Jewish court, is conducted at once (Mk. 14:53-65); and another meeting is held in the morning (Mk. 15:1). Matthew follows the account in Mark. Luke, on the other hand, implies that an informal meeting before the High Priest that night was followed by a formal meeting of the full Sanhedrin in the morning (Lk. 22:54-71).

But the pattern is clear enough. The religious authorities felt the need to move swiftly, and there is every indication that they had decided what to do even before Jesus appeared before them. If the Gospel accounts are dependable, then, to call Jesus' hearing a trial would be misleading, for the formal procedures of Jewish law appear to have been bypassed.[10] Obviously the Gospel accounts of the hearing are open to question, since none of the disciples was there. It is not inconceivable, however, that news of what transpired might have leaked out, and it is entirely possible that some of those who were present, or at least their friends or relatives, might have entered the Christian church later on. It has frequently been pointed out that the account in the Gospel of John contains information that seems to have come from

---

[10] This is a highly debatable question. For an excellent summary of the various solutions see Vincent Taylor, *The Gospel According to Mark,* pp. 644-646. London: Macmillan, 1952.

someone who had access to priestly circles. Most scholars agree that the description in the Synoptics is highly credible in spite of additions made by the early church and the lack of eye-witness details. In fact, the absence of such details enhances the credibility, since no effort was made to claim or pretend that the tradition is an eye-witness account.

Evidently witnesses were planted in the hearing whom Mark calls "false" (Mk. 14:56). A confused charge was made, stating that Jesus had claimed he would destroy the Temple (Mk. 14:58). This charge was probably based on a garbled version or a misunderstanding of Jesus' prophecy of the destruction of the Temple. In any event, the testimony was far from unanimous, and Jesus made no response to the accusation. The final question of the High Priest was: "Are you the Christ, the Son of the Blessed?" (Mk. 14:61). The High Priest was hoping to extract a confession from Jesus that would provide a charge serious enough to arouse Pilate's concern; a confession of Messiahship could be construed as treason to Rome. According to Mark, Jesus answered, "I am" (Mk. 14:62). In Matthew, the reply is "You have said so" (Mt. 26:64). In view of Jesus' reluctance to claim Messiahship, Matthew's words are probably closer to the original, and Jesus may have permitted the High Priest to make a claim he would not make for himself. Whatever words he used, he clearly assented.

Why did Jesus do here what he had refused to do before? Any answer that we make to this question must be very hypothetical. Could it be that he believed that a denial of the claim would be interpreted as a clear rejection of his whole mission? He must have been convinced that he was about to be executed, and that his willingness to die was proof that Messiahship as he understood it was a far cry from the popular expectations. So he refused to deny his mission now, even at the risk of being misunderstood if he assented to the charge that he claimed to be the Messiah.

We are told that after a silence Jesus spoke out again: "You will see the Son of Man sitting at the right hand of Power and coming with the clouds of Heaven" (Mk. 14:62). This answer would have been in keeping with Jesus' teaching and preaching, for he understood his mission as inextricably related to the coming of the Son of Man. Although Jesus did not say that he was the Son of Man of whom he spoke, the High Priest obviously interpreted his words that way, for when the priest heard the words "sitting at the right hand of Power" he "tore his mantle" and accused Jesus of blasphemy. In this way he fulfilled the legal requirement of tearing the clothes when blasphemy was heard. The others present joined in his condemnation and spat upon Jesus.

It is difficult to say just what the High Priest meant by his charge of blasphemy, for it is not at all certain that the claim of Messiahship was blasphemy in itself. Whatever the specific charge was at the time of the hearing, it must be understood against the background of all the charges that had been made against Jesus throughout the ministry. In the eyes of the religious authorities, his attitude toward the Law and the Temple had already brought their condemnation. He clearly represented a threat to the unity of the people as they conceived it, for to destroy the Law and to belittle the Temple was to threaten the life stream of the Jews. As such, he was threatening not only the nation but God himself.

Only when we remember the background of the hearing can we understand the action and reaction of the religious authorities. It was far more than any one statement of Jesus that brought the charge of blasphemy against him. But perhaps the closest we can come to identifying the word that set off the charge is to turn to the statement of Jesus that the Son of Man would be at the "right hand of Power." If we grant that the authorities believed Jesus used Son of Man as a self-designation, and interpreted the words "at the right hand of Power" as Jesus' claim for an unholy relation to God, then the charge of blasphemy makes sense. And in the eyes of the Law he would have condemned himself through blasphemy.

But whatever the religious charges were, the most important charge was that on the grounds of which Jesus was delivered over to Pontius Pilate, the Roman procurator (Mk. 15:1-5),—namely, that he claimed to be Messiah. Pilate asked him one question: "Are you the King of the Jews?" (Mk. 15:2). From this we would infer that the Jewish authorities had delivered Jesus to Pilate for judgment on the charge that he had claimed to be the Messiah. A Roman procurator would not know many Hebrew words—but Messiah he would recognize. To a Roman unfamiliar with the subtleties of Jewish religious thought, the term could mean only one thing: rebellion and treason. There had been messianic pretenders before, and each of them had been a threat to the peace of the land. To a Roman, the Jewish word Messiah would have had only a political meaning, and could be translated as "King of the Jews." Jesus' answer to Pilate must have sounded elusive: "You have said so" (Mk. 15:2).

According to Mark, Pilate was reluctant to condemn Jesus. There are also other passages in the Synoptics that stress Pilate's reluctance, but they have no foundation in fact. Instead, they developed out of the church's later attempt to lay the blame for Jesus' death on the Jews and to exonerate Rome. When the church entered upon its

The Via Dolorosa, the traditional route through which Jesus carried his cross to Golgotha. In the basement of the building on the right are enormous paving stones that are believed to have formed the courtyard of the Roman fortress that adjoined the Temple area. The arch over the street was probably part of a building erected by Hadrian in the second century A.D.

broader mission to the Roman world, it tried in every possible way to prove that its founder had not been treasonable to the Roman government. But even when we make allowance for this influence in the development of the Gospel accounts, it may still be that Pilate really did show reluctance, out of his own doubt about the charge. Certainly, if he had known anything about Jesus' mission or his teaching he would have had a difficult time putting his finger on any overt act of Jesus that could have been called politically dangerous. And during the hearing Jesus must have appeared quite harmless. The Synoptic Gospels all report that Pilate offered to release Jesus if the crowds desired him to (Mk. 15:9), in keeping with the Roman procurator's custom of releasing a prisoner at the feast of the Passover (Mk. 15:6; Mt. 27:15; Lk. 23:17). Although there are no other historical references to this practice, it may actually have existed. But the people were relentless in their cry, "Crucify him!" (Mk. 15:13). The best explanation of the people's attitude is that they were disappointed by Jesus' failure to

G 173

prove to their satisfaction the validity of what they believed to be his messianic claims. In their eyes, he was an impostor.

So Pilate sentenced Jesus to death.[11] After the Roman soldiers had scourged him and mocked him as "King of the Jews," they led him away to a place called Golgotha, where they crucified him (Mk. 15: 22-32). In true Roman fashion, a *titulus*, an inscription stating the crime, was fastened to the cross over Jesus' head: "King of the Jews." Jesus' accusers had succeeded in persuading Pilate that Jesus was a pretender to the "throne of David," a disturber of the peace, and hence guilty of treason.

The disciples had long since scattered. Peter had followed Jesus as far as the High Priest's house, and had then denied any acquaintance with Jesus when a young maid accused him of being a follower (Mk.

---

[11] Scholars have debated whether or not the Sanhedrin had the power in Jesus' day to invoke the death sentence. Although there is still difference of opinion, the consensus is that it had not. In any event, Jesus died under the sentence of the Roman procurator and by the Roman method of execution, crucifixion.

The Garden Tomb, located outside the wall of the Old City of Jerusalem. Though it probably dates from the late first or early second century A.D., it is thought by some to have been the tomb in which Jesus was laid.

14:66-72). Then he too disappeared. Jesus died alone and deserted. A few women who had known him watched the last scene from afar (Mk. 15:40). When death came at last, a man who appears in the Gospels for the first time, Joseph of Arimathea, having received permission from Pilate, prepared the body for burial and placed it in a tomb (Mk. 15:42-47).

There can be little doubt that the handful of disciples and friends who had followed fearfully but hopefully felt nothing but bewilderment and despair. Their only bond was a memory—a memory that was fast being swallowed up in the memory of a cross. It was a fearful, death-dealing finale for the little community that had gathered together in expectation of a great new day for the people of God. The miracle they had expected had not come. Now it was too late!

CHAPTER SIX

᠉ᨆ

THE LIFE OF
THE EARLIEST COMMUNITY

Unlike many modern religious movements, there was never any planning stage in the life of the Christian community. There were antecedents, of course, in the experience of the little band of Jesus' followers during his career, but the Christian community appears to have sprung suddenly into existence, sharing from the outset a basic framework of convictions and practices. This enthusiastic group immediately

---

New Testament readings relevant to this chapter are Acts 1:1-8:40; 9:31-12:19.

found itself bound together by strong ties. As time went on, its members developed doctrine in an effort to understand what had happened, and found it necessary to delineate responsibilities and procedures. But the experiences that created the community came first.

The Risen Lord

(Acts 1:3)

THE ORIGIN OF THE RESURRECTION FAITH

Some scholars have suggested that the disciples recuperated slowly from their tragic disillusionment, and then, as the group began to regain momentum, invented the idea of the resurrection and other beliefs in an effort to justify their actions and to authenticate their claims for Jesus. All our records agree, however, that the sorrow and bitterness that overwhelmed the disciples at the time of the crucifixion were rapidly transformed into confident joy without any interim of scheming or reconnoitring. What could have effected so great and sudden a change? The obvious answer is that the community had become convinced that Jesus had been victorious over death and was alive! We must turn, then, to the evidence for such claims.

The oldest written record of the resurrection of Jesus is that given by Paul in his first letter to the Corinthians (15:3-8), where he lists the appearances of the resurrected Jesus to the various leaders of the early community. First on the list is Peter, and last is Paul himself. This chronological listing of the appearances is in keeping not only with the strategic role that Peter played in the circle of the twelve disciples, but more specifically with the Gospels' repeated emphasis on the fact that Christ appeared to Peter. The most primitive of the resurrection accounts, at first transmitted orally and much later written down, is the one found in Mark (16:1-8). Although this account does not state that Jesus appeared to Peter (also known as Cephas, Simon), it clearly implies that he shortly would do so (Mk. 16:7). The accounts of the post-resurrection appearance in Luke 24 and John 21 state directly that Peter saw the Risen Lord. In the story of Jesus' coming to the disciples gathered behind closed doors (John 20), as well as in Matthew's account of the appearance of Jesus to the disciples in Galilee (28:16-18), Peter is assumed to be among the number, although he is not singled out for specific mention as he is elsewhere. There is a clear implication in the statement of Jesus recorded in Luke 22:31—a prophetic word spoken on the night of his betrayal—that Peter is to be the one who will rally the community around his leadership.

The Church of the Holy Sepulchre, erected by the Crusaders on the site of an earlier church that was built by the Emperor Constantine. Under its roof are the traditional sites of Golgotha, the tomb of Christ, and the cave where the Empress Helena, mother of Constantine, believed she found the true cross of Christ.

It is evident, therefore, that the appearance to Peter of Christ risen from the dead was a basic element in the cluster of traditions circulating in the early church about the strange and wonderful days that burst upon the followers of Jesus shortly after his shameful execution. Small wonder that Peter should be the one to speak for the group in making the first public proclamation that "This Jesus ... whom you crucified ... God has made both Lord and Christ" (Acts 2:23, 36).

As Paul's list makes clear, however, and as the other traditions testify, Peter was just one among many who saw Jesus risen from the dead. Of these others, Paul mentions the twelve disciples, the "more than five hundred brethren," "all the apostles," and James. But the Gospels mention other appearances as well: the beautiful account of the unknown traveller on the Emmaus road, who in breaking bread reveals himself to be the Risen Christ (Luke 24:13-35); and John's record of

178

the famous scene in which Mary Magdalene mistakes Jesus for the gardener (John 20:11-18).

Still another set of traditions current in the early days of the community is concerned with the empty tomb. In contrast to the tradition of Christ's appearance to Peter, which Paul explicitly mentions but which the Gospels only imply, the tradition about the empty tomb is not referred to at all by Paul. But it is described in one form or another by all four of the Gospels. Perhaps the Gospel of Mark originally ended with an account of the appearance of the Risen Lord to Peter, although the most reliable manuscripts extant end with a reference to the empty tomb.[1] The simple, straightforward account of the empty tomb given in Mark is supplemented with vivid detail by Matthew and Luke: the young man in Mark's account is described by Matthew as an angel with an appearance like lightning; Mark says his robe is white, but Luke calls it dazzling. Still further expansion of detail occurs in the apocryphal gospels, such as the Gospel of Peter.[2]

Paul's silence concerning the empty tomb has been interpreted as proof that he knew nothing about such a tradition. Such an inference, however, is precarious, since Paul's argument in I Corinthians 15, where he deals with the subject at great length, is designed to prove the *bodily* resurrection. What is placed in the grave is raised, although it is raised in a transformed condition (I Cor. 15:43, 44). There is no suggestion that Paul believed that the body decayed and the soul or spirit was raised. His insistence on the identity of what is buried with what is raised suggests that he would have expected the tomb of Jesus to have been empty after the resurrection. Whether Paul believed in the empty tomb or not cannot now be determined; that he did not consider the emptiness of the tomb a significant question is evident from his silence on the subject. For him, the indispensable and indisputable fact was that Jesus *had appeared* to chosen witnesses after his resurrection. Later generations of Christians were to appeal to the empty tomb as proof of the resurrection; Paul was much more concerned with the implications of the resurrection for human salvation and for the coming of the kingdom of God than he was with the circumstances surrounding the event.

The appearances of Jesus risen from the dead were for Paul the final proof that the new age had dawned. This unshakable conviction was shared by James, Jesus' brother, and by the "more than five hundred brethren" of whom Paul speaks who saw the Risen Lord. Such,

[1] See M. Dibelius, *From Tradition to Gospel*. New York: Scribners, 1935.
[2] See *The Apocryphal New Testament*, trans. by M. R. James. Oxford: Clarendon Press, 1950.

then, was the belief about the resurrection of Jesus. What could have happened to create such a conviction?

RATIONAL EXPLANATIONS OF THE RESURRECTION

Several explanations are possible. The one that is most tempting at first sight is the theory that the impact of Jesus' personality was so powerful and real that his followers sensed that death had not separated him from them, and that he was still present in their midst. This feeling of continuing presence, however, is to be observed whenever a forceful person dies. *Rebecca*, a popular novel of a few years ago, is built around just this theme. Yet in spite of the universality of this experience, no one has ever made the kind of claims for a departed friend whose presence continued to be felt that Jesus' followers made for him. If the disciples had not thought Jesus was with them in a unique sense, they would scarcely have regarded the resurrection as the keystone of their faith and their gospel.

Students of comparative religion have suggested that the belief in the resurrection was invented to enable incipient Christianity to compete more effectively with other religions that worshipped a god who had died and had risen again.[3] It has been demonstrated, however, that this analogy is not appropriate, since none of these deities is anchored in concrete historical and geographical situations as Jesus was. Moreover, their dying-and-rising is part of a recurrent series—often closely related to the cycles of the seasons—and not at all the once-for-all event that Christianity claimed for its saviour.

One matter-of-fact way to account for the resurrection faith without sharing it is to assume that the women and the disciples found the tomb empty because in their excitement they simply went to the wrong one,[4] and that from this innocent mistake arose the whole movement that we know as the Christian church. It is difficult to believe, however, that even such a great emotional stress as the one through which Jesus' followers passed would cause them to forget where he had been buried. Especially would this have been true of the brave women who stood by him when all others had fled. Even the ancient claim of the enemies of the Christian community—that the disciples had removed the body secretly (Mt. 28:11-15)—though scarcely credible, is more acceptable than the notion that the women forgot in which grave Jesus had been placed.

---

[3] A. C. H. Drews, *The Christ-Myth*. Chicago: Open Court, 1911. On the dying-and-rising gods see Chapter 1, above.

[4] K. Lake, *The Historical Evidence for the Resurrection of Jesus Christ*, p. 250. London: William and Norgate, 1907.

More nearly convincing than any of these suggestions is the theory that the story of the empty tomb was not a part of the most primitive tradition at all, but that it was presented by the early church to make external and concrete the inner experience of the resurrection that had come to the apostles and other witnesses of the Risen Lord. Some who follow this line of thought are convinced that the appearances were wholly subjective, and that they arose out of the conviction that God's justice would not permit such an exemplary and important career as that of Jesus to come to such an ignominious and fruitless close. Others claim that the Spirit of the Risen Christ sent these visions to the disciples, so that they *were* inner experiences, though not merely mental images projected by the minds of credulous followers.

Such an explanation, rationally appealing as it may be, cannot account for what is called a *resurrection* without doing violence both to the New Testament evidence and to the biblical view of the nature of man. Jewish thinking rarely, if ever, portrays a separate, immaterial part of man, such as we usually mean when we speak of *soul* or *spirit*, as the enduring part of man in contrast to his mortal body. Except among the Essenes, it did not conceive of man as existing apart from his body. The Platonic notion was that the body was the prison of the soul, but this idea was not acceptable to the Hebrew mind. The body of man was created first, and then the breath of life was breathed into him (Gen. 2:7). Just as the breath was essential to life, so the body was indispensable if there was to be a living person. Death did not bring release for the soul; it transported man to a shadowy half-existence in Sheol, or Hades, the subterranean realm to which all the dead descended, and from which man could escape only when his soul and body were reunited in the resurrection.

DISTINGUISHING RESURRECTION FROM IMMORTALITY

Paul makes clear his conviction, however, that the body which man will have in the resurrection is not merely a resuscitated corpse; it is a body that is identifiable with the body that was laid to rest. But it is at the same time distinctively different, in that it is "imperishable," "glorious," "powerful," and "spiritual." Paul nowhere explains what he means by the phrase "spiritual body," but he does declare emphatically that "flesh and blood cannot inherit the kingdom of God" (I Cor. 15:50). He states flatly that he does not believe in the resurrection of the physical body (I Cor. 15:44). We are left with the conclusion, then, that the "spiritual body" was Paul's way of saying that in the resurrection the whole man was transformed in the new age of God. He would never have subscribed to the theory that man's body, like that of John

Brown in the old song, "lies moulderin' in the grave, but his soul goes marching on." But neither would he have accepted the flesh-and-blood conception of the future life which expects little more than an endless extension of the life in this world.

In a well-known controversy with the Sadducees, Jesus rejected the idea that life "in the resurrection" would be under the same circumstances as earthly life as it is now known. When the intentionally absurd question was raised by the Sadducees about the marital status in heaven of the woman who had lost seven successive husbands, Jesus' reply was negative ("... when they rise from the dead, they neither marry nor are given in marriage"). But the inference is clear that life in the new age is a transformed existence, and not merely survival after death (Mk. 12:18-25). Both the reply of Jesus just quoted and the Pauline concept of the "spiritual body" are attempts to affirm (1) that man is a unity, and (2) that there is a future life for man in his wholeness. The second affirmation would stand over against those who deny eternal life or who regard only the immaterial part of man as capable of survival after death.

Nowadays psychologists and physicians alike are stressing the interrelation of mind and body in man. The term "psychosomatic," used to describe diseases that have physical symptoms but are mental in origin, is formed by transliterating precisely those Greek words which Paul uses for soul (*psyche*) and body (*soma*). Even though we still distinguish abstractly between man's *body* and his *mind*, the growing recognition of the way in which the two interact leads to an understanding of man closely akin to the New Testament idea of man as a unity. The real man is not just a physical organism, nor is his real nature a soul that can be abstracted from the body in which it has taken up residence. Man is a body and a soul in their interrelations, and not just the two added together.

Paul could not believe that the future life would consist merely in a continuation under improved circumstances of life as he knew it; the moral and physical weakness he saw within himself convinced him that his body must be transformed before entering eternal life. But at the same time, he could not imagine human existence apart from a body. As a middle way between these unacceptable alternatives, Paul developed his doctrine of the spiritual body. The old would not simply pass away; it would be transformed in becoming a part of the new creation to which he looked forward with eager longing. The certainty of man's entering the life of the new age had been established when God raised Jesus from the dead, as guarantee and prototype of man's resurrection.

Proving the resurrection

Toward the end of the first century, certain heretical elements in the Christian community began to deny the reality of Jesus' body. This heresy—called docetism, from the Greek word for *seem* (since its adherents claimed Jesus only *seemed* to have a body)—was quite properly rejected, because it denied the reality of the incarnation, and because it failed to include the transformation of the whole man in its concept of the resurrection. The community would settle for nothing less than the full manhood of Jesus, the reality of his body, and the resurrection of the whole man.

The community's insistence on the bodily nature of the resurrection was shaped in part by current Jewish notions of the after-life. But it was also an essential element of the basic concept that in Jesus, God was revealed in history. The culmination of God's revelation through Jesus was the resurrection. But if the resurrection transported Jesus to a sphere totally unrelated to the historical situation, or if it changed him into something that was no longer identifiable as human, then the phrase "revelation in history" had lost its meaning. But the church insisted that the Risen Lord and Jesus of Nazareth were the same person. The Christ who was raised from the dead was a risen man, not a spirit assuming human form. The resurrection was looked upon, not as a miracle performed to prove that Jesus was divine, but as proof that through him a new kind of human existence—the life of the new age—had become a reality.

Since the resurrection was so central to the faith of the community, the early church was eager to demonstrate that there was abundant evidence for the claim that it continued to make that Jesus had risen from the dead. The prologue to Acts (1:3) mentions the "many proofs" of the resurrection, by which it means the appearances of Jesus to his disciples in order to confirm to them that he had been raised and in order to commission them to proclaim the gospel. In all four Gospels and in the Acts, the privilege of seeing the Risen Lord carried with it the weighty responsibility of serving as a herald of the Good News. The disciples were to go everywhere preaching; Peter was to feed Jesus' sheep; the chosen ones were to be witnesses "to the end of the earth." The resurrection is far more than a marvellous event, interesting for its own sake as a unique phenomenon; it is interpreted by the community as God's public declaration that Jesus is Son of God; it provides a living example of the life of the new age; it is the well-spring of the earliest Christian proclamation, the *kerygma*.

WITNESSES OF THE RESURRECTION

Perhaps it was the sacredness of the number twelve in the Hebrew tradition, added to the Christian identification of the twelve disciples with the twelve tribes of Israel, that led to the conviction that there had to be twelve apostles. The defection of Judas had left a gap in the inner circle of the followers of Jesus, and the community decided to choose a man by lot to replace Judas. The man chosen was Matthias, of whom nothing is known beyond the report in Acts of his being chosen. If he did not gain the fame of Peter or John, he at least avoided the infamy of his predecessor, Judas. Early Christian writers, including the author of Acts, took morbid delight in recounting the gory details of the death of Judas, the unlamented traitor. According to Matthew (27:3-10) he hanged himself; Acts says that he swelled up and burst (1:18); another account reports that he swelled to such an enormous size that he became wedged in a narrow street and was run down by a chariot!

The requirements for membership in the circle of the apostles were two: (1) that each man should have been a follower of Jesus from the beginning of his public ministry following the baptism; (2) that each should have seen Jesus risen from the dead. In later years, it was the second of these qualifications that really mattered. Paul had obviously not been a follower of Jesus from the beginning, but because he had seen the Risen Lord he could qualify for apostleship (I Cor. 9:1). On the basis of their commission from the Risen Christ, the twelve witnesses of the resurrection—later joined by Paul—set about their task of preaching the gospel in Jerusalem and in ever-widening circles to the ends of the earth (Acts 1:8).

The Coming of the Spirit
(Acts 2:4)

The hope and the promises that the Risen Christ gave to his followers were not directed solely toward the indefinite future when God's purpose would be fulfilled. Rather, the promises included equipping them for the task to which they had been called. Acts reports that Jesus told his disciples that the Spirit would come upon them in manifestation of the powers of the new age, just as it had come upon him at baptism and had worked through him when he performed his mighty works (Lk. 4:18 ff.). In Jesus' ministry the forces of evil had been overcome through the power of the Spirit, and the reign of God over his creation had begun to dawn (Lk. 11:20). Similarly, the community was to be the channel through which the coming of God's kingdom was to be announced, and through which its ultimate triumph was to be anticipated. The mighty works that the Spirit would perform through the church were continuing signs of the coming kingdom.

THE RELATION OF THE SPIRIT TO CHRIST

The coming of the Spirit was not viewed in isolation from the resurrection or even from the person of Christ himself. The community believed that the Risen Lord had sent the Spirit, but that he could not have done so until after he had Risen from the dead and Ascended to the Father. In the Gospel of John, this conviction is explicitly stated (16:7): "If I do not go away, the Counsellor [i.e., the Spirit] will not come to you; but if I go, I will send him to you." But not only did Christ send the Spirit; the Spirit was regarded as instrumental in the resurrection, as Paul affirms (Rom. 1:4). Furthermore, Paul associates the Spirit and the Risen Christ so closely that he at times identifies the two (II Cor. 3:17, 18). Although elsewhere in the New Testament it is possible to distinguish between the Spirit and the one who sends the Spirit, the important point in closely relating the two is that there is no discontinuity in the life of the community after the resurrection appearances end. Christ is still present with his people, because his Spirit is there; the work of God in triumphing over the evil powers goes on in constantly enlarging areas as the Spirit continues to work through the growing community. What God had begun to do through Jesus is being carried on by the Spirit that he has sent to dwell in and to energize his people.

THE COMING OF THE SPIRIT

The author of Acts dramatizes the coming of the Spirit by narrating a series of spectacular events that take place in Jerusalem on a feast day called Pentecost. The term "Pentecost" is transliterated from the Greek word for fifty—i.e., the feast came fifty days after the harvest began. In later rabbinic tradition—and perhaps in the first century—the Day of Pentecost was regarded as the day on which God gave the Law to Moses on Mt. Sinai. At that time, the tradition claimed, a miracle was performed, by which the words of God to Moses were simultaneously translated into all the languages of the world. This Jewish tradition offers a striking parallel to the Christian account of the Day of Pentecost, at which time the whole community of Christians was commissioned to carry the gospel to "every nation under heaven" (Acts 2:5). In anticipation of the world-wide spread of the new faith, representatives gathered at Jerusalem are reported to have heard the message "each . . . in his own native language" (Acts 2:8). The miracle that attended the commissioning of the people of the Old Covenant is matched by the extraordinary circumstances that accompany the first convocation of the people of the New Covenant. Although there were in the early church other accounts of the coming of the Spirit (e.g., John 20:19-23, and possibly Acts 4:23-31), it is in Luke's narrative of the Pentecost experience that the significance of the event is most vividly expressed.

As Luke describes it, there had gathered in Jerusalem on the occasion of the great Feast of Pentecost men from all parts of southwestern Asia, Asia Minor, North Africa, and from as far west as Rome itself. There were Jews, proselytes, and (if we follow the Greek text of one ancient manuscript, which omits the word "Jews" in Acts 2:5) devout Gentiles who were interested in Judaism, although they were not a part of the Jewish community. In any case, there were representatives from the entire area throughout which the Jews of the Dispersion had scattered. Some had taken up residence in Jerusalem; others were simply visitors who had come for the festivities. We shall see later that one of the best-known Jews of the Dispersion, Paul of Tarsus, risked his life in order to be in Jerusalem at festival time (Acts 20:16).

In full view of a great crowd of these pious worshippers—perhaps in the courts of the Temple itself—there had also gathered the little band of enthusiasts who were convinced that Jesus of Nazareth was Messiah. The rushing wind and darting fire that accompanied the coming of the Spirit attracted the crowd's attention (2:2, 3), but curiosity gave way to amazement when the men possessed by the Spirit began to speak in strange languages. Luke is careful to point out that the importance of this phenomenon was that people from such a wide area heard and understood the message, as though the words of Peter were miraculously translated into the native languages of his hearers.

Two comments are in order here: (1) Actually, many of the crowd could have understood Aramaic, the native tongue of Palestine, which had served since the fifth century B.C. as the commercial language of the entire area from the Indus to the Nile. (2) The account that follows in Acts (2:14-15) makes clear that the most striking feature of this manifestation of the Spirit was not a miracle of translation, but the ecstatic condition of those possessed by the Spirit. Both Peter here and later Paul, in dealing with problems in his churches (I Cor. 14:23), feared that the Spirit-induced excitement might be mistaken for drunkenness. The practice known as "speaking in tongues" (which is still found in some Christian sects) was a prominent feature of life in the early community. The man who had the gift of "tongues" would be seized with a kind of fit, during which he would babble incoherently. Others in the community were thought to have the gift of interpretation; their job was to explain the meaning of the ecstatic speech for the spiritual enlightenment of the church. None of the later references to tongues mentions the miraculous translation aspect, but the gift of "tongues" seems to have been common in the community down at least to the end of the apostolic age, the period during which the apostles themselves were the leaders of the church.

In the Acts narrative, Peter's word about the misinterpretation of the strange speech of the Spirit-filled disciples serves to introduce his main theme; the coming of the Spirit heralds the dawning of the long-awaited and oft-announced Day of the Lord. The same Jesus who had been rejected and killed "by the hands of lawless men" (2:23) has now been raised from the dead and exalted by God as Lord and Christ (Messiah). The risen and exalted Lord has sent the Holy Spirit to carry on the mighty works that characterize the coming of the new age, which Jesus' work had inaugurated. In the light of the compelling demonstration of God's activity in human history that his hearers have just witnessed, and in the light of the age that is now dawning, men are to repent and to believe the Good News. The coming of the Spirit, therefore, is eschatological in that it heralds the end of the present order and the dawn of the new age.

THE SIGNIFICANCE
OF THE SPIRIT'S COMING

The way in which Acts links this dramatic event with the prophecy of Joel shows that the community believed that it was simply witnessing the fulfilment of the great day that had been long-awaited by ancient Israel. This was new, in the sense that it had never happened before; but it was not novel, since it was for the followers of Jesus the beginning of the Day of the Lord that had been promised through the prophets. In order to be prepared for the Day of the Lord, men must repent and be baptized.

Repentance and baptism are but the inner and outer aspects of a single religious change. The only appropriate response to the *kerygma*, which Peter has just pronounced, is repentance (Acts 2:37, 38); the fitting way to give public expression to inner repentance is to submit to the purifying rite of baptism. There was nothing magical in the community's practice of baptism; it did not of itself effect a moral change in the person baptized. It was a symbolic act, like those performed by the Old Testament prophets and men of God. Such acts not only symbolized what the prophet declared would come to pass, but were believed to help bring about what was prophesied. For example, Moses raised his hand over warring Israel (Ex. 17:8-13) not merely as a sign that the nation would triumph, but as a human channel through which God could work to give Israel the victory. The yoke that the prophet Jeremiah put around his neck (Jer. 27 and 28) was regarded as more than a symbol of the nation's subjugation to Babylon; since Jeremiah was the one through whom the word of the Lord was being revealed, his act was regarded as helping to bring about the predicted judgment. Similarly, to submit to the rite of baptism as a sign of one's desire to be cleansed from sin was looked upon as helping to accomplish the purification that the act symbolized.

THE HOLY SPIRIT AND BAPTISM

Superficially, there is a similarity between the Christian baptismal rite and the ceremonial washings performed by the worshippers in the hellenistic mystery cults. As a result, some observers have assumed that baptism was not a part of primitive Christianity, but that it was introduced when the church moved out onto Greek soil. Among the devotees of the mysteries, participation in a rite of purification was in itself enough to guarantee the desired objective of being cleansed. In the New Testament, the Spirit does not come automatically, however, but is sent by Christ only to those who have revealed a repentant spirit at the same time that they have submitted to the baptismal rite.

Not only is baptism thus different from the mystery rites; it appears to have been a part of Christian practice while the community was confined to Jewish soil. The adoption of the rite was probably influenced both by Jesus' association with John the Baptist, who demanded that all men be baptized, and by Jesus' example in submitting himself to this sacred washing.

In first-century Judaism, baptism was the normal way by which Gentiles prepared themselves for membership in the Jewish community. After being cleansed of their Gentile pollution by ceremonial purification, they were circumcised, and thus became members of the covenant people of God. Although all Jews were circumcised, only Gentile converts, who were called proselytes, were required to be baptized. John the Baptist, however, seems to have been so thoroughly convinced of the corruption of the Jewish nation in his day that he implored all Jews to be baptized as a symbol that the nation needed moral cleansing as much as the converts from heathendom.[5] Although

---

[5] For the view that John's baptism was intended as preparation for the judgment day, see C. H. Kraeling, *John the Baptist*, pp. 95-122. London : Scribners, 1955.

Jesus himself seems not to have felt a need for purification, his desire to associate himself completely with an errant and corrupted people led him to submit to baptism. The practice carried on unbroken the Jewish tradition of ceremonial cleansing and epitomized the new community's consciousness of itself as the New Israel.

The original disciples, having once been baptized by John, did not baptize each other again, even though the resurrection and the coming of the Spirit gave them a sense of sharing in the new people of God which they did not have when John baptized them. From the first occasion on the Day of Pentecost and always thereafter, as Acts reports it, all who joined the circle of the community in response to the gospel were required to undergo baptism. At Pentecost, those who were baptized in water at the same time received the "baptism" of the Spirit—that is, the Spirit filled them with a new sense of purity and power. The performance of the rite and the coming of the Spirit were not simultaneous in every case, however; the original disciples had not received the Spirit until years after their baptism, and other early believers knew only of John's baptism and had heard nothing of the Spirit baptism (Acts 19:1-7). Normally, the practice of baptism was the initiatory rite which signified not only the desire for moral cleansing, but also the desire to be prepared through the Holy Spirit for carrying out the responsibilities that each member had in the life of the community. Baptism was given additional meanings in the church, as we shall see in our study of Paul, but the rite seems to have meant from the beginning purification and empowering.

The Common Life of the Community
(Acts 2:44)

As the writer of Acts pictures it (2:43-47), the little band of disciples gathered in Jerusalem enjoyed an intense community of spirit. They were together daily in worship and in missionary activity. They were united in prayer and praise; they ate their meals together; they pooled their possessions in order that all might live and work unhindered by the need for gainful employment. The force that brought them together and created this sense of oneness was, of course, the Holy Spirit that had recently come upon them under such spectacular circumstances on the Day of Pentecost. But complete unity did not survive for very long. The record of subsequent disputes among the apostolic leaders themselves and the allusions in Paul's letters to controversies within the churches under his care emphasize the uniqueness of the peace and the complete accord that first prevailed. Whether "having all things in common" means that the community took literally the warnings of Jesus against the rich (e.g.Mk.10: 17-31) and hence organized a programme of systematic charity for the poor within the group, or whether it was an experiment in full-fledged communal living is difficult to determine. In either case, however, the arrangement failed and was remembered chiefly as a symbol of the pristine unity that prevailed after the coming of the Spirit. The first major breach in the unity, which resulted from failure to agree on the terms of admission to the Christian community, was of such far-reaching significance that we shall devote a later section of this chapter to it.

Sharing common meals was so closely linked with the celebration of the Last Supper that our sources do not enable us to distinguish sharply between the two. The sharing of bread and wine that had brought to a climax the last meal of Jesus with the Twelve is described in the Synoptics as having taken place "as they were eating" (Mk. 14:22; Mt. 26:26). It is not surprising, therefore, that the common meal and the Eucharist, or the Breaking of Bread, should be so intimately related in the thought and life of the community. As Paul knew it, the Eucharist included a ceremonial sharing of a cup, as a symbol of the sacrificial death of Jesus (blood in Hebrew thought was a synonym for the life of a sacrificial victim; cf. Lev. 17:11). We have no way of telling whether this significance originated with Jesus, as Mark's account of the Last Supper suggests, or whether the common meal was originally just a fellowship meal, as the story in Acts suggests. We shall discuss this development when we consider the problems that arose concerning the Lord's Supper in the church at Corinth (see Chapter 8, p. 260).

THE POWERS OF THE NEW AGE

Obviously the group considered itself to be a part of Israel, since it continued to participate daily in the worship being carried on in the Temple, and made it a practice to be on hand at the times of prayer. It was on such an occasion that the healing at the Temple gate, which is recounted in Acts 3, took place. Peter explained that the same power of God that had been at work through Jesus, triumphing over the powers of evil as they were represented by the diseases of men, was now to be seen operating through Jesus' faithful followers. The successful outcome of Jesus' conflict with the evil powers had been declared by him to mark the beginning of the new age, in the establishment of God's rule over all his creation. What happened at the Temple gate, in the healing of a man "in the name of Jesus of Nazareth," confirmed that the work of overcoming the evil powers that Jesus had begun was going forward with vigour through the members of the community who shared his power and his conviction that the reign of God was dawning. This act of healing is not an isolated miracle; it is one in a series of signs that God is at work bringing his creation into subjection to his purposes. The newness of the age that is about to dawn was demonstrated supremely by the fact that the evil intentions of those who had put Jesus to death had been completely thwarted by God's raising him from the dead (Acts 3:13-15). In the light of the new situation, the coming of which is attested by the healing of the lame man, men are to turn from their former ways, and to prepare themselves in faith for the coming of God's kingdom (Acts 3:17-26).

THE NEW COMMUNITY AND THE OLD

Any activity that produced such spectacular results, and that openly proclaimed the coming of a new era, could not fail to incur the displeasure of the religious authorities, who were eager to maintain the *status quo*. The disciples could have inferred this reaction from the

The tomb on the left, here in the Kidron Valley, is one of the few objects now in Jerusalem that we can be certain Jesus and the Apostles saw. The lower courses of the masonry in the temple wall (above right) also date back to the first century.

antagonism that the ministry of Jesus had aroused. We shall see in a moment that this opposition pointed up the basic incompatibility of the new community with Judaism in spite of the broad areas of agreement between the two. The early superficial harmony was ended soon and abruptly for those who carried through the implications of the community's faith; for those who clung more tenaciously to the Jewish traditions, the break came slowly over a period of about a generation. It took a major catastrophe—the destruction of the Temple and the sacking of Jerusalem—to bring about the final split.

SIGNS OF DISUNITY

        Almost at the beginning of the communal experiment, an incident arose which showed that not all members of the community were ready for the selfless living that the gospel demanded. In the Acts account, a man and his wife who cheated the community were struck down by divine judgment with a violence that comes as a shock to the reader. The peacefulness of the community's life was suddenly shattered by the death of the deceitful pair, Ananias and Sapphira (Acts 4:32-5:11). The solemnity that came upon the church as a result of this incident is typical of the seriousness with which the community continued to regard any challenge to its sense of mutual confidence and interdependence. In Paul's time, as we shall see in studying his letter to the Corinthians, the most heinous sin besetting the church at Corinth was, in his judgment, divisiveness.

The Rise of Official Hostility
(Acts 4-5)

If the religious leaders had been congratulating themselves on getting rid of Jesus, they soon learned that they had not heard the last of him. It was his name that was being preached by the new sect; in his name healings were being performed that were much like those that had attracted attention to Jesus at the first. The number of adherents to the group was increasing daily. Even worse, the judgment of the religious leaders themselves was seriously challenged by the charge of these street-corner preachers that the leaders had revealed a grievous misunderstanding of God's purposes when they rejected Jesus. All their efforts to halt the activity or to silence the preachers were in vain, however, as the story in Acts 4 makes clear. Neither imprisonment nor threats of worse punishment deterred these enthusiasts for a moment. External pressure served only to bind them closer together. The trials and official denunciations of the group drew the attention of the populace and helped swell the crowds of listeners. A summons before the Sanhedrin (the council before which Jesus was examined and by which he was condemned) was looked upon by the apostles as another opportunity to preach the gospel, which they proceeded to do. Gamaliel, a member of the council, gave a timorous "wait-and-see" answer to the question of how the leaders of the sect should be dealt with (5:33-39), but his advice merely forestalled the inevitable crisis.

The issue quite simply was this: If this sect was right in its interpretation of Jesus, then the rest of Jewry was in grievous error when it rejected the sect's claims. The time was coming when the religious leaders could no longer equivocate; either they must accept the claims or else they could no longer tolerate the sect as a part of Judaism. Quite understandably, they decided that the sect was wrong and took steps to silence its propagandizing. But all efforts to stamp out the community served only to make it grow stronger. The struggle was focused sharply in the trial of an eloquent young preacher named Stephen. His Greek name suggests that he was probably of Jewish parentage from one of the Dispersion communities. It is to the trial and death of this vigorous preacher that Acts draws our attention, because of their significance for Paul and the Gentile mission.

Conflict between Hellenists and Hebrews
(Acts 6 and 7)

Stephen was one of seven men chosen by the community to attend to the material aspects of the life of the group. Their responsibilities included apportioning the food and funds of the common pool of resources. The assigning of certain members to handle these affairs became necessary as the result of a charge by some members of the community that women of non-Palestinian origin were being discriminated against. Although the account in Acts is puzzling, it seems to mean that the Hebrews (i.e., Aramaic-speaking people of Palestinian origin) were being favoured in the sharing of goods at the expense of those who had been born in the Dispersion lands (these people were known as Hellenists—i.e., those who speak Greek).

It is clear from the story of Stephen, following the brief mention of the dispute, that the split between the Hebrews and the Hellenists was more serious than just a squabble over the division of labour according to which the Hebrews devoted themselves to spiritual matters and the Hellenists to material affairs. It is true that the verb used to describe the work of the seven Hellenist leaders (*diakoneo*, meaning "to serve")

is found later in the New Testament in noun form (*diakonos*, transliterated into English as "deacon") as an official title for those assigned
to do menial tasks in the church. But in Acts, the seven men had no
sooner been appointed than they began to preach the Good News to
non-Jews. Since all seven have good Greek names, they were probably
fitted by both language and cultural background for a mission outside
the bounds of the Palestinian Jewish community. What is described by
Acts as a relatively minor dispute within the community was actually
the beginning of a major controversy· Who are proper candidates for
admission to the Christian community, Jews and proselytes only, or
Gentiles as well? A generation would pass before this issue was settled.

Stephen's evangelistic activities met with immediate success. His
message was particularly attractive to the representatives from the
many lands of the Dispersion who were in Jerusalem at the time. His
persuasiveness, coupled with a display of spectacular powers like those
that had attracted popular attention to Jesus and his followers, aroused
the suspicion and finally the hostility of the religious officials.

The Jews who brought charges of subversion against Stephen were
from the Dispersion, just as Stephen and his colleagues were. The fact
that they were not from Palestine seems to have increased the importance that they attached to the Temple, since it provided them with
a visible, durable, world-renowned symbol of the faith adhered to by
only a small minority in the Gentile lands from which they came.
When their Gentile neighbours regarded them as queer because of their
refusal to be assimilated into Graeco-Roman life, the Dispersion Jews
could always point with pride to the Temple at Jerusalem whose splendour, in spite of the absence of images, reminded the whole world of the
enduring power of the religion whose followers refused to "bow down
unto any graven image." Either Stephen in his preaching had recalled
the words of Jesus about the destruction of the Temple (Mk. 13:1-4
and parallels), or else his enemies were convinced that the men who
claimed to be followers of Jesus were working toward the fulfilment
of his prophecy about its destruction. In any case, the charge against
Stephen and his friends resulted in his being called before the Sanhedrin,
the supreme legal and judicial body of the Jewish world, on charges of
subverting Jewish institutions and customs.

On the surface, Stephen's defence before the Sanhedrin, as Acts 7
records it, sounds like an innocuous survey of Jewish history. But a
more careful reading shows that the thesis underlying all that Stephen
said was a serious challenge to the religious structure of first-century
Judaism. His recurrent theme was that God's most important revelations to his people had occurred *outside the Land of Promise*, and

further, that the ideal symbol of God's presence with his people was the ancient mobile tent, called the tabernacle (Ex. 40:34-38), and not the fixed habitation in the Temple so highly prized by the Jews. This attack on the uniqueness of the land of Palestine and on the inviolability of the Temple was too serious to be allowed to pass unchallenged, and the leaders understandably responded by demanding Stephen's death (Acts 7:57-60).

Witnesses and Martyrs

Stephen was the first Christian martyr. The English word "martyr" is a transliteration of the Greek term for *witness*. The change of meaning of the Greek word, *martus*, from "one who tells what he has seen" to "one who dies for his convictions" is easy to trace. The New Testament writers do not use the term in the technical sense of one who is called before a court to give objective evidence; rather, they use it to refer to one who testifies to what he has seen—in this case what he had seen through Jesus of the love and power of God. But, since the testimony of the early Christians to their faith in the God of Jesus Christ met with hostility, the term *witness* began to take on the connotation of testifying to one's faith in the face of persecution. When the opposition to Christianity grew increasingly intense in the early second century, refusal to repudiate one's faith in Jesus as the Christ was punishable by death, and the word *witness* came to mean one who suffered martyrdom for the sake of the faith. The earlier meaning of the word is seen in Acts 1:22 and 2:32, where it is translated "witness," and where the reference is to those who had "witnessed" the Risen Christ. In Revelation, and in the writings of the second century, the Greek word *martus* means the same as our English word "martyr," and the shift of meaning is complete.

A powerful factor in Paul's preparation for his role as Christian preacher was his experience as an observer of Stephen's martyrdom (Acts 8:1). Paul's misguided zeal in trying to exterminate the Christian community had culminated in the scene at Stephen's execution, which became indelibly and hauntingly fixed in his mind. Who could ever forget the confidence and compassion with which Stephen had faced death? What power had converted bitterness and despair into forgiveness and ecstatic contemplation (Acts 7:55, 56)? Who had been victorious, the inquisitors or the victim? Questions like these must have plagued the mind of the devout and vigorous Paul, who in his youth had already gained a reputation for his effectiveness in rooting out this subversive movement (Gal. 1:23). Whatever his misgivings may have been as a result of seeing Stephen die so triumphantly, Paul turned again to the persecution of the church with renewed zeal (Acts 8:3).

Reaching Beyond Judaism

The resistance to Stephen did not in the least deter his colleagues. When the religious leaders drove the other Hellenist preachers out of Jerusalem (Acts 8:1-4), the result was not that the preaching to non-Jews was stopped, but that it was spread over a wider territory than ever before. The preachers evangelized the regions to which they had fled, and new communities of the faithful sprang up.

The leaders of the Jerusalem community had apparently restricted their evangelistic activities to fellow Jews, and continued to do so during and after the time of Stephen's activity and execution. But these Greek-speaking preachers, from lands where contact between Jew and Gentile was more common and casual, felt no restraint about telling the Good News to anyone who would listen, regardless of racial origin or religious heritage.

THE GOOD NEWS IN SAMARIA

The first area of activity outside Judea described in Acts is Samaria, where one of the Hellenists, named Philip, began to preach (Acts 8:4-13). The Jews despised the Samaritans because the Samaritans were thought to have mixed blood as a result of the forced mingling of races during the Assyrian occupation of Israel (eighth century B.C.). The Samaritans, in turn, scorned the Jews because the Jews had added supplements from prophets and poets to the original nucleus of the Five Books of Moses, which were all that the Samaritans recognized as scripture. Many in Jerusalem would have considered it a violation of Jewish convictions to launch evangelistic work among any non-Jews, but for it to begin among the Samaritans was revolutionary!

Philip's success in his work with the Samaritans was tempered by a serious problem. The marvellous works that accompanied his preaching, and which the community regarded as an authentication of its claim that through Jesus the new age had come, were regarded by the Samaritans as no different from the achievements of any other highly skilled miracle-worker. There were many miracle-workers roving about the Roman world, as we learn from the *Satires* of Lucian of Samosata, who tells of a travelling trickster who astounded the crowds with fake dragons and trick eggs. Samaria, however, seems to have had its own magician-in-residence, Simon [6] (Acts 8:9). Impressed by Philip's manifestations of the Spirit, Simon tried to buy the secret of control over the Spirit's power. His attempt to buy an authority that could be given only by God has given rise to the proverbial term, *simony*. This man's name keeps turning up as a living symbol of chicanery and heresy in the early centuries of the church. In an official visit, Peter publicly approved the work of Philip and censured the mercenary Simon (Acts 8:14-24).

The missionary work among the Samaritans received not only the community leaders' stamp of approval, but divine approbation as well. The Holy Spirit came upon the Samaritan believers, not when they received the rite of baptism, but in response to Peter's laying on of hands. Apparently the two stages of the coming of the Spirit are described here in order to draw attention to the new situation that was developing: Non-Jews were being united by the Spirit with the new covenant community. If non-Jews believed the gospel and bore witness to their faith by submitting to baptism, the Spirit was poured out on them—as on "all flesh"—in accordance with the prophecy of Joel (cf. Acts 2:17 ff.).

THE GOSPEL EVOKES FAITH FROM GENTILES

The next phase in the outreach of the community was achieved through the conversion of an Ethiopian courtier (Acts 8:26-40), whose connection with Judaism seems to have been remote. Apparently he was a devout man who had heard of the religion of the Jews and had come to Jerusalem to observe their ceremonies and to learn of their sacred writings. He could have participated in the worship only in spirit, since both his race (Hamitic) and his emasculation disqualified him from admission to the household of Israel even as a proselyte convert. As reported by Acts, the version of scripture that he was reading was the Septuagint, the Greek translation of the Hebrew scriptures made in Egypt in the third century B.C. The quotation reported (8:32,33) corresponds precisely to the Septuagint, but it is not a literal rendering of the Hebrew text. There is evidence that Greek literature had penetrated the Nile Valley as far as Ethiopia by the third century B.C., so it is conceivable that the eunuch had read a copy of the Septuagint in his native land, and had been moved to go to Jerusalem to observe the Jews' worship.

Another possible point of contact between this Ethiopian and

---

[6] Foakes-Jackson and Lake, *op. cit.*, Vol. V, note 13, pp. 151-163.

Judaism would be the Jewish colonies that were established in the Nile Valley by Jewish fugitives who had fled from Palestine in the face of the Babylonian invasion of 586 B.C. Late in the nineteenth century, a vast collection of papyrus manuscripts was discovered at the first cataract of the Nile (near the present border between Egypt and Sudan). These manuscripts consisted largely of correspondence between the Persian officials who were overseeing the flourishing Jewish colony there and the central government of the empire. Perhaps knowledge of the Jewish religion had spread to Ethiopia from this colony or from other similar ones in the valley. Whatever his initial contact with Judaism had been, the eunuch had developed a desire to travel to Jerusalem. He had made the long journey and was now returning, still fascinated by the Jewish religion but perplexed by his inability to understand the Jewish scriptures.

At the strategic moment, a man appeared by the dusty roadside who was able to answer the eunuch's questions, having been sent precisely for this purpose. Philip's explanation of the passage that the eunuch was reading at the moment (Isaiah 53:7,8) is not given by Acts (8:35). But it appears that Philip simply explained that Jesus of Nazareth embodied in his person and acts the culmination of Israel's expectations and the true fulfilment of its national hopes. The eunuch was readily persuaded, and Philip administered the rite of baptism, which by then seems to have become normative procedure for uniting converts with the community.

There are at least two aspects of this story that trouble the modern historian. The first is that the Servant passage of Isaiah 53 should be interpreted as a messianic prophecy at what purports to be the earliest period of the church's life. It is not explicitly used either in Paul or the Gospels to document the messiahship of Jesus, though there is an indirect reference to it in Matthew 8:17, and a possible explanation for the one direct allusion to Isaiah 53 is that it is part of the composition of the author of Acts, who, writing a generation after the time described and lacking a first-hand account of Philip's interview with the Ethiopian, decided that this passage would provide an appropriate base for an evangelistic encounter. The other problem raised by the story is the instantaneous transportation of Philip from the desert road to Ashdod on the seacoast (Acts 8:40), in a manner reminiscent of Elijah's experience (II Kings 2). This vivid story is told, however, not simply to amaze the reader, but to portray in concrete fashion the divinely ordained way in which the gospel spread in ever-widening circles from Jerusalem, as the Risen Christ had said it would (Acts 1:8).

Philip travelled northward along the coast of the Mediterranean to

---

6a J. Jeremias in *The Servant of God* (Naperville, Ill.: Allenson, 1956) has shown, however, that there was almost certainly a messianic interpretation of Isaiah 53 in pre-Christian Judaism.

the city of Caesarea. This was a city of commercial importance, because of its fine harbour; and it was of political importance, since it was the official seat of the Roman governor of the united provinces of Judea and Samaria. It was also one of the most splendid of Herod's grandiose building enterprises. Its harbour, the finest along the coast, had been created artificially by positioning enormous stones to form a breakwater. Its gleaming temples and public buildings were clearly visible from the inland hills of Samaria. The main temple of Caesarea was dedicated to Caesar Augustus, and the city itself was one of the strongest centres of hellenistic culture in Syria-Palestine.

In contrast to the southern coastal cities of Joppa and Jamnia, where the Jews were predominant, Caesarea presented an almost purely Gentile field for Philip's evangelistic work. Evidently he continued to carry on his activities there for a long time, since he was on hand to offer hospitality to the journeying Paul some years later (Acts 21:8). By the fourth century, Caesarea had become the major centre of the church's intellectual life in Palestine. Both Eusebius, the first great historian of the early church, and Origen, the greatest biblical scholar and linguist of the early centuries, lived there. A great library was built up in Caesarea, and it is believed that some of the most sumptuous and carefully prepared manuscripts of the Bible were produced under scholarly supervision in that academic setting.

Peter Preaches to the Gentiles
(Acts 9:32-11:18)

The initial furore that had developed around Stephen and his associates seems to have given way to an interim of peace in the life of the Judean community. This calm may have been the result of the expulsion from Jerusalem of the Hellenists, whose interpretation of the gospel had proved so objectionable to the pious Jews of Jerusalem.

Acts reports that members of the community were residing not only in Judea and Samaria, where the previous narrative would have led us to expect them, but also in Galilee. There is no mention elsewhere of a Christian group in Galilee, either in the canonical writings or in the subsequent histories and records of the church. It may be that the disciples in Galilee, like those in Jerusalem, fled at the time of the Roman invasion in A.D. 66-70, and left no traces behind. It is clear from the Gospels, however, that continuation of the Christian community in Galilee was expected, since mention is made of the appearances of the Risen Christ to his followers there (Mk. 16:7; Mt. 28:7;

John 21). For reasons that cannot now be determined, only passing allusions to the Christian community in Galilee have survived.

In harmony with the setting of cooperation and peacefulness in which the author of Acts seeks to picture the church, the summary in Acts 9:31, with the parallel progress reports in 2:41, 4:4, and 6:7, portrays the steady growth and good relations that the early community enjoyed.

BEGINNINGS OF THE MISSION TO GENTILES

Up until this time, the movement appears to have been largely a Jewish phenomenon, with the exception of a few isolated contacts with non-Jews, as we saw above. Even these excursions outside the pale of Judaism involved people who had some relationship, however tenuous, with the people of the Old Covenant. The Samaritans, for example, honoured the Law of Moses, and were regarded as at least half-brothers of the Jews. Other persons of non-Jewish birth who had joined the Christian community had first become Jewish proselytes, and were therefore regarded as religiously acceptable by the Jews. At the very least, men were brought to Christian faith through the Jewish scriptures. Now, however, a major step in the spread of the community was taken by Peter, a member of the original nucleus of

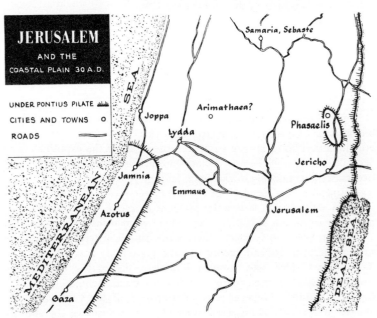

The Mediterranean coast at Jaffa (Joppa), where Peter was summoned to begin a ministry among Gentiles.

Jesus' followers. Previously, the apostles had sanctioned evangelistic activity among the fringe groups and had even participated in that activity (Acts 8:25). But here for the first time one of their leaders actually undertook activity among those who had had no direct contact with the faith of Israel.

The first stop on Peter's journey to the seacoast, according to Acts, was Lydda, a thriving town on the fertile plain of Sharon (9:32 ff.). Although it was later to be a centre of Jewish legal studies, the one inhabitant whose name is mentioned in Acts appears to have been of Gentile birth. His name, at any rate, was identical with that of Virgil's great hero, Aeneas. Since there is no hint of conversion in the story of Peter's healing Aeneas, the important element seems to be that once again—but this time in a Gentile setting—the powers of the new age are evident. It is through the name of Jesus Christ that the forces of evil are routed and that Aeneas is healed. Some of the residents of Lydda and its environs were converted as a result of witnessing this manifestation of divine power.

At the port city of Joppa, an even more remarkable demonstration of the powers of the kingdom took place. A devout widow named Dorcas, who was famed for her charitable acts, was raised from the dead at the command of Peter (Acts 9:36-43). The incident, as Acts reports it, parallels the raising of Jairus' daughter by Jesus (see Mk. 5:21-43, especially verses 40 and 41). The mighty acts that Peter and the others performed in the name of Jesus correspond to Jesus' answer to John's question about the mission. Jesus quoted from the prophecies of Isaiah concerning the new age of God: the blind receive

201

their sight, the lame walk, lepers are cleansed, the deaf hear, *the dead are raised up*, and good news is preached to the poor (Lk. 7:22). The implication is that Jesus was the one anointed of God (Is. 61:1,2) to perform these messianic acts. Clearly, then, the healing ministry that the community was carrying on in the name of Jesus and by the power of the Spirit that he sent was a continuation of the demonstration of the powers of the new age that Jesus had inaugurated.

PETER, THE RELUCTANT PREACHER

From the standpoint of Jewish piety, Peter chose an odd setting in which to live in Joppa, since a tanner's shop with its pig skins was considered unclean by the orthodox. The question of defilement does not seem to have been raised, however, and Peter remained with the tanner until the divine summons came to move on to Caesarea (Acts 9:43). Just as Peter's experiences in the raising of Dorcas paralleled those of Jesus, so the call from Cornelius the centurion reminds us of a similar appeal to Jesus from another Roman officer (Lk. 7:1-10). But Cornelius' appeal was for a word from God, not merely for bodily healing (Acts 10:1-7). Cornelius was granted a vision as a reward for the piety he had practised in the seclusion of his home. Open adherence to the Jewish faith, even to the extent of attending services at a synagogue, might have jeopardized his position in the army. Coordinated with the angel's advice to Cornelius to send for Simon Peter was the vision that came to Peter in which he was instructed to accept the invitation. It may seem to us that Peter was extremely hard to convince, but when we recall the age-old tradition of Jewish separatism and also the reluctance of Jesus himself to mingle freely with Gentiles (Mk. 7:24-30), Peter's hesitancy is easy to understand. Both the bizarre nature of the visions (Acts 10:9-16) and the amount of space devoted to them serve to point up how crucial the question was of the shift of audience for the gospel from Jew to Gentile.

When Peter finally learned his lesson, his change of attitude toward the Gentiles showed up immediately in his preaching (Acts 10:34). His sermon opened with a confession of his belief that God deals with men impartially, and not on the basis of racial preference. At a later time, however, Peter came into open conflict with Paul over an issue closely related to this one: Is it proper for Jewish Christians to eat a common meal with ceremonially unclean Gentile Christians? But in the Acts account, sanction for opening the fellowship of the Christian community to Gentiles was provided by an outpouring of the Spirit in a way that resembled the first such manifestation of the Spirit on the Day of Pentecost (Acts 10:44-48; cf. 2:4 ff.). Even with this divine attestation through the coming of the Spirit, the question of the relationship of Gentile converts to the Jewish law was a problem of the first magnitude that had yet to be worked out.

News that the baptism of the Spirit had come upon the Gentiles soon reached the leaders of the group in Jerusalem, who called for an investigation of this unprecedented event. The retelling of the details seems to the modern reader an unnecessary repetition, but it serves to lay heavy stress on the tremendous importance of this chapter in the history of the church. The signs of divine favour were so unmistakable that even the most rigid advocate of excluding Gentiles could not call them into question. There could be no controversy over the Gentiles' right to be admitted to the circle of those who were awaiting the coming of the kingdom of God. The problems that arose, as we shall see, had to do with the way of life that was to be expected of Gentile converts (see below, Chapter 9).

Herod Agrippa
and the Jerusalem Church
(Acts 12:1-23)

The mention in Acts 11:19 of the "scattering abroad" of the Hellenist members of the Christian community marks a major turning point in Christian history. Because of persecution, the Christian message moved out from the Jewish soil and religious climate to the larger cultural and geographical world. If this message was to be comprehensible to non-Palestinian hearers, it had to be restated and adapted. Had the earliest messengers been unable or unwilling to make such adjustments, the Christian movement might have died out with the sack of Jerusalem in A.D. 70. Before we turn to the story of the community's widening horizons, let us examine the official opposition that was mounting against the Jerusalem nucleus itself.

Agrippa, the grandson of Herod the Great, had first ingratiated himself with the mad emperor Gaius Caligula (A.D. 37-41) and then with the capricious Claudius (A.D. 41-54). As a result of his political manoeuvring, he was declared king of nearly all the region that had once been ruled by his grandfather. Although his blood was largely Idumaean (Agrippa's great-grandfather, Antipas, was a prince of Idumea, a tiny realm south of Palestine), Agrippa was moderate in his attitude toward the Jews, and at times actively sought to gain their favour. In Josephus' *Antiquities*, upon which we must rely for nearly all the information available about Herod Agrippa, there is an account of a famous incident in which the Jews actually acclaimed Agrippa as "brother," in spite of his non-Jewish ancestry. His efforts to win greater esteem from the Jews is reflected in the incident recorded in Acts (12:1-3), in which the popular acclaim that arose after the execution of James, the son of Zebedee, led Agrippa to imprison Peter as well. A tradition of the Eastern Church, coupled with Jesus' prophecy of Mark 10:35 ff., has led some scholars to the conclusion that the Apostle John was martyred at the same time as his brother James. Peter, however, was providentially delivered from the wrath of the mob, according to Acts, and was freed from the royal guard by mysterious means. The author of Acts includes a human touch at this point (12:12-16) when he describes the astonishment of the praying Christians that their petitions for Peter's deliverance are answered!

With the brief notice, "He departed and went to another place" (12:17), Peter disappears from the scene in Acts as a participant in the missionary life of the church. He is mentioned once again, under the name of Symeon in Acts 15, but we are dependent on the letters of Paul for further information about his work and his associations with the church in Antioch.

The account of Herod Agrippa's death following his public acclamation as a divine being by a flattering mob is paralleled in Josephus' account,[7] although the two stories vary greatly in detail (Acts 12:20-23).

The work of preaching the *kerygma* proceeded unhindered in spite of every manner of opposition, and the zealous messengers continued to expand both the scope and the intensity of their work (Acts 12:24 ff.). The result of their diligence was that strong centres of evangelistic activity were soon springing up some distance from the original centre of the community life in Jerusalem. Chief among these centres was Antioch, which had become so strong that it began to develop both missionary and instructional programmes of its own. Foremost in zeal among the workers in Antioch was a man who had once been a prominent opponent of the gospel: Paul of Tarsus. It is to his rapid rise and phenomenal accomplishments that we now turn.

---

[7] Josephus, *Antiquities,* XIX : 7-8.

PART TWO

THE COMMUNITY EXPANDS

H

⫰⫯

CHAPTER SEVEN

PAUL, THE PIONEER

The Judean Christians were understandably sceptical about the sudden, complete transformation of Saul of Tarsus. This man, whose chief avocation had so recently been ferreting out and persecuting the followers of Jesus, now claimed to be one of that despised number himself. As dramatic as his conversion was, we can recognize the powerful forces at work in his environment that prepared him for the change that took place near Damascus. The account in Acts calls him Saul until the point at which he begins his evangelistic work among the Gentiles (Acts 13:9); from then on, he is known by the Roman name,

---

New Testament readings relevant to this chapter are Acts 9, 11-15; Galatians 1-6.

Paul. To avoid confusion, however, the more familiar form of his name is used throughout this account of his life and thought.

Conversion near Damascus
(Acts 9:1-19)

PAUL AS PERSECUTOR

The vigour with which Paul went about his inquisitorial activities before conversion, and his missionary work afterward, make it evident that zeal for God was the consuming passion of his life. Personal welfare, family ties, bodily comfort, material prosperity, social acceptance—Paul brushed them all aside at the call of God. But he did not drive himself just for the sake of activity; his life was shaped by an overpowering sense of religious responsibility. As a devout Jew, his religion centred in Torah; the demands of the God who spoke in Torah could not be evaded by a preoccupation with theological speculation, by legal subterfuge, or by any other dodge. There was no escaping the summons to obedience that came through Torah, and Paul sought earnestly to obey it.

Yet in the midst of striving to obey the voice of God, Paul was constantly harassed by a distressing awareness of his moral impotence. He could not bring himself to do the things that Torah and his own conscience told him he should do (Rom. 7:9-25). Far from motivating him to do right, Torah overwhelmed him with frustration by serving as a gnawing reminder of his failures. He may have sought to compensate for this consciousness of defeat by persecuting others. His frustration would then have contributed powerfully to the fanatical zeal of his attacks on the Christians, whom he regarded as deserters from the pure faith of Judaism.

PAUL'S LIFE AMONG GENTILES

Although Paul's devotion to Judaism was beyond question, some of his contemporaries may have regarded his theological views with suspicion. Born in Tarsus, a cosmopolitan city in the Dispersion, he was subjected from childhood to pagan influences. Strabo, the historical geographer of the period, ranked Tarsus even above Athens and Alexandria as a centre of intellectual life. Athenodorus, the Stoic teacher of Caesar Augustus, had come from Tarsus. It is not surprising, therefore, that traces of Stoic ethics and religious vocabulary may be found in the letters of Paul. Perhaps the sympathy of Paul with the Gentiles is traceable in part to the impression made upon him by the earnestness of the Stoic preachers who stood in the streets and market places of the city, seeking to inculcate virtue in their listeners. Paul's sympathetic attitude toward the Gentiles may have aroused the suspicions of his fellow Jews, but his life in a Gentile city like Tarsus helped to prepare him for his task of communicating a basically Jewish gospel to Greek audiences.

In Tarsus, like other centres of Jewish Dispersion life, the language of the synagogue was Greek, and the Bible of the Jewish community was the Septuagint. It is from this version, rather than from the Hebrew Old Testament, that Paul quotes in his letters. But even more important than Paul's understanding of the Gentiles' language was his firsthand knowledge of the religious aspirations of the Graeco-Roman world. The location of Tarsus helped to bring its inhabitants into contact with the religions of redemption which, though they had developed in the East, were in Paul's day becoming increasingly popular in the West. These oriental religions (described in Chapter 1) promised redemption in the form of deliverance from the physical body so that the soul could ascend to the realm of pure spirit. By rigid asceticism, their devotees believed they could prepare themselves to rise to the heavenly abode of the god of light. Through participation in rites and ceremonies they could overcome the evil schemes of the god of darkness and pass safely through the hosts of evil that inhabited the celestial regions until they reached the presence of their god. Propagandists for these redemptive religions of Iran, and for the cults of the Anatolian plateau, passed through Tarsus, since it lay on the broad Cilician plain near the junction of two main trade routes just south of the Cilician gates, a narrow cleft in the rock that provided the sole pass through the Taurus mountains to the cities of Anatolia and Ionia beyond.

At Tarsus were to be found devotees of other familiar pagan deities: Isis, Zeus, Hermes, Serapis, and Apollo. Paul's letters demonstrate that his familiarity with the terminology of these religions, with their

PAUL'S MINISTRY IN PALESTINE AND SYRIA

ROMAN PROVINCE
CITIES AND TOWNS   o

promise of union with God, was such that he could both state his message in such a way as to appeal to Gentile religious hopes and also combat those who, under the influence of the redemptive religions, sought to pervert his gospel. His emphases on deliverance from the forces of evil, on the coming age of peace, and on the possibility of direct knowledge of God were well chosen for evoking a favourable response from Gentiles who heard his version of the gospel.

PAUL'S LOYALTY TO JUDAISM

In spite of Paul's ability to speak the Gentiles' language (both literally and figuratively), he remained to the last loyal to his Jewish heritage. He was convinced that the Christian gospel was simply the logical fulfilment of Jewish religious expectations. In his Letter to the Philippians (3:5), he stressed the fact that he was a true Hebrew rather than a Hellenist. When the occasion demanded, he could address his audience in Aramaic, the Semitic dialect that had supplanted Hebrew as the language of the Jews (Acts 22:2 ff.). Acts reports further that Paul had studied at Jerusalem under Gamaliel, a famous expert in the interpretation of Torah. Although this statement in Acts has been challenged, the record makes the claim that Paul had enough contacts in the Holy City to obtain letters from the authorities that would help him in his heresy-hunting. He was not, however, well enough known for the Christian community to recognize him on sight (Gal. 1:22). His letters show little interest in the involved methods of interpreting scripture that were commonly employed by the rabbis of his day, although he does use some of the more familiar rabbinic allegories in his letters (I Cor. 10:1-3; Gal. 4:21-31). The general attitude toward the Law expressed in his writings is Pharisaic (Phil. 3:5), but on the other hand he clearly had no sympathy with the rigid legalism often associated with the Pharisees. On the crucial issues of belief in the resurrection, angels, and demons, he stood, of course, with the Pharisees. Like them, too, he made his living in a secular occupation—tent-making—even though his training and certainly his major interest in life may have been in the religious calling of rabbi.

As a result of having been reared in a Gentile environment, but having been trained in the Jewish tradition, Paul was peculiarly fitted for the task of interpreting the gospel to Gentiles. Although in later years he repudiated his former way of life within the Jewish community, he continued to rely heavily on the insights and basic beliefs that Judaism had built into his life and thought. Similarly, his determined resistance to compromise with paganism did not prevent him from using the vocabulary of pagan religion and philosophy and from capitalizing on the yearnings that the pagan teachings expressed. Paul was the apostle of transition, whose work was indispensable in the transfer of Christianity from the soil of Palestine to the larger Roman world

THE CONVERSION EXPERIENCE

It was while Paul was on his way to Damascus, determined to wipe out the Christian community there, that the transforming vision of Christ came to him (Acts 9:1 ff.). If we may judge by Paul's letters, he had little interest in the circumstances surrounding this conversion experience, although his biographer in Acts devotes considerable space to it. Acts has two recapitulations of the conversion story (22:1-21; 26:2-23) in addition to the original account in Acts 9. Paul mentions only that God had chosen to reveal to him the Risen Lord. Clearly the important factor for Paul was the transforming religious experience itself and not the extraordinary features that accompanied it. The revelation of Christ brought about a complete reorientation of Paul's understanding of Judaism, and channelled his zeal into what he was convinced was constructive effort for God. The days of anxiety and uncertainty were past; the thankless role of inquisitor had been exchanged for the rewarding work of evangelist.

Present-day biographers have speculated about the cause of Paul's vision. Some suggest sunstroke, which would be a credible explanation to anyone who has experienced the burning heat of the road leading south from Damascus. Others think they can discern symptoms of epilepsy—a disturbance not uncommonly associated with mystical religious experiences. But such conjectures are valueless in seeking to understand the *meaning* of Paul's vision. He was convinced that God had granted to him a special revelation of the same Lord who had appeared to the disciples in the days immediately following the resurrection. The disciples themselves believed in the reality of Paul's vision, and accepted him on the strength of it as an apostle of the Risen Christ.

Damascus, where Paul was taken in a daze after the revelation (Acts 9:8 ff.), was an important crossroads city of the ancient Near East. Some historians believe it to be the oldest continuously inhabited city on earth. The invigorating climate and the abundance of water, which flows down from the melting snows on Mount Hermon, combine to make the city a verdant paradise on the edge of the Arabian desert. In the days of Abraham, Damascus had been a flourishing caravan city, as it was in Paul's day and still is in our own. Although it had served as an important border outpost for the Roman province of Syria, it had (around A.D. 40) come under the power of Aretas, king of the powerful Arab nation that ruled a great crescent-shaped territory

Damascus, believed by some historians to be the oldest continuously inhabited city in the world. A few traces of Roman times remain in the old covered markets, but most of the city presents the modern appearance pictured here.

stretching from north of Damascus along the edge of the desert to the border of Egypt. These people, who were called Nabataeans, had originally been nomadic. But their strategic location on the caravan routes from South Arabia and India had brought them wealth and a high level of culture, which is attested today by the fragments of exquisite pottery found at Nabataean sites, and by the striking ruins of their rock-hewn capital, Petra.

There were many Jews living in Damascus, including some whose religious views differed widely from those of the major Jewish sects in Judea. Detailed information about one of these unorthodox groups became available some fifty years ago, with the discovery in Cairo of fragments of a book written by a dissident Jewish sect that had made Damascus its headquarters while laying plans to return to Jerusalem and to reform the worship in the Temple. The fact that Damascus would have been considered a safe sanctuary for a persecuted and unconventional branch of Judaism suggests that unorthodox movements normally met no resistance there. But another Jewish sect, a community of Christians, which flourished in the favourable soil of Damascus, met with fierce opposition, as we can infer from Paul's account in Galatians and from the narrative in Acts. Apparently a Christian group had developed among the Damascus Jews within a few years after the resurrection, and Paul, armed with credentials from the Jerusalem authorities, was seeking to exterminate it. The faith of a member of that group, Ananias, was severely tested when he was instructed by the Lord to lend a hand in restoring Paul to health, who was already notorious as the Christians' worst enemy. But Ananias' willingness to obey overcame his fear, and he welcomed Paul into the fellowship of the community (Acts 9:10 ff.).

Training in Arabia and Antioch
(Acts 9:19-30; Gal. 1)

THE PERIOD OF WITHDRAWAL

The impact of Paul's religious experience was so great that he felt the need for a long period of meditation and prayer. So direct was the revelation that had come in this experience that Paul was not content merely to talk it over with someone, but chose instead to withdraw to the desert where he could commune with God in solitude. The area to which he retired, called simply "Arabia" in his account, was probably the section designated by classical geographers as Arabia Petraea. This part of the Arabian peninsula, which was then controlled by the Nabataeans, was semi-arid, but by no means devoid of vegetation. The moisture-laden winds blowing off the Mediterranean drop more rain here than on the somewhat lower hills of Judea on the other side of the Jordan Valley. As a result, this land, which borders the desert proper, is relatively fertile, and in Paul's time was able to support the population of several sizable cities: Gerasa, Philadelphia (ancient Rabbath-Ammon), and Petra. Gerasa and Philadelphia were cities of the Decapolis, a confederation of Greek-style cities east of the Jordan formed in the first century B.C. (see map p. 29). Although these cities were under strong hellenistic influence, there is no evidence that Gentile contacts during this period influenced Paul's formulation of the gospel. He apparently had already had enough contact with Christians at Damascus to have become familiar with the basic elements of the

Christian traditions; now he needed time and solitude to synthesize, from the welter of conflicting influences that had come upon him, his own understanding of the purpose of God that had been made known to him in the revelation of Jesus Christ.

Upon his return to Damascus, filled with zeal for preaching his gospel, Paul was confronted with fierce opposition from fellow Jews, who resented his persuasiveness in convincing hearers that Jesus was the Messiah. Although the chronological reference in Acts is not precise ("When many days had passed...," Acts 9:23), it would appear that after Paul's return to Damascus from seclusion the Jewish leaders and the civil authorities formed a conspiracy to rid themselves of this effective propagandist for the new faith. The crisis came when the ethnarch (the local governor appointed by Aretas) set guards about the city in an attempt to seize Paul. But Paul escaped, as he tells the Corinthians (II Cor. 11:32,33), by an ingenious method. Even today, guides in Damascus delight to point out to gullible tourists the very window from which Paul was lowered to safety. The fact that the relatively modern house in which the window is located is far from the site of the first-century city wall does not disturb the conscience of the guide or the credulity of the visitor! Wherever the wall

The forum at Gerasa, one of the cities of the Decapolis. Its well-preserved ruins bear witness to the efforts of the Greeks and Romans to impose their culture on the eastern world.

and the window were, Paul's nocturnal trip over the wall in a basket enabled him to slip through Aretas' net.

Perhaps Aretas' unsuccessful effort to help the Jews capture Paul was a part of his long-range programme of ingratiating himself with potential allies. If Aretas had been planning a revolt against Rome, as the imperial authorities suspected, his position would have been greatly strengthened by having the Jewish neighbours to the west of Nabataea as his friends. Eagerness to court Jewish goodwill would account for Aretas' joining with the Jews in their efforts to destroy Paul and for the otherwise puzzling recognition by Damascus authorities of documents from the Jewish Sanhedrin in Jerusalem.[1] Whether this was the reason for the coalition or not, the concerted attack on Paul brought to a close his missionary work in Damascus.

PAUL'S RECEPTION IN JERUSALEM

In his letter to the Galatians, Paul describes a journey from Damascus to Jerusalem as having occurred three years after his conversion (Gal. 1:18). Later in the same letter (2:1), he says that his second visit took place fourteen years later. The occasion for the second visit was a famine, which we know from extra-biblical sources to have occurred about the year 46.[2] If 46 is accepted as a fixed date, it is possible to establish the year of Paul's conversion fairly well and to determine how brief the interval was between the death of Jesus and the appearance of the Risen Lord to Paul. Since ancient chronologers included both the beginning and the end of any time series in their computations, and since their years began in the middle of our years (i.e., at September 1), the interval of "fourteen years" mentioned above would be only twelve or thirteen years by modern reckoning. This would take us back, of course, to 34 or 33. The conversion of Paul must have been in 31 or 32—that is, within about a year of Jesus' crucifixion. Although the reference by Paul to "fourteen years" is important to us for determining the chronology of his life, he made it only to indicate how infrequently he had had contact with the Jerusalem leaders and thus to underline his independence of them.[3]

---

[1] This suggestion is made by W. L. Knox in *St. Paul and the Church of Jerusalem*, p. 59, note 47. Cambridge: University Press, 1925.

[2] Cf. F. J. Foakes-Jackson and K. Lake, *The Beginnings of Christianity*, Part I, The Acts of the Apostles, Vol. V, pp. 445-455. London: Macmillan, 1933.

[3] For a detailed examination of the relationship between Acts and Paul's letters, and for another reconstruction of Pauline chronology, see John Knox, *Chapters in a Life of Paul*. London : A. & C. Black, 1954. Knox argues that, since the letters of Paul are the primary sources for reconstructing his life, Acts is to be relied on only where it accords with the biographical information from them. The special

When Paul made his first visit to Jerusalem after his conversion, he was accepted by the leading apostles, Peter and James (the brother of Jesus), on the recommendation of Barnabas (Acts 9:26 ff.; Gal. 1:18, 19). The other members of the community were less willing to receive him, because the memory of his earlier attacks was all too fresh in the minds of those he had sought to exterminate. According to the Acts account, his activity at the time of this stay in Jerusalem was confined to evangelistic work among the Hellenists. His own statement in writing to the Galatians (1:22), that he was not well known among the Judean churches, may be explained by the supposition that his preaching was limited to Greek-speaking groups in Jerusalem proper, so that native-born Jews in and out of Jerusalem would not have come to know him by sight. His presence was clearly embarrassing to the Jerusalem leadership, and his preaching was strongly objected to by the Hellenists among whom he worked. The vehemence of their reaction attests to the effectiveness of Paul's ability to state the gospel in terms meaningful to a Jew reared in the Dispersion. The more convincing he became, the more fierce was the resentment of the Hellenists. It may be that their non-Palestinian origin gave them a sense of inferiority for which they sought to compensate by a burning zeal for orthodoxy.

THE MINISTRY IN ANTIOCH

Clearly, the wise course of action for the Jerusalem leaders was to encourage Paul to go elsewhere. A delegation from the Judean church conducted him to Caesarea, the capital and chief seaport of the province, and from there he sailed to Tarsus (Acts 9:26-30). Paul furnishes no direct information about his activity during the next fourteen years, but from the record in Acts 11:19 ff. it would appear that he joined in the missionary work of the Hellenist Christians among the Dispersion Jews, perhaps in the area of Tarsus itself.

It was, however, in Antioch, the capital city of the province in which Tarsus was located, that the community experienced its most spec-

---

interests of the author of Acts in demonstrating the harmoniousness of the church's life led him to modify his evidence, and his lack of familiarity with the issues at stake in Paul's day led him to describe Paul's relations with the Jerusalem church as more cordial than they actually were. According to Knox, Paul was converted about A.D. 35, carried on his work in Syria, Asia Minor, and Greece for the fourteen-year period mentioned in Gal. 2:1, and made his final visit to Jerusalem about A.D. 55. This hypothesis is developed fully by Donald W. Riddle in *Paul, Man of Conflict*. New York: Abingdon, 1940. M. Goguel, in *The Birth of Christianity* (London: Allen & Unwin, 1953, p. 26), dates Paul's conversion in 29.

Antioch on the Orontes, with Mt. Silpus in the background. Located near the Mediterranean Sea, it was the seat of Paul's operations and one of the most important centres of Christianity in the first three centuries A.D.

tacular growth. And it was there that the derisive epithet, "Christian," was first attached to the followers of Jesus. When news of the community's evangelistic successes in Antioch reached the apostles in Jerusalem, they sent Barnabas to investigate. He observed that the effectiveness of the church's preaching to the Gentiles had brought in so many members who were ignorant of the Jewish heritage of Christianity that a man who combined knowledge of Greek language and thought with a thorough understanding of Judaism was needed to instruct the new converts. The man obviously best fitted for this task was Paul.

Paul's city of Tarsus, although it was not a part of Syria proper, was convenient to Antioch. The coastal area at the north-eastern corner of the Mediterranean Sea is cut off by a mountain barrier from the main part of Asia Minor (the Taurus Range), and forms, therefore, a natural geographical unit with the region to the south and east. Since the border of the Roman province of Syria followed these natural boundaries, Tarsus and Antioch were within the same political unit. Travel between the two cities was easy and rapid, and it was a simple matter for Barnabas to go up to Tarsus in search of Paul and to invite him to assume a place of leadership in the community at Antioch. Paul accepted the invitation, and carried on evangelistic and educational work in Antioch for a year (Acts 11:25, 26).

Antioch, which had been built by the Seleucids as the capital of the eastern half of their empire, had by Paul's day become the third largest city of the Roman empire, exceeded in size only by Alexandria and Rome. Situated near the mouth of the Orontes River, Antioch was famed for its splendid public buildings, its colonnaded streets, and the beauty of its suburbs. The most splendid suburb was Daphne, which was perhaps as widely known as Antioch itself because of the great shrine of Apollo and Artemis that was located there. If Antioch was famous for its splendour, it was also notorious for its superstitions. The religious currents from the East, full of astrological speculation and fantastic mythology, formed a kind of vortex at Antioch, into which were drawn all manner of quack preachers, wonder-workers, and charlatans. The exotic religions that flourished in Antioch were subsequently introduced at Rome, where they gained a large following. The Roman satirist Juvenal described the popularity of these "superstitions" at Rome as the flooding of the Tiber by the Orontes.

ACCEPTING GENTILES INTO THE COMMUNITY

The crucial problem confronting the Christian community in Antioch—and, ultimately, the major issue throughout the entire Christian community—was the question of the basis for admission of Gentiles into the fellowship. The Hellenist Christians had entered the Christian fellowship by way of Judaism. Should all converts be expected to meet the requirements for becoming a Jewish proselyte before being admitted to the Christian community? Although the Jerusalem leaders had on several earlier occasions sent emissaries to report on the evangelistic activity among Gentiles in other localities (e.g., Samaria), they had set up no official policy on the requirements to be made of

Gentiles who sought entrance into the Christian community. A corollary question, also unsettled, was: What adjustments should be made by Jewish Christians within the group in order to permit them to have fellowship with converts from paganism? The Jewish laws concerning diet and ceremonial purity prohibited intimate contact with Gentiles, and even with careless Jews. Although Jesus' laxness on this issue was one of the major criticisms of him by his enemies, the early Jewish Christians were careful to observe the Jewish standards of separateness. Were the Jewish Christians at Antioch to ignore their traditions about purity, or were they to require the converts to purify themselves and live under the Jewish laws of cleanliness?

The issue came to a head in the Antioch area as a result of the successful evangelistic work of preachers who were not from Palestine or Syria, but from Cyprus and Cyrene in North Africa (Acts 11:20). Since these preachers did not feel that the Jewish standards of purity were important, they laid no such requirements on their converts; and neither did the community in Antioch, which welcomed them into its fellowship. Barnabas, impressed by the number of converts and by the evidence of divine favour upon them, had given his blessing and had gone off to secure Paul's help. It was not until after Paul had completed his year of teaching in Antioch and had gone up to Jerusalem with Barnabas on an errand unrelated to this issue that conflict over the question developed.

Paul had so ingratiated himself with the Christians in Antioch that they chose him, together with Barnabas, to carry a contribution from Antioch to the community in Jerusalem. Acts associates the contribution with a famine (11:27-30), but the fact that the contributions continued long after the famine had passed suggests that there were other reasons as well. It may have been that the Jerusalem Christians were impoverished as the result of the failure of their original experiment in communal living. Or it may be that this gift was simply tangible evidence of the respect and kinship that other Christians felt for the original leaders of the community. We do know that Paul continued to make collections for contributions to Jerusalem in later years, even among churches far removed from Palestine. In the working agreement established between Paul and the Jerusalem apostles, as we shall see below, the sole requirement laid on Paul with regard to the Gentile churches was that they continue to make these contributions (Gal. 2:10). This is one of the responsibilities of which Paul was later to remind the church at Rome (Rom. 12:13), and it is stressed in the Letter to the Hebrews as a part of Christian good works (Heb. 13:16). The motive behind the demand of the Jerusalem Christians was not the greed of an indolent church, but the necessity for a concrete expression of unity and loyalty to the original circle of disciples. All the churches felt indebted to the Jerusalem leaders to whom the gospel had first come, and these gifts were expressions of their gratitude.

THE JERUSALEM CONSULTATION

Mention has been made above of Paul's second visit to Jerusalem, at which time he had a private discussion with the apostles concerning the relation of Jew and Gentile in the Christian fellowship (Gal. 2:2 ff.). It seems likely that this informal conference took place at the time of the visit of Paul and Barnabas to present the offering from Antioch. The Acts account makes no mention of this discussion, but perhaps the author has passed over in silence a dispute that was not settled until later, preferring instead to give a full account at the time of the settlement (Acts 15). This would be in keeping with the tendency of the book to minimize the controversies that developed within the community and to give the impression that the harmony of the fellowship was never disturbed more than briefly. But since this conference with the apostles was of prime importance for Paul's side of the argument in the Galatian letter, he related it there in some detail.

If, therefore, we consider the visit mentioned in Acts 11 and 12 to be the same as the one that Paul describes in Galatians 2,[4] Titus must have been a companion of Paul and Barnabas on this trip up to Jerusalem, even though Acts does not mention him by name. Titus figures prominently, both as messenger and deputy, in Paul's correspondence with the Corinthians. He was a Gentile, as both his name and the controversy that revolved around him indicate. Apparently he came from Antioch, since this is where he first appears in the narrative. In spite of Titus' effectiveness as a missionary in Antioch, some of the Jerusalem Christians insisted that he be circumcised before being admitted into their fellowship. The fact that he was accepted by the community in Antioch even though he was a Gentile and uncircumcised seems not to have impressed the Judeans. Paul, however, refused to conform to their wishes, sensing rightly that there was a major issue at stake here: Was conformity to Jewish standards a prerequisite for admission to the Christian fellowship? Titus was a test case for

---

[4] For the theory that the accounts of visits to Jerusalem in Acts 11, 12, and 15 are reports of tne same visit that came to the author of Acts from different sources and were mistakenly interpreted by him to refer to different visits, see Foakes-Jackson and Lake, *op. cit.*, Vol. V, pp. 199-204. See also "The Apostolic Council" in *Studies in the Acts of the Apostles*, by M. Dibelius (London: SCM Press, 1956).

Paul, and the apostles decided that Paul's point of view was the right
one: Circumcision and Jewish standards of ritual purity were not to
be expected of Gentile converts (Gal. 2:3-5).

The Jerusalem leaders recognized that Paul had been called and
divinely endowed for the ministry to the Gentiles, in which he had
already achieved great success. They had before them tangible evidence of his concern for the mother church in Judea, in the form
of the contribution that he and Barnabas had brought from the Christians in Antioch. So they gave Paul their hand as a sign of blessing on
his work among the Gentiles, and he in turn agreed to continue to
solicit contributions for the Jerusalem church (Gal. 2:9, 10). The
leaders of the original Christian community had formulated a policy
concerning the acceptance of non-Jews into the Christian fellowship.
Paul had ostensibly made his point that a man did not have to become
a Jew before he could become a Christian, and peace reigned—for the
moment at least.

Expansion in Cilicia and Cyprus

When Paul and Barnabas left Jerusalem for Antioch, Barnabas took
with him a young relative named John Mark. In the rest of the New
Testament there are occasional references to an associate of Paul by
the name of Mark. If that Mark is the same person as John Mark, then
from youth to maturity this man had a continuing, though relatively
minor, role in the life of the early church. He appears later in the
company of the imprisoned Paul in the Letter to the Colossians and
in the brief Letter to Philemon. There is considerable information
about Mark in the second-century traditions of the church, according
to which he was the companion of Peter in Rome and the recorder
of Peter's memoirs. Other early writers connect Mark with the church
in Alexandria. There is to the present day strong resentment among
the Christians of Egypt toward the Venetians, who, it is said, stole
from Alexandria the bones of St. Mark for their cathedral in Venice!

Judging from the account in Acts (12:12), Mark's contacts with the
Twelve and the other leaders of the Jerusalem community were rather
intimate, since the community met for prayer, perhaps regularly, in
the home of John Mark's mother. The conjecture is often made that
the young man who fled naked from Gethsemane on the night of
Jesus' betrayal (Mk. 14:51) was none other than Mark himself.
Whether or not these identifications are correct, it was probably because of his first-hand contact with the disciples that Mark was asked

to accompany Paul and Barnabas. Grateful for the agreement that had been reached with the Jerusalem church, the three set out for Antioch (Acts 12:25).

Following their arrival, a consultation was held among the leaders of the Christian community. After a period of worship and prayer, it was decided that their missionary work should be expanded by sending evangelists to the island of Cyprus. This island, though it lay more than fifty miles off the Syrian coast, was included by the Romans in the province called *Cilicia et Syria*. For this mission to Cyprus, the community in Antioch chose Paul and Barnabas, who was a native of the island (Acts 4:36). Mark went along as aide (Acts 13:1-5).

They set sail from Seleucia, the port of Antioch, some fifteen miles from the city itself. The port had been named by Seleucus Nicator in his own honour, with an immodesty that was common to hellenistic monarchs. The first destination of Paul and his companions was Salamis, the largest city and the finest harbour on the island. Before the coming of the Romans in the first century B.C., while Cyprus was under Egyptian control, large numbers of Jews had migrated there.

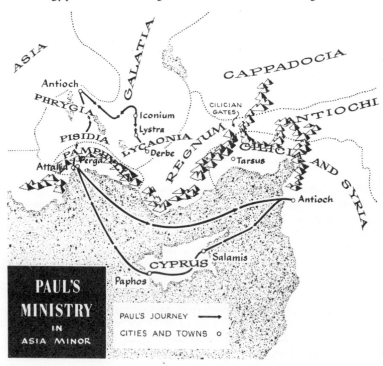

PAUL'S MINISTRY IN ASIA MINOR

PAUL'S JOURNEY ⟶
CITIES AND TOWNS ○

In the reign of Herod the Great (37-4 B.C.), still more Jews had come to work in the copper mines there in which Herod had an interest. Salamis' nearness to the mines may account for the large numbers of Jews who lived there. Several synagogues were needed to house the worshippers, and to these Paul and his friends went to find an audience for the gospel. Whether they made converts among the Jews in Salamis, or whether their preaching tour of the island as a whole met with success, the account in Acts does not reveal.

Although the work in Cyprus may not have gained adherents for the church, it did attract attention to the preachers. At Paphos, the capital city located at the western end of the island, Paul and Barnabas aroused the curiosity of Sergius Paulus, the Roman proconsul. It would appear from the brief mention of him in Acts that he had been interested in the Jewish religion before Paul and his companions arrived. We are told of his curiosity concerning the work of Bar-Jesus, a Jewish wonder-worker. When he heard of Paul and Barnabas, he summoned them to preach for him (Acts 13:6 ff.). Bar-Jesus, who used the name "Elymas" when he was among Greeks, tried to dissuade Sergius Paulus from believing Paul's message. Filled with righteous wrath, Paul denounced Bar-Jesus and called down upon him the judgment of God. Blindness came upon him, as death had overtaken Ananias and Sapphira when Peter invoked divine wrath upon them (Acts 5:1 ff.).

The proconsul seems to have been more impressed by the swiftness of judgment than by the cogency of the gospel. But the Acts account is so compact that we cannot determine its meaning with certainty when it says that "the proconsul believed" (13:12). The translation in the Revised Standard Version is probably the correct one: "Then the proconsul believed, when he saw what had occurred, for he was astonished at the teaching of the Lord." This translation implies, then, not that the proconsul was converted, but rather that he was convinced that a marvellous power was at work through the movement that Paul and Barnabas represented—that is, "the teaching of the Lord." In the New Testament, both Christians and unbelievers are reported as recognizing that amazing powers were operating through the apostles. The unbelievers regarded these powers as demonic, or, at best, as a manifestation of divine activity in some general way. But for the Christians, these acts of healing and judgment were interpreted as an indication that the powers of the new age were already at work. They proclaimed by act the same Good News that was being proclaimed in the sermons by word.

Pioneering in Asia Minor
(Acts 13:13-14:28)

THE INVASION OF NEW TERRITORY

After the missionary tour of Cyprus was completed, the travelling preachers crossed over to the mainland of Asia Minor and landed at Perga in Pamphylia. This Roman province was crowded in between the sea and the precipitous Taurus range, which cut it off from easy access to the Anatolian plateau. The humidity of the climate was aggravated by the water that drained off the mountains and helped to create malarial swamps along the Pamphylian coast. Since neither Greeks nor Romans had been able to establish stable commercial or cultural beachheads there, the population was more nearly of pure native stock than was that of most of the coastal cities of Asia Minor. The silence of Acts about the evangelistic work in Perga suggests that there was no Jewish community there, since Paul's custom throughout his missionary career required him to go first to the synagogues in any town where one was located. Paul and Barnabas simply passed through Perga and went to the higher ground of the inland plateau. John Mark left the other two at the seacoast, perhaps because of his reluctance to go beyond the area in which missionary work had been commissioned by the leaders in Jerusalem—that is, Cilicia and Syria, the province in which Antioch was located. Whatever the reason for the disagreement may have been, Paul flatly refused to use Mark as an aide on his next tour (Acts 15:36-40). Later, however, they were again associated in the work of the gospel (Col. 4:10 ff.).

The puzzling explanation Paul gave to the Galatians for the change in plans that took him into the interior of Asia Minor has given rise to considerable speculation. He wrote: "Because of a bodily ailment I preached...to you at first" (Gal. 4:13). The crucial importance of the tour through the Anatolian uplands has increased interest in the question of why it was undertaken in the first place. One suggestion is that Paul went up into the mountains to seek relief from an illness he contracted on the unwholesome coastal strip.[5] Another possible explanation is that he did not want to make another sea voyage in returning to Antioch, but preferred instead to cross the Taurus Range in order to reach the main highway that led south and east to his native province of Cilicia. Whatever the reason was, Paul made the arduous

---

[5] See William Ramsay, St. Paul, the Traveller, pp. 94-97. London: Hodder and Stoughton, 1897.

climb of about 4,000 feet to the Anatolian plateau, where he launched a new phase of his work.

The central section of Asia Minor was organized by the Romans into a province called Galatia—that is, the territory of the *Galatai*, or Gauls, as they are called in English. The name referred originally to only a small district in which migrants from Gaul had settled in the third century B.C. But the province of Galatia in Paul's day covered an area extending northward from the Taurus range almost to the Black Sea. Paul uses the term to refer to the whole central region in which he founded churches, even though there was no uniformity of language or race in the area that he designated by the general term, "Galatia." [6]

EVANGELIZING THE CITIES OF GALATIA

The first city of the region in which Paul and Barnabas began their preaching mission was another Antioch (Acts 13:14 ff.). In order to distinguish it from the larger and better-known Antioch in Syria, it was called Antioch of Pisidia. Pisidia was an old name that continued to cling to the region around Antioch, even though the official Roman designation of the territory was Galatia. Ethnically, the population was Phrygian, a people famed for emotional excess. And the district was a centre for highly emotional religious cults. A peculiarly exciting type of music that Plato had banned from his *Republic* was known as "the Phrygian mode," and the type of hat that was a necessary part of the costume of an initiate into one of the mystery cults was called a Phrygian cap. Side by side with the strong pagan element in Antioch was a colony of Jews, although the only evidence for its existence, apart from Acts, is an inscription found in the area.

From this point on, Paul and Barnabas are pictured in Acts as following a standard procedure in launching their evangelistic work in a new city. First, they made contact with the Jewish community and obtained permission to address the congregation at a subsequent sabbath session. Following the prayers and lessons from Torah, and at the invitation of the synagogue leaders, Paul gave the sermon or exposition of the scripture. His sermons, according to Acts, followed the prece-

---

[6] A case can be presented for the theory that the "churches of Galatia" to which Paul refers in his letter (Gal. 1:2) were the churches that he established on his next journey through Asia Minor, when he followed a route that took him farther north, through the district north of Iconium that was originally known as Galatia. Against this hypothesis are the facts (1) that the southern territory was officially called "Galatia," and (2) that all the evidence that Paul ever established churches in the northern part of the province is purely inferential. See Foakes-Jackson and Lake, *op. cit.*, Vol. V, pp. 224-240.

dent that had already been established by the apostolic leaders of Jerusalem, especially Peter. A brief summary of Israel's history was used as a springboard for preaching the gospel. In the sermon at Antioch of Pisidia, the point of this historical résumé is that God has always acted beneficently and in accord with his own sovereign purpose toward his people, choosing them, selecting their leaders, delivering them from their enemies. Now, however, the culmination of his dealings has been reached in his sending Jesus, who, though rejected by his own people, has been designated by God as the One through whom remission of sins is granted. Paul is careful to point out to his hearers that the rejection of Jesus was the result of ignorance, not of malice, and that from God's standpoint his death was part of a divine plan, as revealed through the prophets. Man's free decisions, he declares, result in the fulfilment of God's purpose; these decisions are made without any sense of coercion, and in making them man is unaware of how his actions are related to the eternal plan. But the outcome of the decision made by the religious and civil leaders in Jerusalem to execute Jesus was the unfolding of the crucial phase of God's redemptive plan. The sermon closes with a word of warning to those who are indifferent or incredulous (Acts 13:16-41).

The reaction at the synagogue in Antioch to the gospel preached by Paul was mixed, though not mild. In spite of the fervent interest of many of the Jews and proselytes, the opposition of the leaders was so violent that Paul and Barnabas were forced to move on to another city (Acts 13:42-51). The author of Acts saw in this fierce rejection of the message a turning point in the progress of the gospel, especially since it led to an aroused interest among the Gentiles in the district. Although Paul's and Barnabas' dramatic shaking off of the dust of Antioch implies that they had rejected all responsibility for the city, they did in fact return to strengthen the converts there (Acts 14:21, 22). From this point on, the two evangelists devoted more and more attention to preaching the message to interested Gentiles, although Paul never ignored the fact that the Jews had prior claim on the hearing of the gospel (Rom. 1:16; 9:4).

Although the hostility aroused at Antioch toward Paul and Barnabas did not cause them to abandon the city permanently as a field for evangelism, it seemed wise to move on for a time to another city until the furore had subsided. So they turned their attention to another Galatian city, Iconium, located some sixty miles east of Antioch of Pisidia. To reach Iconium, Paul travelled the Via Sebaste, an ancient highway that apparently dated back to pre-Roman times, but that had been rebuilt and renamed by Caesar Augustus in his own honour (Sebastos is the Greek equivalent of the Latin word, Augustus). One of the pair of twin peaks visible from Iconium is still called St. Thecla, in honour of a Christian woman linked with Paul in the popular romance, *The Acts of Paul and Thecla*. This fictional account of Paul and his associates, written apparently in the last half of the second century, includes a vivid picture of Paul's personal appearance: "a man little of stature, thin-haired upon the head, crooked in the legs, of good state of body, with eyebrows joining, and nose somewhat hooked, full of grace: for sometimes he appeared like a man, and sometimes he had the face of an angel." [7] It is conceivable that this imaginative writing incorporates traditions about Paul that circulated in Iconium, but it is impossible to distinguish authentic recollection from pure imagination in the wholly legendary form in which the narrative has come down to us.

According to the brief, stylized account in Acts (14:1-6), the missionary method that Paul followed in Iconium resembled the one he had used at Antioch, and it brought the same results: He converted some Jews and many Gentiles, but in the face of mounting opposition. For the work in the other Lycaonian cities of Lystra and Derbe, however, Acts gives a fuller and more colourful record (14:6-21). The location of Lystra and its status as a Roman colony under Augustus were definitely established in the nineteenth century by the discovery of some coins from the first century and of an inscription identifying the site. The site of Derbe has not been determined with any certainty. The section of the province of Galatia in which Derbe and Lystra were located, though politically part of Galatia and ethnically part of Phrygia, was distinguished from the rest of the province by a dialect called Lycaonian that was spoken there.

While Paul was preaching at Lystra (Acts 14:7-18), he came upon a man who had been crippled from birth, a pathetically familiar sight in cities of the Near East even today. The lame man's response to Paul's preaching showed on his face, and on the strength of his response Paul was able to heal him, as Jesus and the Jerusalem apostles had healed the sick (Mk. 2; Acts 3). The Lycaonians were amazed by Paul's healing powers, just as the onlookers in Jerusalem had been at the healing by Peter and John (Acts 3:9, 10). But the Lycaonians jumped to the conclusion that the two evangelists were gods in disguise. Barnabas, they decided, was Zeus; Paul, the spokesman for the pair, was Hermes, the messenger of the gods. Word of their presence

---

[7] Quoted from *The Apocryphal New Testament*, translated by M. R. James, p. 273. Oxford: Clarendon Press, 1950.

spread to the priests of one of the city's major shrines, and preparations were begun immediately for a procession and special sacrifices. Since the people were speaking Lycaonian rather than Greek, Paul and Barnabas failed to realize at first what was going on. But when the priests began to lead out the animals and bring the garlands preparatory to making sacrifice to them as Zeus and Hermes, the two men were horrified, and vigorously set about trying to persuade the priests of their error.

The address that Paul made to the crowd is of great interest, if in fact it preserves authentic elements of his words on that occasion. This is the first time (of which we have any record) that Paul delivered a Christian message to a thoroughly non-Jewish audience. There is no evidence that there was a synagogue at Lystra or that the citizens were acquainted with the Jewish beliefs about God. Their polytheism and idolatry were especially abhorrent to pious Jews like Paul and Barnabas, and it was to these evils that Paul directed his opening remarks. He followed the same approach that he was later to use at Athens. If we are to judge by the abrupt ending of the speech as summarized in Acts (14:15-18), Paul was unable to finish because of the enthusiasm of the crowd. His themes were (1) the providence and forbearance of God, and (2) the vanity of worshipping anything other than the Creator of the universe. Up to this point, Paul said nothing that would not have been seconded by Stoic preachers of the day. The probability that he went further, and proclaimed convictions that were distinctively Christian, is indicated by the fact that some pious Jews later took the trouble to come all the way from Pisidian Antioch and Iconium to discredit the missionaries and to turn the crowd against them (Acts 14:19). Evidence that the evangelists achieved results in Lystra is provided by the statement that Paul returned to Lystra on a later occasion "to strengthen ... the disciples" there (Acts 14:21, 22).

MOUNTING HOSTILITY

The subversive efforts of Paul's enemies from Antioch and Iconium were partly successful, however, and nearly resulted in Paul's death (Acts 14:19). The fickle crowd, which a short time before had sought to worship Paul and Barnabas, now tried to put Paul to death. He recovered from the stoning, and went on, undeterred, to the city of Derbe, where the gospel was favourably received and where many were converted to the faith (Acts 14:20, 21).

The opposition encountered by Paul and Barnabas in Lystra and the other cities of Galatia may be readily accounted for: From the standpoint of the Jews in Asia Minor, Paul was simply trying to relax the requirements for admission to the community of God's people. They could recognize the kinship of what he said with their own Jewish faith, but the demands he made of the converts were much simpler than those made of Gentiles who wanted to join the Jewish community. Although Paul preached in the name of the God of the Jews, he did not require circumcision or conformity to the Law of Moses. The complaint was valid, then, that he was disregarding the standards of Judaism, and the only reasonable line of action for a devout Jew was to try to put an end to his preaching activity.

The real issue, however, did not come to light in this skirmish between Paul and the opponents of the gospel. Paul was not merely trying to change the standards of admission to the community of faith; he was proclaiming that a God was calling into existence a radically new community, which would supplant the old covenant community, and which would be the New Israel. Within a few years after Paul's initial conflict in the Galatian churches, the issue came to a head as to whether or not the standards of admission to the old covenant community should be required of those seeking admission to the new covenant community. When the crisis came, the immediate provocation was another controversy within these Galatian churches. The ultimate decision reached, although at the time it seemed to have divisive results, resulted in the formal launching of the community's world mission.

Derbe, where Paul and Barnabas went after their harsh treatment in Lystra, was apparently located a short distance to the south-east (Acts 14:20-23). The persecution they had undergone in Lystra served to attract attention to their work and to strengthen the effectiveness of their message. They were careful to explain that the difficulties they were called upon to undergo as ministers of the gospel were not signs of divine disfavour, but rather were a part of the divine plan, and that the new age would come only after the people of God had passed through a series of tribulations like those that the two preachers themselves were undergoing. In Paul's letters there is a recurrent theme that struggles are an indispensable preparation for those who would enter the kingdom of God (Rom. 8:17; Col. 1:24).

RETURN TO ANTIOCH IN SYRIA

Retracing their steps through the cities of Galatia, Paul and Barnabas instructed their converts and appointed leaders to oversee the life of the community in their absence. The practice of fasting, which is mentioned in this account (14:23), originally accompanied national days of mourning among the Jews, but it had become by Jesus' time a form of private moral discipline closely associated with prayer. The early church continued to practise fasting as a means of expressing its devotion to the will of God, but there are signs that at times it became in the church, as it had become in Judaism, a form of religious ostentation rather than a form of private devotion.

The account in Acts of the missionary circuit closes with the report that Paul and Barnabas made to the church in Syrian Antioch, which had commissioned them to undertake this epoch-making journey (Acts 14:24-28). Not only had they met with success in winning converts and establishing congregations, but they had launched a new phase in the history of Christianity by preaching the gospel to persons who had no knowledge of the God of Israel, and who consequently had no inclination to follow the demands of the Jewish Law. How worshippers who entered the community purely on the basis of their response to the *kerygma* were to be accepted into a fellowship whose heritage was that of Jewish ritual purity, was the major problem confronting the infant church. Paul's private agreement with the apostles had really settled nothing. When matters came to a head, as they very soon did in Antioch, the storm that broke was a violent one.

Controversy in Antioch

The leaders in Antioch responded warmly to the report that Paul and Barnabas made of their experiences in Cyprus and Asia Minor. The church at Antioch, which was accustomed to a spirit of freedom in dealing with new converts, had never observed the rigid legal standards for admission to the new community that were characteristic of the Jerusalem Christians. Shortly before Paul and Barnabas returned to Antioch, Peter had come from Jerusalem to observe the progress of the gospel in Cilicia and Syria. Presumably, he was then to report what he found to the leaders of the church in Jerusalem. Even though Peter had found that converts were being accepted into the fellowship in Antioch without having been circumcised and without having undergone proselyte baptism, he entered into the life of the church and seemed thoroughly satisfied with such liberal admission standards (Gal. 2:11, 12). He joined in the common meals of the community, seemingly free from scruples against eating with the Gentiles, and continued to enjoy fellowship with them after Paul and Barnabas arrived.

Some time later, however, other members of the Jerusalem community visited Antioch, and were scandalized by the lax conditions there and by Peter's contacts with defiled Gentiles. These strict disciples rebuked Peter for his infraction of the Jewish laws of separation, with the result that he changed his mind on the subject, and refused any longer to eat with the Gentile converts. So persuasively did the separatist disciples present their case that Barnabas sided with them against Paul on the issue. Others followed the lead of Peter and Barnabas. Ironically, the common meal of the Christians, which was intended to express the unity of the community, had become the major cause of division (Gal. 2:13; Acts 15:1, 2).

Paul reacted violently to all this. He was disgusted with Peter for his vacillation, and with Barnabas for being impressed by the argument of the "Judaizers." The two-fold issue that had disturbed the church in Antioch earlier (Should Gentile converts to Christianity conform to Jewish legal standards? How should Jewish Christians treat fellow Christians who were ceremonially unclean?) now had reappeared in an acute form involving personal conflict among the leaders of the community. It was clearly impossible to reach any decision on this issue in Antioch; appeal had to be made to the leaders of the mother church in Jerusalem.

While the debate was raging in Antioch, word came that the "Judaizers" were at work in the Galatian churches, and that they had met with considerable success in convincing the Galatian Christians that they had to be circumcised in order to be saved. This was the same requirement they had laid down at Antioch (in Syria), as well (Acts 15:1). In the white heat of the controversy, Paul sent a letter to the churches of Galatia in which he told them of the agreement he had reached on this point with the Jerusalem leaders, and in which he outlined what he believed to be the divinely established basis for admission to the community of God's people. Since the issues raised in the Letter to the Galatians had such far-reaching consequences for the subsequent history of the church, we shall examine it in some detail.

Challenge in Galatia
(Gal. 1:1-6:18)

The Letter to the Galatians begins with a brief word of greeting and an expression of astonishment that in such a short time the Galatians had deserted the freedom that Paul had preached to them about (Gal. 1:6). Paul tells them about the crisis that has just developed in Antioch, and how he has denounced Peter publicly for having gone back on the agreement between Paul and the Jerusalem apostles (including Peter). As Peter's actions in Antioch have demonstrated, he can for a time forget the regulations of Torah and live in a manner indistinguish-

able from that of a Gentile, but when the issue is raised, he insists—
quite inconsistently—that Gentile converts must submit themselves to
the requirements of the Law. Such a double standard—of strictness
when the issue was pressed and of leniency when it was not—is hypo-
critical. As a result, Peter, together with the members at Antioch who
had been swayed by the Judaizers, stand condemned logically and
morally.

JUSTIFICATION BY FAITH

Paul turns, rather abruptly, from the narration of what had
just happened at Antioch, to an analysis of the principle underlying the
whole controversy. The basic question was: How can a man come into
right relationship with God? The term for "right relationship" that
Paul uses throughout this letter and the Letter to the Romans is a Greek
word that is usually translated "justification." The cognate verb is
rendered "justify"; the related adjective is sometimes translated "just,"
and sometimes "righteous." Paul challenges the Judaizing Christians
by asking them how they came into the relationship with God in which
they now know themselves to stand. They must admit that living in
conformity with Jewish legal regulations ("works of law," Gal. 2:16)
did not bring them into such a relationship; rather, they entered it
through their faith in Christ. If meeting the demands of Torah had
proved inadequate to give Paul and other Jewish Christians this sense
of standing before God, what made the Judaizers think that obedience
to the rule would "justify" anyone else? Paul's faith in Christ had led
him to identify himself with Jesus in his death and in the new life
beyond the grave. Through this identification with Christ, Paul had
died to the old life, in which he had hoped to gain standing before God
by fulfilling the moral and ceremonial demands of Torah. But "justification" had come by faith in Christ, through whom he now experienced
the new life in relationship with God that the Law did not and could
not bring. The reasons for the impotence of the Law are elaborated in
Paul's Letter to the Romans (see pp. 270-271). If this relationship could
be attained through man's striving after moral achievement, then there
was no point in Christ's having died in man's behalf (Gal. 2:20, 21).

Actually, Paul wrote, man is not dependent on his own strength or
moral urges to gain standing in the eyes of God or to live an upright
life. The power of right living is made available to men of faith through
the Spirit of God. The Galatians had experienced the Spirit in their
midst in the form of wonders done among them through Paul and
Barnabas (Acts 14) and in the form of their own inspiration by the
Spirit (Gal. 3:3-5). They did not suppose for a moment that they had

earned the right to have the Spirit at work among them. Did they now suppose that they could achieve a relationship with God by *meriting* it through good works? The blessing that had come to Abraham, and through him to all men, had not been a reward for pious acts, but had resulted from his trust in God. Because Abraham believed what God told him, he entered a new relationship of intimate friendship with God (Gal. 3:6 ff.); as a result of his faith, even the Gentiles now had the privilege of being accepted by God on the basis of their trust in him.

Conversely, anyone who sought to gain the acceptance of God on the strength of his own moral attainments was automatically cursed. The Law demands total fulfilment of its requirements, and anyone who starts out to obey Torah must either measure up to its demands completely or else fall under its curse (Gal. 3:10 ff.). Obviously, then, no one can be "justified" by trying to obey the Law; the man who tries to earn acceptance with God will be inescapably condemned. But the man whose relationship is established solely by trust in God is the one who, in the fullest sense, "lives." The death of Christ, even though it placed him under the curse that Torah pronounced on all who hang on a tree (Gal. 3:13), brings blessing to men of faith, since it frees them from servitude to a law whose demands they cannot possibly fulfil.

THE TRUE MAN OF FAITH: ABRAHAM

One of Paul's favourite Old Testament figures, Abraham, is introduced into the letter as an illustration of the man of faith. Abraham's friendship with God, established as it was on the basis of faith, began many generations before the time of Moses, under whom the Law was given to Israel; therefore, the idea that is implicit in the Law, that God's favour may be secured by the performance of good works, does not supplant the earlier principle of "justification" by faith that first appeared in Abraham's time (Gal. 3:15 ff.). The Law has had some value, however, for it served as a restraining influence in the period preceding the coming of Christ. Paul demonstrated the inferior nature of the Law by appeal to the rabbinic tradition that Torah was transmitted to men by angels, whereas it is God's Son through whom deliverance from sin is now available, according to the gospel that Paul preaches (Gal. 3:19 ff.). Just as a child needs a "custodian" or pedagogue during his time of immaturity but can dispense with him on reaching adulthood, so man is no longer to be subject to the Law, but may enter the relationship of sonship with God. To change the metaphor, before the child comes of age he cannot participate in what he has inherited, but when he reaches maturity he is freed from the earlier restraints and is able to live as he pleases (Gal. 4:1 ff.).

The time of maturity has come, Paul declares; it came when God sent his Son into the world, born under human conditions to liberate those who were under human limitations and condemned to moral failure. Those who respond in faith to what God has done for men in Christ are accepted by him as sons. They will no longer be ground down by a sense of obligation to fulfil legal obligations that are beyond their moral abilities; they are now free to respond in gratitude to the God whom they know as father, and whose love they have come to know in Jesus Christ (Gal. 4:4 ff.).

MAN'S SUBJECTION TO EVIL POWERS

The helpless plight of man, Paul continues, is not merely the result of human weakness; man is under the domination of superhuman forces of evil at work in the world. Paul's belief in these demonic forces lies behind his words to Gentile hearers about the enslaved condition from which they were delivered by Christ. The hostile spirits that inhabited interstellar space (the elemental spirits of the universe) had held the Gentiles in bondage to the worship of idols. Through their fear of the unknown, and through their belief that the universe was unfriendly, the Galatians had observed the ceremonies and offered the sacrifices that were demanded by the astral divinities whose devotees they were. Now that they had come to know God in Christ, and were by faith children of the Lord of heaven and earth, they were delivered from their terrors, and freed from the obligation to perform the idolatrous rites (Gal. 4:8 ff.). The Judaizers, by urging them to observe the feasts and ritual requirements of Torah, were trying to place the Galatians under the same kind of religious yoke from which they had just been set free. As a means of gaining or maintaining the acceptance of God, the Jewish ritual was as useless as the pagan one had been.

Paul wonders if his entire ministry among the Galatians has not been a waste of time, since they are now trying to desert their newly won freedom for legal tyranny. His argument shifts now to a direct personal appeal. He reminds the Galatians of their eagerness to receive him on his arrival in spite of an embarrassing physical ailment (Gal. 4:12 ff.). He cannot understand why, if they accepted his message so readily then, they are rejecting it now. The Judaizers do not really have the best interests of the Galatians at heart, as Paul did when he was among them. He wishes he could be there in person to see at first hand what has happened, so that he would not have to speak so crossly to them about their surrender of freedom in the faith.

THE ALLEGORY OF FREEDOM

The argument of the letter concludes with a brief allegory, based on the Old Testament story of the two wives of Abraham (Gen. 16:1–17:21; 21:1-21). This narrative is especially appropriate, since Abraham has already figured prominently in the earlier part of the letter. When, in an effort to help God fulfil his promise of a son, Abraham acquired a concubine, the results spelled trouble for all concerned. The son born to the slave woman, Hagar, was not qualified to serve as Abraham's heir. It was through Isaac, the son whose birth came solely by God's grace, that the promise was fulfilled. Similarly, only those who approach God by faith may share in his blessings (Gal. 4:21-31). The detailed significance of this allegory is complex, and Paul's reasoning is not always clear. The main emphasis, however, is unmistakably on the contrast between "law" and "promise" as ways of approach to God.

The Galatians have been set free from the drudgery of trying to earn their way into God's acceptance by doing good works (Gal. 5:1 ff.). They have experienced the release that comes when gratitude and trust replace a sense of obligation and fear. In response to man's faith, God sends his Spirit, which creates in man's heart the desire for right living, and provides the inner strength to fulfil man's moral ambitions. Like the surge of new life that courses through a tree each spring and produces fruit, so the Spirit energizes the man of faith to produce the fruit of good works. Man, unaided by God's Spirit, can produce only evil works, Paul explains. Pressures placed upon him by Torah or by any other religious code only increase his sense of moral weakness. But all the moral qualities that the Law commends are produced in the life of the man in whom the Spirit of God is allowed to work unhindered by selfish aims. It is through the Spirit that the new life has come; it is by reliance on the Spirit that the new life is to be lived. With some advice about the relations among members (Gal. 6:1-6), a word of encouragement about diligence in service (6:7-10), and a warmly personal reminder about the circumcision issue, Paul brings his letter to a close.

This Letter to the Galatians is, by our reckoning, the earliest of Paul's preserved letters. It outlines and sets the tone for most of the major themes that he was to develop during his career as an interpreter of the Christian message. Many of the specific problems that arose in the Gentile churches and with which he was obligated to deal in other letters are not anticipated here. But the main line of argument about acceptance by God through faith in Christ that is presented here is found throughout his letters. The development of the argument is sometimes more systematic (as in the Letter to the Romans), and is sometimes approached from another angle (as in the Letter to the Colossians). A fuller treatment of Paul's message to Gentiles will be found in Chapter 9.

The task of putting his case in writing in this Letter to the Galatians may have helped to crystallize the issues and conclusions in Paul's thinking. Shortly afterward, Paul and Barnabas, together with the other delegates from the church at Antioch, set out for a conference with the leaders of the church in Jerusalem.

Conciliation in Jerusalem
(Acts 15:2-35)

As the travellers passed through Phoenicia and Samaria on their way up to the Holy City, they called on the Christian communities there and reported on the success of the church at Antioch in preaching the gospel to the Gentiles. The brethren whom Paul and Barnabas visited were pleased with the news—not a surprising reaction, since Phoenicia and Samaria were non-Jewish territories and not all the Christians there had Jewish backgrounds (Acts 15:3).

RESULTS OF THE CONFERENCE

At Jerusalem, the welcome extended to Paul and his companions was cordial. But there was a traditionalist wing that was offended by the report that Gentiles had been received into the fellowship without having been circumcised (Acts 15:4, 5). The spokesmen for this group insisted that the community in Antioch be instructed to demand of all its converts conformity to the regulations embodied in Torah.

A lengthy and somewhat formal hearing followed, presided over by the apostles, at which representatives of various points of view were permitted to speak. Peter reminded those in attendance that he was the one who had launched the work of the gospel among the Gentiles, when he preached at Caesarea (Acts 10). He was convinced that the Gentiles should not be obliged to obey the Law, since even those of Jewish heritage had to admit that they were incapable of obeying it (Acts 15:6-11). If, as we are here supposing,[8] the narrative in Acts 15

---

[8] Cf. Note 4 and the discussion of other possible theories about Paul's visits to Jerusalem on p. 220.

is a fairly reliable report of Peter's attitude after the conflict with Paul had taken place in Antioch, Peter had clearly gained his equilibrium in the interim and had come down without equivocation on Paul's side of the argument.

Then Paul and Barnabas were asked to tell about their work among the Gentiles. After hearing of the way God had put his stamp of approval on their activity by performing wonderful works through them, James and the others were reassured. James, agreeing with Peter on the whole, gave the decision that Gentiles must not be required to keep the Law in order to be admitted to Christian fellowship. He quoted words from the prophets (Acts 15:16-18) to show that there was a scriptural warrant for including Gentiles among the beneficiaries of God's redemptive acts. He then proposed a set of minimum requirements for Gentiles: they were to avoid idolatry, unchastity, "things strangled" (that is, they were not to eat flesh of animals that had been put to death by strangling), and "blood" (Torah prohibited the eating or drinking of blood). The first two restrictions are moral or religious; the last two are dietary. One important group of Greek manuscripts of Acts, however, omits the word that is translated "things strangled." If these manuscripts preserve the original form of the decrees, perhaps "blood" should be interpreted as meaning "shedding blood"—that is, murder. Then all the decrees—at least the three authentic ones—would be in the moral category.

It seems incredible, however, that murder could have been common enough in the early church to require a decree against it. "Thou shalt not kill" is repeated in the New Testament only as a part of critical references by Jesus to the Law of Moses, in which Jesus declares that the Law does not go far enough in its demands (Mt. 5:21 ff.).[9] It is perhaps artificial to distinguish between the moral decrees and the ones that have to do with ceremonial purity. Modern theologians continue to claim that Jesus and the early church rejected the ceremonial requirements of Torah but reaffirmed its moral demands. The distinction is one that the Jews of Jesus' day would never have made. Torah was the declaration of the will of God for all of life; religious obligations could not be arbitrarily divided up into moral and ritual sections. Therefore, even if we were to regard the shorter version of the text as the authentic one, the legal demands included in the decrees laid down by James were part of the legal system that Paul had rejected as a requirement for admission to the Christian community.

---

[9] See the discussion of Jesus' attitude toward the Law, pp. 128 ff.

I

THE ISSUE REMAINS UNSETTLED

Was Paul compromising his convictions when he agreed to the rules included in James' decrees? We must bear in mind that these regulations had to do only with the question of fellowship within the church between Jewish and Gentile Christians; the question of justification, or how one might become accepted by God, did not enter the discussion at this point. It is scarcely conceivable that Paul would have surrendered his whole case for "justification by faith" by agreeing to such legal requirements just for the sake of maintaining good relations with Jerusalem. What is more probable is that the leaders were seeking only to proscribe those pagan practices that were most obnoxious to pious Jews. If a Gentile Christian were willing to abstain from these practices, his presence at the common meal of the Christian community would not offend any Jewish Christians who might want to participate. The official silence about a decision on circumcision suggests that Paul may have won his point on that issue, even though controversy about it continued to plague his work.[10]

The most significant part of the official decision reached by the Jerusalem leaders was that the work of Paul and the others among the Gentiles was to continue unhindered. The conference had apparently resulted in a mutually satisfactory working agreement between the Jewish Christians on the one hand and the workers among the Gentiles on the other. But the fact that the problem of the requirements for admitting Gentiles to the fellowship was raised only when Jerusalem Christians raised it, and that it vanished when the Jerusalem community scattered, suggests that the leaders in Jerusalem never really understood Paul. Furthermore, there is no evidence that the decrees had any lasting effect. The requirements embodied in the decrees are mentioned again in Acts 21:25 and are hinted at in Revelation 2:20, but Paul did not introduce them among the churches in Greece. On the other hand, the Jerusalem community never accepted Paul's gospel of justification by faith, although it was his version of the Christian message that swept the Roman world and enabled Christianity to become a universal religion rather than a Jewish sect. As we shall see, the Judaizing wing of the church continued to give a central place to the requirements of Torah, and as a result was eventually declared heretical by the rest of the church (see Chapter 10).

According to Acts, Paul and the others conformed to the wishes of

---

[10] For a full discussion of the Jerusalem Council and the decrees, see Foakes-Jackson and Lake, *op. cit.*, Vol. V, note 16.

the Jerusalem leaders, however, and returned to Antioch with the official bearers of the letter that stated the agreement (Acts 15:22-35). The rejoicing among the Christians in Antioch that is reported to have followed the reading of the letter to the congregation was probably an expression of relief that an agreement had been so easily reached, rather than a sign of pleasure over the additional restrictions. It was clear, however, that the question of circumcision, which the Jerusalem conference had passed over in silence, had not yet been settled, since the issue arose immediately when Paul resumed his work in Asia Minor. It is this phase of Paul's ministry that we shall investigate in the next chapter.

CHAPTER EIGHT

MISSION TO EUROPE

Now that amicable relations had been restored with Jerusalem, Paul was free to turn his attention to the churches in Asia Minor, which had been so disturbed over the controversy about requirements for admission to the community. The representatives who had come down from Jerusalem to convey the decision of the council between Paul and the apostles had returned [1] to the mother church in Jerusalem,

---

New Testament readings relevant to this chapter are Acts 15-19; I and II Corinthians; I Thessalonians.

[1] One major group of manuscripts (the so-called Western text type) adds the information that Silas (one of the Jerusalem delegates) did not return. This is probably an ancient interpolation to account for the fact that in vs. 33, Silas leaves for Jerusalem, but in vs. 40 he—or another man of the same name—is back in Antioch.

apparently satisfied with the reception of the decrees at Antioch. Some time later, Paul proposed to Barnabas that they revisit the churches established on their evangelistic tour of Cyprus and Asia Minor, in order to see how the members were getting on. A bitter dispute developed between Paul and Barnabas over the issue of taking along John Mark, who had proved so unreliable before. Barnabas was inclined to be lenient with his young kinsman, but Paul could not forget the earlier desertion. So it was agreed that they would separate: Paul would go to the churches of Asia Minor; Barnabas and Mark, to Cyprus. Silas was chosen to replace Barnabas as Paul's travelling companion, and together they set out across Syria and Cilicia toward the Cilician Gates and the Anatolian plateau beyond.

"Come over to Macedonia and help us . . ."
(Acts 16:9)

Although there is no evidence on whether or not the breach between Paul and Barnabas was ever healed, Paul continued to associate the name of Barnabas with his own work (cf. I Cor. 9:6). The split seems to have been a purely personal one, and did not spring from the differences between the Jerusalem and Antioch communities on the issue of admitting Gentiles to the fellowship. Silas, who had now become Paul's chief helper, had headed the delegation from the Jerusalem church that had come down to Antioch, and obviously had the complete confidence of the Jerusalem leaders.

STRENGTHENING
THE CHURCHES OF ASIA MINOR

When Paul and Silas reached Lystra, they were confronted by the question of circumcision, which had been troubling the Galatian churches since Paul's first visit there (Acts 16:1-5). Surprisingly, Paul is reported by Acts to have demonstrated a conciliatory attitude on this issue toward those with whom he disagreed. The problem arose over young Timothy, a half-Greek whom Paul wanted to have as a helper on the current evangelistic mission, and who was uncircumcised. Rather than insist on the freedom concerning circumcision that the apostolic decisions had just confirmed, Paul performed the rite of circumcision in order to avoid giving unnecessary offence to Jewish Christians. The churches were strengthened by this peace-making gesture, and they prospered both numerically and spiritually. Later, we shall see that Paul was called on again to demonstrate a conciliatory spirit on the occasion of his last visit to Jerusalem. If the Acts account is reliable, it is paradoxical, and yet perhaps characteristic of Paul, that he was more willing to make concessions to Jewish piety after the controversy had been settled in his favour than he had been before.

After the tour of the Galatian churches was completed, Paul and Silas made an attempt to extend their evangelistic activities to the area north of the province of Galatia, but their effort was thwarted (Acts 16:6, 7). The account in Acts ascribes this failure simply to a prohibition "by the Holy Spirit." What the outward circumstances were that prevented Paul and Silas from entering this territory we do not know. Other Christian missionaries must have carried on effective work there, however, since from the time of Trajan (who reigned from A.D. 98 to 117) the Christians were so strong in the area that they were regarded as a public nuisance by the imperial governor, Pliny. In Chapter 11 we shall examine the charges that Pliny brought against the uncooperative Christians who were undermining the compulsory worship of the emperor.

After turning aside from his destination in the north, Paul journeyed westward to the fabled district of Troy—or Troas, as it is also called (Acts 16:8). More than a generation ago, archaeologists discovered that the ancient mound of Troy contained nine successive levels of occupation, the highest and most recent of which included the ruins of the minor port city that Paul visited. The author of Acts mentions the city, not because of its illustrious past, but because Paul was joined there by the unnamed companion (presumably Luke) whose presence is indicated in the narrative only by a modest shift from "they" to "we" (cf. 16:8 and 16:10). At the beginning of Acts 17, after the author has described Paul's experiences at Philippi, the pronouns shift back from "we" to "they," which suggests that Paul's anonymous travelling companion accompanied him only from Troas to Philippi. When the "we" section takes up again (Acts 20.6), Paul has returned to Philippi. A tempting conjecture, therefore, would be that Paul met someone in Asia Minor—perhaps at Troas—who was attracted by the Christian message and urged Paul to travel across the Aegean to Philippi in Macedonia, in order to preach the gospel there. Paul's dream, in which a man of Macedonia appeals to him to "come over to Macedonia and help us" (Acts 16:9), would be the result of his contact with the man hidden behind the enigmatic "we."

LAUNCHING THE MISSION IN EUROPE

Whatever the accompanying circumstances may have been, Paul determined to cross over to the mainland of Europe and to begin

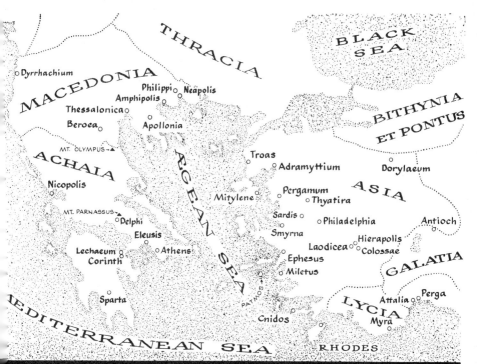

GREECE, ASIA MINOR, (WESTERN HALF) AND THE AEGEAN

his evangelistic activity in Philippi. If our conjecture about the connection between the narrator of Acts and the city of Philippi is correct, there may be a touch of local pride in the description of Philippi as "the leading city of the district" (Acts 16:12). It was, indeed, the centre of a Roman colony, and had been since Octavius Caesar won a decisive battle in the vicinity in 42 B.C. Subsequently, Philippi had become a Roman colony. The custom of the Romans was to settle retired soldiers in outlying cities and to grant them citizenship, thereby fulfilling their obligation to care for veterans while at the same time establishing strong cores of faithful citizens in widely scattered but strategically located centres all over the empire. The first Roman colonists at Philippi included both former followers of Caesar and partisans of Antony. The origins of the city date back before the time of Alexander the Great, whose father, Philip of Macedon, had named the city after himself. Acts prefers to call the city by its simple name, Philippi, rather than to use the official designation, Colonia Augusta Julia Philippensis. The continuing importance of the city, apart from its function as a home for old soldiers, arose from its location astride the Via Egnatia, a vital military and commercial road that stretched

243

across northern Greece from the Aegean to the Adriatic at Corcyra. Its eastern end was Neapolis (Acts 16:11, 12), which served as a port city for Philippi.

Extensive remains of the market place of Philippi have been uncovered, and the western gateway of the city still stands. Beyond the gateway, the Via Egnatia leads toward the bank of the tiny river Gangites. Apparently, the small Jewish community in the city, lacking the resources to erect its own house of worship, met by the bank of the stream, where water was available for the washings that accompanied their worship. At this isolated spot there gathered a number of pious Jewish women, including one named Lydia, whose business was to sell the famous purple dye made from shellfish that was so highly prized in the ancient world. The fact that Lydia is a Gentile name, combined with the description of her as a "worshipper of God" (Acts 16:14)—a term that Acts regularly uses for non-Jews who join in Jewish worship—indicates that this devout woman was one of many Gentiles attracted by the high morality and monotheism of Judaism, rather than a birthright Jew.

On the sabbath following his arrival in the city, Paul sought out this place of worship. Invited to speak a word of exhortation to the assembled worshippers, he took advantage of the opportunity to tell them the good news about Jesus Christ. His message came to Lydia with convincing power, and her submission to the rite of baptism gave public witness that she was a "believer in the Lord"—the first in Europe (Acts 16:15).

Opposition at Philippi

Paul's other recorded encounter with a woman in Philippi led to quite a different experience (Acts 16:16-24). A young slave girl who earned money for her owners by fortune-telling persisted in giving Paul and Silas unsolicited publicity by calling attention to the God and the faith they were preaching. Soothsaying was common enough during that age, and was by no means limited to the ignorant and the uncultured. Military men and heads of state would make no important decision without consulting the oracles.

The term this young soothsayer used to describe the God whom Paul and Silas served, "Most High God," was used by various religions of the day that combined elements of Jewish faith with the worship of angelic and astral beings. On the other hand, it could have been nothing more than the Greek equivalent of the ancient Semitic name for God, El Elyon. Whether her acclaim was mockery, or whether it was a misguided effort to aid these men in their propagandizing, we cannot tell. In any case, Paul, by exorcising the spirit from her, brought her career as a soothsayer to an abrupt end and precipitated an avalanche of opposition, instigated by her owners. The owners, who accused Paul and Silas of insurrection, raised this charge because it stood a better chance of arousing public resentment than the mere announcement that these evangelists had ruined their source of income from the slave girl, which was their real complaint. But the mob's attack on Paul and Silas was as violent as if the charges of insurrection had been justified. The authorities made no effort to hear the defence of these two men, or even to find out who they were. If they had done so, Paul's Roman citizenship would have saved him from the beating and unjust imprisonment, as it was later to do in Jerusalem (see Chapter 10).

Although at first Paul's imprisonment threatened to end his mission, it soon led to the enlargement of the little nucleus of Philippian converts. During the night, an earthquake shook the prison to its foundations, and the fetters of Paul and Silas were unaccountably released. Any ordinary earthquake would have tumbled down the walls of the jail rather than merely setting free its occupants, but the author of Acts credits the quake with freeing the prisoners (Acts 16:25-34). When the terrified jailer saw that his prisoners had been released, he was on the point of committing suicide. But out of the darkness came the reassuring words of Paul: "Do not harm yourself, for we are all here." The jailer's anguished words, "What must I do to be saved?" probably meant only, "How can I escape the penalty for dereliction of duty?" But the answer that Paul and Silas gave led him into the fellowship of the Christian community, and promised deliverance from the powers of evil that he perhaps thought had sent the earthquake. Paul's captor became his debtor.

When the civil authorities realized the perilous thing they had done in scourging and incarcerating Roman citizens, they were quick to apologize for their rash action and to speed the two itinerant preachers on their way. Before Paul and Silas left Philippi, however, the embryonic Christian community met with them for instruction and advice. This group was to become one of the most reliable, generous, and lovable of the churches that Paul established, as we can infer from his Letter to the Philippians—written, appropriately enough, from a Roman prison!

PREACHING IN THESSALONICA

Continuing westward along the Via Egnatia, the travellers reached the thriving seaport of Thessalonica, located at the head of the gulf that bears its name. It is impossible to tell what the city was like in Paul's day, since a series of catastrophes, including a fire early in the present century, have destroyed nearly all traces of the Roman period except for a few remains from the Late Empire. Some inscriptions have been discovered that use the distinctive term for the city authorities that Acts favours, "politarchs" (Acts 17:6). This corroboration for what is otherwise an unimportant detail serves to substantiate the opinion that the author of Acts prepared his record with considerable care.

The presence of a synagogue in Thessalonica provided Paul with a large number of potential converts, both from among the Jews and from among the many pious Gentiles who worshipped at the synagogue. The evidence from Paul's first letter to this church (I Thess. 1:9) suggests that many of the Thessalonian Christians came to the faith straight out of heathendom. This raises the question of how Paul dealt with converts who had none of the preparatory instruction provided by Judaism that supplied many points of contact and mutual understanding as a foundation for the preaching of the gospel. With the Gentiles, Paul could presuppose nothing. We shall deal with this question later in this chapter, and more fully in Chapter 9.

By the time we reach the account in Acts 17, we can almost predict the pattern of events that will occur when Paul visits the various cities: His success in winning converts brings mounting opposition from the Jews who remain loyal to their traditions. In the furore that follows, the civil authorities intervene and the little group of believers urges Paul and Silas to move on to the next town, both to protect the lives of the preachers, and, one suspects, to mitigate the antagonism that has built up against the local converts. At Beroea, the pattern ran true to form, with two exceptions: the Jews were more diligent in consulting Torah to see if the messianic claims that Paul was making for Jesus could be refuted or corroborated, and some upper-class Gentiles were converted along with a considerable number of Jews. Since Paul seemed to be the major source of contention at Beroea, it was deemed wise for him to move on to Athens, leaving behind two of the stalwarts, Silas and Timothy, to strengthen the newly established community.

"Men of Athens, . . . you are very religious"
(Acts 17:22)

Whether Paul travelled from Beroea to Athens by land or by sea, he must have seen two of Greece's glories: the majestic peak of Olympus,

The reconstructed Stoa of Attalos at the foot of the Acropolis. The original was built as a public portico by Attalos II, King of Pergamum, and the marble for the reconstruction was taken from the same quarry that he used in the middle of the second century B.C.

legendary home of the gods, towering over the Gulf of Thessalonica, and the spectacular Acropolis at Athens, crowned with the glistening marble of the Parthenon. A second-century traveller tells us that the light of the sun, reflected from the huge bronze statue of Athena located within the precincts of the Parthenon, was visible to sailors miles away as they entered the harbour of Athens at Piraeus. Among the cluster of buildings that topped the hill were the temple known as the Erectheum, with its famous Porch of the Maidens, and the complex of graceful colonnades and shrines that formed the portal to the temple precincts, the Propylea.

It was, however, not the splendour of Athens' marble shrine that caught Paul's attention; it was the activity in the city centre, several hundred feet below at the foot of the Acropolis. The six acres of open market place (or *agora*, as it was called) had long since become so cluttered with monuments and altars to assorted deities that the Roman rulers had felt obliged to construct annexes in the area to the east. Around the original square were the colonnades and public structures in which were carried on the commercial, political, social, and, to an extent, the intellectual life of this great centre of Hellenic culture. Athens' leadership in the cultural world was declining, to be replaced by that of Alexandria and later the cities of the West. But even in Paul's day the successors of Zeno were to be found teaching in the very public porches (*stoa*) that had given the name Stoic to their philosophical school. To the west of the agora were the imposing council chambers and shrines that had served as public gathering places since before the days of Socrates. Intruding into what was originally the open court of the market place were the Temple of Ares, god of war, and an enormous music hall, which seem in retrospect to have symbolized the devotion to power and pleasure that brought Greece to ruin. The great days of Greek literature and political thought were centuries past, but the pride of culture and the fondness for matching wits remained.

CONVERTING THE INTELLECTUALS

Paul divided his time between the synagogue, where the most fertile field for conversion was normally to be sought, and the agora, where the prospects were dim but the need great. His remarks about Jesus and the resurrection were greeted in the market place with amused interest by some and with open scorn by others. It has been suggested that the Athenians mistook the term "resurrection" for a female deity (the word is feminine in Greek) and thought that Jesus was her consort, after the fashion of such pairs of deities as Isis and

Osiris, and Venus and Adonis. In any case, the excitement that Paul's disputing stirred up led to his being summoned before the council of city officials who were charged with maintaining order in the agora. Originally, this court had convened only in the open-air space carved out of the rock on top of the Hill of Ares (Areopagus in Greek), but in later years it often met in one of the council chambers adjoining the agora. The staircase leading to the summit and the benches carved from the living rock of Areopagus are still to be seen in Athens today. Whether on this occasion the session of the Areopagite council was held on the hilltop or in the stoa is impossible to determine.

If it was from the vantage point of the Hill of Ares itself that Paul spoke to the council, he could have indicated with a single sweeping gesture scores of the idols and altars to which he referred in his opening remarks. Far from condemning the Athenians as irreligious, Paul sought to guide them to the goal of their religious quest, which was epitomized for him in their dedication of an altar to an unknown god. In other Greek cities inscriptions have been found on altars that were dedicated to unknown *gods*, but none to a *single* undesignated deity.

The Acropolis at Athens, with the hill of Areopagus in the foreground. According to Acts 17, Paul preached before the court that traditionally met on the Areopagus.

Two famous travellers of antiquity, Pausanias (around A.D. 150) and Apollonius of Tyana (first century A.D.), are reported to have seen altars to unknown gods in Athens, and an Athenian legend tells how an ancient hero averted a plague by offering a sacrifice to an unknown god. It is not impossible, therefore, that such an altar may have existed in the agora of Athens, even though none has been discovered. In any case, the reference provided an effective opening wedge for the address that Paul is reported to have given.

Scholars have pointed out that neither the style nor the approach of this sermon is quite like what we find in Paul's letters. The famous phrase, "In him we live and move and have our being," sounds pantheistic, as though God were a world-soul that permeated all the universe. What Paul is reported as doing, however, is quoting a familiar passage from Epimenides, a popular semi-legendary figure of ancient Greece. He uses the words to establish a common point of reference with his audience, not as proof for a major point in his sermon. Paul's attack is against idolatry, with its notion that God can be represented in tangible form. He insists on the spiritual nature of God, who is active throughout all his creation, and who is the true goal of those who have erected an altar to the god that they admit they do not know. The god whom they worship without knowing is the one who orders events and fulfils his purpose in his creation. That purpose is a moral one, and in order to prepare themselves for the time when God will fulfil it men must repent. Only through repentance can they be made ready for the end of the present age and the judgment that will usher in the age to come. Paul is not seeking to compete with the philosophers on their own ground by means of an erudite discourse; rather, by using commonplaces of religious verse and sentiment, he is trying to gain a sympathetic hearing from the council before proceeding to controversial matters.

RESULTS IN ATHENS

So long as Paul confined himself to the denunciation of idolatry and the affirmation of the spiritual nature of God, few of his examiners could have felt much antagonism. But when he introduced the notion of a man through whom the world is to be judged, and when he talked about the resurrection, it was too much for most of his listeners. Had Paul spoken of immortality, he would have given no offence; even if he had affirmed only that some dead hero had been revived or deified, the audience would have understood, although they might not have been convinced. But the distinctively oriental (Iranian and later Jewish) idea of the resurrection of the dead seemed an absurdity to the educated

Athenians. The results of Paul's approach were meagre, and he seems never to have used it again.

The narrator has given a tantalizing twist to the account by mentioning that among the converts was a man named Dionysius the Areopagite. This would imply that Paul converted one of his judges in much the same way that the martyr Stephen's courage had contributed to Paul's own conversion (see Chapter 6). Actually, nothing further is known of this Dionysius, although his name was a favourite nom-de-plume for quasi-philosophers in the fifth century and later. As enigmatic as Dionysius is the subsequent history of the community of Christians in Athens; we know nothing more about the Athenian church in the apostolic age.

"You turned to God from idols"

(I Thess. 1:9)

After his mixed success in Athens, Paul travelled westward along the shore of the Saronic Gulf, past the Island of Salamis, which is forever associated with the Greeks' spectacular defeat of the Persian navy in 480 B.C. As he approached the narrow isthmus that separates the Peloponnesus from the rest of Greece, he could see Cenchreae, the eastern port of Corinth and the seat of the famous Isthmian Games. Here goods were transported across the narrow neck of land to Lechaeum, just west of Corinth, where ships carried them on to the ports of Rome. Corinth itself sits on a series of ledges facing out over the gulf that bears its name. To the north-west are the jagged snow-patched slopes of Mount Parnassus, with the famous Delphic oracle nestling at its foot.

Looming up behind the city nearly 1900 feet above the sea is the massive rock known as Acrocorinth. From its summit can be seen the Gulf of Corinth stretching to the west, the rugged hills of the Peloponnesus to the south, and the eastern gulf through which ships sailed to the ports of Asia Minor and the Levant. This impressive vista symbolized the strategic position that Corinth occupied at an important commercial and cultural crossroad.

MORALITY AND RELIGION IN CORINTH

Located atop Acrocorinth was a small structure that dramatized in grosser fashion the cultural mingling at Corinth. It was a temple, ostensibly in honour of Aphrodite, the Hellenic goddess of love and beauty, but actually a centre for the worship of Astarte, the sensual

Phoenician deity whose orgiastic cults had shocked the sensibilities of the ancient Israelites. Strabo, the indefatigable geographer and chronicler of the early first century A.D., reports that at one time more than a thousand temple-prostitutes were maintained in connection with the worship at this shrine.

In the city itself were temples to Isis, the Great Mother, and to other oriental deities. So low was the level of morality in Corinth that the very name of the city had become synonymous with profligacy and degradation. "To corinthianize" meant "to debase."

In addition to all the other eastern cults, there was a colony of Jews in Corinth. The size of the colony had been sharply increased just before Paul's arrival as the result of an imperial decree that banned all Jews from Rome. Suetonius, the Roman biographer, referring to this incident in his *Life of Claudius*, explains that there had been a dis-

Claudius, here pictured on a coin of his reign (41-54 A.D.), was the emperor who drove the Jews from Rome about the year 50. Some of the exiles found their way to Corinth and became Paul's aides.

turbance among the Jews, instigated by a man named Chrestos, which Claudius had sought to settle by dispersing the Jewish community. What Suetonius took for an internal conflict may actually have been caused by the arrival in Rome of preachers of the Christian gospel, which would certainly have stirred up discord among the Jews. Among those who fled to Corinth were Aquila and Priscilla, with whom Paul struck up a lasting friendship (Acts 18:1-3). It may be that this couple had already heard the gospel, or had even accepted it, before leaving Rome, and were thus favourably disposed to cooperate with Paul in his missionary work in bustling, corrupt Corinth. Perhaps the reason Paul does not list Aquila and Priscilla as his first converts in Achaia [2] (I Cor. 16:15) is that they had been converted long before he arrived.

The synagogue in Corinth seems to have been located on the main road that led from the agora down to the port at Lechaeum. More than fifty years ago a heavy stone lintel was discovered with an in-

---

[2] The name Achaia was given by the Romans to the province that included the southern half of the Greek peninsula.

scription that almost certainly reads, "Synagogue of the Hebrews." The crudeness and unpretentiousness of this lintel suggest that the synagogue itself was a modest affair. If so, it would have contrasted sharply with the structures that surrounded the gate a short distance away where the Lechaeum Road ended. The gate itself was an imposing, white marble arch surmounted by a bronze statue of the sun-god in his fiery chariot. Surrounding the archway were glistening colonnaded shops and spacious public markets. Passing through the gate, one entered the agora itself, flanked on the left by the legendary fountain of Peirene, which still supplies water to the little village of Old Corinth. The ruins along the road immediately adjoining the site of the synagogue indicate that the houses and shops that once stood there were of a humble sort; it was in such a house that Titius Justus, Paul's host, must have lived. At this strategic spot, Paul could continue his proselytizing work among the Jews (even though he had made a show of public withdrawal from such work) and could also carry on a programme of open-air preaching in the nearby agora (Acts 18:5-11).

PAUL'S STRATEGY

Judging from the amount of time and attention Paul gave to the Corinthian church both on this visit and on his return, the results of his efforts in such an unpromising city must have been very encouraging. Even criminal charges and a hearing before the civil ruler did not deter him (Acts 18:12-17). The remains of the public rostrum, or tribunal, at which Paul was tried and upon which the proconsul Gallio sat, are still standing among the ruins of the Corinthian marketplace. Gallio is less well known than his brother, Seneca, who achieved fame as philosopher-royal and court adviser until he fell into disfavour with the irresponsible emperor Nero. The date of Gallio's consulship, as we noted in Chapter 2, provides one of the few relatively fixed points for the chronology of Paul's life.

Apart from a mention of Paul's converting one of the leaders of the synagogue and gaining an acquittal before the Roman authority, the account in Acts tells us little about Paul's problems and tactics in founding a church in this predominantly Gentile community. We have to infer his methods from the letters that he later wrote to the Christians there, in which he recalls to their minds what he had told them, how he had lived among them, and how he had anticipated or dealt with difficulties in their corporate life. Since both letters (I and II Corinthians) are written in response to letters from the church in Corinth to Paul, we can see clearly the kinds of problem that developed there in his absence.

Before we consider the internal problems of the community at Corinth and how Paul dealt with them, let us see how he went about proclaiming to a pagan audience a gospel that had originated in a Jewish environment. Along with every other successful missionary to the Gentiles, he endeavoured to show the relation between his message of good news and the aspirations that had arisen in Gentile cultures, without departing from his Jewish heritage or from the basic belief about Jesus that he had "received" (I Cor. 15:3; also see p. 210). Keeping in mind the form and the vocabulary of religious aspirations among the Gentiles, Paul set about "preaching Christ" to those to whom the promises to Israel were both unknown and meaningless. I Corinthians 1 and 2 give us a good illustration of one way in which Paul approached this task.

The gospel in gentile terms

After some introductory remarks (which we shall discuss in Chapter 9), in I Corinthians 1:17 Paul recalls to the Corinthians his objective and the method he had used when he first launched the gospel among them. He made no effort to compete with the popular teachers

The Bema, or public rostrum, at Corinth, with the Acrocorinth in the background. Paul was accorded a hearing on this platform before Gallio, the Roman governor.

of religious philosophy on their own terms. The "wisdom" that Paul proclaimed made no claim to surpass the philosophies in rational appeal. "What we preach" (this translation is a paraphrase for the Greek word *kerygma*) is foolishness by human standards, but through it the true wisdom of God is revealed. What the essence of the *kerygma* was, we have already seen in Chapter 2; but how it was made meaningful to Gentiles is quite another matter.

The first element of the message to which Paul alludes in his convenient, though incomplete, summary in I Corinthians 15:3-8 is Jesus' death on the cross. The cross was a major obstacle in preaching to either Jew or Gentile, and yet it obviously could not be eliminated. The Jews had no theory of a crucified Messiah, and the Gentiles honoured a triumphant redeemer, not a defeated one. Even so, Paul preached to both alike the cross as the symbol of Jesus' having died "for our sins." Here he speaks more in the language of his Hebrew forebears, who believed that God met their priestly representative once a year in the inner sanctuary of the Temple, and there received the offering of a sacrificial victim as an atonement for the sins of the people. The theory implicit in this act was not that of propitiating a wrathful God, but of renewing through this offering the covenant relationship between the people and God, which had been established with Abraham and sealed by a sacrifice (Gen. 15). In just such a manner, Jesus, by sacrificing himself, had removed the barrier of guilt that stood between man and God, and had established a new covenant between God and his reconciled people. This mode of interpreting the death of Jesus is considered more fully in Chapter 9, where we shall examine Paul's most elaborate treatment of the subject (in the Letter to the Romans).

But there is another interpretation of the cross which, though it was rooted in Judaism, was calculated to appeal especially to Gentiles. This is the belief, described briefly in Chapter 2, that Jesus' death and resurrection accomplished the defeat of the evil powers under whose dominion all men were held captive. The idea is found in the Gospels, where Jesus' healing ministry and the exorcisms that he performs are interpreted as launching the battle that will end in the ultimate defeat of Satan (see Chapter 3, pp. 98 ff.). But in the letters of Paul the importance of this aspect of Jesus' messianic mission is spelled out forcefully for the benefit of the Gentiles who lived in constant fear of hostile spirits. Paul affirms that by the divine wisdom embodied in the cross, the evil powers are deceived and decisively defeated. These powers thought to thwart the purpose of God by crucifying Jesus (I Cor. 2:8), but actually they brought about their own downfall. This theme is expanded in I Corinthians 15:24 and again in Colossians

2:15. From Philippians 2 it is clear that even these forces that now oppose God's will submit themselves to God's purposes when the kingdom of God, or the new age, is fulfilled. The crowning proof that the doom of the malevolent spirits is sure has been given in the resurrection of Jesus from the dead.

The all-encompassing, cosmic redemption that Paul preached would surely have been regarded as nonsense by any seeker after an intellectual religion couched in rationally appealing terms, since this message centred in the execution of an obscure Jew in a remote border province. There could be no appeal in the death of a man on a cross, Rome's most brutal and revolting method of punishing criminals. Even if the central elements of the message had been intellectually or aesthetically attractive, its proponents made no effort to present it in language that could compete with that of the popular philosophizers of the day. It was not surprising that few men of prestige or learning in Corinth had allied themselves with the Christian group. But in spite of these seeming hindrances, God had imparted his truth to men who responded in faith to the message of the cross; to such he sent his Spirit, and to them the significance of the cross was seen to be the revelation of divine wisdom (I Cor. 1:18–2:13).

The Gentiles at Corinth, it is apparent, could not be appealed to by a message of moral restitution (as were the Gentiles addressed in the Letter to the Romans), nor by a promise of purification from defilement, such as the Letter to the Hebrews declared was offered through Christ. It was redemption from the forces of evil that they craved, and it was this redemption that Paul preached. Yet he never forgot the reality of the historical life of Jesus, or the desperate need of the Corinthians for the moral cleansing and purification that would make them worthy worshippers of God. Paul could state his message in a way that made sense to his pagan audience, and that would enlist the interest of listeners to whom Judaism was wholly alien. But he could never detach the gospel from the Jewish roots of moral demand and historical consciousness on which his own religious life had been nourished.

"Now concerning the matters
about which you wrote . . ."
(I Cor. 7:1)

More than any of Paul's other letters, I Corinthians gives us a clear picture of the problems that beset the struggling churches whose members were recruited from heathendom. Long before the Corinthians wrote the questions to Paul that he sought to answer in the letter known as I Corinthians, we may be sure that he was aware of the kinds of difficulty that harassed them.

THE PROBLEM OF HERO-WORSHIP

The first of these problems (touched on in I Cor. 1, 4, 12, 13 14) was their reluctance to be a community at all! Pride, hero-worship, and rivalry were stronger forces than the desire for unity. The Corinthian Christians felt a greater sense of loyalty to particular favourites among the men who had founded the church ("I belong to Paul... I belong to Cephas...") than they did to their common Lord. Each man was so inflated with pride over his special spiritual gift ("the utterance of wisdom... the interpretation of tongues...") that he forgot that one Spirit was the source of strength for all these ministries in the life of the church. The ability to serve in any capacity was a "gift"; each gift was necessary to the functioning of the whole Body of Christ, as Paul sometimes called the church. To make matters worse, the Corinthian Christians, among whom the manifestations of the Spirit's power were still novel, chose to parade their newly acquired talents before the unbelieving citizenry, who—far from appreciating the spiritual nature of the gifts—thought the church was an aggregation of madmen. The community in Corinth needed to be reminded that a spirit of order was essential to its corporate life and worship. Divisiveness, disorder, and display must all give way before love, the greatest gift of all.

THE PROBLEM OF IMMORALITY

Quite in keeping with the proverbial Corinthian character, the first of the questions raised by the church there concerned immorality (I Cor. 5). The Christians had come to tolerate among their number a man who had taken his stepmother as his wife. Such flagrant immorality was not condoned even among the pagans. Could the Christians be less severe in condemning it? If the action of such men brought disrepute on the whole community, they were to be rejected by group action. Contacts with them could not be avoided, but fellowship with them was unthinkable! Some Corinthians had exploited their freedom from law to the extent of having sexual intercourse with prostitutes (I Cor. 6). To enter such a union was to ignore the fact that what man does with his body is inseparable from his spiritual condition. The corrupting influence of such an association is completely incongruous with the presence within him of the Holy Spirit, Paul maintained.

Another reason for the ridicule that the city of Corinth heaped on the church was the group's habit of settling internal disputes by airing them in public courts (I Cor. 6). The authority to settle such disputes resided in the community itself, and there was no excuse for stirring up such adverse publicity.

ATTITUDE TOWARD MARRIAGE

Questions regarding sex had been raised in the church on grounds that were more matters of personal piety than of morality (I Cor. 7). Some over-pious members insisted that a Christian was more holy if he did not marry. The issue at stake was not the morality of sex relations, but the piousness of asceticism as demonstrated by sexual self-control. Paul's conviction was that the believer was neither more nor less holy if he married than if he remained single, but that the unmarried Christian had fewer obligations, and thus was freer to devote himself to "the affairs of the Lord." Those in whom the sex urge was so strong that they wasted time thinking of marriage would do well to marry, since their bachelorhood did not actually provide them more time to serve the church. Although Paul felt that freedom from time-consuming marital responsibilities was a great aid to his work, he recognized that everyone could not follow his example. He reminded his readers, however, that the end of the age was soon to come, and that in the light of the shortness of time the Corinthian Christians should avoid doing anything or entering into any relationship that might interfere with their missionary activities. No one was to change his marital status or seek to alter his social position. Rather, each was to serve God in the condition in which he found himself. Paul's belief that the present state of the world would soon undergo a radical transformation made the development of any detailed social ethic unnecessary.

Paul's critics have often maligned him for his alleged woman-hating. Although he shared with his fellow Jews the belief that the woman's place in society was subordinate to that of man, he was happy to welcome women into full membership in the Christian community, and even to give them places of responsibility in the missionary work of the church. It was at Corinth that Paul came to rely so heavily on Priscilla and her husband, Aquila, and in his letters to Corinth he indicates that this couple had major roles in the work at Ephesus as well (I Cor. 16:19). But Priscilla was not the only woman to whom Paul assigned a place of prominence in the churches he established, as we can infer from the numerous greetings and admonishments to women included in his other letters. Although he did believe that the woman's role was a secondary one, his attitude cannot with justice be termed "anti-feminine."

into being the new people of God spoken of by the prophet Jeremiah (Jer. 31:31 ff.). Although the words of Jesus in the Gospels (Mk. 14:22-25) do not refer to the "new" covenant, it seems safe to assume that Jesus was consciously referring to the old covenant established through Moses (Ex. 24:8), which he now looks upon as being supplanted by the new community of the faithful that he established. Paul is warranted, therefore, in referring to the newness of this covenant, even though Jesus may or may not have had in mind the specific words from Jeremiah.

Although Paul sought to correct the exclusive emphasis on fellowship in the common meal, with its sensual excesses, he shared with the Jerusalem community its belief that the communion looked forward to the great supper that the people of God would share in the age to come. Until that time arrived, however, he was insistent that the loaf and the cup should be considered as a memorial of Jesus' death. This solemn note is underscored when Paul points out that the judgment of God has already fallen on those who partook unworthily of this sacred feast.

THE RAISING OF THE DEAD

Judging by the amount of space devoted to it in Paul's first letter to the Corinthians, the resurrection was one of the most perplexing problems for the Gentile Christians. It would appear from Paul's full statement on the subject (I Cor. 15) that some members of the church at Corinth were minimizing the importance of the resurrection, or even denying it altogether. Similar doubts about this cardinal element of Christian faith were expressed by the Thessalonians, as we can infer from Paul's reply to them in I Thessalonians 4. There were all manner of related questions about the resurrection: Is it essential to the faith? How can anyone be sure it will take place? What form does man have in the resurrection? When will the resurrection come? Paul tried to deal with each of these questions in careful, logical fashion.

He recalled to the minds of his Corinthian readers that the resurrection was the foundation stone of the whole Christian faith, and that the authentication of the *kerygma* depended upon the appearance to chosen witnesses of Jesus *risen from the dead*. Because Christ had risen, the dead will indeed rise. Just as the devout Israelite farmer brought the first of his harvest to present before the Lord, so Jesus has now presented himself before God as the first fruits of the great harvest: the new people of God. God's purpose in the resurrection was not to bring the dead back to life, but to bring into being a new order of humanity, which would be characterized by obedience to God, as the old order had been characterized by the disobedience of Adam. The outcome of this renewal of creation is to be the subjection of all the universe to the reign of God. Faith in this divine programme has consequences for the individual Christian's present and future as well. In the present he is to be diligent in service, fearless even in the face of the threat of death, knowing that in Christ death has been conquered. But should death come, he is to have confidence that the same power that brought Jesus from the dead is able to transform his perishable body into one of incorruption. This is not merely resuscitation, as we have seen (p. 182): rather, it involves the exchanging of mortality for an immortal body. Death itself will be utterly defeated. In the light of this confidence, Christians are to be zealous in service, and undeterred by fear of failure or even fear of death. Such faith is the one sure ground of stability and perseverance in the life and work of the community.

"All . . . Asia heard the word of the Lord"
(Acts 19:10)

About two years after his arrival in Corinth, Paul felt either that his work there was done, or that the local resistance to the church might subside if he were to leave. Since he had found Priscilla and Aquila to be his most valuable helpers in missionary activity, he took them with him to Ephesus, which was to serve as a base of operations for the next phase of his work. It was from there that his letters to the Corinthians were written, including the one we have just used as a basis for examining the problems of Gentile churches (I Cor.).

EPHESUS: A CENTRE OF CHRISTIANITY

Before Paul set sail for Ephesus from Cenchreae, the eastern port of Corinth, he cut his hair in performance of a vow. This was a common practice among pious Jews who were about to make a pilgrimage to the Temple. The account in Acts does not mention that Paul went to Jerusalem on this journey, however, even though he travelled as far as Syria after his first brief stay in Ephesus. After visiting the churches in Caesarea and Antioch, Paul returned to Ephesus by land, calling at the cities in Asia Minor where he had founded churches, and seeking to strengthen them.

It was during Paul's circuit of Syria and Asia Minor that Apollos (Acts 18:24 ff.), a learned and eloquent Alexandrian, visited Ephesus and began to preach a colourful, though incomplete, version of the Christian gospel. The gaps in Apollos' knowledge of the faith were filled in by the faithful Priscilla and Aquila. These two, and the other Christians in Ephesus, appreciated Apollos' gifts, and when they had finished instructing him, they sent him off to Corinth with letters of introduction to the church there. The effectiveness of his leadership at Corinth is attested by the wide following that he attracted, and by the words of appreciation for him that Paul voices in I Corinthians 3.

When Paul reached Ephesus (Acts 19), he found that there were other Christians there as ill-informed as Apollos had been. The chief misunderstanding was on the subject of baptism. Some who considered themselves believers were familiar only with the form of the rite practised by John; after Paul enlightened them, they were baptized in the name of Jesus and received the Holy Spirit.

The power of the Spirit continued to be evident in the work of healing and the exorcisms performed by Paul. But in spite of these marvellous works, the majority of the Jewish community refused to believe Paul's message about Jesus. After three months of preaching in the synagogue, Paul was forced to leave; so he hired a public lecture hall to house his audiences. His daily lectures and discussions were so effective, and the following which he developed became so large, that he began to be plagued by both imitators and enemies. Charlatans began to use the name of Jesus as though it were a magic formula. Magicians and fortune-tellers were converted in large numbers, and destroyed their own books of occult secrets.

OPPOSITION IN EPHESUS

So successful was the work of Paul and his helpers in Ephesus that business began to fall off at the civic shrine to Artemis. This temple was far too important an element in the economy of the city for the business and civic leaders to permit its prestige and drawing power to be undermined. The structure erected to house the image of Artemis, patron goddess of Ephesus, was one of the seven wonders of the ancient world, and attracted visitors from all over the empire. The fact that the harbour of the city was filled up with silt caused the amount of commerce that passed through Ephesus to decrease seriously, even though the city was located at the western end of a vital trade route across Asia Minor. As a result, the temple of Artemis became more important than ever to the economic life of the city. Pilgrims to the shrine had to be fed and housed; they deposited treasures in the temple chambers, and bought souvenir replicas of the shrine. It was the artisans who manufactured these miniature shrines that led the opposition to Paul, since they had been hit hardest by the decline in attendance at the temple.

The temple stood on a site that had been sacred to the goddess of fertility from the earliest times. The Greeks had identified this goddess with Artemis, but she more closely resembled Astarte of the Canaanites and the Great Mother of Phrygia. The resemblance to the eastern fertility worship is accented by the fact that both male and female temple-prostitutes were attached to the Ephesian temple to serve in the performance of the orgiastic ritual required by this virgin goddess. The main structure of the temple was considerably larger than a present-day football field, and stood on a huge platform that measured more than 200 by 400 feet. The net effect of the imposing proportions, together with the elaborate exterior decoration of marble, gold, and sculpture, must have been extremely impressive. The image of the goddess, by contrast, was quite simple, as we can judge from representations of it on coins of the era. It had the head and upper parts of a woman, but

The ruins of Ephesus. In Paul's day, Ephesus was one of the great cities of the eastern Mediterranean, but the silting up of its harbour rendered it useless as a port and caused it to be abandoned.

consisted largely of an unworked block of stone. The tradition about its having come down from heaven may indicate that it was originally a meteorite. The copies of the sanctuary that were made and sold by the artisans in Paul's day were models of more primitive shrines antedating the magnificent temple that was standing in the first century. His success in winning the populace away from devotion to Artemis could not go unchallenged by the Ephesians, lest this important source of livelihood for the city be curtailed.

The craftsmen, taking the initiative, inflamed the people against the Christians, or "people of the Way," as the writer of Acts calls them. Two of Paul's helpers, Greeks from Macedonia, were dragged into the amphitheatre before the town assembly. The ruins of this theatre, or, more precisely, of a later reconstruction of it, are still visible today among the marshy remains of Ephesus. In Paul's time, it seated about 25,000. The mob that gathered there refused to listen to one of the Jewish leaders who attempted to bring an accusation against Paul and his followers. They were quieted only at the insistence of the town clerk, who warned them of the peril of taking the law into their own hands. The Roman authorities would almost certainly step in if these men were punished or harmed without due legal process. Since no formal charges had been brought, the clerk refused to allow any action to be taken. It was his duty to record and publish the decision reached by the town council, but under the circumstances there was no basis for deciding anything with regard to these men. Furthermore, the complaints of the artisans raised issues that were not within the province of the assembly to decide.

Paul interpreted this disturbance as a sign that he was to move elsewhere to carry on his work. His sights were set on Rome (Acts 19:21), but he felt an obligation to revisit the churches in Macedonia and Greece first, and then to take an offering to the church in Jerusalem from the Gentile churches before heading westward toward Rome and the unevangelized regions beyond.

"Now concerning the contribution"
(I Cor. 16:1)

There can be no doubt that Paul wrote more letters to the Corinthians than those we now possess. His allusions to an earlier letter (I Cor. 5:9) make it clear that our I Corinthians is at least second in a series of which only two have been preserved. A reasonable case can be made out for the theory that II Cor. 6:14–7:1 is a part of the earlier letter referred to above, and that it became misplaced in the transmission and copying of Paul's letters.[3]

In the interim between Paul's decision to go to Jerusalem via Corinth and his actual departure from Ephesus, he wrote to the Corinthians (I Cor. 16:5 ff.), telling of his intention to visit them and of the collection for the Jerusalem church that they were to have ready by the time he arrived. Unforeseen delays developed, however, and Paul was under attack by some of the Corinthians for failing to come as he had promised. He wrote from Macedonia (II Cor. 9:1-5) to tell the church in Corinth that he was, in fact, coming, and that he was sending some trusted aides ahead of him to help settle matters there before he arrived. He was not eager for a repetition of a painful visit he had made earlier (II Cor. 2:1)—an apparent reference to an otherwise unrecorded quick trip to Corinth taken while he was in Ephesus. It was his hope that this visit would lead to the restoration of peace within the church and between the Corinthians and himself. At the same time, he could complete arrangements for the gift to Jerusalem.

This contribution, as we have seen (Chapter 7), was a part of the obligation that Paul assumed at the earlier, private council with the apostolic leaders in Jerusalem. In his correspondence with the Corinthians (I Cor. 16:1-3), he instructed them to select official delegates to accompany him on his trip to Jerusalem, when he was to deliver the offerings from the Gentile churches. He was careful to commend them for the generosity of which he knew them to be capable (II Cor. 8-9) and at the same time to explain to them fully why this request for money had been made of them. The concluding parts of the last letter (II Cor. 10-12) are taken up with Paul's defence of his apostleship, which had been under violent attack in Corinth. This self-vindication was important, since otherwise the work of his enemies might undermine the results of his years of patient labour. In the course of this defence, Paul penned one of his most beautiful passages, in which he tells how he received the power to carry on his work in spite of physical handicaps and discouragements (II Cor. 12:1-10).

While Paul was still at Macedonia, encouraging reports had reached him of progress in the church at Corinth (II Cor. 7:5-7). Whether the same heartening state of affairs prevailed when he arrived in Corinth we have no way of knowing. At any rate, he remained there for three months, attending to the details of the collection, but also preparing his most systematic statement of faith: the Letter to the Romans. Here,

---

[3] On the whole question of the composite nature of II Corinthians, see Morton S. Enslin, *Christian Beginnings*, Chapters 19 and 20. New York: Harper, 1938.

at the gateway to the West, Paul looked forward with yearning to visiting the thriving community of Christians in Rome, the capital city of the world, and to preaching the gospel among those who had never heard of Christ (Rom. 15:17-25).

We have already observed Paul's way of interpreting the cross to Gentile hearers (p. 232); now let us examine in more detail his message to Gentiles about the nature of man, the redemptive purpose of God, and the nature of the Christian community.

☙❧

CHAPTER NINE

THE
MESSAGE FOR GENTILES

Letter to the Romans

Paul's detractors have described him as a pessimist and a rigid moralist, and his concern over sin might seem to support such an indictment. But if by pessimist we mean one who expects only ruin, and if by moralist we mean one who stresses ethical principles, then neither term is appropriate to Paul. He had no notion of presenting his generation with an ethical code to compete with, much less to supplant, the classical systems of ethics. And far from being a pessimist, he was almost a utopian in the hopes he had for the universe! It was this note of hope, combined with his stress on righteousness, that helped to give Paul's message its universal appeal.

To determine the precise nature of Paul's message is no simple task, even though a sizable collection of his letters is preserved in the New Testament. Since he wrote his letters for specific occasions, they are not in the form of orderly theological treatises. For the most part, the main outlines of his thought have to be reconstructed by inference, and the details arranged into a system only with caution. Fortunately, however, Paul's Letter to the Romans is a fairly systematic presentation of the major aspects of his thought. Written from Corinth to affirm to the church at Rome his intention of visiting them as soon as possible, the Letter to the Romans has no other objective than to introduce Paul and his version of the gospel before he arrives. There are no burning issues to be settled and no questions from the Romans to be answered. As a result, Paul writes in a deeply thoughtful mood, choosing his words with care, and developing his lines of argument as precisely as he can. Adopting this letter as a framework, supplemented by references to his other letters, we shall try to summarize Paul's message to the Gentiles. Using phrases selected from his letters, we shall trace seven major strands that Paul weaves into his discussion and that together provide the structure for his message.

"All have sinned and fall short"
(Rom. 3:23)

In the Jewish world-view, which was a part of Paul's heritage and by which the early church was guided, morality was not a matter of living up to ideals, but of obedience to a living, personal God. Now it is true that in Torah there were many specific precepts by which Israel was expected to live, but these were thought of as concrete expressions of the will of God, rather than as abstract ethical principles. Immoral action, therefore, could be traced to two major causes: (1) rebellion against God's will, and (2) subjection to a power that was opposed to God rather than subjection to God himself. This might be a voluntary subjection to the forces of evil, or it might result from a divine judgment by which God permitted the evil power to possess a person, or it might be a wholly involuntary seizure by an unusually potent demonic power. The one general term to describe a man's condition when he is outside an obedient relationship to God is *sin*. The acts that a man performs as a result of this broken relationship to God and the consequent lack of proper direction in his life are *sins*. Paul devotes the opening

K

section of his Letter to the Romans to a development of the theme of the sinfulness of man.

After a brief introduction, in which Paul outlines the gospel and explains his delay in visiting the community in Rome (Rom. 1:1-15), he plunges into the argument that occupies most of the remainder of the letter. It is clear from the outset that, although he thinks of himself as commissioned to preach primarily to the Gentiles, he is gravely concerned for the Jews and for their status—now apparently forfeited—as the people of God. He believes that both Jew and Greek (i.e., Gentile) are to share in God's salvation—that is, the deliverance of man and the universe from the power of evil, and the fulfilment of God's purpose for man and all creation. The direction that the argument will take is set in the key phrase: "The righteousness of God revealed through faith" (1:17). But before Paul can state what righteousness involves, he must show how it has been revealed and why it can be known only through faith.

The knowledge that God exists, and that he is the power behind the universe, is not the property of any favourite group of men to whom alone it has been revealed; rather, it is an inescapable inference from the majestic order of the natural world. Man, when he ignores the Creator and chooses to worship instead some created thing, is guilty of wilful defiance of God. Paul paints a fearful picture of the moral degradation that results from man's alienation from his Creator (1:18-32). Even though the Jews were given a more direct revelation through Torah, or perhaps *because* they had this unique opportunity of knowing God's will, they are the more reprehensible for failing to fulfil

The Temple of Apollo at Corinth with the Gulf of Corinth beyond.

his demands. Their moral shortcomings are symptoms of the fact that they, like the unenlightened Gentiles, are alienated from God, and hence "under the power of sin" (2:1–3:9). The condemnation under which the human race stands is sweeping, and man cannot possibly escape from it by striving to be better. Torah itself serves only to remind man of his failure, and thus to increase his sense of guilt.

Into this apparently hopeless situation, God himself has come in the person of Jesus Christ. (The relationship between God and Jesus will be considered below.) Through Christ, the enmity of man toward God is overcome, the alienated are reconciled, man's sense of guilt is removed, and he stands delivered from the powers of evil that have kept him enslaved. Once he has been liberated from his condition "under the power of *sin*," man can then turn his attention to the matter of *sins* and ethical demands. Until he is liberated, it is useless to talk to him about ridding himself of any particular sins, since these are only symptoms of his real problem.

Man's failure to gain divine approval is not the result of occasional or even perennial moral lapses: he is simply manifesting his oneness with the entire human race, which has lost the splendour of the image of God in which man was created (3:23). The reference here is to the account of creation in Genesis 1, where man and woman are said to have been created in God's image. That Paul accepts this as the true account of the origin of man and the character God intended him to possess, is evident from the description of man as the "image and glory of God" in I Corinthians 11:7. We shall see later that Paul believed that all mankind shared in the responsibility for Adam's sin of disobedience to God (Gen. 3) and that all men justly suffer under the judgment resulting from that sin. The conviction was a part of the traditional Hebrew belief in the solidarity and inner unity of the nation. In ancient times, all Israel suffered when David, their king, sinned by taking a census. Presumably, the number of God's people was supposed to be a divine secret into which no man could inquire; hence, the judgment fell on David—and on all Israel—for his wicked act.

Since all men stand under condemnation because of their share in Adam's sin, the hope of redemption must involve the creation of a new race. The old race is characterized by Adam's disobedience; the new race will be characterized by the complete obedience of Jesus to the will of God. Simply to tell men they ought to be better is useless; unaided by divine grace, men cannot be good. Conversely, merely to trim off a man's imperfections is not to solve his basic moral problem. A complete reorientation to God and an inner transformation are the prerequisites of goodness.

"A man is justified by faith"
(Rom. 3:28)

JUSTIFICATION BY GOOD WORKS

Paul had respect for the terminology and even the precepts of the moral philosophies of his Greek contemporaries. But he was convinced that to talk ethics to a man bound to a morally impotent race was not only a waste of time, but grossly misleading. Such an approach to righteousness suggested that if man only tried hard enough, he could arrive at the state in which God would be obligated to accept him. Paul, as we have seen, was convinced that the finest moral injunctions that he knew (those embodied in Torah) only frustrated man by reminding him of his shortcomings. The real hindrances to obedience—a sense of estrangement from God, and the lack of inner motivation to do what was right—were aspects of the problem that remained untouched by mere moral appeal. Laws do not make men good; they only remind men of what is wrong (Rom. 3:20).

JUSTIFICATION BY FAITH

Now, however, God has begun to work on an entirely new basis: justification by faith. This possibility for man has been declared with fresh clarity and with finality through Jesus Christ, but it was the basis for the relationship that had existed between God and men of faith as far back as the time of Abraham (Rom. 4), as we have already seen in Paul's Letter to the Galatians (p. 233). The good news of salvation that has come by Jesus Christ is not, therefore, a radical break with the past. It is not as though God had dealt in a legalistic way with Israel, and then had set up faith as a basis for dealing with the church. Throughout Torah it is clear that what God desired was the devotion of his people, not the performance of empty ceremonies or the scrupulous observance of regulations out of a sense of obligation. The burden of the prophets of Israel was to protest against formalism and to issue a summons to loving, obedient trust in God. The essence of Paul's gospel, as stated succinctly in Romans 3:21-26, is that God has acted decisively through Jesus Christ to free men from bondage to sin and the evil forces that held them captive (redemption), to remove the barrier of guilt that kept men from God's presence (expiation), and to restore men to a right relationship with God in spite of their sins (justification). Since this statement is so compact, and since the way of thinking that it represents is so strange, let us examine in some detail the meaning of these words.

The word "righteousness" in English usage usually means a moral quality of uprightness and justice; as such, it could be ascribed either to God or to man. "To justify," which is the cognate verb, would signify "to make right" or "to declare right." To justify God would be to demonstrate his righteousness; and to justify man would be either to declare him to be morally right or to make him right. In any case, righteousness would be regarded as a moral attribute.

In the thought of the Hebrews, however, the concept is quite different. The word that we usually translate as "righteousness" is not primarily a quality, but an activity. When a judge in ancient Israel "justified" a man who had been wronged, he did not instill a quality of uprightness, nor did he publish a decree that the man was innocent of wrong; rather, he rectified the situation, and thus restored the wronged man to his rightful place. In a psalm included in one of the ancient scrolls found in a cave overlooking the Dead Sea in 1947, but dating from the beginning of the Christian era, there is a passage in which both "justification" and "righteousness" are used in the sense of what God does for those who trust in him:

For as for me, my justification belongs to God;
And in His hand is the perfection of my way,
Together with the uprightness of my heart.
Through His righteousness my transgression shall be blotted out....[1]

The emphasis here clearly falls on God's work, by which the oppressed are vindicated; the uprightness of the heart is regarded as a by-product of God's justifying, or vindicating, act. Similarly, when Paul speaks of "the righteousness of God" (Rom. 3:25), he is not merely describing the character of God, nor is he suggesting that God infuses his own qualities into certain persons. He is declaring that God has taken the initiative in restoring man to his proper relation to God and man.

The earlier part of the letter has shown the degradation that man suffers when he is apart from God, and the hopelessness of man's attempts to deliver himself from alienation from God and from enslavement to sin. Now we see that being set right in relation to God is not a condition that man is called on to strive for, but that right relationship results from an action that God has performed in Jesus Christ, the benefits of which are offered as a gift, to be received by faith (Rom. 3:24). God's work of vindication is not dependent upon

[1] Quoted from the translation by W. H. Brownlee in *Bulletin of the American Schools of Oriental Research*, Supplementary Studies, Nos. 10-12, "The Dead Sea Manual of Discipline," pp. 42, 43. New Haven, 1951.

man's fulfilment of law, although Torah and the writings of the prophets bear witness that God's nature is such that he does vindicate the oppressed (Rom. 3:21).

THE GROUND OF JUSTIFICATION BY FAITH

God's justifying activity is focused in the death of Jesus on the cross. That death is looked upon by Paul, as it was by Jesus himself (Mk. 10:45), as a ransom. As we saw in our study of the early *kerygma* of the community, the ransom was thought of as a means of release for one in bondage, not as a price to buy off the captor. The conviction that the death of Jesus was the means for freeing men from subjection to the evil powers is elaborated in the Letter to the Colossians (2:13-15). There, in words that are reminiscent of Jesus' allusion to pillaging Satan's household, Paul declares that in the cross man's bondage to law was broken and the powers that oppress man in this age were decisively defeated. If these powers had realized that the seeming tragedy of the cross would be the means of God's triumph over them, they would not have instigated his crucifixion. (The early church was convinced that behind every temporal authority was an unseen spiritual power, and that it was these invisible powers that plotted against the purposes of God. See Chapter 11.) Later in the Letter to the Romans (6:20), Paul describes the former condition of the Roman Christians as "slaves of sin"; here in a single phrase he proclaims that God has acted to free men from such bondage.

The agent through whom God's justifying act was achieved is Jesus, whom God ordained for this role. When Paul speaks of Jesus as "an expiation by his blood" (Rom. 3:25), it sounds as though God were a vengeful deity whose wrath could be appeased only by the slaughter of a bloody victim. The term "propitiation," which is used in the King James Version to translate the Greek word that is here rendered "expiation," heightens the picture of a God of wrath. Actually, the term in question is used in the Septuagint to describe the removal of the guilt that stands as a barrier between man and God. If guilt is removed by man's action, the proper rendering is "expiation"; if it is simply a matter of God's gracious removal of the barrier, "forgiveness" is the appropriate translation.[2] As we saw earlier, in Hebrew usage blood means life. The point of Paul's phrase, then, is this: Through Jesus' offering up his life to God, obedient unto death, the barrier of guilt that separated man from God has been removed.

---

[2] For a full discussion of the key words in this passage, see C. H. Dodd, *The Epistle to the Romans*, pp. 48-61. London : Hodder, 1932.

The idea that the obedience of Jesus removes the guilt is explicitly stated in Romans 5:19 and is reaffirmed in Philippians 2:8. But the logic of the idea is not clear to a modern mind unaccustomed to thinking of religion in terms of sacrifice. From the gospel records it is clear that the major reason for the determination of Jesus' enemies to have him executed was their belief that he was undermining the moral standards and the institutional structures of their religion. He refused to abide by the regulations that required him to keep separate from defiled people; he persisted in befriending religious outcasts; he would not condemn sinful people; he enjoyed deflating those who, according to accepted standards, excelled in piety. His parables told of a God of grace and forgiveness. So it is not surprising that he was regarded as a religious subversive. It was in large measure because he was the friend of "tax collectors and sinners" (Lk. 7:34) that he was put to death. In spite of the growing opposition to his ministry, Jesus continued to challenge the religious institutions and to proclaim the grace of God, because he believed it was God's will for him to live and teach in this way. Paul was not drawing on his imagination when he said that Jesus was "obedient unto death," or when he connected Jesus' death with the forgiveness of sin; it was part of the tradition he had received.

The initiative of God in bringing men into the right relationship with himself has been fully and finally made known in Jesus Christ (Rom. 3:25, 26). Up until the time of Jesus' coming, God has been forgiving toward man, and forbearing towards man's sins, but man's sense of guilt and spiritual blindness kept him from understanding the true nature of God. Weighed down by guilt, man fled from God's presence and sought peace and safety in the worship of false gods. But now the coming of Jesus in complete dedication to God, even to the extremity of death, has demonstrated once and for all that God is One who vindicates the oppressed, removes the barriers that separate man from him, and brings man into relationship with himself. In response to what God has done, man is expected to trust God and to rely for his salvation on God's justifying act in Christ.

JEW AND GENTILE

There is no place in such a scheme for human pride, since a man is accepted before God not on the basis of what he does, but on the strength of what God has done for him in Christ (Rom. 3:27, 28). So there is no place for any distinction between Jew and Gentile, since both must come to God on the same basis: faith. Even circumcision, which the Judaizers had been insisting on as a requisite for admission to the Christian community, was not required of Abraham until after he had trusted God, and had been accepted by him. There is, therefore, neither reason nor precedent for demanding that the Gentiles be circumcised in order to enjoy salvation. The fulfillment of the promise to Abraham rested solely on faith (Rom. 4:13 ff.).

We might conclude from this line of argument that a man who has faith can live as he pleases. Paul puts the issue in an exaggerated form: If our sins cause God to display his gracious forgiveness, we should sin more so that more grace might be available (Rom. 6:1 ff.). But the answer to such a suggestion is an emphatic no. The believer who is convinced that God has revealed himself in Jesus Christ, and that God has taken the initiative in removing the barrier that separates man from God, comes under the control of an influence which is strong, yet unlike the burdensome necessity of keeping the Law. The new influence is the love of God, as the believer has experienced it in Christ (II Cor. 5:14, 15). Man is free either to respond to God's love or to ignore it. But when he does respond in faith, he feels himself overmastered by Christ's love, which was demonstrated by his willingness to die in order that all men might be reconciled to God. The force, then, which compels the believer to do the will of God is not a sense of obligation, but an overwhelming feeling of gratitude for what God has done for man in Christ.

"God was in Christ"

(II Cor. 5:19)

So far in what we have said about Paul's formulation of the gospel, we have referred only in passing to the relationship between Jesus and God. Actually, Paul never defines this relationship, although he gives considerable attention in his letters to what God has done through Jesus. It is important to remind ourselves that the Hebrew mind does not express itself in abstract concepts, but in terms of action and concrete events. Ancient Israel did not construct a set of ideas or theories about God; she gloried in what God had done for Israel and how he had made himself known in her historic experiences. Similarly, when Jesus was asked to define "neighbour," he did not launch into a lengthy discourse on neighbourliness, or on the ideal qualifications of being a neighbour; rather, he told the unforgettable story of the Good Samaritan, who demonstrated what a neighbour was by what he did (Lk. 10:29-37). It is this action type of thinking, rather than the conceptual or theoretical type, that must be foremost in our minds if we are to understand Paul's belief about the nature of Jesus' relation to God. Before attempting to trace out what it was that Paul believed God to have done in Christ, let us look briefly at the titles that Paul gives to Jesus in his redemptive role.

JESUS AS LORD

Paul never says that Jesus is God. He does, however, so closely identify Jesus and God that it is sometimes difficult to tell to which one he is referring—as in his many references to "the Lord," for example. This title for God, which is *kurios* in Greek, was the one used by the translators of the Septuagint when they found in the Hebrew text "YHWH," the unpronounceable name of God. It was Jewish practice to read this "YHWH" as though it were the Hebrew word, *adonai*, which means "Lord." The Greek translators translated the substitute word, *adonai*, rather than the original Hebrew, YHWH, the meaning of which was no longer known. Therefore to any reader of the Septuagint—and of course every Dispersion Jew was familiar with it—*kurios* was the most common name for God.

As it happened, the term *kurios* was also widely used by the pagans, particularly by the devotees of the mystery cults. In the worship of Osiris or Dionysus, for example, *kurios* was the common designation for the saviour-god. Paul acknowledged in writing to the Corinthians (I Cor. 8:5) that in the Roman world there were many competing "lords" or *kurioi*. The earliest Christian preachers had affirmed that God had made Jesus "Lord" (Acts 2:36); Paul echoes this conviction in his words to the Philippians (Phil. 2:9-11). The affirmation "Jesus is Lord" is the earliest form of Christian confession (cf. Rom. 10:9, 10).

Because this term *kurios* is first widely used in the New Testament by Paul, we must not infer that Paul invented the idea of calling Jesus *kurios* in order to put him into competition with other hellenistic saviours. Paul's quotation (in I Cor. 16:22) of the Aramaic phrase, *Maranatha*, which means, "Our Lord, come!", shows that Jesus was called "Lord" by the earliest Christian community in Palestine; Paul simply adopted the practice from them, translating it into Greek, the language that was meaningful to those among whom he was working. Later theological elaborations of the nature of Jesus were aided by the connotations of the word *kurios* among both Jews and Greeks of the day. But the term was a part of the earliest Christian tradition and was not introduced as part of a process of deifying the man Jesus. Paul goes so far as to apply to Jesus passages from the Old Testament that referred in their original context to the God of Israel. A prime instance of this occurs in the Letter to the Romans, where Paul quotes the promise of the prophet Joel that "everyone who calls upon the name of the Lord will be saved." Here the title "Lord" is clearly taken to mean Jesus (Rom. 10:9-13).

JESUS AS SON OF GOD

Another of Paul's favourite designations for Christ is "Son of God." In the usage of ancient Israel, this phrase was applied to the ideal king, who, because he had been designated by God to reign over God's people, was called the "Son of God" (Psalm 2:7). The term continued to be used throughout Israel's history, although later it was not applied to a historical personage, but rather to the king who would one day come and establish the reign of God over creation. The belief in Jesus as the one anointed to bring in God's reign was clearly in the back of Paul's mind when he applied the title to Jesus. But Paul added to this traditional meaning for "Son of God" the conviction that there was an intimate relationship between Jesus and God which gave Jesus a unique claim to the title (Col. 1:13), even though the term was commonly applied to the saviours of the hellenistic religions. Furthermore, the character of Jesus was such that his concerns for mankind and his selfless attitudes were identified by Paul as divine qualities. He described the death of Jesus on behalf of sinners as "God showing his love" (Rom. 5:8). The fluid way in which Paul shifted from speaking of Jesus to speaking of God is puzzling grammatically, but it is thoroughly compatible with Paul's conviction that Jesus' relation to God was unique.

Paul rarely referred to Jesus as simply "Jesus." He preferred such expressions as "Jesus Christ," or "Christ Jesus," or "the Lord Jesus Christ." The title "Christ," as we have seen, is simply the Greek form of the Hebrew word "Messiah," meaning "anointed." It was often used in referring to the king, as one anointed to rule for God, but it could be used of any man who had a special role to play in the purpose of God. It was used of Cyrus, the Persian ruler who gave orders for the nation Judah to return to Palestine from captivity in Babylon (Is. 45:1). It is applied to the Servant of God through whom the coming of the day of Israel's redemption is announced (Is. 61). When Paul called Jesus "Christ," he meant that Jesus was the one through whom God was working to defeat the forces of evil and to restore man to a right relationship with God.

JESUS AS REDEEMER

In later centuries, after the church had become the official religion of the Roman empire, theologians devoted a great deal of

discussion to questions about the relation of the human to the divine
elements in the person of Jesus. They tried to decide whether Jesus
had a divine will and a human will, or simply one composite will;
whether he had a divine and a human nature, or just one. They strug-
gled with the problem of what happened to the divine characteristics
(for example, omniscience, omnipresence) during the time that Jesus
was on earth and was subject to the human limitations of localization,
hunger, thirst, and incomplete knowledge (Mk. 13:32). Paul, however,
had no such interest in theorizing; for him the important fact was that
God had acted decisively in Christ for the redemption of his creation.
Paul had himself experienced this deliverance, and had taken his stand
within the community that had similarly come to a new understanding
of God's nature and purpose and that felt a new sense of kinship with
him. Paul's task in his letters, therefore, was to inform the members
of the community about what God has done through Christ, and what
the implications of this work of redemption were for the life and
faith of the community.

Paul's classic statement of what God did through Christ is found
in the Second Letter to the Corinthians (5:19): "God was in Christ,
reconciling the world to himself...." The meaning of these words is
developed more fully in the fifth chapter of Romans, where Paul
describes the whole human race as alienated from God, and actually
at enmity with him. Man, conscious of his disobedience and burdened
with a sense of guilt, had fled from God's presence as Adam had in
the Genesis story. In his estranged state, man's resentment against God
had mounted to the point where man became an enemy of his Creator.
It was in this spiritually helpless condition that man had languished
prior to the coming of Christ. In the obedient life of Jesus, man
could see in concrete form what complete dedication to the will of
God meant. Even though Jesus' life had ended in seeming defeat, God
had vindicated him by raising him from the dead and exalting him at his
right hand. There could be no doubt that God in Christ was victor
over both sin and death. But in the extremity to which God went to
achieve his redemptive purpose, the depth of God's love was made
known. There was no limit to the grace of God, since he was willing
to "put forward" (Rom. 3:25) his son to die in order that men might
understand his love and be reconciled to him.

When men responded in faith to God's redeeming act in Jesus Christ,
they realized that Jesus, by his "obedience unto death" (Phil. 2:8),
had removed the barrier of guilt that separated man from God, and
had defeated the powers of evil who had sought to destroy him. The
new relationship with God that results from his work of reconciliation

in Christ is contrasted in detail with the results of Adam's disobedience (Rom. 5:12-21). Adam, the man who typified the old creation, had violated the will of God, and had brought condemnation and death on all humanity as a result. Christ's justifying act will result in the transformation of men from sinners into righteous, obedient people of God.

As the rest of the Letter to the Romans shows, this transformation is not merely a matter of juggling the records, as though God arbitrarily listed as righteous those who believed what he said. Paul makes clear that what God did in Christ was to remove the barriers that stood between man and himself, but that until man responds in faith to God's offer of reconciliation the work of redemption will have no effect on him. When man comes to a realization of what God has done, and responds in grateful trust, God's Spirit will begin to work in his heart, transforming and shaping his desires and aspirations in order to conform them to God's will. (This aspect of Paul's teaching about redemption will be treated more fully below.)

JESUS AS PRE-EXISTENT

Paul did not feel that the importance of Jesus began with Jesus' birth, nor that it was confined to the promise of salvation to all mankind. Paul believed that Jesus had existed before his birth, and that he was God's agent in creating the world. Furthermore, the programme of redemption would not be complete until all creation was restored to the condition that God had intended for it when he brought it into being. The idea of pre-existence was a common one in the Judaism of Paul's day. In the book of Psalms (139:13-16), the belief is expressed that a man's form and the whole pattern of his life are in existence in the plan of God before man is born. The claim to pre-existence would not, therefore, in itself be unique. The uniqueness of Jesus lies in the creative role that he is described as having fulfilled before his incarnation—that is, before he assumed human form.

In the Wisdom Literature of Judaism, of which the book of Proverbs is the most important representative in the Hebrew canon, there is the conviction that God is too sublime and exalted to have been involved in the business of creating the universe, and that this work was done through an intermediary. Usually, the intermediary is Wisdom, personified; at other times, Torah is described in personal terms as the creative agent. Paul adopted this concept of the intermediary through whom the creation was accomplished, and modified it for his own purposes. Jesus Christ was the one in whom "all things were created, in heaven and on earth ... all things were created through him and for him" (Col. 1:16). When the new age has fully come, the whole of creation will share in the benefits of redemption. The powers of evil that have held the created world in subjection will be overcome, and creation will enter a new era of freedom comparable to the freedom that men of faith experience in the new life into which they enter through Jesus Christ (Rom. 8:18-23). Just as believers are called on to suffer in this life so that they may partake of glory in the age to come, so creation itself groans like a woman in childbirth until the day of its deliverance from the powers of evil.

In barest outline, these are the chief meanings behind Paul's phrase, "God was in Christ." Although Paul refrained from saying that Jesus was God, he comes within a hair's breadth of doing so. He speaks of Jesus as "in the form of God" and as refusing to grasp at equality with God (Phil. 2:6). He ascribes to him the qualities and functions of God, as we have seen. He turns with ease from speaking of the grace of God to mention "the grace of our Lord Jesus Christ." Later New Testament writers define the relationship between Jesus and God in terms of virgin birth (Matthew and Luke), or develop the idea that Jesus was the pre-existent Logos of God (John 1). Paul introduces his convictions about the nature of Jesus Christ only incidentally, when they help to drive home a practical point that has arisen in connection with the life of one of his churches. For example, the magnificent passage on Jesus' taking human form appears in Philippians 2 as an encouragement to the Christians to be humble. The description in Colossians 1:15-20 is built up to pave the way for Paul's attack on a serious error that has developed in the Colossian church. Paul's chief concern in all that he wrote about the significance of Christ was to inform his readers of what God had done for them, and to relate to them his own liberating, transforming experience of the Christ who had appeared to him risen from the dead.

"If any man be in Christ"
(II Cor. 5:17)

The man who by faith in Jesus Christ had experienced reconciliation to God, Paul believed, was part of a whole new order of being. He was not just a reformed sinner; he was part of the "new creation" to which everyone belonged who trusted Christ to bring him into right relationship with God. The new sphere of existence that was constituted by Christ's renewal of the creation Paul identified by the simple phrase "in Christ" (Rom. 6).

All believers who have been baptized have, by participation in that rite, attested to their identification with Christ in his death, burial, and resurrection, which the rite symbolizes. Since they share with him by faith in his obedience unto death, they also now share with him in the new life that is brought into being by the resurrection. Here is a form of human existence that is not subject to death, and that is triumphant over sin and the powers of evil which held the old life in subjection. Paul states the concept of the new creation succinctly in writing to the Corinthians (I Cor. 15:22): "As in Adam all die, so also in Christ shall all be made alive." Again, we see the Hebrew conviction of the solidarity of God's people expressing itself in the inclusion of all humanity under two heads: Adam and Christ.

The fact that a man is "in Christ" does not free him from responsibility for his actions. His life should correspond to his spiritual status in the new creation. Even though from the divine perspective the final outcome of the whole scheme of redemption is foreseen, it is man's responsibility to guide his actions and order his life in a manner befitting a Christian. So long as man is in his physical body, temptations to sin will always be present and the possibility of his yielding to the pull of the old life will continue to be very real. Nothing in his new status before God makes it impossible for him to allow sin to control his body. But Paul appeals to those who have discovered the potential for new life in Christ to avail themselves of their spiritual resources, and to allow God to use them for his purposes. We shall see later on that the service of God was a corporate rather than an individual matter, but each member was to see to it that the controlling influence of his life was obedience to God and not a yielding to sinful impulses. To sharpen the issue, Paul speaks as though there were no halfway house between the life of obedience and the life of sin. Either a man devoted himself to the service of God or he became the servant of sin, in spite of his having been set free from the power of sin. If he chose voluntarily to return to his former enslaved condition, God would permit him to exercise his own will in the matter.

But we must not infer from this passage in the Letter to the Romans that Paul thought a man must be either sinlessly perfect or hopelessly sinful. He makes this clear in writing to the Philippians (Phil. 3), when he tells them that he is himself bending every effort to increase in righteousness and to become more like Christ in his unconditional obedience to God's will. But he also warns them that he has not achieved perfection. Although failures have plagued him, he tries to leave them behind, pressing on to the prize that awaits the obedient. Yet the compelling force behind Paul's earnest striving was not "the prize," but an eagerness to express gratitude and devotion for the redemption that he and the whole community had experienced "in Christ."

"We were all baptized into one body"
(I Cor. 12:13)

Paul's favourite metaphor to describe the community is "the body." This is a highly useful figure, since it is obviously familiar to everyone, and since it is capable of being developed in several ways to illustrate various aspects of the corporate life of the community.

THE UNITY OF THE BODY

The first of these aspects—the unity of the body—we have already considered in Paul's dealing with the problem of the schisms that marred the unity of the church at Corinth. But for Paul, the unity of the church was not merely a feeling of togetherness but a belief in a mystical oneness "in Christ," with whom the church was identified in death and resurrection. Developing the figure of "the body" in connection with another illustration, Paul demonstrates that the Christian, because he is a member of the Body of Christ, is free from obligation to the Law, just as a widow has no legal obligation to her husband after he has died (Rom. 7:1-6). And just as she is free to remarry, so the believer is now free to be joined in mystical union with Christ. The marital relationship as an illustration of religious experience is common in the Old Testament (cf. Hosea, Isaiah), but it was also widely used among devotees of the popular religions and mystery cults. Gentiles, then, would find this analogy familiar, even though they were not familiar with Torah.

DIVERSITY WITHIN THE BODY

In Romans 12, Paul speaks of the need for the church to recognize the diversity that must exist within the unity of the body. The one Spirit that came upon all believers in baptism is now at work in their midst to perform through them the various functions that are needed to carry on the work of God. The "gifts"—that is, the duties bestowed or the qualities granted by the Spirit to believers—include both participation in the active ministry of the church (prophecy, exhortation, teaching) and simple good works (contributions, acts of mercy). The body cannot function when every member wants to do the same job, or when any member thinks the others are negligent or unspiritual because their share in the work of the church does not correspond to his. The Spirit is the one who operates within the members to show them their appointed tasks; the diversity of ways in which the Spirit manifests itself must never obscure the fact that there is just one Spirit behind all these differing functions.

The life of the community, like the life of the human body, is dependent on certain central organs. No member of a human body can live independently, although the body can continue to function even after some members have been removed. For Paul the central organ in a human body was the head, which he regarded as the seat of life. Analogously, the life of "members" in the Body of Christ was dependent upon the Head—that is, Christ. The Head (Col. 2:18, 19) is not only the source of life for the entire body; it also determines the form of the body's growth and integrates the life of the whole body. The theme of the oneness of the body and its dependence on the head is developed much more elaborately in the Letter to the Ephesians, which, though it parallels Paul's thought, was probably not written by him (see p. 67).

The community, therefore, cannot consider itself as autonomous. It depends for its existence and for its continuance on Jesus Christ, who called the community into being, who died to seal the covenant on which the community is founded, and who has sent the Spirit to guide and empower its corporate life.

"Walk according to the Spirit"
(Rom. 8:4)

THE SPIRIT AS POWER

In the thinking of the Gentiles to whom Paul sought to interpret the Christian message, the existence of spirits and their power over human life were among the accepted facts of life. The phenomenon of demonic possession was a commonplace: the spirit that took control of a man might be beneficent, as in the case of the inspired prophetess of Apollo at the Delphic oracle, or it might have a ruinous effect on a man's life and personality. The Greek word *pneuma*, like the Hebrew word *ruach*, meant "breath" or "wind" as well as "spirit"; so the evanescent, intangible quality of spirit was emphasized in the word itself. When Paul spoke of "the Spirit," however, he did not mean a generalized, immaterial force. In the thinking of the Stoic philosophers of Paul's day, even *pneuma* was a material substance, though a highly refined one. For Paul, "the Spirit" was the pervasive power of God through which his purposes were fulfilled. It is not surprising, therefore, that in Paul's letters the person of Jesus and the Holy Spirit are very closely related. Occasionally, Paul will shift from one to the other without warning, as for example in Romans 8:10, 11, where he speaks of "Christ . . . in you" and, in the next breath, of "the Spirit . . . in you." It is as though the character and personality of God's continuing work of redemption were demonstrated in the person of Jesus, but as though the unseen yet efficacious power behind the work were defined as the Holy Spirit. In keeping with this relation between Christ and the Spirit, Paul describes the life "in Christ" as a life lived "according to the Spirit."

THE FLESH AGAINST THE SPIRIT

As we saw in our biographical study of Paul above (p. 208), he felt morally impotent so long as he tried to please God by keeping the Law. The injunctions of Torah had proved to be a stimulus to disobedience rather than a means of moral achievement (Rom. 7:5-25). Now that he found himself liberated from the Law, and free to serve God through the new power that the Spirit had brought into his life, he characterizes the life of defeat that he had previously experienced as life "in the flesh." By "flesh" Paul does not mean simply "the material body." Rather, "flesh" is the quality of being human, with such inevitable limitations as transitoriness, apprehension, and weakness. The flesh relies on insecure foundations in its misguided effort to stabilize life. It judges by appearances and fails to understand the nature of reality. It mistakes the worldly standards of wealth, force, and social approval for the real values in life. It was through these susceptibilities in man that the tempter in Eden was able to lead man to disobey God, by arousing his pride and by promising power that was supposed to come through increased knowledge. It is these ethical and religious considerations that Paul has in mind when he contrasts the life "in the flesh" with the life in the Spirit. He is not identifying "flesh" with matter and then simply echoing the dualistic belief that matter is inherently evil and that only spirit is good.

All humanity, or, to translate literally, all "flesh" (Rom. 3:20), stood under condemnation and moral helplessness because of the inability of man to do the will of God even with the aid of Torah, the classic statement of God's purpose for his people. Undeterred by the ineffectiveness of Torah to bring man into right relationship with God, God sent his son, who was identified with humanity in every way, except that he was wholly obedient. Thus the hold which sin maintained upon humanity, through the weakness of the flesh, was broken;

or, as Paul phrases it "[Christ] condemned sin *in the flesh*" (Rom. 8:3). Now, those who are in Christ measure up to the requirements of the Law; but they do so, not by moral striving, but through the power of the Spirit at work within their lives. Men of faith, therefore, "walk, not according to the flesh, but according to the Spirit" (Rom. 8:1-11).

In the life according to the Spirit, Paul testifies that he found peace and a sense of kinship with God that striving to obey the Law had never brought. That feeling of intimacy with God is epitomized in the term of address that Paul uses in prayer: "Abba" (Rom. 8:15), a word that is commonly used by Aramaic-speaking people when talking to their fathers. For Paul, therefore, the working of the Spirit was not some vague, impersonal force, but an intimate experience of closeness to God that his former life in Judaism had never made possible.

Life "in the Spirit" was not, however, free from difficulty or conflict. Paul was able to endure the difficulties that overtook him because he was convinced that they were the prelude to a new age of righteousness that was to come. Here, too, the role of the Spirit was an important one: the presence of the Spirit was an anticipation of the new situation that would obtain throughout creation when the will of God triumphed over all opposition (Rom. 8:23). As he phrased it in writing to the Corinthians (II Cor. 1:22), the Spirit that dwelt within him was a guarantee or a kind of "down payment" on the time of consummation that lay in the future. Until that time came, however, the Spirit was at hand to give guidance to the man of faith in praying to God (Rom. 8:26-27). In the midst of trials, men of faith could look forward to the day when God's purpose for creation would be fulfilled, confident that God was even now at work shaping events to his ends (Rom. 8:28 ff.). But until the time of total victory came, the man of faith might live his life free from guilt and fear, conscious that nothing could separate him from God's love (Rom. 8:31-39).

THE COMMANDS OF THE SPIRIT

Paul recognized, as Jesus had earlier, that it was not enough to tell a man that he should obey God; some specific indications of attitude and actions were needed. As real as Paul felt the power of the Spirit to be, he was careful in his letters to include a set of detailed, practical instructions by which the communities could regulate their corporate and personal lives. "What is good and acceptable and perfect" (Rom. 12:2) had to be spelled out in unmistakable terms. In the concrete ethical injunctions that are given in Romans 12, 13, and 15, there are a few instances in which Paul's language parallels that of the Greek ethical systems of his day, but the whole orientation of Paul's ethics is much more Hebraic than Greek. His appeal rests on love and gratitude to God, rather than on the essential logic of his ethic. He does not discuss the abstract principle of "the good," nor does he even ask what the duty of man is. Rather, the life of service and dedication to which man is called is simply a response to "the mercies of God" that believers have experienced in Jesus Christ.

The nearest that Paul comes to a formal set of ethical precepts is the list of instructions in the Letter to the Colossians. There (Col. 3:5–4:6), Paul gives advice to the various members of the Christian families to guide them in their mutual relations. A similar, though longer, list is found in the Letter to the Ephesians (4:25–6:20). Yet even in these didactic passages, Paul is not merely telling men that they should be better. The whole appeal is set in the context of the forgiveness of God in Christ, the operation of the Spirit in the lives of the faithful, the love of Christ for the church, the need of the church for maintaining the respect of those who are not members. For Paul, the ideal was not conformity to a standard of virtue, but the dedication of oneself to God—that is, sanctification. It was the holy character of God with whom man had, through Christ, been brought into relationship that required purity of life on the part of man; it was not merely that goodness was reasonable, or "according to nature," as the Stoics phrased it. Man's nature led him away from the will of God, but the Spirit of God at work within him both aroused the urge to do right and gave man the moral strength to achieve the right. To experience this inner transformation was to "walk according to the Spirit."

"We shall all be changed"
(I Cor. 15:51)

Christianity has sometimes been described as the religion of individualism, and Protestant Christianity has, in fact, stressed individual freedom throughout its history. But from the beginning, the Christian faith affirmed that God's purpose was to create a *community* of the obedient, not merely to snatch isolated individuals from destruction. Paul was concerned with the establishment of the new people of God, a group that he believed to be already in the process of formation but that would come to its fullness at some time in the future.

HAS GOD TURNED FROM THE JEWS?

This conviction raised for Paul an acute problem, which he dealt with at length in the Letter to the Romans (Rom. 9-11)—namely, the relation of the former people, Israel, to the new people, the church. In this extended passage he acknowledges the place of peculiar favour that Israel enjoyed because the earlier covenant was established with her, the prophets spoke through her, and the promises of future blessings for creation were given to her. But just as God acted in sovereign choice among various descendants of Abraham, choosing some for honour and passing others by, so God has now chosen to pass Israel by temporarily in order to have his message of redemption proclaimed to the Gentiles. Since God is the sovereign creator of his universe, man is in no position to dispute the wisdom or justice of his actions (Rom. 9:14-24). Israel will share ultimately in the blessings that are now being enjoyed by faith among those who, whether Jew or Gentile, respond in faith to the gospel. The tragic mistake of Israel has been her effort to gain standing before God by her own efforts in obedience to Torah (Rom. 9:24–10:4). At this point (Rom. 10:5 ff.), Paul uses a method of interpreting the Old Testament that seems strange to modern readers, but that was an accepted practice among the rabbis of his day. He takes a few phrases from the book of Deuteronomy (30:12-14) which declare in a vivid way how the word of God has been made readily accessible to man in Torah; he then interprets these phrases as referring to the word of the gospel, which has now been proclaimed to all men, whether Jew or Gentile. The one response demanded of man is that he confess "Jesus is Lord." His lips and his heart are to give outward expression to his inner trust.

If men are to be brought into the fellowship of the people of God by response to the *kerygma*, someone will have to serve as a proclaimer of the good news. Faith can arise only when men have heard (Rom. 10:14 ff.). Israel has heard and has not responded in faith, however, because God's purpose is that the Gentiles should be saved as a result of Israel's failure. Israel's rejection of ·the Messiah made redemption possible; her rejection of the message about the Messiah had led the Christian preachers to turn to the Gentiles with it (Rom. 10:18–11:12). But Paul is convinced that Israel will not persist in her unbelief indefinitely; she will return to God. And when she does, the blessings that will follow for all the world will be immeasurably greater than before she turned away in disobedience.

Paul develops an extended allegory of the grafting of branches onto an olive tree. The allegory is difficult from the standpoint of logic as well as of horticulture (Rom. 11:13-24). But the point is clear: that God still will have a purpose for Israel when his work of summoning the Gentiles to obedient trust has been completed. A divinely determined number of Gentiles must come into the fellowship of God's people, and the new age will not come in its fullness until that number has been reached (Rom. 11:25 ff.). The argument in verses 28 to 32 is not clear, and it involves Paul in a series of contrasts that are perhaps overdrawn. But the passage ends in a majestic hymn of praise to God, whose wisdom transcends man's capacity to comprehend. Man may rest assured that God's purpose is effectively at work throughout his creation. From his poetic outburst of praise to God, Paul turns to practical considerations (Rom. 11:33-36).

In contrast to the inconclusiveness of the discussion about the place of the Jews in God's plan, Paul was certain of two things: that he had reason to be proud of his heritage of Jewish faith and piety, and that God had called him to turn from the Jew to the Gentile as the major target of his evangelizing. The passage from Romans 9, 10, and 11 summarized in the preceding pages gives evidence of the importance Paul attached to the whole question of the relation between the community of the Old Covenant in which Paul had been reared, and the community of the New Covenant in which he was now at work in the service of God. He was convinced that "in Christ" there was no place for racial distinction (I Cor. 12:13), and yet he believed that the promises made by God to Israel were not simply abrogated by Israel's unbelief. The Jewish hope of the coming kingdom of God was a strong element in Paul's thinking (I Cor. 15:24 ff.), and, as a result, he made no attempt to legislate for a Christian society or to give instructions for the establishment of a new social order. At "the end," God would restore Israel to favour and to faith, and would defeat his enemies, thereby establishing his rule over creation. Paul longed for the day of peace and deliverance, and laboured for its coming. It was not his task to bring in the kingdom; he was charged with the mission of preaching the Good News, and thus preparing men for the kingdom that God was about to establish.

WHAT WILL ETERNAL LIFE BE LIKE?

Although Paul's major concern was for the future of the community, he did have words of comfort and admonition about the future for individuals as well. It is impossible to reconstruct a neat system out of Paul's thoughts on the theme of the future life. At times, he writes as though he expected to be transported immediately to the presence of Christ when he died (Phil. 1:23). At other times, he speaks of those who have died as being asleep, awaiting the trumpet call at the day of resurrection (I Cor. 15:51; I Thess. 4:13). In one famous passage, he describes a "body" in which the believer is "clothed" at death, when he is transported into the presence of the Lord (II Cor. 5:1-4).

The Appian Way just south of Rome, with the arches of the Claudian aqueduct in the background. Paul travelled this road on his way to Rome.

In I Corinthians 15, however, Paul speaks of the "spiritual body" as though it were bestowed at the time of the resurrection, rather than immediately upon death. Efforts have been made to reconcile these two aspects of Paul's thought by assuming that in II Corinthians 5 Paul was describing an intermediate state. A similar diversity of detail can be seen in a comparison of I Thessalonians 4 and II Thessalonians 2. In the first passage, the return of Christ is expected with little delay, since Paul expected to live to see that event; in the second passage, Paul explains what must happen in the interim before Christ's return. (This question will be dealt with in detail in Chapter 15.) But notice that Paul was not interested in developing a systematic theology; he was living in a time of crisis, during which his job was to preach, to exhort, to instruct, to prepare men for the coming of the new age.

Paul's consistent conviction, which overarches the divergent details, was that Jesus would again appear but this time in triumph, that the resurrection would take place, and that the day of consummation would thus arrive. Man's hope, then, was that God would change his people, so that their present bodies of humiliation (Phil. 3:21) would become glorious bodies. Corresponding to the hoped-for transformation of individuals would be the transmutation of the weak and imperfect "Body of Christ" into the fullness of the community of the New Covenant. Since the coming of this time of "salvation" was near at hand (Rom. 13:11-14), there was no place in the lives of Christians for frivolity or dissipation. Believers belong to the Lord, and are to conduct themselves worthily until the time of fulfillment comes (Rom. 14; 15).

In the concluding chapters of Paul's Letter to the Romans, he told the Roman Christians that he intended to visit them after he had gone from Corinth to Jerusalem to take the contribution from the churches of Greece and Asia Minor to the "saints" in the Holy City (Rom. 15:25 ff.). Rome was to be just a stopping-off place for him on his way to Spain, where he intended to go in order to preach the gospel in territory untouched by Christian evangelists. The fact that Paul here greets by name so many of the members of a community that he never visited has raised a question about whether this chapter is an authentic part of the Letter to the Romans. But Paul's indication that some of the contacts had been made in the Corinth area (16:3), in addition to the ease and frequency of travel between Corinth and Rome, suggests that there may already have been considerable visiting back and forth by Christians between the two cities, although Paul himself had not made the journey to Rome. If this explanation is correct, it would account for his feeling close enough to them to solicit their prayers that he might not be deterred from his projected travels by any opposition in Judea. The seriousness of the opposition that Paul did encounter in Jerusalem, the subsequent history of the Jerusalem community, and the circumstances of Paul's coming to Rome, are matters that we shall discuss in the next chapter.

꧁꧂

CHAPTER TEN

THE DEATH OF PAUL
AND THE END OF THE
CHURCH AT JERUSALEM

Whon the Jewish opposition to Paul began to mount at Corinth, he decided to leave for Jerusalem. He did not go directly, however, for he had to collect contributions from the various churches in Macedonia and Asia Minor as he went eastward toward Palestine. His companions on the journey were representatives from the contributing churches who helped assure the safe transit of the large sum of money that was being carried to Jerusalem (Acts 20:1-5). At Philippi, Paul was joined by the anonymous associate (probably Luke) whose presence in the narrative is marked by the sudden shift from "they" to "we" (Acts 20:5).

New Testament readings relevant to this chapter are: Acts 20-28; Colossians; Philippians; Philemon; and James.

The Crisis in Jerusalem

COLLECTING THE CONTRIBUTION

Although nothing is known of the establishment of the church in Troas (Troy), there was a group on hand there to hear Paul when he arrived. Interest in his sermon was so great that the people remained all night in the upper chamber of the house where the Christian community met. The size of the crowd and the number of lamps raised the temperature and lowered the oxygen content to the point where some of the listeners became drowsy. One young member, Eutychus, who had sat in the window in the vain hope that the fresh air would keep him awake, dozed, lost his balance, and plummeted to the ground three floors below. Paul revived him and continued preaching, undaunted, until daybreak. It appears that the formal ceremony of the breaking of bread was followed by a common meal (Acts 20:11). By prearrangement with the ship's officers, the ship on which Paul was to sail left without him; later, he went by foot to Assos and boarded the ship there. It has been conjectured that Paul made this arrangement in order to avoid the rough passage through choppy waters around the point of land between Troas and Assos.[1] Making several stops along the coast, the party proceeded southward to Miletus, where Paul was met by a group of leaders from the church at Ephesus.

In a touching address (Acts 20:18-35), Paul looked back with mingled humility and confidence over the course of his career and, in particular, at his three years' work in Ephesus. Since he had earned his own way during his stay in that city, no one could accuse him of having profited in any material way from his preaching the gospel of the kingdom among the Ephesians. But Paul had two premonitions: He felt that he would probably never return to Ephesus, and he feared that discord and false teaching would arise after his departure. After joining with the Ephesians in prayer, he bade them farewell (Acts 20:36-38) and returned to the ship.

As Paul and his companions travelled toward Jerusalem, they stopped off for brief visits with various Christian communities, notably in Tyre, Ptolemais, and Caesarea. In Caesarea lived Philip, the evangelist whom we have already met in connection with the launching of the Christian message in the territory outside Jerusalem. The fact that Philip's daughters are described as "virgins" (Acts 21:9) suggests that

---

[1] Lake and Cadbury in Foakes-Jackson and Lake, *The Beginning of Christianity*, Part I, Vol. IV, pp. 257-258. London: Macmillan, 1933.

certain wings of the church were already commending celibacy, although we have seen that Paul himself thought that abstinence from marriage was a practical rather than a moral question. Philip's daughters later moved to Ephesus and were counted among the luminaries of the church in Asia Minor, as we discover from the account of Philip's work given by Eusebius of Caesarea (who died in A.D. 339) in his *Ecclesiastical History* (Bk. III, xxxi).

At Tyre, and again at Caesarea, men who claimed to be inspired by the Spirit tried to dissuade Paul from going up to Jerusalem. They seem to have had a sense of foreboding about the treatment Paul would receive there. Their anxiety may have been based on information about the plotting against him that was going on in Jerusalem, or it may have been a premonition of some sort. In reading Acts, we cannot be sure whether Paul doubted their claim to be speaking "in the Spirit" when they tried to discourage him from going to Jerusalem, or whether he was convinced that the Spirit was simply trying to test his faith by these words of discouragement. In either case, he would not be deterred. In spite of the tearful protests of his loyal friends (Acts 21:10-14), he went up to the Holy City, accompanied by disciples from Caesarea and Cyprus.

THE JEWISH LEGALISTS

According to the account in Acts (21:17 ff.), Paul was in a conciliatory mood from the moment of his arrival in Jerusalem. The old question about the necessity for Christians to keep the Law of Moses was still the major issue in the minds of the leaders of the Jerusalem church in spite of the agreements they had made in the past. Paul's reputation for laxity on this matter of keeping the Law was so notorious that James and the other leaders were embarrassed by their association with him. They suggested that he might ease the Jewish opposition against him if he would make some public demonstration of his willingness to conform to Jewish ritual requirements. As it happened, Paul had already taken a step in the direction of conformity to ritual requirements by cutting his hair in preparation for his pilgrimage to the Temple (Acts 18:18). The practice of cutting the hair or shaving the head as a part of an act of consecration had its roots in the rites of ancient Israel (Num. 6), and a man consecrated in this way was called a Nazirite. The most famous Nazirite was Samson, although in his case the vow of dedication made by his parents demanded that his hair should never be cut. Why Paul performed the rite at this time is impossible to determine. Now, when the leaders of the church suggested that Paul should pay the expenses for a group of four other Christians who had shaved their heads as a part of their vow of consecration, Paul agreed. It was considered an act of piety for a man of means to pay the expenses of a poor man who wished to take a vow but could not afford to do so.

The logic of Paul's position on the question of Torah should have led him to refuse to cooperate in this scheme, since his action gave the impression that he was a strict observer of the Law when in fact he was not. Critics have raised the question of whether this incident may not have been invented by the author of Acts to document his thesis that peace prevailed in the relations between Paul and the Jerusalem church. Even if we were to assume that the account as we have it is substantially accurate, we should still be unable to decide whether Paul's motivation was a desire for peace-making, or a surge of sentiment for the traditional practices of Judaism, or a strategic compromise with his own convictions. But whatever his objectives may have been, they were not fulfilled. Instead of gaining the favour of the Jews by this attempt at conciliation, Paul brought the wrath of the mob down upon his head.

MOB VIOLENCE IN JERUSALEM

One day toward the close of the seven-day period of ritual obligation, Paul was in the Temple preparing to complete the offerings for himself and the others who were consecrating themselves. Some of his enemies—perhaps including men who had been active in the opposition to him in Asia Minor (Acts 21:27)—spread the word that he had brought a Gentile, Trophimus, into the inner courts (see Temple plan, p. 161).

The Temple area was divided into a series of courts and terraces, mounting upward to the innermost sanctuary, and Gentiles were permitted to enter only the outermost of these courts. Separating the Court of the Gentiles from the more sacred sections was a carved stone screen on which were placed at intervals stone tablets bearing the following warning: "No stranger [is permitted] to enter within the screen and enclosure around the sanctuary. Whoever is seized will be answerable to himself for his death which will follow therefrom." Two of the blocks of stone bearing this inscription have been discovered in Jerusalem. The punishment that followed a violation of the sacredness of the Jewish Temple was carried out by the crowd of the faithful gathered in the precincts; no formal trial was held.

Word of the alleged desecration spread instantly through the throngs gathered for worship. Paul's notoriously liberal attitude toward Gentiles made the charge seem plausible, and the crowds rushed to the scene of the riot, eager to witness, if not to share in, the death of this enemy of the traditional religion.

The mob had already begun to beat Paul when word of the melee reached Claudius Lysias, the tribune in command of the Roman garrison stationed in the massive Tower of Antonia, which overlooked the Temple area from the north. The tribune rushed down the stairway leading from the tower into the outer court of the Temple and tried to quell the riot. His first impression was that Paul was an Egyptian trouble-maker who was wanted by the Roman authorities for an earlier insurrection. But, since the noise of the mob was so great that the tribune could not hear Paul's defence against the charges, he decided to take the prisoner up into the fortress, away from the excitement and shouting (Acts 21:27-36).

As they were mounting the stairs, Paul spoke in Greek to the tribune, who concluded immediately that he had been wrong about Paul's identity. Thereupon, Paul identified himself as a citizen of the Roman colony of Tarsus, and asked permission to speak to the people. Standing high on the stairs, he spoke to the crowd in Aramaic—a choice that helped him command the crowd's attention. Hebrew was no longer spoken by the Jews, although both Jews and Christians continued to refer to Aramaic, the Semitic dialect that had replaced Hebrew by the beginning of the Christian era, as "Hebrew" (Acts 21:40).

In diplomatic fashion, Paul began his address by telling the crowd of his Jewish background and training, and of his former violent opposition to Christianity (Acts 22:1-6). The story of his conversion seems to have entranced the people, but when he began to identify himself with Stephen and the mission to the Gentiles that developed as a result of Stephen's death, the fickle mob again demanded his death (Acts 22:6-22). So violent was the hatred of the crowd toward Paul that the tribune concluded there must be some more serious charge against him, and that Paul might be forced to confess if he were scourged. Before the ordeal began, Paul reminded the centurion, a minor officer who was supervising the scourging, that extorting a confession by such means from a Roman citizen was illegal. When Paul's remark was relayed to the tribune, he stopped the proceedings immediately, fearful of the punishment that he might suffer for such a careless violation of Roman law (Acts 22:22-29).

Because of all the confusion, the real nature of the Jewish accusation against Paul had never come through clearly. Now, determined to get all the evidence he could, the tribune permitted the Jewish council to examine Paul. But there was no opportunity for a fair hearing, for the leaders had already decided before they heard his case that Paul must be destroyed. Paul's strategy, therefore, is understandable even if it is not commendable. Sensing that he would receive no justice at the hands of the council, he seized the opportunity to set the two major factions within the group against each other. By taking his stand with the Pharisees on the questions of the resurrection and the messianic hope, he stirred up an internal conflict that diverted attention from the real reason for the trial: his alleged violation of the sanctity of the Temple precincts. Finally, through the intervention of the tribune and his troops, Paul escaped (Acts 23:1-10).

THE PLOT ON PAUL'S LIFE

But the Jewish religious leaders' determination to kill Paul continued to mount. At last, upwards of forty men plotted to ambush him. Paul learned of the plot and had it reported to the tribune, who decided to take Paul secretly to Caesarea, where it would be easier to protect him from his enemies. Since Caesarea was the capital of the province, the governors spent most of their time there on the coast, travelling inland to Jerusalem at festival times when peace was threatened by the throngs of excitable pilgrims. With an escort of guards and cavalrymen, and with an explanatory letter for Felix, the governor, Paul was sent off by the tribune to Caesarea (Acts 23:16-32).

Once Felix had ascertained that Paul was from Cilicia, and that the case was therefore within his jurisdiction, nothing more could be done until the accusers had arrived from Jerusalem. Meanwhile, Paul was imprisoned in "Herod's Praetorium" (Acts 23:35), which was evidently the palace built by Herod that the Romans had taken over as the seat of imperial authority in the province. There has been a good deal of speculation over what Paul did with his time during his two years (Acts 24:27) of imprisonment. The mention of the "praetorium" here, combined with Paul's statement about the "praetorium" in Philippians 1:13, might suggest that it was while Paul was in prison that he wrote his letter to the Philippians. If this were so, we might infer that the other prison letters—Colossians, Philemon, and possibly Ephesians —were also written at this time. "Praetorium" was a general term, however, that was applied to the imperial headquarters anywhere in the empire. If any of Paul's correspondence from this period has survived, it is probably limited to the few personal notes addressed to young Timothy and incorporated by a disciple of Paul into the post-Pauline writing we know as the Second Letter to Timothy (4:16 ff.), in which Paul tells that all his associates deserted him at the time of his trial.[2]

When the priests and elders arrived from Jerusalem, they made their charges through an official spokesman or advocate, who gave evidence of his training in rhetoric by the flowery and flattering words he used to address the governor (Acts 24:1-8). The accusation was that Paul was a trouble-maker, and a leader of the Nazarene sect. The very fact that Jesus had come from the obscure Galilean village of Nazareth was enough to discredit his followers, since Galileans were considered to be lacking in culture and in religious and racial purity. Paul did not deny his connection with the Nazarenes, but he pointed out that he had come to Jerusalem solely as a bringer of alms and as a pious worshipper in the Temple. Charges that he had disturbed the peace were simply not true. The real issue—Paul's success in preaching a law-free gospel in Asia Minor—was not raised by the Asiatic Jews (Acts 24:18, 19) who had roused the mob against Paul in Jerusalem. Such an accusation, resting on a point of mere theological disagreement, would not be weighty enough for Rome to take punitive action. So Felix postponed taking any action at all until he could talk again with Lysias, the tribune in Jerusalem. Meanwhile, Paul was permitted to visit with and receive assistance from his companions.

THE INCONCLUSIVE TRIALS

Felix already had become interested enough in the new Christian sect to learn for himself what they taught and what their practices were (Acts 24:22). But he arranged for his young wife, Drusilla, to hear Paul, perhaps supposing that her own Jewish background would give her a basis for estimating the worth of Paul's claims more accurately than his own Gentile training. His liberal attitude toward Paul during his imprisonment (24:23) and the haste with which he dismissed Paul after Paul had preached to him about the judgment (24:25) suggest that he was attracted by the gospel, even though he could not bring himself to accept its claims. It may be that the reports of the large sum Paul had brought from Greece and Asia to Jerusalem had reached Felix's ears, leading him to believe that Paul was personally wealthy and that he might bribe Felix to release him. The acceptance of bribes from prisoners, though forbidden by Roman law, was not uncommon.

---

[2] Another theory, which claims that Ephesus is the place of origin of Colossians, Philippians, and Philemon, is considered below (p. 305). For a full statement on the theory that the verses from II Timothy originated during the Caesarean imprisonment, see P. N. Harrison, *The Problem of the Pastoral Epistles*, pp. 121, 122. Oxford: University Press, 1921.

In any event, at the end of two years, Felix was still unconverted; Paul was still in jail; and no bribe had been paid (Acts 24:24-26).

Felix's successor, Porcius Festus, sought to ingratiate himself with the leaders of the Jewish people in Jerusalem by keeping Paul imprisoned. The leading Jews requested that Paul be brought back from Caesarea to Jerusalem for another hearing, intending to ambush and kill him en route (Acts 25:1-3). But Festus refused to comply with the request, announcing instead that the hearing would take place in Caesarea and that Paul's accusers might come and bring charges against him there. At the hearing, the same charges that had been made at the earlier trials were repeated before Festus. And Paul's defence took the same line as it had before; only on this occasion he decided to extricate himself and his case from the web of petty, provincial politics by appealing to Caesar, as was the privilege of any Roman citizen. Festus agreed to have the case brought before the emperor—pleased, no doubt, to have the matter off his hands.

Before arrangements were made to take Paul to Rome, however, Festus was visited at Caesarea by Agrippa II, the puppet king of Batanea, Gaulanitis, and Trachonitis, arid regions north and east of the Sea of Galilee. Agrippa was accompanied on this official welcoming visit by his sister, Bernice, who completely dominated her fawning, pomp-loving brother. Agrippa had secured from the emperor Claudius authority to appoint the High Priests and to oversee the Temple in Jerusalem, and because of his royal blood and his connection with the Hasmonean dynasty [3] through his great-grandmother, Mariamne, he had deemed it his right to occupy the Hasmonean palace when he was in Jerusalem. In order to get a good view of the activity within the Temple courts nearby, he had erected a tower on top of the palace, which provided an unsurpassed vantage point. But the priests, who detested him for his pagan ways and for his connivance with Rome, had built a high wall that completely obstructed his view. Agrippa's complaints to the Roman authorities were unavailing, and he had to find other pastimes during his Jerusalem visits.

During the course of Agrippa's extended stay in Caesarea, Festus mentioned to Agrippa that he had inherited from his predecessor a curious case of a prisoner against whom no civil charges, but only religious accusations, had been brought by the leaders of the Jews. Since Agrippa had a Jewish heritage, Festus thought he might be able to clarify some of the religious issues involved. Agrippa was pleased to

---

[3] The Hasmonaeans were the royal line of the Jewish nation from 162 B.C. until the Roman invasion in 63 B.C. See pp. 26, 27.

have been asked, and agreed to hear Paul's case. Agrippa's reputed concern about Jewish religious practices and the sectarian differences among Jews seems to have been more a matter of curiosity than piety, however. And his own participation in Jewish religious life seems to have been motivated more by politics than by conviction. It is reported that Bernice also tried to keep up an appearance of piety by performing a Nazirite vow, but her moral standards were so low that they raised even Roman eyebrows. The show of fidelity to Judaism that this pair made was more than counterbalanced by the thoroughly profligate lives they lived.

In Agrippa's presence, Paul recounted his conversion and the conflict that had developed around him at the instigation of the Jewish leaders (Acts 25:23–26:23). He took care to include a brief statement of the gospel, in which he emphasized the resurrection and the mission to the Gentiles. Festus' reaction was one of astonishment, since Paul's words sounded to him like those of a madman. Turning to Agrippa, Paul tried to press him for a decision regarding the validity of the Christian belief in Christ as the fulfilment of the prophets, but Agrippa quickly terminated the hearing (Acts 26:24-30), disturbed and perhaps moved by Paul's eloquence.

In private, Agrippa told Festus that his earlier decision had been correct: there was nothing in what Paul had done that would justify executing him. There was not even any reason to keep him in prison, except that he had appealed to Caesar, and the law required that he be kept in custody until the hearing before the emperor could be arranged (Acts 26:31, 32). This was a safe conclusion. It gave Agrippa the appearance of a man of insight and mercy, but it saved him from possible trouble with Rome or Jerusalem, since Paul could not be freed under the circumstances. The craft and political acumen of the Herodians [4] surely flowed in Agrippa's veins. No further delay was possible: Paul must go to Rome. Along with several other prisoners, he was assigned to a centurion named Julius, whose task it was to escort his charges to Caesar.

THE JOURNEY TO ROME

The account of the journey to Rome and the shipwreck en route is the most vivid and detailed section of the book of Acts (27:1–28:16). There is a ring of authenticity in the allusions to such navigational problems as the prevailing winds in the various parts of the Mediterranean. Shipping was a dependable means of travel in those

---

[4] See Chapter 1, pp. 28-30, for details about Herod the Great and his family.

A mural of a harbour on the Campanian coast, probably Puteoli, where Paul landed in Italy. The painting was on the wall of a house that was destroyed by the eruption of Vesuvius in 79 A.D.

days, but only during the summer months. Paul and his party were late in starting, and their early progress was so slow that it was late September or early October [5] by the time the ship reached Crete. Paul's advice against going any farther was ignored. What was at first a helpful breeze from the south became a raging north-easter that threatened to drive them across the Mediterranean to the shoals off North Africa. Actually, they drifted westward, across the opening of the Adriatic, and finally ran aground on the island of Malta. In a vision, Paul had received a promise that he would in fact stand trial before Caesar. Not all the factors that contributed to Paul's deliverance from disaster were of the miraculous kind, however, for the centurion was instrumental in saving Paul's life when the soldiers, fearful of the

---

[5] This dating is based on the assumption that "the fast" in Acts 27:9 is a reference to the Day of Atonement, which came after the autumn equinox.

consequences if any prisoners escaped, were about to put Paul and the other prisoners to death.

While Paul was on the island of Malta, his life was miraculously preserved, according to Acts, after he had been bitten by a poisonous reptile. The Maltese natives had concluded that the goddess of justice, Dike, had sent the viper to strike him down even though he had survived the storm and the shipwreck. But when he came through unharmed, they concluded that he was under the special protection of the gods, or perhaps he was a divine person in human form. The admiration of the natives increased when Paul was able to heal the sick, especially when he cured the father of the "chief," as the man designated by Rome to rule the island was known. When the weather began to clear —early the following spring—the centurion, the prisoners, and the friends of Paul who had accompanied him all the way from Caesarea set out for the Italian mainland, reaching the harbour of Puteoli, near Naples, after stops at Syracuse and Rhegium. At Puteoli there was already a community of Christians, founded, we may assume, by the missionary activity of the thriving church in Rome. A delegation from the community in Rome travelled southward along the famous Appian Way to meet Paul and to escort him into the imperial city (Acts 28:1-15).

Paul in Rome

THE EVANGELISTIC ACTIVITY

Having arrived in Rome, Paul extended the usual courtesies to the Jewish community. First, he invited them to hear his version of the conflict with the Jews in Jerusalem, and then he arranged a time for them to hear a statement of the Christian message. Since there had as yet been no adverse reports on Paul from Jerusalem, the Roman Jews came in large numbers to hear what he had to say. As on similar occasions in the past, the response to Paul's preaching of the gospel was mixed. But to those who rejected it, Paul had a word of warning: The prophet Isaiah had predicted that the people of Israel would not receive his message to them. It was in accord with the word of the prophet, therefore, that Paul had turned his attention to the Gentiles, confident that they would continue to respond in faith to the *kerygma*.

During Paul's imprisonment in Rome, he was permitted considerable freedom, both in personal activities and in the preaching of the gospel. According to the account in Acts (28:30, 31) he lived at his own expense, although he was attended constantly by a Roman guard (28:16). The record in Acts ends inconclusively, without telling us whether or not Paul came to trial, much less whether he was acquitted or sentenced at the trial.[6] Since the words in 28:31 sound like the formal statements with which the author closes the other sections of his book (5:32; 15:35; 19:20), it does not appear that the text has been artificially broken off at this point. It has been conjectured that the author intended to write a third book (in addition to Luke and Acts), but it seems odd that he should have left unresolved such an important issue as the outcome of the trial while he shifted from one volume to another. A more plausible explanation is that the book was to serve as an apology for Paul and the Christian movement, by presenting evidence (1) that the Jewish rejection of Paul and his message was arbitrary and contrary to their own scriptures, and (2) that the Roman authorities had dealt fairly with Paul, and had never found him guilty of violating Roman law. If this was the author's purpose, he closed his account at a dramatic moment. The "two years" (Acts 28:30) of waiting may refer to a statute of limitation, during which period either the accusers of a prisoner were obliged to appear in court or else the

---

[6] For full discussions of the trial of Paul and the end of Acts, see Foakes-Jackson and Lake, *The Beginnings of Christianity*, Part 1, Vol. V, Additional Note XXVI; and G. H. C. Macgregor in *The Interpreter's Bible*, Vol. 9, pp. 349-352. New York: Abingdon, 1954.

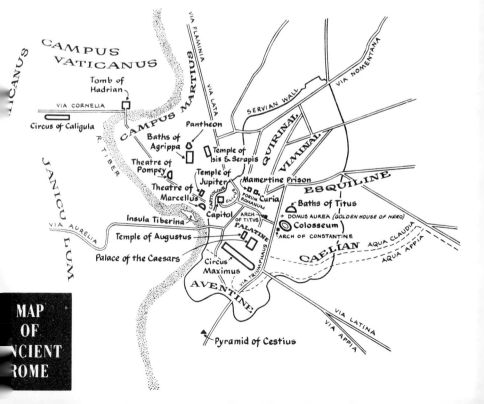

MAP OF ANCIENT ROME

The Roman Forum and the Arch of Septimius Severus from the Palatine Hill. The plain, squarish building across the Forum is the Curia, where the Senate convened. At the lower right are the steps and column-bases of the Basilica Julia, one of the colonnaded porticos used for transacting business in ancient Rome. Behind the arch appears the flat roof of a small church that was built over the ruins of the Mamertine Prison, where, according to tradition, Peter and Paul were imprisoned.

prisoner could be set free. We may infer from the absence of any mention of Paul's accusers appearing in Rome that the Jewish leaders from Palestine who originally brought the charges against Paul must not have appeared in the two-year period. But what happened to Paul afterward, we do not know.

CORRESPONDENCE WITH THE ASIAN CHURCHES

The matters that occupied Paul's mind can be inferred from the letters he is believed to have written during this time of imprisonment: the Letters to the Philippians, to the Colossians, and to Philemon (and possibly the Letter to the Ephesians). These letters contain clear references to the fact that Paul is in prison (Phil. 1:12; 1:17; Col. 4:10; 4:18; Phm. 23; Eph. 4:1). The fact that Paul mentions several times his hopes of visiting friends in Philippi and Colossæ (Phil. 2.24; Phm. 22) has given rise to the theory that it was from an Ephesian rather than a Roman prison that Paul was writing. Would he have told his friends in Colossæ to prepare the guest chamber for him when he was 1200 miles away? On the other hand, if he were only 100 miles away (that is, in Ephesus) the possibility of a visit would seem more likely. There is no direct evidence of Paul's having been imprisoned in Ephesus,[7] and, conversely, the personal references in the imprisonment letters fit well into the probable course of events at the close of Paul's life. In the following paragraphs, we shall attempt to reconstruct the situation.

While Paul was waiting in Rome for his accusers to appear, information came to him from Asia Minor about the church in Colossæ and the sister church in Laodicea. These were both vigorous communities, the report ran, but certain unnamed adversaries were trying to convince the Christians there that Paul's gospel was incomplete. As we have observed (p. 209), central Asia Minor was fertile territory for religious speculation. Under the influence of the Iranian belief in intermediaries, false teachers had been telling the Colossians that they must purify themselves by means of certain ritual observances (Col. 2:16, 20-23) in order to prepare themselves for the presence of God, and that they must aspire to more complete knowledge of the other intermediary beings—in addition to Christ—if they were to travel the path that leads

---

[7] The fullest statement of the hypothesis of an imprisonment in Ephesus is in G. S. Duncan, *St. Paul's Ephesian Ministry*. New York: Scribner's, 1930. A summary of the whole question is given by M. S. Enslin, *Christian Beginnings*, pp. 273-275. New York: Harper, 1938. The arguments based on the difficulty of travelling from Rome to Philippi or Colossæ are weakened by the evidence of the relative speed and dependability of sea travel in imperial Rome. See *Cambridge Ancient History*, 1927, Vol. 10, p. 387.

from the earthly world of darkness to the heavenly realm of light. It was in answer to these false teachings and practices that Paul wrote the Letter to the Colossians.

After expressions of commendation and gratitude (Col. 1:1-12), Paul tells the Colossians that they have already been transferred through Christ to the realm of light, and have already been purified. There are no angelic agents of creation of whom they must gain knowledge: Christ is the one through whom God made the universe, and Christ is superior to all other beings. The whole *pleroma* (that is, the totality of God's means of disclosing himself to man) dwells bodily in Jesus Christ (1:13-19). He has already, by his death on the cross, brought man into relationship with God (1:20-23). To Paul, and through him to the Colossian Christians, has been committed the task of declaring the message of what God has done in Christ. There is no need to seek further wisdom about God; it has all been made known in Christ. The effort to delve into religious mysteries is futile; the "mystery" has been revealed, and its meaning is now to be proclaimed (1:24-2:4). The Colossian community is to use its own spiritual resources; it is to shun involvement in ascetic ritual, which subjects the participant to the hostile spiritual powers from which Christ has set men free (2:8-23). The legitimate task of the Colossians is to develop the corporate life of the community, in the power of the Spirit and under its guidance, so that their unity in Christ will appear in their church life as well as in their personal relationships (3:1-4:5).

The concluding paragraphs of the letter tell us the means by which Paul was carrying on correspondence with distant churches. He was sending Tychicus and Onesimus to carry to the Colossians a first-hand report on his condition and on his prospects for the future. Presumably Paul was reluctant to put in writing his opinions of Rome and its judicial system, lest his comments fall into the hands of the authorities. (We shall see in Chapter 15 how a Christian from Asia Minor veiled his denunciation of Rome in elaborate symbolic imagery.) The names of Paul's companions who aided him during his imprisonment are of interest to us: Mark has already appeared in association with Paul's early work (p. 221); Aristarchus was one of the delegates who carried the offering from the Greek churches to Jerusalem (Acts 19:29; 20:4); and Luke has been identified traditionally as the author of Acts and the Gospel that bears his name (4:7-10, 14).

In addition to the Letter to the Colossians, Paul sent two other letters with Tychicus. One of these was a letter to the Laodiceans, which Paul mentions (Col. 4:16), but which has not survived. Marcion, a learned heretic of the second century, believed our "Letter to the Ephesians" was the letter to the Laodiceans mentioned by Paul. Curiously, several of the oldest and best manuscripts of the New Testament omit the phrase "at Ephesus" in Ephesians 1:1. It has been inferred that the Letter to the Ephesians was originally an encyclical, intended for general circulation among all the churches founded by Paul.[8] The other letter that Tychicus took with him was a personal note to Philemon, in whose house the Colossian church assembled (Phm. 2). The purpose of the letter was to plead with Philemon to accept with gracious forgiveness Onesimus, a slave of Philemon's who had run away. Onesimus had found his way to Rome, where he had come in contact with Paul and had become a Christian (Phm. 16). Paul had found him valuable as a helper in his work, but felt that justice demanded he be returned to his rightful owner. If Onesimus has taken anything from his master, Paul offers to repay it. It is tempting to conjecture that Onesimus, the bishop of Ephesus mentioned by Ignatius (a writer of the early second century) may have been this same runaway slave!

In writing to Philemon, Paul speaks as though he hoped soon to visit his friends in Colossæ, which would imply that he expected to be released from prison. But apparently Paul's earlier hopes for release had begun to weaken. He may even have been set free for a time, at the expiration of the waiting period prescribed by Roman law, and again imprisoned—perhaps in connection with Nero's persecution of Christians in A.D. 64—and finally executed. Since both the language and the point of view of the Pastoral Letters (see p. 67) show that they were not written by Paul, but in the closing decades of the first century, we have no evidence at all that Paul undertook any further journeys. The wish that Paul expresses in Romans 15:24, that he might preach the gospel in Spain, probably went unfulfilled. It seems likely that the charges brought against the Christians in Rome during the reign of Claudius (see p. 252) were revived during the early years of Nero's reign, and that Paul was executed as a disturber of the peace. This must remain, however, a mere conjecture. The whole series of questions about Paul's death should serve as a reminder that the Christian movement, which was later to play such an important role in the history of the empire, was at this time nothing more than a minor nuisance.

[8] This theory is defended by Edgar J. Goodspeed in *The Meaning of Ephesians*, Chicago: University of Chicago Press, 1933. In the same author's *Introduction to the New Testament* (University of Chicago Press, 1937, pp. 238, 239), it is further suggested that Onesimus is the compiler of Ephesians and the one who first brought together all Paul's letters into a single collection.

PAUL'S FINAL WORD

It was probably during the closing months of Paul's life that he wrote his most personal message to one of the churches: the Letter to the Philippians. His hope for freedom is not extinguished (Phil. 1:19, 26), but at the same time he has faced up to the fact that death awaits him (1:20; 2:17). He reminds the Philippians (2:8) that it was Jesus' obedience unto death that led to his exaltation by God, and he prays that he may be made like Christ, even in his death (3:10). For Paul, death has no terrors; it will be "gain" (1:21) for him, although his removal by death will be a loss for the Philippians and for all other communities among whom Paul has worked.

The letter begins with words of profound gratitude for the participation of the Philippian Christians in Paul's work through the gift they have sent (1:3-5), and to his thanks he adds a heartfelt prayer for their continued growth in understanding and spirituality (1:6-11). He urges them not to be alarmed by the fact that he has been imprisoned as a result of the schemes of his enemies: his presence in prison has brought the message of Christ into the imperial household itself; the work he has carried on in prison has helped to strengthen the Roman Christians. Even Paul's opponents are "preaching Christ" by their acts of opposition, since they are drawing attention to the movement and its claims, and are providing Paul with an opportunity to bear witness to Christ in such unexpected places as the imperial establishment itself.

It is at this point in the letter that Paul expresses the hope that the prayers of the Philippian Christians for his deliverance from prison will be answered, even though his personal preference would be to die and so enter the presence of the Lord (1:19-23). He feels, however, that it is more important for the work of the gospel that he live, and in the light of this conviction he hopes to visit Philippi again (1:24-26). Meanwhile, it is his prayer that they continue steadfast in the face of opposition and even suffering, free from selfishness and factionalism. The supreme illustration of humility and dedication to the welfare of others is Christ, who did not grasp at equality with God even though he possessed the divine qualities characteristic of God. Instead, he humbled himself in obedience to God, to the extreme of dying on a cross. God had publicly acclaimed this complete obedience by exalting Christ as Lord, and by bringing all creation in subjection to him, so that all the universe confesses that "Jesus is Lord."

In the light of Christ's obedience, the Philippians are to be earnest in service to God, pure in mode of life, faithful as witnesses to the truth. Paul hopes to see them again, and is sending messengers to tell them of his own fate (2:23). He warns them against men who take pride in Jewish legalism, and reminds the community at Philippi that he has as enviable a heritage in Judaism as any of the Judaizers. Unlike those who are trying to impose Jewish ritual on the Gentile Christians, Paul is not relying on his religious credentials, but is earnestly striving to live and serve acceptably before God. He is conscious that his new life was given him by God, and that he cannot pride himself on his spiritual achievement; rather, he presses on, longing for the day when the transformation that God has begun in him through Christ will be complete (3:3-21).

The letter closes with a series of warm, personal exhortations and an expression of profound gratitude for the contribution that the church at Philippi has made to his work. There is something unexpected and poignantly powerful about a man who is facing possible death and who can still write: "Rejoice ... always. Have no anxiety about anything...." (4:4, 6). If the closing lines of II Timothy are authentic notes from Paul's last days, we can see that his confidence never wavered: "For I am already on the point of being sacrificed; the time of my departure has come.... Demas has deserted me.... Luke alone is with me.... But the Lord stood by me and gave me strength.... To him be the glory for ever and ever. Amen." (II Tim. 4:6, 10, 11, 17, 18).

Growing Conflict Between Judaism and Christianity

EVIDENCE FROM LITERARY SOURCES

The hostility of official Judaism toward the Christian community was not limited to Paul; shortly after Paul's death, antagonism arose even toward the church in Jerusalem, which had once enjoyed such friendly relations with the Jewish leaders. But the animosity was by no means confined to Jewish attitudes toward Christians; the strain of anti-Jewish polemic found in all the Gospels reflects clearly the situation in the last half of the first century A.D. in which conflict between Jew and Christian developed. On the other hand, some Christians sought a solution to the problem of the relation of Judaism to Christian faith by seeking to mould Christianity according to the patterns of Jewish life and thought. Since the conflict reached a crisis in connection with the fall of Jerusalem to the Roman army in A.D. 70, we shall consider the antecedents and consequences of the city's fall in some detail. At the end of the chapter we shall examine the literature pro-

duced by the branch of the Christian community that was more favourably disposed toward Judaism.

The evidence for the mounting hostility between Jew and Christian
in the later first century is found in both Jewish and Christian sources.
The rabbinic traditions that have been preserved from this period regularly refer to Christians as heretics, and heap scorn and slander on Jesus
and his followers. For example, the story that Jesus was the illegitimate
son of Mary by a Roman soldier appears to have originated with Jewish
polemicists of this time.[9] Concurrently, the Christians were modifying
the stories in the Gospels to intensify the hatred against the Jewish
leaders by portraying them as having assumed full blame for the death
of Jesus. Matthew quotes the Jews as saying at Jesus' trial, "His blood
be on us and on our children" (Mt. 27:25). The fact that these words
condemn the Jews in such strong terms, coupled with the fact that
they are found in none of the other Gospel accounts of Jesus' trial,
suggests that they were added as a polemic against the Jews at or
shortly before the time Matthew wrote his Gospel.

Similarly, the harsh treatment that Jewish converts to Christianity
received at the hands of the leaders of the synagogues throughout the
empire during this period is reflected in the Gospels in various ways:
the Jewish-Christian tension appears in the heightening of the element
of conflict in the accounts of Jesus' encounters with the Pharisees; it is
included in the predictions of persecution for faithful disciples in the
apocalyptic section of Mark (13:5 ff.) and in the stories of Jesus' sending the disciples out to preach (Mt. 10:17-25). In three different passages the Gospel of John speaks of the practice of putting a man out
of the synagogue if he confesses that Jesus is the Christ (9:22; 12:42;
16:2). These specific warnings of Jewish opposition were probably
added by the early church to Jesus' predictions of the general resistance
that preachers of the gospel would meet, and the additions were probably made just when Jewish hostility to Christianity was mounting.

The high point of animosity between Christian and Jew in the New
Testament is reached in the Gospel of John, especially in the story of
the Passion. Although it is true that Matthew is the writer who has
added to the Markan tradition the dreadful words, "His blood be on us
and on our children" (Mt. 27:25), the whole movement of the trial
scenes in John points up the belief that Pilate could find no cause for
condemning Jesus, but that he yielded to the pressure of "the Jews."
The very phrase "the Jews" demonstrates that the wide differences

---

[9] For a survey of the anti-Christian elements in the rabbinic tradition, see J.
Klausner, *Jesus of Nazareth*, pp. 18-54. London : Allen & Unwin.

between the Jewish sects that prevailed in Jesus' day no longer existed in the time of the writing of the Gospel of John, but that all opposition from Jewish quarters could be lumped together as traceable to "the Jews." Even Jesus is quoted in John as putting the major blame on his own people: "He who delivered me to you has the greater sin" — that is, the Jews are really responsible. Further evidence of conflict between Jew and Christian in the time in which John's Gospel was written is probably to be found in the questions that appear throughout the book, always on the lips of Jewish antagonists: "Is not this Jesus, the son of Joseph, whose father and mother we know?" (6:42); "How can this man give us his flesh to eat?" (6:52); "Are you greater than our father Abraham?" (8:53); "How can you say that the Son of Man must be lifted up?" (12:34). From the words of the prologue (John 1:11), "His own people received him not," throughout the book the theme recurs that "the Jews" were obstinate and blind in their failure to accept Jesus as the Christ.

EVIDENCE FROM HISTORICAL SOURCES

The mutual ill-will between Christian and Jew that developed at this time is apparent not only in the literature of the period, but also in direct reports of events from Christian and non-Christian sources. As we noted earlier (p. 204), Herod Agrippa had gained favour with the Jews in Judea by executing James (and possibly his brother John), though it seems unlikely that the idea of persecuting the Christians originated with Herod. At any rate, he continued the persecution primarily to please the Jews (Acts 12:3), and quickly lost interest in the undertaking when one of his victims escaped (Acts 12:19). With Peter, James, and John removed as leaders of the Jerusalem community (about A.D. 44), the tension between Christians and Jews seems to have relaxed. When James, Jesus' brother, took over as head of the church in Jerusalem, he was eager to maintain good relations with the Jewish leaders, especially since his own convictions and practices were strongly legalistic. It was he who took the initiative in demanding that Gentile Christians respect certain aspects of Jewish regulations (see p. 237), and it was he who was most embarrassed by Paul's presence in Jerusalem, since Paul was notorious for his contacts with Gentiles and for his concessions to their way of life. The Jerusalem Christians were, until A.D. 62, zealous to demonstrate their loyalty to Judaism.

There is no evidence of any further conflict between Judaism and the Jerusalem church until A.D. 62, when James, the brother of Jesus, was put to death by order of the High Priest. Even the riot stirred up by Paul in A.D. 55 does not appear to have resulted in any unfavourable reaction against the Jerusalem Christians; in any case, they remained aloof from the incident, and made no effort to come to Paul's aid. There are two independent—and probably irreconcilable—accounts of the execution of James.[10] Josephus, the Jewish historian of the period, tells in his *Antiquities* that Annas, the High Priest, sentenced James to death on an alleged violation of Jewish law. The sentence was passed and the execution performed during the interim between the death of Festus (A.D. 62) and the arrival of Albinus, his successor; so the absence of a Roman governor provided Annas with an opportunity to act independently. Probably Annas wanted to destroy James out of resentment for his popularity with the people, who seem to have admired James for his piety. Since James was famous for his fidelity to the Law, the charge brought against him by Annas was almost certainly false. There was a strong reaction to Annas' plot, both from the Jewish officials, who sought to have Annas deposed, and from the procurator himself, who did in fact remove Annas from the high priesthood.

The other account of the death of James comes to us in two forms from Eusebius, who quotes from two of the church fathers, Clement of Alexandria (around A.D. 200) and Hegesippus (around A.D. 180). According to these stories, James was first thrown down from a pinnacle of the Temple and then beaten on the head with a laundryman's club until he died. The details of the story are what we would expect to find in a legend of the death of a martyr. Although Josephus' more sober version of James' death is to be preferred to the accounts in Eusebius, the stories agree that James was executed by official Jewish action in spite of, and in part because of, his popularity with the people of Jerusalem.

THE CLIMAX

In the years 66 to 70, the position of the church in Jerusalem became increasingly difficult as a result of the Jewish revolt against Roman occupation. The cruelty and corruption of the Roman procurators had been increasing. Nero had made important concessions to the Gentiles in Palestine, and they had begun to interfere with Jewish worship in the synagogues. In the year 66, as a reaction against maltreatment at the hands of the Roman administrators, the Jews refused to permit the sacrifices to the emperor to continue, although these sacrifices were required by Roman law throughout the empire. Riots broke out in every city; Gentile towns were burned; the Roman gar-

---

[10] These accounts are quoted and analysed in detail by M. Goguel in *The Birth of Christianity*, pp. 124-132. London : Allen & Unwin, 1953.

risons were attacked in cities where they were weak; and Jews were slaughtered in reprisal in cities where the garrisons were strong. At first, the Jews succeeded in liberating parts of the land from Roman control; the independence of the Jewish nation was declared, and Jewish coinage was issued. But the poorly armed bands of revolutionaries could not withstand the 60,000 seasoned troops that Rome sent in to quell the revolt. By the year 69 all of Palestine, except for Jerusalem and some outlying fortresses near the Dead Sea, was once again under Roman control.

Vespasian, who commanded the Roman troops, could have quickly destroyed all resistance, but his mind was occupied with other matters: the emperor, Nero, had died under mysterious circumstances in 68, and Vespasian's chances of succeeding him were excellent. Accordingly, Vespasian held back from the fighting for a time to see what the outcome of the contest for the imperial throne would be. When it became clear that the army in the east would declare for him, he returned to Rome. His rivals faded from the scene, and he became emperor in 69. His son, Titus, who had been left in charge of the troops in Palestine, pressed the siege of Jerusalem.

The city's resistance might have been greater if the people had not been torn by internal dissension. At the start of the revolt there had been two main parties: the peace party, whose members believed God would free the nation from Rome in his own time and by his own methods; and the resistance party, whose adherents were convinced that the time had come for them to take the initiative in driving the Romans out. With the advent of the Roman troops, the peace party was overwhelmed by the rebels, but any prospect of success for the revolt was ended when the rebels began to fight among themselves under rival leaders. The civil strife continued within the city even during the siege. Although the revolutionaries had killed Annas, who had caused James' death, the Christians appear to have been in sympathy with the peace party. They believed that the hope of the nation

A shekel of Israel, minted by the Jews during the Jewish Revolt of 66-70 A.D. The reverse side is inscribed "Jerusalem the Holy."

A bust of Vespasian. He invaded Palestine in 67 A.D., let his son Titus capture Jerusalem, and returned to Rome to be acclaimed emperor in 69.

lay in the return of their Messiah to establish the reign of God, not in military victory. The siege, which began in April of the year 70, lasted five months, and during this time thousands died of starvation. Then, when the city fell, the Romans laid it waste and demolished the Temple. A generation later, during the reign of Hadrian, the Jews attempted a second revolt (A.D. 132-135), but at the order of Hadrian the city of Jerusalem was levelled and a pagan city called Aelia Capitolina was built on the site.

Presumably it was just before the siege began that the Christians decided to flee to a place of safety. At first glance, it seems clear that the reason they fled was to escape destruction at the hands of the Romans, but Eusebius tells us that they went to the Gentile city of Pella, east of the Jordan in the region of the Decapolis, in response to a divine oracle. Certain questions immediately arise: What was the

314

The Mausoleum of Hadrian on the west bank of the Tiber River, with the dome of St. Peter's in the background. In Christian times, the top of the structure was rebuilt and served both as a fortress and as a chapel.

nature of the oracle? Why did it tell them to go to a despised Gentile city like Pella, which had been among those attacked by the Jewish nationalists only a few years earlier? Why were the Jewish Christians—traditionally so fastidious about maintaining separateness from Gentiles—willing to seek refuge in a Gentile stronghold? Considering these questions in reverse order, the probability is that the Jerusalem Christians were willing to compromise their religious scruples for the sake of saving their own necks. The only place of safety in the whole area for Jews who had opposed the revolt would be a place like Pella, which was Gentile and hence free of Jewish nationalist feeling. There they would be safe from the Romans, who might have taken them for

315

rebels in Jerusalem, and safe from the rebels, who might have killed them as traitors.

Eusebius gives another theory to explain the flight of the Christians from Jerusalem. He suggests that the Roman emperors, from Vespasian on, sought out all descendants of David in an effort to exterminate the Jewish hope of a revival of the Davidic dynasty. Since Jesus was from "the seed of David" (Rom. 1:3), he and his relatives would have been in the royal line, and his brothers and other surviving relatives would have been the victims of Vespasian if they had remained within his reach at Jerusalem. On this theory, the flight to Pella would have been a communal effort to protect Jesus' family, to whom had passed the leadership of the Jerusalem community. This story of Eusebius, like the ones about James alluded to above, bears the marks of legendary embroidering, and really conveys little more than the general impression that (1) the Romans did not understand the nature of Christian messianic beliefs, and mistakenly identified them with the nationalistic hopes

A bas-relief on the Arch of Titus in Rome, erected to celebrate Titus' triumph over the Jews. The victors are carrying off from the Temple at Jerusalem the seven-branched lampstand, the sacred trumpets, and the table where the sacred bread was kept.

of Judaism, and (2) the Jerusalem wing of Christianity had already lapsed into such complete obscurity by the end of the second century that there were no precise recollections of what had happened to it after the city of Jerusalem fell to the Romans.

As for the oracle that instructed the Christians to flee, there is a possibility that it may be embedded in the apocalyptic section that precedes the Passion story in each of the Synoptic Gospels (Mt. 24; Mk. 13; Lk. 21). The phrase in Mark 13:14, "let the reader understand," is often interpreted as referring to the reader of the oracle, which Eusebius tells us was circulated in Jerusalem at the time of the Roman invasion. The possibility of identifying the oracle mentioned by Eusebius with the Little Apocalypse in the Synoptic Gospels is discussed at some length in Chapter 15, where the nature of the Christian hope is considered.

Although we do not know what happened to the Christians after they fled from Jerusalem, we do know that the destruction of Jerusalem by the Romans was interpreted by Christians generally as a divine judgment on Judaism for its rejection of Jesus as the Christ. This conviction is plainly and repeatedly stated in Eusebius, and it is easy to read it between the lines of the Gospels. The very fact that the apocalyptic section mentioned above was incorporated into the Synoptics shows that the fall of Jerusalem was considered a major event in the unfolding of the purpose that God had begun with the coming of Jesus. The destruction was understood to be the final proof that the old dispensation had come to an end; the new age was already beginning to dawn.

The Heritage of Jewish Christianity

JEWISH CHRISTIAN SECTS

Although we have no direct knowledge of the fate of Jewish Christianity after A.D. 70, certain developments both inside and outside the main body of the church are probably a heritage from this vanished wing of Christianity. Writers in the second, and again in the fourth, centuries tell of various groups living east of the Jordan who may have been the survivors of Jewish Christianity. One of these sects, known as the Ebionites (meaning "poor"), appears to have been directly related to the Jerusalem community, which also called itself "the poor" (Gal. 2:10; Rom. 15:26; cf. Lk. 6:20). The Ebionites are reported to have regarded Jewish Law and tradition as the basis for their outlook and practices. From all the Christian writings, they accepted as scripture only the Gospel of Matthew, although they denied the virgin birth of Jesus. Later writers speak of another group, called "Nazorenes" or "Nazarenes," who were also more Jewish than Christian in character, and who spoke a Semitic dialect rather than Greek. But these Jewish Christian groups east of the Jordan did not retain unchanged the Jerusalem type of Christianity; under the influence of the unorthodox Jewish sects in the Jordan region, they engaged in the wildest kind of elaboration of the faith. Early in the second century there appeared a prophet named Elxai (Alexis in Greek), who insisted on the observance of the full Jewish ritual, but who recognized Christ as Son of God. Elxai had first-hand knowledge of Christ, since he had seen him in a vision in which Christ appeared as a mountain ninety-six miles high!

Fortunately for the subsequent history of Christianity, this type of bizarre speculation never became a dominant force in the church. Like the rivers of Damascus, it flowed out to the edge of the desert and vanished. The church buildings that have survived in this territory east of the Jordan date from the time of Constantine (fourth century) or later, and demonstrate by their form and decoration that the orthodox type of Christianity eventually prevailed here as elsewhere. Jewish Christianity simply died out.

JUDAISTIC CHRISTIANITY IN THE LETTER OF JAMES

The powerful appeal of certain aspects of Jewish Christianity, however, is apparent in writings that were included in the Christian canon. Significantly, it was the Jewish moral law and not the ritual that continued to exert an attraction among Christians. The Epistle of James, although it is strongly hellenistic in style and is written in smooth Greek, is thoroughly Jewish in its ethical appeal. Many of its illustrations on moral points are drawn from the Old Testament, and it has no doctrine of the cross or even any developed teaching about the role of Christ. In spite of its insistence on obedience to the Law as a requisite for salvation, it does not demand fulfilment of the ritual aspects of Torah. The outlook on religion that the book represents, therefore, is quite different from that of James, the brother of Jesus. James, as we learn from the account in Acts 15, demanded that even the Gentiles make concessions to the ceremonial purity of Jewish Christians by avoiding certain practices that by Jewish standards were defiling. It is unthinkable, therefore, that James, the brother of Jesus, could have written this book, since he would surely have included ritual purity among his themes, and since it is most unlikely that an Aramaic-speaking peasant would write in such polished hellenistic

Greek. Apart from the fact that it has no concern for Jewish ritual requirements, the Letter of James, however, is so thoroughly Jewish in its ethical tone and moralistic approach to religion that it has been suggested that the book was originally a Jewish ethical treatise to which a brief Christian introduction was added.[11] This theory, however, has not gained wide acceptance.

There is no theme or controlling purpose in this little book; rather, the author strings together a series of moral injunctions with little or no connection between them. It is probable that some of the sayings included here were drawn from a common store of proverbs—for example, those in 1:13; 4:5. The repeated mention of "wisdom" recalls to mind the Wisdom Literature of the Old Testament (1:5 ff.; 3:13 ff.). There are warnings to the rich, the self-indulgent, the contentious, the talkative, the proud, the complaining, the deceitful. The book ends abruptly, with no concluding remarks.

The attitude of the author of James toward the Law and faith is the most puzzling feature of this book, and the one aspect that has been most discussed. Theologians like Martin Luther, for whom Paul's formulation of the Christian faith was normative, have regretted publicly that the Epistle of James was ever included in the Christian canon. The author seems to reject flatly the idea of justification by faith, and insists that the Law must be obeyed in its totality (2:10). Faith alone is inadequate to render a man acceptable to God. In a passage that seems to be a direct criticism of Paul's statement (Rom. 3:28), "James" sternly opposes the claim that faith alone can save (2:24): "You see that a man is justified by works, and not by faith alone." As we shall note in Chapter 11, the Christians of the second and third generation tended to lose something of the sense of faith as a relationship to God and to regard it more as a set of beliefs that could be set down in formal fashion as "the faith." When Paul uses the word "faith," he implies a trust in God that demonstrates itself in obedience to God's will. If the author of James uses the word "faith" to mean only doctrinal beliefs, then Paul would surely have agreed with him that faith of that sort does not justify a man. "James" had undoubtedly seen men who claimed to believe the doctrines that the Christian community affirmed, but whose lives gave no indication of an inward change by the Spirit. In James 2:14-16, for example, there is a gently ironic account of some poor members of the community who lack both clothing and food. Instead of helping to provide for their needs, the wealthier members

---

[11] For a concise statement of this theory, see M. S. Enslin, *Christian Beginnings*, p. 327. New York: Harper, 1938.

of the church—undoubtedly orthodox in faith—wish the poor folk well and send them away empty-handed. Paul would surely have concurred in "James' " judgment that this was a neglect of Christian responsibility, and that these people, though they claimed to subscribe to the Christian faith, had never entered into the new way of life that was to characterize Christians. Although they professed to have faith, they were religiously dead (2:26).

It seems probable, therefore, that "James' " real quarrel is not with what Paul meant by justification by faith (Chapter 9), but with what Christians of the later part of the first century mistakenly understood Paul to have meant. But even when we make allowance for the change in the meaning of faith from "trust" (as in Paul) to "belief" (as in the Letter of James), there remains a wide divergence between the book of James and the earlier books of the New Testament. Originally, the emphasis was on what God had done in Jesus Christ for man's redemption, but "James" puts his whole stress on what man must do for God.

Similar to the book of James in its Jewishness, and in its stress on the moral aspect of religion, is the *Didache*, or *Teaching of the Twelve Apostles*.[12] This book, which was discovered for modern readers in 1883, gives details about the ritual, moral, and organizational rules of the church. Although it is clearly a Christian book of regulations, it reproduces the ethical and even the liturgical forms of Judaism. For example, it incorporates Jewish prayers, with only the slightest modification, into Christian worship (see Chapter 12, p. 373).

THE JEWISHNESS OF MATTHEW'S GOSPEL

A third book that shows strong Jewish influence is the Gospel of Matthew. Paradoxically, Matthew at times indulges in polemics against the Jews and at other times assimilates ideas that are more Jewish than Christian into his formulation of the Christian faith. When we compare the Parable of the Marriage Feast as Luke records it (Lk. 14:16-24) with Matthew's version (Mt. 22:1-14), it becomes obvious that Matthew has changed the point of the story to make it a prophecy of the destruction of Jerusalem. Luke reports that the disappointed host invited the outcasts after the original guests refused to come, but Matthew introduces an unmistakable polemic against the Jews by saying that the invited guests murdered the messenger, whereupon the "king was angry, and he sent his troops and destroyed those murderers and burned their city." This parable, which was intended to show that

---

[12] Cf. Chapter 2, pp. 75-76. For a brief description of the *Didache*, see M. Dibelius, *A Fresh Approach to the New Testament and Early Christian Literature*, pp. 234-237. New York: Scribner's, 1936.

God's invitation to fellowship is extended to all, has here been converted into a detailed prediction of the judgment on Jerusalem for its rejection of Jesus as Messiah.

In the Sermon on the Mount, and elsewhere throughout the Gospel, Matthew shows by his devotion to Jewish ethics and by his use of rabbinic methods of scriptural interpretation that he has by no means repudiated the whole of Judaism. His antagonism was only to official Judaism, and not to the underlying principles of Jewish religion. Matthew's Gospel is organized, as we have seen (Chapter 2), in such a way as to parallel the five Books of Moses. Just as the rabbis of that day were eager to document their teachings by appeal to the Law and the prophets, so Matthew often reminds his readers that what Jesus was doing was fulfilling the promises made in the scriptures. An example of this mechanical documentation is found in the story of Jesus' entry into the city of Jerusalem on Palm Sunday (Mt. 21:1 ff.), which is understood by the church to have occurred in fulfilment of prophecy. The actual words of the prophet Zechariah (Zech. 9:9) mention an ass and a colt as the animals on which the King of Israel rides into Zion, rather than just an ass alone, as in Mark's account of the story (Mk. 11:1 ff.). Matthew failed to understand that Hebrew poetry is written in couplets in which each of the lines describes the same thing—for example, "Who shall ascend the hill of the Lord? And who shall stand in his holy place?" Accordingly, Matthew seems to have decided that to have Jesus ride into Jerusalem only on an ass would be to fulfil only half of Zechariah's prophecy, and so he added the colt as well in his version of the incident. Words ascribed to Jesus in Matthew 5:17-20, but which are not found elsewhere (except for verse 18, which appears in a milder form in Mark 13:31), are quoted in order to make clear that Torah is the eternally abiding basis of true religion (see the discussion of Jesus and the Law in Chapter 4).

During the last decades of the first century, the Christian community represented in the Gospel of Matthew was under the influence of rabbinic Judaism. Just as the rabbis were constructing a code for living based on Torah, so rabbinic-type Christians were developing a code for Christian living based on the teachings of Jesus. Although institutionally Judaism and Christianity were far apart from A.D. 70 on, the impact of Judaism on the Christian movement continued to be strong.

In spite of the community of interests and convictions between Judaism and Christianity, the Christian claim that the faith of Judaism had found its fulfilment in Jesus Christ was, to the pious Jew, arrogant and perverted. From the earliest times, Christians had been convinced that Jesus and his redemptive work had been the fulfilment of Jewish prophecy, as is attested by the recurrence in the oldest form of the *kerygma* (I Cor. 15:3-8) of the phrase, "according to the scriptures." As we noted in Chapter 2, the church was convinced that it was the authentic heir of the promises made by God to Israel, and that therefore it alone was in a position to interpret the Hebrew scriptures. When, toward the end of the first century, Christian writers began to quote as authoritative the books that were later incorporated in the New Testament, it became evident that Judaism must draw up a list of those religious books that alone were to be considered authoritative for Jews. This it did, when the rabbis met at Jamnia in the year 90 to establish the Jewish canon; as a result of their action, the line of demarcation between Jew and Christian was sharply and unalterably drawn.

By this time, Rome had come to recognize that, since Christianity was not merely another Jewish sect, it was not automatically to be included among the legal religions of the empire. The resulting conflict between church and empire, and the struggle of Christianity to define itself and to withstand the inroads of alien concepts and practices, forced the church into a period of consolidation. In the next chapter, we shall look more closely at this phase of the community's experience.

PART THREE

❧

THE
COMMUNITY MATURES

CHAPTER ELEVEN

ᕽᘺᕽ

THE

COMMUNITY IN CONFLICT

The Christian church was born in the midst of conflict. Even before its inception, Jesus had carried on his mission in conflict with the Jewish leaders, and he was finally brought into head-on conflict with the Roman procurator. Then the young church immediately found itself in conflict with Judaism from without and with Judaizing Christians from within, as we have just seen. Conflict with Jews and occasionally with Gentiles during Paul's missionary journeys had led him into trouble with local Roman officials, and at Corinth and elsewhere he found himself in conflict with Christians who were making strange

New Testament readings relevant to this chapter are Revelation 12-18; I Peter 3:8-4:6; 4:12-5:11; Hebrews 6:4-8; 10:32-39; 11:29-40; 12:1-17; I and II Timothy; Titus; I and II John; Jude; II Peter; Ephesians.

interpretations of the gospel. Although the conflict with Judaism finally abated, that with the Roman government and with false teaching increased in intensity. These conflicts had a profound effect on the life and thought of the Christian community as it began to mature.

Conflict with the Roman Government

The Christian attitude toward the Roman government was fixed in the Christian tradition by a teaching attributed to Jesus. When the Pharisees and Herodians questioned Jesus about paying taxes to Rome (Mk. 12:13-17), Jesus is reported to have said, "Render to Caesar the things that are Caesar's, and to God the things that are God's." Jesus did not challenge the existence of the Roman government, yet he steadfastly refused to ally himself with the Jewish radicals who longed to revolt against Rome. So the logical answer to the question about taxes was simply to "pay them."

In part, Jesus' attitude can be explained on the grounds that, like most of the Pharisees, he believed that Israel's immediate destiny was distinctly religious rather than political. And to Jesus and the other Jews who refused to revolt, it was sheer common sense to recognize that Rome was providing the human institution of government, and that she obviously deserved taxes to carry on her operations.

But it is also clear that Jesus, like the moderate Pharisees, by no means looked upon Rome's authority as ultimate. Jesus said, "Render unto God the things that are God's." What God as Creator possessed was the earth and all its people, for he had a claim upon all creation as its Sovereign Lord. The day was coming when he would reveal that claim to all men in the final coming of his kingdom, when the earthly order of existence would be no more. All human beings and institutions were ultimately subject to God's will and God's judgment. Rome's power was real, but it was in no sense absolute. The Roman government was one of the temporary institutions that were to be recognized and accommodated as long as they did not claim what God alone could claim: absolute sovereignty and worship. This attitude toward Rome was not determined by political theory—with which no Palestinian Jew was concerned in Jesus' day—but by biblical tradition, theological perspective, and pure common sense.

This same view persisted in the early church. Paul, for example, advised the Roman Christians to accept the governing authorities (Rom. 13:1) and to pay taxes to whom they were due. He explicitly states that the authority of the state had been instituted by God for the purpose of executing judgment on the wrong-doer. Paul, like Jesus, could look to Jewish biblical tradition to find support for his position, for in Israel's past God had often used rulers, such as Cyrus the Persian, for his purposes. Paul looked upon the state, in so far as it maintained peace and order, as a servant of God. It was not the authority and judgment of the state, however, but the will of God that finally determined Christian obedience. This is implied in Paul's statement that Christians should be subject to Rome "for the sake of conscience" (Rom. 13:5).

The fact that the state existed by God's sufferance did not mean that the will of the state was always identical with God's will. It was a human institution, subject to demonic powers. And so Paul could write to the Corinthians that the rulers who had put Christ to death were instruments of the evil powers of this age (I Cor. 2:6). Paul believed that the Roman authorities, like all other human beings, would one day be called to account. Like Jesus, then, Paul accepted the authority of the state to execute law and order even though he acknowledged that it was only to God's ultimate will that Christians were responsible. In obeying that will, Paul found himself imprisoned over and over again, and finally executed.

Ostensibly, there was nothing in the church's attitude toward the state that could be cited as politically dangerous. What was it, then, that finally led to the conflict between them?

We have already seen in Paul's epistles and in Acts that Paul was often in trouble with the Roman government because his religious arguments with the Jews had a tendency to turn into wild riots. The charge against him was usually disturbance of the peace—an offence that was never tolerated by Rome. Since Roman officials looked upon Christianity as a sect of Judaism, and as such a fully recognized religion (*religio licita*), the questionings, arrests, and imprisonments of Christians were personal matters, and the charges against them were not religious but civil. It was probably the riots between Christians and Jews that led to the expulsion of the Jewish community from Rome under the emperor Claudius (A.D. 41-54). If Christians were actually involved in this action, it is certain that the emperor and his officials thought of them as Jews.

THE FIRST GREAT CRISIS

It was in the time of the emperor Nero (A.D. 54-68) that the first severe encounter between Christians and the Roman state took place. In July of A.D. 64, a fierce fire raged through Rome for six days, devastating large areas of the city. According to the Roman historian

Tacitus, there was a persistent report that Nero himself had been responsible for the conflagration. When Nero looked around for someone on whom to lay the blame, his attention fell on the Christian community—an indication that the Christians had already become unpopular enough with the people to be used as scapegoats. In his report, Tacitus tells us that they were convicted of the outrage not on the grounds of clear evidence, but on the grounds of "sullen hatred of the human race."

> First, Nero had self-acknowledged Christians arrested. Then, on their information, large numbers of others were condemned—not so much for incendiarism as for their anti-social tendencies. Their deaths were made farcical. Dressed in wild animals' skins, they were torn to pieces by dogs, or crucified, or made into torches to be ignited after dark as substitutes for daylight.[1]

There is a strong tradition in the ancient church that both Peter and Paul met their death at this time.

The persecution under Nero was limited to the Christians living in Rome; it did not extend to the provinces, and in no sense did it reflect

[1] Tacitus, *Annals*, XV, 40, 44. Translated by Michael Grant, *Tacitus: The Annals of Imperial Rome*, p. 354, London : Penguin, 1956.

The emperor Nero, under whose reign the first persecutions of Christians in Rome began.

The obelisk on the right, brought from Egypt by the emperor Caligula, originally stood on the dividing strip of the circus he built between the low hills of the Vatican. It was in this circus, according to strong tradition, that Peter was martyred under Nero.

a settled policy of the Roman government. Although it seems to have sprung from the irresponsible action of the unstable Nero, the whole action shows the general hostility that was felt toward the Christians and the relative ease with which this feeling could be transformed into hostile action. Apparently, the one charge that Nero felt might appeal

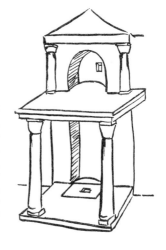

A sketch of the Martyrion, or shrine, erected over the probable burial place of Peter. The remains of this shrine, which date back to the beginning of the second century, were discovered directly below the high altar of St. Peter's Church in Rome. The fact that the shrine is in the midst of pagan tombs tends to confirm its authenticity, since it is unlikely that Christians would have invented a burial place for Peter on unholy ground.

to the populace in his laying the blame on the Christians was that of
odium humani generis (hatred of the human race). The vigorous monotheism and morality of Christianity, and its denial of all other deities
were offensive to this loose-living and polytheistic age, and Christianity's attack on idolatry was interpreted as an attack on those who
worshipped the gods. At this time, religious formalities had a way of
intruding into all sorts of activities—even civil festivals—so the Christians had cut themselves off from much of the daily routine of the
other Romans. Nero obviously capitalized on the popular resentment
against their stand-offishness to divert attention from himself. His attacks
on the Christians were so brutal that sensitive Romans like Tacitus were
offended.

Even if Nero believed that Christianity was a sect of Judaism, his
action against the Christians served to single it out to the world, for no
Jews were persecuted in the Neronic fury. Shortly after the persecutions in Rome, the Jewish revolt flared up in Jerusalem, and the break
between Jews and Christians grew sharper than ever. So it was merely
a matter of time before the question of Christianity's legal status would
arise.

THE ISSUES BECOME CLEAR

The next information we have of strife between the Christians
and the government is from the time of Domitian (A.D. 81-96). The
letter traditionally attributed to Clement of Rome, I Clement, begins
with a reference to the sudden and repeated misfortunes and calamities
that have befallen the church in Rome. The letter, which is usually
dated about A.D. 95, at the end of Domitian's reign, seems to refer to
troubles the Christians in Rome were having with the government. To
determine the nature of these troubles, we must look more closely at
Domitian's activities.

During the latter part of his reign, Domitian is known to have dealt
harshly with various individuals and groups of people.[2] In the year 89,
for example, he ordered all the philosophers and astrologers to leave
Rome, and in the year 95 he accused many persons of godlessness and
of loyalty to Jewish customs. The Roman consul, Flavius Clemens, was
accused of godlessness and was executed, and his wife, Flavia Domitilla,
who was Domitian's niece, was ordered into exile. The archaeological
discovery of an early Christian cemetery in Rome that was the gift of
a Flavia Domitilla has led some to believe that Clemens and Domitilla
themselves were Christians.

---

[2] See Robert M. Grant, *The Sword and the Cross*, pp. 55-60. New York: Macmillan, 1955.

The emperor Domitian, first of the Roman rulers to command that he be acclaimed as "Lord and God." It was probably during the latter part of his reign (81-96 A.D.) that the Book of Revelation was written as an encouragement to Christians to defy his demand for divine honours.

To account for Domitian's behaviour we must understand something of his ambitions.[3] He was the first of the Roman emperors to seek divine honours openly for himself, and he wanted to be known as the son of the Roman god Jupiter. He actually had his bust placed on the statue of Jupiter on the Capitol. He doted on elaborate processions, festivals, and games, and on each occasion he claimed for himself the place of central honour. He struck coins inscribed with the words of homage to himself, and was the first Roman emperor to demand that his subjects call him "Lord and God" (*Dominus et Deus*).

But it was not only in Rome that Domitian's honours were celebrated, for a sanctuary was built at Ephesus to house his statue, and the influence of the imperial cult undoubtedly spread throughout Asia Minor. At annual games and festivals Domitian was honoured through acclamation and probably through liturgical rites supervised by priests of the imperial cult.

It was inevitable that a man who made such extravagant claims for himself would offend certain people. Many of those who were accused

---

[3] We follow the excellent discussion in E. Stauffer, *Christ and the Caesars*, trans. by K. and R. Gregor Smith, pp. 147-191. London : SCM Press, 1955.

of "godlessness" and were executed or exiled had undoubtedly refused to acknowledge Domitian's claim to divinity. And surely those who were condemned for their Jewishness—among whom must have been many Christians—were attacked because they had refused to pay homage to Domitian as Lord and God. It appears that in Domitian's time Christians were still considered by the government to be a sect of the Jews, and since the Jews themselves were apparently abused because of their religious beliefs, the Christians probably were too. Nevertheless, the government does not seem to have taken any official position on the status of Christians. Although the records restrict Domitian's persecution to the city of Rome, the cult of emperor worship was also popular in Asia Minor, and it seems reasonable to assume that strife between the early church and the Roman state had begun to spring up there as well.

THE STORY BEHIND THE ISSUES

A long story, going back to the founding of the empire under Augustus, lay behind these claims of Domitian. When Augustus became the first *princeps*, one of his first moves had been to revitalize the traditional Roman religion. He assumed the title *pontifex maximus*, high priest of the official state religion, and laid the foundation for the worship of the reigning Julian house. Ancestor worship had its roots in ancient Roman history, but under Augustus there was a new tendency for the cult of the imperial family to take its place alongside other state cults. The deceased Julius Caesar was deified, and Augustus was hailed universally as Saviour and Son of God for his success in bringing peace to the world. Although claims to divinity were alien to traditional Roman thought, the poets Vergil and Horace acclaimed Augustus as a divine being, and hailed the new peace and harmony as the dawn of a golden age surpassing all others in glory. Throughout the provinces temples were built to Augustus and divine honours were heaped upon him.Even in the Jewish Temple at Jerusalem sacrificial prayers were regularly offered for the emperor, although Augustus himself provided the money for the sacrifices. People everywhere responded enthusiastically to Augustus' accomplishments.

This marked the beginning of the emperor's cult in which reverence for the Roman state as represented in its gods was brought into close relation with reverence for the emperor, who was not only the symbol of Roman empire but actually the one in whom that power resided. It was through this cult that Rome tried to create a religious bond of allegiance throughout the empire to match the political unity created by her vast system of law. Consequently, political loyalty as expressed

The Colosseum from the air. Built by Vespasian and Titus as an arena for great public spectacles, it seated more than 50,000 people. In the later years of the empire, many Christians were slain here by Roman gladiators and wild animals.

by obedience to the law gradually became inseparably bound to religious loyalty as expressed by participation in the imperial cult. In Rome, only the dead emperors received divine worship. But in the oriental provinces, where divine kingship had been accepted for centuries, divine honour was given to the living Caesar, and temples, priests, and sacrifices became a normal part of the cultic rites.

As we have seen, Domitian was the first living emperor to claim for himself the title Lord and God not only in the provinces but in Rome itself. And because the line of demarcation between political loyalty and reverence for the imperial family had by this time been effaced, Domitian could interpret as treason any refusal to recognize his claims against the state. He dramatically brought to its logical conclusion an assumption that had been present from the beginning: Rome's power was divine power, and was embodied in the emperor.

It is perfectly clear, then, why the Christians could not avoid a head-on clash with Rome. Once the test of loyalty to the state became a willingness to worship the emperor, rather than just a willingness to

M 333

pay taxes and obey the laws, then the Christians were in trouble, for they could not render unto Caesar what belonged only to God.

THE CHRISTIANS ON THEIR OWN

The first certain historical evidence we have of the showdown comes from the reign of Trajan (A.D. 98-117). It is preserved in a body of correspondence between Trajan and Pliny the Younger, who was Trajan's imperial legate in Pontus and Bithynia around A.D. 110. Pliny came into conflict with the Christians because Trajan had forbidden secret meetings of unapproved societies. The reason for this ban is clear: Rome was threatened with invasion from Parthia to the east, and Trajan could not have Asia Minor riddled by secret societies that might become wartime tools of political disruption. Since Pliny uses the term Christian in his correspondence, it is apparent that Christianity had become recognized as distinct from Judaism, and hence no longer enjoyed the status of *religio licita*.

Pliny, who had had no experience with this sort of thing, wrote to Trajan for information about how to examine and punish the Christians. By way of report, he outlined the procedure he had been following so far: First he asked the accused if they were Christians. If they said yes, he asked a second and third time, threatening them each time with punishment. If they persisted, he executed them. In dealing with those who had been accused by the townspeople, sometimes anonymously, of being Christians, he again asked whether the accusation was true. If the accused denied it, he demanded that they invoke the gods and worship the emperor's statue with incense and wine, and then curse Christ. Some of the accused said that though they had been Christians in the past they were not any longer. But they claimed that even when they were Christians they had done nothing more than meet together, sing hymns to Christ, bind themselves by an oath not to commit theft or robbery or adultery, not to break their word, and not to refuse to pay a debt. Beyond that they had simply participated in eating a harmless meal of harmless food.

Trajan replied that Pliny had taken the right course, and that no general rule or fixed form of action could be laid down. Christians were not to be sought out actively, but if they were accused they would have to be punished. If anyone denied that he was a Christian and agreed to worship the gods, he was to be pardoned even if he had been under suspicion. And certainly no one was to be charged anonymously.

It is perfectly clear from all this that Trajan's primary interest was political, and that, unlike Domitian, he was not making wild claims for his own divinity. But it is also clear that the Christians, whenever they were put to the test, would either have to renounce their faith or suffer punishment. To the man on the street, the Christian point of view must have been impossible to understand, for polytheists could not see how recognition of the state gods in any way threatened individual religious loyalties. But for the Christians there could be only one God and one Lord, who alone was the object of their worship. So they persisted in their refusal to worship the emperor, even though it meant being accused of treason. It was at this time, for example, that Ignatius, Bishop of Antioch, was arrested and taken to Rome for execution.

The Persecution Literature

Many of the New Testament writings reflect this tension and potential conflict between Christianity and the state. The author of Luke-Acts, for example, was in part motivated by a desire to defend the church against charges of disloyalty to Rome or of treasonable activity. And Paul's discussion of relations between church and state in his epistle to the Romans (13:1-7) may have been prompted by his uneasiness over the seething rebellion of the Jews either just before or after their open revolt in A.D. 66. We have already seen that certain interpolations in the Gospel narratives of Jesus' trial and execution tend to exonerate Pilate and condemn the Jews, partly in an attempt to show that Jesus was not a revolutionist. The Gospel of Mark, with its strong emphasis on Jesus' victory through suffering and death, may have been written in part to encourage Christians who had grown fearful under Nero's persecution. But three writings in particular reflect either actual conflict or a threat of conflict; these are Revelation, I Peter, and Hebrews.

THE EXTREMIST POSITION: REVELATION

A Christian prophet by the name of John once found himself stranded on a lonely, barren island called Patmos, in the Aegean Sea. According to later tradition, he had been banished as a political prisoner. In the book called Revelation,[4] which he wrote during his stay on Patmos, he has this to say to his readers: "I John, your brother, who share with you in Jesus the tribulation and the kingdom and the patient endurance, was on the island called Patmos on account of the word of God and the testimony of Jesus" (Rev. 1:9). The word "tribulation" implies that both John and the Christian communities in Asia Minor

---

[4] Revelation is discussed fully in Chapter 15.

to whom he was writing (1:11 ff.) had experienced persecution—his own as a result of his having borne faithful testimony to Jesus.

The central theme of Revelation is a call to Christians to stand firm in their faith even though they are threatened with suffering or death. John's message is cloaked in symbolic language, through which he portrays a great war going on in the heavenly places between the powers of evil (Satan) and the powers of good (God). In one vision, John describes a great dragon that appears in the heavens and threatens the life of a woman who is about to give birth to a child (Rev. 12:1-6). The dragon, whose power is revealed by the fact that his tail sweeps a third of the stars from the skies, seeks to devour the child, who is to rule all the nations with a rod of iron. Each of John's readers could recognize immediately that the child was Jesus Christ, whom the forces of evil (the dragon) had sought to destroy in the crucifixion. But the "child was caught up to God and to his throne" (Christ's resurrection and exaltation), and the woman (the church) fled into the wilderness (the world), where she was nourished by God.

The great war in heaven (Rev. 12:7-12) dramatically portrays God's decisive defeat of the dragon through Christ's death and resurrection. But although God's victory has been won in heaven, the dragon (Satan) has been cast down to the earth and continues to plague the woman and her offspring (the church). Those "who keep the commandments of God and bear testimony to Jesus" are the particular foes of the dragon (12:17).

In Revelation 13, John describes the battle that is being waged on earth. A beast with ten horns and seven heads rises out of the sea and is given the power and authority of the dragon. This beast is none other than Rome, who wages war as the chief agent of Satan. The people of the earth are deceived and worship the beast, saying, "Who is like the beast, and who can fight against it?" (13:4). The beast, aided by a second one, who exercises the authority of the first (13:12), makes war on the Christians and kills them. The second beast performs great signs, deceives men, inspires them to make an image of the first beast, and then slays those who will not worship the image.

Most scholars identify the first beast with Domitian, and the second with the priests of the imperial cult. The historical setting seems clear enough, in the light of our understanding of Domitian's ambitions and activities in Rome, and in the light of the spontaneous reaction of the provinces to his claims. The prophet John says that Christians in Pergamum, the centre of the imperial cult, live "where Satan's throne is," and that one of the brethren, Antipas, has already suffered martyrdom in this city (2:13). Against Domitian's claims to divinity, John reminds his readers that Jesus Christ is "the ruler of kings on earth" (1:5), and that Christians can bow their knee to the claims of no other.

John's position is uncompromising, in contrast to the usual attitude of Christians toward the Roman government. To him, Rome is no servant of God, but rather the embodiment of the devil himself. In the whole structure of the Roman empire he sees nothing but evil—it is doomed to fall even as Babylon fell (Rev. 17). John prophesies Rome's fall as one of the inevitable consequences of Christ's complete establishment of the kingdom throughout the earth. More clearly than any other early Christian, John foresaw with prophetic insight the inevitable showdown that must come between Rome and the church. Domitian had brought together the power of empire and the claim of personal divinity, and John recognized the inevitable conflict that such claims held in store for the church. The ultimate question was to become: Caesar or Christ? And long before the emperor Constantine recognized that loyalty to both could not exist side by side, John had prophetically defined the issues. Although his writing did not call for active revolt, it undoubtedly had a disturbing influence on the church, which up to that time had not identified Rome so closely with evil. John did not conceal his burning hatred for Rome, and his emphasis on the nearness of God's kingdom could very easily have incited the harassed Christians to take desperate action. At the end of the second century, Irenaeus referred to Revelation as a writing that had done harm to the Christian cause. But the prophet John was not concerned with the consequences of his message; his only concern was to strengthen Christians in their faithful resistance.

THE MODERATE POSITION:
I PETER AND HEBREWS

Not all the advice that was given to the Christians under the threat of oppression, however, was so inflammatory and irreconcilable as John's. The author of I Peter, for example, shows considerable moderation. This writing, which dates from the last half of the first century A.D., was sent to Christians in Asia Minor (Pontus, Galatia, Cappadocia, Asia, Bithynia; I Pet. 1:1) who were threatened by persecution.[5] The central part of the writing has to do with matters of Christian conduct (1:3–4:11), but the writer concludes with a strong appeal for Christians to stand fast in the face of a "fiery ordeal" that was coming upon them (4:12-19; 5:6-11). He urges them not to be

---

[5] For a discussion of authorship, date, and general content, see Chapter 14, pp. 433 ff.

surprised if as followers of Christ they are faced with suffering, for Christ himself had suffered. Although the "fiery ordeal" clearly refers to the threat of persecution, the author avoids any specific attack on Rome, such as we find in Revelation. He does speak of Rome as Babylon (5:13), and refers to the "devil" prowling around like a lion looking for someone to devour, which is certainly an allusion to Rome. But earlier in the writing he calls upon Christians to recognize the emperor and the government officials as supreme and worthy of honour (2:13-17).

The author of I Peter sees this period of suffering as a time of judgment for the church (4:17, "household of God"), during which the faith of Christians is being tested. He implies that those who persecute Christians (4:17, "those who do not obey the gospel") are also subject to judgment, and that God will be the judge. So Christians are to entrust their souls to God and be humble in the face of their persecutors (4:17-19; 5:6). Although he expects the end to come in "a little while" (5:10), he does not, as John does in Revelation, picture the conflict with Rome as the final battle, and in no sense tries to incite Christians to a hatred of Rome. Perhaps the author's approach can be accounted for in part by the fact that he was a presbyter (5:1, "elder") in the church, and felt a responsibility for helping Christians avoid unnecessary conflict with Rome.

The author of I Peter speaks of Christians as being reproached "for the name of Christ" and suffering "as a Christian" (4:14,16). There has been considerable debate over whether or not these words indicate that Christianity had already become recognized as a sect separate from Judaism. Scholars who interpret them in this way tend to date the writing during the time of Trajan. Others, however, interpret the phrases more loosely, pointing out that regardless of Rome's understanding of the relation of Christianity to Judaism any Christian who suffered persecution would feel that he was suffering in the "name of Christ" or "as a Christian." These scholars feel that the writing might very well refer to the situation under Domitian.

The interesting suggestion has been made that I Peter was written to the Christians in Asia Minor to correct the disturbing effects that Revelation had produced in that area. The author is just as earnest as John in insisting that Christians should endure suffering rather than yield to emperor worship, but he also states the traditional Christian position of loyalty and moderation toward Rome, as John does not. In any event, the position represented in I Peter was to characterize the second-century church, which went on trying to work out a way of co-exist-

ing with the empire. Most of the emperors, in fact, were as reluctant
to do battle as was the author of I Peter.

The same moderation is found in the third of the persecution documents—the Epistle to the Hebrews. Like I Peter, it contains the exhortation of a church leader to a community threatened by persecution
(6:4-8; 10:32-39). He warns his readers that they must hold fast to
their faith, since there is no hope of repentance if they abandon it in the
face of danger (6:4-8). There is good reason to believe that the writing
was sent to Rome in the time of Domitian,[6] and that the troubles confronting the Roman church were those referred to in I Clement, which
we have already mentioned. The author's reminder that the community
had endured struggle, public abuse, affliction, and plundering in the
past (10:32-34) may be a reference to the earlier persecution under
Nero. He calls upon his readers to find new courage in the steadfastness
of their predecessors, and not to throw away their confidence because
they are confronted with suffering.

There is no trace in Hebrews of the radical attitude toward Rome
that we find in Revelation. Like I Peter, Hebrews implies that suffering
must be expected by Christians, and that they are to accept it as God's
discipline (Heb. 12) rather than as an occasion for venomous hatred of
Rome or unseemly action. In due time, God will shake the very foundations of the heavens and the earth in the revelation of his kingdom
(12:26-28), but that time has not yet arrived. Until it has, Christians
must stand firm and leave the final judgment to God.

Through conflict to maturity

The conflict with the Roman state made a deep impression on
the life and thought of the early Christians, and provided a rigorous
test of the true faith of every member of the community. True, there
is no evidence that during the first or even the second century Rome
sought to eliminate Christianity outright. Nevertheless, over and over
again in the past the Christians had been charged as a threat to the well-
being of the state, and the same charge might be made against them at
any time in the future. Every Christian knew that he might find himself
under suspicion at any moment. Since the Christians made up a minority group, highly vulnerable to social ostracism and political disfavour,
anyone who chose to enter the church knew beforehand that he might
be called upon to suffer for his faith. This threat of action by the state
helped to bring the members of the community together into a closely

---

[6] For a discussion of date, authorship, and content see Chapter 14, pp. 415 ff.

knit group, and served as a test of strength and courage to those who sought to enter.

The very nature of the times meant that most Christians were serious in their intentions and well informed about their convictions. Through baptism, they entered into a way of life that they had to be willing to die for as well as live for. Obviously the death of Christ could not become an abstraction to Christians who were constantly faced with the possibility of dying with him. Faith and life were inseparably related, and the meaning of each was illumined by the other.

One of the important lessons that the Christians learned from the conflict with the state was the meaning of patience and humility. In a sense, this was a lesson they had to learn if they wanted to survive. But their patience was far more than a matter of expedience, for patience and suffering were deeply ingrained in the very structure of the church's thought and life. Christ had overcome the world through patient and humble submission to suffering, and the church was realizing in its own life this great truth that it proclaimed in its gospel. Long before the church arrived at mature theological thinking, it had matured in the discipline of patient suffering. The precedent of patient endurance established by the early Christians was one of their greatest contributions to the maturing church, and it contributed profoundly to the final triumph of the church over the empire in the fourth century.

The Conflict with False Teaching

Very early in the life of the church, the mission to the Gentiles had opened the door to hellenistic influences, as the message of Paul reveals; these influences became even more pronounced in the last half of the first century, when the Gentiles had begun to outnumber the Jews in the Christian community. The forces that led to discord within the community originated not so much in the traditional religions of Greece and Rome, however, as in the general religious movement called gnosticism (see p. 20). The impact of gnosticism on Christianity came not only through Jewish gnostic sects (for gnosticism had already influenced Judaism), but also through direct encounter with Gentile converts who had been affected by gnostic ways of thinking.

The principal threat of gnosticism was its radical dualism. According to the gnostic mythology the visible world was a mixture of light and darkness, spirit and matter, good and evil. The world had been created not by the true God who existed in the heavenly realm, unsullied by contact with the lower world, but by a lesser being who himself shared in the imperfections of the lower order. Between the high god and the lower world, there was a series of intermediate beings, the purest of whom were nearest the high god and farthest removed from the world of matter.

The gnostics believed that man was made up of two parts, flesh and spirit. The spirit, which was man's one point of potential contact with the higher world, was hopelessly imprisoned in the evil body of flesh. Not all men could escape this bondage. Some, the "spiritual," were predestined to everlasting felicity; others, the "fleshly," were predestined to everlasting imprisonment in the corrupt world. Some gnostics spoke of a third class of men who were predestined to an intermediate state of blessedness, though not as high as that of the spirituals.

According to the gnostic view, salvation from bondage in this material world could be won only through a redeemer sent by the high god. This redeemer was of the same nature as the high god, uncontaminated by the lower world of fleshly matter. By revealing knowledge of the high god and their own destiny, this redeemer could promise spiritual men eventual return to the heavenly realm from which their imprisoned spirits had once come.

Once the gnostic had been released by the redeemer from his imprisonment in the material world, he could show his freedom in one of two ways: He could demonstrate his superiority over flesh and matter by practising rigorous asceticism, and by mortifying his body through the denial of the senses—through dietary rules, sexual abstinence, refusal to marry, and rejection of the normal pleasures of life. Or he could show his freedom by means of excessive indulgence in sensual pleasure. Since he was already assured of emancipation, he could flaunt his freedom in indulgence (antinomianism—the tendency to deny the validity or necessity of moral law for those who have been "saved," especially as found in the Old Testament).

This was the sort of religious belief and practice then, that intruded itself into the Christian faith in the late first and early second centuries A.D. Naturally, the leaders of the church were quick to combat such false teaching.

THE CONFLICT LITERATURE

A number of the later New Testament writings show marked evidence of this struggle with false teaching—I and II Timothy, and Titus, for example. These writings, which are commonly called the Pastoral Epistles, were traditionally attributed to Paul (see p. 72). It is generally acknowledged today, however, that they were written later than the time of Paul, although they may contain fragmentary phrases from lost Pauline writings. The language and theology of these epistles show some similarity to Paul, but the differences are far more striking, as we shall see later. Above all, these writings reflect a concept of the church and the ministry that more nearly represents the situation at the end of the first century than at the time of Paul. A study of the outline of these books shows that they are really manuals composed by some church leader to aid in the development of rules and regulations at a time when the church was of necessity seeking to organize (see p. 363). But throughout, these writings show a deep concern for right teaching and the dangers of false teaching.

The author, clearly a great admirer of the apostle Paul, wrote in Paul's name not only because he believed that what he said fully accorded with Paul's thought, but also because he wanted the apostle's authority for his message. Traditionally, these writings were associated with Rome, for they were believed to have been written by Paul during his Roman imprisonment. If we discount the possibility that Paul wrote them, however, it seems likely that the author lived in Asia Minor, perhaps in Ephesus, where the type of false teaching that he combats is known to have emerged at an early date.

A second group of letters that shed light on the early church's struggle with false teaching is I, II, and III John, especially the first two. The authorship of these writings, along with that of the Gospel of John, was traditionally attributed to the apostle John, but they are now believed to have been written by a church leader in Asia Minor—again, perhaps, in Ephesus. Although they deal to some extent with other matters, they are primarily concerned with combating false teaching of the gnostic type, as is the Gospel of John (see Chapter 13).

Jude and II Peter (see p. 73) complete this group of conflict epistles. The former was written in the name of Jude, the brother of Jesus, but it is now denied that Jude was actually the author. Since the false teaching the author combats so vehemently seems to have reached an advanced stage, the historical setting of the epistle was probably the early second century. And, although the letter is addressed to Christians everywhere, it is likely that it was first written to the communities in Asia Minor.

II Peter is partly a word-for-word restatement of the Epistle of Jude, which obviously dates the writing later than Jude in the second century A.D. and eliminates the possibility that Peter himself composed it. The author, probably a resident of Asia Minor, attacked with even greater vehemence the same false teaching that had disturbed his predecessor, the author of Jude.

These are the New Testament writings, then, that provide us with our information for reconstructing the early period of the church's conflict with false teaching. It is not surprising that most if not all of them originated in Asia Minor, for it was from Asia Minor and neighbouring Syria that the first known gnostics of the Christian church emerged in the second century: Cerinthus from Syria and Asia Minor; Basilides from Syria; Marcion from Pontus; Menander from Syria; and Saturninus from Syria. Let us look at these writings more closely to see what evidence we can find of gnosticism's influence on the early church.

THE CONFLICT WITH DOCETISM

Shortly after the year 110 A.D., Ignatius, Bishop of Antioch, made a forced trip through Asia Minor on his way to Rome, where he was to die as a martyr. En route, he wrote letters to the churches in Ephesus, Magnesium, Tralles, and Smyrna, and one to Polycarp, the Bishop of Smyrna. These letters, which were written at the same time as or shortly after our New Testament conflict writings, provide us with invaluable historical information about the life of the churches in Asia Minor. One problem that seemed to be bothering Ignatius a great deal was a strange teaching about Jesus that was being circulated. He writes to the Smyrnaeans:

> For what does anyone profit me if he praise me but blaspheme my Lord and do not confess that he was clothed in the flesh? But he who says this has denied him absolutely and is clothed with a corpse. Now I have not thought right to put into writing their unbelieving names; but would that I might not even remember them, until they repent concerning the Passion, which is our resurrection.[7]

Apparently certain Christians refused to acknowledge that Jesus had been flesh and blood, and thereby denied his humanity. Those who held this view were called "docetists," a word derived from a Greek word meaning "appear" or "seem." The docetists claimed that Christ only *seemed* to be corporeal, but that he really was not. The docetists were gnostics, and they found it easy to accept this view because of the radical dualism that characterized gnostic thought. They regarded the material world as evil and alien to God, so it was inconceivable to them that Christ, who was a spiritual and heavenly redeemer, could have been associated with flesh in any real way. The gnostics tried to explain the relation between the heavenly Christ and

---

[7] Ignatius, Epistle to the Smyrnaeans, V, 2-3.

the man Jesus by saying that the spiritual Christ had descended upon the man Jesus at baptism, had used his body temporarily, and then had left him before the crucifixion. But he was in no sense to be identified with the earthly man.

Ignatius was understandably offended by this view of the suffering and death of Jesus. To deny the true humanity of Jesus meant to reject the reality of his sufferings, which Christians from the beginning had proclaimed as central to God's saving act.

In combating a similar teaching among the Trallians, Ignatius insists on the humanity of Jesus and its essential importance for salvation:

> Be deaf therefore when anyone speaks to you apart from Jesus Christ, who was of the family of David, and of Mary, who was truly born, both ate and drank, was truly persecuted under Pontius Pilate, was truly crucified and died in the sight of those in heaven and on earth and under the earth; who also was truly raised from the dead, when his Father raised him up, as in the same manner his Father shall raise up in Christ Jesus us who believe in him, without whom we have no true life.[8]

This is the same false teaching that is attacked in the Johannine epistles. In I John, for example, the author warns his readers that "Many false prophets have gone out into the world" (4:1). These men are spokesmen for the docetic teaching who have refused to acknowledge "that Jesus Christ has come in the flesh" (4:2). The warning appears again in II John: "For many deceivers have gone out into the world, men who will not acknowledge the coming of Jesus Christ in the flesh" (II John 7). Like Ignatius, the author of I John counters this false teaching by insisting on the humanity of Jesus. The very opening words of I John carry overtones of the conflict:

> That which was from the beginning, which we have heard, which we have seen with our eyes, which we have looked upon and touched with our hands, concerning the word of life—the life was made manifest, and we saw it, and testify to it, and proclaim to you the eternal life which was with the Father and was made manifest to us.

> —I JOHN 1:1-2

The author does not hesitate to affirm that the life of Jesus (the Word) was a manifestation of divine life, but he insists that this manifestation took place through the full human life of Jesus. He points out

---

[8] Ignatius, To the Trallians, IX; see also, To the Ephesians, VII; To the Magnesians, XI; To the Smyrnaeans, I-II.

that the false teaching threatens not only the Christians' understanding of the nature of Jesus Christ, but their understanding of the nature of God himself. For unless God had truly acted and revealed himself in history through the man Jesus Christ, then he was not really the kind of God the Christians had proclaimed him to be. John admonishes: "Any one who goes ahead and does not abide in the doctrine of Christ does not have God; he who abides in the doctrine of Christ has both the Father and the Son" (II John 9).

THE CONFLICT WITH ANTINOMIANISM

Although this conflict over the humanity of Jesus was basically theological, it had very practical implications. For just as the gnostics drew a sharp line between the spiritual Christ and the man Jesus, between God and the world, between the spiritual and the material, so they made a sharp division between individuals—between fleshly and spiritual men. The gnostics, of course, counted themselves among the spiritual men, and insisted that they possessed divine knowledge that had not been granted to others. In part, this knowledge consisted of bizarre interpretations of the Old Testament and the Jewish apocalyptic writings, in which they found support for their peculiar views. In part, it consisted of esoteric teachings that they claimed had been secretly handed down from Jesus through one or more of the twelve apostles. During the second century A.D., the gnostics actually produced a number of apocryphal writings to which they ascribed apostolic authorship. A portion of one of these writings, the Gospel of Peter, was discovered in Egypt in the nineteenth century. The attacks on "fables and genealogies" (I Tim. 1:4; Titus 3:9) and "old wives' tales" (I Tim. 4:7) that we find in the post-apostolic writings no doubt were prompted by gnostic writings of this sort.

In addition to producing apocryphal writings, the gnostics took great delight in interpreting the Old Testament in the light of their own peculiar mythologies, and they looked with disdain upon anyone who refused to accept or was unable to appreciate and understand their esoteric speculations. The author of I Timothy attacks their erroneous teaching regarding the "law" (I Tim. 1:3 ff.), claiming that they are wandering away from true doctrine and do not understand what they are saying. It was this highly subjective interpretation of the Law (Old Testament) and the traditional teaching of Jesus that enabled the gnostics to exercise unusual freedom from the ethical demands of the Christian faith (antinomianism).

The gnostics' attitude of superiority, and their tendency to deride others as second-class Christians, opened up sharp rifts in the fellowship of the Christian church. It was to counteract the gnostics' unsettling influence in the church in Asia Minor, for example, that the author of I John wrote: "If anyone says, 'I love God', and hates his brother, he is a liar" (4:20). And it is no accident that the author of II John, immediately after stressing the central importance of the commandment that Christians should love one another, writes: "For many deceivers have gone out into the world, men who will not acknowledge the coming of Jesus Christ in the flesh" (II John 7). The allusion to the gnostics is unmistakable here, and it is clear that the author was criticizing men whose allegedly superior knowledge had separated them from fellowship with other Christians—men who felt that Christians were bound together by esoteric knowledge rather than by love.

Here is how Ignatius describes the attitudes that this feeling of superiority produced in the gnostics:

> But mark those who have strange opinions concerning the grace of Jesus Christ which has come to us, and see how contrary they are to the mind of God. For love they have no care, none for the widow, none for the orphan, none for the distressed, none for the afflicted, none for the prisoner, or for him released from prison, none for the hungry or thirsty.[9]

The author of the Pastoral Epistles repeatedly states that love of the brethren is the very essence of the Christian life (I Tim. 1:5, 14; 2:15; 4:12; 6:11; II Tim. 1:13; 2:22; 3:1-10), and that where there is faith there must be love. Those who looked disdainfully on their fellow Christians were clearly flaunting the principal commandment given by Christ: love for God and for fellow men.

But some of the gnostics were not concerned with any law, even the law of love, for they felt that they had been freed from sin. Typically, the author of I John charges that if any man says he has no sin he makes God a liar (I John 1:10). Sometimes the gnostics carried this feeling of emancipation from the Law to great extremes, and the little epistle of Jude vigorously attacks Christians who live by their instincts like emotional animals (Jude 10). To show their superiority over fleshly desires, they turn their Christian fellowship meals into carousals; by following only their passions, they cut themselves off from other Christians who deny that freedom from the Law means freedom to indulge in sensual desires (Jude 14-19).

Earlier, in Corinth, Paul had encountered similar problems among Christians who completely misunderstood what he meant by free-

---

[9] Ignatius, To the Smyrnaeans, VI, 2.

dom from the Law. Now, in the second century A.D., the author of
II Peter was forced to combat gnostic Christians who were mis-
interpreting both Paul's teachings and the Old Testament to their
own detriment (II Pet. 3:15-16). The author warns that these gnostic
Christians, who deny the humanity of Christ, are false teachers (2:1).
They have decided that the interpretation of Old Testament scripture
is an individual matter, and then have gone on to use their interpretations to substantiate their mythologies (1:16). Believing themselves free
from bondage to the flesh and the Law, they indulge themselves in
revels, dissipation, and carousing (2:13-14). The author warns his
readers against making the mistake of following them (3:17), for although they promise freedom they are slaves of corruption. Christians
who claim to have escaped defilement through knowledge of Christ
and then become entangled in corruption are worse off than if they
had never believed (2:18-20): "For it would have been better for them
never to have known the way of righteousness than after knowing it
to turn back from the holy commandment delivered to them"(2:21).
Only judgment and destruction await the victims of this false teaching
(2:4-10).

What was at stake, then, in the struggle with these antinomian
gnostics was not only right understanding of the Christian faith but
the Christian way of life itself. The Christian concept of morality, and
the morale and unity of the community, were all threatened, and the
leaders of the church fought vigorously against this threat.

THE CONFLICT WITH ASCETICISM

Not all gnostic Christians flaunted their freedom from material
and sensual matters by extravagant indulgence, however. Some, by
despising the body and treating it with the ruthlessness that all evil
matter deserved, felt that a man could win a foretaste of the time when
his soul, freed from his body, ascended to its spiritual home. These
ascetic Christian gnostics abstained from certain foods and from marriage, both of which they believed were evidences of man's bondage
to the material world and sensual passions (I Tim. 4:1-10). Arguing
against such tendencies, the author of I Timothy insists that they are
a denial of the truth that the material world is good, because God
created it (4:4-5). Christians are not to discipline themselves by ascetic
practices but by godliness (4:7-9).

In combating the gnostics who advocate strict celibacy, the author
of I Timothy urges young women to marry (5:9-15), and bishops to
have children (3:2-5). The physical world and the realities of human
existence are not impure in themselves, for God made them good. It is

the ends to which a man puts them that determine whether his relation to them is pure or impure: "To the pure all things are pure" (Tit. 1:15).

So the author of the Pastorals struggles against the separation of God from his creation and his creatures. God is not only the Creator of the material world but the Saviour of all men (I Tim. 4:10; 2:3-4); God is not the special divinity of a few men who claim to possess superior knowledge and who exercise ascetic discipline over their physical appetites.

RESULTS OF THE CONFLICT

This conflict over false teaching drove the leaders of the church to scrutinize and reaffirm their fundamental beliefs. In the conflict writings, we find no evidence that the authors entered into any profound theological argumentation in response to the false teaching, however; rather, they seem content to reiterate what they believed to be the truth and to condemn the teachings they believed to be erroneous. They drew upon the truths that they regarded as central to traditional teaching: that God was the Creator of the material world; that God had sent Jesus Christ in the flesh to save all men; that salvation from sin meant living a life according to God's righteous will revealed in the life and words of Jesus Christ.

There is, however, a significant change in the meaning of certain key concepts in the conflict writings when compared, for example, with Paul's teaching. One of the principal changes is in the meaning of faith. For Paul, faith is primarily trust and commitment to God in response to the gospel and God's revelation in Jesus Christ. But in the Pastoral Epistles the emphasis shifts to faith as "sound doctrine" (I Tim. 1:10; Tit. 2:1), the "pattern of the sound words" (II Tim. 1:13), "the truth that has been entrusted to you" (II Tim. 1:14). All these phrases place the emphasis on faith as right understanding about God and Jesus Christ. To be "sound in the faith" (Tit. 1:13) is to think in accordance with right teaching. In this sense there is "a common faith" (Tit. 1:4), a body of truths that Christians share in common. Christians are able, then, "to contend for the faith which was once for all delivered to the saints" (Jude 3), and the church is understood to be the "pillar and bulwark of the truth" (I Tim. 3:15).

This emphasis on faith as sound doctrine includes not only right teaching about God but also right teaching about the ethical conduct of Christians. To hold the faith is to maintain a good conscience (I Tim. 1:19) by following the sound words of Jesus Christ and by obeying the teaching that is in accordance with godliness (I Tim. 6:3).

Here we have a decided shift from the concerns of the church leaders in the early days. During the first few decades of the church's existence —the apostolic age—there were no standards of orthodoxy to use in identifying false teaching. There were many disputes, of course, but this was a time of freedom of spirit and thought, and authority rested pretty much on the persuasiveness of each interpreter of the faith. Toward the end of the first century, however, the situation was changing rapidly.

Forced by the gnostic influence to review their basic beliefs, these later church leaders felt an increasingly urgent need to firm up not only the content of the faith but also the basis of authority for distinguishing truth from error. It was no mere academic problem or fondness for theological speculation that drove them to call on the community to contend for the true faith, for these were practical men. Rather, it was their awareness that the church was being threatened with disunity that led them to close the ranks against false teaching.

At the turn of the century, then, the church was in bitter conflict with forces which, if victorious, would have submerged the essential truth of the gospel under popular hellenistic modes of thought. The church leaders lacked the intellectual competence to deal with the deeper aspects of the problem, but they reasserted the fundamental truths of the *kerygma* and sought to organize the community into a semblance of unity in belief and ethical conduct against those who would pervert the gospel and subvert the common fellowship (see Chapter 12).

A Call to Unity:
The Epistle to the Ephesians

During the latter half of the first century, one of the most eloquent pleas for unity in the history of the church—the Epistle to the Ephesians—was written. The writing purports to be an epistle of Paul, and there is certainly a similarity in language and thought between Ephesians and Paul's epistles. But there is reason to doubt that Paul was really the author, for, in spite of the similarities, careful study shows that words are often used in Ephesians with different shades of meaning from what they have in the epistles of Paul. Furthermore, there are several significant terms in Ephesians that do not occur in Paul's writings. This alone would not be reason enough to doubt Paul's authorship, but there are other significant differences. For example, in Ephesians the conflict with Judaism lies in the past, whereas in the Pauline epistles it was still a burning issue. Also, the author of Ephesians speaks of the "apostles and prophets" as the foundation of the church (2:20), whereas Paul had said there could be no other foundation than Jesus Christ (I Cor. 3:5-17). Ephesians also refers to the "holy apostles" (3:5), a phrase that would be almost inconceivable for Paul to use in referring to himself.[10]

According to one theory, the author of Ephesians put together the first collection of Paul's letters, and then appended his own writing as an introduction.[11] Since Ephesians shows clear literary dependence on Paul's epistle to the Colossians, it has been suggested that the author was very familiar with it and used it as his model. Whatever we think of this suggestion, there can be no doubt that Paul did serve as the author's inspiration, and by writing in Paul's name he showed his profound gratitude and admiration for Paul's life and thought.

Ephesians is the most Pauline of all the later writings of the New Testament, for its emphasis on justification by faith, the in-dwelling of Christ, and the Spirit is highly reminiscent of Paul. (The fact that from the earliest times Ephesians was associated with the church in Asia Minor points to that region as the place where it was written.) Unlike the genuine Pauline epistles, which were written to specific churches to deal with specific problems, Ephesians, like some of the other later New Testament writings, appears to have been written for general reading by a number of churches. It is a general call to Christians to consider anew the unity of the Christian church.

THE UNITY IN CHRIST

Two great themes dominate the thought of Ephesians: the unity of all things in Christ, and the church as the visible symbol of that unity. The author unfolds these two themes (1:3-23) in a long benediction and thanksgiving, with many liturgical phrases. In Jesus Christ, God has revealed his purpose, which was present from the creation of the world; through Christ men were destined to be sons of God and in him all things were destined to find their ultimate unity. Although the author speaks of unity in cosmological terms ("things in heaven and on earth"), it is perfectly clear that he does not regard the disunity of the world as some tragic flaw in creation. Rather, the cause of the disunity is man's sin (1:7), which prevents

---

[10] For an excellent discussion of the authorship of Ephesians, see Francis Beare, *The Epistle to the Ephesians, Interpreters' Bible*, Vol. 10, pp. 597-601. New York: Abingdon-Cokesbury, 1953.

[11] See Edgar J. Goodspeed, *An Introduction to the New Testament*, pp. 222-239. Chicago: University of Chicago Press, 1937.

him from realizing the unity God has intended from the beginning. But those who have been laid hold upon by God through the Holy Spirit (1:13) have been enlightened; to them the power of God has been revealed in the death and resurrection of Christ. God has given Christ dominion over all powers in heaven and earth, evil or good, in order that now and forever all things may be subject to him. The evil powers that disunite the world have been overcome by Christ, who is the head of the church, the body in which this unity is made known to the world.

This unity that the author speaks about is not just a theoretical concept, however (2:1-21). In the first place, he reminds his readers that before they were Christians they were enslaved to the evil powers of this world and that through their sin they have contributed to the disunity of mankind. But through the mercy and love of God, Christ has released them from this dead past and has re-created them for good works (2:1-10). The sin that made them servants of the evil that disunites mankind has been marked out and declared dead through Christ. The grasp that evil powers had on their lives was broken.

In the second place, the author points out that through Christ the greatest division among men has been healed (2:11-21). The Gentiles, who were not the chosen people of God, who did not worship the true God, and who were separated in hostility from God's people (the Jews), have now been made God's people through Jesus Christ. A new household of God has been created through the preaching of the aₚostles and the Christian prophets. Men from all nations have been knit together into a community in which God dwells through his Spirit and in which all men are united in one great family.

THE WORLD MISSION OF THE CHURCH

Ephesians emphasizes that God has revealed through Christ the mystery of creation: in Christ, mankind is to find power to overcome its divisions and to be united in a new community, the church, which God has called into being. The church's sole reason for existence is to bear witness to the world to this purpose of God (2:9-13).

The author concludes his declaration of the unity of the church with one of the most beautiful prayers in the New Testament (3:14-21). This is a petition to God, who is the Father of all nations, that his Spirit may so prepare Christians in mind and heart that Christ may dwell in them, and that Christ's love may become the bond that unites them. In the doxology that concludes the prayer (3:20-21), the author acknowledges the power of God that is at work in Christ and in the church and is accomplishing his purposes in ways that surpass understanding. Above all, the author has in mind the unity of mankind that God is bringing about through Christ and the church.

But again, the author emphasizes that there must be tangible evidence of this unity in the church if the world is to believe its message (Eph. 4-6). The church testifies to the truth that its unity is founded upon its belief in one God who has been revealed through one Lord (Jesus Christ) and one Spirit (4:1-6). But God has given the church a ministry that is to lead it to an ever-increasing unity of thought and action (4:7-16). Through knowledge of Christ, it is to move toward ever greater maturity: it must overcome the strange teachings that disunite it (4:14) and make it appear foolish to the world, for it cannot proclaim unity while a conflict rages within. The church must grow strong in the bond of love—the true basis of its unity—as it fulfils its mission in the world (4:16).

In the final section, the author speaks of Christian unity in terms of specific ethical conduct (4:17–6:9). Since God, through Christ, has recreated Christians in newness of life (4:22-24), they are to put aside their former way of life, especially those vices that disrupt rather than unite the community (4:25-32). Since Christians are called to be "imitators of God," they must shun all immorality and walk in the light whereby God has revealed to them what is good and right (4:7-10). All their relationships—marriage, family, and social—must bear single testimony to the new life in Christ (5:21–6:9) that they share in common.[12]

The Epistle to the Ephesians does not reflect the polemical mood that we have found in other epistles, for the author was convinced that implicit in the Christian faith was a unity of thought and action that must find expression in the daily life of Christians in the world. As we have seen, he believed that the leaders of the church had been given the special task of leading Christians to a manifestation of this unity. We shall next see how the church advanced toward this unity by organizing its internal life.

---

[12] For a discussion of the search for a common ethic, see Chapter 14.

☀

CHAPTER TWELVE

THE
COMMUNITY ORGANIZES

From the very start, the Christian community took its unity for granted. Those who entered the church believed that they were becoming members of the new community that God had called into being through the Messiah Jesus, and together they awaited Christ's coming and the consummation of God's purposes. They felt they had a sure sign that they were the people of God: the presence of the Holy Spirit or the Spirit of Jesus Christ in their midst. They were living in the last days that had been proclaimed long ago by the prophets of Israel.

New Testament readings relevant to this chapter are I and II Timothy; Titus; I and II John; Revelation 4-5; I Clement; Didache; Ignatius' epistles to Ephesians, Philadelphians, Smyrnaeans, Magnesians, Trallians.

The missionary efforts of the new religious sect were remarkably successful, and whenever men responded to the Christian gospel they did so with spontaneity and enthusiasm. Throughout the Roman world, little communities of Christians sprang up, bound together by faith and hope. The feeling of unity among these communities was largely unpremeditated and spontaneous.

The Spontaneity of Early Organization

We find this same spontaneity in matters of organization—in the form of worship, for example. The first Christians were either Jews or converts from among Gentile "godfearers" who had been accustomed to worshipping in synagogues. So without giving the matter much thought, they simply took over the form of worship they had been used to. This consisted of prayers, the reading of the scriptures (Old Testament), the interpretation of the scriptures, and the singing of hymns and psalms. Obviously, the Christians chose to interpret the Old Testament in the light of the *kerygma* and the traditions regarding the life and teachings of Jesus, but in form the service was very much like that of the synagogues. The central rite of the church, the fellowship meal and Lord's Supper, was a continuation of the meal that had been inaugurated by Jesus himself, but even this was thought of as closely related to the Jewish Passover meal. Not that Christian worship was in no sense unique; but the early Christians did not worry themselves with complicated questions about either the form or meaning of their worship.

The same was true of the way in which the ministry of the apostolic church was organized. Naturally enough, the men who were looked to as leaders were the eleven disciples of Jesus (Judas was gone), who had been intimates of Jesus during his lifetime. It was they to whom the Risen Lord had first appeared (I Cor. 15:5), and it was they who had inaugurated the mission of the church.

In his epistles, we find Paul stressing the importance of the *charismatic* ministry (see p. 283), which arose as a spontaneous response to the action of the Spirit (I Cor. 12). First in this ministry there were the apostles, who had been given a direct commission by the Lord for their task. Then there were the prophets, who through the inspiration of the Spirit delivered prophecies to the churches. And last there were the teachers, who were charged with instructing converts on the Old Testament and the traditions of the church. The prophets and teachers were often itinerants who travelled from church to church. Paul also speaks of some who worked miracles, some who healed, some who spoke in tongues, and some who interpreted. Although there were many varieties of service, all were the gift of the same Spirit, and all emerged spontaneously within the church under the impetus of the Spirit. As Paul speaks of the ministry of his day, then, we get a picture of a very loose organization.

True, Paul does mention "governments" as one of the charismatic ministries, no doubt in reference to members of local congregations who handled administrative details and served as leaders of community meetings. Only in his letter to the Philippians does Paul give us a title for these administrators—there he calls them "bishops and deacons" (Phil. 1:1). The word "bishop," which comes from the Greek word *episcopos*, means primarily "overseer"; [1] the word "deacon," which comes from the Greek word *diakonos* (see p. 193), means "servant." The deacons, then, assisted the bishops in their work. Acts reports that Paul appointed "elders" in the churches of Asia Minor; this term is a translation of the Greek word *presbuteros* (English, presbyter). As we will see later, it was probably used as an alternate title for bishop, and the presbyter himself probably had the same functions as the bishop. It is likely that all these offices were present in most of the Pauline churches, and that the men who filled them had shown themselves, in one way or another, to be peculiarly endowed with the Spirit. In any event, although these offices seem to have been more or less permanent, and although their functions seem to have included some degree of administration, we can still surmise that the organization of the early church was very loose.

Drawing the Lines of the Ministry

This loose organization seems to have been satisfactory enough in meeting the needs of the early communities, and certainly the church showed remarkable cohesion and rapid growth in spite of the forces that threatened its unity. But the post-apostolic period brought changes that created a drastically new situation. By A.D. 70, the twelve apostles and Paul, who from the beginning had exercised unusual authority throughout the churches, were probably all dead. We have already seen Paul's influence in the churches he founded, and there can be no question that apostolic authority was acknowledged in all the churches,

---

[1] A more detailed discussion of the office of bishop will be given later in this chapter.

even though at times they argued about which apostle's authority was to prevail.

After the passing of the apostles, more and more second- and third-generation Christians found their way into the community, and their ardour was not always so strong as that of their predecessors. For one thing, the intense expectation of the imminent coming of the Lord was beginning to diminish. Although the hope of his coming had by no means been lost, the feeling that it was near at hand had become less intense, and as the years passed the coming of the Lord tended to recede further and further into the future. At times of stress and suffering, of course, like the period during which the book of Revelation was written, the coals of expectancy were fanned to white heat. But there was a growing feeling that things were probably going to continue pretty much as they were, at least for a time. Since the church was apparently to be in the world for an indefinite period of time, then, there was an increasing need to recognize and adjust to historical facts.

The increasing predominance of Gentiles in the church—both among the community members and the leaders—led to another new situation, for no longer could the strong influence of Jewish ethics and theology be presupposed, as it had been in the early years. The church was faced with the necessity of almost completely re-indoctrinating converts who came into the community with an outlook on God and the world, on good and evil, that was quite alien to the Jewish-Christian heritage. Some of the new converts even tried to force erroneous teaching on the Christian church, and the question of discipline became critical in the post-apostolic period.

These new conditions pointed clearly to one fact: The loosely knit organization of the apostolic age had become obsolete. Now the post-apostolic church began to move, with a certain spontaneity, to cope with the new problems that had arisen. Not that the Christians of that day were conscious of departing from established practices, however, for, as we shall see, they believed they were following the lines that had been set down from the beginning. But to historians of the twentieth century it is perfectly clear that new paths were being broken.

The later writings of the New Testament provide ample evidence of the development that was taking place. We have an excellent example in I John, whose author was deeply exercised over certain prophets who he believed were disrupting the life of the churches to which he sent his letter. He calls upon his readers to "test the spirits to see whether they are of God" (I John 4:1), and urges them to "test" the prophets' claim that they were speaking under the influence and in the name of the Holy Spirit. One of the main tests he suggests is this:

Do they or do they not acknowledge that Christ came in the flesh? Now a test of this sort has certain implications. For one thing, it implies that there must be standards for testing those who claim a charismatic ministry, and also that there must be someone with the authority to set up or approve such standards. Further, although the author does not specifically deny the validity of the prophetic office, he implies that it should not be left free from rigorous examination.

The author of I John warns that "many false prophets have gone out into the world" (I John 4:1). The serious offences that these false prophets committed indicate how easy it was to use the charismatic ministry to promulgate strange teachings. And they committed a good many less serious offences as well. The author of the *Didache*, for example, warns his readers that "no prophet who orders a meal in a spirit shall eat of it." [2] From the beginning, the Christian churches had received wandering prophets warmly and had provided them with food and lodging, but now false prophets were abusing this Christian hospitality. So when a prophet orders a meal "in a spirit," says the *Didache*, the time has come to draw the line. The writing adds that a true prophet is known by his behaviour, the behaviour of the Lord. And even though a prophet teaches the truth, if he does not do what he teaches he is a false prophet. On the whole, the *Didache* still holds the prophetic office in high esteem, but the fact that it formulates specific tests indicates that the office was being abused and that restraints were deemed necessary. Clearly, the charismatic ministry was in danger of degenerating, and norms were badly needed for its control.

The Movement Toward Regularization

So long as the apostles were still living, they provided a ready court of appeal for problems confronting the church, and members of the community expected them to formulate the important policies for the Christian mission. The Christians were confident that the apostles were in possession of the tradition that had been delivered to them by Jesus Christ. Paul himself, though often at odds with the apostles in Jerusalem, insisted that he was faithful to this tradition. [3] From the beginning, then, the office of the apostle and the tradition of the church were intimately related. The apostle was the one who had received the tradition from the Lord and then transmitted it faithfully to the community. In fact, the major debate between Paul and the apostles Peter,

---

[2] *Didache* 11:9. See Chapter 2, p. 75, for a discussion of the *Didache*.
[3] See Chapter 2, p. 51, for the meaning of tradition.

James, and John centred on whether or not Paul's teaching was true to the tradition.

Understandably enough, in the post-apostolic period there was a growing tendency to idealize the authority of the twelve apostles—a tendency that was not altogether unfounded, since the apostles exercised a good bit of control over the church in their own day. We find evidence of this trend in the Synoptic Gospels, where the title, "the Twelve," is already used to refer to the apostles. This title reflects the honour in which these men were held in the church, and also shows that the apostolic office was tending to be limited to these twelve. Paul, in his epistles, however, does not limit the office to the twelve, for he obviously affirms his own apostleship and mentions several others (for example, in Rom. 16:7). Moreover, the book of Acts makes it clear that the other apostles considered Barnabas as an apostle too. The mention of "apostles" in the *Didache* must mean that there were Christians known as apostles about the turn of the first century, at least in the region where the writing was first circulated (*Didache* 11:3). But the fact that the *Didache* provides a test for apostles, and speaks of them in the same breath with prophets, suggests that a great gap has opened between these latter-day "apostles" and the original twelve. Indeed, the full title of the *Didache*, "The Teaching of the Twelve Apostles," which it purports to be, shows the superior esteem in which the twelve were still held. So it is likely that the "apostles" mentioned in the *Didache* were really missionaries, although the title had already fallen from general use in most of the churches, except in referring to the Twelve and Paul. In the book of Revelation, the prophet John reveals the level to which the church had elevated the original apostles when he describes the heavenly city, which has twelve foundations "and on them the twelve names of the twelve apostles of the Lamb" (Rev. 21:14).

One of the most significant witnesses to the growing authority of the twelve apostles is found in Matthew's version of Peter's confession at Caesarea Philippi. Here it is reported that after Peter's confession of Jesus' Messiahship, Jesus said to him: "And I tell you, you are Peter, and on this rock I will build my church, and the powers of death shall not prevail against it. I will give you the keys of the kingdom of heaven, and whatever you bind on earth shall be bound in heaven, and whatever you loose on earth shall be loosed in heaven" (Mt. 16:18-20). Many scholars feel that this passage, as it stands, represents an interpretation by the church at a fairly late date, by which time Peter's authority was held in high esteem. Whatever its origin, to the post-apostolic church this tradition would have been valued highly as a testimony to the authority, not only of Peter, but of all the twelve apostles whom he represented. When we remember that by the turn of the century the Gospel of Matthew was rapidly becoming the favourite Gospel among the churches, we can be sure that this passage played a major role in further enhancing the authority of the twelve.

So the real question confronting the post-apostolic church was this: Who were the rightful successors to the apostles? This question was never actually asked, however, since in the very process of development the church found an office ready at hand that assumed the privilege and responsibility of the apostles. This was the office of presbyter.

The Acts account of the important council held in Jerusalem mentions that the "apostles and elders were gathered together" (Acts 15:6), and, in another place, that on Paul's missionary journeys he appointed "elders" (presbyters) from among the permanent residents of the local churches. When the book of Acts was written, the office of presbyter had become well established throughout the church, but that does not necessarily mean that wherever the term occurs the author is reading back into past history conditions prevailing in his own time. In fact, the office of presbyter in the Christian community has its antecedents in the organization of the synagogues, where a body of elders—older, respected members of the community—were responsible for the business affairs of the community and the exercise of discipline in matters regarding the Law. In the Christian community, the presbyters represented the local churches in negotiations with governmental authorities, and were probably appointed to office through the laying on of hands. It was to these leaders of the local churches that the book of Acts refers, not only in the Jerusalem church but in the Pauline churches as well. Paul himself refers to the presbyters in I Thessalonians, when he calls upon his readers to "respect those who labour among you and are over you in the Lord and admonish you" (5:12). Here it would seem that the presbyters were not only responsible for the general administration of church affairs but also were involved in the work of preaching, teaching, and officiating in the worship of the church.

It is only when we turn to the later literature of the New Testament, however, that we begin to get a clear picture of the role of the presbyters. The author of II and III John, for example, specifically refers to himself as a presbyter, and it is reasonably certain that I John was also the work of a presbyter. In each writing, the unknown author assumes the authority to warn and admonish his readers. And the author of I Peter writes as one presbyter to others, urging them to "tend the flock of God that is your charge, not by constraint but willingly, not for shameful gain but eagerly, not as domineering over those in your charge but being examples to the flock" (I Pet. 5:2-3). As we have seen, the Johannine epistles have traditionally been connected with the churches in Asia Minor, and the author of I Peter definitely addresses his writing to this same area (I Pet. 1:1). By this time then (probably about the year 95), the presbyters must have assumed a very important role in the region, and their importance in many of the visions of Revelation further substantiates their increasing prominence.[4] Here they appear as a permanent fixture in the heavenly scenes, an indication of the esteem in which they were held by the author and the churches to which he wrote.

A disturbance in the church at Corinth about A.D. 95 brought forth a letter, *I Clement,* from the church at Rome that sheds valuable light on the office of presbyter at this time. According to tradition, the author of this letter was Clement, a leader in the church at Rome, who reproached the Corinthian church because "on account of one or two persons the stedfast and ancient church of the Corinthians is being disloyal to the presbyters." [5] Apparently the church at Corinth, at the instigation of a few members, had ousted certain presbyters from their office, and Clement calls on those who were responsible to "submit to the presbyters, and receive the correction of repentance, bending the knees of your hearts" (I Clem. 57:1). The arguments that Clement uses are very illuminating:

> The Apostles received the Gospel for us from the Lord Jesus Christ, Jesus the Christ was sent from God. The Christ therefore is from God and the Apostles from the Christ. In both ways, then, they were in accordance with the appointed order of God's will. Having therefore received their commands, and being fully assured by the resurrection of our Lord Jesus Christ, and with faith confirmed by the word of God, they went forth in the assurance of the Holy Spirit preaching the good news that the Kingdom of God is coming. They preached from district to district, and from city to city, and they appointed their first converts testing them by the Spirit, to be bishops and deacons of the future believers.
>
> —I CLEMENT 42:1-4

Later on, we shall see that Clement uses the titles bishop and presbyter interchangeably in his epistle, and that the deacons were apparently

---

[4] Rev. 4:4, 10; 5:5, 6, 8, 11, 14; etc. We have seen in Chapter 11 that Revelation was written to churches in Asia Minor.

[5] I Clement 47:6. For a discussion of I Clement, see Chapter 2, p. 75.

assistants to the presbyters. Clement proceeds to establish the validity of the office of presbyter-bishop on the grounds that the first to hold the office had been appointed by the apostles themselves, and that a direct line reaches from God through Christ to the apostles and hence to each presbyter-bishop. So the appointment of presbyter-bishops is in accordance with the will of God. Again he reasons:

> Our Apostles also knew through our Lord Jesus Christ that there would be strife for the title of bishop. For this cause, therefore, since they had received perfect foreknowledge, they appointed those who have been already mentioned, and afterwards added the codicil that if they should fall asleep, other approved men should succeed to their ministry. We consider therefore that it is not just to remove from their ministry those who were appointed by them, or later on by other eminent men, with the consent of the whole church, and have ministered to the flock of Christ without blame, humbly, peaceably, and disinterestedly, and for many years have received a universally favourable testimony. For our sin is not small, if we eject from the episcopate those who have blamelessly and holily offered its sacrifices. Blessed are those Presbyters who finished their course before now, and have obtained a fruitful and perfect release in the ripeness of completed work, for they have now no fear that any shall move them from the place appointed to them. For we see that in spite of their good service you have removed some from the ministry which they fulfilled blamelessly.
>
> —I CLEMENT 44:1-6

Here Clement moves his argument forward another step: It was because the apostles had foreseen conflict that they appointed the first presbyters. And these first presbyters in turn appointed other presbyters to succeed them with the consent of the church. So it is a sin to eject presbyters who have blamelessly performed their duties. By regarding the presbyters as the appointed successors of the apostles, Clement makes their authority stronger than ever.

By the time Clement wrote (A.D. 95), the presbyters in the church at Rome were probably already regarded as successors of the apostles by virtue of their having been appointed in an endless succession from the apostles themselves. Clement does mention that each of the appointments was accompanied by a "testing by the Spirit" and the consent of the church, but it is perfectly clear that to him the all-important test was whether or not they had been duly appointed by other presbyters who in turn had been duly appointed by the apostles. The fact that he had to go to such lengths to persuade the Corinthians of the validity of this tradition suggests that it had not been completely accepted by the church there. This resistance to growing authority and discipline in Corinth indicates that not all the churches moved at the same speed toward regularizing ministerial authority.

Clement's argument seems to limit the charismatic conception of the ministry, for the presbyters have obviously assumed a position of authority and influence beyond that of any of the older orders, especially the prophets. Clement clearly implies that the presbyters are the ministers who officiate at the rites of worship (I Clem. 40:1-5), and that only those who have been duly appointed possess the authority to do so. Since Clement writes in the name of the church of Rome, and since later Christian literature suggests that his epistle helped settle the disturbance at Corinth, it seems reasonable to assume that the general outlook of both the churches was probably about the same at the turn of the first century A.D.

Clearly, the church was witnessing the gradual passing of the charismatic ministry as it had been known earlier in the century. But not everyone was pleased to see it go, as we can infer from this instruction in the *Didache* (15:1-2):

> Appoint therefore for yourselves bishops and deacons worthy of the Lord, meek men, and not lovers of money, and truthful and approved, for they also minister to you the ministry of the prophets and teachers. Therefore do not despise them, for they are your honourable men together with the prophets and teachers.

This passage states that the presbyter-bishops and deacons are taking over the functions of the prophets and teachers, but its tone is downright apologetic on behalf of these officials. It reflects the respect that some Christians still had for the older charismatic offices of prophet and teacher.

As time passed, however, the presbyters came to be accepted throughout the church as the rightful heirs to the apostles. Not all the Christian communities arrived at this conclusion simultaneously, or along the same path, but rather general agreement seems to have been reached by the end of the first century A.D. As the recognized successors of the apostles, the presbyters were becoming the guardians of the Christian teaching and tradition of which the apostles had been the first custodians.

One further step was taken in the development of the ministry in the post-apostolic period. In some of the communities, one of the presbyters began to emerge as head of the college of presbyters, and as head of the local church itself. This leader came to be known as *episcopos,* or bishop, to distinguish his office from that of presbyter.

The distinction is clearly indicated in the Pastoral Epistles (I and II Tim., Titus), where the author delineates the responsibilities and obligations of the ministry. I Timothy, for example, deals with the duties and qualifications for the offices of bishop, presbyter, and deacon (I Tim. 3:1-13; 5:17-22), and the author, in the name of Paul, apparently intends to set up Timothy and Titus as "types" of the perfect church leader. As a bishop, Timothy is portrayed as having both the obligation and the authority to exercise leadership. He is to charge certain people to desist from heterodox and speculative teaching (I Tim. 1:3 ff.); he is to place a whole series of instructions before the church (I Tim. 4:6); he is to command and teach (I Tim. 4:11); and he is to guard what has been entrusted to him—that is, the faith conceived in terms of a body of accepted doctrine (I Tim. 6:20). The fact that Timothy is to preach and teach and read the scriptures indicates that he is to conduct public worship and supervise the instruction of new converts. But above all he is to "entrust to faithful men" what he has heard from Paul (II Tim. 2:2). Since in the author's mind Paul was the representative of the apostles, this is a plea to the bishop to make sure that the tradition of the apostles is safeguarded.

This organization, in which one man, the bishop, serves as the head of the church, is called the *monarchical episcopacy*. To explain just how the monarchical episcopacy emerged is impossible, for we simply do not know enough about the events of the time. Some scholars contend that the office of bishop began to be distinguished from the office of presbyter at a very early date in some of the churches, although the evidence of the New Testament indicates that the distinction came later. It has been said in jest that at the end of the apostolic age the church was like a locomotive going into a dark tunnel and that it emerged in the post-apostolic period with a bishop on its cow-catcher. All we can say with certainty is that at some point one of the presbyters rose to the position of "president" or representative of his colleagues, and to distinguish his office from the rest of the presbyters he was given the title of bishop.

As we have seen, the monarchical episcopacy did not emerge in all the churches at the same time. Apparently it already existed in the churches addressed in the Pastoral Epistles, and in the epistles of Ignatius it is clear that Ignatius is the monarchical bishop of Antioch. Moreover, Ignatius addresses other bishops by name in some of the churches of Asia Minor to which he writes: Damas in Magnesia, Polybius in Tralles, Polycarp in Smyrna, and Onesimus in Ephesus. He implies that there is a bishop in Philadelphia, but he fails to mention the bishop in either Rome or Philippi. This seeming omission may very well mean that the monarchical episcopacy had not yet emerged in these two cities at this time (A.D. 110).

It is in these letters of Ignatius that we find the monarchical episcopacy in its most advanced state. To understand Ignatius' earnest pleas to the churches to recognize the authority of the bishop, we must remember that it was at this time that the battle against false teaching was disrupting the unity of the church. Since to Ignatius the church is a fellowship joined together by faith in Christ in a perfect unity of love and obedience, any members who promulgate or accept false teaching or withdraw from fellowship with the community are a threat to the church's unity. The churches were faced with the practical problem of how to know God's will, and it is in terms of this problem that Ignatius deals with the role of the bishop. Just as Jesus Christ is the will of the Father, so the bishop is the will of Christ (Ephesians 3:2); and Christians are to respect the will of the bishop just as Christ follows the will of the Father (Smyrnaeans 8:1). So to deceive the bishop is to deceive God (Magnesians 3:2), and to belong to God and Jesus Christ means being in agreement with the bishop (Philadelphians 3:2).

When Ignatius seeks to deal concretely with what is meant by unity of faith, he speaks in terms of the teachings and ordinances of the Lord and the apostles (Magnesians 13:1; Trallians 7:1-2)—in other words, in terms of the apostolic tradition. It is because the bishop is the custodian of the traditions that he is able to fulfil the will of Christ and lead his people into obedience to God. And it is within the context of this plea for the unity of the church and for faithfulness to the tradition that Ignatius stresses the authority of the bishop.

Ignatius regards the office of bishop as closely related to the offices of the presbyter and the deacon. For example, he writes to the Trallians to "submit yourselves to the bishop as to the commandment, and likewise to the presbytery" (Trallians 13:2), and admonishes them that "whoever does anything apart from the bishop and the presbytery and the deacons is not pure in conscience" (Trallians 7:2). He goes so far as to say that where there are no deacons and presbyters there is no church (Trallians 3:1), and warns the Magnesians to do nothing without the approval of the bishop and presbyters (Magnesians 7:1). This warning was prompted by Ignatius' knowledge that some of the false teachers were welcoming Christians into separate religious gatherings of their own—a danger that is mentioned frequently throughout his letters. Scholars differ on whether these false teachers were Christians, or non-Christians who had some sort of appeal for certain members of the community. In any event, Ignatius argues that just as Jesus Christ in unity with God's will once worked through the apostles, so now he is working through the bishops and presbyters, the successors of the apostles. When they are in doubt about the truth, Christians are to go to legitimate ministers of the church for guidance; and when they worship, their services must be presided over by duly constituted officers.

The picture of the ministry that Ignatius gives us was not true of every Christian church, of course—in fact, his lengthy arguments imply that not even the communities to which he wrote agreed with him completely. Otherwise, there would have been no point in his arguing. But his position surely represents the pattern of organization that was gradually becoming dominant in the churches of Syria and Asia Minor. Even though the monarchical episcopacy had not yet been instituted in all the churches, the authority of the presbyters—and of the bishops in the churches that had them—was certainly gaining increasing respect. The threefold ministry of bishops, presbyters, and deacons was well on the way to recognition, and all the functions of the ministry—preaching, teaching, administration, and conduct of worship—were being relegated to these officers in more and more churches as time passed. We can see, then, that a well-organized system of leadership was being developed, even though there was still no universally accepted rationale for its function and authority.

Expanding Responsibilities of the Ministry

Earlier in this chapter, we mentioned some of the changing conditions that speeded up the process of organizing the ministry of the church, and observed that these changes brought with them the danger that the meaning of the church's faith and message would be misinterpreted. Over and over again, pleas for recognition of the ministry's authority were based on the claim that the ministers were the true custodians of "right teaching" and the guardians of the church's unity. But there were other forces at work that hastened the development of a more formal organization. From the very beginning, the church had assumed certain responsibilities for its members, but when it began its rapid expansion in the post-apostolic age it found that it could no longer carry them out without better organization. These responsibilities had emerged from teachings that went back to Jesus himself. At the heart of these teachings were those dealing with the love and care of the brethren, and in earlier chapters we saw that the earliest Jewish Christian communities and the Pauline churches took seriously the obliga-

N

tion of caring for the less fortunate brethren. The post-apostolic church did not neglect this practice.

In I Timothy, for example, there is a long section dealing with the care of widows (I Tim. 5:3 ff.). The book of James defines pure religion as caring for orphans and widows (James 1:27), and in the Shepherd of Hermas care for orphans and widows is a cardinal virtue.[6] Cornelius, a bishop of Rome late in the second century A.D., reported that the Roman church was supporting no less than 1500 widows and poor people. There can be no doubt that even in the late first century the number of widows and needy persons in the community was always large.

A prayer incorporated in I Clement reveals how keenly the church felt its responsibilities:

> We beseech thee, Master, to be our "help and succour." Save those of us who are in affliction, have mercy on the lowly, raise the fallen, show thyself to those in need, heal the sick, turn again the wanderers of thy people, feed the hungry, ransom our prisoners, raise up the weak, comfort the faint-hearted.
>
> —I CLEMENT 59:4 ff.

For Christians to have prayed in this way without trying to do something themselves to meet these needs would have been contrary to the whole purpose of the early church. About a hundred years after I Clement was written, a Carthaginian Christian theologian, Tertullian, recorded this description of Christian practices:

> Each man deposits a small amount on a certain day of the month or whenever he wishes, and only on condition that he is willing and able to do so. No one is forced; each makes his contribution voluntarily. These are, so to speak, the deposits of piety. The money therefrom is spent not for banquets or drinking parties or good-for-nothing eating houses, but for the support and burial of the poor, for children who are without their parents and means of subsistence, for aged men who are confined to the house; likewise, for shipwrecked sailors, and for any in the mines, on islands or in prisons. Provided only it be for the sake of fellowship with God, they become entitled to loving and protective care for their confession. The practice of such a special love brands us in the eyes of some. "See," they say, "how they love one another"; (for they hate one another), "and how ready they are to die for each other." [7]

---

[6] Shepherd of Hermas, Mandate 8, 10.

[7] Tertullian, *Apology*, ch. 39, trans. R. Arbesmann, *The Fathers of the Church*, Vol. 10, pp. 98-99. New York: Fathers of the Church, Inc., 1950.

The practice of voluntary giving to which Tertullian refers was nothing new, for from the very beginning the church had cared for its sick, aged, poor, and disabled in this way.

In the first century, Christians had already begun to be jailed as a result of their belief, and others were imprisoned because of debts that they were too poor to pay off. The Epistle to the Hebrews contains this exhortation: "Remember those who are in prison, as though in prison with them; and those who are ill-treated, since you are also in the body" (Heb. 13:3). The church assumed responsibility for visiting prisoners, for providing them with food, and for trying to get them released. It also took steps to aid Christians in disaster areas. In the book of Acts, for example, we are told that money was sent from Antioch to help the Jerusalem church at a time of famine. The church also tried to help unemployed members to find jobs. In the *Didache* we have instructions on how to receive fellow Christians arriving from other cities: "And if he wishes to settle among you and has a craft, provide for him according to your understanding, so that no man shall live among you in idleness because he is a Christian" (12:3-4). Finally, each local church was obliged to provide hospitality to fellow Christians travelling through the city. Again, the Epistle to the Hebrews exhorts: "Do not neglect to show hospitality to strangers, for thereby some have entertained angels unawares" (Heb. 13:2). And in I Clement the Corinthian church is commended for its generous hospitality to strangers.[8]

As the church grew in size, the problem of carrying out all these responsibilities increased proportionately. The bishop, where there was one, and the presbyters no doubt found themselves responsible for overseeing these activities, although the deacons probably had more to do with actually carrying them out. Individual Christians continued their own private works of charity, of course, but by the end of the first century A.D. the responsibilities had often grown too great to be met piecemeal. Large sums of money were involved in carrying out these duties, and we find that the presbyters were not always above reproach. In I Peter, for example, the presbyters are warned to tend the flock "not for shameful gain" (I Pet. 5:2). Nor should bishops and deacons be greedy (I Tim. 3:8; Titus 1:7).

In general, however, the men who filled the church offices were dependable and faithful. We have no evidence that they were profound thinkers, but they were loyal to Christ and to what they believed to

---

[8] For a full discussion of the charity of the early church, see A. Harnack, *The Mission and Expansion of Christianity in the First Three Centuries*, trans. J. Moffatt, Vol. I, pp. 147-198. New York: Putnam's, 1908.

be the tradition of the apostles. The measure of their faithfulness is the dedication with which they led the church in contending for the faith and in assuming the responsibilities that were implicit in the teaching of Jesus Christ. These were the men who helped forge a strong community just when the first enthusiasm of the primitive community was fading, and with it the effectiveness of the charismatic leadership. They saw the church as the guardian of truth in a world not always receptive to the truth or capable of understanding it. They sought to make the teachings of the church and the Christian way of life relevant in a world that seemed less likely to come to an end than it had a few decades earlier. In its efforts to fulfil its responsibilities, the ministry gradually became better organized to take concrete action in a variety of circumstances, and in the process the foundations of the new community were greatly strengthened.

There was as yet no overarching ministry to bring local and regional churches together into a universal organization, for the ministry was still pretty much local both in function and authority. True, various bishops and presbyters did try to influence churches other than their own. But they had no well-defined authority, and their chief weapon was that of persuasion. Rather, it was the cultus that provided the formal bond among Christians throughout the Roman empire. Wherever Christians lived, they first entered the community through the rite of baptism, and they joined together in common worship and to eat the common meal. We must turn to certain developments in these rites in order to understand how the community managed to maintain a real homogeneity of life and thought as it continued to expand.

The Community's Rites

BAPTISM

The earliest description we have of Christian baptism appears in the *Didache* (7):

> Concerning baptism, baptise thus: Having first rehearsed all these things, "baptise, in the name of the Father and of the Son and of the Holy Spirit," in running water; but if thou hast no running water, baptise in other water, and if thou canst not in cold, then in warm. But if thou hast neither, pour water three times on the head "in the name of the Father, Son and Holy Spirit." And before the baptism let the baptiser and him who is to be baptised fast, and any others who are able. And thou shalt bid him who is to be baptised to fast one or two days before.

Baptism had been one of the central rites of the church from the earliest days, and this description from the *Didache* shows that its importance had not diminished. In fact, there was increasing concern in the church that baptism be administered properly. Both the baptizer and those to be baptized, according to the *Didache*, were to discipline themselves by a period of preparation. Obviously the rite was regarded as a very serious matter, an impression that is heightened by the use of the threefold formula "in the name of the Father, Son and Holy Spirit." This formula, which is found in the New Testament only in Matthew (28:19), expressed more adequately to the post-apostolic church the real meaning of the earlier formula, "in the name of the Lord Jesus" (Acts 2:38; 8:16; etc.).

The instructions from the *Didache* also contain the phrase "having rehearsed all these things," an indication that by this time candidates for baptism were being instructed in the Christian faith and life. The first six chapters of the *Didache*, for example, contrast the conduct expected of one who has entered the "way of Life" through baptism with his behaviour in the "way of Death" out of which he has just passed. A set of instructions very similar to this is found in the *Epistle of Barnabas*, and was no doubt used for baptismal instruction in the community where the writing originated.

How long had the church been giving instruction in connection with baptism? The accounts of baptism in Acts and the Pauline epistles leave the impression that in the early days the rite of baptism was less formal than is suggested by the *Didache*. Take for example the baptism of the Ethiopian eunuch by Philip (Acts 8:36-37). Philip meets the eunuch, tells him "the good news of Jesus," and baptizes him in the first water they see. Other passages in Acts give us the same picture: The gospel is preached and hearers are immediately baptized. In Paul's epistles, the faith that leads to baptism is response to the proclamation of the gospel (Rom. 10:14-15). In none of these accounts is there any explicit hint of instruction for baptism; they mention only response to the *kerygma* under the influence of the Spirit.

And yet even in the New Testament we find indications of a development toward the formal statement of baptismal instruction that we have in the *Didache*. Recently, scholars have suggested that in the Pauline epistles there are brief doctrinal statements that represent efforts to summarize the principal tenets of the faith [9] for use in instructing new converts, especially Gentiles.

---

[9] See P. Carrington, *The Primitive Christian Catechism*. Cambridge: University Press, 1940.

Some of the later writings of the New Testament give further evidence that the development of baptismal instruction was under way. In I Peter, for example, there is good reason to believe that we have preserved a type of discourse that was delivered in connection with baptism (I Pet. 1:3–4:6). This discourse includes both a definition of baptism as a sacrament of regeneration (1:3-12) and a lengthy section of instructions on the character and conduct that God expects of one who has been baptized (1:13–4:11). We shall look more closely at the details of this description in a later chapter (14), but here we can note that it does give us evidence that baptismal instruction was practised at this time, and that such instruction included both a summary of theological beliefs and moral instructions (catechism). There was probably no catechism in the sense that converts were required to be examined before being baptized, for that was a later development. Rather, the instruction was probably delivered either at the time of baptism, or to converts recently baptized. Although no set form for instruction had been developed in the post-apostolic period, baptismal catechisms were being worked out, and they provided one more means of promoting a strong communal life.

Just why did this development take place? First, there was the influence of Judaism, in which Gentile proselytes were instructed before they submitted to baptism. We have seen that the Jewish Qumran sect required new members to be instructed before they were admitted, and the Manual of Discipline of this sect includes a section in some ways similar to the first six chapters of the *Didache* and to *Barnabas*. Such practices may very well have influenced the Christian community. Second, the increase in the number of Gentile converts who had no previous knowledge of Judaism may have led the leaders of the Christian community to provide a more formal means of instruction. Third, the serious intention to keep the new life after baptism unspotted from sin would have heightened the need for clearly defined instructions. Baptism was not taken lightly, for through it the Christian entered into salvation (I Peter 3:21). Only fearful consequences would ensue should he through sin neglect the salvation bestowed on him in baptism (Heb. 10:31). This problem of post-baptismal sin became acute in the post-apostolic period. The logical solution was to abstain from sin after baptism. But the new convert would have to be given instruction in how to avoid sin. What better time than baptism was there to give such instruction? Then, to the question of how a man could guard against neglecting the salvation promised in baptism, there was a ready answer: Follow the instructions given to you in baptism.

Since all baptismal instruction had to be based on teaching that was common to all the Christian churches, its development forged another strong bond in the chain of common life. Christians were bound to-gether in baptism not only by one name and one Spirit, but also by one faith and a common effort to define how this faith was to be ex-pressed in conduct and character. Emerging norms of conduct gave concrete expression to the faith and tended more and more to identify the church as a cohesive social organism in the Roman world. The fact that this indoctrination in the new way of life came to be linked so closely with the rite of baptism provided a powerful motivation for following the new way, for to neglect it meant judgment (Heb. 10:26-27).

CHRISTIAN WORSHIP

The prophet John informs his readers in the book of Revelation that his first vision came to him on the "Lord's Day" (Rev. 1:10). In the time of Paul, Christians regularly assembled "on the first day of the week" (I Cor. 16:2). The *Didache* (14:1) and Ignatius (Magne-sians 9:1) also refer to the "Lord's day," and Barnabas (15:9) mentions a meeting on the eighth day. The first day of the new week was obvi-ously the day after Saturday, the Jewish sabbath, the eighth day from the first day of the Jewish week. Justin Martyr, a Christian theologian who wrote about the middle of the second century A.D., refers to it as the "day of the sun," [10] the pagan name for Sunday. According to tradition, Sunday was the day of Christ's resurrection, and from the earliest apostolic time it had been a special occasion for the gathering together of all Christians wherever they might be. Long before there was an annual celebration of Christ's resurrection on Easter, the church celebrated the resurrection weekly on Sunday. At first, that was the chief significance of the day, but its importance increased with time.

In the early days of the church, when there were relatively few Christians, the members of the community were together daily. Then, as the years passed, these daily meetings became less feasible—if not impossible. The uniqueness of Sunday sprang not only from the fact that it was a celebration of the resurrection of Christ, but also from the fact that the Christians, like the Jews, ascribed special religious signifi-cance to one day of the week by making it a day of assembly. No other religious cult in the ancient world shared this practice. When the prophet John had his vision, he knew that Christians were gathering together throughout the churches of Asia Minor for worship on that very day. Sunday, the Lord's day, dramatized not only to John, but

---

[10] Apology I, 67, 3.

to Christians everywhere, the unity that each professed. By providing a regular, consistent occasion for the worship of the Risen Lord, and for instruction in the faith and in the way of life the Lord required from each worshipper, the Lord's Day was a vital factor in making the unity of the church concrete and immediate to Christians.

The elements of the Sunday worship service were pretty much the same as they had been in apostolic times: prayer, reading from the scriptures and other writings, preaching, instruction, and the singing of hymns and psalms. The climax of each service was the fellowship meal in which, like members of the early church, the participants believed the Risen Lord was present with them, and during which they renewed their hope for his coming again. It was the faith in the Risen Lord that gave meaning to all Christian worship.[11]

The Old Testament, which formed the "scriptures" of the church, was read as a regular part of the service. Since books were costly and scarce, and since not everyone knew how to read, this reading aloud was for many the only way in which they could become familiar with the scriptures. No doubt the readings were often lengthy; Justin Martyr said that went on "as long as there was time." [12] We do not know whether or not there was any set order of reading from the Old Testament. In the service of the Jewish synagogue, from the third century A.D. on, the reading of the Law and the prophets was planned in such a way that the entire Old Testament was completed in one year. Moreover, the readings were correlated with important religious festivals. Many scholars believe that this practice dates from a much earlier period; if so, it is possible that some such arrangement was practised in the Christian church as well, under the influence of the synagogue. Christians would have been particularly interested, of course, in the messianic passages of the Old Testament that they believed had been fulfilled in the events of their Lord's life.

In addition to the Old Testament, other writings were read in the church service. We know, for example, that Paul wrote his letters to be read in the local churches, though of course they were not then regarded on the same level as the "scriptures." Later, Revelation was written to be read in the churches of Asia Minor; *I Clement* to be read in Corinth; the *Shepherd of Hermas* to be read in Rome; and I, II, III John, I Peter, and Hebrews to be read in one or more churches.

In recent years some scholars have theorized that the literary struc-

---

[11] For a complete discussion of Christian worship, see O. Cullmann, *Early Christian Worship*. London : SCM Press, 1953.

[12] Apology I, 67.

ture of some of the New Testament writings reveals that they were composed for liturgical reading—the Gospels of Matthew, Mark, and John, in particular. This would mean that even the writing of the Gospels was controlled to some degree by the needs of Christian worship. But whether or not we accept this thesis, it is quite probable that the Gospels were read in the churches. At first, some of the churches would have preferred one Gospel over another. The first specific reference to the reading of several in one church comes from Justin Martyr, who says that the "memoirs of the apostles" were read regularly along with the Old Testament.

The reading of the scriptures was always followed by preaching, teaching, and exhortation. The author of the Pastoral Epistles calls upon the church leaders to attend to the "public reading of scripture, to preaching, to teaching" (I Tim. 4:13). He also writes: "All [Old Testament] scripture is inspired by God and profitable for teaching, for reproof, for correction and for training in righteousness, that the man of God may be complete, equipped for every good work" (II Tim. 3:16). The scripture reading was intended to give some helpful word to the gathered congregation, and the sermon was an interpretation of "the word."

We have a good example of just this use of the scriptures in the Epistle to the Hebrews. Careful study shows that this writing is a sermon or homily of some early church leader intended to be read to the church to which he wrote. Based largely on Psalms 2, 8, 95, 110, and on Jeremiah 31:31-34, it follows a regular outline, in which an Old Testament passage is first cited and then interpreted in the light of the revelation in Christ. Then certain practical implications are drawn for the Christian reader on the basis of which he is exhorted to action. The writing is called a "word of exhortation" (Heb. 13:22), a term that the author of Acts used to describe this kind of preaching (Acts 13:15).

Prayer was also an important element in the worship. As we have seen earlier, spontaneous and free prayers were common in the Pauline churches, especially among the Christian prophets. Under the influence of the synagogue and Jewish Christianity, however, the more traditional corporate or liturgical prayer gradually took precedence over spontaneous prayer. In I Timothy it is urged that "supplications, prayers, intercessions, and thanksgivings be made for all men" (I Tim. 2:1), and men are urged to pray "lifting holy hands" (I Tim. 2:8). Fortunately, two of these liturgical prayers have survived from the post-apostolic period. One, used in the church at Rome, is found in *I Clement,* and the other, probably used in Antioch, is found in the

Didache.[13] Each is a good illustration of how prayers that were un-doubtedly used in the hellenistic synagogues of the Diaspora were adapted to Christian usage. The liturgical prayer in *1 Clement* opens with the following words of glorification of God:

> Grant us to hope on thy name, the source of all creation, open the eyes of our heart to know thee, that thou alone art the highest in the highest and remainest holy among the holy. Thou dost humble the pride of the haughty, thou dost destroy the imaginings of the nations, thou dost raise up the humble and abase the lofty, thou makest rich and makest poor, thou dost slay and make alive, thou alone art the finder of spirits and art God of all flesh, thou dost look on the abysses, thou seest into the works of man, thou art the helper of those in danger, the saviour of those in despair, the creator and watcher over every spirit; thou dost multiply nations upon earth and hast chosen out from them all those that love thee through Jesus Christ thy beloved child, and through him hast then taught us, made us holy, and brought us to honour.

This prayer and the prayer from the *Didache*, which we shall consider later, are examples of the content of the liturgical prayers of the post-apostolic church. In addition to such prayers, the worship service in-cluded doxologies, or brief ascriptions of praise to God, some of which are already found in the Pauline epistles (Rom. 9:5; 11:36; 16:25-27; etc.). We have a doxology, for example, in I Timothy, where the author speaks of God in these words: "The blessed and only Sovereign, the King of kings, and Lord of lords, who alone has immortality and dwells in unapproachable light, whom no man has ever seen or can see. To him be honour and eternal dominion. Amen" (I Tim. 6:15-16). The writings of the New Testament abound with both doxologies and benedictions, giving us glimpses into the worship of the church.

Of particularly great importance in Christian worship was the Lord's Prayer, which in the Gospel of Matthew is already presented as the one prayer that Jesus taught his disciples. Certainly it was in general use in the worship of the church from an early period. The *Didache*, after instructing Christians to pray the Lord's Prayer, adds: "Pray thus three times a day" (8:3), an indication that it was used not only as a part of corporate prayer, but as a personal prayer as well.

Finally, part of the worship service was given over to psalms and hymns. In several places Paul had already mentioned the use of hymns among Christians (I Cor. 14:26; Col. 3:16). Most of the psalms were taken from the Old Testament, but other psalms were probably used

---

[13] I Clement 59-61; *Didache* 10.

too. The recent discovery of many non-biblical psalms among the
Qumran scrolls shows that the Jews continued to compose psalms
long after the canonical book of Psalms was closed. The discovery
of a Christian gnostic book of hymns, called the Odes of Solomon,
written to Christ, faith, hope, and love, shows that the Christians too
were interested in this form.[14]
We have in the New Testament some of the hymns that were actually used in these early Sunday services. Three of them, found in the
opening chapters of Luke, are known as the *Magnificat* (Lk. 1:46-55),
the *Benedictus* (Lk. 1:68-79), and the *Nunc dimittis* (Lk. 2:29-32).
All three were probably adapted from original Jewish compositions.
Fragments of other hymns are found throughout the New Testament. Many scholars believe that Paul, in his letter to the Philippians,
drew at one point on a hymn to Christ (Philip. 2:5-11), and there is
another hymn to Christ in I Timothy:

> He was manifested in the flesh,
> vindicated in the Spirit,
> seen by angels,
> preached among the nations,
> believed on in the world,
> taken up in glory.

—I TIMOTHY 3:16

The fragment of yet another hymn is found in Ephesians:

> Awake, O sleeper, and arise from the dead,
> and Christ shall give you light.

—EPHESIANS 5:14

All through the post-apostolic age, the church continued to develop
the liturgical mode of worship that had been present from the beginning. Since individual churches undoubtedly enjoyed a good bit of
freedom in selecting the forms to be used, we find considerable variation from one church to another. The best example of the role of
liturgy in the worship service of the post-apostolic church is found
in the book of Revelation. Recent research has established that the
author of this writing was deeply influenced by Christian worship, and
his use of prayers, doxologies, responses to prayers, hymns, and halle-
lujah choruses reveals that the church was not only deeply indebted to
Jewish liturgy but had already developed a liturgy of its own. Nowhere is this better illustrated than in Revelation 4 and 5, which have

14 R. Harris and A. Mingana, *The Odes and Psalms of Solomon.* Manchester:
University Press, 1916.

been interpreted as the setting for a Christian worship service. In fact, the heavenly scene described is visualized on the basis of its earthly counterpart—the church at worship. In outline, the elements of the church service would appear as follows: [15]

Call to worship	4:1 ff.	(Leader)
Singing of trisagion	4:8	(Congregation)
(Holy, Holy, Holy)		
Ascription of praise to God as Creator	4:11	(Choir)
Reading from scripture	5:1 ff.	(Leader)
Psalm	5:9	(Leader)
Response	5:12	(Congregation)
Doxology to God and Christ	5:13	(Congregation)
Amen	5:14	(Choir)

It is not strange that the book of Revelation should have been so strongly influenced by Christian worship, for the heart of John's message is the victory of God revealed through Christ, and the expectation of its consummation in the near future. He visualizes all the heavenly hosts worshipping God and Christ for this victory. But in a sense all Christian worship was a service of joyous thanksgiving in gratitude to God for the victory in Christ and in expectation of his coming again, and the event that John describes was continually celebrated in Christian worship.

THE CHRISTIAN EUCHARIST

In Chapters 6 and 8, we saw the central place that the Lord's Supper held in the worship of the early church. The later New Testament writings do not provide us with any explicit records of the service itself, but from other sources it is clear that the rite maintained its central importance throughout the post-apostolic age. It was called by several names at this time. The *Didache*, for example, refers to it as the "breaking of bread," a name that had been used from the earliest times (Acts 2:42; 20:7). Ignatius and the Epistle of Jude (12) call it the *agape*—a Greek word meaning love, and, in this connection, "love feast." Both terms suggest the rite was related to the fellowship or social meals that Christians had shared together from the beginning. But as time went on, a new term gained increasing usage: *eucharist*,[16] a Greek

---

[15] This reconstruction is suggested by Lucetta Mowry in "Revelation 4-5 and Early Liturgical Usage," *Journal of Biblical Literature*, Vol. LXXI, Part II, June, 1952, pp. 75-84.

[16] *Didache* 9 and 10; Ignatius, To the Philadelphians 4; Justin Martyr, Apology I, 66, 1, etc.

term meaning "thanksgiving." The rite itself was characterized by thanksgiving to God for his gift of salvation in Jesus Christ. As in the earlier period, the primary meaning of the meal was Christ's presence in the midst of those who ate, and the hope it brought for his final coming.

There is some difference of opinion among scholars as to whether or not the Eucharist was ever observed apart from the fellowship meal in the first century A.D. It is perfectly clear from the *Didache* and from Ignatius, as we have just seen, that the fellowship meal had not completely disappeared, and we have further evidence to this effect in a letter written early in the first century by Pliny the Younger to the Emperor Trajan concerning Christians in Bithynia and Pontus. But the first certain evidence we have for the separation of the two is found in Justin Martyr.[17] What probably happened was that the separation took place gradually in different churches during the late first and early second century A.D. As the churches grew in size, it must have become more and more difficult to manage a social meal in somebody's home. But the church continued to observe the Eucharist, which enabled Christians to go on celebrating the presence of the Lord in a common meal.

Yet the separation cannot be explained solely on these grounds. It came about only after long years in which the Eucharist had achieved increasing importance in relation to both the fellowship meal and other elements of Christian worship. From the beginning, even when the Eucharist was closely integrated with the fellowship meal, its religious significance was undoubtedly conveyed by certain words or prayers at an appointed moment in the meal—probably the words that Jesus had uttered at the Last Supper.

By the end of the first century A.D., liturgies for the Eucharist were being developed, one of which we can reconstruct—partially, at least—on the basis of the *Didache*. The writing instructs Christians to come together on the Lord's Day, break bread, and hold the Eucharist "after confessing your transgressions" (*Didache* 14), an indication that a prayer of confession was already in use in the service. The writing also states that concerning the cup the following words are to be repeated: "We give thanks to thee, our Father, for the Holy Vine of David thy child, which thou didst make known to us through Jesus thy child; to thee be glory for ever" (*Didache* 9). And concerning the bread, "We give thee thanks, our Father, for the life and knowledge which thou didst make known to us through Jesus thy child. To thee be glory for

---

[17] Apology, I, 67.

SOME TYPICAL PLACES OF WORSHIP IN THE FIRST FOUR CENTURIES

(Left) *A chapel in a Roman villa at Herculaneum. Since the city was destroyed by Vesuvius in 79 A.D., wealthy Romans must have been converted to Christianity before the end of Vespasian's reign and have been using the cross as a Christian symbol.*

(Below) *An underground chapel in what is now known as the Catacomb of Saint Sebastian. Originally a pagan tomb, it later came to be used for Christian burials. A strong tradition affirms that the bones of Peter and Paul were kept here temporarily during a period of persecution.*

(*Above*) *The Church of the Nativity, one of the first churches built by Constantine after his conversion. Considerably rebuilt, it stands at the far end of the open court and is located over a cave where, according to local tradition, Jesus was born.*

(*Right*) *The baptistry of a tiny chapel at Dura Europos, on the Euphrates River in north-eastern Syria. The walls of the chapel, which was destroyed in 258 A.D., were covered with paintings of biblical scenes, traces of which are still visible. The person to be baptized stood in the shallow pool and had water poured over his head.*

ever. As this broken bread was scattered upon the mountains, but was brought together and became one, so let thy Church be gathered together from the ends of the earth into thy kingdom, for thine is the glory and the power through Jesus Christ for ever."

Then the author gives the final prayer for the Eucharist (10:2-6):

> We give thanks to thee, O Holy Father, for thy Holy Name which thou didst make to tabernacle in our hearts, and for the knowledge and faith and immortality which thou didst make known to us through Jesus thy child. To thee be glory for ever. Thou, Lord Almighty, didst create all things for thy Name's sake, and didst give food and drink to men for their enjoyment, that they might give thanks to thee, but us hast thou blessed with spiritual food and drink and eternal light through thy Child. Above all we give thanks to thee for that thou art mighty. To thee be glory for ever. Remember, Lord, thy Church, to deliver it from all evil and to make it perfect in thy love, and gather it together in its holiness from the four winds to thy kingdom which thou hast prepared for it. For thine is the power and the glory for ever. Let grace come and let this world pass away. Hosannah to the God of David. If any man be holy, let him come! if any man be not, let him repent: Maran atha, Amen!

We can see, then, that the Eucharist was gradually receiving a more extensive liturgical setting. There were undoubtedly variations from church to church, of course; we cannot say how representative the form in the *Didache* was, since there was still considerable freedom in practice. Even the *Didache*, after giving the liturgical prayer for the Eucharist, says: "But suffer the prophets to hold Eucharist as they will" (*Didache* 10:7). Here we have an acknowledgment of the prophets' right to engage in free and spontaneous prayer. Side by side in this passage we have evidence of the continuing freedom of expression under the impetus of the Spirit, and of the tendency toward a more formal liturgical service. The post-apostolic church apparently sensed no conflict between the two.

The increasing tendency toward the more liturgical type of service resulted from the gradual passing of the charismatic ministry and the ascendancy of the bishops and presbyters. As we have seen, one of the principal reasons for this development was the church's battle against the strange teachings that were being promulgated by false prophets. These teachings were as dangerous to the Eucharist as to any other aspect of Christian faith and practice, and in his letters Ignatius repeatedly insists that the Eucharist can be held only where bishops, presbyters, and deacons are present. Ignatius knew that in some churches members were partaking of the Eucharist isolated from the main body of Christians and under unauthorized ministers. Others were refusing to participate at all. He sensed a real danger here, for once the rite stopped being shared by all Christians, the unity of the community would be threatened. So Ignatius attacked the misconceptions about the meaning of the Eucharist that were being disseminated by false teachers, and insisted that there was only one Eucharist—the one shared in by the whole church, and interpreted by its recognized leaders.

The Christian cultus played a fundamental role in developing a community strong enough to withstand the pressures of an alien world. For in baptism, worship, preaching, instruction, and the Eucharist, not only did the Christians know themselves to be one in the Spirit, they also shared more and more a common understanding of the content and meaning of their faith which found expression in their daily conduct. The close relationship between Christian worship and daily conduct in the world is disclosed in Pliny the Younger's letter to the Emperor Trajan, where, referring to a meeting of Christians in Bithynia (Asia Minor) in a way that strongly suggests a eucharistic service, he writes:

> On a certain day before sunrise they were accustomed to meet and recite antiphonally a hymn to Christ (as to a God); they bound themselves by an oath, not for any crime, but not to commit theft or robbery or adultery, not to break their word, and not to refuse to repay a deposit.[18]

Another example is recorded by Justin Martyr, who, after describing the Eucharist, continues:

> And they who are well to do, and willing, give what each thinks fit; and what is collected is deposited with the president, who succours the orphans and widows, and those who, through sickness or any other cause, are in want, and those who are in bonds, and the strangers sojourning among us, and in a word takes care of all who are in need.[19]

These two passages are from the second century, but they are firmly rooted in the practice of the apostolic church—indeed, in the teachings of Jesus himself.

---

[18] Pliny the Younger, Letter to Trajan (No. 97). Translated by R. M. Grant, *The Sword and the Cross*, pp. 66-68. New York: Macmillan, 1955.
[19] Apology I, 67. Translation from A. Roberts and J. Donaldson, editors, *The Ante-Nicene Fathers*, Vol. I, p. 186. New York: Scribner's, 1925.

It was in worship that the church found both its motivation and its guidance for life in the world. Here Christians confessed their hope in the Lord's coming, and sought the meaning of their common faith and the common action that it involved. In the chapter that follows, we shall see how the church was influenced by the religious thought of the Graeco-Roman world as it entered upon this search.

✂

CHAPTER THIRTEEN

THE COMMUNITY
IN RAPPROCHEMENT
WITH THE WORLD: I

The Gospel of John

S o far, we have been concentrating on the conflicts that engaged
the Christian church as it pursued its mission in the Graeco-Roman
world. But the whole story is not one of conflict. In order to interpret
the Christian message to non-Jews, for instance, the early church used
religious language and concepts that would be meaningful to them.
Paul was among the first of those who tried to communicate the gospel
in religious terms that were already popular in the non-Jewish world
(see Chapter 8), and this effort was continued throughout the post-
apostolic age. Although the church was in conflict with the world.

New Testament reading relevant to this chapter is the Gospel of John.

then, it also entered into rapprochement with the world. For the church to have done otherwise would have meant renouncing its mission to the Gentiles.

In all the post-apostolic writings we find hellenistic language and concepts adopted for Christian use in communicating the message of the gospel. But the practice is particularly clear in the Gospel of John.

Around the turn of the first century A.D., a gospel was written in Ephesus that later became known as the Gospel of John. By the late second century A.D., this gospel was traditionally believed to have been written by the Apostle John, but the earliest testimony on its authorship does not necessarily lead us to this conclusion. In fact, most scholars today agree that it was not written by one of the original twelve apostles.[1]

Who was the author, then? His knowledge of the Septuagint, of Jewish customs, and of rabbinic modes of scriptural interpretation suggests that John was a Jewish Christian. But if he was a Jew, he was a product of a Judaism that had been strongly influenced by hellenistic religious thought. Because of this mixed background, John was able to interpret the Christian gospel in language and concepts that were more meaningful to his Gentile readers than more purely Jewish terms would have been. John himself obviously did not feel that he was clothing the Christian message in strange garb, however, and it is likely that this manner of interpretation was probably already established when he wrote.

John's subject was Jesus Christ and the eternal life he had brought to men. At the conclusion of the Gospel,[2] John states that he has written his book "that you may believe that Jesus is the Christ, the Son of God, and that believing you may have life in his name" (20:31). This was also the purpose of the authors of the three Synoptic Gospels, which had already been written by this time. John probably knew Mark, and possibly Luke, but he was unacquainted with Matthew. He was clearly familiar with the traditions about Jesus that were circulating in the church in his day, and he assumes that his readers were familiar with them too. For example, he writes as though his readers knew about John the Baptist and his message, about Jesus' family and ministry in Galilee, and about the call of the disciples. And he includes familiar stories from the Synoptics: the account of John the Baptist's preaching, the Feeding of the 5,000, the Stilling of the Storm, the Last Supper and the Passion Narrative. In addition to these specific refer-

---

[1] For a discussion of authorship and date see Chapter 2, p. 72. For convenience, the author will be referred to here as John.

[2] Critics agree that John 21 is a later addition to the original text.

ences, there are scores of passages that echo the tradition as found in the Synoptics. In short, John wanted to write a Gospel that was faithful to the church's memory of Jesus as recorded in the Synoptic Gospels.

But the differences between John and the Synoptic Gospels are more striking than the similarities. For one thing, John changes the chronology of events. He puts the Cleansing of the Temple at the beginning of Jesus' ministry rather than at the close, and he has the last meal with the disciples take place a day earlier than in the Synoptics. In John, the ministry of Jesus lasts about three years rather than one or two, as implied by the Synoptics, and the scene of much of Jesus' activity is shifted from Galilee to Judea and Jerusalem.

Even more noticeable are the changes that John makes in the form and content of Jesus' teaching. The parables, similes, and short prophetic utterances are gone, and in their place we find long discourses on recurring themes. These are not the familiar themes of the Synoptic Gospels: the kingdom of God, righteousness, repentance, forgiveness, and so forth. Rather, they are the themes of eternal life, light, truth, blindness, darkness, sight, and glory. John prefers symbolical language, and he gives words and events a double meaning. In two series of sayings, one introduced by the words "I am," and the other by the words "Verily, verily, I say unto you," Jesus makes striking pronouncements about himself and his mission. He explicitly affirms his divine Sonship in terms that never occur in the Synoptic Gospels.

How can we account for these differences? In the first place, we must realize that John wanted to write a theological interpretation of the life and death of Jesus. Though he makes use of the gospel as a literary form, his main concern is not to repeat the story of the ministry of Jesus as found in the Synoptics. Rather, he aims to *reinterpret* the ministry in the light of his faith that Jesus was the Eternal Son of God. And so it is that Jesus speaks and acts as the divine Son of God throughout the Gospel. John assumes that his readers are familiar with the total ministry of Jesus, and then proceeds to reinterpret the words and deeds of Jesus as remembered in the tradition, in order to discover their deeper meaning. This is an important point for the modern reader to keep in mind, for at first glance John's use of the gospel form suggests that he meant simply to record events, rather than an interpretation of those events.

In the second place, John draws more heavily than do the Synoptics on the terminology and concepts produced by the syncretism of Greek and oriental religions in the hellenistic age. In particular, he reflects the dualism of Iranian religion and of popularized Platonic thought.

John, like Paul, was trying to build a bridge between the message of the earliest Jewish Christian community and a church that was becoming increasingly Gentile. Yet, again like Paul, John never lost sight of the primitive *kerygma* and the early traditions of the life and ministry of Jesus.

The Prologue of the Gospel of John

John begins with a Prologue that sets forth the subject of his Gospel (1:1-18)—namely, the Word of God (1:1-5). This is the Word that was with God from the beginning and through which all things were created and life was given to man. And this life, in turn, is the light that alone dispels the darkness of the world, the light to which John the Baptist had borne witness. But when the light of God came to "his own" (the Jews), many of them rejected him (1:10). Yet some of them received him and believed in him; to these Jews was given the power to become children of God (1:12). It was not, however, because they were earthly descendants of the Jewish people that they became children of God; rather, it was by an act of God's will. And God's will was accomplished when his Word became flesh and lived as a man among men (1:14), thereby revealing the "only Son" from the Father. Everyone who shared the "fullness" of Jesus' Sonship with those who believed in him also became children of God. Moses had given the Law, but it is only through the Son, Jesus Christ, that God's grace and truth are revealed. Since only the Son has seen the Father, only he can reveal the grace and truth through which men become children of God.

In short, then, John announces in his Prologue that he is going to tell his readers how God brought into being a new community through his only Son, Jesus Christ, through whom his life-giving Word was revealed. And he is also going to explain how the Jews' rejection of Christ was paralleled by the Gentiles' acceptance of Christ.

The terminology of the Prologue reveals how close John's religious thought was to that of the hellenistic world in which he lived. For example, he describes the world as a place of darkness into which men are born and from which they can escape only by being born anew by one who brings light and truth from the divine world (Jn. 3). Immediately we are reminded of the hellenistic practice of dividing reality into two realms of existence—the divine realm of light, truth, and life, and the lower world of darkness, falsehood, and death (see pp. 19-23 and 341-344).

And yet John differs from hellenistic religious thought in important respects. In the first place, he modifies the absolute distinction between the realm of light and the realm of darkness by affirming that God, through his Word, had actually created the lower world. Moreover, he asserts that the divine Son of God "became flesh"—that is, he dwelt as a man among men. Clearly, then, if the divine Son himself was clothed in a material body, there could be no absolute distinction between the realm of spirit and the realm of flesh. And John is emphatic on this point, for he affirms Christ's true manhood (2:3; 4:6-7; 11:35; 19:26-27), refers to Jesus' "flesh and blood" (6:53-55), and vividly describes his death as a human being by referring to the blood that poured forth on the cross (19:34). There is no doubt that in emphasizing Jesus' humanity John was combating the same docetic tendencies that were rampant in the churches to which I John was written (see pp. 341-344). John was as eager as the docetists to acknowledge that Christ was a divine being, but he vigorously rejected any refusal to acknowledge that the divine Christ was also the man Jesus of Nazareth.

No term in John's Prologue is more pregnant with meaning or richer in religious association than the term *logos* (Word). This term had many shades of meaning in the hellenistic world. The Stoics, for example, had popularized the *logos* as the rational principle that pervaded and constituted and ordered the universe. And the term had come to have a particular religious significance to Greek-speaking Jews who read their Scriptures in the Greek translation (Septuagint), for here *logos* was used to refer to the creative Word of God through which he had created the universe. The account in Genesis (1:3 ff.) records that the creation came into being when God *spoke*, and as time passed men decided that it was by God's *logos* that he had brought forth his creation.

Logos took on additional meaning in connection with the development of another concept in Judaism: wisdom. The Wisdom Literature of the Old Testament and the Apocrypha shows a growing interest in the place of wisdom in the creation of the world. There was even a tendency to personify wisdom, although the rigorous monotheism of the Jews kept them from suggesting that wisdom could exist independently. Later, however, under the influence of Greek speculation, *logos* was sometimes identified with wisdom as God's agent in creation. And, since the Law (Torah) was the embodiment of God's wisdom and his Word, there was also a tendency to ascribe to the Law all the attributes of Wisdom and Word.[3]

---

[3] For a complete discussion, see J. Coert Rylaarsdam, *Revelation in Jewish Literature*. Chicago: The University of Chicago Press, 1946. See also above, Chapter 9, p. 280.

In the Old Testament, the Word of God appears not only as the means by which God created the world, but also as the vehicle by which God revealed his purposes for Israel and the world. The Old Testament prophets, for instance, often preface their prophecies with the phrase, "The Word of the Lord." Here the revelation consisted not merely of what the prophets had to say, but in the series of events that was set in motion by the prophets' words and actions. This use of *logos* as a vehicle of revelation was also common in popular hellenistic philosophy and religion. Philo, for example, sees the *logos* as the divine instrument whereby is revealed the knowledge of God, and in hellenistic religious thought it is through the *logos* that salvation is disclosed to man.

But what does all this have to do with John's use of *logos* in the Prologue to his Gospel? Simply that he was consciously using a term that had broad associations in the hellenistic world among both Jews and non-Jews. Many efforts have been made to explain John's usage in terms of his dependence on either the Jewish or hellenistic usage, but it would be more historically correct to recognize a common influence.

There is one sense, however, in which John's use of *logos* is unique, for when he says, "the Word became flesh," he *identifies* the *logos* with Jesus Christ. This means that John conceived of the *logos* primarily in personal and historical terms rather than in mythological or cosmological terms. His understanding of the *logos* is determined by his understanding of the life and work of Jesus. True, John opens his Gospel by naming the *logos* as the agent of creation, a reference that would be familiar to both Jews and non-Jews. But he quickly turns to the *logos* as the personal revealer of God, the one through whom salvation is revealed and given. And in the rest of the Gospel, though the word rarely occurs, John retains this emphasis on its religious significance.

The Revelation in the World

Like the Synoptists, John begins his story of the ministry of Jesus with an account of John the Baptist (1:19-34), though he completely subordinates the Baptist's role to that of Jesus. In several passages he depreciates John the Baptist's mission (1:6-8; 1:35-37; 3:25-30; 10:40-42), and from the very beginning ascribes words to him to indicate that the Baptist himself was aware of his subordination to Christ (1:15). John's account of Jesus' baptism completely omits the Baptist's message, and leaves him simply to proclaim Jesus as the "Lamb of God who takes away the sin of the world" (1:29-34) and as the Son of God.

In the Synoptics (except for Matthew) John does not recognize Jesus, but in the Gospel of John God reveals Jesus' identity to the Baptist through the Spirit. It is Jesus upon whom the Spirit comes and permanently abides who will baptize with the Spirit. In interpreting Jesus' relation to John the Baptist, John is utilizing a theological principle that he will develop more fully in the rest of the Gospel—namely, that knowledge of Jesus' identity is revealed by God through the Spirit only to those who believe. Although John is deeply concerned with the historical foundation of Jesus' ministry ("the Word became flesh"), his primary interest is in reinterpreting that ministry in the light of the theological truths it has revealed.

In playing down the role of John the Baptist, John was undoubtedly hitting out at a rival sect in Asia Minor made up of the Baptist's followers. But quite apart from this motive, John's subordination of the Baptist was consistent with his tendency to treat everyone in his Gospel as lesser actors in a drama that was played out for only one purpose: to reveal to the world the central figure, Jesus Christ. The Baptist speaks for every character in the Gospel when he says: "He must increase, but I must decrease" (3:30). It is this emphasis that helps to account for the artificiality of the dialogues between Jesus and the rest of the *dramatis personae* throughout the Gospel; the others are important only in providing a setting for Jesus' words and deeds. This approach contrasts with that of the Synoptics, where hints of the historical tensions of the times often break through. John's purpose is not to reproduce the tradition represented in the Synoptics but to interpret it.

With the Baptist's proclamation that Jesus is the "Lamb of God," John introduces a subject that he later develops in interpreting the death of Jesus as the sacrificial lamb. Here at the very beginning, he alludes to the death as crucial to an understanding of the revelation and the mission of Jesus, the one who alone baptizes in the Spirit. While in the Prologue Jesus' divine Sonship was affirmed on the basis of his having been with God from the beginning and having seen God (1:1, 15-18), here his Sonship is affirmed on the basis of the fact that he will baptize through the Spirit. As John proceeds, he will disclose how the Sonship of Jesus was revealed in history and how the Spirit was imparted to men through Jesus Christ.

In John's version of the call of the disciples, he differs decidedly from the Synoptics (1:35-51), for here Jesus is recognized as the Messiah from the beginning. And Peter is named the Rock (Cephas) at his call rather than later in the ministry (Mt. 16:18). The climax is the story of Nathaniel's call. This is the first of a series of dialogues between

Jesus and certain persons who take on symbolical significance. Nathaniel, the Jew "without guile," finds no basis in Jewish tradition for believing that Jesus is the Messiah ("Can anything good come out of Nazareth?"). But in spite of his doubt, he is willing to "come and see." For John, this is the essence of faith: the openness of mind that leads a man, in spite of doubt, to approach Christ to be shown. When Nathaniel approaches Christ, he is amazed by a knowledge that he cannot account for in human terms (1:47-48), and on the basis of this experience he believes. Christ responds by promising Nathaniel that a day will come when his belief will be founded on something far more profound than Christ's superhuman knowledge—the day when he will see "heaven opened, and the angels of God ascending and descending upon the Son of Man." This is John's way of saying that a greater revelation will come to Nathaniel when he realizes that it is Jesus Christ through whom God has access to man on earth and through whom man has access to God in heaven. John is referring here to the death and resurrection of Christ, the moment in which this full revelation will be given. Nathaniel stands in vivid contrast to the unbelieving Jews who are later pictured as unwilling to open their eyes to the possibility that in the words and works of Jesus God is revealed (Jn. 7-9).

John divides his narrative of the ministry of Jesus into two phases. The first twelve chapters deal with Jesus' public ministry, which reaches its end when certain Greeks come to Christ. Beginning with chapter 13, John portrays the final period, during which Jesus privately instructs the twelve disciples (13-17); this section is concluded with the Passion Narrative (18-20) and reaches its climax with the coming of the Spirit. In general, this twofold division resembles the Synoptic outline, in which the public ministry is followed by a withdrawal during the last days. But John's account of the conduct of the public ministry and the nature of the teaching is decidedly different from that in the Synoptics.

THE NEW LIFE GIVEN BY CHRIST

In the first twelve chapters, John reconstructs the story of Jesus' public ministry around the framework of seven miracle stories and a series of discourses and dialogues. The first of the miracles sets the theme for the entire ministry of Christ (2:1-11). During a wedding feast attended by Jesus in Cana, a village in Galilee, the wine is depleted. At his mother's request, Jesus provides a superabundant supply. He takes six large vessels normally used for Jewish purificatory rites and has them filled with water, which he then miraculously changes into wine. This miracle, which is found only in John's Gospel, may derive from an independent tradition.

But John's interest is not primarily in the physical miracles as such, and, in contrast to the Synoptic Gospels, he uses the term "signs" in referring to them. To John, Jesus' signs are manifestations of the power of God, and they help to bring salvation to those who believe. In this sense, the miracle itself, met by faith, discloses the glory of God to the disciples (2:11). In John, the symbolic term "glory" refers not only to the transcendence and ineffable power of God, as in hellenistic religious thought, but also to the power revealed in Jesus Christ (1:14, "We have beheld his glory")—the power that brings salvation. In the seven signs, Christ reveals God's power by doing God's works (5:36; 9:3). But the full manifestation of God's glory must include the death and resurrection of Jesus, and for John this is the greatest of all the signs, the one through which the meaning of all the others is revealed.

The word "sign" carries a second meaning in John's Gospel, for each of the physical miracles serves as the vehicle for an unobservable truth. To put it another way: The signs are manifestations of God's power to the naked eye, but at the same time they are symbols of truth that cannot be observed directly. In the miracle at Cana, for example, the wine that Christ miraculously produces from the water is symbolic of the new life that he brings to mankind. It is the new life of the Christian community as contrasted to the old life of Judaism, symbolized by the water jars intended to be used for the ritual purifications required by Jewish Law. What the miracle really says is that Jesus is already engaged in the work through which man is purified and is thereby given access to salvation. Here, as in each of the succeeding six signs, we find a double meaning, for the observable deed carries with it a symbolic meaning.

In referring to the miracles as "signs," John differs from the Synoptic Gospels, in which the term "signs" generally refers to the apocalyptic events that were to mark the final coming of the kingdom. But since it is a basic theological belief for John that in Jesus Christ the true life of the kingdom was already revealed, he readily refers to the works of Jesus as manifestations of that life in history. This underlying belief also accounts for John's symbolical use of the term "hour." At Cana, for example, he tells his mother, "My hour has not yet come" (2:4). This is the hour of death and resurrection when God's revelation will be fully consummated (12:23-25), and when Christ will accomplish all that his signs foretell. But for John, who stands beyond that event in time, the term "hour" refers to that moment in history when the Eternal Word was made incarnate in Jesus Christ—that is, the time of

Jesus' ministry. Since it was only with the death and resurrection that the meaning of all Jesus' words and deeds was finally revealed, John here refers to that last event as the "hour." But in so far as the coming of Christ into the world is the beginning of that hour, John can also say that the hour "now is" (4:23).

The miracle at Cana is followed by the Cleansing of the Temple (2:13-22). Here again John differs from the Synoptic Gospels, which place this event in the final days of Jesus' ministry. Some scholars believe that the passage originally came late in the Gospel, but that at some point it was displaced. In fact, for a long time scholars have debated the possibility that several passages in John have been shifted about.[4] But it is generally agreed that John put the Cleansing of the Temple where he did because the change of order served his theological purpose. By placing it at the opening of the ministry, John emphasizes that the Spirit that was bringing into being a new community of worshippers was present in Jesus Christ from the very outset, but that the full coming of the community had to await the resurrection and the consequent coming of the Spirit.

The climax of the story comes in Jesus' words: "Destroy this temple, and in three days I will raise it up" (2:19). John explains this saying symbolically: Jesus is really prophesying his resurrection, when the Risen Christ will replace the Temple as the place where man finds God. Those who worship in his Spirit are the true worshippers (Jn. 4). As the changing of the water into wine symbolizes the new life that Christ gives, so the cleansing of the Temple symbolizes the spiritual worship of the new community of Christ that is brought into being through faith in the Risen Lord.

This act, which heralds the day when the Temple worship will be superseded, fits into the over-all scheme of John's Gospel. John builds the chronology of Jesus' ministry around a series of Jewish festivals, beginning with the Cleansing of the Temple at Passover (2:13), and closing with the crucifixion at Passover (19:14). Between these events, Jesus makes significant pronouncements in or near Jerusalem at other festival seasons. John has invented this chronology in order to show that Jesus has supplanted all the old festivals of Judaism. He has revealed a new way to worship God, a way open to all men.

THE NEW BIRTH

John 3, which purports to be a conversation between Jesus and a prominent Pharisee, Nicodemus, may be John's reinterpretation

[4] For a complete discussion, see James Moffatt, *An Introduction to the Literature of the New Testament*, pp. 550 ff. New York: Scribner's, 1911.

of Jesus' conversation with the Rich Young Man (Mk. 10:17-22). Here, however, the dialogue runs off into a discourse (3:16-21), which is obviously John's commentary on the conversation. The subject, entrance into the kingdom, is reminiscent of Jesus' teaching in the Synoptic Gospels. But when Jesus begins to discuss *how* one enters into the kingdom, he uses language and concepts that are peculiar to John's Gospel. To enter into the kingdom one must be "born anew" (3:3,7). The Greek phrase that is translated "born anew" can also be translated "born from above," and John undoubtedly intended that the phrase should convey this double meaning. To be born anew is to be born of the Spirit (3:6). All men are born of the flesh in their physical birth, but only those who are born anew by the Spirit enter the kingdom. Since the Spirit comes from "above," those who are born anew are also "born from above." This new birth has been made possible by the Son of Man, who has descended from heaven and ascended again (3:13). Those who believe in him "have eternal life" (3:15). This passage could readily be taken for a commentary on the statement in the Prologue: "But to all who received him, who believed in his name, he gave power to become children of God; who were born, not of blood nor of the will of the flesh nor of the will of man but of God" (1:12-13).

The entire dialogue with Nicodemus presupposes not only the earthly ministry but the death and resurrection of Jesus, and the faith of the church. This is evident in the shift from the first person singular to the first person plural in the words, "we speak of what we know, and bear witness to what we have seen; but you do not receive our testimony" (3:11). Here we have the Christian church speaking through John; the birth through "water and the Spirit" (3:5) clearly refers to Christian baptism, which John considered the sacramental rite in which rebirth was consummated. Furthermore, the death and resurrection is presupposed when John says that the Son of Man has descended and ascended again, making this rebirth possible (3:13). John contrasts the Old Testament story of Moses, in which a bronze serpent is set up so that Israelites who were bitten by snakes could be restored to physical health (Num. 21:4-9), with the lifting up of the Son of Man "that whoever believes in him may have eternal life" (3:15). The words "lifted up" in John are symbolical, for they refer to both the elevation of Christ on the cross (death) and to the elevation of Christ to heaven (resurrection).

In the discourse that follows, John gives the purpose of Christ's mission to the world (3:16-17). It is because God "so loved" the world that he sent his only Son, and the ultimate purpose of that love is that the world might be saved through the gift of eternal life. But Christ's coming has brought judgment as well as salvation, for those who do not believe in him are already condemned. The judgment is this: the light (Christ) has come into the world and men have preferred darkness to the light because their deeds are evil (3:18-20). In their blindness they bring judgment on themselves.

For John, the great sin is unbelief, a logical outgrowth of his conviction that in Jesus Christ God's truth ("I am the way, the truth, and the life") has been revealed. Unless a man knows the true way of life as revealed in Jesus Christ, he will inevitably walk the way of darkness or sin. In part, then, faith is belief in the proposition that Jesus is truly the Son of God. But John does not make faith simply an intellectual matter. He insists that the knowledge that Jesus is the Son of God cannot be verified by reason alone; it is revealed through the Spirit. This revelation is possible only when men open their minds and hearts (as Nathaniel did) to Jesus Christ. Involved here is an act of trust and commitment to the possibility that God was revealing himself through Christ. In short, faith means not just accepting certain propositional truths about Christ; it means entering into a personal relationship with Christ in which trust and obedience become the controlling factors in a man's life, thought, and action.

Moreover, belief in the truth that eternal life is given through Christ is possible only to those who enter into that life. In so far as God alone is the truth, his truth can be known only as it is communicated directly by him to man. But the truth he communicates is not truth *about* himself, but rather *himself*. John believes that God communicated through Jesus Christ and that through him God's love and eternal life are communicated to man. To know the truth, then, is to know God, who reveals himself in Jesus Christ as the one who loves and who gives his Spirit to man. Such truth and knowledge can be comprehended only by entering into a union with God through his only Son, Jesus Christ.

In the discourse with Nicodemus, we have an example of how John transformed the eschatological teachings of Jesus and of the early Christian community. For John, life in the kingdom is primarily a *present reality* and not a *future expectation*, since eternal life has already entered into history with the coming of Jesus Christ. Baptism is not a baptism of repentance in expectation of the coming of the kingdom; it is being born anew as a child of the heavenly world of the Spirit. This approach recalls a phrase that was common in hellenistic religious thought—"reborn into eternity."

Further, although John uses the title "Son of Man" to designate

Jesus Christ, he no longer pictures an apocalyptic figure coming on the clouds of heaven to effect final judgment. The final judgment has already begun with the coming of the Son of Man; it is an event that is now occurring in history as a result of the coming of Jesus Christ. The Jewish apocalyptic concept of the Son of Man has been appreciably modified in John by his concepts of the heavenly Son of God and the pre-existent *logos*. And all these concepts have been given new meaning through the work and words of Jesus Christ.

THE SAVIOUR OF THE WORLD

In the dialogue with the Samaritan woman (Jn. 4), John develops the theme of the new life bestowed by Christ. When Jesus asks for a drink from Jacob's well, the woman is puzzled not only by the fact that a Jew would ask a Samaritan for a drink (John explains that the Samaritans and Jews were not on the best of terms), but also by Jesus' statement that he gives "living water" that becomes a "spring of water welling up to eternal life" (4:14). The water metaphor appears frequently in the Old Testament as a symbol of God's activity in giving life to men. In an eschatological passage in Zechariah, for example, it is prophesied that when the "day of the Lord" comes, "living waters" will flow out of Jerusalem and the Lord will become king over all the earth (Zech. 14:8-9). But John uses water as a metaphor for the Spirit, as he explicitly says (7:38-39). With the coming of Jesus the Messiah, all the expectations of the final "day of the Lord" are being realized; not the least of them is the coming of the Spirit (7:38-39) and the life it brings.

When Jesus discloses intimate details of the Samaritan woman's past life, she calls him a prophet and asks him to answer the question that has divided the Jews and the Samaritans for centuries: Where is the proper place of worship—the Temple in Jerusalem, or Mt. Gerazim in Samaria where the Samaritans worshipped (4:20)? Jesus answers that true worship occurs neither in Jerusalem nor on Mt. Gerazim, for the "hour is coming and now is" when worship "in Spirit and truth" shall prevail. The woman realizes that this answer is more than a prophecy, and replies that only the Messiah could possibly "show us all things" (4:25). Then, in response to her dawning faith, Jesus tells her, "I who speak to you am he" (4:26). This characterization of Jesus as the revealer of all things has associations both with Jewish speculation about the Messiah and with the gnostic concept of a divine revealer who leads men into knowledge of truth.

In this dialogue between Jesus and the Samaritan woman, John explicitly links together the new life and the new worship that he has already alluded to in the sign at Cana and the Cleansing of the Temple. It is no accident that the setting for this dialogue is Samaria, for the coming of the Samaritans (4:39-42) demonstrates the universal nature of eternal life and true worship. The disciples would postpone the true and universal worship of God until the coming of the kingdom (four months until the harvest, 4:35); but Jesus declares that the hour has already come when the true God is being worshipped universally. While salvation is from the Messiah of the Jews (4:22), Jesus, who is that Messiah, has proved to be the universal saviour of all men. So the Samaritan friends of the woman confess "this is indeed the Saviour of the world" (4:42). In calling Jesus Saviour, John is using a term that would have greater religious significance to Gentiles than the strictly Jewish term Messiah would have. Jesus has come to accomplish God's work (4:34), and that work is no less than the salvation of the world.

In the second of Jesus' signs, which follows immediately after the dialogue with the Samaritan woman, John illustrates the work that God has sent Christ to perform (4:46-54). Jesus heals a Roman official's son who is at the brink of death, and by so doing elicits the faith of the Roman official and his entire household. The fact that the man is a Roman emphasizes again the universal scope of the salvation

The Roman forum and part of a temple at Sebaste, the Greek-style city of Samaria built by Herod the Great and named in honour of Augustus ("Sebastos" in Greek).

THE COMMUNITY AND THE WORLD: I

Jesus brings. This sign points to the ultimate work of Christ—the healing of men at the brink of spiritual death through his life-giving word and through faith in its power. In the very hour that Jesus utters his healing word (4:53), the official's son recovers from his illness. But just as Christ's word restores physical life, so also is his word the source of eternal life to all who believe—Jew, Samaritan, or Roman.

THE WORK OF THE FATHER AND THE SON

The third of Jesus' signs, the healing of the man in Jerusalem at the sheep-gate pool (5:2-18), is a reinterpretation of one of the Synoptic healings (Mk. 2:11; Mt. 9:6; Lk. 5:24). In the Synoptic account, however, it is Jesus' forgiveness of the man's sins that arouses a dispute with his Jewish opponents, whereas in John it is the fact that he makes himself "equal with God" by calling God Father. Even the argument over his performing the miracle on the Sabbath is subordinated to this central difficulty.

In the long discourse that follows the miracle (5:16-47), the true meaning of the sign is given. Jesus heals the man according to the Father's will, not his own; and the sign points to the final work of the Father, which is raising the dead and giving eternal life (5:20-21). Since the Father loves the Son and has sent him to accomplish his work, whoever hears the Son's word and believes God who sent him has eternal life, does not come into judgment, and has already passed from death to life (5:24).

In the fifth chapter, John develops several themes that he is to elaborate further in the rest of the Gospel. Earlier, he had used mythological language in commending Christ's authority and power. Christ is the unique Son of God who has come from heaven (1:11; 3:13, 17, 31, etc.). Though John continues this theme, he speaks more and more of Christ's Sonship in terms of his doing the work of the Father. The Father has sent the Son to give eternal life to the world (3:16; 5:21, 26), but the Son's coming also involves judgment (3:17-21; 5:22-23). Those who believe the Son have eternal life; those who do not, stand under judgment. The crucial point of later discussions is whether or not Jesus was "sent" from God.

The Greek word that John uses for "sent" is significant. In the Old Testament, it was used to refer to the office and work of a prophet or any other man who was believed to have been commissioned by God to speak or act in his name. One who was "sent" by God bore the authority and represented the power of the sender, and it is in this sense that the word is used elsewhere in the New Testament. The noun "apostle" comes from the same root, and means one sent with a com-

o

mission from God to speak and act on his behalf. This use of the term was also familiar to hellenistic religious thought—in gnosticism, for example, divine agents and their earthly disciples are "sent" as messengers of divine truth. But John claims that Jesus, being the Son, not merely represents the authority of God and speaks the word of God, but actually bears *in himself* that authority and power. The words he speaks *are* God's, and the works he does *are* the work of God. This is because he is himself God's Word.

This identity of Christ's work, authority, and will with God's leads to increasing conflict with the Jews. They continue to seek for eternal life through their scriptures (Torah) (5:39), while all the time the living Word is in their midst. John argues that if the Jews understood their scriptures, they would recognize Christ as the one prophesied by Moses (5:45-47). Their failure to understand their own scriptures, in which Moses himself wrote of Christ (5:46-47), is proof that they do not understand who Christ is.

The fourth (6:1-14) and fifth (6:16-21) signs, also reinterpretations of Synoptic miracles (Mk. 6:34-44; 45-52), further emphasize the divine power manifested in Christ's work. The fourth sign is John's version of the Feeding of the 5,000. When Jesus has finished feeding them, the people declare that he is "the prophet who is to come into the world" (6:14), and they wish "by force to make him king." The crowds do not understand the true meaning of the sign—they do not realize the nature of the one with whom they deal, and hence they fail to recognize that his kingship is "not of this world" (18:36).

The fifth sign is Jesus' walking on the water, and the climax comes in his words to the disciples "It is I" (6:20). The English translation of these words does not convey the full significance of the Greek *ego eimi*, which literally means "I am." This was a technical phrase that had already been used as a name for God in the Greek translation of the prophet Isaiah. John uses it to signify the presence of God himself in the person of Jesus. Although the crowds saw in the miracle of the Feeding the power of an earthly king, here, in the words "I am," Jesus discloses to the disciples that God himself is with them. But even the disciples do not fully understand.

In the lengthy discourse that follows (6:25-65), John tries to explain the meaning of the Feeding of the 5,000. The crowds have seen it only as a miraculous work that reveals Christ's power to establish an earthly kingdom (6:26-27). But Jesus tells them that the Son of Man has not come to supply material needs but to give food that is the source of eternal life. The contrast between Moses and Jesus, already suggested earlier by John (1:17; 5:46), is further drawn when Jesus recalls that Moses miraculously gave the Israelites manna to sustain them in the wilderness, and yet they all died (6:49). Now Christ does what Moses could never do; he gives the "true bread from Heaven" which affords eternal life to the world.

In answer to the request that he produce some of this bread, Jesus says, "I am the bread of life; he who comes to me shall not hunger, and he who believes in me shall never thirst" (6:35). This is the first of a series of sayings that are prefaced with the words "I am," and are followed by a phrase with symbolic meaning, such as "bread of life," "the light" (8:12), "the door" (10:7), "the good shepherd" (10:11), "the resurrection and the life" (11:25), "the true vine" (15:1), "the way, the truth, and the life" (14:6). Although this form of pronounce-ment is not found in the Synoptic Gospels, it had been used from ancient times in the Orient as a mode of speech for a divine being. According to one Jewish view, when the Messiah came the heavenly manna would again descend from heaven as it had in Moses' day and would provide food for the faithful. According to another view, the manna was a symbol for the Law that was given through Moses.[5] But in John the heavenly food has a unique meaning, for here Jesus Christ is the "true bread." Just as he gives the living water (Jn. 4) that brings eternal life, so he offers the food that gives "life to the world." He accomplishes this by doing the will of the Father (6:38), by giving his flesh for the world. When John identifies the true bread with the "flesh" of Jesus, he emphasizes that it is through the words and deeds of the historical person Jesus Christ that God has given man eternal life.

This discourse on the true bread is followed by a dispute among the Jews, who ask how Jesus can give his flesh to be eaten (6:52). Jesus replies, "He who eats my flesh and drinks my blood has eternal life, and I will raise him up at the last day. For my flesh is food indeed, and my blood is drink indeed." This answer seems to confirm the Jews' misunderstanding rather than to resolve it. But to his disciples Jesus explains that the flesh avails nothing; it is the "Spirit that gives life" (6:63). Only when they have seen the Son of Man "ascending where he was before" will they be given this food. In speaking of the ascent of the Son of Man, John refers once again to the resurrection of Jesus, which is necessary before the Spirit is sent; the Spirit alone reveals the truth of Christ's words and deeds and is the source of eternal life to those who believe.

---

[5] See C. H. Dodd, *The Interpretation of the Fourth Gospel*, pp. 333-345. Cam-bridge: University Press, 1953.

John's account of the Feeding of the 5,000, and the discourse that follows, obviously reflect the eucharistic teaching of the early church. As the community ate the bread and drank the wine, it was conscious of the fact that Jesus, the Son of God, the Messiah who had lived as a man among men, now shared his life through the gift of the Spirit. Although the Son truly revealed himself in the flesh, the full revelation came only when he sent the Spirit after the resurrection. For John, the ultimate meaning of the sign of the Feeding of the 5,000 was the death and resurrection of Jesus Christ, through which eternal life was given to the world. And John interprets the feeding as the sign in Jesus' ministry of the eucharistic meal of the early church. Through participation in the meal, the believers shared in the spiritual life bestowed by the risen Son of God.

John's language here is close to that of certain hellenistic religious cults, which believed that through a sacred meal they entered into the life of the deity (see Chapter 1). Jesus says, "He who eats my flesh and drinks my blood abides in me, and I in him" (6:56), and the phrase "abide in" occurs with increasing frequency in the latter part of the Gospel. John uses this term to express the mystical union between Christ and the believer, in a sense that is close to Paul's concept of being "in Christ." But unlike Paul, John explicitly interprets the Eucharist through this concept of mystical union. When John later deals more extensively with what he means by mystical union (Jn. 14-17), the difference between his understanding of the concept and the notions popular in his day becomes obvious. In John, the man is not absorbed by the deity, nor is there any deification of the man in which the distinction between man and God is broken down. And in his teaching about the Eucharist he avoids identifying the bread and wine as the body and blood in a way that would suggest they had some magical power when consumed ("The flesh is of no avail," 6:63). The words and the spirit are the source of life.

Since John's language was so closely associated with hellenistic religious ideas, however, it was often subjected to superstitious and magical interpretations. Ignatius, for example, who was influenced by the type of theology we find in John, referred to the Eucharist with the easily misunderstood phrase "medicine of immortality." [6] But John's doctrine of the Spirit (as also Ignatius') stands clearly against such misinterpretations. Although John uses hellenistic terminology and ideology in interpreting the Eucharist, he insists that it is the presence of the Spirit that determines the meaning and efficacy of the Eucharist.

---

[6] *To the Ephesians* 20:20.

THE CHILDREN OF GOD
AND THE CHILDREN OF THE DEVIL

John 7 and 8 are concerned largely with the controversy between Jesus and the Jews, especially the Pharisees. Actually, the controversy reflects the later antagonism between the synagogue and the church, though ostensibly it is over the Law (7:24) in general and the Sabbath observance in particular (and to this extent recalls the Synoptic reports of the actual conflict during Jesus' ministry). But the real issue is over Jesus' Messiahship (7:40-55) and unique Sonship (Jn. 8). In his second "I am" saying, Jesus declares: "I am the light of the world; he who follows me will not walk in darkness, but will have the light of life" (8:12). The Pharisees charge Jesus with bearing witness to himself (8:13); and they insist that his testimony is invalid in light of the Old Testament requirement that more than one witness is needed to establish a case (Num. 35:30; Deut. 17:6). But Jesus claims that the Father also bears witness to him. The very fact that the Jews do not recognize Jesus' claim is proof that they do not know the Father, since Jesus has come from the Father (8:14) and all he declares is what he has heard from the Father (8:26). Contrary to the Jews' claim, they are neither children of Abraham nor children of God, for they seek to kill him (8:39-43); rather, their unbelief and hatred show that they are children of the devil. They do not hear the words of God spoken by Jesus because they "are not of God" (8:47). Consequently, they are slaves of sin (8:34ff.) and will die in their sins (8:24).

As John develops this conflict between Jesus and the Jews, he seems to build up a rigid determinism—for example, in such sayings as "no one can come to me unless it is granted him by the Father" (6:65; cf. 6:44). John seems to say that God has predetermined who can and will believe in Christ. John's determinism springs, not from any tendency to indulge in speculation about man, but rather from his firmly held concepts of faith and revelation. For John, faith is that trusting response to God's Word and action that is the only means of arriving at knowledge of and communion with God. John clearly understands that faith depends on both God's act *and* man's response. But throughout his Gospel he emphasizes the divine side of the relationship: God's revelatory act in Christ. Unless God acts, man cannot know him. It is this emphasis that accounts for the many references to the fact that no one comes to God except he lead them, and except they be his children. Since John believed God's complete revelation was in Christ, God's true children are those who believe in Christ.

Conversely, John says that those who do not respond to Christ are not children of God but children of the devil. Their actions reveal not the truth of God, but the lies of the devil, who is the "father of lies" (8:44). John gives two reasons for the Jews' failure to believe in Christ, and thus for their subservience to the lies of the devil. First, they judge by "appearances" rather than by right judgment (7:24); John means they place their traditional beliefs—that is, what *appears* believable to them—above God's revelation in Christ. Second, they seek "their own glory" (5:44; 7:18; 12:43)—that is, they take more delight in the pride that comes from being Abraham's children, the chosen of God, than in the glory revealed in Christ, through whom Abraham's hope that all men become God's children by faith was fulfilled. Men become children of the devil because **their** desires are his desires (8:44ff.): they seek their own glory and close their eyes to the revelation of God's truth.[7]

In spite of John's apparent determinism, it is evident that all men, without distinction, are potentially children of God. Though all are born in sin (Jn. 9) and must be born again (Jn. 3), God sent his Son to be the Saviour of the whole world. But only those who in faith are "taught by God" will recognize him as Saviour (6:45).

In the sixth sign (Jn. 9), John deals with the cardinal sin of unbelief. The occasion is the miraculous restoration of sight to a man who had been born blind. In the extended controversy with the Pharisees that ensues, two themes are dominant. On the one hand, there is the Pharisees' blindness to the possibility that Jesus' healing act can be in God's power, since Jesus is a sinner who has broken the sabbath laws. On the other hand, there is the blind man's confidence; his recovery is evidence enough that Jesus is from God and has acted according to God's will.

As with the other signs, however, it is only when we grasp the symbolism of this sign that we can understand its ultimate meaning. The clue is found in the man's confession that Jesus is the Son of Man whom he worships (9:38). The true miracle is not the man's recovery of his physical sight, but rather the opening of his "spiritual eyes" when Jesus reveals in faith that he is the Son of Man. John uses physical sight as a metaphor for the faith whereby man sees God in Christ (14:8-11). With the other signs, this sign anticipates the death and resurrection; it was only the Risen Lord who fully opened men's eyes and was worshipped by them.

In contrast to the healed man's faith and sight stands the blindness of

---

[7] For an explanation of John's vehement attack against the Jews, see Chapter 10, p. 310.

the Pharisees. To them Jesus says: "For judgment I came into this world, that those who do not see may see, and that those who see may become blind" (9:39). What does John mean by this cryptic statement? He is saying that in reality all men are blind from birth, not physically but spiritually. The man who was born blind is a symbol of all men, for no man has the power within himself to penetrate the darkness in which he walks. He knows not where he goes, because he knows not where his true life is to be found (8:12). Only God's light can dispel the darkness and reveal the true life, for it is only in God that men have life. But only those who acknowledge their blindness can have their spiritual eyes opened; this acknowledgment is the beginning of faith and sight. On the other hand, those who claim that they see do not know they are blind. They walk in the light of their own knowledge, believing it to be the true light. This is the sin of the Pharisees: Christ cannot open their eyes to who he is because they already claim to know who he is—a demon-possessed man (8:48). Their judgment derives from their own preconceptions of what the Messiah will do and say. It is their claim to sight (their own understanding of how God will reveal himself) that brings judgment upon them. The Pharisees are symbolic of the children of the devil who walk in darkness; the man born blind is symbolic of the children of God who walk in the light. For Christ is the "light of the world" (8:12ff.), without which men do not know whence they go.

In contrast to the Pharisees, who are blind leaders of the blind (as evidenced by their maltreatment of the blind man), Jesus is portrayed in the tenth chapter of John as the "Good Shepherd" who cares for the sheep. This shepherd-sheep metaphor is commonly used in the Old Testament, where God frequently is called the Shepherd of his people (Ps. 23; Is. 40:11; etc.). King David, the ideal ruler, is also described as a shepherd (Ps. 78:70; Ezek. 37:24). And in Ezekiel 34 the prophet utters God's promise that he will give his people a shepherd in the Davidic line who will lead them to salvation from the false rulers who are destroying them. Here the shepherd is a messianic figure. John was clearly influenced by the Old Testament in his use of the shepherd-sheep metaphor.

But the metaphor was also common in the non-Jewish world, for it had been used as a divine title in the religions of Egypt, Babylonia, and Persia. It also appears in the Hermetic literature, where one book is entitled *Poimandres*, a Greek word meaning "shepherd of mankind." The shepherd is *nous* (personification of mind), who reveals all truth to mankind. So the metaphor had associations for Jew and non-Jew alike.

Jesus, however, is the "good shepherd," the *true* shepherd of the sheep. All who came before him are robbers who would lead the sheep astray (10:8). He alone gives life to the sheep, through laying down his life (the crucifixion) and taking it up again (the resurrection). His sheep include not only the Jewish disciples who first believed, but others who are not of this fold (10:16). John refers here to the Gentiles who accepted Christ when the Jews rejected him, and who made up most of the early communities. These sheep know the Father and the Shepherd, since the Father and the Shepherd are one (10:29). It is ultimately God who calls the sheep through Jesus to the eternal life that no one can take from them, for he is the source of all life (10:25-30).

THE LAST SIGN—RESURRECTION AND LIFE

John brings Jesus' public ministry to its close with the seventh sign, the raising of Lazarus from the dead (Jn. 11). This is clearly intended to be a climactic finale, the greatest of the signs. Each of the preceding six signs points to this seventh, in which Jesus actually restores life to a dead man in the most dramatic demonstration of his divine power. As with the other signs, this miracle is seen as a manifestation of the glory of God (11:4) and the glorification of the Son.

This miracle is found only in John, and there are obvious problems over the historicity of the event. If this striking miracle was known to the other Gospel writers, it is very difficult to explain why they omitted it; only two other accounts of raising the dead are reported (see pp. 101-102), and the early church would hardly have overlooked this one. As it stands, the story is typical of John's language and theology. Furthermore, it is not incidental to the public ministry but actually serves as the climax. The most that can be said is that John was working with traditional materials, on the basis of which he presented Jesus as the giver of eternal life. One explanation suggests that John is reinterpreting as a literal event the parable of the Rich Man and Lazarus (Lk. 16: 19-31), where the point is made that the Jews would not be persuaded even if someone returned from the dead to tell them the truth that Moses and the prophets had spoken. And indeed the raising of Lazarus does not convince the Jews that Jesus is the expected Messiah; rather it leads to the final conflict.[8] Whatever its background in tradition, it is the symbolic meaning of this miracle that is important to John.

Lazarus and his two sisters, who live in Bethany, are pictured as

---

[8] For an excellent discussion, see Alan Richardson, *The Miracle-Stories of the Gospels,* pp. 120 ff. London: SCM Press, 1941

close friends of Jesus (11:3, 5). When Jesus receives word that Lazarus is ill, he says that it is not an "illness unto death" and delays two days before going to his friend. Only when it is certain that Lazarus is dead does Jesus go to Bethany with his disciples (11:14-15). As he approaches Bethany, Martha greets him with the pitiful words that Lazarus would not have died had Jesus been there sooner. When Jesus assures Martha that Lazarus will rise again, Martha shows her belief in the traditional Jewish view of a future resurrection, saying that she knows Lazarus will "rise again in the resurrection at the last day" (11:24). But Jesus corrects this misunderstanding with his reply: "I am the resurrection and the life; he who believes in me, though he die, yet shall he live, and whoever lives and believes in me shall never die"(11:25-26). This saying summarizes the view of eternal life that has been evident throughout the Gospel. Jesus gives eternal life *now* to those who believe in him; those who believe, though they suffer physical death, will never lose the eternal life already bestowed by Christ. When Jesus asks Martha if she believes this, she replies, "Yes, Lord; I believe that you are the Christ, the Son of God, he who is coming into the world." To believe that Christ is the resurrection and the life is to believe that he is the Christ, the Son of God.

The "I am" saying of Jesus, followed by Martha's confession, forms the climax of the story and provided a clue to the symbolical meaning of the sign. For the glory of God that is revealed in the restoration of Lazarus to physical life is but a partial manifestation of the glory that is disclosed in God's gift of eternal life through Christ. The ultimate revelation of this life is to be given only in the death and resurrection, not of Lazarus, but of Jesus. Lazarus is the symbol of all men: Apart from Christ, they are already dead; through him, even in this world, they share in eternal life. John now has the High Priest unwittingly prophesy the gathering together of the true children of God through the death and resurrection of Christ: "You do not understand that it is expedient for you that one man should die for the people and that the whole nation should not perish" (11:50). Not only the Jews who believe, but also the Gentiles (the children of God scattered abroad), are to be gathered into one community (11:51-52) of life.

The Fulfilment of Christ's Hour

The events following the raising of Lazarus take place under the shadow of the imminent death of Christ. John concludes his account of the ministry of Jesus with a series of brief semi-public incidents. As in the Synoptic Gospels, the action occurs during the Passover Season (12:1). In the home of Mary and Martha in Bethany, Jesus is anointed by Mary. But John, unlike Mark, has the anointing take place immediately before the Triumphal Entry (12:12ff.; cf. Mk. 11:7-10). Whereas in Mark the anointing is interpreted as preparation for burial, in John the event symbolizes Jesus' anointment to kingship. After the anointing, Jesus enters Jerusalem and the people proclaim him "King of Israel" (12:13). Neither the crowd nor the disciples understand Jesus' kingship (12:16); it is only after his resurrection that they understand ("when Jesus was glorified"). He dies as the king of the Jews (19:12); but again the terminology is symbolic, for his kingship is "not of this world" (18:36).

In consternation, the Pharisees cry: "Look, the world has gone after him" (12:19). Again John places an unwitting prophecy on the lips of the Pharisees, for John writes from the vantage point of one who has seen men from all over the world, mostly Gentiles, enter into the church. The coming of the Greeks to "see Jesus" (12:21) is John's dramatic way of announcing that Christ's death is near. With their coming, "the hour" in which the Son of Man will be fully glorified is near. The hour of Christ's death is the hour of judgment on this world whose ruler (the devil) is cast out (12:31), and the death is the doorway to the resurrection in which the victory over death and darkness (the realm over which the devil presides) is completely manifested. The world is judged for its unbelief; by their rejection of Christ, the Jews have shown themselves sons of the devil (the ruler of this world, 8:44). At the same time, the "hour" of Christ's glorification is the moment when "all men" will be drawn unto him (12:32)—that is, when the whole world will acknowledge him as the *logos* who came to "his own" but was rejected (1:11). Christ is glorified by God because through him the whole world is given a share in the life of the Father.

THE MEANING OF DISCIPLESHIP

After the Triumphal Entry, Jesus withdraws for a period of intimate association with his disciples (13:1 ff.). The evening meal is clearly John's version of the Last Supper recorded in the Synoptics, but John has it take place the day before the Passover eve. Whether or not John's dating is more correct than that of the Synoptic Gospels is not of great importance, for John was not primarily concerned with historical accuracy. By placing the meal the day before Passover eve, he has synchronized the crucifixion of Jesus with the traditional slaying of the lamb on the day of the Passover. John the Baptist had announced Christ to be the "Lamb of God who takes away the sin of the world" (1:29). Now as the Lamb of God Christ dies in fulfilment of John's proclamation. His bones are not broken on the cross (19:36), just as scripture had enjoined that the paschal lamb's bones be not broken (Ex. 12:46; Num. 9:12). In contrast to the Passover, which celebrates God's leading of the Israelites safely out of their Egyptian bondage, John sees the death of Christ as the event through which God leads all men out of death and darkness into eternal life.

John, like the Synoptics, includes in his narrative of the last meal a reference to Judas' betrayal and the prediction of Peter's denial. But unlike them he omits any account of how the Lord's Supper was instituted.[9] In place of the account of the Last Supper, John substitutes the narrative of the Foot-Washing (13:2-20). The clue to the meaning of this act lies in the introductory words, "Having loved his own who were in the world, he loved them to the end" (13:1). The phrase "the end" may mean either "completely" or "to the point of death." John undoubtedly intends both meanings. The Foot-Washing must be understood against the background of Jesus' death, in which he completely revealed his love. In washing the disciples' feet, Jesus was performing a menial task that was usually the duty of the Jewish slave in the household. This act of humility surprised Peter, who wanted to stop Jesus from performing it. Peter's reaction is reminiscent of his rebuke to Jesus for announcing his coming death, as recorded in the Synoptics (Mk. 8:32ff.). Peter is told that he does not know what Jesus is doing but that someday he will (13:7). Jesus' words to Peter, "If I do not wash you, you have no part in me" (13:8), are a symbolical reference to Christ's death, for it is through Jesus' death, resurrection, and the gift of the Spirit that Christians are washed and have a part in Christ.

John's account of the Foot-Washing recalls the image of Jesus as the Suffering Servant that is so vivid in the Synoptic Gospels. John's interest in presenting Christ as the divine Son has led him to a portrayal that conveys the heavenly glory of Christ, but only at the expense of the profound human emotions and sympathy with which Jesus entered into the sorrows and afflictions of a troubled people. And yet in this brief episode John makes it perfectly clear that the divine Son is none other than the Suffering Servant. In this one dramatic moment John recalls the lowly path trod by Jesus, a path that John has all but obliterated in his desire to show that Jesus has revealed the glory of God.

It is significant that when John refers to the humble Servant he

---

[9] For a discussion of this omission, see A. J. B. Higgins, *The Lord's Supper in the New Testament*, pp. 75-78. London: SCM Press, 1952.

turns his attention momentarily from Christ to the disciples. He speaks of discipleship in the terms of lowly Servant, and points out that there are implications for the disciples in the Foot-Washing. For to call Jesus teacher and Lord means that the disciples must follow the example of Jesus, since "he who is sent [the disciple] is not greater than he who sent him [Jesus]." The true disciple is recognized not only by his faith in the divine Son but also by his following the path of love and humble service trod by the historical Jesus; the disciples must love one another (13:35) even though this means death (15:13), as it did for Jesus. Again we see that although John often used the language of hellenistic mythology, his divine redeemer is no mythological figure who inhabits the heavens. Rather, he is the historical person, Jesus, who saved men by entering into history. And eternal life is not a victorious journey through heavenly space; rather, it is a journey, here and now, along the path that Jesus has trod.

John sets up a vivid contrast between this description of the true disciple and his portrait of Judas, the false disciple. Judas is present through it all, already planning the betrayal. Paradoxically, he will help bring about Jesus's death, through which all men are washed clean, but he himself will not be made clean (13:11). That is why John remarks, "It was night," when Judas leaves (13:30). He is referring not to physical darkness but to the darkness of unbelief of one who fails to see that in Jesus is to be found light and life.

Judas' departure marks the first in the final sequence of events leading to Jesus's death, the moment of the glorification of the Son of Man and God himself. For by his death the Son of Man reveals the love of God for man. In anticipation of his death, Jesus leaves his disciples with one commandment: "That you love one another" (13:34). This is not a "new commandment," except in the sense that the love enjoined is for the first time revealed in Jesus Christ. The disciples are to love "as I have loved you"(13:34),a love that is revealed in the life of humble service dramatized by the Foot-Washing and the death that it symbolically anticipated. Although there were tendencies in the early church to interpret Jesus as a new lawgiver (see pp. 319-321), John presents Jesus as the giver of eternal life that may be shared by entering into union with him. Like Paul, John believes that the ethical life is the "fruit of the Spirit," not the product of rigid adherence to legal prescriptions.

THE FAREWELL DISCOURSES

The last meal provides the setting for a series of long discourses (Jn. 14-16) and a lengthy prayer (Jn. 17). There is some question about whether we have these chapters in their proper sequence, since the words at the close of chapter 14 suggest a departure from the meeting ("Rise, let us go hence"). Yet it is clear that chapters 14-17 stand in close relationship and must be read and interpreted as a unit. These discourses deal with Christ's departure from his disciples and his coming again. Although there is nothing comparable to them in the Synoptic Gospels, they undoubtedly represent John's interpretation of several Synoptic passages. Chief among these is the apocalyptic discourse in Mark 13, which speaks of the coming of the Son of Man on the clouds of Heaven. John's farewell discourses represent his interpretation of these expectations.[10]

In John's Gospel, the discourses are delivered to the original disciples on the last night of Jesus' life. There can be no doubt, however, that it is the Risen Lord who is speaking and that the hearers are Christians living in John's own day. All that is said presupposes the death and resurrection of Jesus, the coming of the Spirit, and the Christian community's long history of experience. True, Jesus' words often seem to refer to the future, but this is because John continues to write within the dramatic framework of this historic ministry.

Several themes recur throughout the discourses. Chief among these is the relationship between Jesus and God, the Father. Jesus enjoys a mystical union with the Father, for he is "in the Father" and the Father is in him; the Father dwells in Jesus (14:11), and is with him in his hour of death (16:32). But this union of Jesus with the Father is not a mystical absorption in which the identity of either is lost. As he has throughout the Gospel, John continues to recognize the distinction between Father and Son: the Father is greater than Christ (14:28). Rather, it is a union grounded in the love of the Father for Christ and Christ's love for the Father; the love of the Father is manifested in his faithfulness to the Son to the end (16:32); Christ's love is manifested in his perfect obedience to the Father's will (14:31; 15:10), finally sealed by his death. And so the words Christ speaks and the works he performs are not his alone but the Father's (14:10-11). John has continually emphasized that in Christ's words and works he was saying and doing his Father's will. But now it is the Father's last work, the death of Christ, that is on John's mind. The seven "signs" were mighty manifestations of power, but the death is to all outward appearances only a show of weakness. And yet, only those who see it as the perfect revelation of God's love can understand the true meaning of the signs and the words that Christ spoke.

---

[10] For a discussion of John's eschatology in relation to the eschatology of the Synoptic Gospels, see Chapter 15.

This revelation is possible, however, only if Christ goes to the Father. And so Jesus repeatedly refers to his going to the Father (14:28; 16:7, 17, 28), in reference to both the death and the resurrection. For John, Christ's going is important as the event by which Christ sends the Spirit. After his death there will be momentary sadness. But then there will be joy (16:16-24), for when the Spirit comes he will reveal the truth of life, death, and resurrection.

Jesus promises to come again. Unlike those Christians who thought of the coming largely in terms of some future event, John speaks of Jesus' coming in the Spirit to the community. In several passages Jesus promises that he will send the Spirit. When the world is no longer able to see Jesus because he is not physically present, the Christian community will see him in the coming of the Spirit (14:18). The Spirit, being the Spirit of truth, will bear witness to the truth about Christ. (15:26). He will reveal all the truths that the disciples could not "bear" (understand) during Jesus' ministry (16:12). Christ will speak to the community through the Spirit, because the Spirit will faithfully declare Christ's words; and, because these are also God's words, they will be true (16:14-15). Since it is only with the coming of the Spirit that all truth is revealed, it is only the Spirit who can reveal that Jesus is "the way, the truth, and the life" and that "no one comes to the Father" except through Christ (14:6). Only those who possess the Spirit will understand that to know and see Christ is to know and see God (14:7-9).

Clearly, it would be impossible to over-emphasize the significance that the concept of the Holy Spirit had for John. Like Paul, John thought of the Spirit in terms of God's pervasive power through which God carried out his purposes in the world. It is as Spirit that God is present in the world. But since God fully revealed himself in Christ, it was in Christ that the meaning of Spirit was revealed. John speaks of the Spirit as "Counsellor," a term that is not found anywhere else in the New Testament.[11] In Greek, this term may mean "advocate" or "comforter," and in John the term has both meanings, as we shall see. The Spirit is present as one who pleads for the community before God, and who comforts the community in its troubles.

Apart from the Spirit, there could have been no community, for it is through the Spirit that the community knows that Christ lives and that the community itself lives by sharing in his life (14:19). And it is

---

[11] A strong argument has been made that these "Counsellor" passages were the additions of a later editor. See W. F. Howard, *Christianity According to St. John*, pp. 74-80. London: Duckworth, 1943.

through the Spirit that the community knows that it shares in the union of Christ with the Father. But, as Christ's union with the Father is grounded in mutual love, so must the union of the community with Christ and the Father. It is by loving Christ and by keeping his commandment of love for the brethren that the community comes to know the love of the Father. Where such love is present, Jesus and the Father come to make their home (14:21-24). This is eternal life as John sees it: life motivated and sustained by trust in the love of God revealed in Christ.

In the discourse on the vine, John allegorizes the union of Christ and the church (15:1-17). Christ is the vine, and Christians are the branches that depend on the vine for life. This allegory is meant to help the church understand the meaning of the union, for if the branches do not bear fruit they are cast forth. To "bear fruit" has a double meaning: in the first place, the church must obey Christ's commandment of love in order that God may be glorified. In this the fruits of discipleship of the church are demonstrated (15:8). But in the second place, it is through this love that the church witnesses God's love to the world, with the result that other disciples are led to God (fruits). As the Great Prayer of Jesus (Jn. 17) reveals, the only reason for the church's existence is to bear witness to the Father's love in word and deed. The church realizes its union with the Father as it bears witness to that love through the Spirit given by Christ.

The church can expect persecution in the world (15:18-22), because the world does not know the Spirit and does not receive it (14:17). The Spirit passes judgment on the world's sin (hatred) in the light of God's righteousness (love); in so far as the world does not desire forgiveness for its sins it turns away from God (16:7-11; 3:19-21). The sin (hatred) of the world, manifested in rejection of Christ's words and love and its persecution of him (16:18-24), has come under God's judgment. But as Christ loves to the end, so the church, even though persecuted, must continue to manifest Christ's loving Spirit so that all the world may believe (17:20).

THE GREAT PRAYER

The farewell discourses conclude with a long prayer ascribed to Jesus. But the language and thought are typically John's and at one point John even has Jesus refer to himself in the third person (17:3). The prayer is a résumé of what John believes Jesus had actually done for the church through his life, death, and resurrection and through the gift of the Spirit. John formulates all this as a great petitionary prayer to God on behalf of man. In the deepest sense, the prayer was not an invention of John, for it was inspired by what Christ had accomplished in obedience to the Father's will. Just what did John consider Christ's accomplishments to have been?

In his "hour" of death, Christ had glorified God by revealing God's love to man (17:1). By dying in obedience to God's will, Christ had finished his work; and when he was raised up into the presence of the Father, he had revealed through his Spirit that to know the only true God was to have eternal life (17:2-5). He had manifested God's name —that is, he had revealed the will, purposes, and love of God to the church, and the church had treasured and proclaimed this revelation (17:6). The Christian community knew that everything Christ said and did was a revelation of God, for it believed he had been sent with the commission and authority of God (17:7-8). Through the continuing presence of the Spirit, the community knew that it was under God's watchful care, and this knowledge was a source of joy (17:11-13). Because of its faithfulness to God's word revealed in Christ, the community had been separated from the world and had come to know its hatred (17:14). Yet confident of God's victory over the world and its evil, the community had been kept from the grasp of evil power (17:15). Instead of being removed from the world, the community had actually been sent by Christ into the world to proclaim the truth that he himself had revealed (17:17-19). The tiny community of disciples had through their proclamation of the word led many new believers into the community of Christ, and there they had come to know the love of God, which is eternal (17:20-24). They believed that Christ would continue to reveal this love throughout all the future (17:26).

This prayer has sometimes been called Christ's "High Priestly Prayer," a term that indicates what John seems to imply—namely, that in the prayer Christ consecrated the church to its life and task in the world. But John clearly shows that it was not through any single word or prayer of the historical Jesus that this consecration took place, but rather through his *total life*. And the consecration did not cease with Jesus' death; rather, it continues to be consecrated through the Spirit throughout the life and history of the church.

THE COMING OF THE SPIRIT

This prayer is the climax of John's Gospel. The speaker is Jesus, the Word of God, who is known not only through the words and deeds of his historical ministry, but also as the living Christ who is present in the community and who leads it to understand the meaning of his ministry for the world. It is through the inspiration and revelation of this Spirit that John has seen Christ's life as a prayer for his people, and it is this Christ whom John has been portraying throughout the Gospel. The ultimate truth about Christ and his works does not spring from a recounting of the literal words he spoke or of the literal works he performed; the truth is disclosed only by interpreting the historic ministry in the light of the meaning that the living Christ continued to reveal to the community in the days beyond the resurrection right up to the time John wrote. We can now understand why John's portrait of Christ differs so decidedly from that of the Synoptics. Even the portrait in the Synoptics reflects the theological interpretation of the early community,[12] but John has carried the interpretation much further. It is as though John had said: Let us re-tell the story of the life and work of Jesus on the basis of the meaning that has been revealed to the present day. Let him speak in language that will be meaningful to us. And let us reinterpret the events of his ministry from the standpoint of later happenings that have unfolded new meaning.

It has been said that John gave the Gospel to all the ages—that is, he freed the life and ministry of Jesus from its narrow Jewish setting and presented him as the Saviour of the world in language that would be familiar to non-Jews. But there is a more profound sense in which John gave Christ to the ages. By implication, John says that the historical Jesus is meaningful to men only when he is known as the Christ who lives in all ages, revealing himself and the Father to the church.

This does not mean that John fails to affirm the significance of the Word become flesh, the historical ministry of Jesus. As we suggested earlier, he constantly presupposes the memory of the apostles as recorded in the Synoptic tradition. Nowhere is this more clear than in John's Passion Narrative (Jn. 18-20), which agrees with the Synoptic record on point after point. In fact, John may even include invaluable historical data that are not found even in the Synoptics. But here again John's interpretative mind is at work. He uses Jesus' trial before Pilate as an occasion for the pronouncement, "My kingship is not of this world" (18:36). And on the cross the last words are "It is finished" (19:30), words that have John's typical double meaning: it is not so much that Jesus' life is ended as that his work as Incarnate Word has been accomplished. And the accomplishment is not marked by the death on the cross, though that is the conclusion of the earthly ministry. It is the gift of the Spirit that marks the accomplishment. John's version of Pentecost is intimately related to Jesus' death and

---

[12] See Chapters 3, 4, 5. Also see discussion on history and interpretation, Chapter 2, pp. 63 ff.

the resurrection appearances of Jesus,[13] the time at which the disciples receive the Spirit (20: 19-23).

And the last word of John is consistent with his position throughout the Gospel: "Blessed are those who have not seen and yet believe." These words are intended for the readers of John's own day. It is not those Jewish disciples who saw Jesus in the days of his flesh who are blessed, nor even those who experienced the post-resurrection appearances; blessed are those in all places and all ages who through their faith know Christ as present in the Spirit in the community of believers.

---

[13] See Chapter 6, pp. 177 ff., for a discussion of the resurrection account in John. See Chapter 6, pp. 185 ff., for John's version of Pentecost.

CHAPTER FOURTEEN

THE COMMUNITY IN RAPPROCHEMENT WITH THE WORLD: II

The Community Seeks a Religious Philosophy: The Epistle to the Hebrews

Some time in the latter part of the first century a Christian leader wrote a "word of exhortation" (Heb. 13:22) to a group of Christians who were threatened by persecution. His writing later came to be called "To the Hebrews," and eventually it was accepted into the New Testament canon as an epistle of Paul. But Paul's authorship was questioned in the first few centuries, was later doubted by Calvin and Luther, and is generally denied today, for the language and theology differ markedly from that of Paul. Numerous other authors have been suggested (Luke, Barnabas, Silas, Apollos, Clement of Rome, and

New Testament readings relevant to this chapter are Hebrews; I Peter.

others), but the question of who wrote the epistle to the Hebrews remains one of the unsolved riddles of the New Testament.

The writing itself reveals a great deal about the unknown author, however. He was at home in the Greek language, and his vocabulary and style compare well with good literary prose of the period. The writing is not an epistle in the proper sense, for although it has an epistolary ending (13:24) it does not begin with the normal salutation. The ending may have been added later in an effort to enhance the claim for Paul's authorship. The epistle closely parallels a type of discourse common to hellenistic rhetoric,[1] but the literary form has been modified under the influence of a type of Christian preaching. The author develops his argument within the framework of a series of quotations from the Old Testament; he interprets the quotations in the light of the revelation of Christ; and then he exhorts his readers to specific action.

The language, style, and form of the writing indicate that the author had been educated in the hellenistic tradition. For example, he uses terminology and concepts that show some familiarity with Platonic thought, as in his tendency to see earthly forms and phenomena in contrast to heavenly and eternal realities. Here he shows affinity to the writings of Philo, and some scholars have argued that the writing originated in Philo's home city, Alexandria. The author also resembles Philo in his method of interpreting scripture, in his dependence on the Jewish Wisdom literature, and in his fondness for tracking down the derivations of words. On the other hand, he seems familiar with the rabbinical principles of interpreting scripture. In short, the author could have been either a Jewish Christian or a Gentile Christian; in either case, he had come to know Christianity as it was interpreted under the influence of hellenistic Judaism.

Since the author tells us that he was a second- or third-generation Christian (2:3), the writing can be dated some time in the late first century A.D. And it is addressed to a community that is threatened by persecution (see pp. 377 ff.) and is in danger of apostasy. Only in the closing salutation, "Those who come from Italy send you greetings" (13:24), do we find any clue to the actual destination of the writing. This phrase has generally been interpreted to mean that the writing was first sent to Rome, and that there were Roman Christians with the author who sent greetings to their friends back home. The phrase may be a later addition to the text, but even so it would reflect a tradition

---

[1] See A. H. McNeile, *An Introduction to the Study of the New Testament*, 2nd ed., pp. 225 ff. Oxford: Clarendon Press, 1953.

that had already related the writing to Rome. Our surmise that the epistle was sent to Rome is strengthened by the fact that the first writing that shows acquaintance with Hebrews is *1 Clement*, which is traditionally believed to have been written in Rome about A.D. 96. And it is true that toward the end of the reign of Domitian (A.D. 81-96) the Christians of Rome experienced some hostility from the government.

The writing has a very practical end in view: to strengthen the readers in their faith. The author strives earnestly to lead his readers to a fuller understanding of the truth for which they are being called upon to suffer. They have been called to share in eternal salvation in Jesus Christ, and he summons all the theological insights at his command to help them stand firm in their faith. It is this purpose that leads him to picture Christ as the great High Priest whose sacrificial death is the doorway to salvation. He embodies his appeal in a sermon to be read in the church to which the epistle was sent.

THE SUPERIORITY OF THE SON OF GOD

In his magnificent prologue, the author proclaims the finality of God's revelation in Jesus Christ (1:1-4). In ages past, God had revealed himself through the prophets, but now in the "last days" he has given his full revelation in his Son. The Son is the "heir of all things"; all God's promises to man are being realized through Christ (6:12, 17). Philo had referred to the *logos* as the "heir"—the divine, immanent principle that guides the world to its appointed ends. By heir, our author has primarily in mind God's Son who brought salvation to the world. The author, like Paul and John, is clearly influenced by the wisdom and *logos* speculation of hellenistic Judaism when he attributes to Christ pre-existence and a mediating role in creation (1:3). But his major concern is not with cosmological speculation about Christ or the creation, but with God's purposes in creation as they are revealed in the salvation accomplished through the Son: *the end of creation is redemption.*

He speaks of the finality of God's revelation in two senses: First, in the eschatological sense that with the coming of the Son the "last days" of this age have been entered. And second, in the more philosophical sense that the Son has fully revealed the nature of God. To the hellenistic mind, the very title "Son of God" would have suggested a unique relation of oneness with God. But our author is very explicit on this point. Christ reflects the glory of God, and bears the very stamp of God's divine nature. The Greek word translated as "reflects" is a hellenistic term that was borrowed both by Philo and by the Jewish

Wisdom literature. A favourite analogy to explain how the transcendent God could manifest himself in the world was that of the sun and its rays. As the sun's rays (reflections) participated in the very essence of the sun's light, yet without diminishing that essence, so the divine life was mediated in the world without diminishing or disturbing the source from which it came. The author adopts this analogy to illustrate the unique relation between God and Christ.

The author comes to the crucial point of God's revelation in Christ when he refers to "purification for sins" and Christ's having "sat down at the right hand of the Majesty on high" (1:3). Here he turns to God's act of salvation in the historical death of the Son through which purification was accomplished, and to its consummation in the Son's exaltation to heaven. These are to be the subjects of the main section of his writing. The reference to the historical work of the Son, standing as it does in the midst of quasi-philosophical terminology, clearly relates God's final revelation to the historical person Jesus. In the death and exaltation of this historical person, God's salvation has been accomplished and Jesus' unique relation as Son has been revealed.

The author now elaborates on Christ's superiority to all other beings; he considers angels first (1:5–2:9), using Old Testament passages to support his thesis. Like other Christians of his day, our author regards the Old Testament writings as prophecies looking forward to Christ. Turning to a passage from the Psalms (Ps. 2:7) and to a passage from II Samuel, he points out that Christ has been called "Son" by God (1:5), whereas the angels have not. On the contrary, angels have been commanded by God to worship the Son (1:6), and according to Psalm 45 the Son has been anointed by God as the righteous ruler of God's kingdom (1:8-9). The author interprets Psalm 45, which was originally an enthronement psalm written to celebrate the anointing of a Jewish king, as a reference to God's appointment of Christ as the Messiah-King. This same theme of the victorious rule of the Messiah-King is also found in his next statement—namely, that God has promised that all the enemies of righteousness will be put in subjection to the Son (1:13); in contrast to Christ, angels are not to be served, but rather are to act as ministering servants to those who are to obtain salvation (1:14; 1:7).

But what practical point are the readers of the epistle to gather from this discussion of Christ's superiority to the angels? This is just what the author tries to make clear in the first of his series of exhortations to his readers (2:1-4). Since their salvation is given only through the Son himself, who is superior to all heavenly beings, he asks them how they can escape judgment if they neglect "such a great salvation."

Clearly, they must pay close attention to this salvation, which was declared first by the Lord (Jesus), attested to by those who heard him (perhaps the apostles), and later by Christians. By making this reference, the author is firmly grounding his own message in the *kerygma* of the Church. Whatever his own interpretation of the *kerygma*, it is clear that he believes he is remaining true to its content and intent.

In developing this argument, the author is making use of a rabbinic principle of interpretation called *a minore ad majus* ("from the lesser to the greater"). If breaking the Torah that was given by lesser beings (according to Jewish tradition God had given the Torah through angels) brought judgment, a far worse judgment will result from disobeying the word of the Son of God, who is far superior. Later on in his writing, the author uses this same principle over and over again.

Now the author quotes from another Psalm, which he interprets as God's promise that in the age to come (the new age) all things will be put in subjection to man, and not to angels (2:5-8). But anyone can see that all things are not yet subject to man; in particular, our author has in mind the power that death still seems to hold over man. The author calls upon his readers to fix their gaze on Jesus (2:9-18), who has suffered death but who has been exalted and crowned with honour and glory. It is to Christ that they must look for evidence of the new age and of man's victory over death. Jesus has tasted death for every man. The author believes that the promises God gave to man have been fulfilled in the man Jesus, who through his suffering became the pioneer of salvation to many "sons" who share in his "sonship" and in the promises. This fulfilment was made possible because Jesus was a man ("partook of the same nature") and through his death destroyed the devil who holds man in the power of death. Here the author has preserved the apocalyptic mythology of the conflict between the Messiah and Satan that is found elsewhere in the New Testament.[2] But he concentrates on the victory over death—or the "fear of death," as he puts it—perhaps remembering that his readers are under threat of persecution.

The author does not say just how this victory has been won. But later on he speaks of Jesus' being "made perfect" through obedience (5:8-9), and we may assume that it was in Jesus' perfect obedience to God's will that he overcame the power of evil and the death that is the inevitable consequence of sin. But this mode of thinking about the meaning of Jesus' death is not central to the author's argument, for his major concern is not the destruction of the devil but the expiation of

---

[2] See Chapter 2, pp. 56 ff.; Chapter 3, pp. 88 ff.

sins by Christ acting as a faithful High Priest (2:17). Although the term "High Priest" is injected here, its meaning is not discussed until we come to the main theological argument of the writing (4:14–10:25).

Next, the author shows the superiority of Christ to Moses (3:1–4:13). Christians share in a "heavenly call" given by Jesus, who is the "apostle" and High Priest. This is the only place in the New Testament where Jesus is called "apostle." The term here has its usual technical meaning of one sent with the commission and authority of the sender (God).[3] But notice that it appears side by side with the term High Priest—a fact that may give it added meaning. According to rabbinic tradition, on the Day of Atonement the High Priest entered the Holy of Holies as the apostle of the people and represented them before God. Since the author later pictures Christ in these very terms (9:24), he may purposely be using the word apostle in an ambiguous way here.

In contrast to Christ's call, Moses had called the house of Israel into being. But Moses, as the representative of the house of Israel, was merely a servant; the author believes that what Moses said and did merely testified to, or foreshadowed, what Christ was to say and do (3:5). Since the true household that Christ built was merely foreshadowed by Moses and Israel, the author argues that Christ is far superior to Moses.

Again the author exhorts his readers to hold fast to their confidence in Christ, through whom the true household of God (the church) has been built, in order that they may remain members of that household (3:6–4:13). Quoting Psalm 95, he calls to his readers' mind the story of how Israel disobeyed Moses in the wilderness when they doubted God's promises that he would lead them to a new land (Num. 12:7 ff.). From the Psalm, he recalls how Moses warned them that unless they refrained from rebellion "today" they would not enter into God's "rest." Then he interprets the word "today" as actually foreshadowing the day in which Christ has called the true household into being. The author uses the term "today" in an eschatological sense to refer to "these last days" (1:2) when the Messiah, the Son of God, has come to lead God's people to God's "rest."

The "rest" that was promised to the Israelites was entrance into the Promised Land. But here again the author uses a term to foreshadow something that came later—the "rest" foreshadows the better promise that the author refers to variously as entrance into the heavenly sanctuary (10:19), into the city of the living God (12:22), or simply salvation (2:3). He is depending here on Jewish speculation about the

---

[3] For a discussion of the term see Chapter 13, pp. 397 ff.

statement in Genesis (2:2 ff.) that when God had finished the creation he rested. But it was inconceivable to the Jews that God had ceased his divine activity after creation. Philo, for example, insisted that the "rest" merely referred to God's continuing work; since it was of the very nature of God to create, this rest was a symbol of his effortless, unhindered, divine activity. One rabbinic interpretation was that the rest referred to God's completion of his work in judgment and salvation. All these interpretations were related to the meaning of the Sabbath, which commemorated the creation. And the author of Hebrews says there remains "a Sabbath rest for the people of God" (4:9). This is the true rest, the heavenly sanctuary, into which Jesus Christ, having been perfected through suffering, has already entered. It is the rest into which the people of God will enter if they are obedient and hold fast their confession of faith (4:11-14). To fall short of that "rest" is to come under the judgment of God, who discerns the inward thoughts of men (4:12-13).

CHRIST, THE TRUE HIGH PRIEST (HEB. 4:14–7:28)

The author now turns to his central teaching about Christ, in which he compares and contrasts Christ's work with that of the Levitical priesthood. In his typical rhetorical style, he again introduces a subject that he will elaborate later on (Heb. 8-10). Throughout the early stages of the argument he emphasizes two points: first, because Christ was a man, and therefore was tempted as all men are, he can sympathize with men's weakness and give help in time of need (4:14-16). This point would be particularly meaningful to his readers, who were facing a threatening historical situation. In one of the few references to the historical ministry of Jesus found outside the Gospels, the author recalls the Synoptic story of Jesus' agony in the Garden of Gethsemane (5:7-9): "In the days of his flesh, Jesus offered up prayers and supplications, with loud cries and tears, to him who was able to save him from death, and he was heard for his godly fear." The second point is that through Christ's obedience to God even unto death he fulfilled his own destiny as Son by becoming the source of eternal salvation to all who obey him (5:8).

Like the Levitical priests, Jesus is human, and so he can understand and sympathize with human weakness. This is a truth that must not be lost in face of the belief that he is a great High Priest who "has passed through the heavens, Jesus, the Son of God" (4:14). And just as the High Priest in the Levitical line is appointed by God to act on behalf of men in their relations to God, offering gifts and sacrifices for sins, so Christ is appointed by God and offers a sacrifice (5:1). But there is a difference: The Levitical High Priest is beset by human weakness and has sinned, and he must offer sacrifices for himself as well as for the people (5:2-3). But Christ, though a man, is without sin (4:15), and so does not need to offer sacrifices for himself.

There is also a difference in the way in which Christ was called to his ministry. Just as Aaron and his descendants in the Levitical line of priests were appointed by God and not self-appointed, so Christ was appointed by God (5:5-6). But Christ was called to his ministry as Son (5:5). The author again quotes Psalm 2, which he, along with other Christians, believed was a prophecy of Jesus' appointment as Messiah. This is an important point, for it shows that it is *as Messiah* that Jesus exercises his priestly role. But the author also quotes Psalm 110:4, "Thou art a priest for ever after the order of Melchisedek," which he also interprets as a reference to Christ. Now the first verse of this Psalm, "The Lord says to my Lord: sit at my right hand, till I make your enemies your footstool," was commonly interpreted by Christians as referring to Christ's exaltation to heaven as Messiah (Mt. 22:44; Mk. 12:36; Acts 2:34; I Cor. 15:25; Eph. 1:20; etc.). But our author is the only New Testament writer to use the reference to the order of Melchisedek. What he intends to do is to show the superiority of Christ's order of priesthood (Heb. 7) to the Levitical order; but before he does that he again exhorts his readers (5:11–6:12).

He reprimands them for their dullness of hearing (5:11) and for their sluggishness in faith and conduct (6:11-12). Although they ought to be teachers, they themselves are in need of being taught again the first principles of God's word. But he proposes to leave elementary doctrines and go on to mature teaching (6:1-3), despite their need to be fed with milk rather than solid food (5:12). Exactly what the author means by "milk" and "solid food" is not clear. Usually the solid food is taken as the author's interpretation of Christ as a priest after the order of Melchisedek (5:10). It has even been suggested that the author, under the influence of gnosticism, thinks of solid food as esoteric knowledge about Christ that only the mature (5:14) are able to receive.

When the author uses the terms "dullness" or "sluggishness," he is not referring simply to his readers' understanding of doctrine. The meaning of "dullness" depends upon the meaning of the word "mature," which is a translation of the Greek word meaning "perfect." As used in the mystery cults, this term referred to the state of those who had been initiated. In gnostic circles, it referred to those who were in possession of the secret knowledge whereby the gnostic was guaranteed salvation from the material world. Paul uses the term to refer to

Christians who through the Spirit have come to know the Wisdom of God revealed in Christ (I Cor. 2:6-10).

But in Hebrews, "perfection" has a somewhat different connotation. Essentially, it refers to the status of one whose sins have been forgiven through the sacrificial death of Christ (9:26). "For by a single offering he has *perfected* for all time those who are sanctified" (10:14). The author stresses that as a consequence of this forgiveness the believer has had his conscience purified (9:14; 10:22). Once he has been purified he must sin no more, for a Christian who sins after baptism can expect no further forgiveness for sins (10:18, 26). The perfecting that is accomplished by Christ through the forgiveness of sin and the cleansing of the conscience demands a moral purity of life. What is "hard to explain" because they are "dull of hearing" is the truth that having been forgiven they must maintain moral purity of life or they will forfeit their salvation. This is implied by the author's statement that those who live on milk are "unskilled in the word of righteousness" (5:13), whereas solid food is for those who have been trained "by practice to distinguish good from evil" (5:14). In this latter passage, the author is using a philosophical term for the capacity of a person to distinguish between right and wrong.

What is "hard to explain" is also implied in his warning that it is impossible to "restore again to repentance those who have once been enlightened, who have tasted the heavenly gift, and have become partakers of the Holy Spirit, and have tasted the goodness of the word of God and the powers of the age to come, if they then commit apostasy . . ." (6:4-6). Here the author refers to the forgiveness of sins received in baptism and the power to live according to the new life bestowed upon them. According to the author, this includes the power to refrain from apostasy. Apostasy may include the actual denial of Christ under persecution but it also has the figurative meaning found in the Old Testament of denying God through immoral action. Bearing "thorns and thistles" (6:8) may refer to moral corruption as well as to an outright renunciation of faith in Christ. In short, the author is insisting that there is no further repentance for those who deny Christ in word *or* deed.

The author now turns to his interpretation of Christ's work in terms of priesthood. Although Hebrews is the only New Testament writing to speak of Christ's work in these terms, the author may not have been the first to do so. Jewish speculation had already proposed that the Messiah would come from a priestly line. We find evidence of this in the Jewish apocalyptic writing, *The Testament of the Twelve Patri-*

archs, and in the recently discovered Dead Sea Scrolls a Messiah from the line of Aaron is expected.

The thesis of Christ's priesthood is developed in relation to the mysterious Old Testament personage, Melchisedek (Heb. 7), who is mentioned in two Old Testament passages, Genesis 14:18-20 and Psalm 110:4 ff. According to the account in Genesis, Melchisedek, king of Salem and priest of the Most High God, had met Abraham returning from his battle to release Lot from captivity. Melchisedek blessed Abraham and took from him a tenth of all he had.

By a method of interpretation common in the author's day, though it seems far-fetched today, he seeks to establish the superiority of Melchisedek over both Abraham and the Levitical priesthood descended from Abraham. This superiority clearly shows, he argues, that perfection was not attainable through the Levitical line; otherwise the other order of priesthood through Melchisedek would not have been necessary (7:11). The point of the author's involved interpretation is to show that it is in the priesthood of Melchisedek alone that the priesthood of Christ is foreshadowed. Melchisedek was not from the tribe of Levi, nor was Christ (7:13). Melchisedek was made a High Priest for ever, and so was Christ (7:3; 7:24). Christ's priesthood was not validated by his being in the line of Levi but by his "indestructible life" (7:16). The Lord, as the scripture testifies, swore that Christ was a High Priest for ever (7:21).[4]

There is one other important line in the author's argument. If Jesus, in the order of Melchisedek, represents a priesthood that supersedes the Levitical priesthood, then the Law that established that priesthood is superseded (7:12), and a former commandment is set aside (7:18). The author, like Paul, believes that with the coming of Christ the Law has been set aside. But there is a difference in the two views. Paul thought of the Law in terms of its unrealizable ethical demands, and so the Law held him in bondage to sin and death. With the coming of Christ, the power of the Law was broken, for man is justified by faith and not by works of the Law. The author of Hebrews thinks of the Law in terms of the cultus, with its priesthood, sacrifices, and sanctuary, none of which he believes can provide forgiveness of sins. But with the coming of Christ, the true priesthood, sacrifice, and sanctuary are revealed, and through them true forgiveness is made possible. With Christ a new covenant is given that is superior to the old one that established

---

[4] For a discussion of the complicated problems raised by the author's reference to Melchisedek and of previous speculation about this figure, see Alexander C. Purdy and J. Harry Cotton, *The Epistle to the Hebrews, The Interpreters' Bible*, Vol. II, pp. 660 ff. New York: Abingdon, 1955.

the cultus (7:22). And a better hope grounded in better promises is given whereby man is able to draw near to God (7:18; 25). It is to establish the superiority of the new priesthood, sacrifice, sanctuary, covenant, promises, and hope that the author now compares Christ and the Levitical priesthood.

THE HEAVENLY SANCTUARY (HEB. 8:1–10:18)

Having established Christ as a priest after the order of Melchisedek (Heb. 7), the author mentions Melchisedek no more. His purpose has been served, for he has shown that in Christ a priesthood that supersedes the Levitical priesthood has found its fulfilment. The author now turns to the climax of his theological argument, in which he explains how Christ's priesthood is superior to the Levitical priesthood.

The author draws his comparison in terms of a High Priest in a heavenly sanctuary built by God (8:1-2), and in terms of the setting up of an earthly priesthood and the building of an earthly sanctuary according to the Law revealed to Moses on Mt. Sinai (8:5). Here the author alludes to the instructions regarding the tent (tabernacle) in the book of Exodus (24-27). According to this account, Moses was to "make everything according to the pattern which was shown you in the mountain" (Ex. 25:40). Throughout his discussion, the author has in mind this tent that was set up in the wilderness rather than the Temple at Jerusalem, which he had probably never seen. His description of the sanctuary is clearly drawn from the biblical account.

There had been a good bit of speculation among the Jews about this statement to Moses. The word "pattern" had led them to the conclusion that the earthly Temple was a copy of an invisible heavenly sanctuary in which angels continually interceded for the sins of men. The author of Hebrews was undoubtedly influenced by such speculation. But he was also influenced by hellenistic dualism, which tended to think of earthly phenomena as copies or shadows of heavenly realities. He uses the words "copy" (8:5; 9:23, 24) and "shadow" (8:5; 10:1) in contrast to the "true" (8:2; 9:24; 10:1), the "perfect" (9:11), the "real" (10:1). Philo spoke of the Temple as a symbol of the true temple, the invisible world of ideal forms whose Holy of Holies is the heaven, and whose High Priest is the *logos* who leads men to understand that the material world is patterned after the immaterial world.[5]

And yet the author of Hebrews is not primarily interested in the

[5] See E. R. Goodenough, *By Light, Light*, pp. 108 ff., 116 ff. New Haven: Yale University Press, 1935.

cosmos or a replica of the tent in the heavens, but rather in the revelation of the true priest Jesus Christ and the heavenly sanctuary that God has made through him. Not only has Christ obtained a priesthood that is more excellent than the old; he has also mediated a covenant that is better. The author finds his authority for this new covenant in a prophecy of Jeremiah (8:8-12). From the beginning, Christians had believed that this promise of a new covenant prophesied by Jeremiah had been fulfilled in Christ (Mt. 2:18; 26:28; Mk. 14:24; Lk. 22:20). The author of Hebrews is peculiarly interested in the promise of the "forgiveness of sins" (8:12) that will bring about a new relationship between God and man through the true sacrifice of Jesus Christ.

He describes the earthly sanctuary with its ineffectual priesthood and sacrifices (9:1-14). Here he is dependent on the Exodus account (Ex. 25 ff.). Obviously he was not aware that this description (9:1-5) derives from an idealized account by priestly scribes who wrote long after Moses' time. Nor was he apparently aware of certain discrepancies between his own description and that in the Exodus account.[6] But, as he himself says, he is not concerned with details (9:5). The major features that are important for his interpretation are the two inner tents. The outer of the two, known as the Holy Place, was open to all classes of priests, though not to the people; in this area the daily sacrifices were offered. The inner tent, the Holy of Holies, only the High Priest was allowed to enter, once a year on the Day of Atonement (9:7). This great occasion, described in Leviticus 16, preoccupies our author and he deals with it as representative of the whole Levitical system of sacrifices. On that occasion the High Priest entered through the curtain to sprinkle sacrificial blood upon the mercy seat. The sacrificial blood of a bull was sprinkled for the sins of the High Priest himself and of the other priests, for, being human, they too were liable to sin. And the sacrificial blood of a goat was sprinkled for the sins of the people. The author argues that these animal sacrifices could only guarantee ritual cleansing after some infractions of the laws dealing with ritual purity (9:10), such as those found in Leviticus 11. But he contends that none of these sacrifices could perfect the conscience (9:9).

Now the author explains that the outer tent is actually a symbol of the present age, and that as long as it stands it is impossible to enter into the inner sanctuary—the heavenly sanctuary (9:8-9). He seems to mean that until the "new age" came no matter how often the High

---

[6] For these discrepancies, see Purdy and Cotton, "The Epistle to the Hebrews," *Interpreter's Bible*, New York: Abingdon, 1955, pp. 685-687.

Priest entered the Holy of Holies he never actually entered into the presence of God. But with the exaltation of Christ to the right hand of God (8:1), the new age has come (9:26) and the true High Priest has entered the heavenly sanctuary, into the presence of God himself (9:24). And in entering that sanctuary he offered himself and not the blood of goats and bulls (9:11-12).

The superiority of Christ's offering of his life is that it purifies the conscience from dead works through forgiveness of sin. His offering of a life without blemish (sin), through the Spirit, was able to purify men from all sins (9:14; 2:9-18) and so perfect those who were consecrated by that offering (10:14; 10:29). The superiority of Christ's sacrifice is also substantiated by the fact that it was a single sacrifice that could never be repeated (7:27; 9:25-26; 10:10, 12, 14), whereas in the tent sacrifices had to be continually offered, showing that the conscience was never purified from sin. By implication, this single offering was sufficient for all time, since it need not, indeed it could not, be repeated. It marked the end of the old age of sin and the beginning of the new age in which sin and death were overcome by Christ, who was now seated at the right hand of God (10:12-13; 2:9-15). Interpreting words from Psalm 40 as words of Christ, the author can say that Christ himself came to do away with all other kinds of sacrifice (10:5-7) by doing the "will of God," and in his death he consecrated those who believe once and for all.

Christ's sacrifice was superior in yet another sense, for through his sacrificial death he had become the mediator of the new covenant. Alluding to his earlier statement that through Christ the believers are led into God's "rest" (3:7-4:10), the author now declares that the promises of the new covenant are better than those of the old, for those whose sins are forgiven will receive the promised eternal inheritance; they will enter into the heavenly sanctuary with Jesus Christ (9:15, 19). As the former covenants were ratified by the sprinkling of blood (9:15-22), so Christ, through his death, has ratified the new covenant; those who are consecrated by Christ's offering of himself in perfect obedience to God's will are heirs of the better promises.

The author concludes this section with an exhortation (10:19-39) in which he shows the implications of Christ's priesthood for the reader. Although in the Jewish cultus only the High Priest was allowed to enter the Holy of Holies (which was believed to be the peculiar place of God's presence), Christ's "brethren" have confidence that they may enter into the heavenly sanctuary (10:19)—that is, into the heavenly presence of God himself. This is the climax of the author's argument, and he urges his readers to hold fast their confession of Christ and to remain faithful. For having had their conscience cleansed in baptism (10:22), if they now sin deliberately there is no longer any sacrifice for sins; only judgment awaits them (10:26-31). They must continue steadfast in good works and in confidence lest they lose their reward (10:23-25; 35-56).

No matter how elegant this rhetorical argument may have seemed to the first century, to the modern reader it inevitably sounds rather strange. But the patient reader cannot fail to discover the main point of the discourse. The author's basic conviction is remarkably clear: Because man is sinful, his relationship to God is broken, and man himself cannot restore the relationship. Jesus Christ, through his sacrificial death, accomplished what no man could do for himself: He made forgiveness of sins possible and opened the doorway to a new relationship with God through the promise of salvation.

Our author never explicitly explains why a sacrificial death was necessary. In this he resembles the earliest Christians, who, though they proclaimed a relationship between Christ's death and the forgiveness of sins, never explained that relationship. There is certainly nothing in the writing that suggests the concept of an angry God who must be appeased before man can be forgiven. Nor is there any explicit suggestion, as in John and Paul, that it is through Christ's death that God's love is revealed and the believer is made a new creature or is born again.

Two questions stand unanswered: Why was the sacrifice necessary? How did it benefit man? In answer to the first question, the most we can say with certainty is this: The author of Hebrews seems to accept the Old Testament principle that in the relationship God had established with his people (through covenants) and in the people's continuing effort to maintain that relationship (through worship) sacrifice was of primary importance. What was true of the Old Covenant foreshadowed the situation under the New Covenant established through Jesus Christ.

It is equally difficult to decide just how man is to benefit from Christ's sacrifice. The author seems to presuppose that his readers will accept the crucial significance of sacrifice for establishing relations with God. On the basis of this presupposition, he is content to argue the finality of Christ's sacrifice and to summon them to faith that through his sacrificial death their sins are forgiven. The primary benefit seems to be found in the assurance that the believers experience through this acceptance of the effectiveness of Christ's death and the power this faith gives them to endure temptations and to maintain a pure conscience.

The distinctiveness of our author's teaching about sacrifice perhaps can be seen best in relation to Paul. Paul also agrees that Christ's sacrificial death was necessary for man's salvation. But he explicitly sees that death as a revelation of the love of God. Furthermore, man appropriates the benefits of that sacrifice as through faith he enters into Christ's sufferings through the Spirit of Christ who dwells in him.[7] It is the absence of the Pauline concept of faith and of the indwelling Spirit that, among other things, distinguishes our author's teaching on sacrifice, as well as on many other points, from that of Paul.

THE WAY OF FAITH (HEB. 11:1–13:21)

Chapter 11 is one of the best-known passages in Hebrews. It is a roll call of the heroes of the Old Testament who followed the way of faith. The author hopes to strengthen his readers by reminding them that they are not alone in their struggles, and to inspire them to faithfulness by recalling the example of their forebears in the faith.

In his opening lines he gives the only explicit definition of faith that appears in the New Testament (11:1-4). When he says that faith is the "conviction of things not seen," and that through faith we know the world is made out of things that do not appear, he is speaking in language that was common in hellenistic philosophical thought. This is the way of thinking that conceived of the material world as the shadowy and passing image of the heavenly world of reality. This heavenly world is what is in the author's mind when he says it was through faith that Abraham looked forward to "the city which has foundations, whose builder and maker is God" (11:10). Into this scheme of thought the author inserts Jewish apocalyptic language when he refers to the "city of the living God, the heavenly Jerusalem" (12:22). And earlier he has spoken of the heavenly world of reality in terms of a heavenly sanctuary, the true tent, the Holy of Holies. All this metaphorical language points to unseen realities. So he pictures the great Old Testament heroes of faith as "strangers and exiles on the earth" (the material world) looking for a "homeland," "a better country, that is, a heavenly one" (11:13-16). It is into this heavenly world that Christ had gone when he "passed through the heavens" (4:14).

Our author says that it is through faith that we understand the existence of such a world. A philosopher like Philo would have said it was through the mind (*nous*) or *logos* (reason) that man knew of its existence. But our author, deeply influenced by the Christian understanding that all truth is a revelation of God, uses the term *faith*. Nevertheless,

---

[7] See Chapter 9, pp. 283 ff.

P

in so far as the author speculates about an invisible world he clearly reflects the concern of hellenistic philosophy for a rationally acceptable interpretation of reality understood in terms of a transcendent order beyond this world of time and space.

But when our author calls the Old Testament roll of those who have been approved by God for their faith, he stresses another aspect of the meaning of faith: the more familiar biblical concept of faith as that immediate, trusting response to the word of God and to the promises substantiated by that word. Abel, Enoch, Noah, Sarah, and especially Abraham are examples of this faith. Abraham responded obediently to God's call and journeyed into a strange country, trusting only in God's promise that he would lead him to a new land. The author comments that all these heroes were really seeking for something far more than the partial fulfilment of the promise, such as Abraham's arrival in Canaan. It was really the city of God toward which they journeyed, though they did not know the way. Here the author uses faith very nearly in the sense of hope, since in his mind the entrance into the city of God had to await the fulfilment of the promise in Christ.

In the last list of persons (11:23–38), faith has the meaning of patient endurance, a meaning that we have frequently met earlier in the epistle. In this list, which covers the period from Gideon to the Maccabeans, he recalls men and women who risked their lives, suffered, or died a martyr's death in obedient response to God's word. All these, though faithful, did not receive what was promised (11:39-40). This was because God intended for them the promise that was revealed and fulfilled only through Jesus Christ.

The author summons up this host of witnesses before his readers in order to encourage them (12:1). Having given them grounds for faith, he now gives them living examples of faith. And in the centre once more he places Jesus Christ, the pioneer and perfecter of faith. Like the faithful in all ages, Jesus suffered; but by his suffering and elevation to the right hand of God he has revealed the true substance and meaning of faith.

Now the author calls his readers to recognize that, in view of the suffering of the faithful people of the old covenant and of Christ himself, they must expect to undergo the discipline of suffering in resisting sin and abuse (12:5-11). The Greek word for discipline literally means "education" (*paideia*). The author develops the thesis, found frequently in Jewish Wisdom literature, that it is through the discipline of suffering that God educates his people in righteousness. The Stoics had also emphasized that a man must endure suffering as part of his education into true manhood. This was in contrast to the classical Greek concept of *paideia,* which was concerned more with the full-rounded education of the mind, body, and soul according to the ideal of the true, the good, and the beautiful. Quoting from Proverbs 3:11-12, the author says it is through endurance that Christians realize their sonship to God even as Christ did (5:8). The present pain, if endured, will lead to a share in God's holiness when they reach the heavenly city. So they must stand firm (12:12) under affliction lest they fall into sin, for which there is no more repentance (12:17). For they do not have to do with the covenant of Moses delivered on Sinai (12:18-21), awesome as that event was; they have to do with the covenant mediated by Jesus Christ (12:22-24), and with those of all ages who have been faithful to the promises, and with God who is the judge of all men. If those did not escape who failed to obey Moses, who was merely a man, what chance of escape do they have who reject God, who speaks from heaven through his own Son, Jesus Christ (12:25-29)? For what they confront is not the lightning and thunder on Mt. Sinai, but rather the shaking of the foundations of the heavens and the earth in judgment; in this finale only those who have received God's unshakable kingdom will not be consumed. In thankfulness for such a kingdom, Christians are to offer acceptable worship to God with awe and reverence (12:28-29). The author refers not only to worship in the formal sense, but to worship of God through good deeds (13:15).

In this last exhortation and warning, the author reveals his own belief in a final apocalyptic cataclysm and a judgment on mankind. In this he retains the two-age view of the primitive Christian community, a view that stands in strange juxtaposition with the hellenistic dualism that we have found in the writing. But it reveals his Christian understanding that the divine world and the human world (history) are not ultimately two separate realms. The one God who has created all things has revealed himself in history through Jesus Christ. He is not only the One through whom all things had their beginning, but through whom all things have their end. The whole created world moves to a single appointed end, which Jesus Christ has already inaugurated in bringing in the new age.

The author concludes his writing with a series of specific admonitions on the treatment of fellow Christians, and on marriage, money, and respect for leaders, together with statements of doctrine (13:1-17). If this chapter was actually a part of the original writing, he undoubtedly was directing his remarks to specific problems confronting the church to which he wrote. And they were problems that were being faced by all the churches in the first century. He concludes his writing with one of the most beautiful of New Testament benedictions

(13:20-21), in which he reminds his oppressed readers that they are in the care of "Our Lord Jesus," the great "Shepherd of the Sheep" who will provide them with the strength to do what is pleasing in his sight.

We can imagine how encouraging this message must have been to its first afflicted readers. And its message, in a time of social confusion, must have brought hope to Christians in other communities as well. But it would have had a particular appeal for the hellenistic world, for men were wandering in a strange land (the world) of sin and imperfection, and were looking for a saviour who could lead them to a heavenly home (see Chapter 1). The forgiveness of sins, the universality of Christ's salvation, the familiar dualistic teaching, even the persuasive style of the author's argument, would have made a strong appeal. In an age when men sought desperately for a sense of community, our author's presentation of a great company of people gathered together in a fellowship of suffering, journeying toward the heavenly city, must have been peculiarly stirring. And the portrayal of the great pioneer and perfecter of faith as a historical person, not a mythological figure, provided a clearer image of the God whom they had worshipped from afar.

The Community Seeks an Ethical Code: The First Epistle of Peter

To the early church, its primary vocation was to proclaim the message of salvation to the world. And since this was a message of the final revelation of God in Christ, it was by implication a judgment upon all other ways of thinking about God, man, and the world. And yet we have seen in the Gospel of John and the Epistle to the Hebrews that the church did not hesitate to adopt language and concepts that would help it speak more intelligibly to the world. The problem was always how to proclaim the message relevantly without at the same time perverting or distorting it.

In order to proclaim its message, the church found it necessary to live in the world. Its message was concerned with a new life and it believed that its deeds testified as much to that life as did words. This life of the new age, bestowed by God through the Holy Spirit, was radically different from the life of the world and the institutions, customs, and practices that gave expression to it. Nevertheless, since Christians found that they had to live in that world, they realized that they somehow had to relate themselves to its customs and practices without perverting or distorting the new life. They were driven to find an ethical code whereby they might share the new life and at the same time preserve its unique qualities. As we have seen (p. 370), the need was heightened when the church became flooded with Gentiles whose ethical views were radically different from those of Christianity. The church obviously did not weave its norms of conduct out of thin air. There were five main sources from which it drew them, though quite unconsciously and spontaneously. First, there was the Old Testament, which the church believed to be its sacred scripture. Second, there was the ethical tradition of various apocalyptic sects in Judaism which depended on the biblical tradition, though in an altered form. The newly discovered Dead Sea Scrolls have shed new light on this whole movement. Third, there were the teachings of Jesus, preserved by oral tradition and finally written into the Gospels. Although no other New Testament writing actually quotes from the Gospels, it is certain that these teachings were everywhere remembered and were basic to Christian teaching. But, since Jesus had not tried to give a systematic code of ethics, later Christians were confronted by many ethical decisions for which they had no ready answers. This was particularly true when the church found itself living in a Gentile environment, rather than in the Palestinian environment in which Jesus had taught. Evidences of reinterpretation reflecting this need to adapt Jesus' teaching to a new environment are found in the Gospels themselves.[8] A fourth source of ethical standards was the instruction used in the hellenistic synagogues for the training of proselytes. Hellenistic Judaism was indebted not only to the Old Testament but also to the ethical teaching of hellenistic philosophy, the influence of which is evident throughout the New Testament. A fifth source was the common store of hellenistic ethical instruction, though it is difficult to ascertain when the borrowing was direct and when it was mediated through the hellenistic synagogue.

No writing in the New Testament shows more clearly the influence of all these sources than does I Peter. Here we have a revealing glimpse into the mind of the early church as it sought to understand its ethical responsibilities in the world.

EXHORTATION AND INSTRUCTION

Early tradition attributed the authorship of I Peter to the Apostle Peter, but his authorship is generally questioned today.[9] The strongest argument against it is the author's excellent command of the Greek language; the Greek of I Peter, like that of Hebrews, judged by

---

[8] See Chapter 4.
[9] For the best recent defence of Peter's authorship, see E. G. Selwyn, *The First Epistle of St. Peter*, pp. 7-38. London: Macmillan, 1952.

literary and grammatical standards is the finest in the New Testament. It is inconceivable that an uneducated, Aramaic-speaking, Galilean fisherman, even though he spoke Greek, could have written in a style like Paul's. Sometimes it is argued that the excellent Greek can be accounted for by the fact that Silvanus (Paul's former travelling companion, Silas) served as Peter's amanuensis (5:12). But this leaves other questions to be answered: Why was Peter writing to Gentile communities in Asia Minor (1:1), when we have no record of Peter's activity in this area, but do have a specific record that his apostleship was to the Jews? More important, how can we account for the absence of any specific personal references to Jesus, or of any specific mention of his teaching, from a disciple who was one of his closest companions? Furthermore, the author's assimilation of Paul's concepts and his occasional use of Stoic terminology are difficult to explain if this is the work of Peter, for they seem to reflect a later period in the development of Christianity. Finally, the persecution referred to in this writing more nearly fits the historical situation in the time of the Roman emperors Domitian (81-96) or Trajan (98-117).

In any event, some time around the year A.D. 95, a Christian presbyter (5:1) wrote to the Christians in the Asia Minor provinces of Pontus, Galatia, Cappadocia, Asia, and Bithynia (1:1) to encourage them in the face of persecution. There is general agreement today that the latter part of the writing (4:12–5:13) is in some way independent of the major section (1:3–4:11). In particular, the reference to persecution in 4:12-17 clearly implies an immediate and more acute situation than the more general references to persecution in the first part of the writing. Furthermore, the structure and content of the major section (for reasons discussed later) appear to be that of a catechism for new converts. It is highly probable that in part, or in full, we have preserved in the central section a type of baptismal discourse providing instruction for new Gentile converts to Christianity. That is why I Peter is so valuable for our study of the church's ethical teaching, for it provides us with an actual example of what was taught and the form of the teaching.

What seems to have happened was this: In seeking to strengthen the persecuted Christians in Asia Minor (1:1), the presbyter called to mind the teachings they had received at baptism. He added a formal epistolary introduction (1:1-2), and a letter (4:12–5:11), in which he dealt with the immediate threat of persecution and with more general matters, and concluded with a salutation (5:12-14). He wrote in the name of Peter to give his writing the added authority of the famous apostle.

On the basis of the mention of "Babylon," a cryptic term used by
Christians to designate Rome, and of Mark, who according to tradition
was associated with Peter in Rome, I Peter is believed to have been
written from Rome. No better alternative has been proposed. As we
saw earlier, there is reason to believe that I Peter was written in part
to counteract the more violent and incendiary attack made by Revelation on the Roman government.

NEW FAITH AS THE FOUNDATION
OF NEW ETHICAL LIFE

What gave the early community its distinctive character was
its faith more than the conduct of its members. That is why the author
of I Peter prefaces his instructions with a statement on faith, which
lies at the heart of all ethical action (1:3-12). In baptism, Christians
enter into a new life, they are "born anew." Our author, like the author
of the Gospel of John, emphasizes the radical nature of this new life
by speaking in terms of rebirth.

What is the source and substance of this new life? The source of
the new life is God himself, who is the Father of Jesus Christ—the
Lord to whom the Christian has committed his life. The substance of
this life consists of a living hope. This hope is a gift from God that
was made possible when God raised Jesus Christ from the dead and
thereby revealed that men will inherit salvation. But it is only through
faith—that is, through trust in God's revealing act in Christ—that life in
this hope, and the ultimate fulfilment of that hope in salvation, become
a possibility. Since faith and hope are the source of Christian joy (1:6),
Christians will not sidestep ethical decisions that bring them trials
and hardships; their actions are not directed toward temporal ends
such as pleasure, but toward proving their faithfulness to God, who is
the source of their joy (1:6-7). The new life is also characterized by
love for Christ, through whom salvation has come, whom Christians
have not seen, whom the prophets looked for. But Christians have come
to know him through the proclamation of the good news (gospel) that
the Holy Spirit revealed as true (1:8-12). It was the church's faith as
known through the gospel that was the source of the new life.

This, then, is the foundation that the author lays for his ethical
instruction—a sure knowledge that the new life is not to be measured
primarily by what the Christian *does*, but by what he *hopes, believes,*
and *loves*. This approach to ethical teaching is essentially the same as
that of both Jesus and Paul.[10]

---

[10] See Chapter 4 and Chapter 9.

A HOLY NATION,
GOD'S OWN PEOPLE (1 PETER 1:13–2:10)

But the Christian's primary concern with faith does not free him from responsibility for his actions. Faith makes vigorous moral demands. And the Christian's mind must be alerted to these demands; he must be capable of making sober judgments in his daily life if he is not to betray the hope that is to be fulfilled when Christ is finally revealed (1:13). This means that Christians can no longer follow their desires (passions) as they did before they knew the God revealed through Jesus Christ (1:14). The God who has called them out of their aimless ignorance is holy, and he demands that Christians be holy in all their conduct as he is holy (1:16). For God's holiness is expressed not only in love and mercy; he is also the judge of all men, and he judges them according to their deeds (1:17). Through Jesus Christ, God has not only given Christians a new hope and a new life; he has also released (ransomed) them from their bondage to pagan idolatries and from the futile dissipation of the way of life they had inherited from their fathers (1:18-21). But since God has delivered (ransomed) them from all other ways of life, they have really become exiles in the world (1:17). God's holiness has revealed the futility of any way of life (1:18-21) except that lived in faith and hope in the God who raised Jesus Christ from the dead. And Christians can no longer be at home with the world's ways.

What is the way of holiness? It is the way of love. Christians who have obediently responded to God's gracious act of love proclaimed in the gospel (the truth) have been purified through God's holy love; they have been given a new birth in a new community of love. This community's life is born out of and sustained by one thing: the active power of God's creative and redeeming Word disclosed in the gospel. All other grounds of life are transient (perishable seed). And the substance of the new life in the new community is the sincere love of the members for one another (1:22-25).

Notice how logically the author has proceeded through this opening discussion. First, he announced that the new life is grounded in faith (1:3-12). Then he emphasized that faith inevitably demands holiness (1:13-21). And now he concludes that faith and the new life it brings are the foundations of a new community (1:22-25). This community is called "a chosen race, a royal priesthood, a holy nation, God's own people" (2:9).

This concept of community is essential to the author's approach to ethical instruction. The concept was deeply rooted in Jewish tradition and had been stated in different terms by the early church. In the Old Testament, we have a people chosen by God to bear witness to him through word and through obedience to his holy laws. Jesus himself had tried to recall Israel to her mission with his message of the kingdom and the new life of the kingdom. And the early church came into being in the faith that through the death and resurrection of Jesus, and through the coming of the Spirit, God was finally calling his people together and fulfilling his promises to them. Paul, for example, had thought of the church as the spiritual Israel called out of the world by God to live in obedience to his Holy Spirit revealed through Christ.

As a holy nation, then, the church is in exile in the world and Christians are aliens (2:11). This feeling of separateness was heightened by the belief that the Christian's ultimate inheritance (salvation) was a gift of God and not of the world; indeed, salvation would mark the end of this world order. And as long as the community lived in this world, its one authority for action was God's holy will as revealed through Jesus Christ. This meant that the most the church could do was to adjust itself to the world for the time being. Political, social, and economic institutions, and the temporal purposes for which they were set up, were all part of a life that would soon pass away. Consequently, the church worked out no programme of social or political reform. It accepted the social order as it was, although its acceptance did not imply absolute approval. The primary obligation of the church was to live in the world according to the will of God. Sometimes this meant separating itself completely from the practices of the world—as it did on matters involving pagan worship and the rather loose attitude toward sex relations. But on other points the church accommodated itself to the world—as in its relation to government and to social institutions like slavery.

The ethical instruction in I Peter reflects the teaching of the early church on these matters. Beginning with 2:1, and continuing through 4:11, we have a series of exhortations. Study of the Greek text shows that each instruction begins with a technical phrase derived from a Hebrew formula.[11] This phrase is used in the same way elsewhere in the New Testament, especially in Paul's epistles to the Colossians and Romans, in I Thessalonians, in Ephesians, and throughout the Pastoral Epistles. In fact, all these passages, including those in I Peter, show a similarity in content as well. For example, in Colossians (3:8–4:12) we

---

[11] See D. Daube, *The New Testament and Rabbinic Judaism*, pp. 90-105. London: Athlone, 1956.

find a series of exhortations to put off certain vices, worship God, submit to certain people, and be watchful. When we look at Ephesians (4:22–6:18), we find similar exhortations regarding putting off, worshipping, submitting, and watching. And in I Peter we find instructions to put away (2:1), worship (2:4-5), abstain (2:11), be subject (2:13), submit (2:18; 3:1; 3:7), and watch (4:7, keep sane and sober). Further, each of these epistles contains a brief statement about the new life of the Christian in terms of new creation (Col. 3:10ff.; Eph. 4:24), and we find the same reference to the new life in I Peter in terms of regeneration (1:3). Apparently we have embedded in all these epistles a definite type of instruction defining the nature of the new life given in baptism, and governing the conduct of Christians [12] in the world. Each teacher used a definite type of instruction and expanded the materials according to the needs of the local situation. The forms themselves were borrowed from Jewish instructions to proselytes, though they were expanded and revised to give them full Christian significance. The context in I Peter implies that the instructions were intimately related to the baptism of new converts (1:3; 3:21).

The Christians, like the Jews of an earlier day, felt an urgent need to define the unique life of the new community in distinction from the world, and at the same time to provide definite instructions on how members of the community should conduct themselves in the world. There are interesting parallels here with the Dead Sea Sect, which also looked upon itself as a community set apart from the world with its own covenant faith and its own rigorous discipline. But there are important differences too. For although the Dead Sea Sect laid great stress on ethical purity, it strongly emphasized ritual purity. And it attached great importance to withdrawal from normal intercourse with the outside world.

According to I Peter, the one law that determines the life of the Christian community is the law of love. But this is not a vague or sentimental quality; basically, it is love for Christ as Lord (1:8). And to love Christ means to love what he loved—hence Christians are to love one another. Now the author goes on to spell out in greater detail just what is meant by love. Since love is always concerned with the welfare of the brother, any words or deeds that harm him must be put aside (2:1). Like new-born babes (through their new birth), Christians should long for the holy life of love (spiritual milk) in order to be nurtured in preparation for their coming salvation. Obvi-

---

[12] See P. Carrington, *The Primitive Christian Catechism*. Cambridge: University Press, 1940.

ously, since it was within this community that "the kindness of the Lord" (2:3) was known, it is here and not in any other community of the world that the life of love can be nurtured.

The Christian community is likened to a spiritual house whose cornerstone is Christ; the building itself is made up of those who trust Christ (2:4-8). Then, mixing his metaphor, the author refers to Christians as a "holy priesthood" who offer "spiritual sacrifices acceptable to God through Jesus Christ" (2:5). Here he is talking about the ethical life of Christians, for what they offer God are really works of love done in his name. And, like their prayers, these are offerings of thanksgiving to God. Paul too, in Romans (12:1-2), had spoken of Christian ethical action as sacrifice, and so had the author of Hebrews (12:28).

The instruction in I Peter on how Christians should conduct themselves in the pagan environment begins with an exhortation to abstain from passions that war against the soul. Here we must remember that the level of personal morality in the Graeco-Roman period was generally low, especially in sexual matters. Paul had had his troubles in Corinth,[13] and conditions had improved very little in Asia Minor. But the ultimate purpose of restraint is not the self-glorification of the community, but in order that Christians may "declare the wonderful deeds of him who called you out of darkness into his marvellous light" (2:9). Christians are to behave ethically, then, in order to bear witness to God himself. It is this emphasis that distinguishes Christian ethics from other ethical codes, as we shall see from the way in which the author interprets his instructions.

CHRISTIAN ACTION IN A NON-CHRISTIAN WORLD

Having dealt with faith and the new life as the basis of ethical action, and with the new community as the place in which the new life is nurtured, the author now turns to the Christian in relation to the pagan world. The instruction takes the form of a catechism dealing with various relationships: government, slavery, marriage, and family. These were relationships in which Christians, like all men in the Graeco-Roman world, were involved, and both Jews and thoughtful Gentiles had tried to formulate principles of action to govern them. The formula and content of the various duties prescribed in I Peter and in many other epistles of the New Testament show a dependence on pre-Christian codes of ethical action. These codes are commonly referred to as "household tables," because they describe the duties of

[13] See Chapter 8, pp. 251 ff.; Chapter 1, pp. 16 ff.

the average person in his relationship at home and in the world. The Christians probably borrowed from the hellenistic synagogue, which had already been influenced by the ethical teaching of hellenistic philosophies.

The instruction begins with an exhortation to abstain from the "passions of the flesh that wage war against your soul" (2:11), a reference to the base and selfish impulses that lead to words, thoughts, and actions incompatible with the new life. To all such impulses, Christians must be strangers (aliens and exiles). But they are to abstain not as an end in itself; they are to show good conduct so that Gentiles may recognize it as good and glorify God "on the day of visitation" (2:12). This phrase is primarily eschatological, and refers to God's final revelation at the end of the age.

The first specific instruction deals with the Christian's relation to the Roman government. Since we have given a more complete discussion of this relationship elsewhere (Chapter 11), we need only summarize it here (2:13-17). The Christian accepted the Roman government as part of the structure of this world's order, which was passing away. But so long as the Christian was a member of Roman society, he was obligated to respect its laws and the officials who enforced them. His obligation, however, was not primarily to the emperor or to any other official, but to the will of God. He was free from the emperor, for through the gospel he had been emancipated from bondage to all human institutions. But in his freedom he was bound by the will of God; and, since the early Christians believed it was God's will to live in harmony with all men, they complied with the laws. But notice that they did not abide by the law out of any political conviction, for actually they denied to the Roman empire any ultimate authority or allegiance. They were simply accommodating themselves to the times, although their decision to do so was based on what they believed to be the will of God—that is, to do no moral evil. Ultimately, the Christian was a servant, not of the emperor, but of God. And his allegiance became evident at times of crisis when the government violated God's will by demanding divine honours for the emperor. Then the Christian defied the government and died or went to prison. The instruction in I Peter says "Honour the Emperor"—only God is to be feared.

This same principle came into play when the Christian community tried to work out an ethical decision on the relationship between slaves and masters. This was an acute problem, for there were many slaves in the Christian community. The fact that the instruction in I Peter makes no mention of the masters' obligations to their slaves—like that found in Ephesians 6:9 and Colossians 4:1, for example—may mean that this instruction was intended mainly for slaves. Paul had already defined the relation of slaves and masters in the church. There was no distinction among those who were in Christ. But this freedom was a gift of God and not of the world. The Roman world had its own definitive laws regarding freemen and slaves; and Christians, who were subject to the Roman state, might even possess slaves. Paul even wrote a letter (Philemon) to a fellow Christian urging him to permit a runaway slave to return without punishment.

So the instruction reads, "Servants, be submissive to your masters with all respect, not only to the kind and gentle but also to the overbearing" (2:18). Now from the standpoint of the Christian faith, slavery was just as transient an institution as the Roman government itself. Consequently, the government's approach to the ethical relationship between slaves and masters was different from the Christian approach. According to Roman law, the slave was chattel in the hands of his master. He had no civil rights and his master could punish him even with death. The instruction here obviously implies that the slave should fulfil his obligations to his master in accordance with customary law and practice, and that he should be a good slave. But the ultimate sanction for this action is not the law of Rome but the approval of God. And the slave must go beyond what is expected of him and be kind and gentle even to a master who abuses him, for he is ultimately obligated to the will of God. The pattern for his conduct is none other than Christ himself: "When he was reviled, he did not revile in return; when he suffered, he did not threaten; but he trusted to him who judges justly."

Here we see clearly how the Christians conformed to convention while searching for an ethical code. For while the slave fulfils his obligations to his master, his conduct is not governed only or primarily by law but by the Spirit of Christ. It is not surprising that in the early centuries many masters were led into the church through the examples of their Christian slaves.

Unfortunately, this early Christian instruction was to be used centuries later as a justification for slavery. In America during the early nineteenth century, many sermons were preached on this very text to justify slavery as a divine institution established by God's will as revealed in the New Testament. Nothing could have been further from the mind of the early church. Slavery, like every other human institution, existed by God's sufferance as long as this world order continued. Christians made no effort to justify slavery on the grounds of philosophical or social theory, for they did not expect the present order to last much longer, and they were not political theorists any-way. Like almost everyone else in the Roman world, they accepted the institution of slavery. They did not try to defend it as a divine in-stitution; they merely asked themselves the question: Given this relationship between Christians and the world, how can we act to bear witness to God's will?

The instruction in I Peter next deals with another common institu-tion—marriage (3:1-7). The requirement that the Christian wife "be submissive" to her husband was in no sense peculiar to the Christian community. Both Jewish and Gentile teachers pictured the ideal wife as faithful and obedient. And yet in the Graeco-Roman world this ideal was not always attained. The unfaithfulness of the wives of em-perors and of other well-known persons was common knowledge and could not fail to set the tone. Some of the most moving epitaphs dis-covered from the period are those of husbands praising their wives' faithfulness—evidence, perhaps, of their rarity.

The wife's submission to her husband was the ideal of the Graeco-Roman world, but again we find the ideal interpreted in a peculiarly Christian way. The instruction implies that the wives who are being addressed are married to non-Christian husbands. Now according to the hellenistic philosopher Plutarch, the ideal wife should accept her husband's religion. But for a Christian wife to renounce her faith would be to act contrary to the will of God. And yet she was not to withdraw from the relationship altogether. In all other respects, she was to live up to the common ideal of the good wife so that her husband would be won to Christ "without a word" from her about her faith (3:1), sheerly on the basis of the new life into which she had entered.

Here again we see how the Christian, though following a pattern of conduct not peculiarly Christian, in a relationship not peculiarly Chris-tian, is to act in such a way to transform the whole relationship. When we recall that Christianity was commonly despised, we can imagine how little peace there must have been in homes where Christian wives were regarded as insubordinate by their non-Christian husbands. It must have taken all the power at her disposal for a Christian wife in such a situation to maintain a "gentle and quiet spirit." But through the manifestation of the new life of holy love into which she has entered, she was to give new meaning to marriage so that her husband might be won to Christ. And the ultimate sanction for her fulfilling the role of wife was not in order to satisfy convention but in order that she "do right" in the sight of God (3:6).

The instruction to husbands again brings up what was regarded as the proper conduct of husband toward wife (3:7). The Christian husband is not to submit to his wife, for he clearly has the authority in the household. But he is to "live considerately" with his wife. This translation does not quite do justice to the original Greek, which literally reads "live with her according to knowledge." This phrase undoubtedly refers to the "knowledge of God" that the husband has been granted through his new faith. That the husband sees this relationship with his wife in a new light is further substantiated by the reason given for his new way of life: "since you are joint heirs of the grace of life." Although the husband is to maintain his traditional authority, through his faith he is to regard his wife as a joint partner in eternal hope and life. He is no longer to think of her as simply the woman who bears his children or who acts as steward in the household. Their life together is to be transformed into a Christian relationship within the context of an institution that was in no sense peculiarly Christian.

The instruction concerning ethical action in relation to the world ends with a plea for love and humility (3:8-9). Humility is essential to Christians who are to be loyal to their responsibilities in the world, especially in a world that is hostile to their hopes and sceptical of their new faith and life. The instruction then brings together two qualities of the new life that are most difficult to hold in balance: humility on the one hand, and acting in accordance with the will of God on the other (3:8-21). True humility means that Christians must return a blessing when they are reviled (3:9). It means defending their faith, not in arrogance, but in gentleness (3:13-15). Humility will often lead them into undeserved suffering, but acting in accordance with the will of God will keep their conscience clear (3:15-16). This passage almost certainly refers to the conduct of Christians who are brought before magistrates for questioning. They are to conduct themselves in such a way that their accusers will be shamed. And the pattern for humility is to be found in the example of Jesus Christ, who himself stood before the Roman procurator Pilate and then suffered on the cross (3:17–4:1).

Once again the instruction reminds the Christian converts that they must put aside the old life they had known in the world: "living in licentiousness,passions,drunkenness,revels,carousing,and lawless idolatry" (4:3). On matters such as these, the church was uncompromising, for conduct of this sort violated the teachings of Jesus and the whole Hebrew tradition. The Christians are warned that their old friends will abuse them now (4:4), but they must remember that the judge of their actions is the will of God (4:2,4-6) and not the whims of their former companions. And it is to God that they must account for their actions.

The instruction now relates all this ethical teaching to the expected end of the world order (4:7). It was this expectation that made Christian action so unusually earnest. They were not to become excited but to remain sane and sober, and they were to be constant in the prayer through which their knowledge and strength were given. The final end might come any minute, and in a hostile world they might be called upon any time to make sound decisions under unusual pressure. They were to place their love for one another above all else, and to show hospitality toward one another. This demand for love and charity is emphasized not only because it is the all-encompassing law of the new life, but also because in an unfriendly world the community's very existence depended on a strong bond of fellowship. This bond was to be further strengthened by the sharing of spiritual gifts (4:11), and by encouraging and enlightening one another in their faith as they worshipped together.

To the final section of I Peter the author adds a letter dealing with the crisis in which his readers found themselves and a note to the leaders of the community. Here again the author urges that even if acting according to God's will leads to suffering they should rejoice, since they suffer for Christ and thereby glorify God (4:12-19). He reminds them that their humility in suffering is before God and not before man (5:6); and they are not alone, since Christians throughout the world suffer with them (5:9). God, who has called them to a life that involves suffering, will provide them with the strength to endure (5:10).

I Peter, then, helps us understand how the early Christians tried to live as a holy people in the world without being assimilated by the world. Indeed, they were under an obligation to transform the world's ways. The author clearly shows that Christ's command of love for God and for their neighbour was the undergirding ethical principle that guided all their decisions. But he also shows how Christians tried to define their actions as they entered into relations with the world. It was the will of God that ultimately determined how they should conduct themselves in new situations. And their constant hope was that through their actions in the world men might be led to glorify God. Underlying all these ethical decisions was their hope in the coming manifestation of God's righteousness in all the world. We turn now to a consideration of this hope of the Christian church.

⋙⋘

CHAPTER FIFTEEN

THE HOPE
OF THE COMMUNITY

From the very beginning, the Christian community had looked forward eagerly to the time when God would complete the work of transforming his creation. This mood of hopefulness and expectancy had been strong in the Hebrew prophetic tradition, from which Christianity inherited so much. But now, at the very time when the hope of redemption seemed to be waning among many of the leaders of Judaism, it was becoming more and more powerful in the Christian community. Jesus, by his wonderful works and his teachings about the kingdom of God, had set off this surge of expectancy, and the convictions of his followers kept it swelling.

New Testament readings relevant to this chapter are I Thessalonians 4; II Thessalonians 2; Mark 13; Revelation; Hebrews 9.

Appropriately enough, it is in the last book of the New Testament (though not the last book to be written) that this Christian hope is most fervently expressed. This is the Revelation to John. Probably no other book of the Christian canon has caused so much confusion or given rise to so much unbridled speculation as this. From time to time, leaders of the church have expressed regret that this book was even included in the canon. But Revelation is by no means unique among the Jewish-Christian writings of the period. Although its style is quite different from that of the rest of the New Testament, nearly all the author's convictions are shared by one or more of the other writers, and its basic perspective is in some respects like that of Jesus himself.

The Hope According to the Synoptics

THE KINGDOM AS PRESENT REALITY

At the very beginning of our study, when we were considering the nature of the kingdom of God (Chapters 2 and 3), we saw how strongly the Christian community was convinced that, with the coming of Jesus and through the works he performed, a new era in God's dealings with men had been inaugurated. The promises made by God to his ancient people Israel were now believed to be in the process of fulfilment. Since this fulfilment took on forms that the prophets themselves seem not to have anticipated, only a minority of Jesus' Jewish contemporaries believed that their hopes were being fulfilled in him. But to those to whom the Spirit revealed the meaning of the *kerygma*, it was clear that Jesus had established the New Covenant promised through Jeremiah (31:31 ff.), and that he had sealed it by offering his life in obedience to God. The new age for which Judaism longed had now begun to dawn. The powers of evil were already being overcome by the power of Christ and his Spirit. Manifestations of God's redemptive power had first appeared in Jesus' ministry of healing, and were continued through the Spirit-filled leaders of the primitive church. Jesus himself had said: "If it is by the finger of God that I cast out demons, then the kingdom of God has come upon you" (Luke 11:20). The establishment of God's sovereign rule over his creation had already begun, and the time of fulfilment was near.

THE KINGDOM AS YET TO COME

On the other hand, the community was fully aware that the reign of God had not yet come in its fullness. Most men were still resisting the will of God, and the forces of evil were still flourishing.

Satan's hold had been undermined, but by no means destroyed. The mass of men had not acknowledged Jesus as Lord and Christ. His coming had been in humiliation, and had not been attended by the glory that befitted one of his worth. Human wickedness continued its unrequited way, and evil men still harassed the people of God and plotted the church's destruction. In short, most men were still alienated from God and oblivious of his mighty acts of redemption on man's behalf. There was only one ultimate solution: The Son of Man must appear again, this time in glory and triumph. The deeds of men must be judged by the God of righteousness, and the work of redemption must one day be consummated by the transformation of the universe into the state for which God intended it when he created it.

Jesus had often spoken of the coming of the Son of Man (Mk. 8:38; 13:26; 14:62; Lk. 17:24, 30), both by direct statement and in parables. Scholars have disputed whether he thought of himself as the coming Son of Man, or whether he was simply speaking of a Messiah who was yet to come. But whatever the original significance of Jesus' words may have been, it is clear that the early church found in his remembered words assurance that he would reappear to the world in glorious exaltation. Although Jesus predicted the coming in triumph, he refused categorically to set any date for this event (Mk. 13:32). He had also spoken of the coming judgment, and again the church was convinced that he would play a key role in the final reckoning before God (see especially Mt. 25:31-46). The fact that the Son of Man in his role as judge is called "King" in Matthew's Parable of the Last Judgment suggests that the word "judge" is used in the Gospels in the Old Testament sense of "ruler," rather than in a strictly judicial sense. It appears, therefore, that the coming kingdom, the work of the judge, and the appearance of the Son of Man are closely related to one another and to the expected day of consummation. The world could never be set to rights until Messiah came again and the work of redemption and judgment was completed.

Living between the time when God's reign had dawned and the time when it would arrive in its fullness, the community found itself in a state of tension. Through the cross and the resurrection, God had already given assurance of his final victory over the forces of evil. The presence of his Spirit in the hearts of men of faith gave continuing promise of the time when his will would be sovereign over all creation. But this tension between the present state and the future state did not originate with the community; it marked an emphasis in the message of Jesus himself. The familiar words of the prayer, "Thy kingdom come, Thy will be done on earth, as it is in heaven," reminded the church then, as now, of the incompleteness of its experience of redemption. The community lived in confidence that what had been inaugurated would be carried to completion; fulfillment of the promise had now been guaranteed, but it had not yet been achieved.

In the sermons in Acts, as in the Gospels, the same two themes recur: the appearance of Jesus from heaven, and the judgment that will follow (Acts 3:19-23; 10:42). But there is no hint of what is to take place in the interim, except that the Christian witnesses are to be diligent in proclaiming the gospel. In the light of what God has done in Christ for man's redemption and in view of the coming judgment (Acts 2:37-40), the wicked are urged to repent and believe.

The Hope According to Paul

THE RETURN OF CHRIST

Paul was converted only a few years after the crucifixion of Jesus, when the hope of Jesus' coming again was still strong. Yet he lived long enough to see serious problems arise in the church when the hopes for Jesus' return failed to materialize. Writing to the Thessalonians at the time of his first stay in Corinth, Paul offered a word of reassurance to those who were troubled by the fact that some of the members of the Christian community had died before "the coming of the Lord" (I Thess. 4:13 ff.). Paul urged his readers not to fear that those who had "fallen asleep" would be left out on the day of glory when the Lord appeared in triumph, for the faithful dead would have priority over the living Christians, and the dead and the living would together meet the Lord in the clouds of heaven. The summons of the archangel and the sounding of the heavenly trumpet as accompaniments of the coming of the end (I Thess. 4:16; I Cor. 15:52 ff.) were common themes in the Old Testament and in the non-canonical Jewish writings of the pre-Christian period. The resurrection was to accompany the appearance of Christ, and the entire number of the faithful were then to be united with him for ever.

Later, in writing to the Corinthians, Paul described in fuller detail the series of events that would lead to the end of the present age and the coming in fullness of the long-awaited new age (I Cor. 15:22-28; 51-54). The disobedient universe will be brought by Christ into subjection to the will of God. Every force opposed to God will be destroyed, and all his enemies will then acknowledge his lordship over his creation. But Paul also had words of assurance for individual believers. For the details of his description of the day of resurrection, he again draws upon the vast fund of apocalyptic tradition. The fact that Paul does not include this kind of apocalyptic detail in his later letters has suggested to some scholars that with the passing years he moved away from the strong sense of expectancy that he had had at the beginning of his career.[1] It is true that his earlier letters indicate that he expected the Lord to appear almost immediately, and that his later letters, written from prison as he awaits trial, face quite frankly the possibility that he may be executed. But Paul still clings to his hope of the Lord's coming. In one of the last of his letters, he describes himself as "awaiting . . . the Lord Jesus Christ" (Phil. 3:20). He concluded that, since his citizenship was in heaven, his ultimate loyalty was to God and not to Rome.

THE FINAL CONFLICT BEFORE CHRIST'S COMING

In Paul's letters, side by side with the theme of quiet waiting for the coming of Christ, are statements that show the extent to which he was influenced by apocalypticism, a type of thinking that is interested in action. The terms "apocalypse" and "apocalyptic" are transliterated from the Greek word, *apokalupto*, which means to reveal what has previously been hidden. The term "apocalypse" has a more precise meaning than this, however; it is the name given to a unique type of literature that purports to reveal the future through visions and elaborate symbolism. Apocalypticism is a primitive type of philosophy of history in which the convictions are expressed that (1) the writer is living near the end of the present age, (2) that God will soon intervene to deliver his people from their difficulties, and (3) that the situation must deteriorate before it can improve. Paul shows the influence of apocalypticism when in Romans 8 he speaks of the birthpangs through which the world must pass before the coming of the new age.

An unmistakably apocalyptic passage occurs in Paul's second letter to the Thessalonians (2:3-12), where he anticipates a final outburst of satanic activity before the arrival of the day of redemption. A report had been circulated among the Thessalonian Christians that Paul believed that the day of the Lord had already come. He countered this false rumour by reminding them of the time of stress that must precede the final release of the world from the power of the adversary. Attempts have been made by interpreters since Paul's day to identify "the man of lawlessness" (II Thess. 2:3) and "he who now restrains"

---

[1] See especially C. H. Dodd, *New Testament Studies*, pp. 108-118. Manchester: University Press, 1953.

(2:7) with known figures of Roman history. If Paul was writing in the early 50's, the emperor would have been Claudius, whose decree against the Jews seems to have hindered the work of Christian missionaries in Rome (see p. 252). Caligula and Nero have been suggested as the persons alluded to as the "man of lawlessness," and both Claudius and Seneca have been identified as the restraining influences. Paul himself gives no clue to their identity, and none would be needed for those living in the midst of the situation. Speculation is futile, however, since the point that Paul was making is simply this: The operation of the Roman government, whether it aided or hindered the work of the gospel, was simply the outward aspect of the invisible working of the hidden spiritual forces that were contesting for mastery of the universe.

The unseen forces, which Paul elsewhere refers to as "principalities and powers" (Col. 1:16), have the potentiality for either good or evil. At times they may be regarded as beneficent (Rom. 13:1 ff.); but when they act independently, in defiance of the fact that they were created by God to do his will and share in the governing of his creation, then they became demonic, and are to be denounced and defied as such (Rev. 13). The contest between the power of God and the powers of evil could have no decisive outcome until God himself had intervened, defeated the rebellious powers, and established his righteous rule. The growing movement toward elevating the emperor to the rank of divinity was undoubtedly interpreted by Paul as proof that the conflict with evil was nearing its climax.

DID PAUL CHANGE HIS MIND?

Perhaps the differences in Paul's statements about the future mean simply that he changed his mind with the passage of time, but they may also indicate that he felt it necessary to stress different aspects of his beliefs in response to the various questions about the future that came to him from the churches. In spite of these changing emphases, Paul remained throughout his life confident that the decisive act of God in reconciling the world to himself was already in the past—in the cross and resurrection of Jesus—and yet he continued to be filled with longing for the day when the work of reconciliation would be completed. Paul believed himself to be living between two times: the time when God's victory over evil had been made certain by the resurrection of Jesus, and the time when the victory would be finally achieved. Even though Paul shared with apocalyptic writers their expectation of a catastrophic end to history, he did not adopt their practice of setting dates for the end or creating a time schedule for the coming of the new age.

The Hope Stated as Specific Predictions

There were others in the early church who, unlike Paul, were quite willing to outline the series of events that must come to pass before the end of the present age. We have seen that Paul was content to sketch out a sequence of events that would come at "the end," without taking the further step of announcing when the series would begin to take place. But other New Testament writers identified events in their own time with the apocalyptic happenings that would usher in the new age. They employed the elaborate imagery traditionally used by apocalyptic writers to disguise the meaning of their words about the future from the prying eyes of the uninitiated.

MARK'S PREDICTIONS

The oldest of these Christian apocalypses is the one included in the Gospel of Mark (13:3-27; possibly 28-31 also). Although the apocalypse is included by all three Synoptic writers, there are strong reasons for doubting that Jesus spoke these words, or rather that he spoke all the words attributed to him in this passage: (1) The comment in Mark 13:3 that the words were spoken in secret to the inner circle of the disciples seems to have been a favourite device used by the writers of the Gospels to explain why certain words they were attributing to Jesus were not well known, or why, if generally known, they were not really understood.[2] (2) The predictions included in the passage do not really answer the question posed by the disciples at the start of the discourse (13:2) about the time of the destruction of the Temple. (3) The inclusion of the phrase, "let the reader understand" (13:14), suggests that these remarks were originally part of a written document, not an oral statement. (4) It is difficult to harmonize the series of specific predictions about signs preceding the end (13:7-25) with Jesus' explicit denial of any knowledge of the time when the end would come (13:32). A plausible theory about the original form of this passage was discussed in connection with the fall of Jerusalem (Chapter 10, p. 317), where it was suggested that the "Little Apocalypse" was part of a tract circulated among the Christians in Jerusalem before the destruction of the city in A.D. 69-70.

One possible hint concerning the historical circumstances out of which the apocalypse emerged may be the phrase, "the desolating sacrilege" (13:14). This phrase is quoted by Mark from Daniel 9:27 and

---

[2] For a discussion of this device as used in the Gospels in connection with the parables, see J. Jeremias, *The Parables of Jesus*. London : SCM Press, 1954.

11:31, where it is used in referring to the desecration of the Temple by Antiochus Epiphanes, who erected an altar to Zeus over the altar of burnt offering, and had a pig sacrificed upon it. It may be that the Emperor Caligula's threat in A.D. 40 (reported by Josephus in his *Antiquities*) to set up a statue of himself in the Jewish Temple and to institute pagan sacrifices there was interpreted by Palestinians as a recurrence of the earlier "desolating sacrilege." Since Caligula's death prevented the threat from being carried out, this apprehensive reference to it in Mark might have been written between the time Caligula issued the order and the time when word of his death reached Jerusalem —that is, early in A.D. 41. There is other evidence, however, that this date is too early. Luke's version of the Synoptic apocalypse mentions the armies that will surround the city of Jerusalem (Lk. 21:20), an event that did not occur until A.D. 69-70. It would seem likely, therefore, that the Synoptic apocalypse assumed its present form after the fall of Jerusalem and was interpolated into the genuine sayings of Jesus concerning the destruction of the Temple.

In all probability, the apocalypse as it now stands in the Gospels is composed of three layers: (1) authentic words of Jesus about the destruction of the Temple and the downfall of the city of Jerusalem (Mk. 13:1-2, 32-33); (2) details added to Jesus' words as the conflict between the Christian community and Judaism, and between Judaism and Rome, began to increase (e.g., Mk. 13:9-13); and (3) further details attached to the earlier nucleus after the destruction of the Temple had taken place, with the intent of heightening the power of Jesus' prophetic words (e.g., 13:14-30). Whether we consider the apocalypse to be, in its entirety, an authentic report of the words of Jesus or to have developed by accretion, the place of prominence given to this theme in the Synoptic Gospels testifies to the continued vitality of apocalyptic thought in the church down toward the closing years of the first Christian century.[3] If the Synoptic apocalypse is to be considered a composite document, its present form bears witness to the willingness of the community to revise and rework its prophetic oracles in order to make them relevant to a changing situation. Since apocalyptic writing is characteristically composite, it is not surprising to find a single unit like the Synoptic apocalypse containing materials that have probably emerged from at least three different historical contexts, as suggested above.[4] Although for some in the community the

---

[3] For a full-scale treatment of the Synoptic apocalypse, and a defense of its authenticity, see G. R. Beasley-Murray, *Jesus and the Future*. London: Macmillan, 1954.

passage of time and the non-fulfilment of the promised return of Christ may have modified, or even quenched, the hope for the end of the age, for many the hope continued with unabated fervour.

BACKGROUND OF THE BOOK OF REVELATION

One circle in which hope for the consummation of God's purpose continued to be strong was the Christian group in Asia Minor that produced the prophet, John, the author of the book of Revelation. Tradition has identified this prophet with John the Apostle, and has ascribed to him the authorship of the Gospel of John, the Letters of John, and the book of Revelation. If this tradition were reliable, it would mean that we have an extended body of literature that comes to us from the hand of one of Jesus' most intimate followers and that might be presumed therefore to represent a point of view very close to Jesus' own.

In fact, however, there are serious difficulties connected with the theory that John the Apostle wrote the books with which he has been credited. Since he was a Galilean fisherman, uneducated and perhaps even illiterate (Acts 4:13), it is most unlikely that he could have written—in Greek—a work of the theological subtlety of the Gospel of John. Efforts to demonstrate that the Gospel of John was originally written in Aramaic have not been particularly convincing to most scholars. The skill of the apologetic that the Gospel of John contains suggests that it was written by a man who had had protracted contact with and intimate knowledge of the Greek world. It has been argued that the Gospel and the Letters of John, which both language and theological content show came from the same circles, were written by John when he was very old and had had a lifetime in which to theologize. Even if this proposal were to be considered plausible, there is some evidence in the New Testament that the disciple John was martyred at the same time as his brother James—i.e., A.D. 44. If this evidence is valid, then none of the books bearing the name of John could have been written by John the son of Zebedee, the disciple of Jesus. It would have been a simple matter for the early traditions of the church to confuse a notable leader named John from the church in Ephesus, or from some other city of Asia Minor, with the disciple of the same name.

The book of Revelation, which is the only book in the New Testament that claims to have been written by John, differs radically in style

---

[4] For a full demonstration of this thesis, see the analysis of the Books of Enoch in R. H. Charles, *The Apocrypha and Pseudepigrapha of the Old Testament*. Oxford: Clarendon Press, 1913.

and perspective from the Gospel and Letters of John. In the Gospel, the emphasis falls on the spiritual life of the church as a continuing fact, free from time-bound considerations. In Revelation, the author is gravely concerned to stress the crisis that is now impending. For him there is no indefinite or unlimited period of time stretching out into the future, but rather a conviction that very soon the conflict of the powers of evil against God and his people will reach its climax. We might conclude from this that Revelation was written by a disciple, since this understanding of God's purpose would be likely to exist among the followers of Jesus. But John the Prophet also looks backward with veneration to the times of "the twelve apostles of the Lamb" (Rev. 21:14)—a phrase more appropriate to one who, with awe and reverence, has heard about the apostolic leaders than to one who was himself a member of the twelve.

PURPOSE OF THE BOOK OF REVELATION

The book was written at a time when efforts were being made to cripple the church, as we have seen (Chapter 11). The community was ill prepared to meet the crisis precipitated by the Christians' refusal to participate in emperor worship, for it had become half-hearted in matters of Christian faith and life. "Because you are lukewarm, and neither cold nor hot, I will spew you out of my mouth," John reports Christ as saying to one of the Asian churches (Rev. 3:16). The genius of John the Prophet, as the author of Revelation may fittingly be called, was not primarily foresight, but insight into the real nature of the problems confronting the Christian community. He saw with clarity the issues on which the Christians must make decisions, and the far-reaching consequences of those issues. John's ultimate concern, therefore, was not for a solution to the immediate problem of the empire's demand that Christians worship the emperor. Rather, he viewed the immediate crisis as a crucial stage in the final conflict between God and the evil powers. Steadfastness in this crisis would lead the community on to complete victory in which God's purpose for his creation would be achieved. We must examine the book of Revelation again, therefore, not from the viewpoint of the community in conflict, as in Chapter 11, but with the aim of understanding how through this conflict the community saw the fulfilment of its hope.

PROMISES AND PREDICTIONS

After a brief but impressive introduction (Rev. 1:1-8), John addresses in turn seven of the churches of Asia Minor, pointing up in each case the church's weaknesses, strengths, and prospects. Some had been lulled to sleep and needed to be aroused; some had flirted with paganism and needed to be warned in the strongest terms of the consequences of such behaviour. John himself had been exiled to the tiny, barren isle of Patmos as a result of his courageous testimony to the faith, and the faithful Christians in the churches addressed could expect the same fate or worse.

The Letters to the Churches. The words addressed to the individual churches are not merely general comments; in each case, the remarks are peculiarly appropriate. For example, Pergamum is warned about Satan's throne, an apparent reference to the fact that the emperor was worshipped as divine in Pergamum long before the emperor cult was begun in Rome. Pergamum had been from the beginning the setting for "Satan's throne"—i.e., the seat of imperial worship in the East. To Sardis, John wrote a warning of the coming of the Lord "like a thief," an unmistakable reference to a famous incident in which the seemingly impregnable city of Sardis had been captured by the Persians, who entered the acropolis through a tiny crevice while the fabulous King Croesus sat in complete confidence in his splendid palace. The spiritual blindness of Laodicea is stressed because, ironically, it took pride in its great hospital dedicated to Asclepius, the god of healing, and in its famed eye salve, which was supposed to cure blindness. It is fitting for John to heap scorn on this city for its pride of riches, since at a time of earthquake when other cities had had to ask for financial assistance from the empire, Laodicea had, in proud self-sufficiency, announced

A reconstruction of the Great Altar of Zeus at Pergamum. With its grand proportions and its magnificent sculpture, it was one of the wonders of the ancient world. The allusion to Satan's throne in the letter to the church at Pergamum (Rev. 2:13) may have been a reference to this altar.

that she had ample resources to meet the emergency.[5] In spite of these words of warning to the churches of Asia Minor, and in spite of the troubles that were soon to fall upon these churches, the Christians were to remain confident in God's love for them, and in the fulfilment of his purpose through these difficulties. The new age could not come without these birthpangs, and the people of God must meet them informed and confident.

The Visions. The ingenuity of the writer is nowhere more apparent than in the series of apocalyptic visions that occupy the rest of the book (Rev. 4:1–22:19). The recurrence of the number seven is one of the most striking features of this section: there are seven seals (6:1–8:1), seven trumpets (8:2–11:15), seven visions of the kingdom of the dragon (11:16–13:18), seven visions of the coming of the Son of Man (14:1-20), seven bowls (15:1–16:1), seven visions of the fall of Babylon (17:1–19:10), and seven visions of the end (19:11–21:4).[6] Perhaps the greatest difficulty in interpreting this book has resulted from the effort to discover a chronological sequence in this series of visions. This method of interpretation has appeared in two forms: the futuristic, which sees in these visions pictures of the successive situations that will arise in the last days; the historical, which relates the visions to the contemporary history of the church, and identifies the symbolic figures of the book with historical personages. The futuristic method ignores the clear historical allusions of the writing. And the historical method must

---

[5] Tacitus, *Annals*, 14:27.
[6] Based on Ernst Lohmeyer's outline.

constantly be revised with the passage of time, since as historical crises pass it becomes clear that there was no basis for seeing in them the fulfilment of John's prophecies. There is scarcely a demagogue of international fame who has not been identified by interpreters of prophecy as the beast of Revelation 13. Napoleon and Hitler were awarded this label, to name only two. In the 1930's biblical literalists opposed to President Roosevelt's New Deal even claimed that the Blue Eagle which all merchants were required to display under the terms of the National Recovery Act was "the mark of the beast" (Rev. 13:17)!

The most plausible approach to the apocalyptic section, and hence to the entire book, requires (1) an awareness of the historical crisis—actual or impending—that was the immediate provocation for the book, and (2) a recognition of the cyclical structure of the writing. The historical situation that gave rise to the book was the empire's opposition to Christianity. The Christians of Asia Minor had come under suspicion of subversion because of their refusal to join in the worship of the emperor. On the eastern edge of Asia Minor were located the Parthians, a warlike people who remained a constant threat to the peace of Rome, and whose border was the one perennially unsettled boundary of the entire empire. There can be no doubt that any show of disloyalty to the emperor in the region of Asia Minor would be viewed with special suspicion, since it might indicate collusion with those perennial trouble-makers, the Parthians. The involved and highly figurative language of a book like Revelation would serve to communicate a message of resistance to those who understood the imagery, but would at the same time conceal the message from eyes for which it was not intended. Since this kind of writing had become common in late Judaism, neither the form nor even some of the specific images had to be invented. The author simply had to rework these well-known materials in terms of the new crisis of faith that he saw looming on the horizon.

It is misleading to suppose that the series of visions of the end is intended to describe a sequence of events in strict chronological fashion. Rather, the images and prophecies are presented in cyclical form in order to bring out the full implications of the end in a manner in which a single set of visions could not. It is as though the author were saying to the reader: "I have described the end under the figure of the trumpets; now, lest you have missed something of the fullness of meaning, I shall go back over the same territory, but this time I shall use the figure of the kingdom of the dragon."

The apocalyptic section begins with a magnificent vision of the throne of God (Rev. 4). With typical Jewish reluctance to picture God, only the throne and its surroundings are described (4:2). But this description conveys a sense of the awesome majesty of God, surrounded by the symbols of his universal authority. Clearly, however, God's authority is not limited to heaven, since John outlines the things which, it has been revealed to him, "must take place after this" (4:1). There can be no mistaking that the author shares the apocalyptic viewpoint which is characteristically deterministic: these things *must* take place. But the author is not a fatalist. He regards the history of the world as moving by divine will and in fulfilment of a wise and gracious purpose, and not as proceeding by chance. The ultimate outcome of this determined course of history will be the achievement of God's programme of redemption for his creation. Unlike Paul, however, John does not expect the redemption of all things; he looks forward to the unending punishment of the wicked spirits and of the dragon, their leader.

For his imagery in the description of the divine throne, John draws heavily on Old Testament resources. The living creatures resemble the cherubim, which are designated as the guardians of God's throne both in the historical shrines of ancient Israel (Ex. 25:18 ff.; I Kings 6:23) and in the prophetic visions (Ezek. 1:5 ff.). The twenty-four elders seem to represent the people of God of every generation, who fall in adoration before him. The prose descriptions break over periodically into poetry, as in the ascription of praise with which Revelation 4 closes:

> Worthy art thou, our Lord and God,
> to receive glory and honour and power,
> for thou didst create all things,
> and by thy will they existed and were created.

The Victor. At the opening of Revelation 5 there appears a figure, both majestic and humble, both conquering and submissive, who dominates the apocalypse, and, according to John's conviction, dominates the unfolding of God's purpose. Although this figure is not named, the opening words of the book make it clear that it is Jesus Christ, who is both Lion (5:5) and Lamb (5:6). He comes in humility, yet he is the one through whom victory over the powers opposed to God will be won. He is the only one worthy to unroll the seven-sealed scroll, which is a symbol for the unfolding purpose of God (5:2). What follows in the rest of the book is an elaboration through complicated symbolism of what will be achieved according to God's plan. Fearful conditions will arise on earth: war (6:2, the white horse), civil strife (6:3-4, the red horse), famine (6:5-6, the black horse), and plagues (6:8, the pale horse). There will be astronomical disturbances (6:12-

17)—reminders that, as the New Testament writers understand it, the fate of the whole universe is involved in the fulfilment of man's destiny.

In the midst of this destruction and misery, however, God is at work bringing together his faithful witnesses. They look forward with eagerness to the final deliverance of the creation from its subjection to the control of the evil powers (6:9-11), even though they know that their fidelity to God will bring about their martyrdom. The word "martyr" is simply a transliteration of a Greek word meaning "witness"; the implication is that the Christian who is faithful in his witness to what he believes to be the truth will meet a martyr's death. These witnesses are considered by John to be the special objects of God's loving care; they are granted the privilege of everlasting shelter in the presence of God. It is at moments like this that the prophet shifts over to poetry:

> Therefore are they before the throne of God,
>   and serve him day and night within his temple;
>   and he who sits upon the throne will shelter them with his presence.
> ... The Lamb in the midst of the throne will be their shepherd,
>   and he will guide them to springs of living water;
> and God will wipe away every tear from their eyes.
>
> —REVELATION 7:15, 17

Terrifying as some of John's visions are, there can be no doubt that the primary intent of his book was not to frighten but to comfort the Christians living under the shadow of persecution. No matter how oppressive the situation might become, they were to have confidence that beyond tribulation lay peace and God's victory.

The Vanquished. New pictures of the struggles with the evil powers are presented under the figure of the seven angels with the trumpets (Rev. 8:1-2). The angels announce the scourges that are to come upon the earth, and release fearful, fantastic creatures that spread death and destruction on the idolaters of the world. As numerous as locusts, and more horrible than dragons, these creatures torture with their scorpion-like stings, and kill with sulphurous fumes and fire (Rev. 8 and 9). Even though a third of mankind is slaughtered, the suffering is still not at an end (9:18). The holy city itself is to be visited with judgment, and the prophets of God bring drought upon the surrounding land (Rev. 11). The wicked try in vain to destroy the witnesses, just as the dragon (Satan) tries to destroy the child who is destined to rule over the earth (Rev. 12). In cunning fashion, the dragon gives supernatural powers to "the beast" (Rev. 13), who is a symbol of the emperor, with his demands for divine honours. The special powers are designed to lure the unwary into worshipping him, on the supposition that he is divine.

The prophet reveals the beast's identity by a cryptic number, 666. This figure must have had meaning for John's original readers, but now we can only guess at what it meant. Probably the number was arrived at by adding the numerical values of the letters in the emperor's name. This would be an obvious kind of cryptogram, since in Greek and Hebrew the letters of the alphabet also served as numbers (alpha was 1; beta was 2; iota was 10; and so on). Since the number of combinations to give the sum of 666 is almost infinite, it is impossible to determine with certainty which emperor the author had in mind. One likely conjecture is Nero: the letters of Nero Caesar add up to 666, if spelled in Hebrew. The fact that Domitian was probably emperor at the time of John's writing raises no serious problem, since it was customary for apocalypticists to re-use materials from earlier times without recasting them and bringing them up to date. Although the identity of the figure hidden behind the number cannot be known, certainly the intent of the symbol is unmistakable: it is a veiled allusion to an emperor claiming divine honours—in all probability, Domitian.

In contrast to all these demonic figures, John now turns to a seven-fold picture of Christ, through whom the promise of victory is fulfilled. He is portrayed as the Lamb in its purity (14:1-5), as the herald of the gospel throughout the earth (14:6-7), as the herald of doom for the emperor-worshippers (14:8-11), as the Son of Man who both announces the judgment (14:14-16) and executes it. In vivid imagery based on Isaiah 63, he is pictured as tramping out the grapes of God's wrath just as the ancients pressed out the wine from the grapes with their feet in the winepresses. His feet and garments are spattered with the blood of the fallen as a man in a winepress would be stained with the juice from the grapes (14:17-20; cf. Isa. 63: 3, 4).

Following a magnificent hymn of praise to God for his might and majesty ("Great and wonderful are thy deeds, O Lord God the Al-mighty!" 15:3), John introduces two new series of seven woes each: one series is to fall on all the earth, in a vain effort to bring it to repentance (Rev. 15-16); the other is to fall on Babylon—that is, Rome— the scourge of God's people in John's day as Babylon was in the days of the ancient prophets (Rev. 17). The proud splendour and moral cor-ruption of Rome are described under the unforgettable figure of a harlot, gorgeously clad in scarlet, trying to entice all the world to engage in emperor worship. John, like the Hebrew prophets, looks upon idolatry as closely related to adultery. The harlot was seated on seven hills (Rev. 17:9), which are the seven hills of Rome.

The seven heads of the beasts are almost certainly seven emperors,

but which seven are meant is difficult to determine. Since three emperors sat on the throne in a single year (Galba, Otho, and Vitellius, in
68-69), it is impossible to tell whether or not the writer included all
three in his computation. Estimates are further affected by the weight
we attach to the theory that the king who "was and is not" (17:11) is
the same as the one who was earlier pictured as mortally wounded and
healed (13:3). Perhaps both these references are allusions to the belief
prevalent in the first century that Nero would come back from the
dead to lead Rome's traditional enemies on the eastern border, the Parthians, against Rome. Since Nero died under mysterious circumstances,
reportedly by suicide, there was much speculation about his death. The
rumour spread that perhaps he was not really dead, but would return.
Finally, the theory arose and became widespread that he would be
raised from the dead to lead the attack on Rome. If Nero is the man
behind John's symbol here, we have additional evidence of the prophetic insight that saw in the purely local persecution of Christians
under Nero the first rumblings of a tremendous conflict that was later
to develop between the church and the empire. The completeness of
the destruction of the city of seven hills (Rev. 17:9) is celebrated in
an awesome dirge (Rev. 18):

> Fallen, fallen is Babylon the great!
> It has become a dwelling place of demons,
> a haunt of every foul spirit,
> a haunt of every foul and hateful bird;
> for all nations have drunk the wine of her impure passion. . . .
> Alas, alas, for the great city
> that was clothed in fine linen, in purple and scarlet,
> bedecked with gold, with jewels, and with pearls!
> In one hour all this wealth has been laid waste.
>
> —REVELATION 18:2, 3, 16, 17

The Final Victory. The final chapters of the Revelation portray
in majestic fashion the finale of the present age and opening of
the new. Conflict and judgment are at an end; the adversary and his
demonic aides are banished and enchained for ever; the hostile nations
are destroyed in the great battle of Armageddon, after which the birds
of prey swarm over the field of the fallen warriors to gorge themselves
on their flesh (Rev. 19). Then begins the period of one thousand years
(Rev. 20), which is an initial stage of the reign of God over his creation. But even under these ideal conditions, man continues to disobey
God. The period ends in a final judgment of man, the destruction of
death itself, and the renewal of the entire creation (Rev. 21). The book

Q

closes with a description of the serenity and plenty that come upon God's creation when, at last, it is subject to his will:

> Then I saw a new heaven and a new earth; for the
> first heaven and the first earth had passed away.
> ... And I heard a great voice from the throne
> saying, "Behold, the dwelling of God is with men.
> He will dwell with them and they shall be his people."
>
> Then he showed me the river of the water of life,
> bright as crystal, flowing from the throne of God
> and of the Lamb ... ; also, ... the tree of life with
> its twelve kinds of fruit, yielding its fruit each
> month, and the leaves of the tree were for the healing
> of the nations.
>
> And night shall be no more; they need no light of
> lamp or sun, for the Lord God will be their light, and
> they shall reign for ever and ever.
>
> —REVELATION 21:1, 3; 22:1, 2, 5

The Hope Is Modified

Not all members of the Christian community accepted this apocalyptic restatement of the church's hope for the coming of God's kingdom. Undoubtedly John's words provided great comfort and encouragement to the community in Asia Minor, where persecution was threatening, but others, who felt pressures from different quarters, adopted quite different ways of re-interpreting the hope.

HOPE FULFILLED IN HEAVEN

The author of Hebrews, for example, writing at a time when the community's zeal was seriously declining, felt obliged both to re-affirm the ancient hope of the church in the ultimate fulfilment of God's purpose, and also to provide a new structure that would enable the intelligentsia to account for the imperfections of earth in the light of the perfections of heaven. As we have seen before, the Letter to the Hebrews weaves a quasi-Platonic strand into the Christian understanding of history. According to this scheme, things on earth are only imperfect copies of the true realities, which are to be found in heaven. Thus the Hebrew system of Temple worship is to be discarded, not because it is bad, but because the true worship, of which it was only an imperfect copy, has now been revealed through Jesus Christ. The tension connected with the Christian hope, then, would not be between the imperfect Now and the perfect Future, but between the earthly imperfection and the heavenly perfection. This modification in perspective is not consistently carried through by the author, however; rather, he urges his readers to await with eagerness the fulfilment of the hope of the church in the future, when Christ will "appear a second time" (Heb. 9:28), and at the same time to realize that the ultimate fulfilment of God's purpose is to be found only in heaven.

Ever since New Testament times, the church has had a tendency to ignore the fact that the Gospels report Jesus to have prayed that God's kingdom would come *on earth* (Mt. 6:10), not in some other-worldly sphere. Other-worldly interpretations of the Christian hope have been so common in later centuries that the viewpoint of Hebrews may not seem at all unusual. But the Gospels, the letters of Paul, and the Revelation to John, all look to the transformation of *this* world, not merely to some transfer to a heavenly realm. This proposal to shift the tension involved in the expectation of fulfilment from a temporal basis (this age—the age to come) to a philosophical basis (the earthly shadow —the heavenly substance) has proved to be an appealing one down through the history of the Christian community. Once it has been accepted, one need not be concerned over whether the Christian hope is fulfilled in a matter of years or centuries or millennia, or whether the fulfilment is to be looked for, not in the future at all, but in some celestial realm. Various tricks of interpretation have been used to try to prove that Jesus and the apostles did not really expect the end of the age in the near future, but these arguments remain quite unconvincing. Paul expected it within the lifetime of his contemporaries (I Thess. 4:15); Jesus expected it within a generation (Mk. 13:30). Even in Hebrews itself, although a new motif is introduced, the writer is confident that the time is not long, and that "the Day" is drawing near (Heb. 10:25).

HOPE FULFILLED IN THE PRESENT

Another modification of the hope of the community is found in the Gospel of John. In the Synoptic Gospels, Jesus is represented as saying that the kingdom has been inaugurated with the mighty works he is performing, and that it will come in its fullness at some future time. The expectation of a future kingdom was common among Jesus' Jewish contemporaries, but the idea that it had already begun to dawn was a major new element in the Good News of the gospel. In the Gospel of John, however, the emphasis has shifted from the sense of expectation of *future* fulfilment to confidence that the promises of

God have already been fulfilled in the form of resources *presently* available to Christians. For example, eternal life is not regarded in the Gospel of John as a reward to be bestowed at some future time, but as a present possession of the believer. The resurrection is not a future event, but a symbol of the present enjoyment of new life in Christ.

In a sense, this modification of the Christian outlook is no more than a shift of emphasis. But it did serve to relax the tension created by the non-fulfilment of the promise that the new age would come soon. It tended to redirect attention to what the Christian now possessed, rather than to what he did not yet have.

Yet the community would not be true to its heritage if it forgot that God's purpose for it was not yet accomplished. And so there remains in the Gospel of John a significant strand of expectation about the future, which recognizes that there will still be a "last day"—a day when resurrection and judgment will take place, and the moral disorder of man and the universe will be rectified (John 5:29). In the discourse on the Bread of Life (John 6), the promise is repeated four times: "I will raise him up at the last day." Similar references to a future day when redemption will be completed are found in John 5:28, where the resurrection is yet to come, and in John 12:48, where judgment will come "on the last day." The suggestion is sometimes made that the passages in which John uses references of this sort are interpolations by someone who tried to correct John's theology. But it seems (1) that these passages fit well into their contexts and (2) that the paradoxical way in which John claims that the promises of redemption have been fulfilled and his predictions that they will be fulfilled in the future differ only in emphasis from the viewpoint expressed throughout the New Testament. Neither disappointment over the failure of the end to come, nor concern to provide an explanation for the non-fulfilment, could alter the basic conviction of the community that with the coming of Jesus the new age had dawned, but that the full splendour of that day was yet to come in the indeterminate future.

The Hope Persists

REVISIONS IN THE SCHEDULE

Probably the last book of the New Testament to be written was II Peter. Proposed dates for its writing range from A.D. 100 to as late as the close of the second century. For our present purposes, the significant feature of the book is the way in which it seeks to solve the troublesome question of the non-fulfilment of the Christian hope by proposing a new time scheme. Since "with the Lord one day is as a thousand years, and a thousand years as one day" (II Pet. 3:8), the passing of a century or more between the time of the promise and the present time was no more than a brief moment judged by God's time standards. There can be no doubt that this line of reasoning gave, and has continued to give, comfort to many who would otherwise be troubled by the fact that the promised end had not come.

In the works of other Christian writers, not included in the canon but of great importance in the developing thought of the second-century church, there is abundant evidence that the hope of Christ's return continued to flourish in spite of the protracted delay. As a matter of fact, there was a strong tendency among the writers of the late first and early second centuries to concentrate on the future fulfilment of their hopes, and to ignore the belief of the primitive community that the new age had dawned with the coming of Jesus. The first epistle written by Clement, an early and able bishop of Rome, speaks of the suddenness of the end, and of the judgment that is to follow. In the so-called Epistle of Barnabas, a clumsy allegorical essay on the abrogation of the Old Covenant and the establishment of the New, there is a heavy reliance on such apocalyptic classics as Daniel and Enoch. Like Daniel, Barnabas shows a fondness for setting the dates of the eschatological events in cryptic fashion. The author of II Clement takes ill-concealed delight in the prospect of the impending punishment of the wicked.

THE PLEASURES OF THE NEW AGE

Other writers of the post-apostolic era turned their attention to conjectures about the material benefits that were to come to God's people in the new age. Chief among these celestial speculators was Papias, Bishop of Hierapolis (near Colossae) in the first part of the second century. In a famous passage, quoted by several later leaders of the church, Papias claims the authority of the Lord in the following picturesque description of the abundance of the earth in the age to come:

> The days will come in which vines shall grow, each having ten thousand branches and in each branch ten thousand twigs, and in each twig ten thousand shoots, and in each of the shoots ten thousand clusters, and on every cluster ten thousand grapes, and every grape when pressed will yield five-and-twenty measures of wine. And when any of the saints shall lay hold of a cluster, another shall cry out, "I am a better cluster, take me!" [7]

[7] Quoted in Irenaeus, *Against Heresies*, V, 33.

The vividness of the picture and the frequency with which it was quoted by others indicate that hope for the end of the present age and the coming of the next continued to thrive in the church even though more than a century had passed since Jesus had first pronounced the promises of the end.

THE GREAT REDEMPTIVE DRAMA

One of the most powerful restatements of the Christian hope— and of the whole range of Christian faith as well—was given by Irenaeus, Bishop of Lyons (in what is now France) during the last quarter of the second century. He was convinced that God's purpose for man, which had been thwarted by man's disobedience and by the powers of evil, would ultimately be fulfilled. God had intended that man should be immortal; in the new age, God would bestow on man immortality. Man would receive immortality, not as a reward for his fidelity, but because of Jesus Christ, who identified himself wholly with man, and who as a man had been victorious over death, sin, and the evil powers. Analogously, man might gain immortality by identifying himself with Christ. The new possibility for mankind, which Jesus had opened up by a life and death of obedience, would in that day become an actuality. Irenaeus, who is one of the greatest theologians of his century, shares with enthusiasm the eschatological hope of the coming kingdom in its most literal form, and even quotes with approval the colourful words of Papias in which the physical pleasures of the new age are described. So it is evident that even by the end of the second century, the hope for the end was still flourishing within the church, both among simple believers and in the minds of the era's great thinkers.

Perhaps the mounting threat of persecution on the part of the later emperors and the growing hostility of the pagan mobs toward the church provided the pressure which kept alive the expectation that God would intervene in history suddenly on behalf of his people. One of the fullest statements of this expectation in the language and imagery of apocalypticism is Lactantius, a teacher of rhetoric who lived at the end of the third century during the reign of Diocletian, the last and fiercest persecutor of the church. In addition to drawing freely on the Revelation to John, Lactantius supports his picture of the end with quotations from such unlikely sources as the Sibylline Oracles—curious prophetic writings compounded of Jewish and pagan speculation—and from the Fourth Eclogue of Vergil, the Latin poet who hailed the coming of Augustus in terms closely resembling the messianic hopes of Israel. The ferocity of the persecution under Diocletian was sufficient reason for Lactantius and his contemporaries to look upon their fearful experiences as the final birthpangs of the new age.

THE HOPE IS ECLIPSED

As it happened, a new era did come on the heels of Diocletian's persecution, though it was surely not the coming of the kingdom of God. With the accession of Constantine to the imperial throne, Christianity was for the first time officially tolerated (in 313), and was subsequently regarded as the official state religion. The abrupt relaxation of pressure with the ending of the persecutions, added to the intense preoccupation of church leaders with a rapidly developing theological crisis, diverted their attention from questions about the end. The new crisis was the result of sharp controversy over the proper way to state in the creed the relation of Jesus to God. The problem had been posed unintentionally by a great Christian scholar, Origen, of Alexandria (185-253), whose writings were the outstanding intellectual product of the church during the second and third centuries.

Although Origen was deeply interested in the future life, and often engaged in speculation on the subject, his greatest influence on subsequent Christian thought arose from the ambiguity of the language he used in describing the relation of Christ the Son to God the Father. At times, when he was combating those who identified the Father and the Son, Origen spoke as though they were completely separate persons. When he was opposing those who talked as though Christ had been created like any other being, he ascribed to Christ all the attributes of God in such a way as to make him almost indistinguishable from God the Father.

The effort to find some creed that would do full justice to the divinity of Christ, but would recognize him as distinct from the Father, was the major concern of the church in the days of Constantine. This problem quite eclipsed that of the non-fulfilment of the Christian hope. Eusebius of Caesarea, an adviser to Constantine and his biographer, believed that the present age would reach its end in the year A.D. 500. But of course that was far enough away from his time (early fourth century) to remove any sense of urgency. Few Christians could become excited about the future when the present had brought imperial recognition and undreamed-of power and prestige to the church leaders.

THE HOPE AMONG THE SECTS

More and more during this period, speculation about the age to come passed by default to various sects. For example, the followers of a second-century church leader in Asia Minor, named Montanus, attracted a wide following for their theory that the history of the world could be written in three phases: the age of the Father, which lasted from creation until the coming of Christ; the age of the Son, which lasted from the time of Jesus until the coming of Montanus; and the age of the Spirit (who, it was believed, had become incarnate in Montanus), which would last until the coming of the thousand-year kingdom of God. The end was near, the Montanists taught, and great enthusiasm was generated by those who were preparing themselves for the return of Christ that would inaugurate the millennial kingdom. Irenaeus, the bishop of Lyons mentioned above, was astounded to find on his arrival in Rome that the Pope himself had been converted to these teachings. Tertullian, one of the most influential thinkers of the church in Africa, in later life (around A.D. 200) repudiated orthodox Christianity and became a Montanist. A Syrian bishop announced that Christ was about to begin a reign of a thousand years, and led all his people out into the desert to meet him at his return. They would all have died there if the police had not forced them to return.

The Montanists were extreme in their rejection of this world. They demanded rigid asceticism and rejected all efforts to harmonize Christianity with the intellectual life of the day. They were emotional people, given to visions and subject to fits and seizures during which special revelations were received. Since the movement flourished at a time when the church was at last gaining long-sought recognition from political and intellectual leaders, the main body of the church rejected Montanism vehemently. Theologians tended to shy away from any emphasis associated in the popular mind with Montanism, lest the stigma attached to that sect fall on the whole church. So, since eschatology was the major concern of the Montanists, it fell into the background of Christian thought.

THE HOPE IN A THEOLOGICAL FRAMEWORK

The whole question of the goal and meaning of history was raised in a profound manner, however, when another major crisis occurred in the history of the empire. The sacking of the city of Rome by barbarian invaders from the north in 410 made it unmistakably clear that Rome was not eternal, and that it could not stand for ever as the stronghold of culture and stability in a barbarian world. The sense of security that men felt in the durability of the Roman imperial system was now shown to be utterly false.

A brilliant, philosophically trained bishop in North Africa named Augustine saw with prophetic insight that Rome was living on borrowed time, and that the miseries which were coming upon her were the fruits of seeds of destruction sown centuries earlier when imperial despotism began. In a book which he called *The City of God*, he contrasted with the earthly city (actually, the Latin term for city, *civitas*, means a political structure and a cultural system, not just a single city) the heavenly *civitas* that God would one day establish upon the earth. The goal of history was the fulfilment of this divine purpose: the tottering of the earthly *civitas*, sad as it was to those devoted to the splendours of Roman civilization, was a sign of the coming of God's kingdom. Although Augustine did not take the prophecies of the Revelation to John literally, he did take them seriously. By suggesting various figurative interpretations of the prophecies found in Revelation, he explained in detail what these predictions meant for the future of the church and the world. He believed, for example, that the thousand-year kingdom spoken of in Revelation was the age in which he then lived, and that it would stretch from the time of Christ's birth to the Day of Judgment in the year 1000. His own time (354-430), according to this scheme, would be just short of the midway point of the age preceding the coming of the eternal kingdom.

Augustine was careful to point out in his *City of God* that, although the heavenly city was gaining its citizens on earth through their being converted, these chosen ones would not enter the kingdom until the day of resurrection. The suggestion that the divine *civitas* was already operative in the midst of the terrestrial *civitas*, coupled with the fact that in the declining years of the empire the church was the major force providing social and political stability, led the church to identify itself increasingly with the kingdom of God on earth. The conviction grew that there was no need to pray for and work toward the coming of the kingdom of God, since it was already present in the church. In spite of Augustine's classic restatement of eschatology, doctrines of the Christian hope fell more and more into disuse, until finally they were of interest mainly to fanatical sectarian groups. In fourteenth-century England, for example, John Wycliffe had to remonstrate with the peasants who, believing that in the coming kingdom of God Christians would possess all things in common, set about stealing produce from neighbouring farms. In sixteenth-century Germany, as a by-product of the Reformation, the peasants took literally the promise of Jesus that the meek should inherit the earth. They rose up in the name of the coming kingdom and seized the land, in the conviction that they were laying claim to their inheritance as the true people of God.

There was, however, some continuing interest in eschatology among theologians, since it was a part of the biblical and theological heritage of the church that it was their task to explain. In the encyclopedic works of Thomas Aquinas (*ca.* 1225-1274), for example, there was a place in the development of the theological system for such subjects as the resurrection and the millennial kingdom, but they were presented as part of a body of knowledge for academic study by learned theologians, not as a challenging hope for simple believers.

PHILOSOPHICAL AND CRITICAL THOUGHT

With the rise of biblical criticism (that is, the application of the same kind of analytical historical and literary methods to the Bible that were used in the analysis of any other works of literature or history) in the late eighteenth century, the way was opened for the student of the Bible to select those parts that he believed to be authentic or authoritative. By careful analysis, the critics sought to reconstruct the historical situations out of which the stories about Jesus originated. They chose from among the sayings and stories those that were considered to be authentic and assigned the others to their respective sources. Applied to the Gospels, this method made it possible to dismiss as unimportant those parts that speak of the return of Christ, the throne of judgment, and the resurrection. They could be regarded as either accommodations by Jesus to the primitive outlook of his time, or as misconceptions that originated in the early church and were fictitiously, though piously, ascribed by the Gospel writers to Jesus. Then the critic could proceed to reconstruct, along the lines of his own presuppositions, his portrait of the *real* Jesus. Accordingly, Jesus has been variously represented as a poetic dreamer, a social reformer, a moral idealist, and a gentle prophet and messenger of the love of God.

Coupled with the development of the critical method, and strongly influenced by it, was the rise of the progress theory.[8] Largely under the influence of the German philosopher Hegel (1770-1831), historians (including biblical historians) set about rearranging history to conform to the dogma of inevitable progress. According to this theory, man moved through conflict upward toward realization of the Absolute— that is, the fulfilment of the perfect, predetermined goal of the historical process. According to Hegel, as unchangeable as the law of gravity was the principle that man's history was a story of unceasing progress from error to truth, from incompleteness to complete fulfilment of man's potentialities. Such "primitive" elements of the biblical

---

[8] For a full treatment of this theme, see John Baillie, *The Belief in Progress.* Oxford : University Press, 1950.

record as eschatology could be written off as expendable antiques, or as figurative representations of the very goal of which the philosophers were speaking in more sophisticated language. In either case, eschatology was no longer to be taken at face value as an important part of the biblical faith. The "Kingdom of God" was at best an archaic symbol for the culmination of the process of inevitable progress.

THE RECOVERY OF ESCHATOLOGY

This great confidence in progress was shattered early in the present century by mounting international tensions and by growing evidence of man's inhumanity to man. The "progress-theory" interpretation of the New Testament was dealt a severe blow by the publication of Albert Schweitzer's epochal *Quest of the Historical Jesus*. (The original German edition was published in 1906; the English translation followed four years later.) After surveying the various attempts to establish by objective historical methods who Jesus was, Schweitzer concluded that all efforts have ended in futility, except that those that have taken seriously the eschatological element in Jesus' teaching have come closer to understanding what he was like. Schweitzer proposes a reconstruction that puts the announcement of the impending new age at the centre of Jesus' whole life and message: the fact that the new age is about to dawn provides Jesus with his understanding of his mission, and it provides the perspective in which all his teachings are set. Since eschatology was an integral part of Jesus' outlook, it cannot be eliminated from the record without distorting beyond recognition the picture of what Jesus historically was. He was not a preacher of morals. He was not propounding a higher ethic. He was the herald of the coming kingdom of God, and of the judgment that would accompany its coming.

Since the appearance of the *Quest*, few scholars have accepted Schweitzer's position in detail, but none have been able to ignore the convincing case that he presented for eschatology as the key to understanding Jesus. Schweitzer himself thinks Jesus was mistaken in expecting the end of the old age and the coming of the new soon afterward, and that Jesus died loyal to his convictions, though disillusioned. But there can no longer be a serious claim that Jesus taught the gradual triumph of good over evil and the eventual transformation of this world into the kingdom of God. Schweitzer demonstrated clearly that Jesus expected the new age to come in a catastrophic manner, all at once.

Now that eschatology has been rediscovered in the outlook of Jesus and the early church, it has become necessary to think through anew such basic concepts as the Messiahship of Jesus,[9] the nature of Christian ethics,[10] the nature of the Christian community Perhaps the most important result of the revival of interest in eschatology is the recognition that the church as it is pictured in the New Testament does not regard itself primarily as an organization, though it does organize in order to assign responsibilities. Nor is it a closed corporation, established to serve as the protector of the body of truth committed to it by God. Rather, the church is the community of those who are convinced that the God of history has acted decisively in Jesus Christ to achieve the redemption of his creation, to overcome the evil at work in it, and to bring the whole into subjection to his sovereignty. In spite of periodic lapses into complacency, in the long run the community of the New Covenant has never been willing to accept the *status quo*, since it has believed that its destiny lay not in this age, even at its best, but in the age to come. Although the community's history has been one of conflict within and hostile pressure from without, it has refused to die in despair, but has continued through the centuries to live in hope.

---

[9] As was noted in Chapter 3, a masterful study of the Messiahship of Jesus is found in Rudolf Otto's *Kingdom of God and Son of Man*. London: Lutterworth, 1938.

[10] For an excellent survey of recent efforts to relate eschatology and ethics, see A. N. Wilder, *Eschatology and Ethics in the Teaching of Jesus*. London : SCM Press, 1954.

Chronological Chart

	Roman Emperors	Procurators of Judea	Christian Writings
	Augustus, 30 B.C.		
I B.C. A.D. I			
A.D. 10		Coponius, A.D. 6-9 Ambibulus, A.D. 9-12 Annius Rufinus, A.D. 12-15	
	Tiberius, A.D. 14	Valerius Gratus, A.D. 15-26	
A.D. 20		Pontius Pilate, A.D. 26-36	
A.D. 30	Gaius Caligula,	Marcellus, A.D. 36-37	
A.D. 37	Marullus, A.D. 37-41		
A.D. 40	Claudius, A.D. 41	Cuspius Fadus, A.D. 44-46 Tiberius Alexander, A.D. 46-48	
A.D. 50		Ventidius Cumanus, A.D. 48-52 M. Antonius Felix, A.D. 52-60?	Galatians, A.D. 48-50? I Thessalonians, A.D. 50 II Thessalonians, A.D. 50-51 I Corinthians, A.D. 52-54 (Galatians, A.D. 52-54) II Corinthians, A.D. 52-54 Romans, A.D. 55-56
	Nero, A.D. 54		
A.D. 60		Porcius Festus, A.D. 60-62?	Captivity Epistles, A.D. 60—
	Galba, A.D. 68		
	Otho, A.D. 69	Albinus, A.D. 62-64?	
	Vitellius, A.D. 69	Gessius Florus, A.D. 64-66	
	Vespasian, A.D. 69		
A.D. 70			Gospel of Mark, A.D. 70 James, A.D. 75-100 (Ephesians, A.D. 75-100)
A.D. 80	Titus, A.D. 79		Gospel of Matthew, A.D. 85-100
	Domitian, A.D. 81		Gospel of Luke-Acts, A.D. 85-100
A.D. 90			I Peter, A.D. 90-95 Hebrews, A.D. 90-95 Revelation, A.D. 90-95 I Clement, A.D. 95
	Nerva, A.D. 96		
A.D. 100	Trajan, A.D. 98		Didache, A.D. 100-130 Pastoral Epistles, A.D. 100-130 Shepherd of Hermas, A.D. 100-140
A.D. 110			Epistles of Ignatius, A.D. 110-117
	Hadrian, A.D. 117-135		Jude, A.D. 110-130
A.D. 120			
A.D. 130			II Peter, A.D. 130-150

(Captivity Epistles, [Ephesians?], Colossians, Philippians, Philemon, A.D. 52-54?)

Gospel of John, A.D. 90-110
Epistles of John, A.D. 90-110

Important Events in Early Church	Important Events in Jewish History	
	Maccabean Revolt, 167 B.C.	
	Dead Sea Sect at Qumran, 105 B.C. (?)-A.D. 66	
	Pompey takes Jerusalem, 63 B.C.	
	Herod the Great (King of Judea), 37 B.C.-4 B.C.	
Birth of Jesus, 6-4 B.C.?	Herod Antipas (Tetrarch of Galilee), 4 B.C.-A.D. 39	I B.C.
	Archelaus (Ethnarch of Judea), 4 B.C.-A.D. 6	A.D. I
	Philip (Tetrarch of Iturea), 4 B.C.-A.D. 34	
		A.D. 10
	High Priest Caiaphas, A.D. 18-36	
Preaching of John the Baptist, A.D. 27-29?		A.D. 20
Ministry of Jesus, A.D. 29-33?		A.D. 30
Crucifixion, A.D. 30-33?		
Conversion of Paul, A.D. 33-35?		A.D. 40
Peter imprisoned by Herod Agrippa, A.D. 41-44?	Theudas' revolt, A.D. 40?	
Execution of James, son of Zebedee, A.D. 44	Herod Agrippa I (King of Judea), A.D. 41-44	
	Jews banished from Rome by Claudius, A.D. 41-49?	
Paul in southern Galatia, A.D. 47-49?		A.D. 50
Paul in Corinth, A.D. 50-51		
Paul in Ephesus, A.D. 52-54		
Paul arrested in Jerusalem, A.D. 56		
Paul in Rome, A.D. 60—		A.D. 60
Death of James, brother of Jesus, A.D. 62		
Flight of Christians to Pella, A.D. 66-67	War with Rome, A.D. 66-73	
	Jerusalem and Temple destroyed, A.D. 70	A.D. 70
		A.D. 80
	Council of Jamnia, A.D. 90?	A.D. 90
		A.D. 100
		A.D. 110
Martyrdom of Ignatius, A.D. 117?		A.D. 120
		A.D. 130

SUGGESTIONS
FOR ADDITIONAL READING

General

For a general survey of the history of critical study of the New Testament, and for discussions of the origins of the individual books of the New Testament, the best recent, non-technical book is *An Introduction to the New Testament*, by Richard Heard (London: A. & C. Black, 1950). A more technical discussion is *An Introduction to the Study of the New Testament*, by A. H. McNeile, which was revised by C. S. C. Williams and published in a second edition in 1953 (London: Oxford University Press). Part III of M. S. Enslin's *Christian Beginnings* (London: Harper, 1938), written in Professor Enslin's own brand of colourful prose, includes concise statements on the date and authorship of the New Testament books. Perhaps the finest brief survey of the history of the first-century church is *The Beginnings of the Christian Church*, by H. Lietzmann (London: Lutterworth, 1953).

CHAPTER ONE: *The Search for Community*

For surveys of the history of Judaism during Greek and Roman domination, see Part I of M. S. Enslin, *Christian Beginnings*, and ch. 1 of R. H. Pfeiffer's *History of New Testament Times* (London: A. & C. Black, 1954). One of the best concise studies of the complex nature of Judaism in the first century A.D. is C. Guignebert's *The Jewish World in the Time of Jesus* (London: Routledge and Kegan Paul, 1939). A detailed description of the religions of the Graeco-Roman world may be found in H. R. Willoughby, *Pagan Regeneration* (Chicago: University of Chicago Press, 1929). For a balanced discus-

SUGGESTIONS FOR ADDITIONAL READING   477

sion of the significance of the Dead Sea Scrolls and for a readable translation of the major documents, see Millar Burrows, *The Dead Sea Scrolls* (London: Secker & Warburg, 1956).

CHAPTER TWO: *The Community and Its Convictions*

The one book that, more than any other, has drawn attention to the centrality for the New Testament of the *kerygma*, or the primitive Christian message, is C. H. Dodd, *The Apostolic Preaching and Its Developments* (London: Hodder & Stoughton, 1944). The fullest study of the book of Acts in relation to the rise of Christianity is the five-volume work, *The Beginning of Christianity*, Part I, "The Acts of the Apostles," by F. J. Foakes-Jackson, K. Lake, H. J. Cadbury, and others (London: Macmillan, 1920-33). Primarily historical in interest are Vol. 4, a commentary on Acts, and Vol. 5, a series of essays on various problems relating to the beginning of the Christian church.

The discussions of the origin of the New Testament books in the introductory books listed above will supplement the brief treatment of these matters given in these volumes. In addition, the *Introduction to the New Testament* by E. J. Goodspeed (Chicago: University of Chicago Press, 1937), offers a readable discussion of the origin of the New Testament writings, and includes a development of Professor Goodspeed's theory that the books were organized into smaller units (e.g., a collection of the letters of Paul) before being joined to form what we now know as the New Testament.

CHAPTER THREE: *The Conduct of Jesus' Ministry*

A helpful, brief introduction to the life and ministry of Jesus may be found in "The Life and Ministry of Jesus," by Vincent Taylor, in *Interpreter's Bible*, Vol. VII, pp. 114-144. The author has expanded this article into a book, *The Life and Ministry of Jesus* (London: Macmillan, 1954). The introductory chapters of two other books set the ministry of Jesus in the context of the contemporary Jewish world: T. H. Manson, *The Servant-Messiah*, chs. 1-4 (Cambridge: University Press, 1953); Martin Dibelius, *Jesus*, trans. by C. B. Hedrick and F. C. Grant, chs. 1-4 (Philadelphia: Westminster, 1949). Helpful studies of the miracles in the Gospels are: Alan Richardson, *The Miracle-Stories of the Gospels* (London: SCM Press, 1941); and S. Vernon McCasland,

478   SUGGESTIONS FOR ADDITIONAL READING

By the Finger of God (London: Macmillan, 1951). The latter, though
concerned with demon possession and exorcism in the light of modern
views of mental illness, also tries to see these phenomena in relation to
Jesus' own mission and message.

CHAPTER FOUR: *The Content of Jesus' Teaching*

A classic discussion of the form and method of Jesus' teaching is that of
M. Goguel, *The Life of Jesus*, trans. by Olive Wyon (London: Allen
& Unwin, 1933). A valuable little book on the same subject is E. C.
Colwell, *An Approach to the Teaching of Jesus* (New York: Abing-
don, 1947). Three articles in Vol. VII of *Interpreter's Bible* are help-
ful introductions to Jesus' teaching: C. T. Craig, "The Proclama-
tion of the Kingdom," pp. 145-154; A. Wilder, "The Sermon on the
Mount," pp. 155-164; W. R. Bowie, "The Parables," pp. 165-175. An
excellent, extensive treatment of the Sermon on the Mount is H.
Windisch, *The Meaning of the Sermon on the Mount*, trans. by S. M.
Gilmour (Philadelphia: Westminster, 1951).

  Of the many excellent books on the parables none is better than
J. Jeremias, *The Parables of Jesus*, trans. by S. H. Hooke (London:
SCM Press, 1954). An indispensable tool for the serious study of Jesus'
teaching is T. W. Manson, *The Teaching of Jesus* (Cambridge: University Press, 1948). Brief but lucid interpretations of Jesus' proclamation
of the kingdom of God are found in A. Wilder, *New Testament Faith
For Today*, ch. 3, "The Proclamation of Jesus" (New York: Harpers,
1955); and M. Dibelius, *Jesus*, ch. 5 (Philadelphia: Westminster,
1949). The most complete study of the interpretation of Jesus' proclamation of the kingdom, his ethical teaching, and his mission in
relation to their eschatological context is A. Wilder, *Eschatology and
Ethics in the Teaching of Jesus* (London: SCM Press, 1954). For a
more systematic treatment of the ethics of Jesus, see L. H. Marshall,
The Challenge of New Testament Ethics, chs. 1-6 (London: Macmillan, 1950).

CHAPTER FIVE: *The Crisis in Jesus' Ministry*

For a helpful interpretation of the problem of the "messianic consciousness" of Jesus based on a study of his message, mission, and death,
see chs. 3-5 in T. W. Manson, *The Servant-Messiah* (Cambridge: University Press, 1953). Three varying but suggestive interpretations of the

meaning of Son of Man are found in R. Otto, *The Kingdom of God and the Son of Man*, trans. by F. V. Filson and B. Lee-Woolf (London: Lutterworth, rev. ed., 1943); G. S. Duncan, *Jesus, Son of Man* (London: Nisbet, 1948); and R. Fuller, *The Mission and Achievement of Jesus*, Studies in Biblical Theology No. 12 (London: SCM Press, 1954). There is a brief, lucid interpretation of the meaning of Son of Man in M. Dibelius, *Jesus*, ch. 7 (Philadelphia: Westminster, 1949). The same book (ch. 9) provides a concise summary of the nature of the opposition leading to Jesus' death. The events of the last days (Passion Narrative) are given a dependable historical reconstruction and suggestive interpretation in W. E. and M. B. Rollins, *Jesus and His Ministry*, chs. 12-14 (Greenwich: Seabury, 1954). A highly illuminating effort to see Jesus' death in relation to his total mission and message is found in W. Manson, *Jesus the Messiah*, ch. 7, "The Passion and Death of the Messiah" (London: Hodder & Stoughton, 1943).

CHAPTER SIX: *The Life of the Earliest Community*

In addition to the general works on the beginning of Christianity listed above, two commentaries on the book of Acts provide supplemental information on the earliest Christian community: *The Acts of the Apostles*, by F. J. Foakes-Jackson (London: Hodder & Stoughton, 1931), which, though much briefer than the five-volume study of Acts described above, has the great advantage for the non-technical reader of being based on the English text rather than on the Greek text; Vol. IX of *Interpreter's Bible* includes a valuable study of Acts by G. H. C. Macgregor (New York: Abingdon, 1954). These commentaries include a great deal of material that is relevant to Chapters Six to Ten of this book.

CHAPTER SEVEN: *Paul, the Pioneer*

For an excellent brief reconstruction of the life and thought of Paul, see *Paul*, by M. Dibelius and W. G. Kuemmel (London: Longmans, 1953). A fuller statement of Paul's thought, based on his religious experience, is a reverent work by James S. Stewart, *A Man in Christ* (London: Hodder & Stoughton, 1935). A fresh and illuminating, though highly technical, analysis of Paul's thought is given in Vol. I of Rudolf Bultmann's *Theology of the New Testament*, trans. by

Kendrick Grobel (London: SCM Press, 1952), pp. 187-352. For a technical study of Paul's thought against the background of first-century rabbinic teaching, see *Paul and Rabbinic Judaism* by W. D. Davies (London: S.P.C.K., 1948). A detailed reconstruction of the issues and developments in Paul's relationships with the Jerusalem Christians is given in *St. Paul and the Church of Jerusalem*, by W. L. Knox (Cambridge: The University Press, 1925). Paul's break with Jewish Christianity is the recurrent theme in *The Birth of Christianity*, by M. Goguel (London: Allen & Unwin, 1953), which also includes descriptions of the historical situations out of which the books of the New Testament emerged.

CHAPTER EIGHT: *Mission to Europe*

In addition to the relevant sections of the commentaries on Acts, the reader will find more detailed analysis of life in the Gentile churches in such commentaries on the Corinthian Letters as *The First Epistle to the Corinthians*, by James Moffatt (London: Hodder & Stoughton, 1938), and the exegesis of I and II Corinthians by C. T. Craig and F. V. Filson, respectively, in Vol. X of *Interpreter's Bible* (New York: Abingdon, 1953).

CHAPTER NINE: *The Message for Gentiles*

Two of the finest commentaries on the Letter to the Romans (based on the English text) are *The Epistle to the Romans*, by C. H. Dodd (London: Hodder & Stoughton, 1932), and the exegesis of Romans to be found in Vol. IX of *Interpreter's Bible*, by John Knox (New York: Abingdon, 1954).

CHAPTER TEN: *Death of Paul and End of Church at Jerusalem*

For a careful reconstruction of the fall of Jerusalem and the end of the apostolic age, see M. Goguel, *The Birth of Christianity* (London: Allen & Unwin, 1953), Part II, chs. 2 and 3. Macgregor, in *Interpreter's Bible*, Vol. IX, pp. 349-352, gives a concise statement of the various theories about the fate of Paul in Rome. The best commentary on the

English text of James is by James Moffatt, in *The General Epistles* (London: Hodder & Stoughton, 1928). An excellent brief introduction to the book of James is given by Goguel in *The Birth of Christianity* (London: Allen & Unwin, 1953), Part IV, ch. 6.

CHAPTER ELEVEN: *The Community in Conflict*

An excellent treatment of the relation of the church and the Roman government is O. Cullmann, *The State in the New Testament* (New York: Scribner's, 1956). A similar study, though dealing more extensively with non-Christian sources and covering a period up to the beginning of the fourth century, is R. Grant, *The Sword and the Cross* (New York: Macmillan, 1955). A series of historical essays dealing largely with various Roman emperors up to the fourth century is Ethelbert Stauffer, *Christ and the Caesars*, trans. by K. and R. Smith (London: SCM Press, 1955). An interesting discussion of the "false teaching" confronting the early church may be found in M. Goguel, *The Birth of Christianity*, trans. by H. C. Snape, pp. 393-435 (London: Allen & Unwin, 1953). A thorough treatment of false teaching, especially as it relates to the Pastoral Epistles, appears in the introduction to the commentary on I and II Timothy and Titus by F. H. Gealy, *Interpreter's Bible*, Vol. II, pp. 350-360 (New York: Abingdon, 1955).

CHAPTER TWELVE: *The Community Organizes*

An illuminating book on the development of organization in the early church is J. Knox, *The Early Church and the Coming Great Church* (New York: Abingdon, 1955). An older important work on the origins of the Christian ministry is B. H. Streeter, *The Primitive Church* (London: Macmillan, 1929). A balanced non-technical chapter dealing with worship in the New Testament may be found in D. H. Hislop, *Our Heritage in Public Worship*, pp. 59-92 (Edinburgh: Clark, 1935). An important work on the subject of the Eucharist is A. J. B. Higgins, *The Lord's Supper in the New Testament* (Studies in Biblical Theology No. 6) (London: SCM Press, 1952). For a general survey of the historical development of the New Testament church, see H. Lietzman, *The Beginnings of the Christian Church*, trans. by B. L. Woolf, esp. pp. 191-221; 236-248 (London: Lutterworth, 1952). The most thorough study of the development of the church in relation to its environment is A. Harnack, *The Mission and Expansion of Christianity in the First Three Centuries*, trans. by J. Moffatt, Vol. 1 (London: Williams & Norgate, 1908). For a theological interpretation of the development of organization, see R. Bultmann, *Theology of the New Testament*, trans. by K. Groebel, Vol. 1, pp. 133-152; Vol. 2, pp. 95-126; 231-236 (London: SCM Press, 1952).

CHAPTER THIRTEEN: *The Community and the World: I*

For a concise discussion of the problems confronting the interpreter of the Gospel of John, see the article by W. F..Howard on The Gospel According to St. John, Vol. VIII, pp. 437-462, *Interpreter's Bible* (New York: Abingdon, 1952). Two short books dealing topically with the Gospel of John are E. C. Colwell and E. L. Titus, *The Gospel of the Spirit* (New York: Harper, 1953), and W. F. Howard, *Christianity According to St. John* (London: Duckworth, 1943). Among the many excellent longer commentaries in English on John none is more important than E. C. Hoskyns, *The Fourth Gospel*, ed. by F. N. Davey (London: Faber and Faber, 1947). One of the most successful efforts to provide guidance on the theological perspective and literary method of the author of John is found in A. Wilder, *New Testament Faith For Today*, pp. 142-164 (New York: Harper, 1955).

CHAPTER FOURTEEN: *The Community and the World: II*

A concise discussion of the historical, literary, and theological problems posed by Hebrews is the introduction to Hebrews by A. C. Purdy, *Interpreter's Bible*, Vol. XI, pp. 577-594 (New York: Abingdon, 1955). In a recent study of Hebrews, *The Epistle to the Hebrews* (London: Hodder and Stoughton, 1951), W. Manson propounds some unusual theories about the purpose of the book. A short non-technical commentary influenced by Manson's book is W. Neil, *The Epistle to the Hebrews* (London: SCM, 1955). For a discussion of the historical problems connected with I Peter, see F. W. Beare, *The First Epistle of Peter*, pp. 1-41 (Oxford: Blackwell, 1947). An important article dealing with the ethical teaching of I Peter is W. C. van Unnik, "The Teaching of Good Works in I Peter," *New Testament Studies*, Vol. 1, No. 2 (Nov., 1954), pp. 92-110. For a theological interpretation of the development of ethical teaching, see R. Bultmann, *Theology of the*

New Testament, trans. by K. Groebel, Vol. 2, pp. 203-231 (London: SCM, 1955), and W. Beach and H. R. Niebuhr, *Christian Ethics*, pp. 46-57 (New York: Ronald, 1955).

CHAPTER FIFTEEN: *The Hope of the Community*

The most complete survey of the historical setting of the book of Revelation is that of W. Ramsay, in *The Letters to the Seven Churches* (London: Hodder & Stoughton, 1904). An excellent commentary on Revelation is *The Revelation of St. John*, by M. Kiddle (London: Hodder & Stoughton, 1940). The fullest technical analysis of Revelation is *The Revelation of St. John*, by R. H. Charles (Edinburgh: T. & T. Clark, 1920). For an illuminating survey of the changing interpretations of New Testament eschatology in the present century, see chs. 1-3 of A. N. Wilder, *Eschatology and Ethics in the Teaching of Jesus* (London: SCM Press, 1954). For a brief analysis of the development of eschatology in the New Testament, see H. A. Guy, *The New Testament Doctrine of the Last things* (London and New York: Oxford, 1948).

INDEX

Aaron, 422
Abel, 59, 430
Abraham, 19, 38, 59, 81, 123, 211, 233, 235, 255, 272, 276, 288, 311, 401-2, 424, 429-430
Achaia, 252
Acrocorinth, 251
Acropolis, 248
Acts of the Apostles, 2, 49-50, 52-4, 56, 61-2, 65-6, 68, 71-2, 74, 76, 176-8, 183-7, 189-208, 210-232, 236-246, 252-3, 260-265, 292-303, 306, 311, 318, 355, 358-9, 367, 369, 373, 376, 422, 448, 453
Adam, 57, 262, 271, 279, 280, 282
Adonis, 249
Adultery, 112, 257
Aelia Capitolina, 314
Aeneas, 201
Aenon, 79
Agape meal, 376
Agrippa II, 299-300
Albinus, 31, 312
Alexander Jannaeus, 27, 43
Alexander the Great, 10-14, 25, 243
Alexandria, 12, 13, 19, 24, 71, 208, 221, 416
Allegory, 115, 210. 235, 259, 288, 411
Amos, 32, 34, 59
Ananias and Sapphira, 192, 223
Ananias of Damascus, 213
Andrew, 105
Annas the High Priest, 312-3
Antinomianism, 341, 345-7
Antioch : Pisidian, 225-8 ; Syrian, 71-2, 93, 204, 216-222, 224-5, 230-232, 236-7, 239-241, 262, 367, 373
Antiochus Epiphanes, 25-7, 33, 452
Aphrodite, 251
Apocalypticism : Christian literature of, 451-2 ; definition of, 38, 449 ; in *Hebrews*, 462-3 ; in Jewish literature, 38-9 ; in *Revelation*, 456-462
Apollo, 209, 218, 284
Apollonius of Tyana, 98, 250
Apollos, 262-3, 415
Apostasy, 423
Apostle : meaning of term, 397-8, 420 ; ministry of, 354-9 ; qualifications of, 184
Apostolic succession, *I Clement* on, 360-362
Apostolic tradition : Paul's dependence on, 260
Appian Way, 302
Apuleius, 22
Aquila, 252, 258, 262-3
Aquinas, Thomas, 470
Arabia Petraea, 213
Archelaus, ethnarch, 30

Areopagus, Paul's speech on, 53, 249-251
Ares, temple of, 248
Aretas, king, 211, 214-5
Aristarchus, 306
Armageddon, 461
Artemis, temple of, 218, 263-5
Asceticism : and the Colossian church, 306 ; conflict of church with, 347 ; in gnosticism, 341 ; in mystery religions, 209
Asclepius, the god, 20, 455
Asia, province of, 337, 434
Assos, 293
Astarte, the goddess, 251, 264
Astrology, 19
Athenodorus, 208
Athens, 13, 16, 23, 53, 62, 208, 246-251
Atonement : Day of, 36, 60, 301, 420, 426 ; of Jesus, 59
Attis, 23
Augustine, Saint, 54, 468-9
Augustus Cæsar, 9-11, 15, 28, 30, 46, 71, 199, 208, 226-7, 332, 466

Babylonian captivity, 24, 25, 32-3, 150
Baptism : of Jesus, 83-8, 388 ; in *Didache*, 368-9 ; in early church, 187-9, 263, 368-370 ; in *Gospel of John*, 393-4 ; in *Hebrews*, 423 ; in *I Peter* 370, 434-5, 438 ; John the Baptist's, 81-2 ; Paul's view of, 282, 283
Bar-Jesus, 223
Barnabas : and Paul, 216-232, 236-7 ; disputes with Paul, 241 ; regarded as apostle, 358
Barnabas, Epistle of, 369-371, 465
Baruch, 67, 145
Basilides, 343
Benedictus, The, 375
Berenice, 299, 300
Beroea, 246
Bethany : beyond Jordan, 79 ; in Judea, 155-6, 162, 404-6
Bethphage, 155
Bethsaida, 143
Birth stories : of Jesus, 9, 79, 83-4, 281, 310 ; of John the Baptist, 79
Bishops, 355, 360-365, 367-8, 380
Bithynia, 334, 337, 377, 381, 434
"Body of Christ", Paul's concept of, 283-4
"Breaking of Bread" (*see also* Common meals, Eucharist), 178, 190, 260, 293, 376

Caesarea, 71, 158, 199, 202, 216, 236, 262, 293, 294, 297-9
Caesarea Philippi, 87, 91, 146-8, 152-4, 358

484

authorities, 48, 122, 128-132, 143, 159-172, 401-3, 406 ; interpretation of rejection of mission, 162-4 ; meaning of Last Supper to, 165-8 ; messianic consciousness of, 86-8, 147-154, 471-2 ; "mighty works" of, 98-103 ; prophecies of death of, 152-4 ; relation to John the Baptist, 49, 83-8 ; sinlessness of, 86 ; Suffering Servant concept of, 87, 150, 198, 278, 407 ; *ministry of :* crisis in, 141-175 ; *Gospel of John's* outline of, 390-406 ; in Jerusalem, 154-175 ; journeys to north, 91, 145-6; manifestation of Kingdom in, 122-8 ; place and date of, 91-3 ; *teaching of :* ethical content of, 127-8, 131 ; Fatherhood of God in, 120-122, 126 ; final, 162-5 ; forgiveness in, 132-9 ; form and method of, 114-7 ; *Gospel of John's* representation of, 385 ; humility in, 134-5 ; Jewish Law in, 128-132 ; Kingdom of God in, 117-128 ; love in, 132-6 ; new life in, 127-8, 132-8, 395-7 ; problem of authority in, 97-8 ; radical character of, 135 ; Son of Man in, 147-152

Jewish Christians, 193, 207, 218-9, 230-238, 317-322

Jews *(see also* Diaspora) : faith of, 32-3 ; hostility towards early church, 192-5, 228-9, 295-300, 309-317 ; under foreign domination, 12, 24-32

Joel, 50, 56, 61, 187, 197, 278

John, Gospel of : authorship and date of, 67-8, 72, 384 ; church in, 411 ; coming of Christ in, 410 ; communion with God in, 401 ; conflict with Jews in, 310-311, 398, 401 ; dating of Last Supper in, 165, 406 ; death of Jesus in, 406-414; determinism in, 401-2 ; differences from *Synoptics,* 385, 413 ; discipleship in, 406-8 ; divine revealer in, 395 ; eschatology of, 393, 463-4 ; eternal life in, 393-4, 397-9, 404-5, 408 ; ethical life according to, 408 ; Eucharist reflected in, 400 ; faith in, 394, 401-2 ; Holy Spirit in, 389, 392, 399, 407, 410-414 ; "I am" sayings in, 398-9, 401, 405 ; judgement in, 394-5, 464 ; kerygma in, 386 ; logos in, 387-8 ; ministry of Jesus in, 93, 390 ; mystical union in, 400 ; rebirth in, 393 ; resurrection in, 399, 405, 414 ; sin in, 394 ; Son of Man in, 394-9 ; Suffering Servant in, 407 ; symbolism in, 385, 391 ; theological interpretation in, 385, 413 ; work of Christ in, 386, 388, 397, 411-2 ; world saviour in, 395

John, The Epistles of (I, II, III) : charismatic ministry in, 356-7, 359 ; date and authorship of, 67, 72, 342 ; false teaching attacked in, 344-6

John Hyrcanus, 27

John, son of Zebedee : call of, 105 ; death of, 204, 311, 453 ; discipleship of, 105, 134, 153, 168-9 ; question of authorship, 67, 72, 384, 453

John the Baptist : as forerunner of Jesus, 84 ; birth of, 79 ; disciples of, 83, 189, 263, 389 ; *Gospel of John's* interpretation of, 384, 388-9 ; imprisonment and death of, 88, 90-91, 125, 143 ; message of, 80, 96 ; relation to Jesus of, 49, 83-8, 188-9

Joppa, 199, 201-2

Joseph of Arimathea, 104, 175

Josephus, 41-2, 44, 78, 90, 91, 203, 204, 312, 452

Judaizers, 231-4, 275-6, 294-5

Judas Iscariot, 166, 170, 184, 354, 407-8

Judas Maccabaeus, 26-7, 47

Jude, Epistle of : attack on antinomianism in, 346 ; authorship and date of, 73, 342 ; faith in, 348 ; "lovefeast" in, 376

Judgement *(see also* Eschatology) : early church's expectation of, 61-2, 259, 347, 418, 431, 461 ; in *Gospel of John,* 395, 403 ; in teachings of Jesus, 96, 123, 126-7, 163-4, 447 ; Jewish view of, 32, 37-9

Julian, emperor, 23

Julius Cæsar, 10, 243, 332

Justification by faith : in Dead Sea Sect, 273 ; misunderstood in *James,* 319-320 ; Pauline concept of, 232-5, 272-5

Justin Martyr, 371-3, 381

Kerygma : death of Jesus and, 59-60 ; defended by post-apostolic writers, 349 ; definition of, 52-4 ; reaction of Gentiles to, 255 ; resurrection of Jesus and, 183, 261

Khirbet Qumran, 42-3

Kingdom of God : as coming event, 123-4 ; as symbol of progress, 471 ; gift of, 122 ; in *Gospel of John,* 394 ; Jesus' proclamation of, 94-7, 117-127 ; Jewish hopes for, 37, 118-9 ; life of, 122 ; "mighty works" as manifestation of, 100-101 ; Paul's teaching about, 289 ; present reality of, 124-7 ; radical demands of, 127-139 ; righteousness of, 138-9

Kingdom of Satan, 38

Kingship, divine, 10, 332-3

Kurios ("Lord"), 277

Lactantius, 466-7

Laodicea, 305, 455

Laodiceans, Letter to the, 306-7

Last Supper : *Gospels* account of, 165-8, 406-8 ; Pauline tradition of, 260-261

Law *(see also* Torah) : identification with wisdom and logos, 387 ; in

Praetorium, 297
Pre-existence of Christ : according to Paul, 280-281 ; in *Gospel of John*, 386-8 ; in *Hebrews*, 417
Presbyter : authority and function in Ignatius, 364 ; function in *I Clement*, 361-2 ; in early church, 355 ; Jewish origin of, 359 ; relation to bishop, 355 ; successor to apostles, 359
Priesthood : and Dead Sea Sect, 44, 80 ; and John the Baptist, 80 ; of second Temple, 36-7
Priscilla, 252, 258, 262-3
Procurators, 30-31
"Progress-theory ", 471
Pronouncement stories, 113
Prophets : and post-exilic Judaism, 32-3 ; in early church, 354 ; testing of, 357
Proselytes : among early converts, 194, 200 ; baptism of, 81, 438 ; instruction of, 370, 433, 438
Psalms, 87, 278, 280, 373, 375, 403, 418-420, 422, 424, 427
Ptolemais, 293
Ptolemy, 13
Puteoli, 302

Qahal ("church "), 69, 70
Quelle (Q source), 70, 72, 80, 82, 85, 88-90, 100, 111, 113-4, 120, 148, 155, 164
Qumran Scrolls, *see* Dead Sea Scrolls
Qumran Sect, *see* Dead Sea Sect

Rabbi, Jesus called, 109
Rabbinic interpretation, influence of : on *Gospel of John*, 384, 399 ; on *Hebrews*, 416, 419, 425 ; on Paul, 210, 259
Rabbinic tradition : attitude towards Jesus in, 310 ; influence on *Gospel of Matthew*, 321
Ransom, Jesus' death as, 59, 274
Rebirth : in *Gospel of John*, 393 ; in hellenistic religion, 21-3, 386 ; in *I Peter*, 435
Reconciliation, Paul on, 279, 281
Redeemer, Jesus as, 278-280
Redemption : church's belief on, 54, 57-62 ; in mystery religions, 209 ; Paul's concept of, 209, 256, 278
Reformation, The, 469
"Religio licita ", 327, 334
Remnant of Israel : disciples symbolize, 107 ; in Dead Sea Sect, 43
Repentance : as response to kerygma, 187 ; as sign of Kingdom, 126 ; Jesus proclaims, 97 ; John the Baptist's preaching of, 80
Resurrection (*see also* Eschatology, Hope) : and immortality, 181-2 ; early church's belief in, 61 ; *Gospel of John's* concept of, 405, 464 ; *Gospel* traditions regarding, 177-180 ;

Jesus' belief in, 124, 128 ; Jewish belief in, 38 ; Kerygma based on, 59, 61, 183 ; Lord's Day celebration of, 371 ; Paul's teaching regarding, 289-291, 448-450 ; Paul's understanding of, 179, 18 , 248, 261-2 ; rational explanations of, 180-181
Revelation : Jesus as God's, 56, 386, 388, 417 ; Torah as divine, 33-4
Revelation, Book of : attitude towards state in, 2, 335-7 ; beast in, 457, 459-460 ; Christ in, 458 ; date and authorship of, 73, 335-6, 453-4 ; final victory in, 461-2 ; interpretation of, 446, 455-462 ; liturgical worship reflected in, 375-6 ; purposes of, 336-7, 453-4
Rhegium, 302
"Right teaching ", 349
Righteousness of God, 131, 138, 273
Roman empire, structure of, 14-5
Roman state : church in conflict with, 326-335 ; Jesus' attitude towards, 2, 326 ; Paul's attitude towards, 2, 326-7
Romans, Letter to the, 59-60, 66, 185, 208, 219, 226, 229, 232, 266-291, 307, 327, 335, 358, 369, 374, 439

Sacrament (*see also* Baptism, Eucharist) : baptism as, 187, 368, 370, 393 ; common meal as, 50, 260-261, 376-381, 399-400 ; in mystery cults, 24
Sacrifice : in early church, 59-60 ; in Eucharist, 190, 260 ; in *Hebrews*, 426, 428 ; Jewish view of, 35-6, 59 ; Paul's teaching on, 259-260
Sadducees : beliefs of, 39-40 ; disappearance of, 40 ; Jesus in conflict with, 158-162, 172, 182 ; John the Baptist attacks, 82
Salamis, 222-3, 251
Salvation (*see also* Eschatology, Hope, Redemption) : in mystery cults, 21-4 ; through Jesus Christ, 59, 275, 341, 391, 395-7, 417-8, 420, 432, 435, 437
Samaria : Philip's mission to, 196-9 ; woman of, 395-6
Samaritans : attitude of Jews towards, 196 ; Christian mission to, 196-202 ; in *Gospel of John*, 395-7 ; Jesus' visit to, 155
Sanhedrin, 36, 52, 147, 170-172, 193-4, 215
Sarah, 430
Sardis, 455
Satan, 38, 57-9, 89, 100, 142, 152, 255, 274, 336, 419, 447, 455, 459
Saturninus, 343
Schweitzer, Albert, 471
Scribes, 34
Sects, Jewish, 39-45
Seleucia, 222
Seleucus, house of, 13, 15, 25-7, 37, 39, 47, 218
Seleucus, Nicator, 222

GALLIA

ITALIA

ADRIATIC SEA

ILLYRICUM

DANU

● Roma

● Puteoli
● Pompeii?

Philippi ●
Thessalonica ●
Beroea ●

Nicopolis ●

AE
SEA

MEDITERRANEAN

Athens ●
Corinth ●

MALTA

CRETE

Cyrene?

The Church at the Close of the First Century A. I